# TOMARE!
## STOP

## You're going the wrong way!

## Manga is a completely different type of reading experience.

## To start at the beginning,
## Go to the end!

hat's right! Authentic manga is read the traditional Japanese way—
rom right to left, exactly the opposite of how American books are
ead. It's easy to follow: Just go to the other end of the book and read
ach page—and each panel—from right side to left side, starting at
ɛ top right. Now you're experiencing manga as it was meant to be!

A Kodansha Trade Paperback Original.

*Pretty Guardian Sailor Moon* volume 5 copyright © 2003 Naoko Takeuchi
English Translation copyright © 2012 Naoko Takeuchi

Published in the United States by Kodansha Comics, an imprint
of Kodansha USA Publishing, LLC, New York.

Publication rights for this English edition arranged through
Kodansha Ltd., Tokyo.

First published in Japan in 2003 by Kodansha Ltd., Tokyo, as
*Bishoujosenshi Sailor Moon Shinsoban*, volume 5.

ISBN 978-1-61262-001-5

Printed in Canada.

www.kodanshacomics.com

9 8 7 6

Translator/Adapter: William Flanagan
Lettering: Jennifer Skarupa

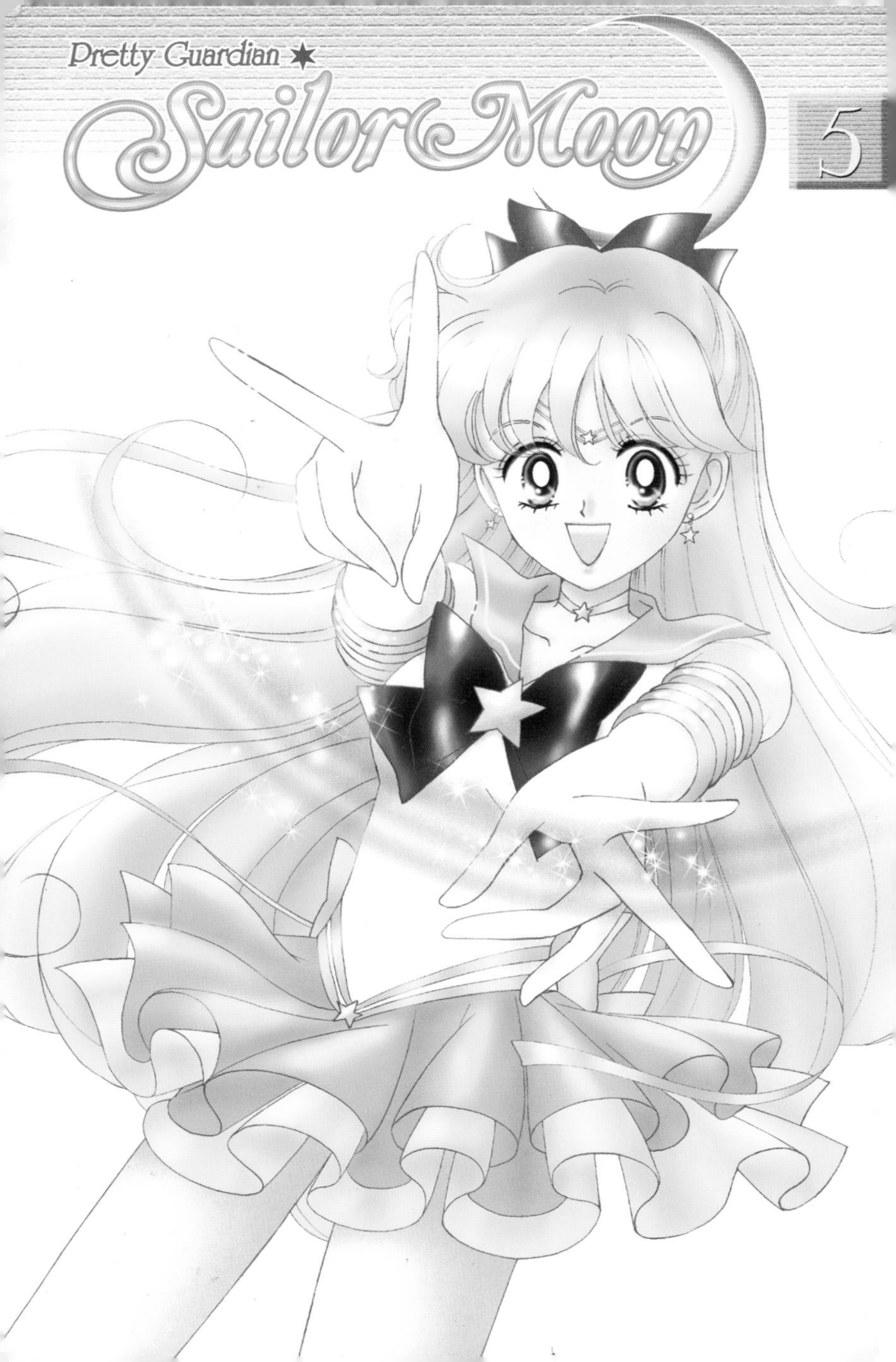
Pretty Guardian ★
Sailor Moon
5

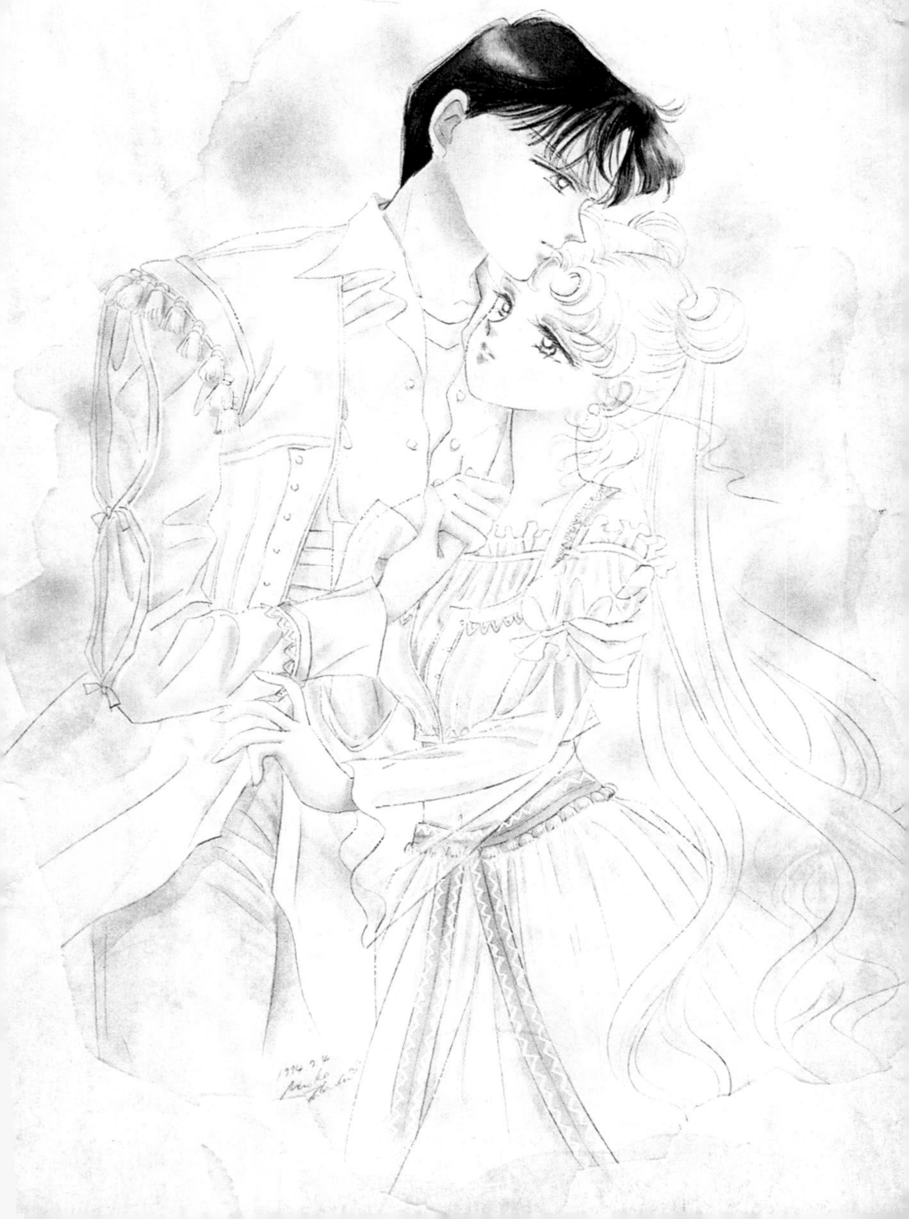

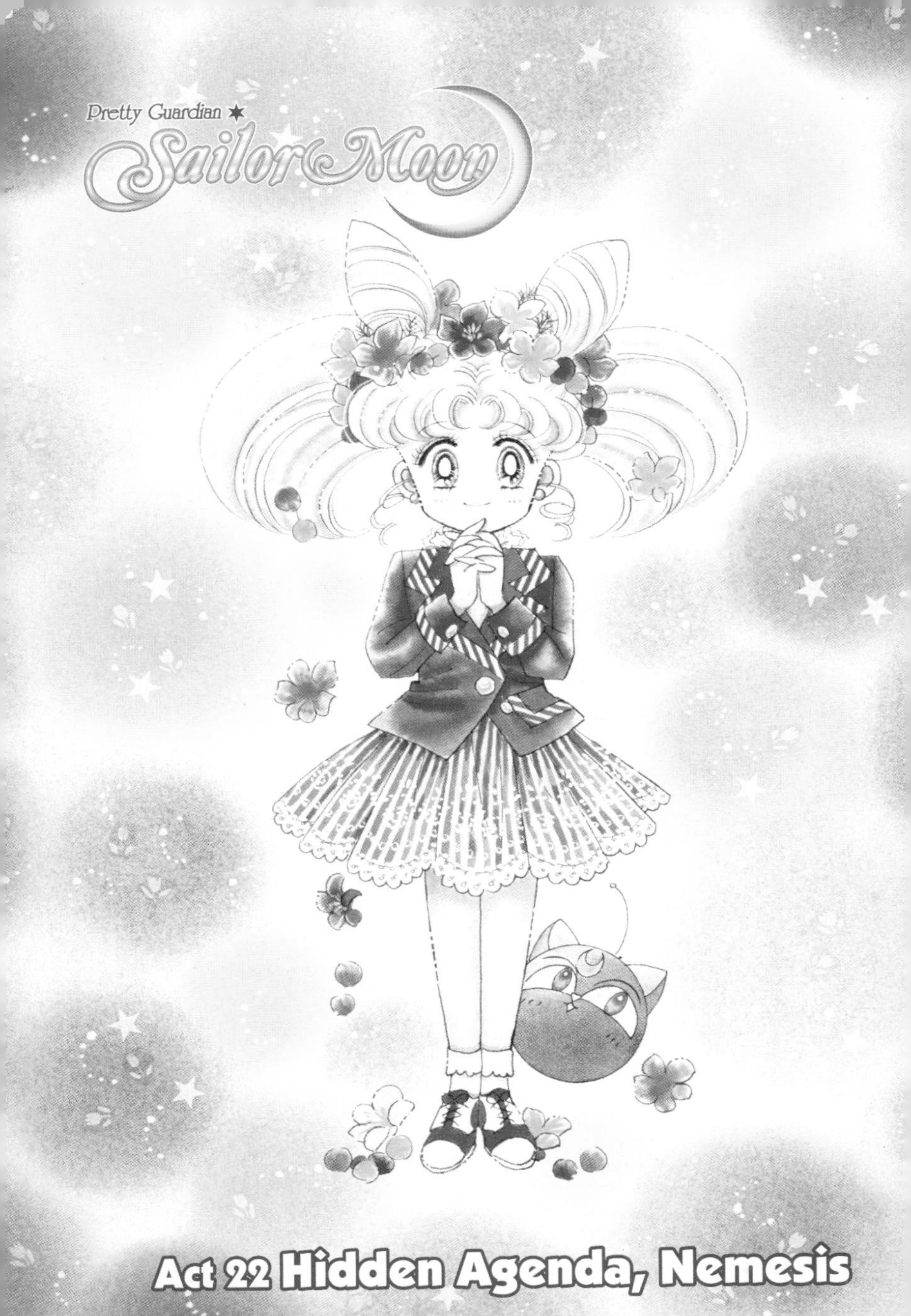
Pretty Guardian
Sailor Moon

# Act 22 Hidden Agenda, Nemesis

# CONTENTS

Pretty Guardian SAILORMOON

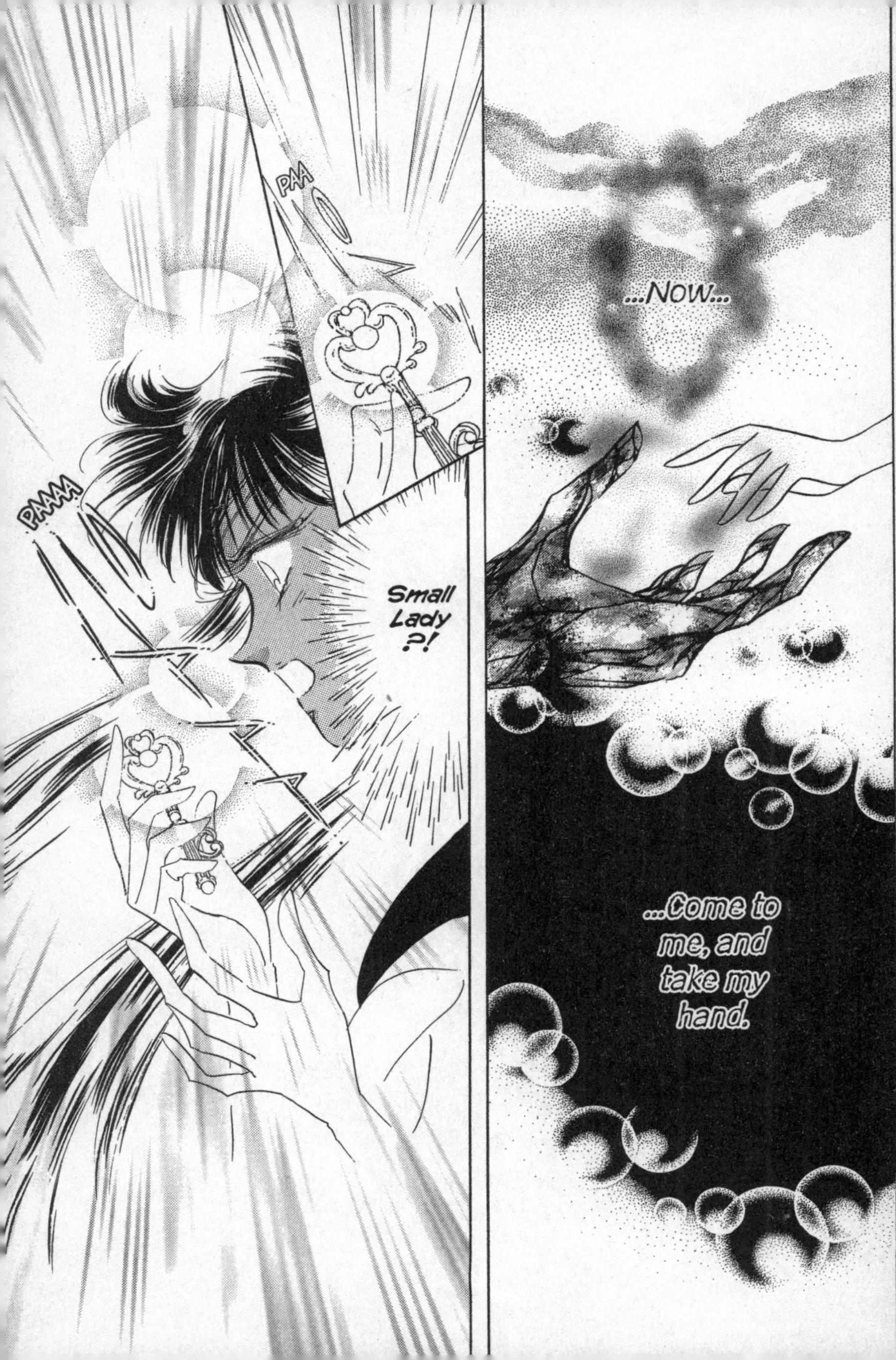
...NOW...
...Come to me, and take my hand.
PAA
PAAAA
Small Lady ?!

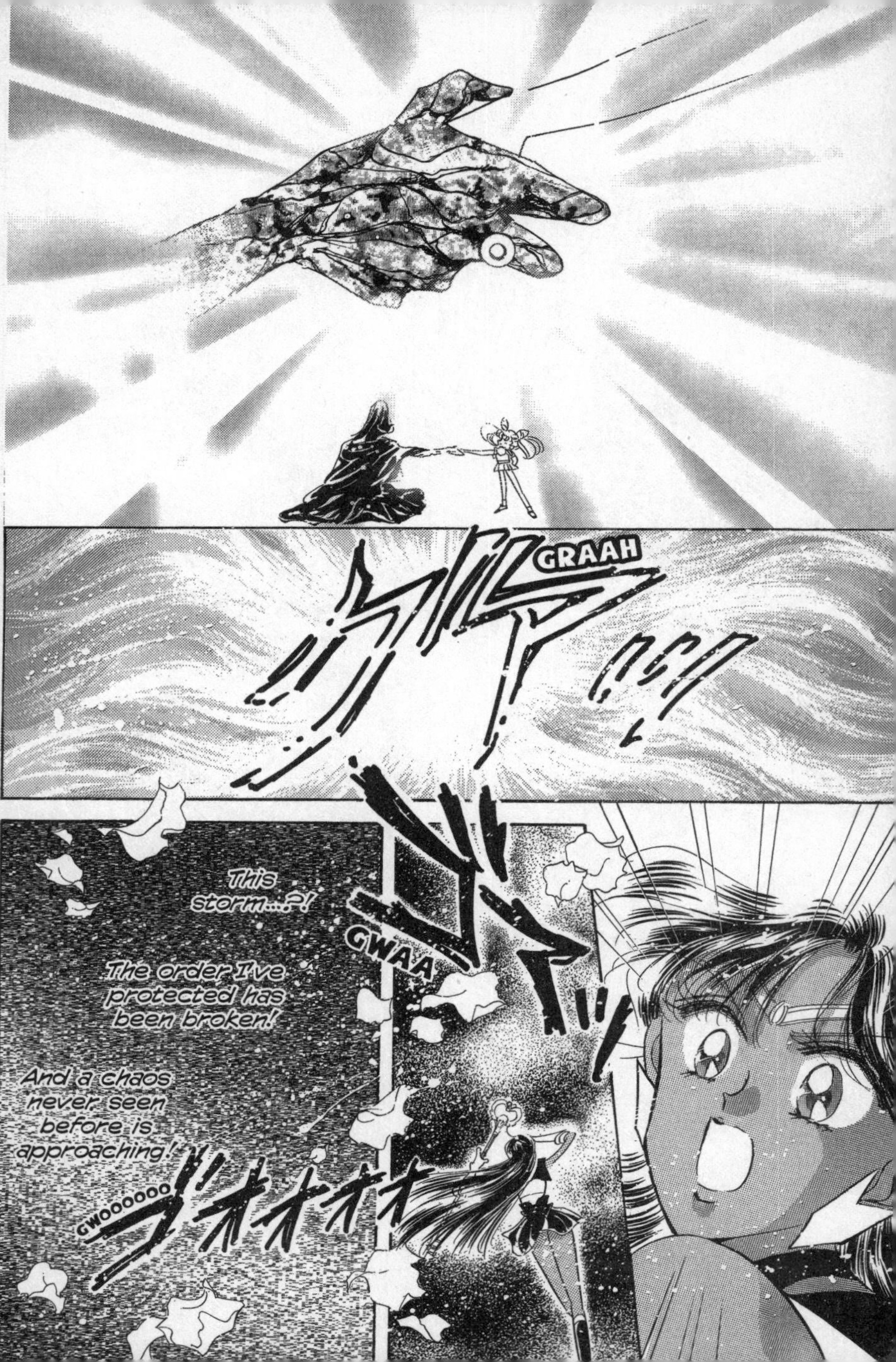
GRAAH
This storm...?!
GWAA
The order I've protected has been broken!
And a chaos never seen before is approaching!
GWOOOOOO

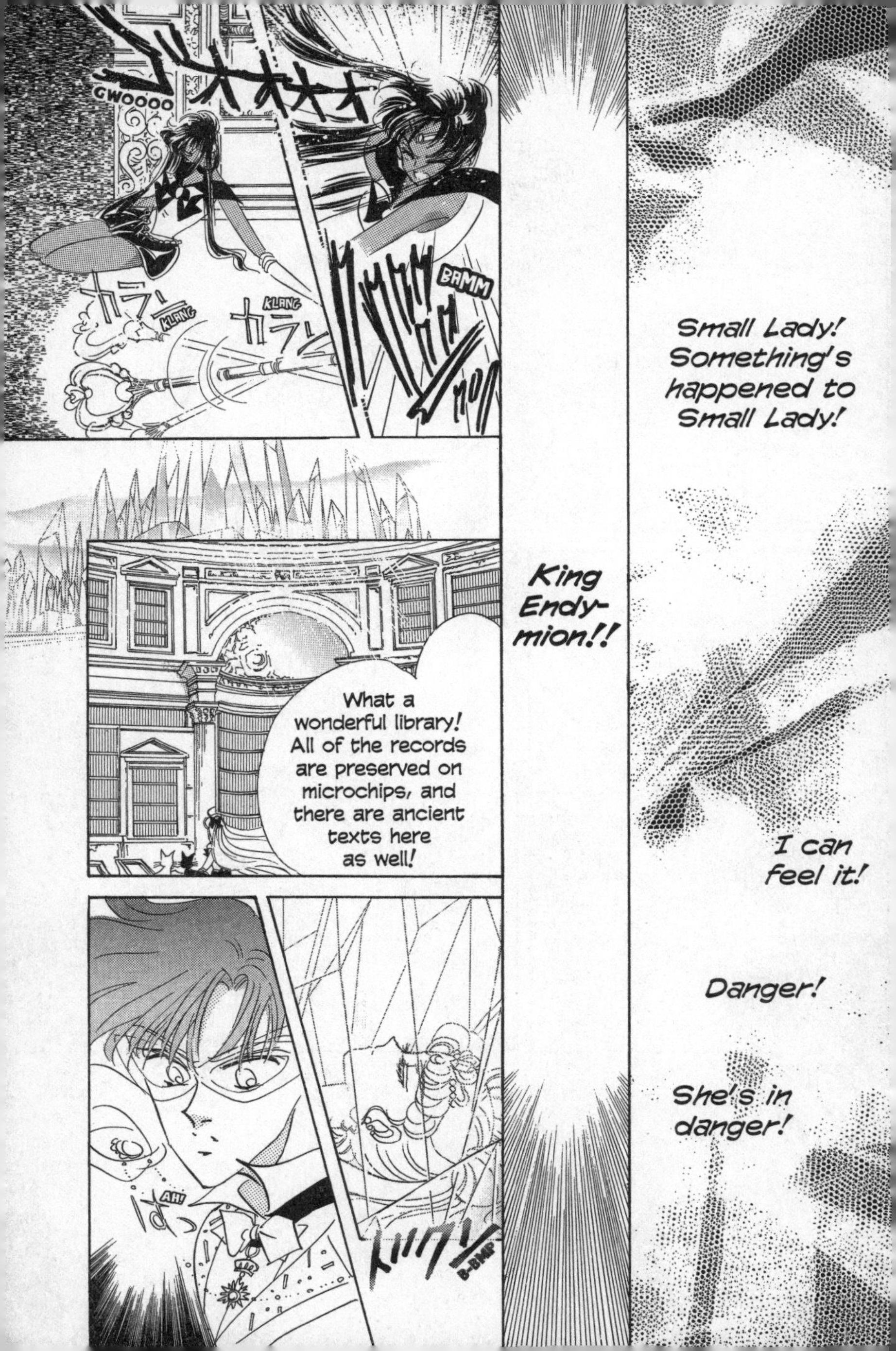
Small Lady! Something's happened to Small Lady!
I can feel it!
Danger!
She's in danger!
King Endymion!!
GWOOOO
BAMM
KLANG
KLANG
What a wonderful library! All of the records are preserved on microchips, and there are ancient texts here as well!
B-BMP
AH!

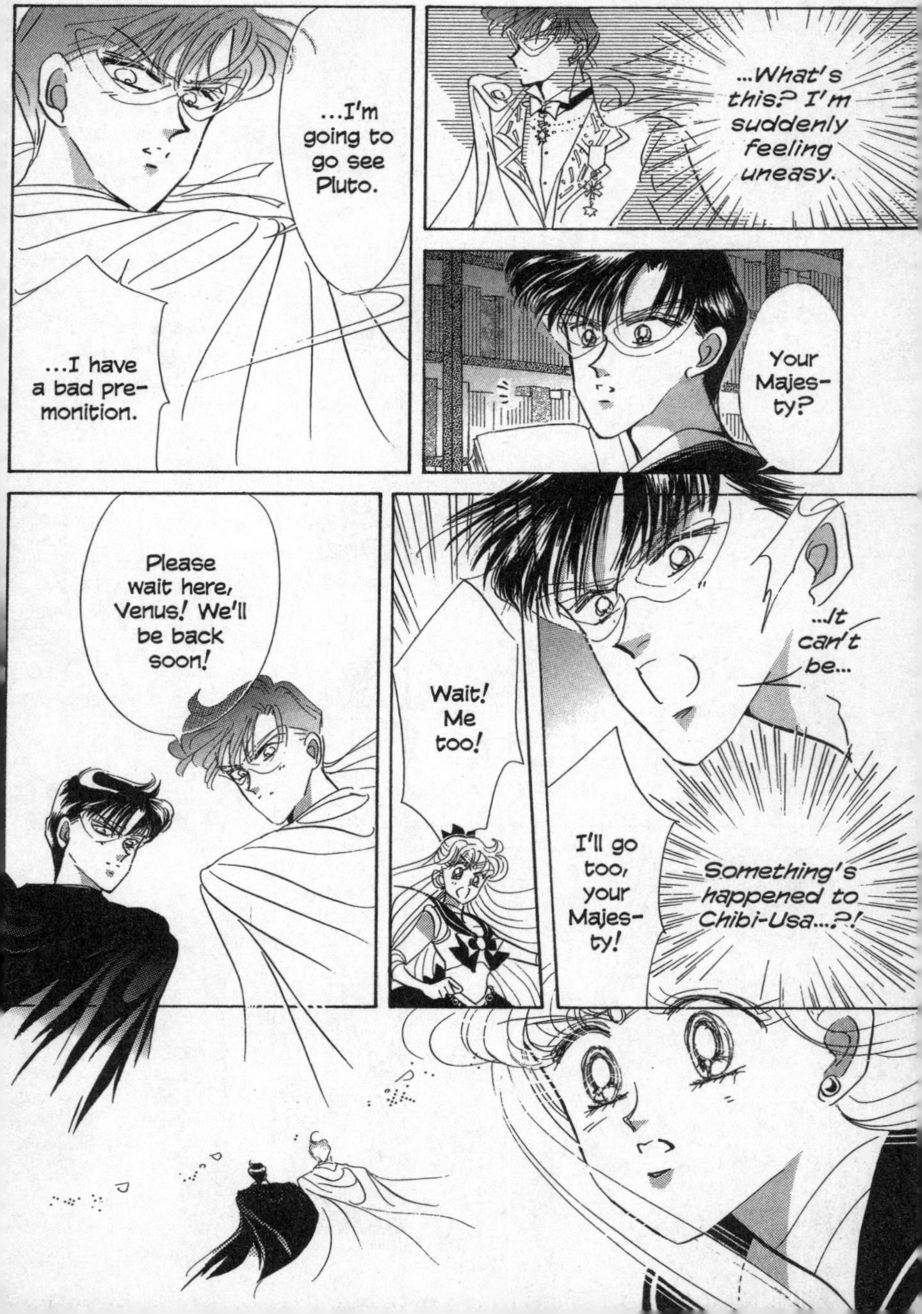
...What's this? I'm suddenly feeling uneasy.
Your Majes-ty?
...I'm going to go see Pluto.
...I have a bad pre-monition.
...It can't be...
Something's happened to Chibi-Usa...?!
I'll go too, your Majes-ty!
Wait! Me too!
Please wait here, Venus! We'll be back soon!

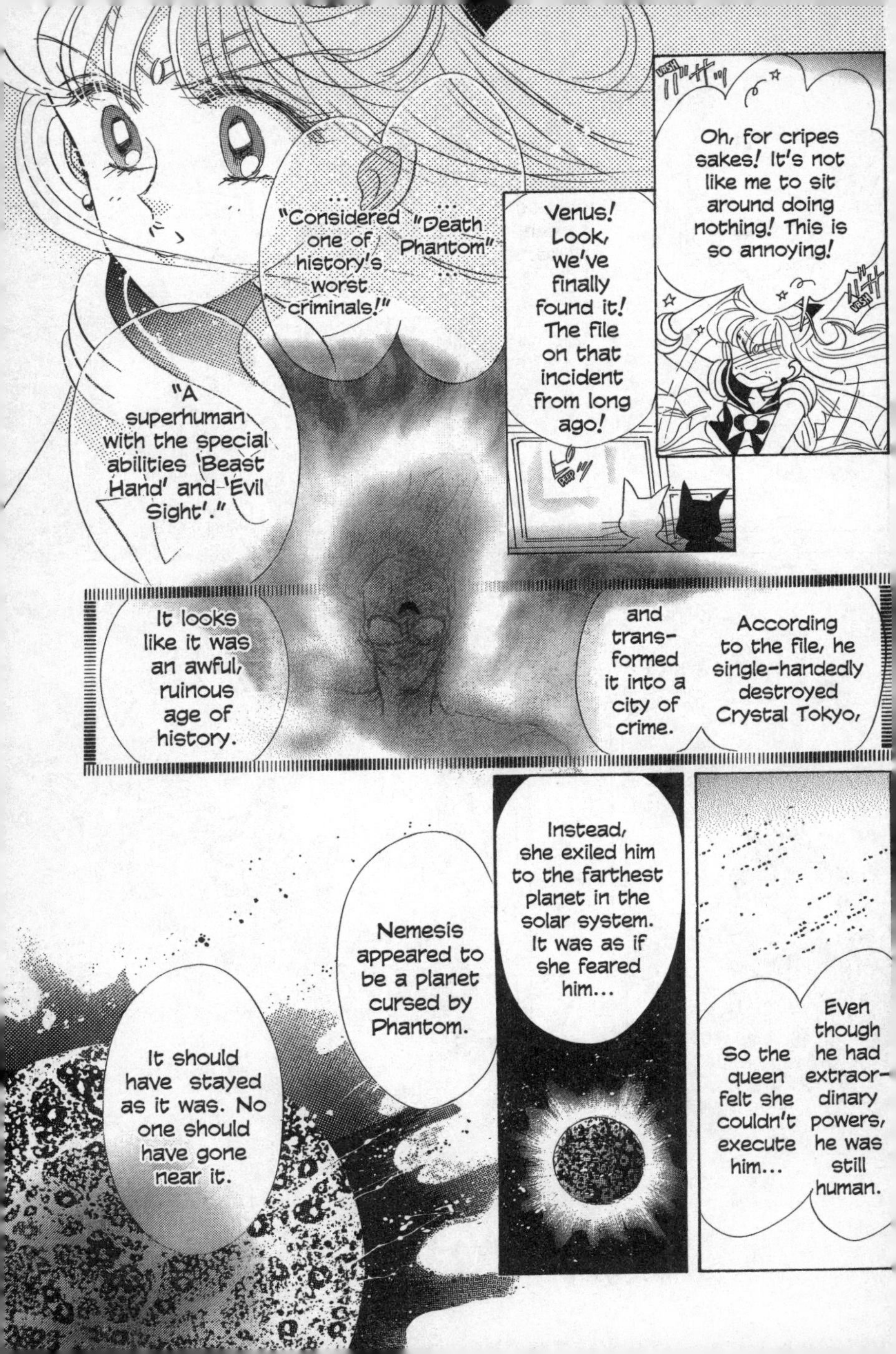

VRSH
Oh, for cripes sakes! It's not like me to sit around doing nothing! This is so annoying!
VRSH
Venus! Look, we've finally found it! The file on that incident from long ago!
..."Death Phantom"...
..."Considered one of history's worst criminals!"
"A superhuman with the special abilities 'Beast Hand' and 'Evil Sight'."
According to the file, he single-handedly destroyed Crystal Tokyo,
and trans-formed it into a city of crime.
It looks like it was an awful, ruinous age of history.
Even though he had extraor-dinary powers, he was still human.
So the queen felt she couldn't execute him...
Instead, she exiled him to the farthest planet in the solar system. It was as if she feared him...
Nemesis appeared to be a planet cursed by Phantom.
It should have stayed as it was. No one should have gone near it.

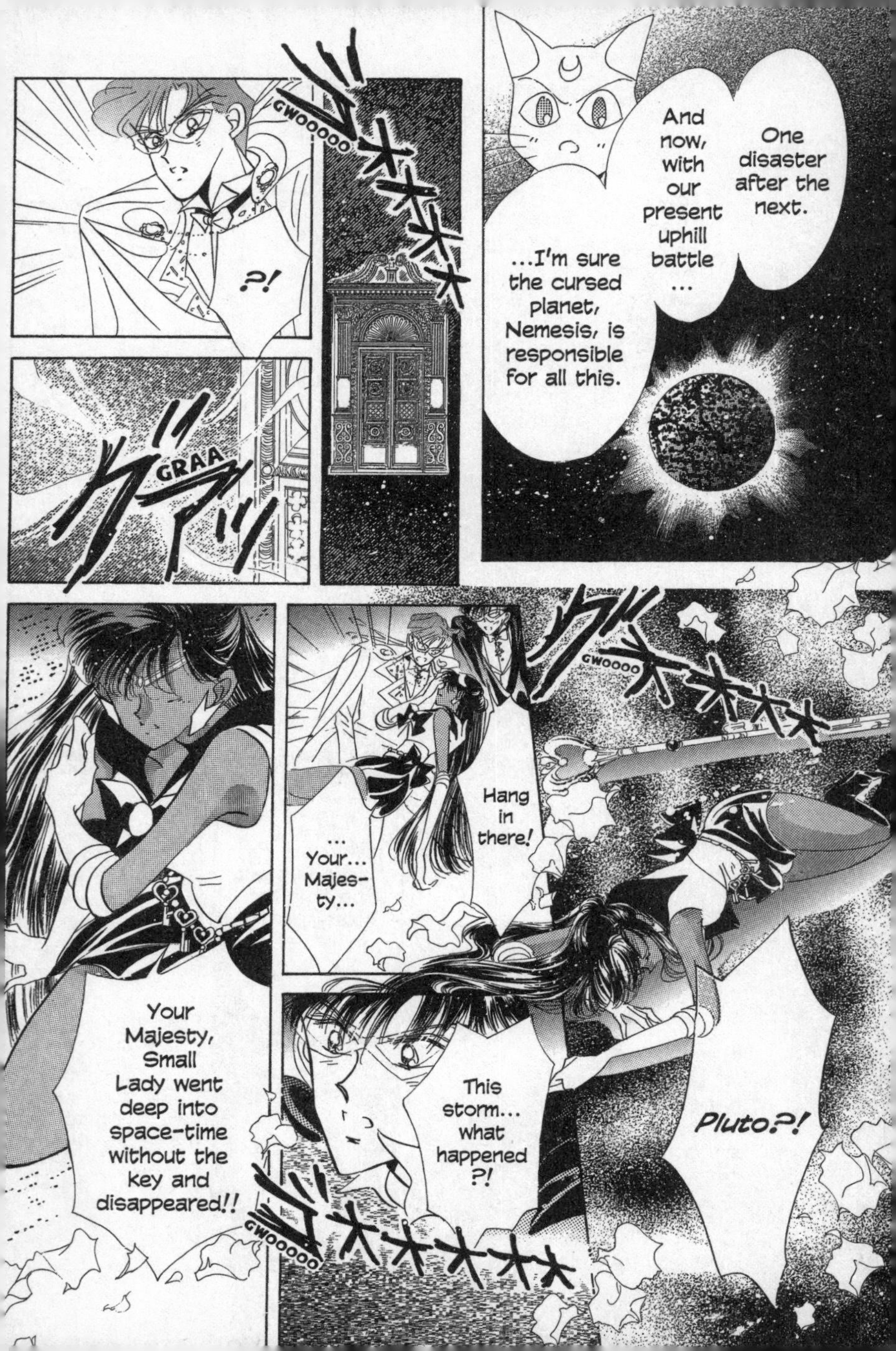

One disaster after the next.
And now, with our present uphill battle ...
...I'm sure the cursed planet, Nemesis, is responsible for all this.
GWOOOOO
?!
GRAA
GWOOOO
Hang in there!
... Your... Majesty...
Pluto?!
This storm... what happened ?!
Your Majesty, Small Lady went deep into space-time without the key and disappeared!!
GWOOOOO

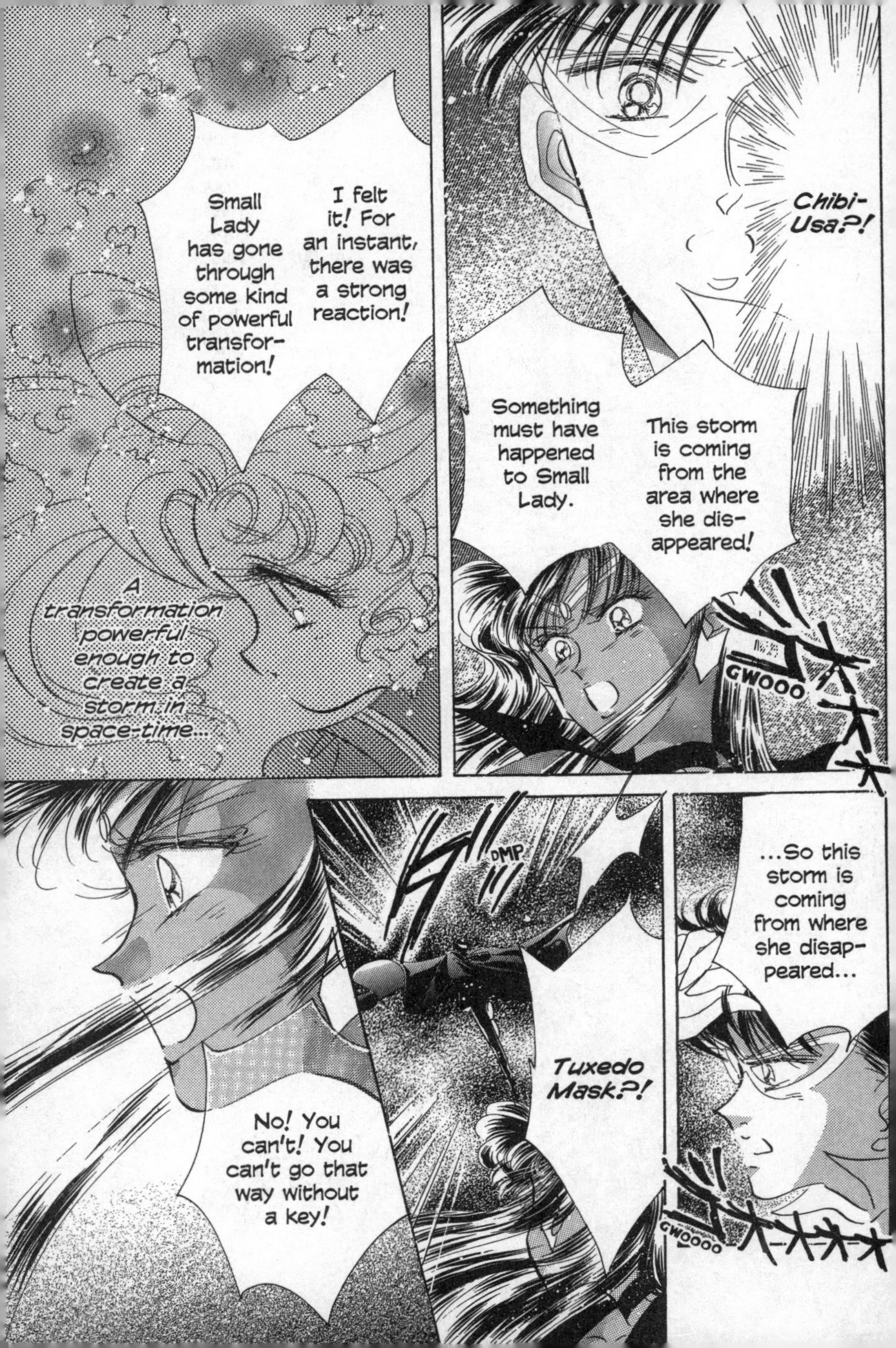
Chibi-Usa?!
This storm is coming from the area where she disappeared!
Something must have happened to Small Lady.
GWOOO
I felt it! For an instant, there was a strong reaction!
Small Lady has gone through some kind of powerful transformation!
A transformation powerful enough to create a storm in space-time...
...So this storm is coming from where she disappeared...
GWOOOO
DMP
Tuxedo Mask?!
No! You can't! You can't go that way without a key!

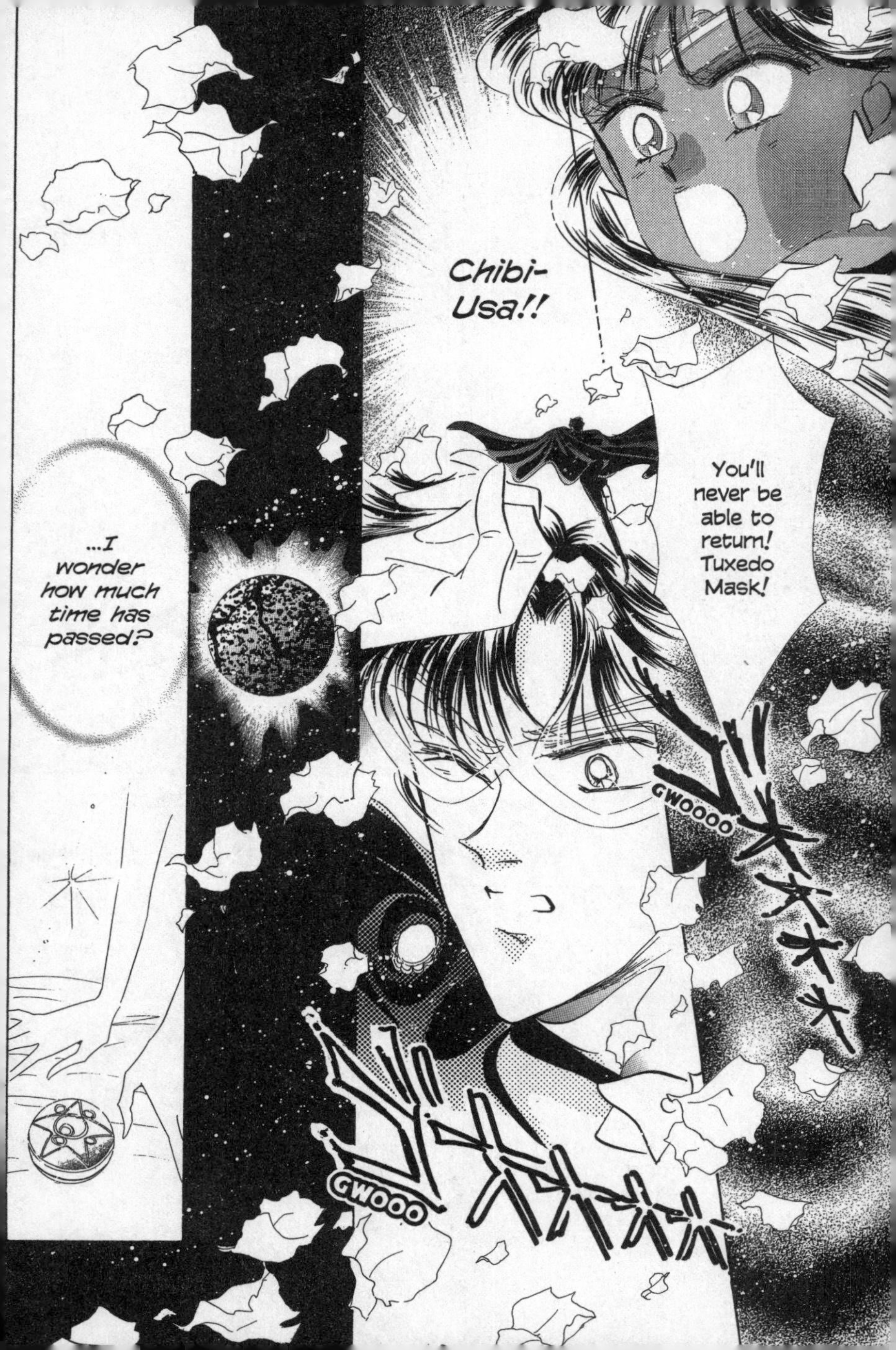
Chibi-Usa!!
You'll never be able to return! Tuxedo Mask!
GWOOOO
GWOOO
...I wonder how much time has passed?

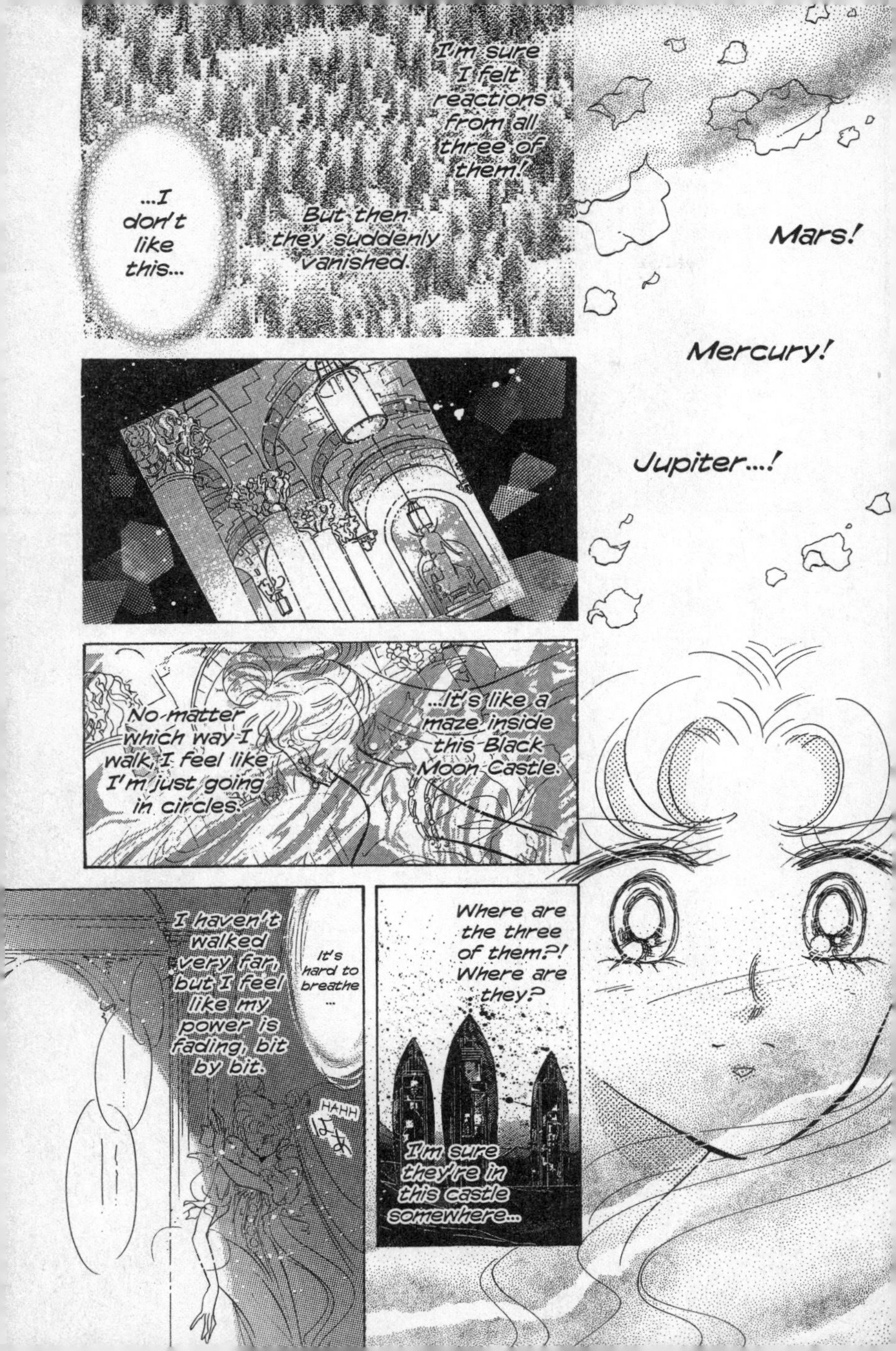
Mars!
Mercury!
Jupiter...!
I'm sure I felt reactions from all three of them!
But then they suddenly vanished.
...I don't like this...
...It's like a maze inside this Black Moon Castle.
No matter which way I walk, I feel like I'm just going in circles.
Where are the three of them?! Where are they?
I'm sure they're in this castle somewhere...
I haven't walked very far, but I feel like my power is fading, bit by bit.
It's hard to breathe...
HAHH

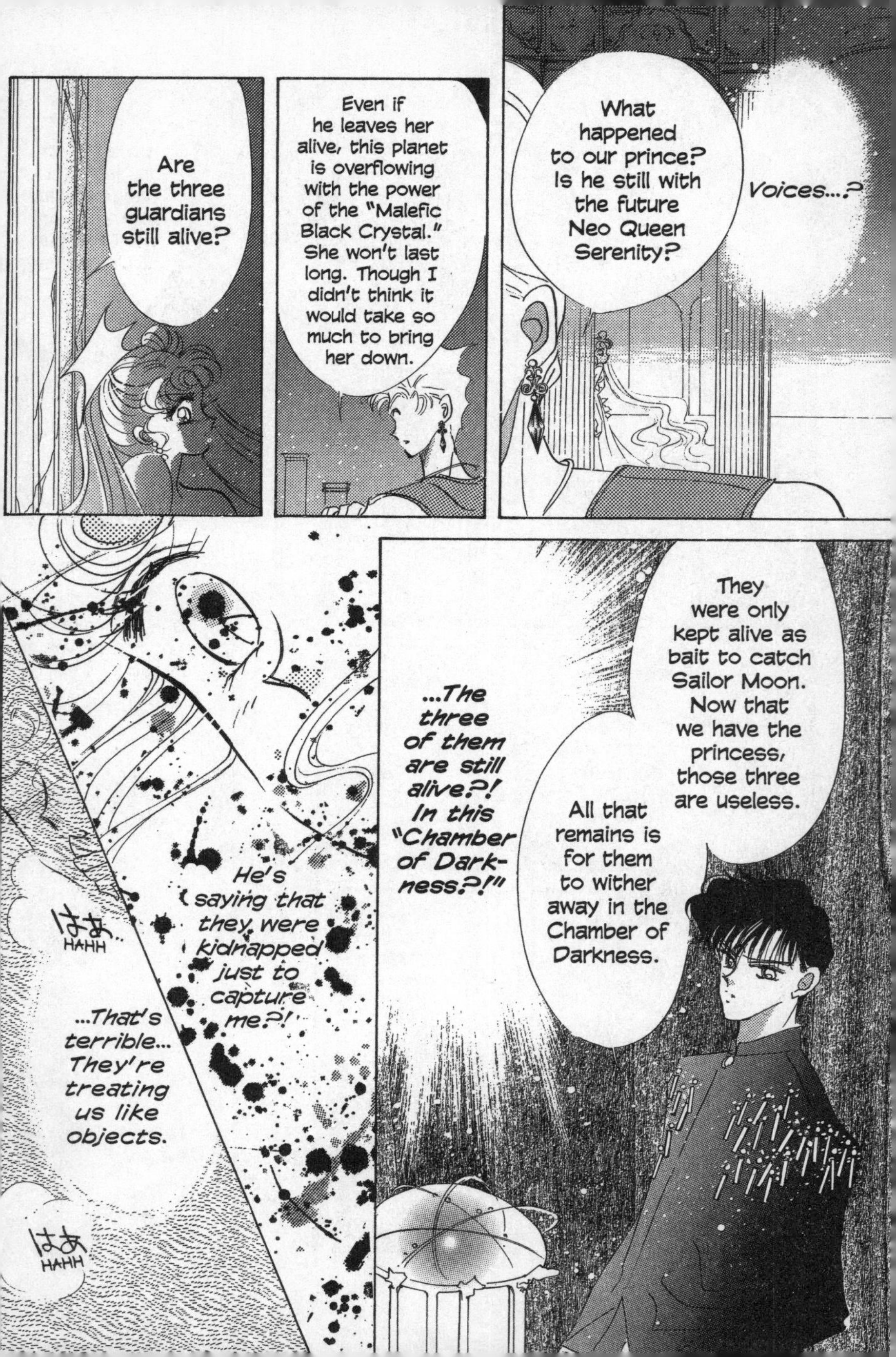
What happened to our prince? Is he still with the future Neo Queen Serenity?
Voices...?
Even if he leaves her alive, this planet is overflowing with the power of the "Malefic Black Crystal." She won't last long. Though I didn't think it would take so much to bring her down.
Are the three guardians still alive?
They were only kept alive as bait to catch Sailor Moon. Now that we have the princess, those three are useless.
All that remains is for them to wither away in the Chamber of Darkness.
...The three of them are still alive?! In this "Chamber of Dark-ness?!"
He's saying that they were kidnapped just to capture me?!
はあ HAHH
...That's terrible... They're treating us like objects.
はあ HAHH

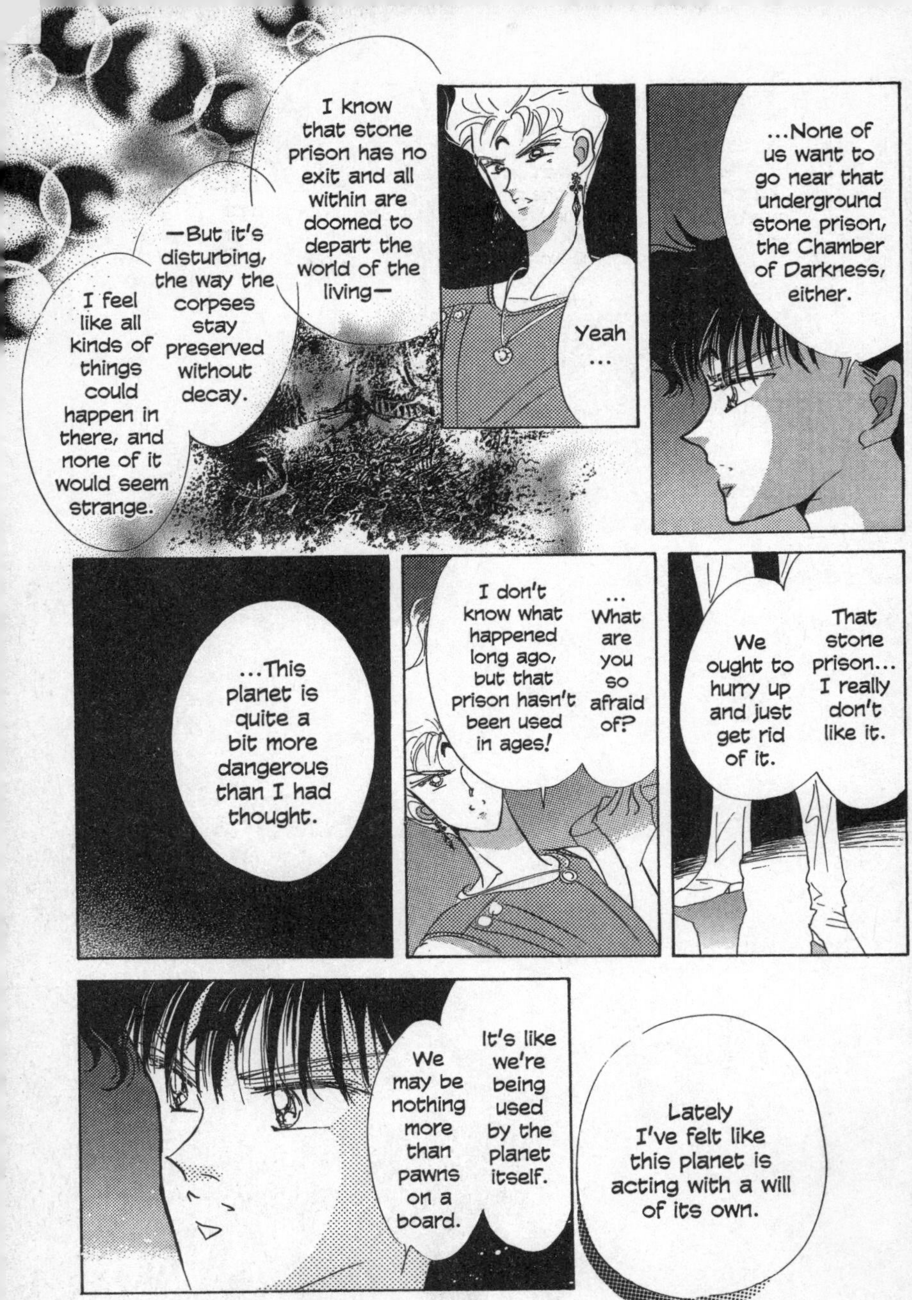
...None of us want to go near that underground stone prison, the Chamber of Darkness, either.
Yeah ...
I know that stone prison has no exit and all within are doomed to depart the world of the living—
—But it's disturbing, the way the corpses stay preserved without decay.
I feel like all kinds of things could happen in there, and none of it would seem strange.
That stone prison... I really don't like it.
We ought to hurry up and just get rid of it.
... What are you so afraid of?
I don't know what happened long ago, but that prison hasn't been used in ages!
...This planet is quite a bit more dangerous than I had thought.
Lately I've felt like this planet is acting with a will of its own.
It's like we're being used by the planet itself.
We may be nothing more than pawns on a board.

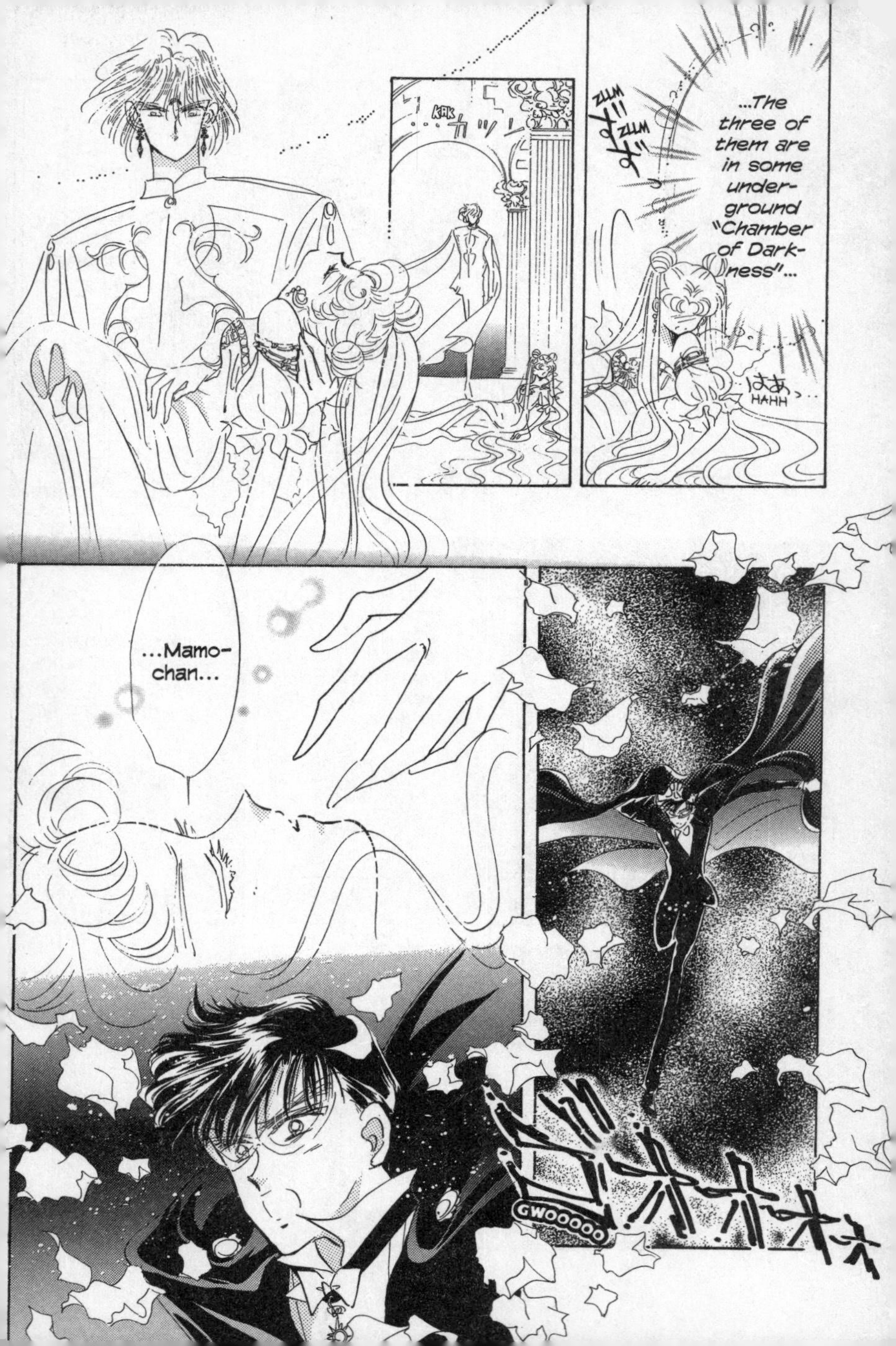
...The three of them are in some under-ground "Chamber of Dark-ness"...
ずず
ZUUM ZUUM
はあっ
HAHH
カツン
KAK
GWOOOOO
...Mamo-chan...

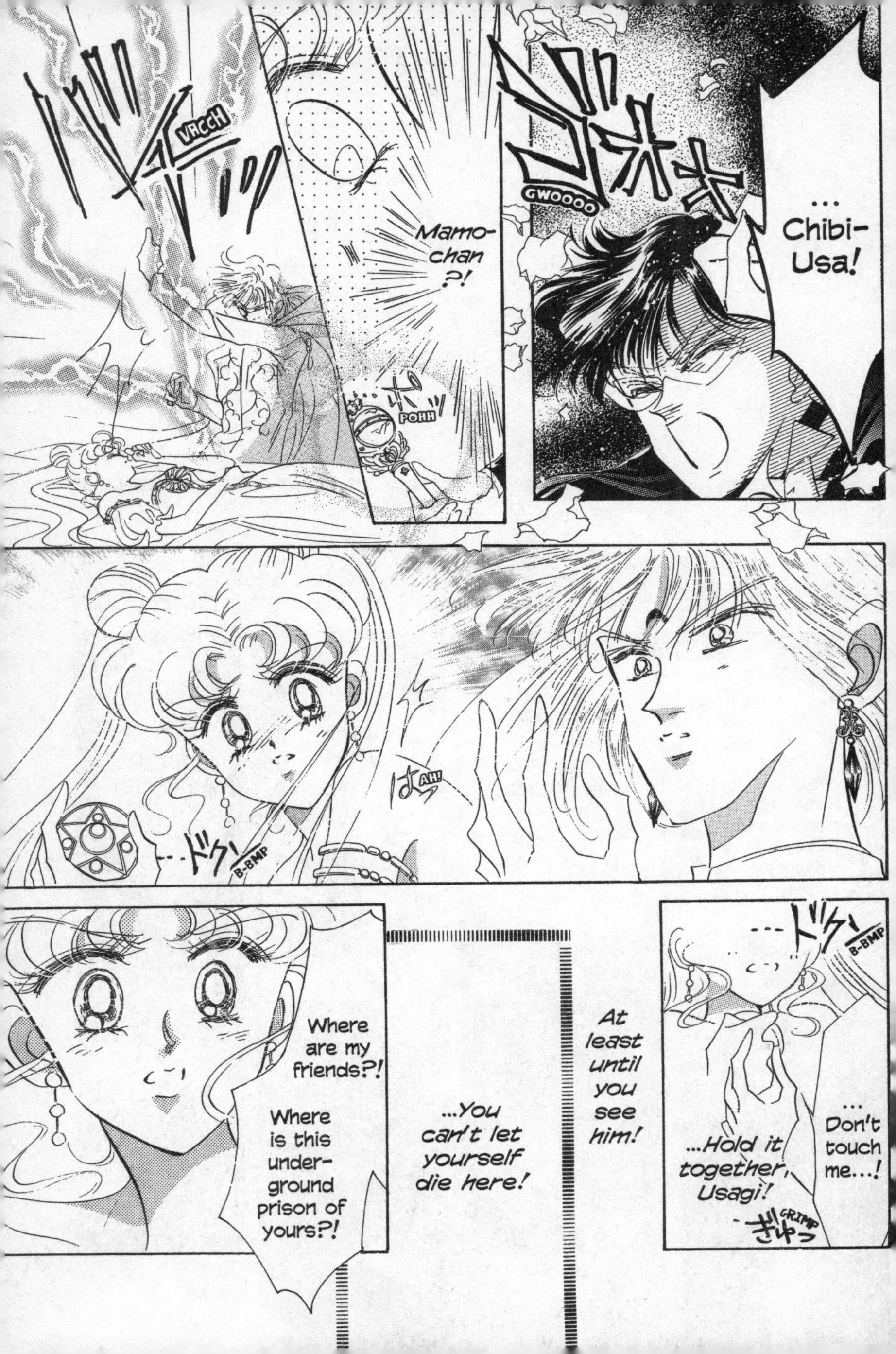
GWOOOO
... Chibi-Usa!
Mamo-chan ?!
POHH
VACCH
AH!
B-BMP
B-BMP
... Don't touch me...!
...Hold it together, Usagi!
GRIMP
At least until you see him!
...You can't let yourself die here!
Where are my friends?!
Where is this under-ground prison of yours?!

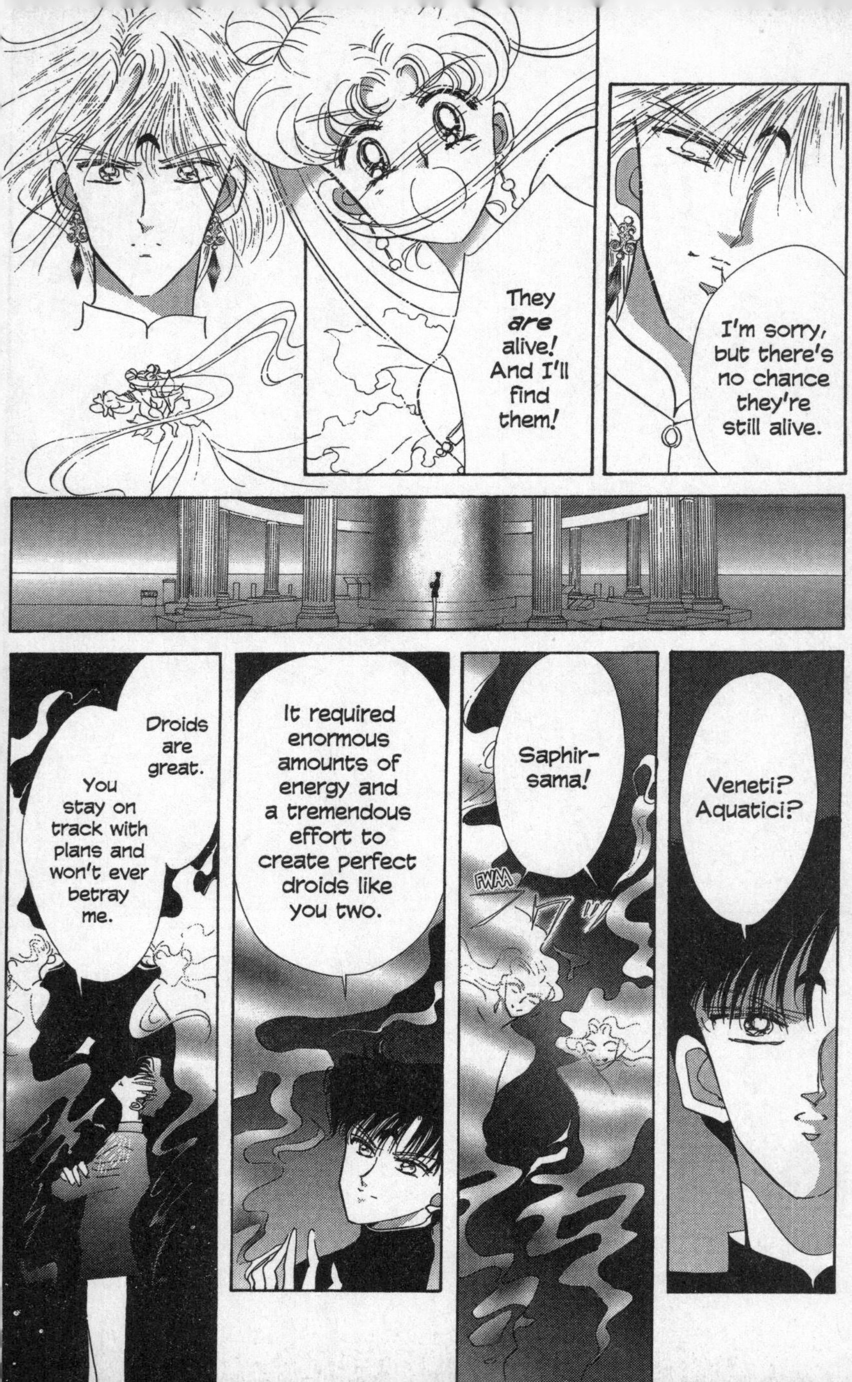
I'm sorry, but there's no chance they're still alive.
They *are* alive! And I'll find them!
Veneti? Aquatici?
Saphir-sama!
FWAA
It required enormous amounts of energy and a tremendous effort to create perfect droids like you two.
Droids are great.
You stay on track with plans and won't ever betray me.

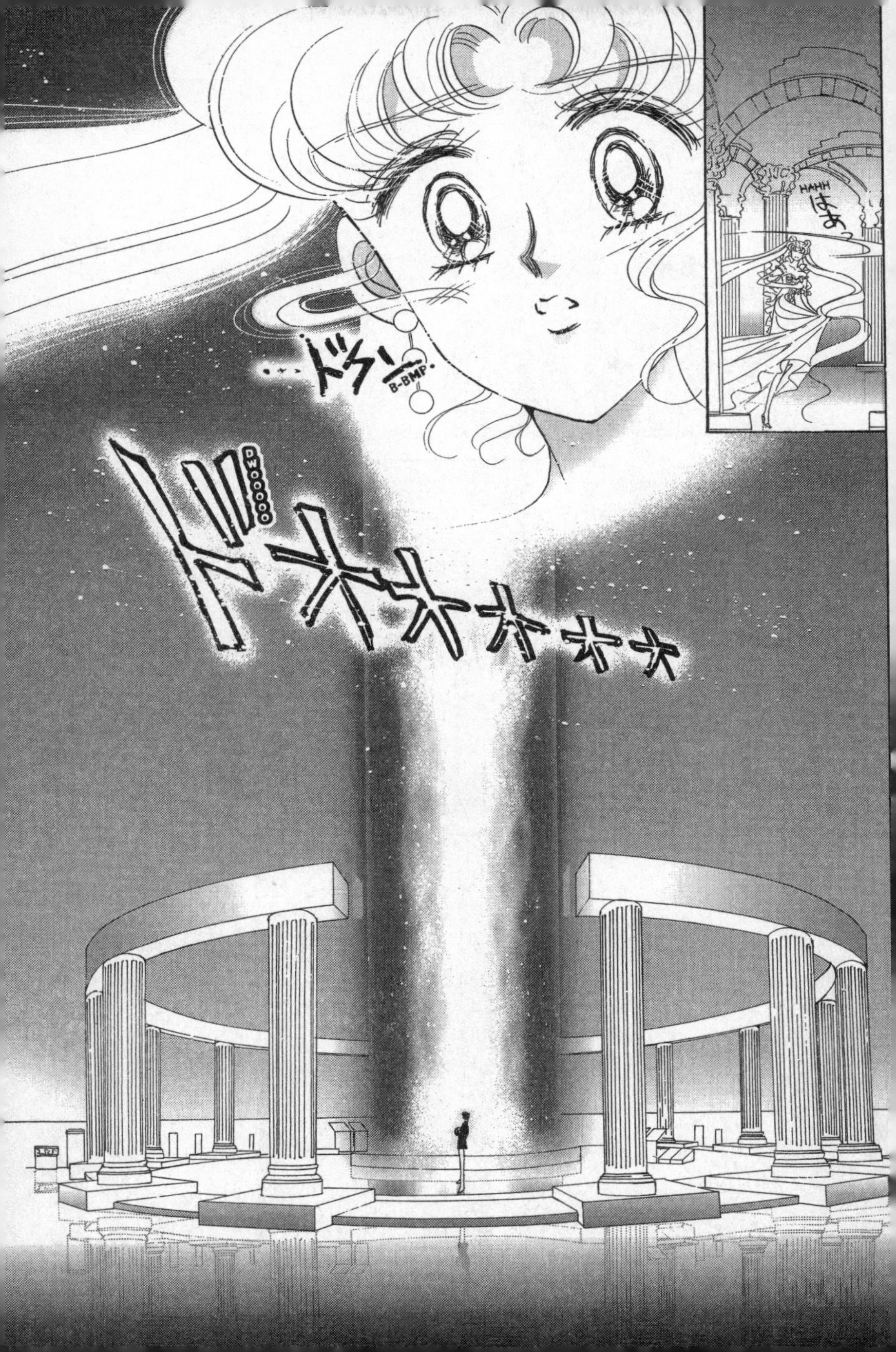
HAHH
はあっ
ドクン
B-BMP.
ドオオオオオ
DWOOOOO

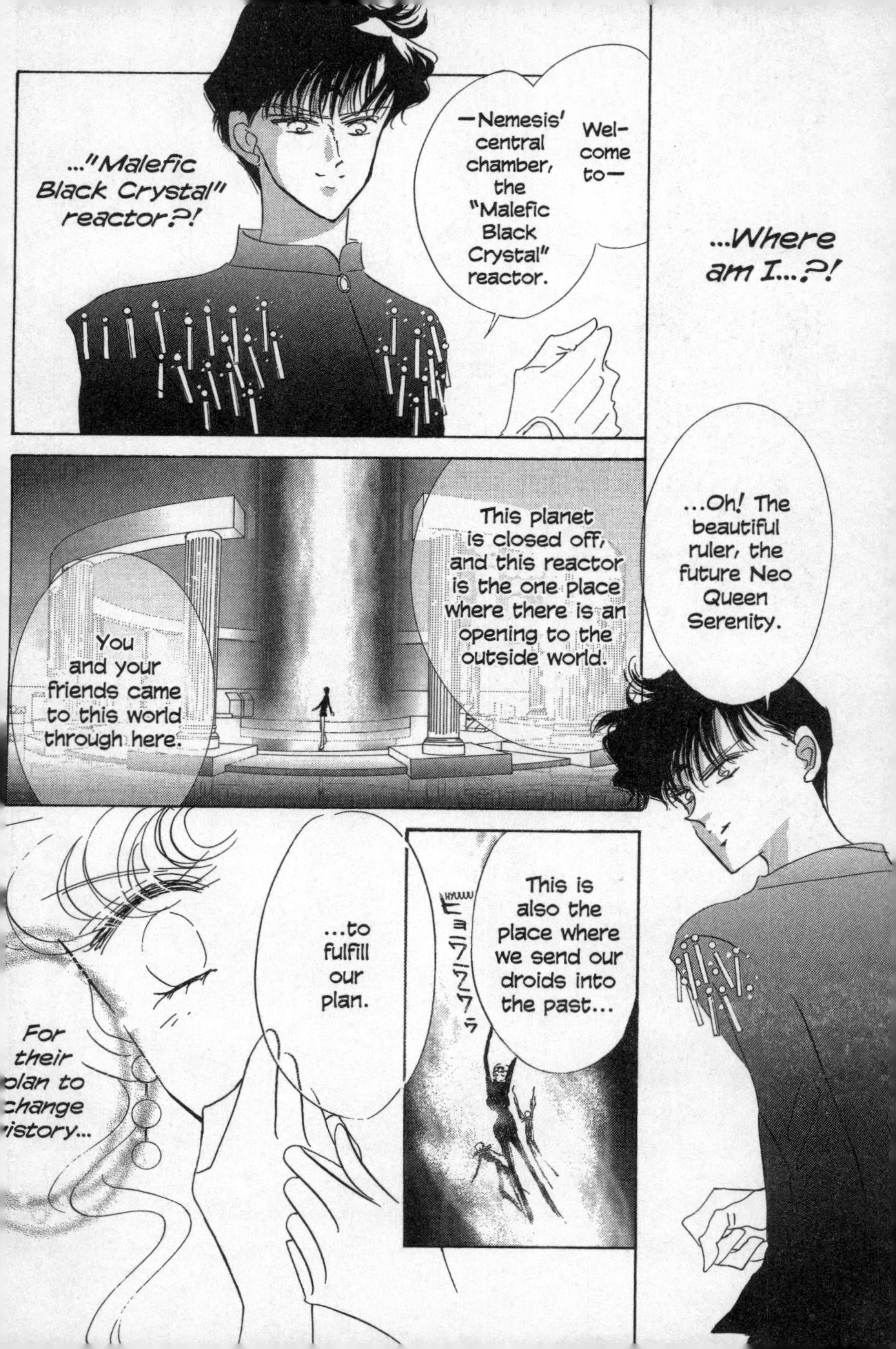
...Where am I...?!
...Oh! The beautiful ruler, the future Neo Queen Serenity.
Wel-come to—
—Nemesis' central chamber, the "Malefic Black Crystal" reactor.
..."Malefic Black Crystal" reactor?!
This planet is closed off, and this reactor is the one place where there is an opening to the outside world.
You and your friends came to this world through here.
HYUUU
This is also the place where we send our droids into the past...
...to fulfill our plan.
For their plan to change history...

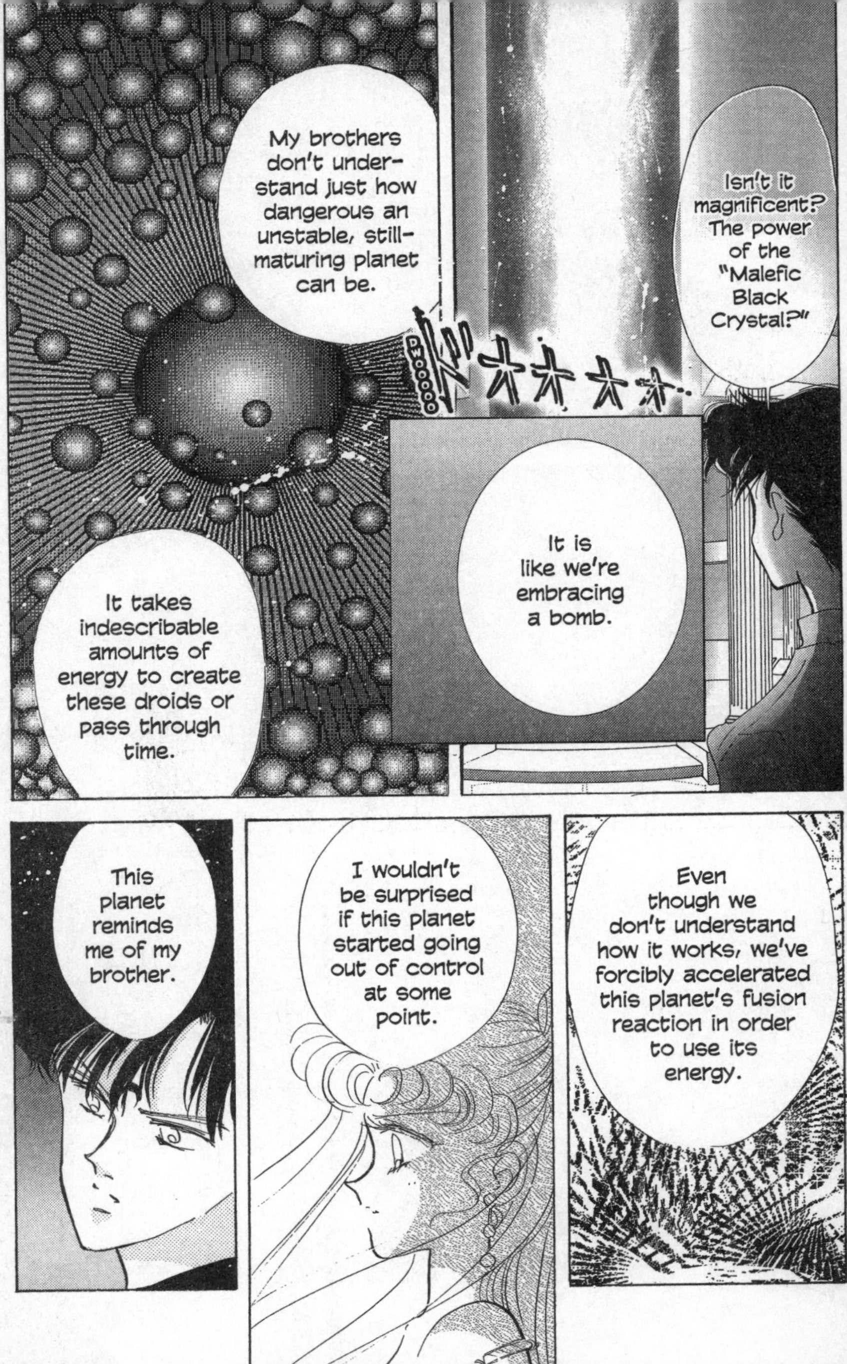
Isn't it magnificent? The power of the "Malefic Black Crystal?"
DWOOOOO
It is like we're embracing a bomb.
My brothers don't under-stand just how dangerous an unstable, still-maturing planet can be.
It takes indescribable amounts of energy to create these droids or pass through time.
Even though we don't understand how it works, we've forcibly accelerated this planet's fusion reaction in order to use its energy.
I wouldn't be surprised if this planet started going out of control at some point.
This planet reminds me of my brother.

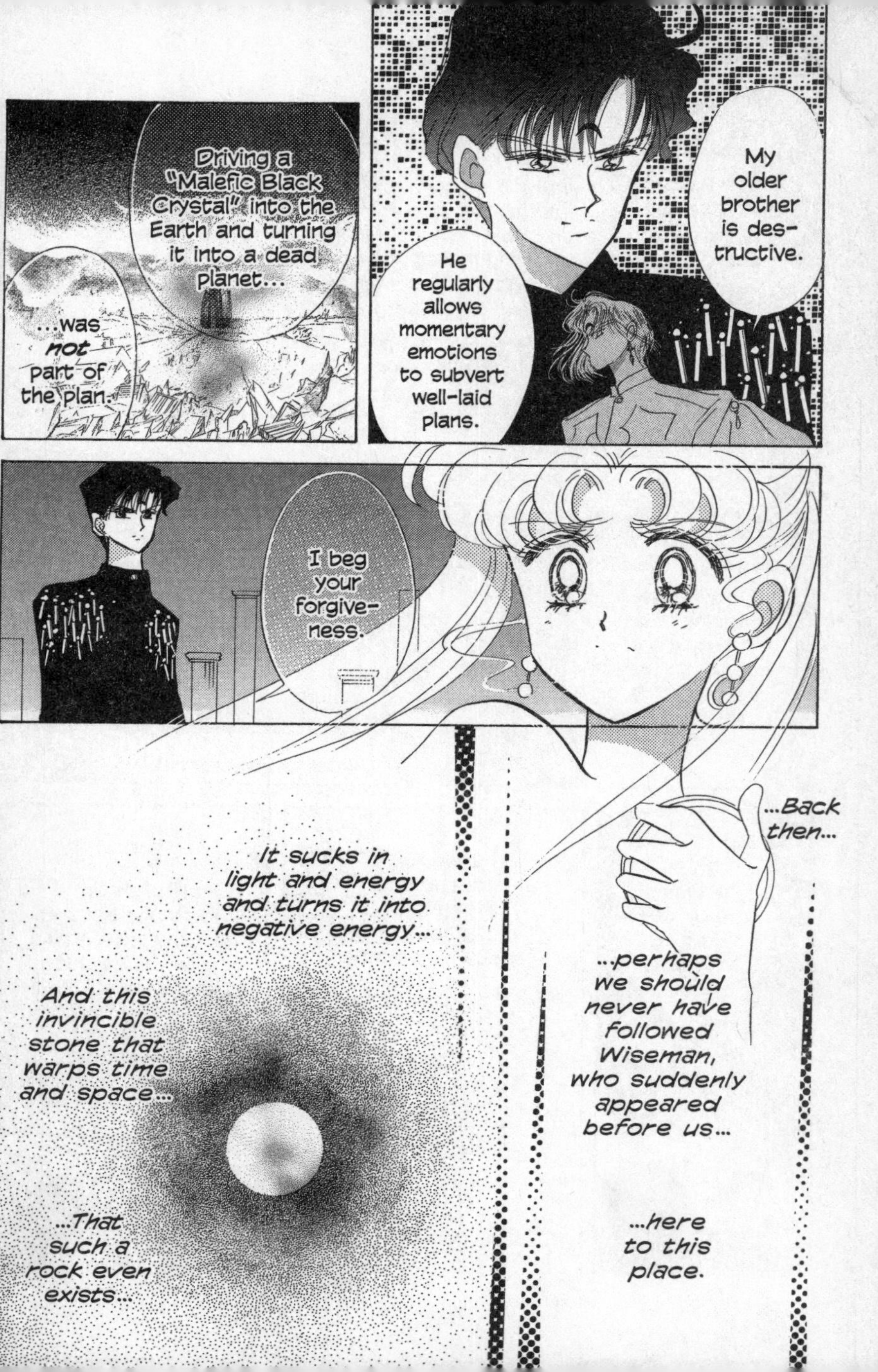

My older brother is destructive.
He regularly allows momentary emotions to subvert well-laid plans.
Driving a "Malefic Black Crystal" into the Earth and turning it into a dead planet...
...was **not** part of the plan.
I beg your forgiveness.
...Back then...
...perhaps we should never have followed Wiseman, who suddenly appeared before us...
...here to this place.
It sucks in light and energy and turns it into negative energy...
And this invincible stone that warps time and space...
...That such a rock even exists...

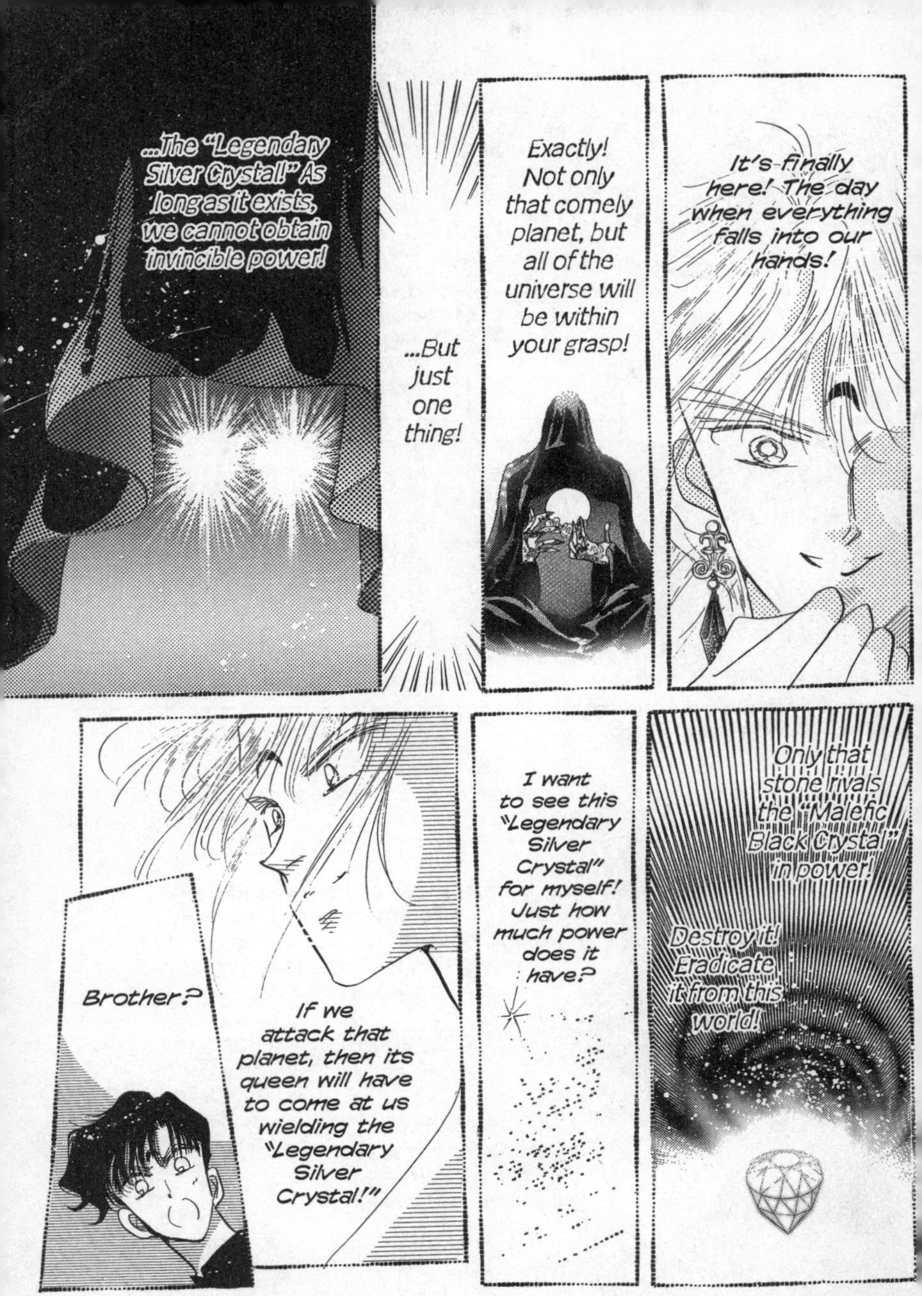
It's finally here! The day when everything falls into our hands!
Exactly! Not only that comely planet, but all of the universe will be within your grasp!
...But just one thing!
...The "Legendary Silver Crystal!" As long as it exists, we cannot obtain invincible power!
Only that stone rivals the "Malefic Black Crystal" in power!
Destroy it! Eradicate it from this world!
I want to see this "Legendary Silver Crystal" for myself! Just how much power does it have?
If we attack that planet, then its queen will have to come at us wielding the "Legendary Silver Crystal!"
Brother?

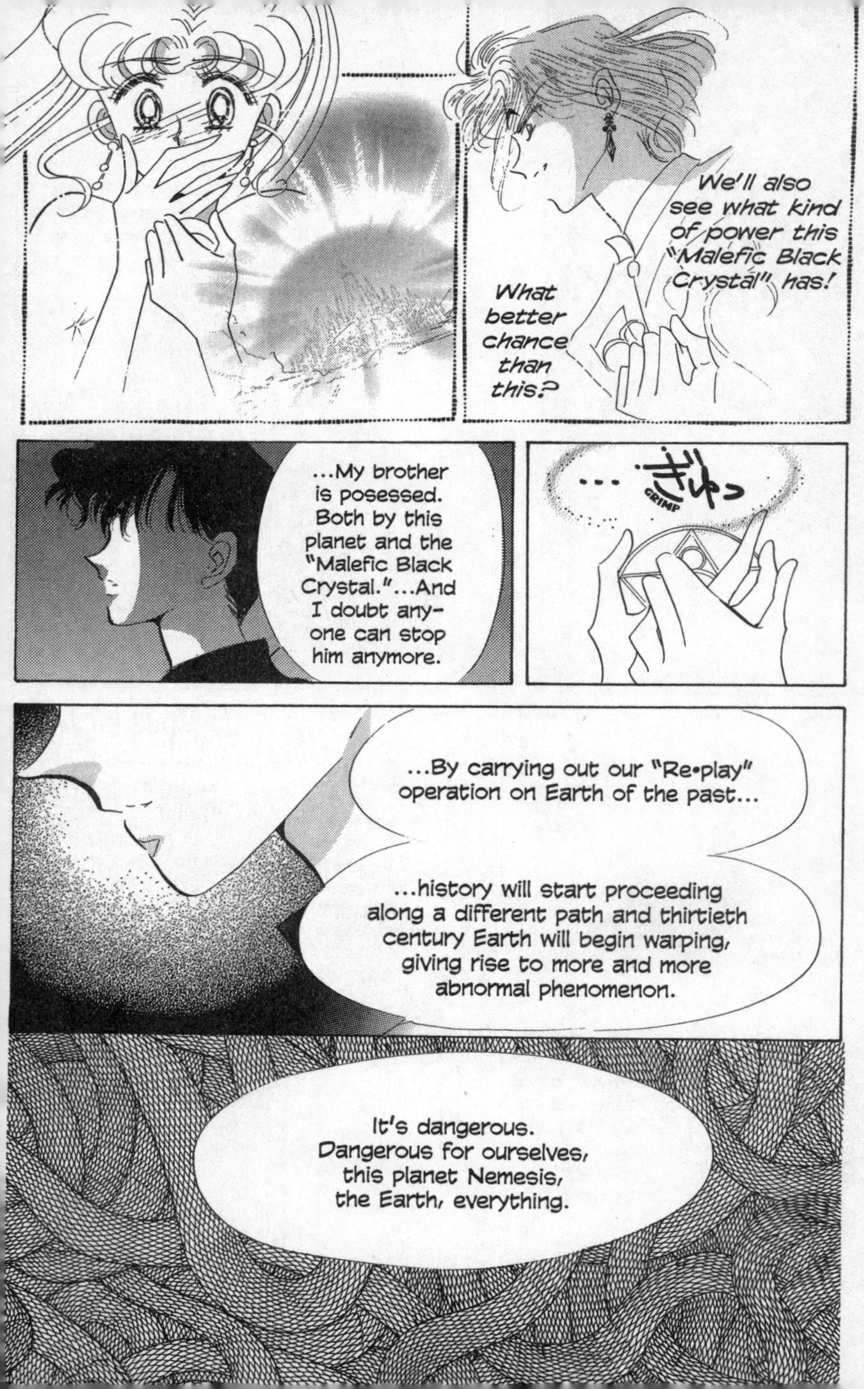
We'll also see what kind of power this "Malefic Black Crystal" has!
What better chance than this?
...
ぎゅっ
GRIMP
...My brother is posessed. Both by this planet and the "Malefic Black Crystal." ...And I doubt any-one can stop him anymore.
...By carrying out our "Re•play" operation on Earth of the past...
...history will start proceeding along a different path and thirtieth century Earth will begin warping, giving rise to more and more abnormal phenomenon.
It's dangerous. Dangerous for ourselves, this planet Nemesis, the Earth, everything.

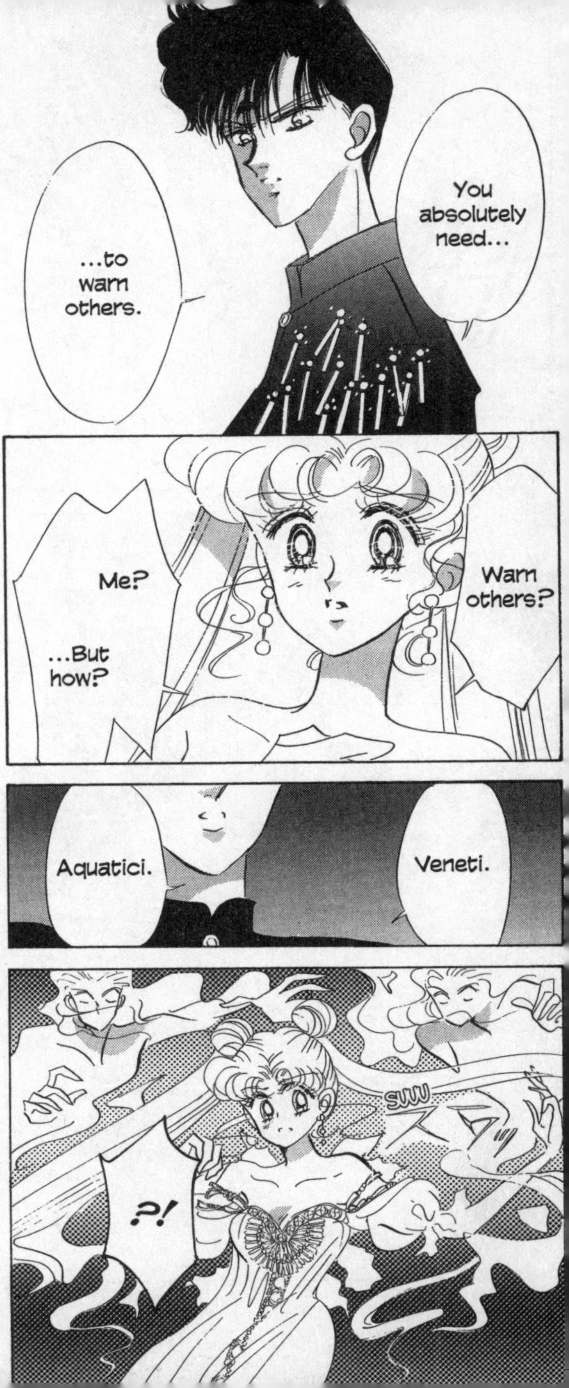
You absolutely need...
...to warn others.
Warn others?
Me?
...But how?
Veneti.
Aquatici.
SUU
?!

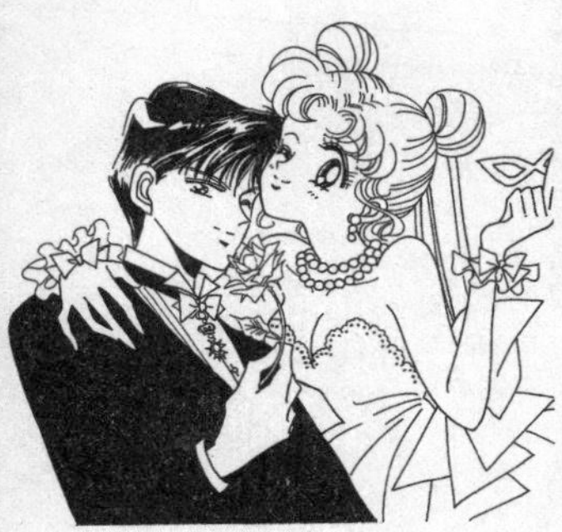

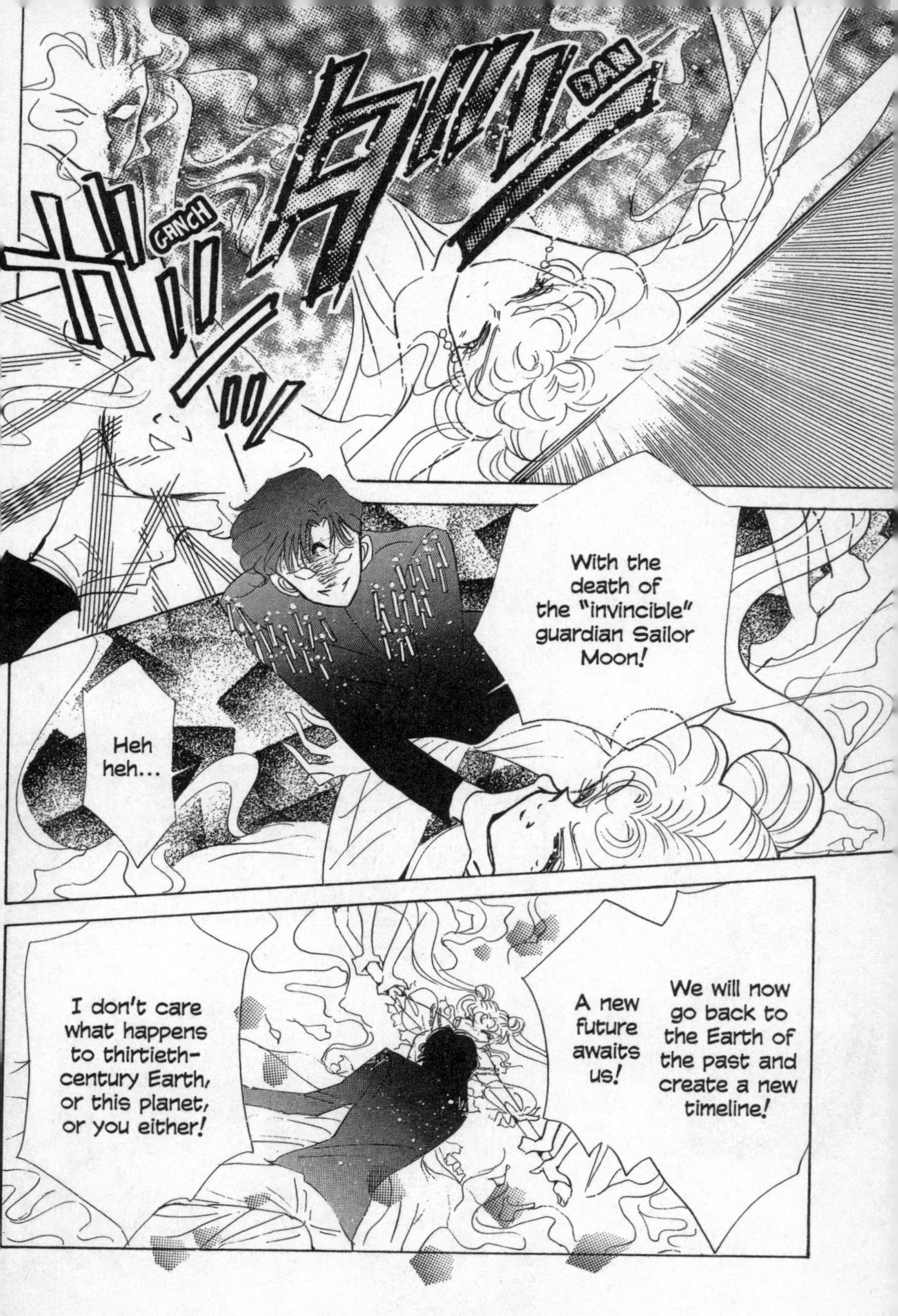
DAN
GRNCH
With the death of the "invincible" guardian Sailor Moon!
Heh heh...
We will now go back to the Earth of the past and create a new timeline!
A new future awaits us!
I don't care what happens to thirtieth-century Earth, or this planet, or you either!

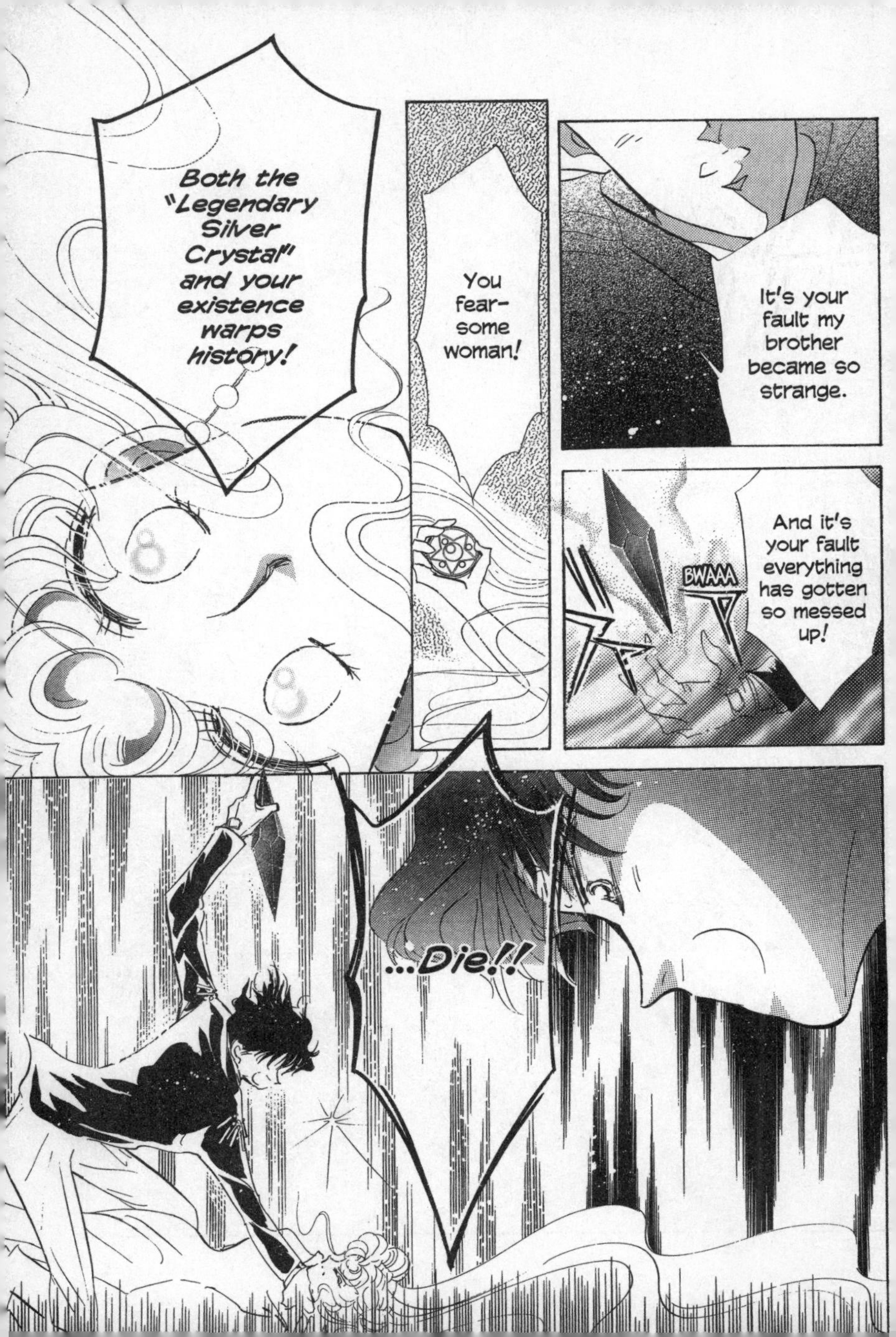
It's your fault my brother became so strange.
And it's your fault everything has gotten so messed up!
BWAAA
You fear-some woman!
Both the "Legendary Silver Crystal" and your existence warps history!
...Die!!

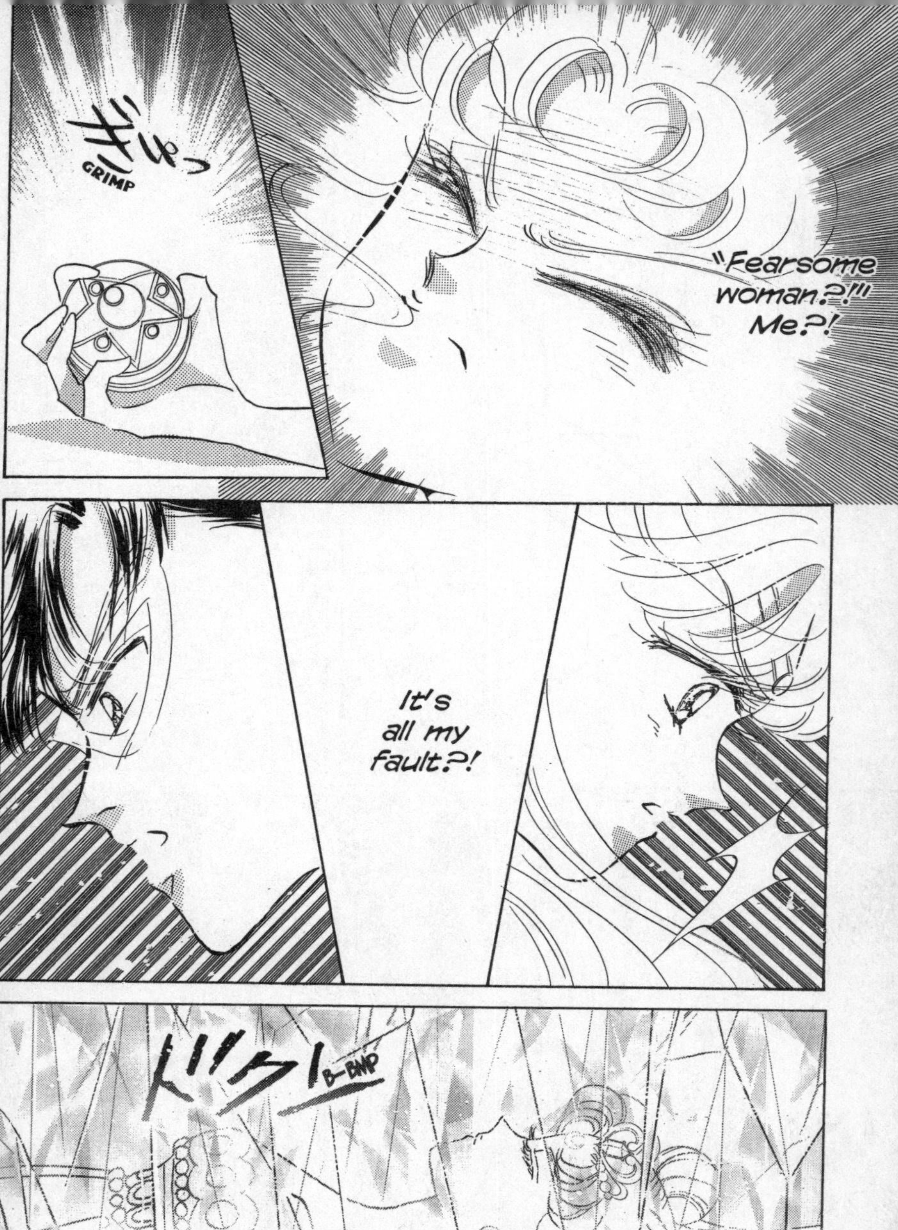
"Fearsome woman?!" Me?!
ぎゅっ
GRIMP
It's all my fault?!
B-BMP

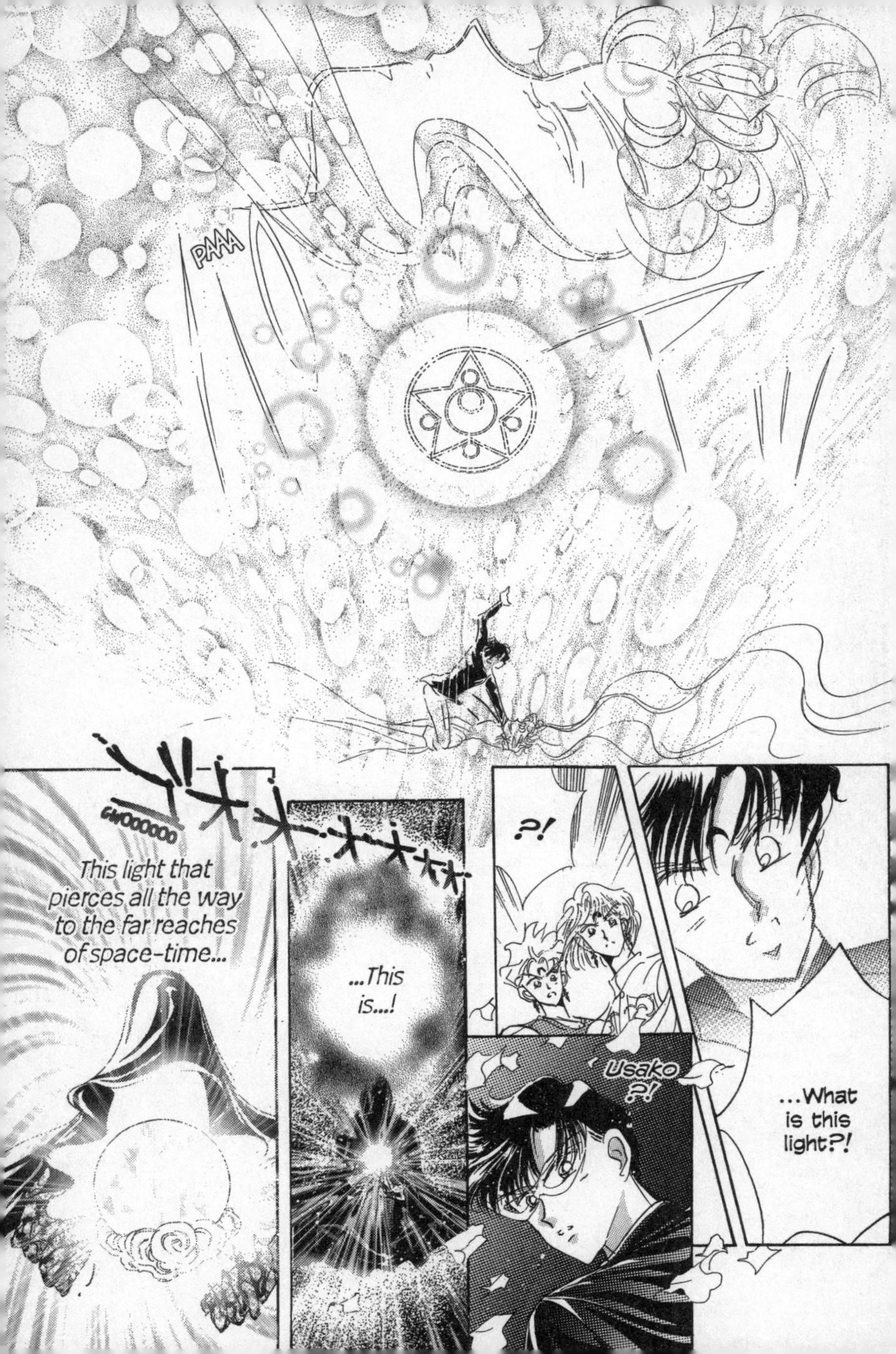
PAAA
GWOOOOOO
...What is this light?!
?!
Usako ?!
...This is...!
This light that pierces all the way to the far reaches of space-time...

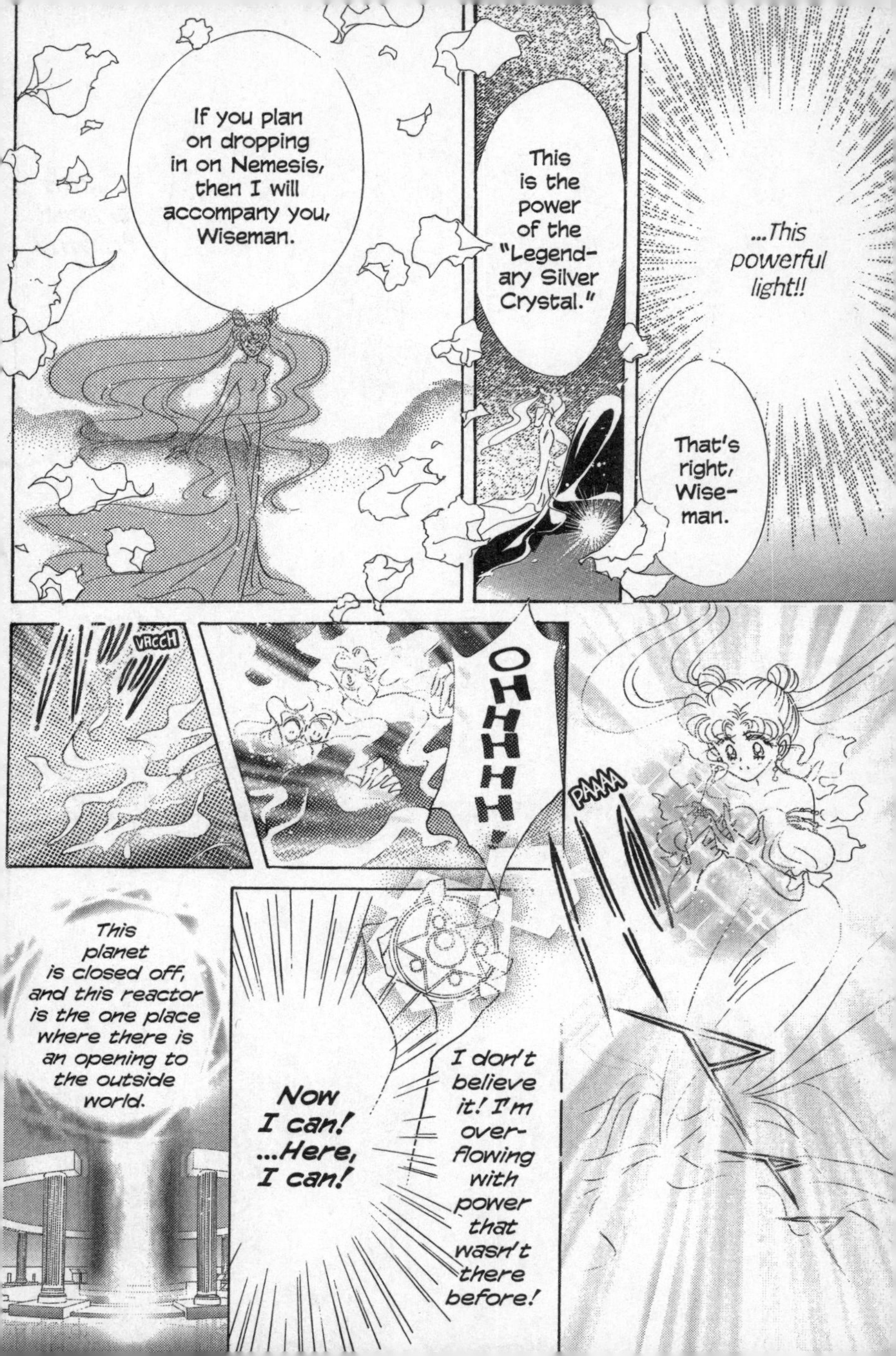
...This powerful light!!
That's right, Wiseman.
This is the power of the "Legendary Silver Crystal."
If you plan on dropping in on Nemesis, then I will accompany you, Wiseman.
PAAAA
OHHHHH!
VRCCH
I don't believe it! I'm overflowing with power that wasn't there before!
Now I can! ...Here, I can!
This planet is closed off, and this reactor is the one place where there is an opening to the outside world.

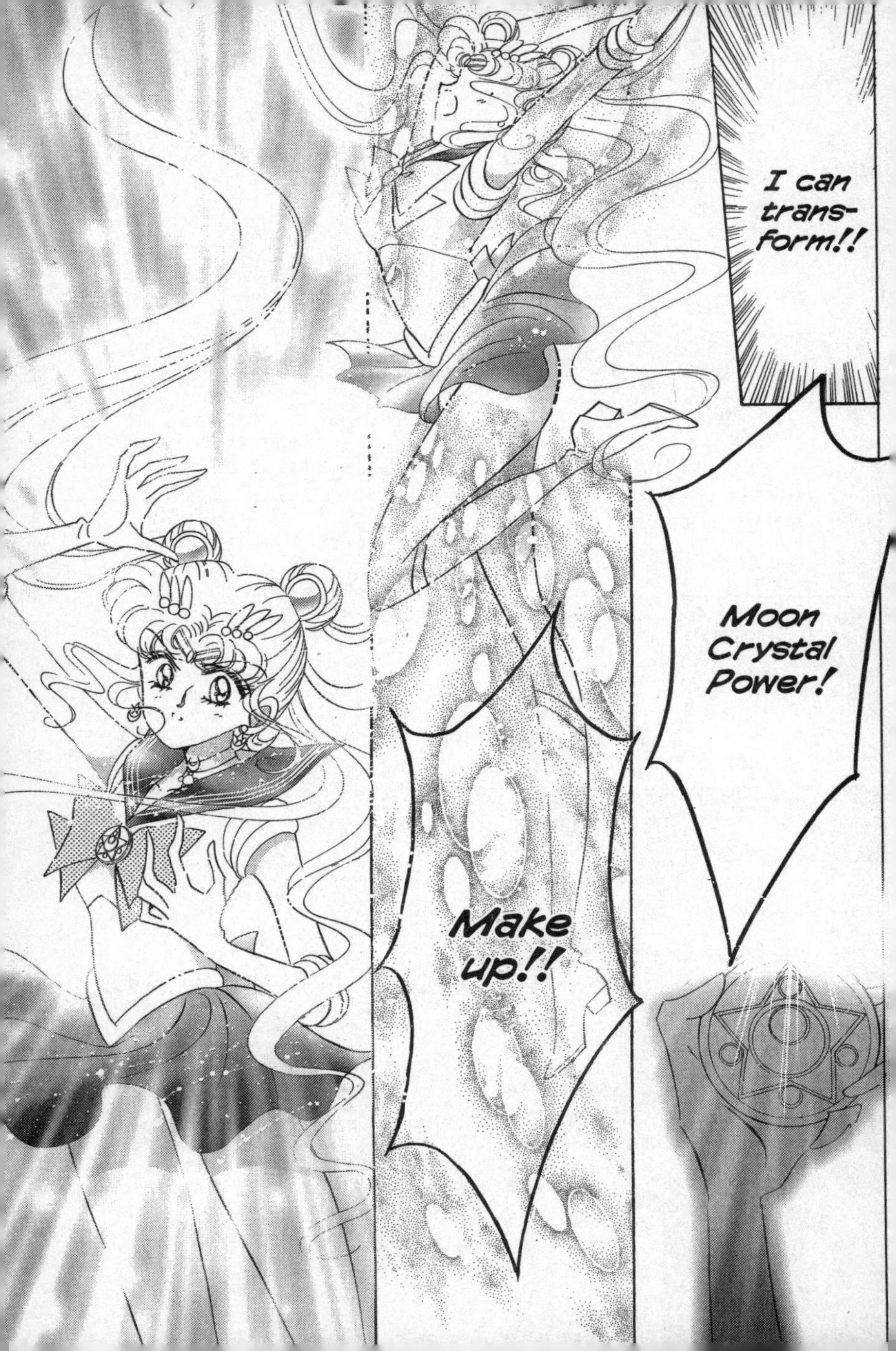
I can trans-form!!
Moon Crystal Power!
Make up!!

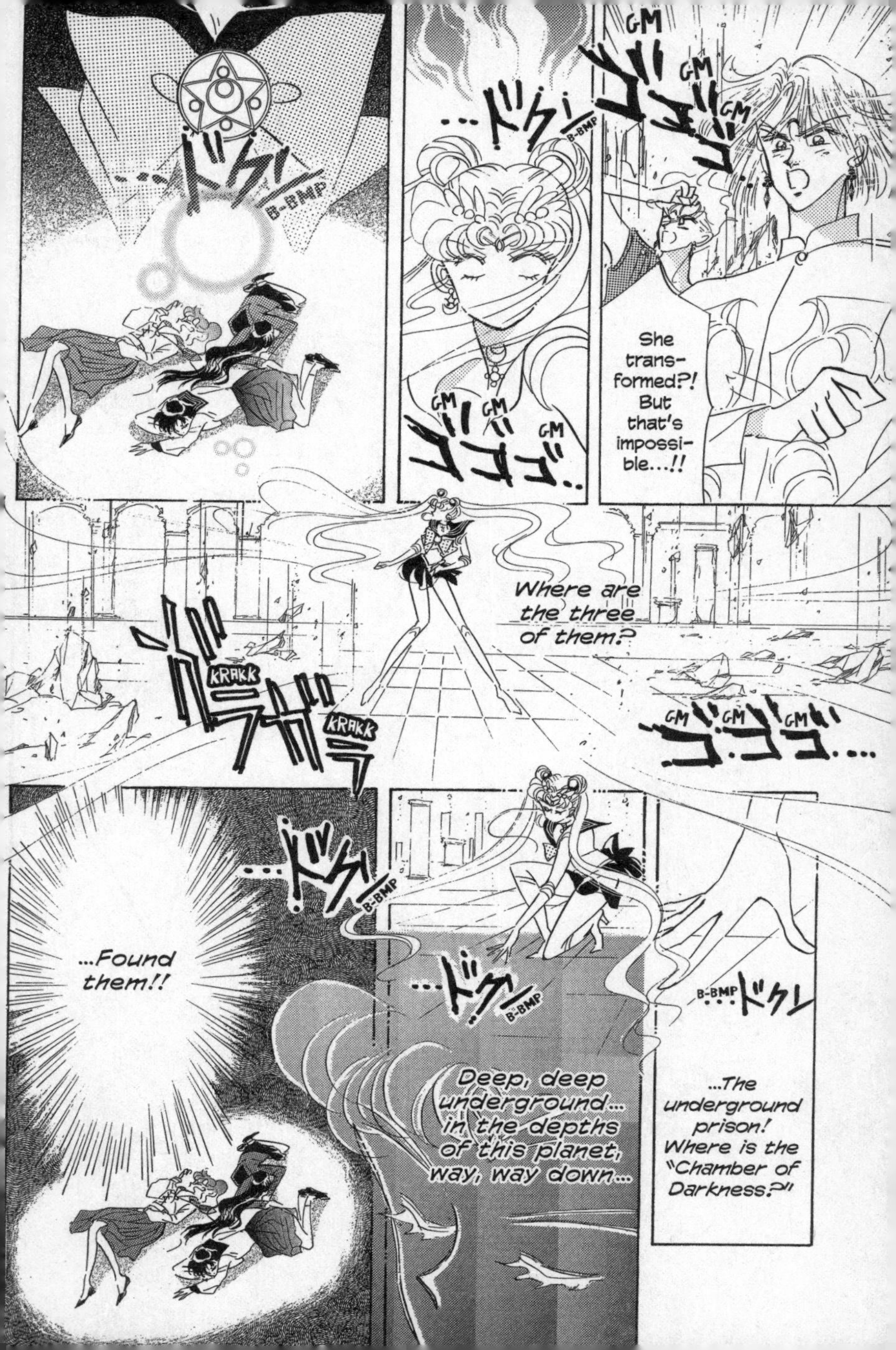
GM
GM
GM
She transformed?! But that's impossible...!!
B-BMP
GM
GM
GM
B-BMP
Where are the three of them?
GM GM GM
KRAKK
KRAKK
...The underground prison! Where is the "Chamber of Darkness?"
B-BMP
B-BMP
B-BMP
Deep, deep underground... in the depths of this planet, way, way down...
...Found them!!

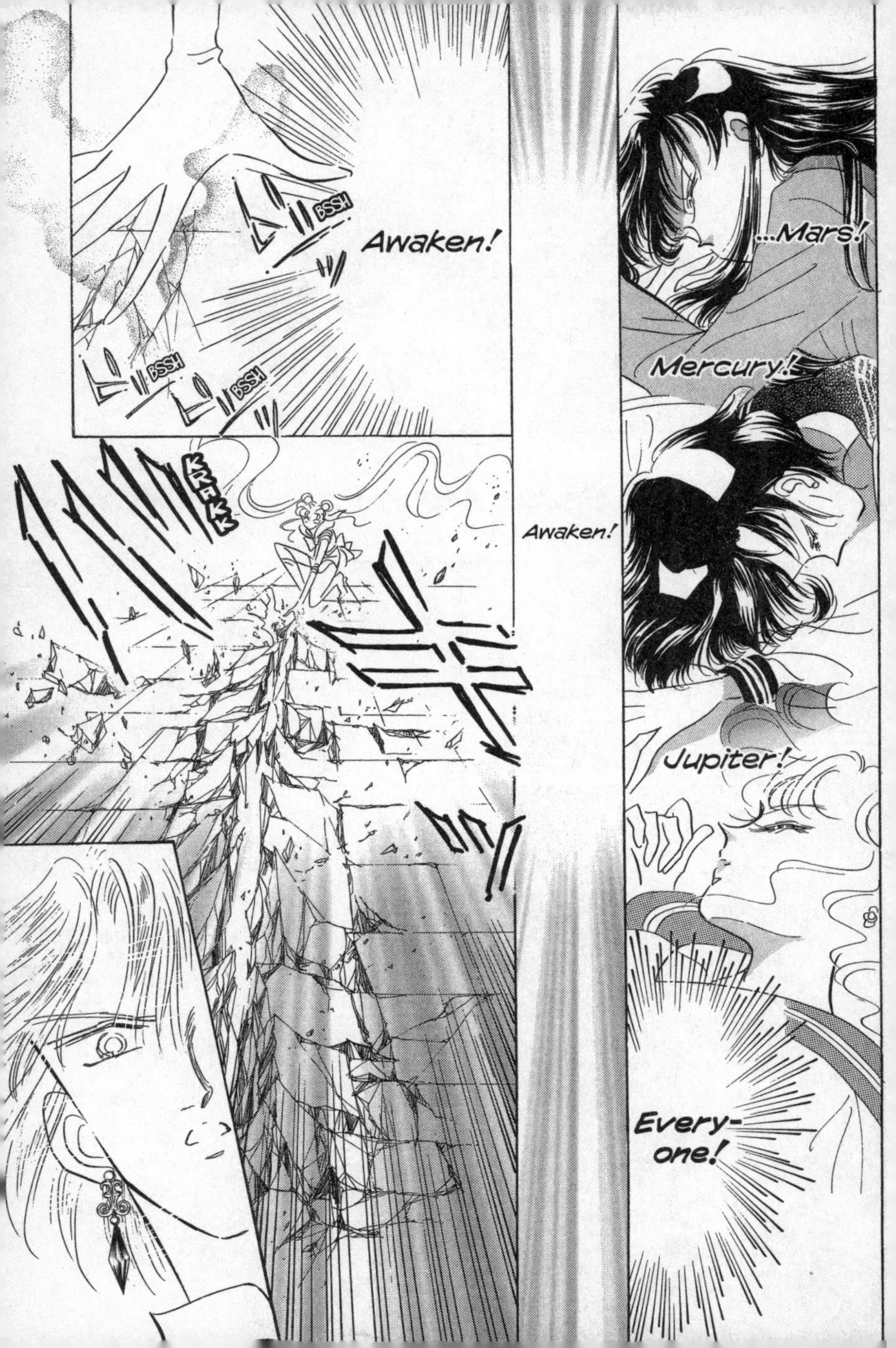
...Mars!
Mercury!
Jupiter!
Every-one!
BSSH
Awaken!
BSSH
BSSH
KRAKK
Awaken!

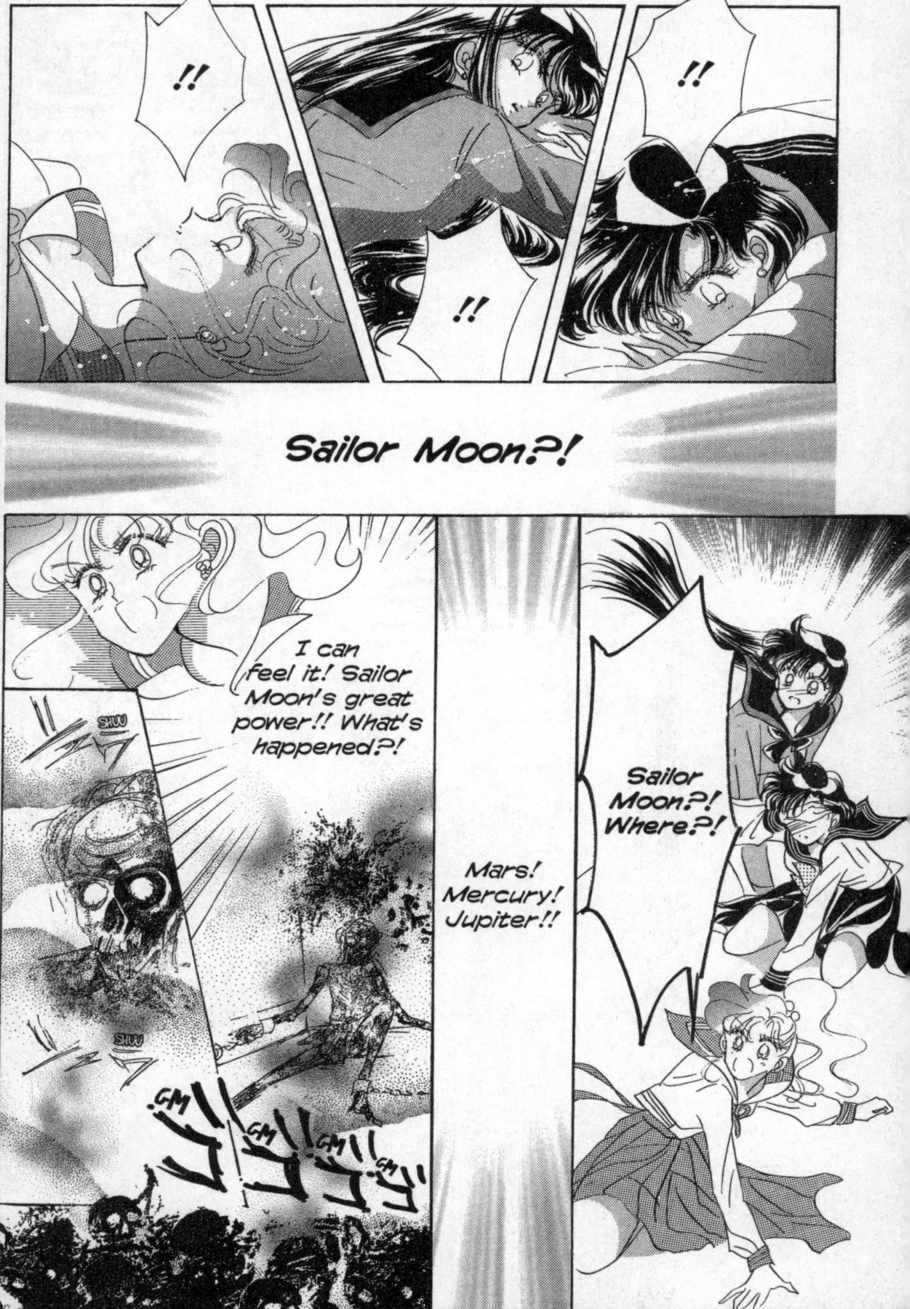
!!
!!
!!
Sailor Moon?!
Sailor Moon?! Where?!
Mars! Mercury! Jupiter!!
I can feel it! Sailor Moon's great power!! What's happened?!
SHUU
SHUU
GM
GM
GM
GM

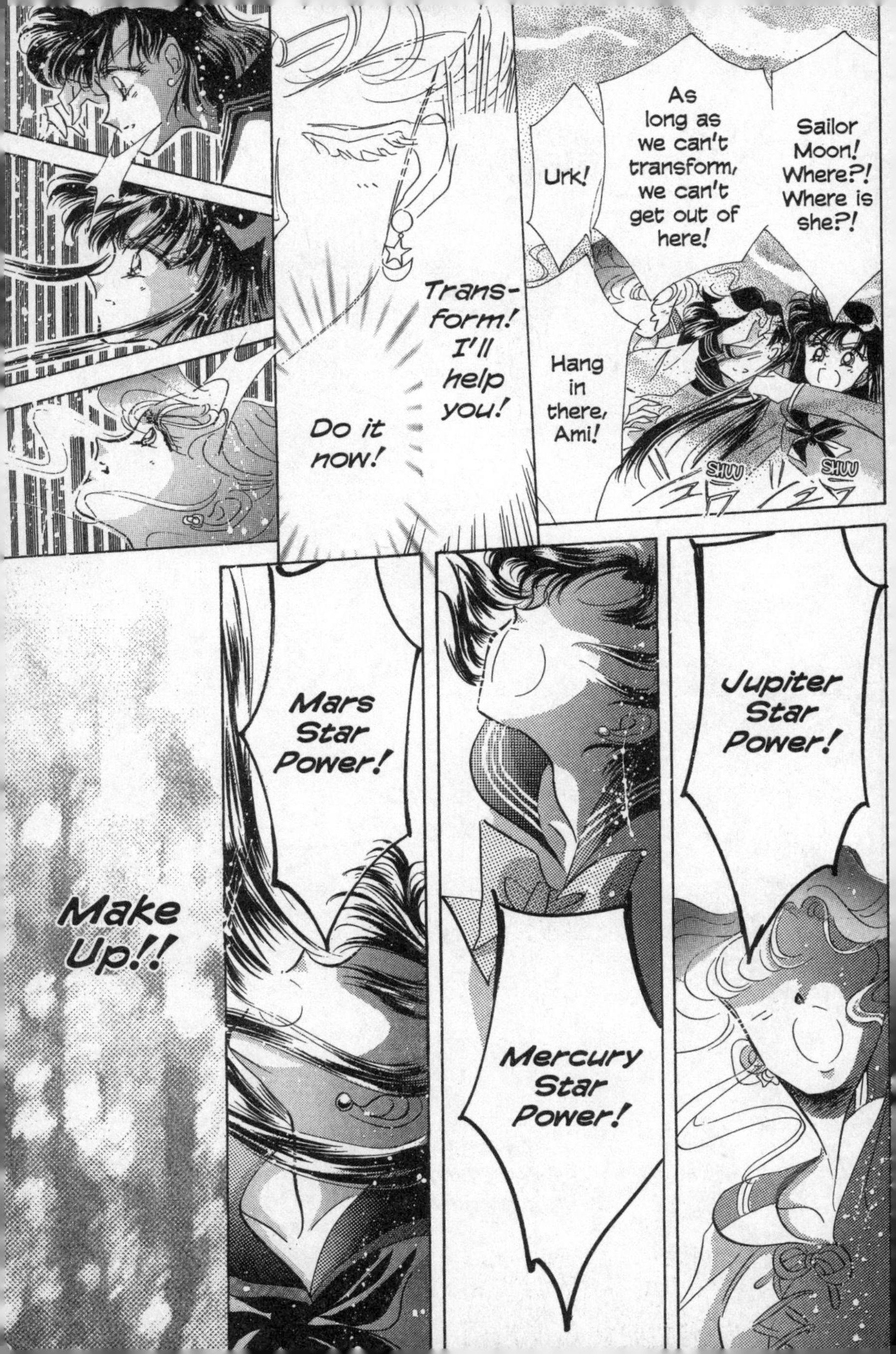
Sailor Moon! Where?! Where is she?!
As long as we can't transform, we can't get out of here!
Urk!
Hang in there, Ami!
SHUU
SHUU
...
Transform! I'll help you!
Do it now!
Jupiter Star Power!
Mercury Star Power!
Mars Star Power!
Make Up!!

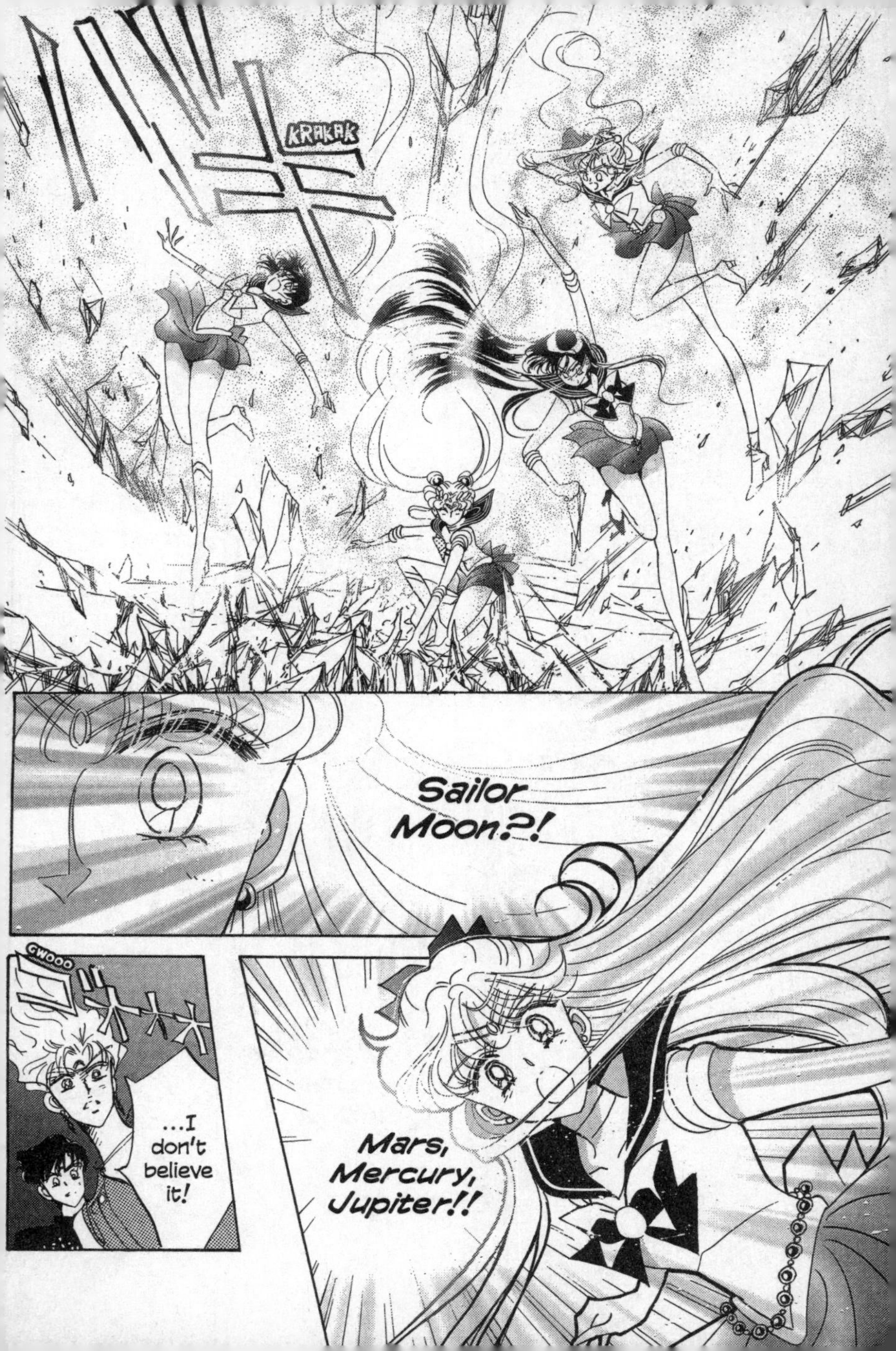
KRAKAK
Sailor Moon?!
Mars, Mercury, Jupiter!!
GWOOO
...I don't believe it!

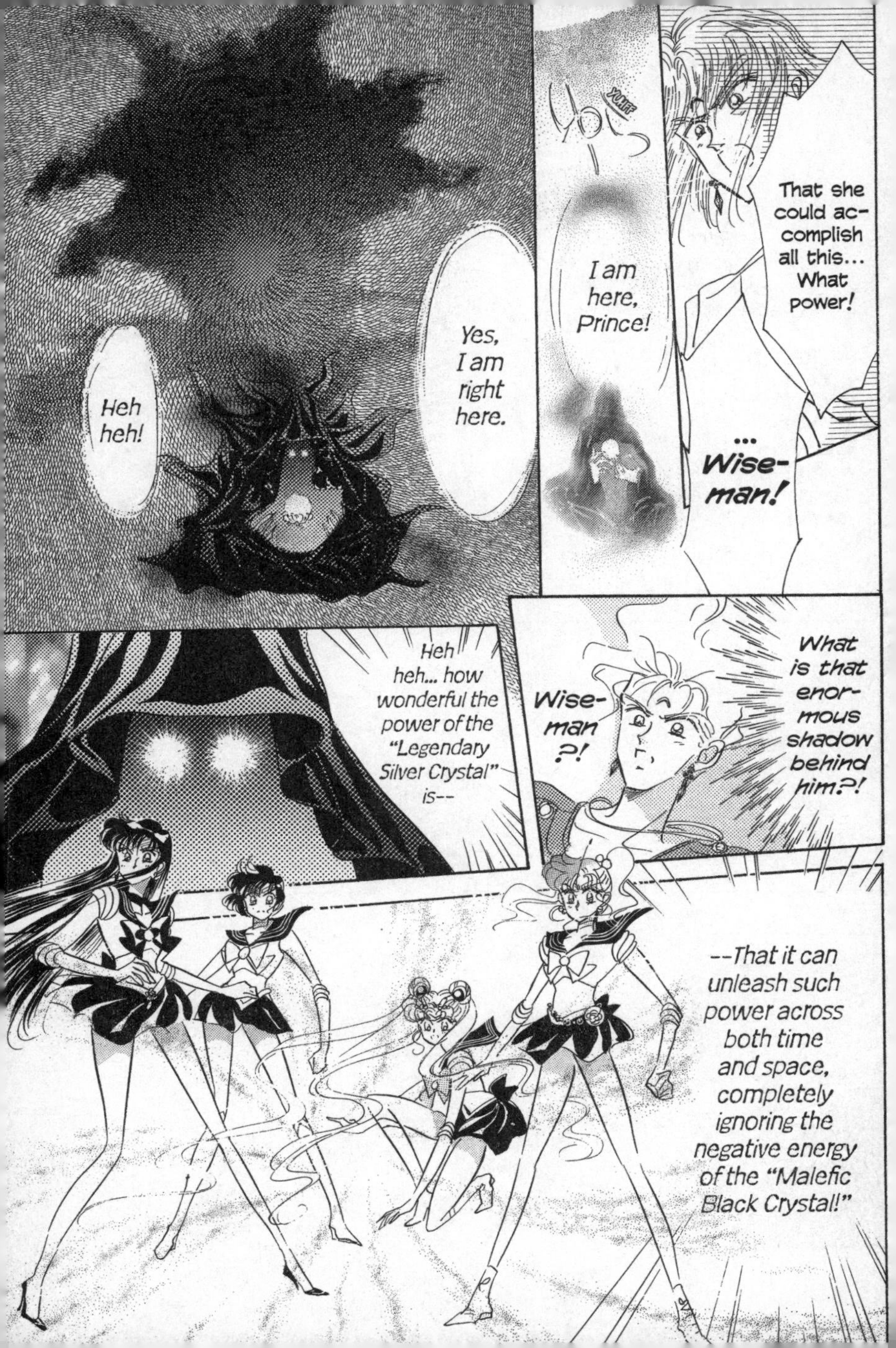
That she could ac-complish all this... What power!
...Wise-man!
I am here, Prince!
Yes, I am right here.
Heh heh!
What is that enor-mous shadow behind him?!
Wise-man?!
Heh heh... how wonderful the power of the "Legendary Silver Crystal" is--
--That it can unleash such power across both time and space, completely ignoring the negative energy of the "Malefic Black Crystal!"

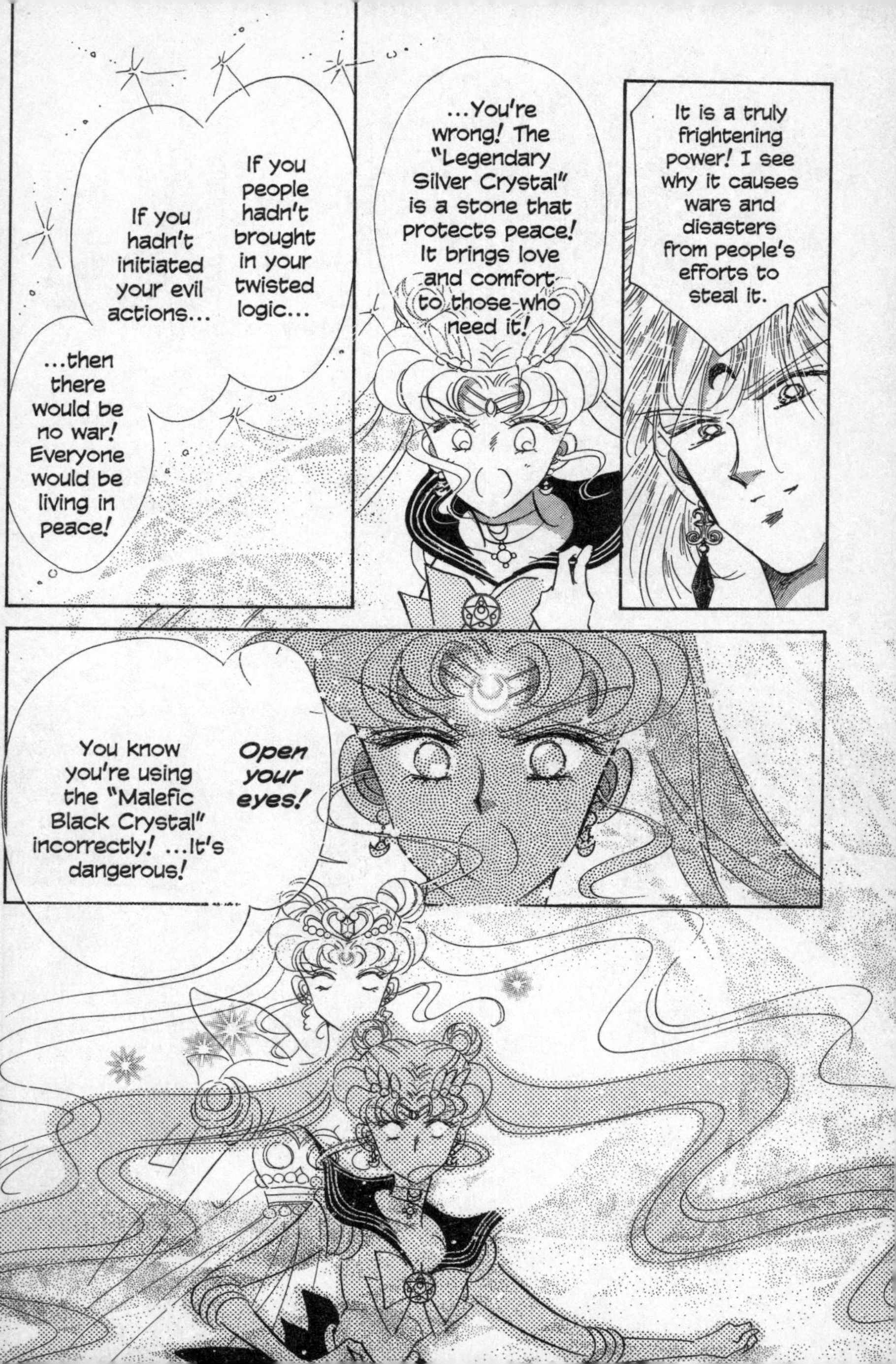
It is a truly frightening power! I see why it causes wars and disasters from people's efforts to steal it.
...You're wrong! The "Legendary Silver Crystal" is a stone that protects peace! It brings love and comfort to those who need it!
If you people hadn't brought in your twisted logic...
If you hadn't initiated your evil actions...
...then there would be no war! Everyone would be living in peace!
Open your eyes!
You know you're using the "Malefic Black Crystal" incorrectly! ...It's dangerous!

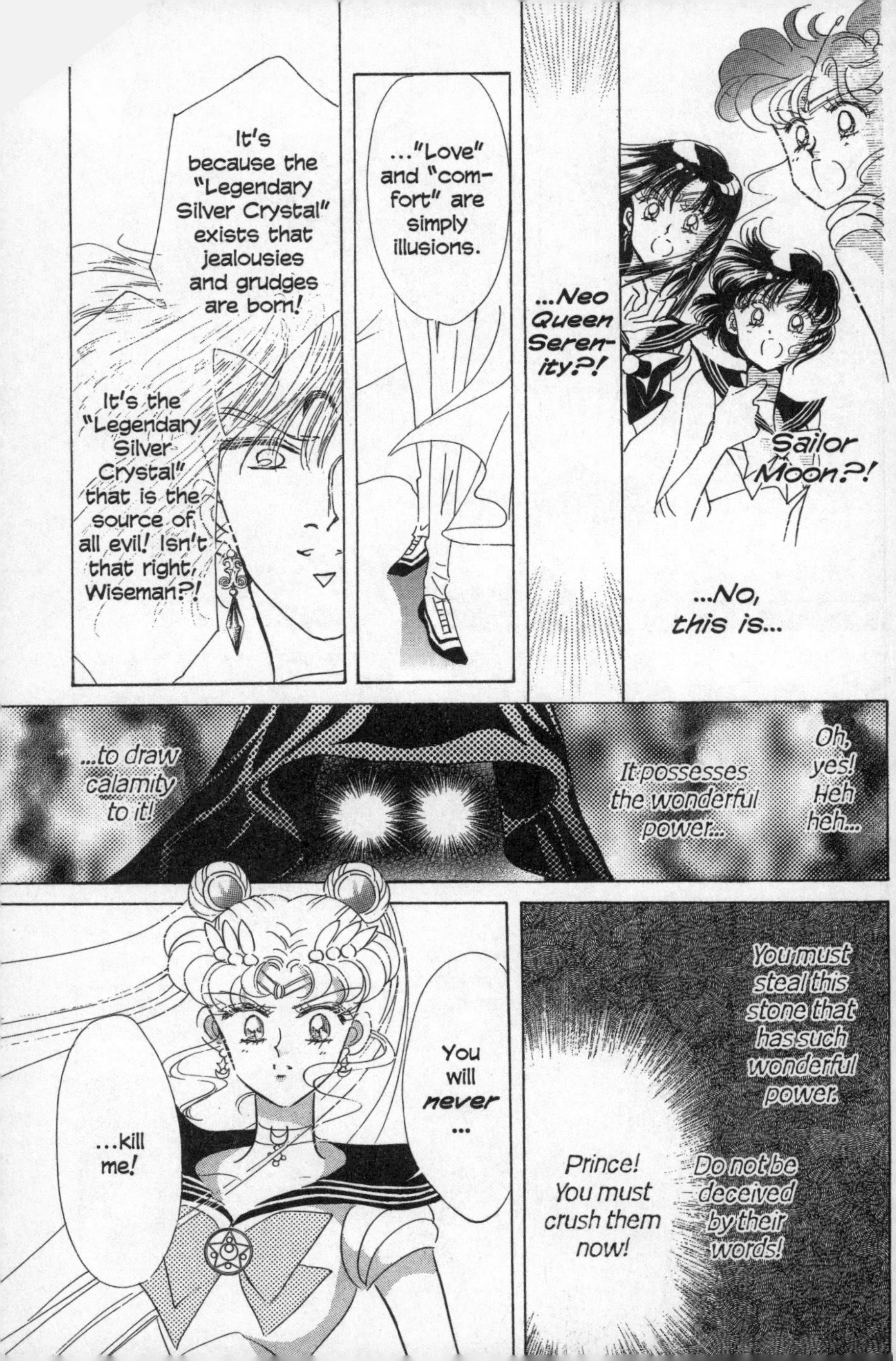
Sailor Moon?!
...Neo Queen Serenity?!
...No, this is...
..."Love" and "comfort" are simply illusions.
It's because the "Legendary Silver Crystal" exists that jealousies and grudges are born!
It's the "Legendary Silver Crystal" that is the source of all evil! Isn't that right, Wiseman?!
Oh, yes! Heh heh...
It possesses the wonderful power...
...to draw calamity to it!
You must steal this stone that has such wonderful power.
Do not be deceived by their words!
Prince! You must crush them now!
You will never...
...kill me!

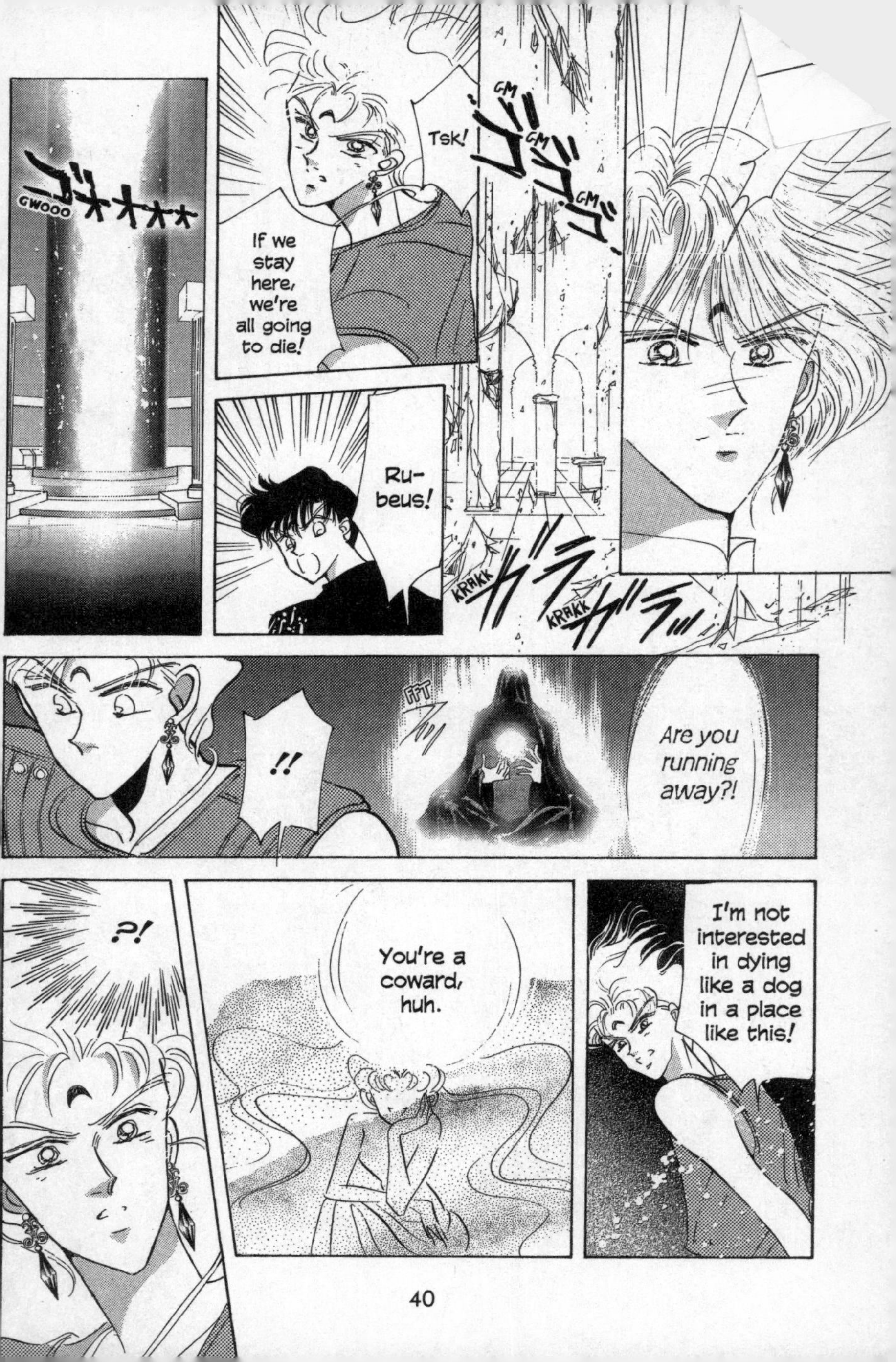
GM
GM
GM
KRAKK
KRAKK
TSK!
If we stay here, we're all going to die!
Ru- beus!
GWOOO
Are you running away?!
FFT
!!
I'm not interested in dying like a dog in a place like this!
You're a coward, huh.
?!

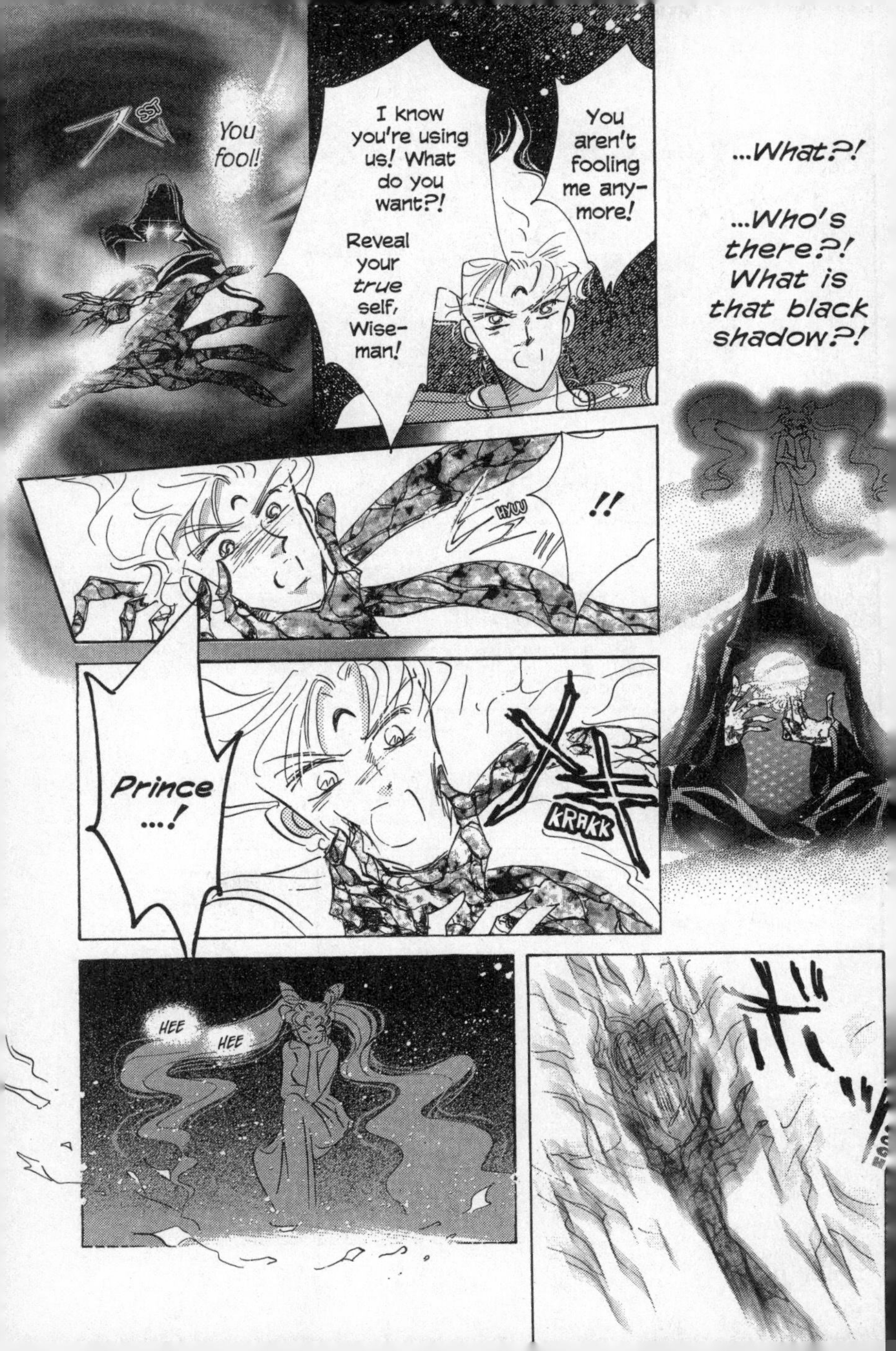

...What?!
...Who's there?! What is that black shadow?!
You aren't fooling me anymore!
I know you're using us! What do you want?!
Reveal your *true* self, Wiseman!
SST
You fool!
!!
HYUU
Prince ...!
KRAKK
HEE
HEE

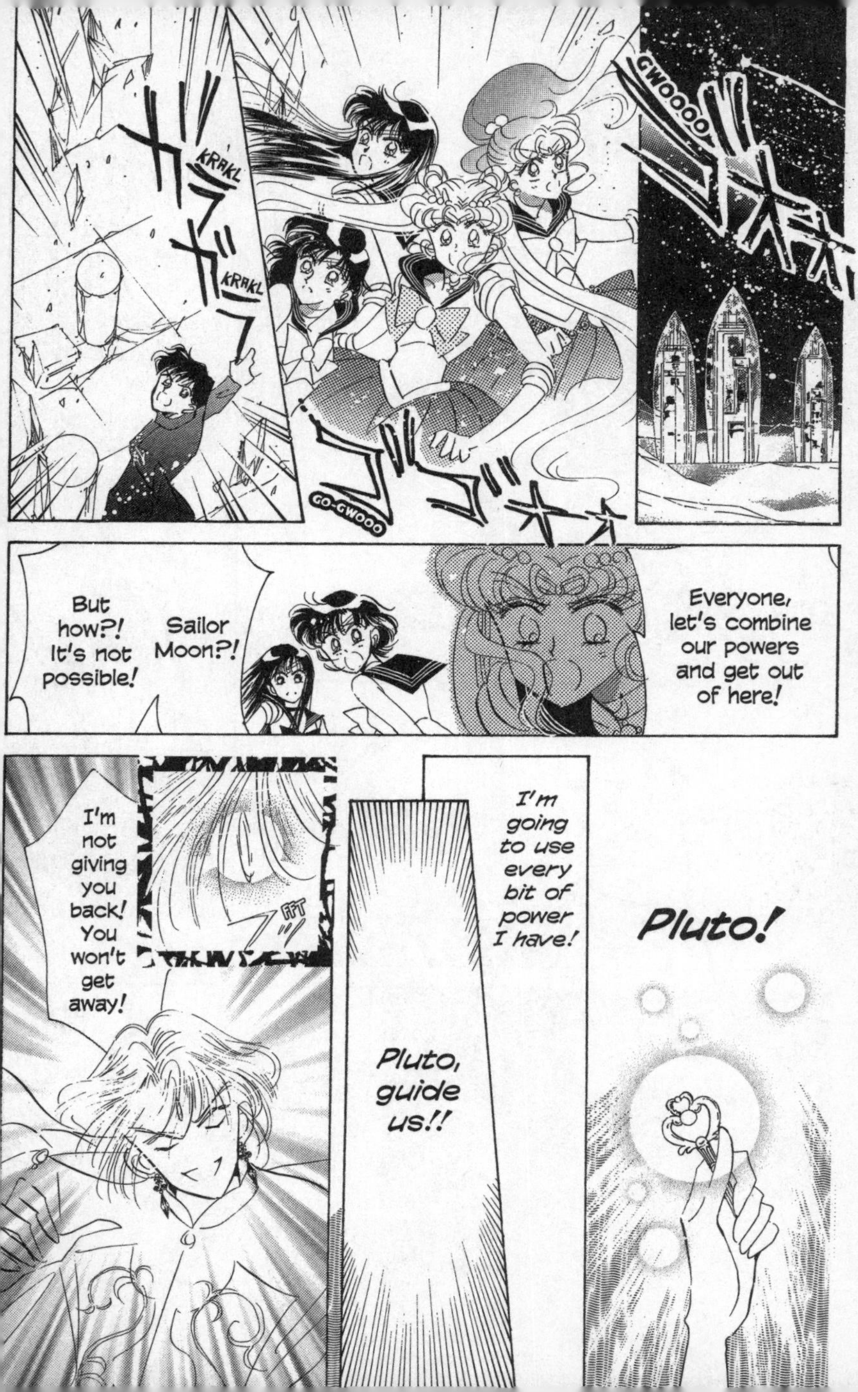
GWOOOO
GO-GWOOO
KRAKL
KRAKL
Everyone, let's combine our powers and get out of here!
Sailor Moon?!
But how?! It's not possible!
Pluto!
I'm going to use every bit of power I have!
Pluto, guide us!!
FFT
I'm not giving you back! You won't get away!

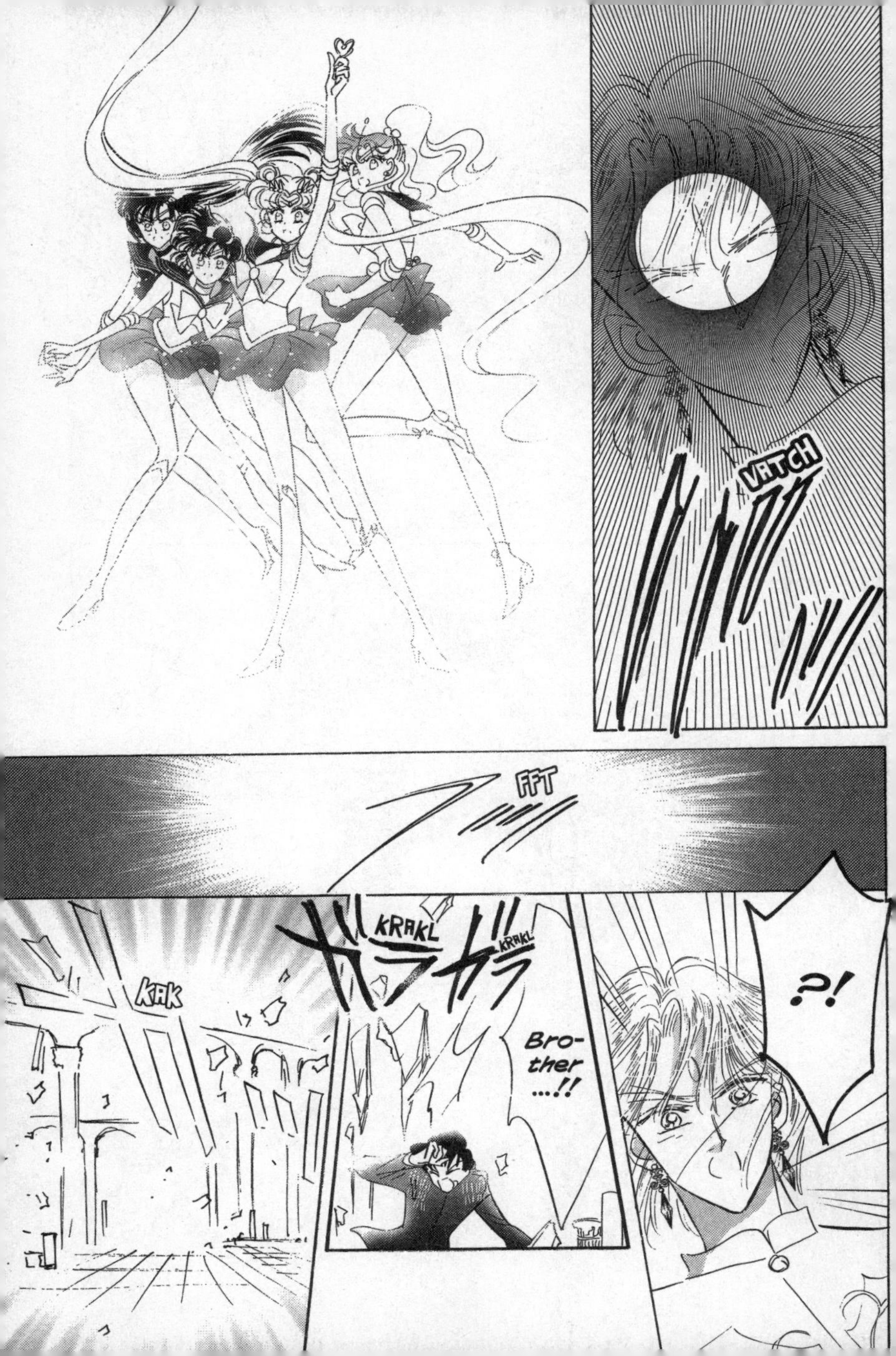
VATCH
FFT
?!
Brother...!!
ガラガラ
KRAKL
KRAKL
KAK

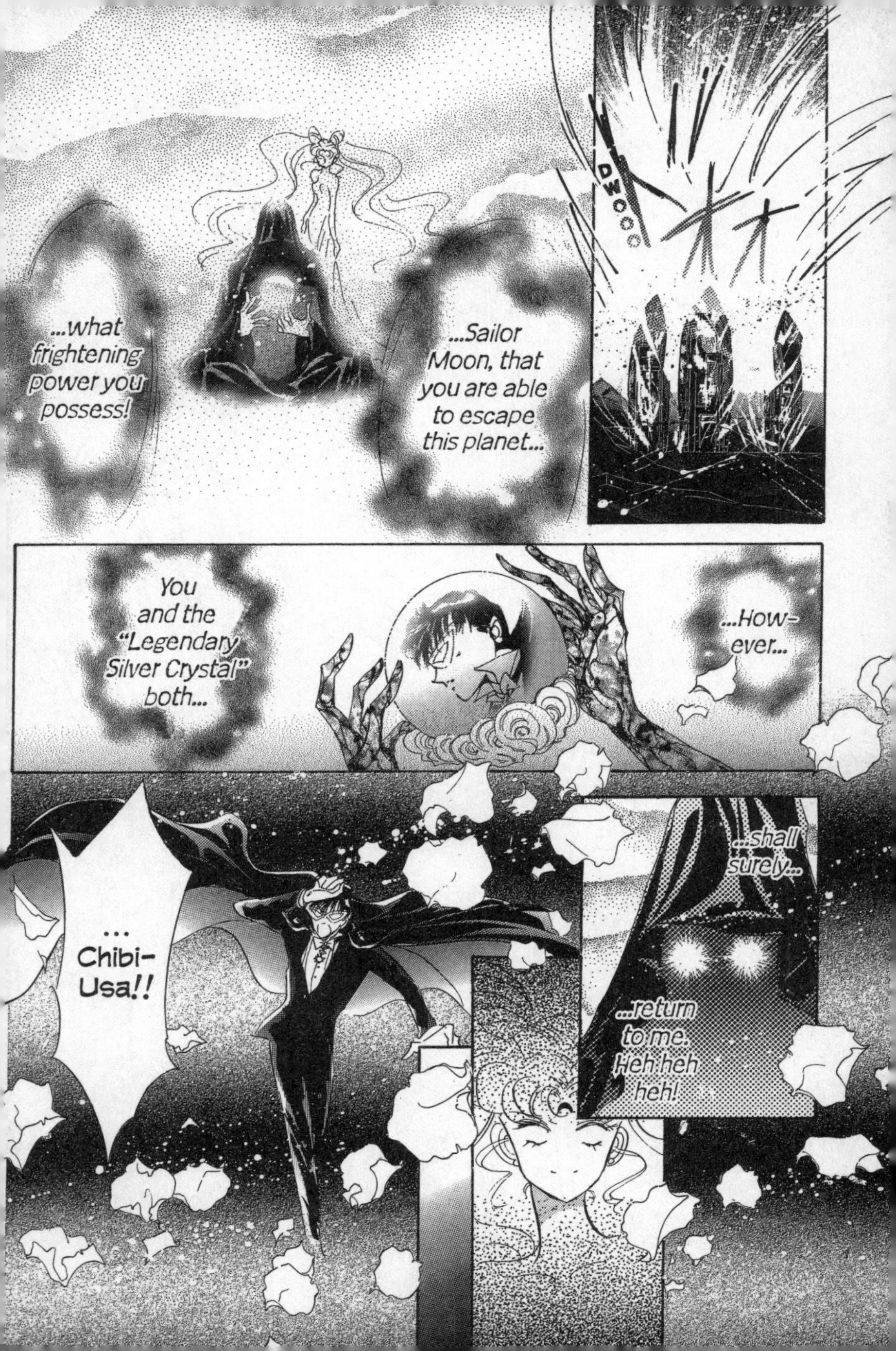
DWOOOO
...Sailor Moon, that you are able to escape this planet...
...what frightening power you possess!
...How-ever...
You and the "Legendary Silver Crystal" both...
...shall surely...
...return to me. Heh heh heh!
... Chibi-Usa!!

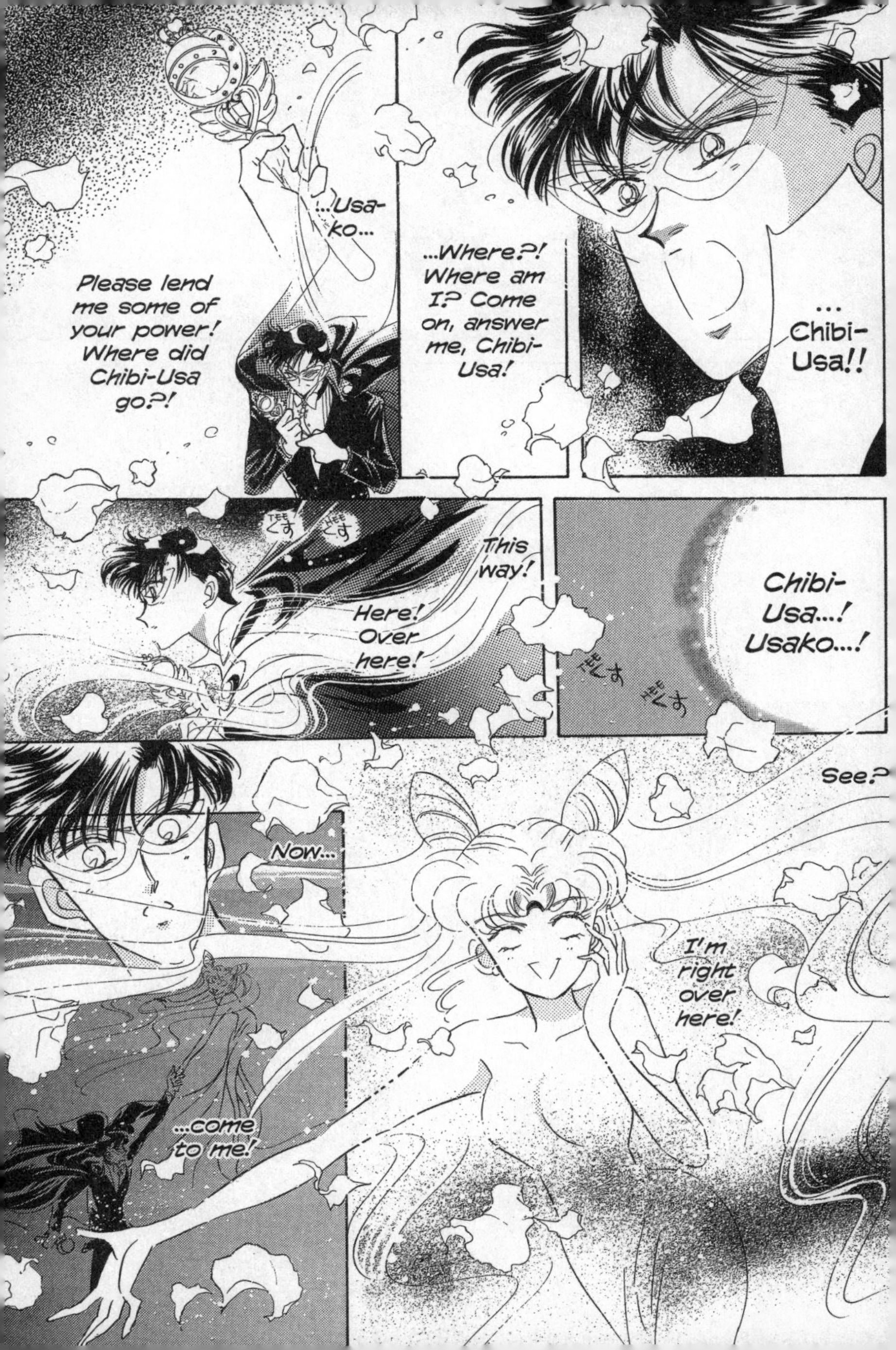

... Chibi-Usa!!
...Where?! Where am I? Come on, answer me, Chibi-Usa!
...Usa-ko...
Please lend me some of your power! Where did Chibi-Usa go?!
Chibi-Usa...! Usako...!
くすくす
This way!
TEE くす
HEE くす
Here! Over here!
See?
I'm right over here!
Now...
...come to me!

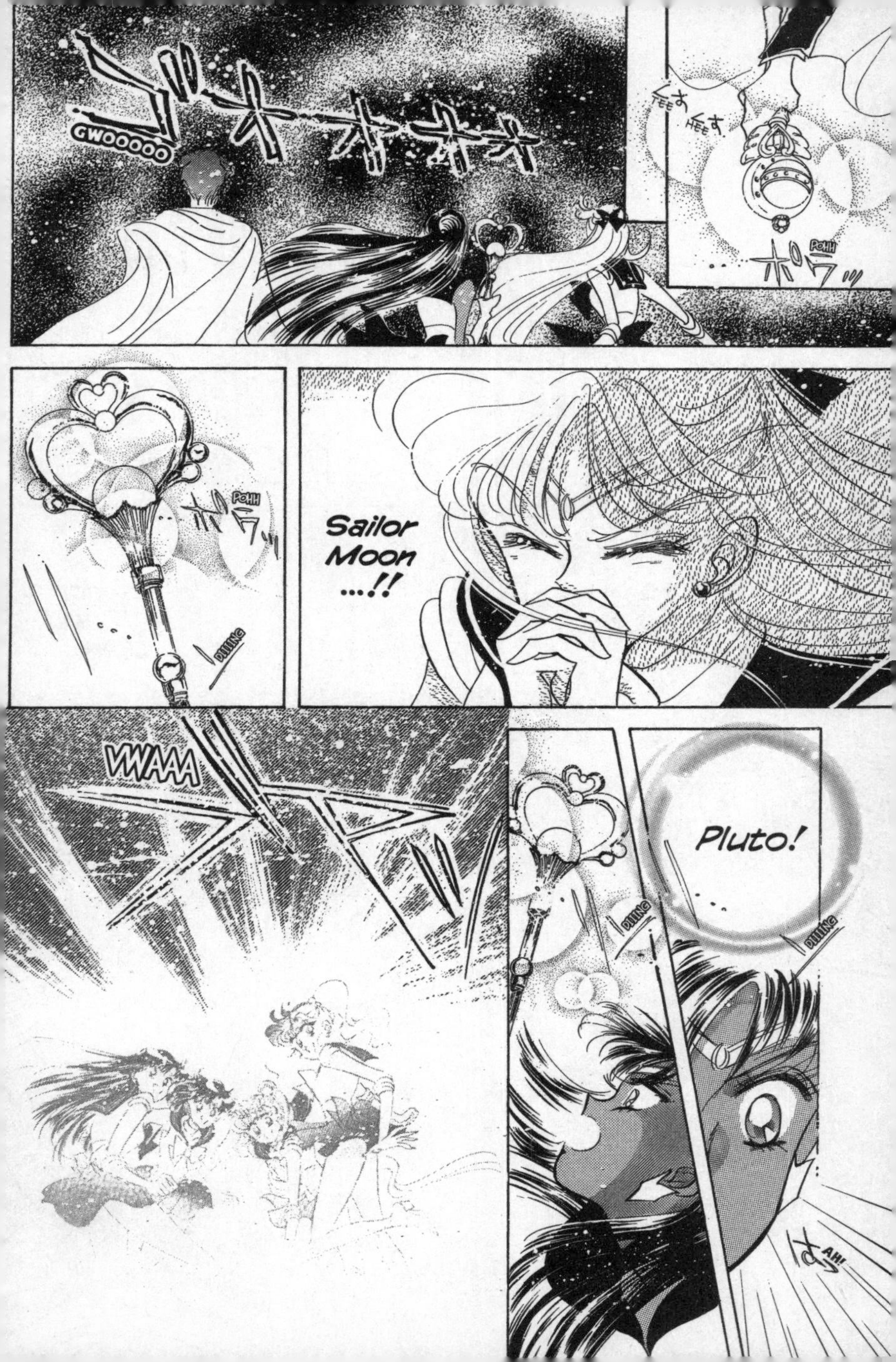

FEE
HEE
...
POHH
GWOOOOO
Sailor Moon ...!!
POHH
...
DIIING
Pluto!
...
DIIING
DIIING
AH!
VWAAA

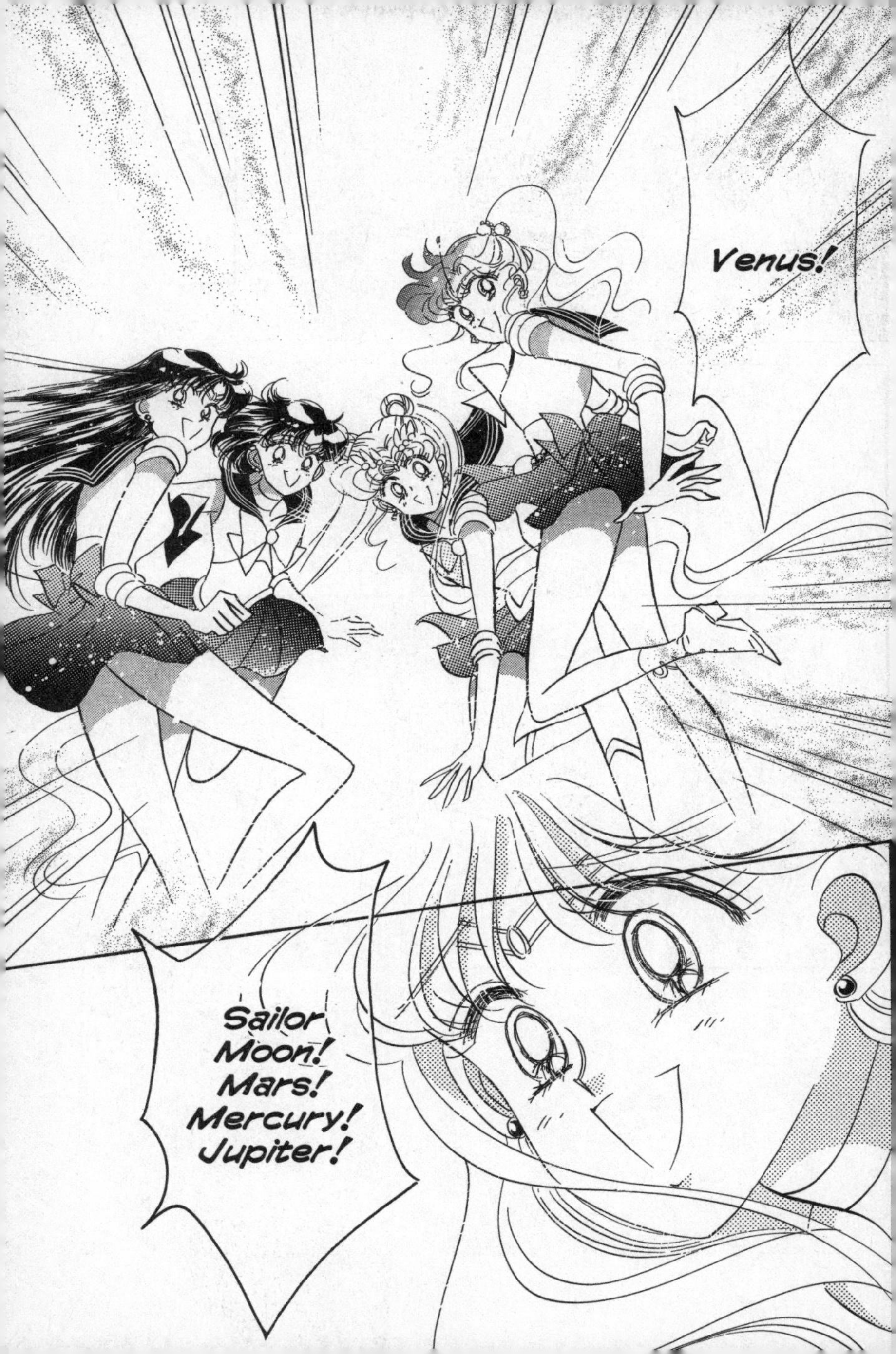
Venus!
Sailor Moon! Mars! Mercury! Jupiter!

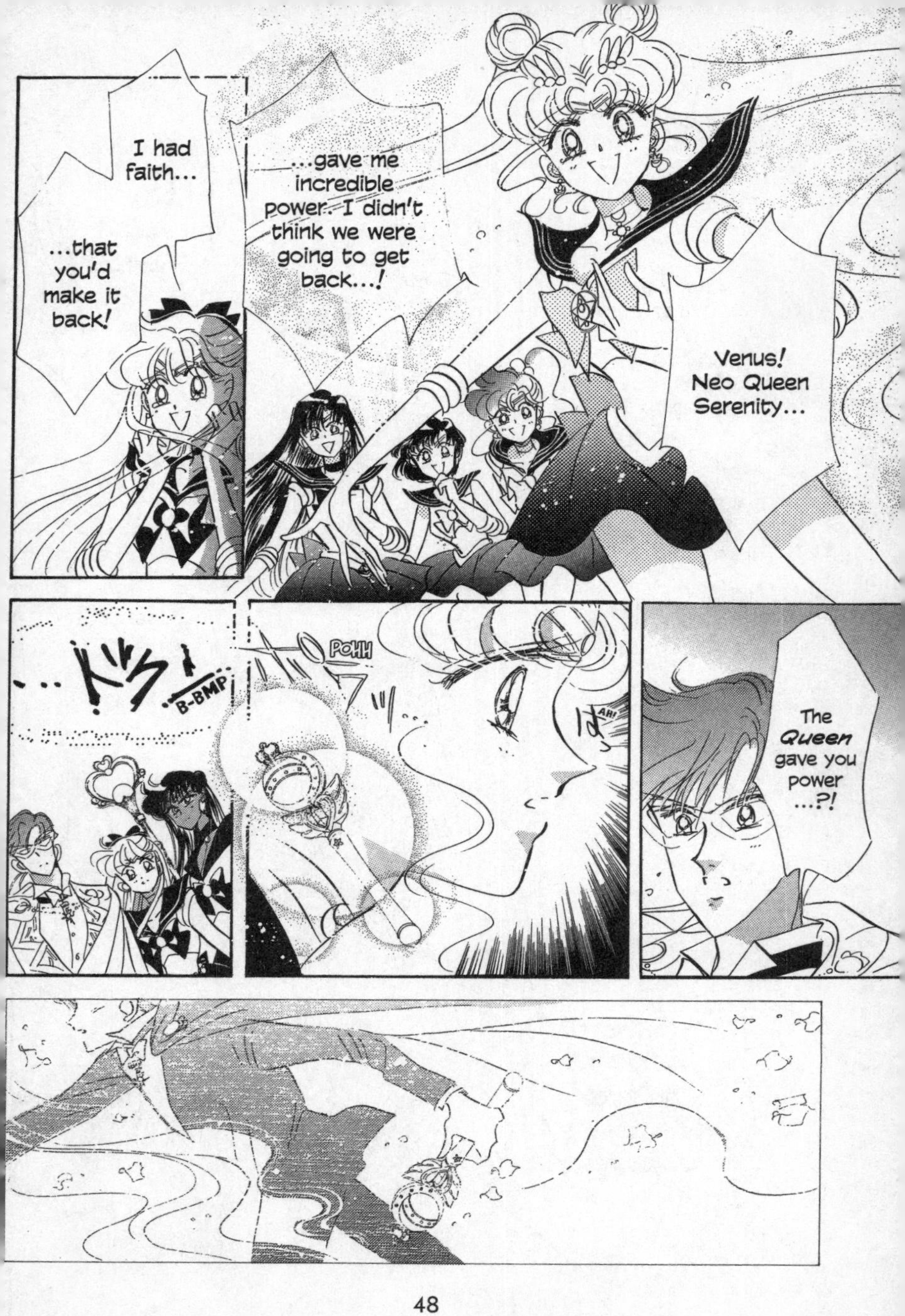

Venus! Neo Queen Serenity...
...gave me incredible power. I didn't think we were going to get back...!
I had faith...
...that you'd make it back!
The *Queen* gave you power ...?!
POHH
AH!
...
B-BMP

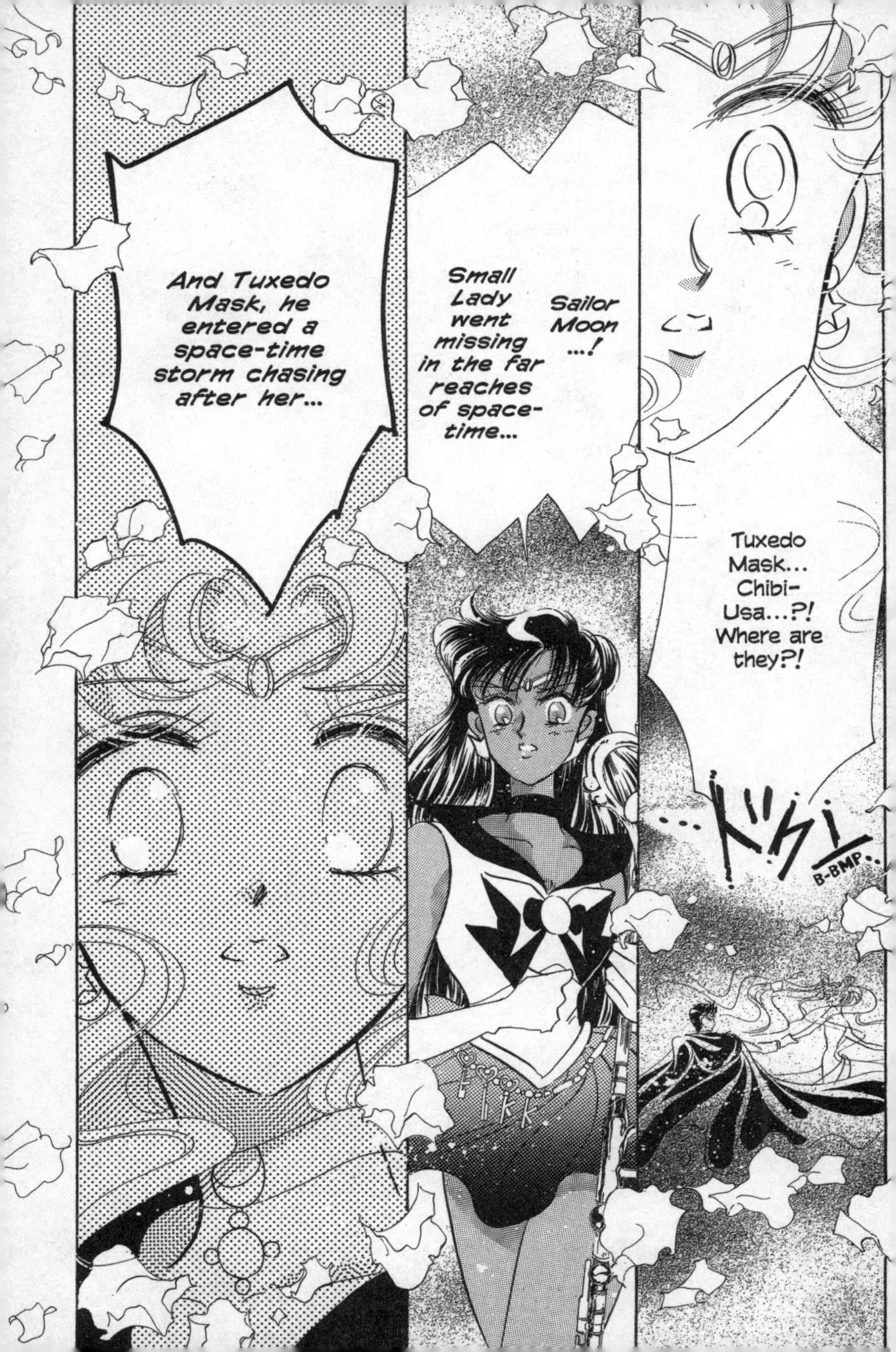
Tuxedo Mask... Chibi-Usa...?! Where are they?!
B-BMP..
Sailor Moon ...!
Small Lady went missing in the far reaches of space-time...
And Tuxedo Mask, he entered a space-time storm chasing after her...

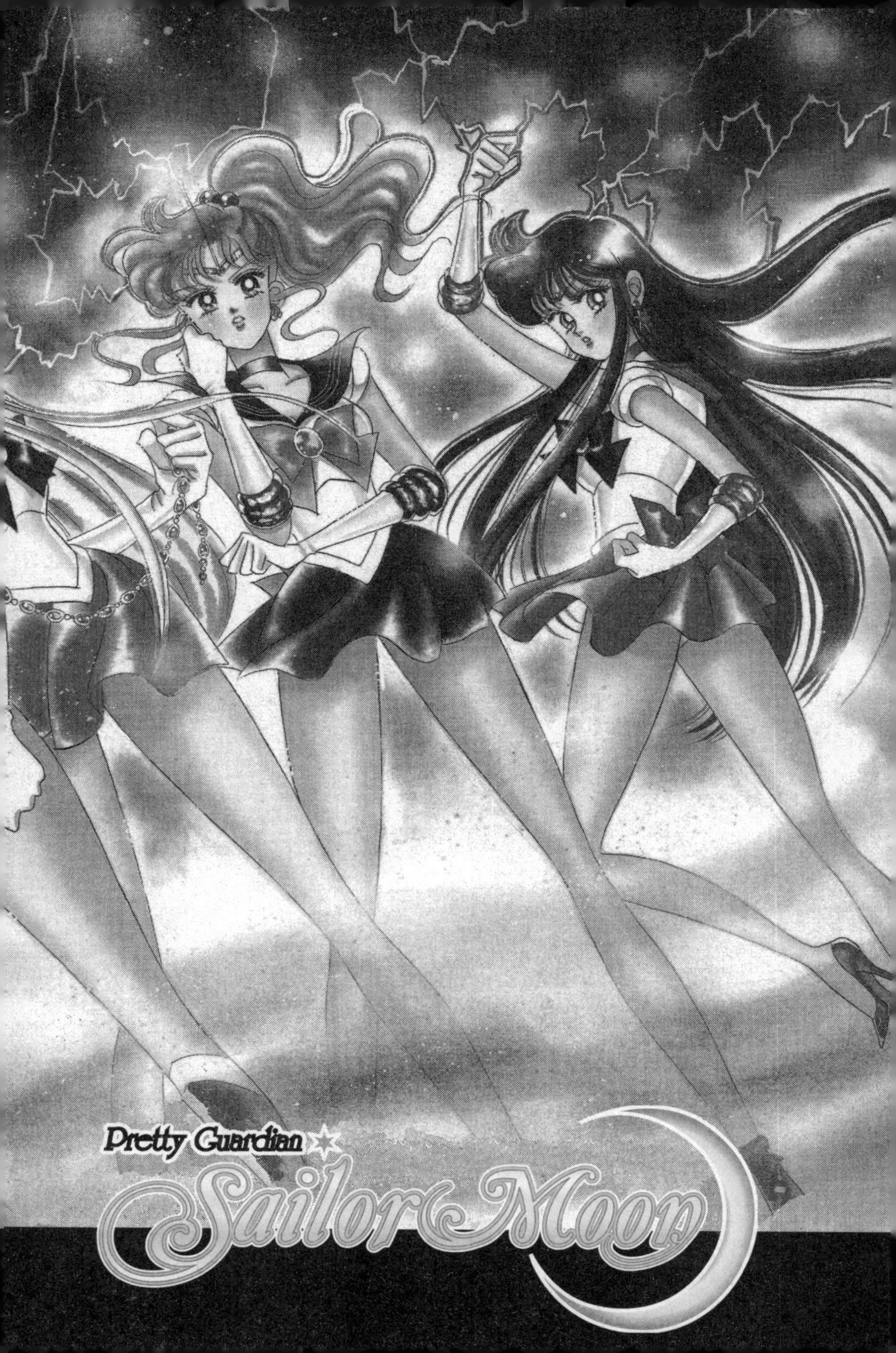
Pretty Guardian
Sailor Moon

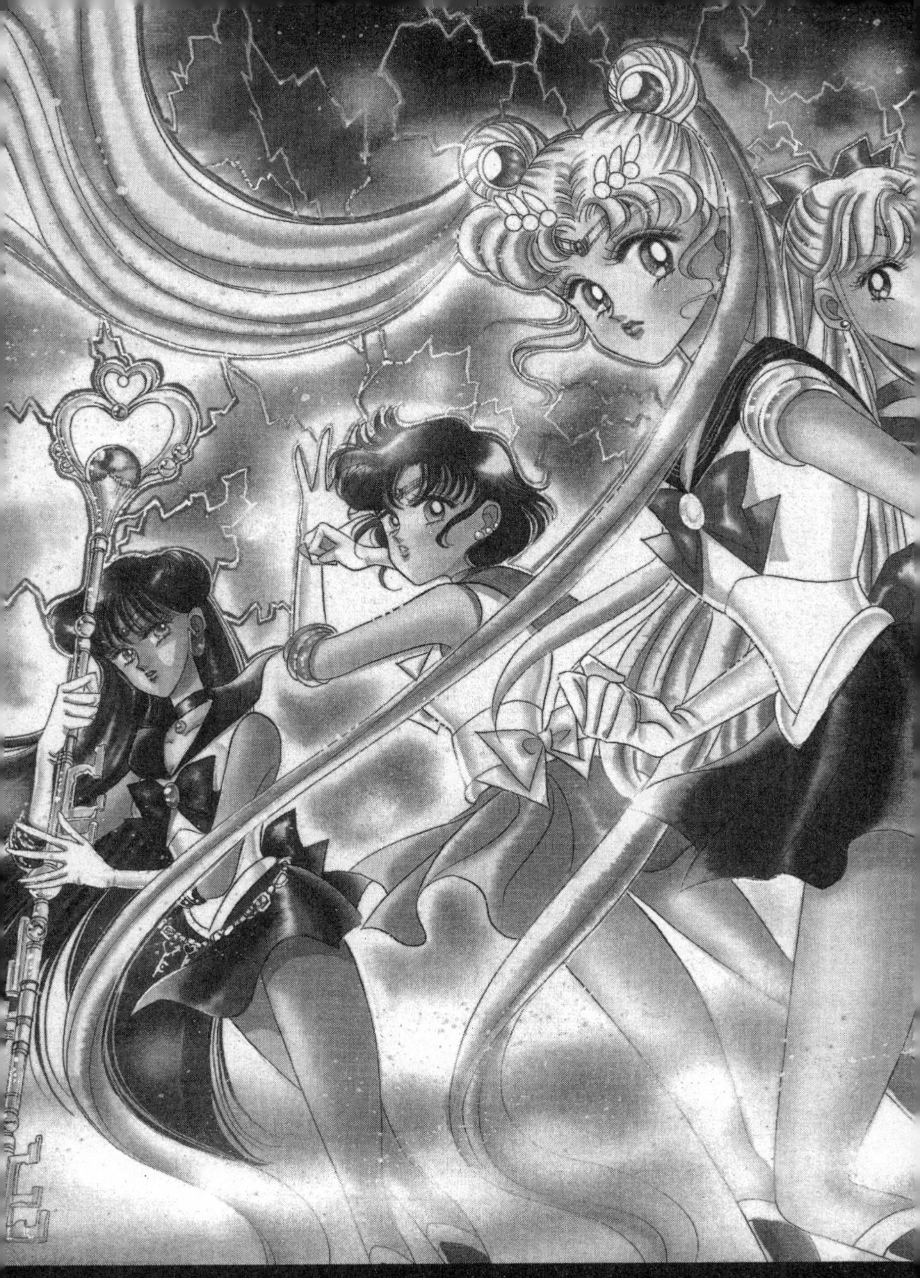

# Act 23
# Covert Maneuvers, Wiseman

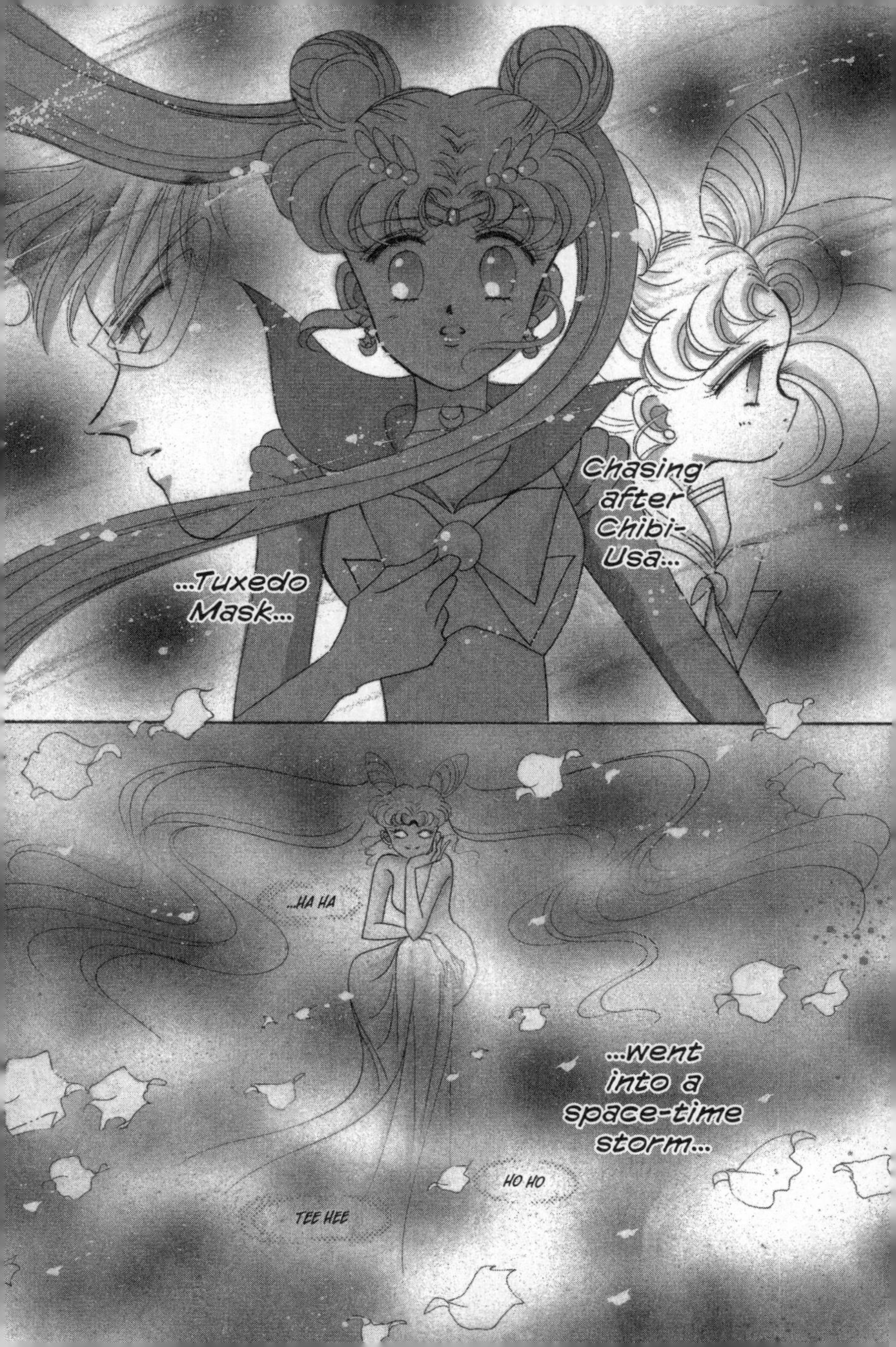
Chasing after Chibi-Usa...
...Tuxedo Mask...
...went into a space-time storm...
...HA HA
HO HO
TEE HEE

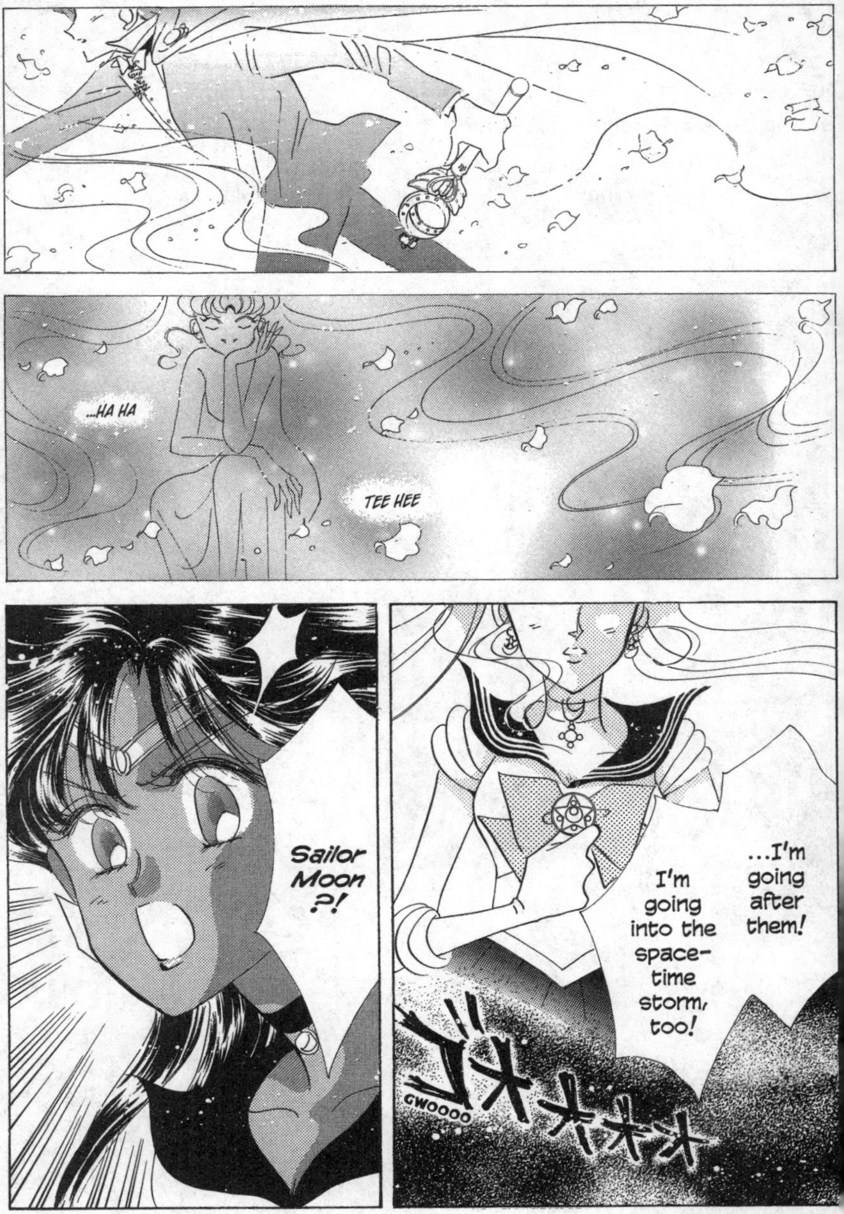

...HA HA
TEE HEE
...I'm going after them!
I'm going into the space-time storm, too!
GWOOOO
Sailor Moon ?!

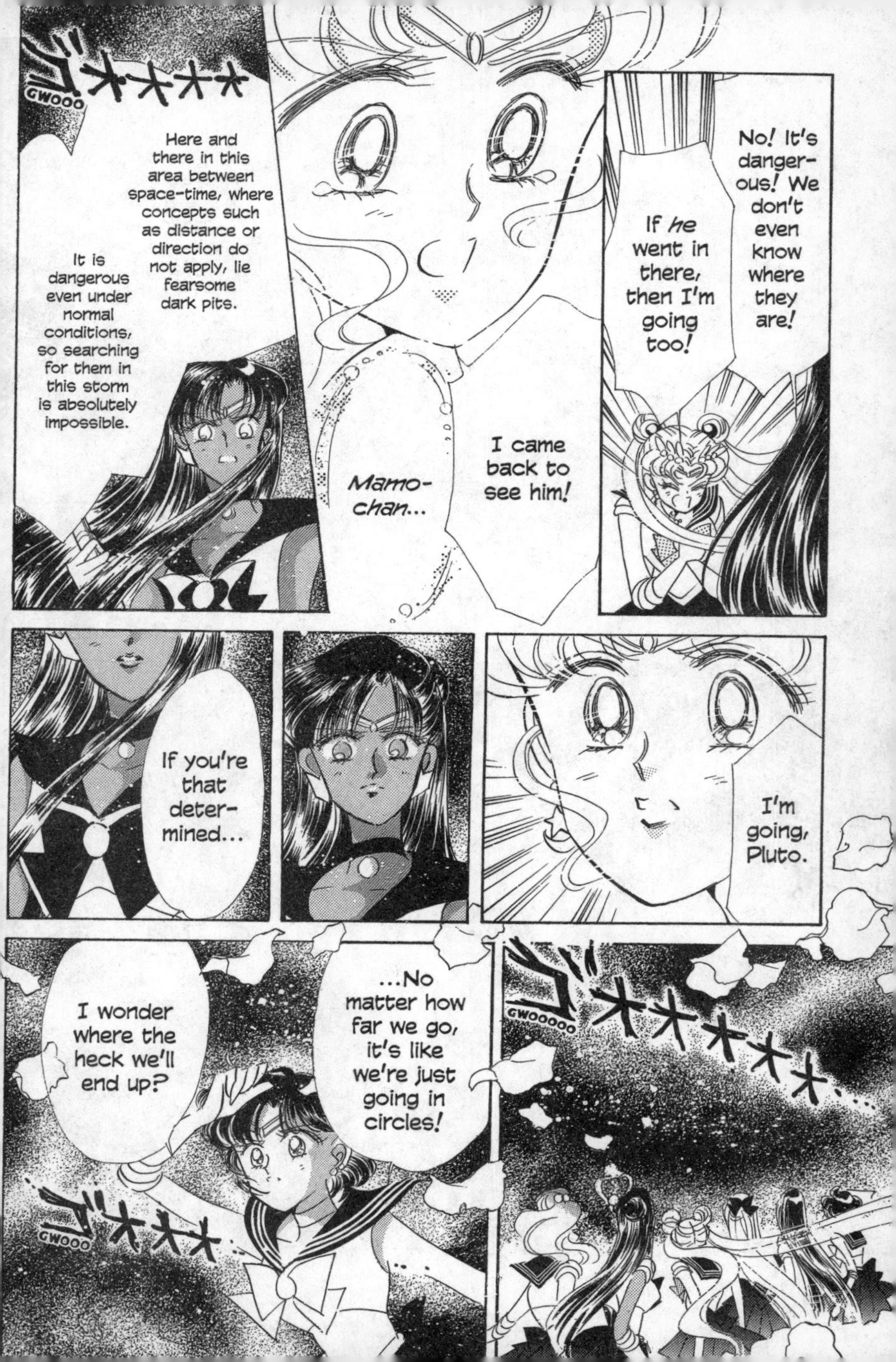
No! It's danger-ous! We don't even know where they are!
If *he* went in there, then I'm going too!
I came back to see him!
*Mamo-chan...*
GWOOO
Here and there in this area between space-time, where concepts such as distance or direction do not apply, lie fearsome dark pits.
It is dangerous even under normal conditions, so searching for them in this storm is absolutely impossible.
I'm going, Pluto.
If you're that deter-mined...
GWOOOOO
...No matter how far we go, it's like we're just going in circles!
I wonder where the heck we'll end up?
GWOOO

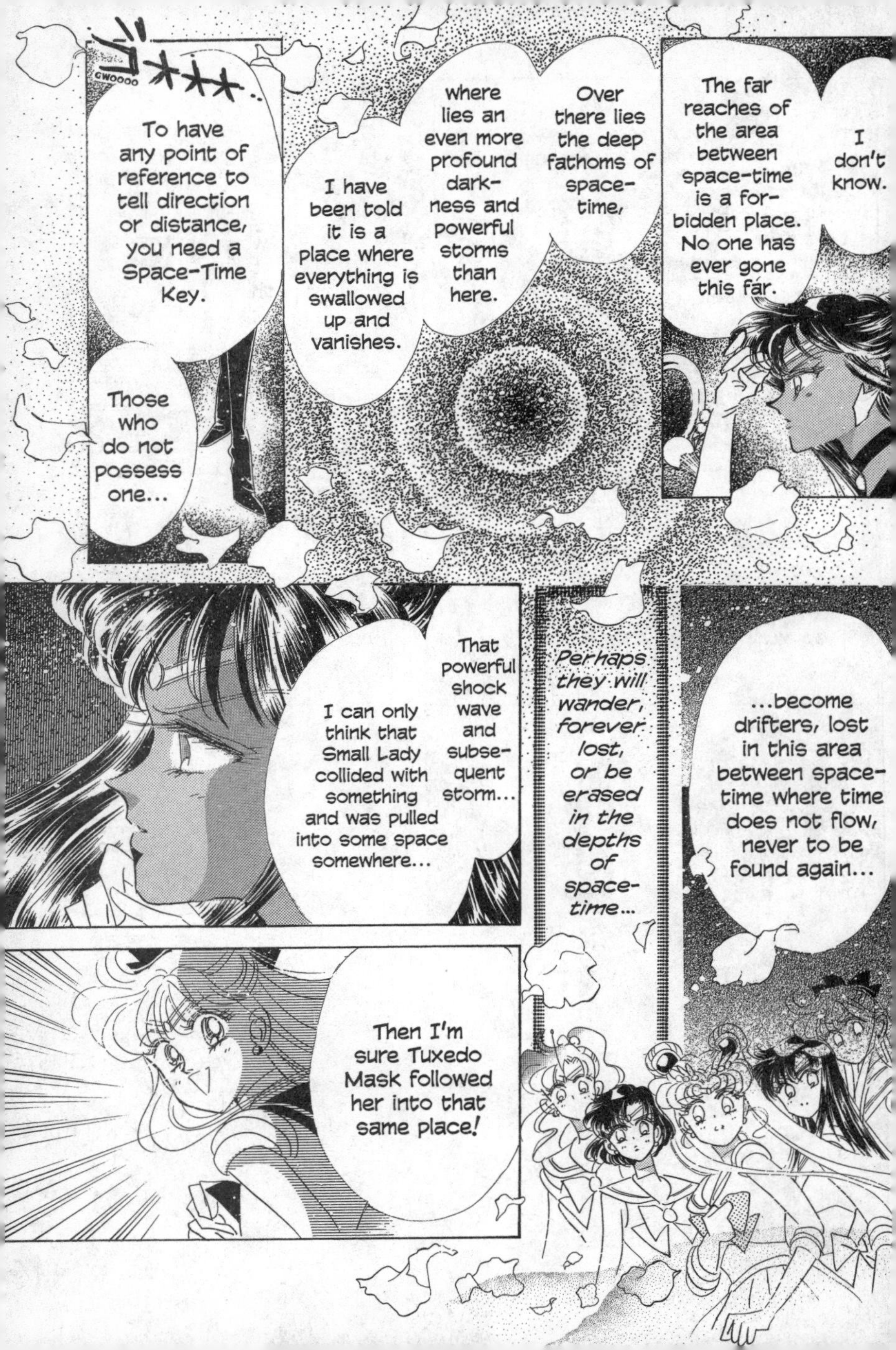

I don't know.
The far reaches of the area between space-time is a forbidden place. No one has ever gone this far.
Over there lies the deep fathoms of space-time,
where lies an even more profound darkness and powerful storms than here.
I have been told it is a place where everything is swallowed up and vanishes.
GWOOOO
To have any point of reference to tell direction or distance, you need a Space-Time Key.
Those who do not possess one...
...become drifters, lost in this area between space-time where time does not flow, never to be found again...
*Perhaps they will wander, forever lost, or be erased in the depths of space-time...*
That powerful shock wave and subsequent storm...
I can only think that Small Lady collided with something and was pulled into some space somewhere...
Then I'm sure Tuxedo Mask followed her into that same place!

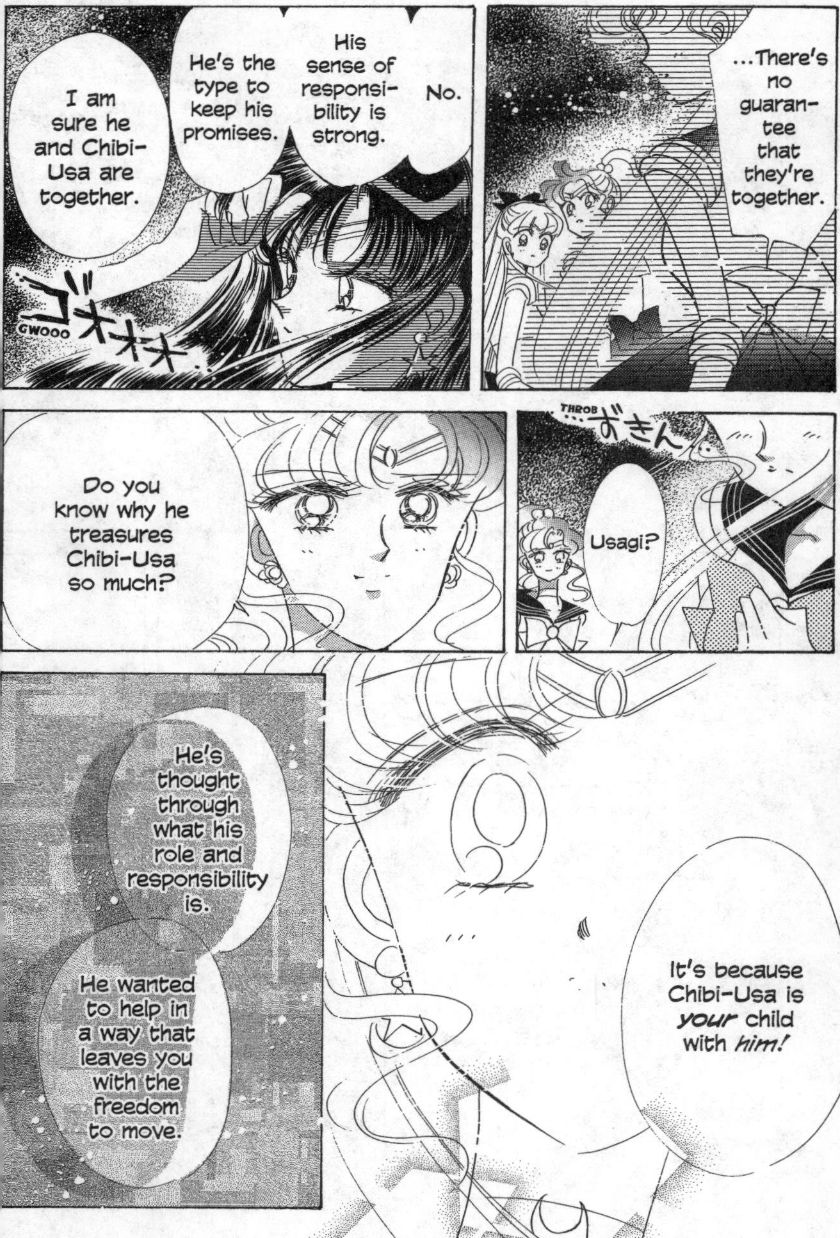
...There's no guarantee that they're together.
No.
His sense of responsibility is strong.
He's the type to keep his promises.
I am sure he and Chibi-Usa are together.
ゴオオオ
GWOOO
THROB
ずきん
Usagi?
Do you know why he treasures Chibi-Usa so much?
It's because Chibi-Usa is *your* child with *him!*
He's thought through what his role and responsibility is.
He wanted to help in a way that leaves you with the freedom to move.

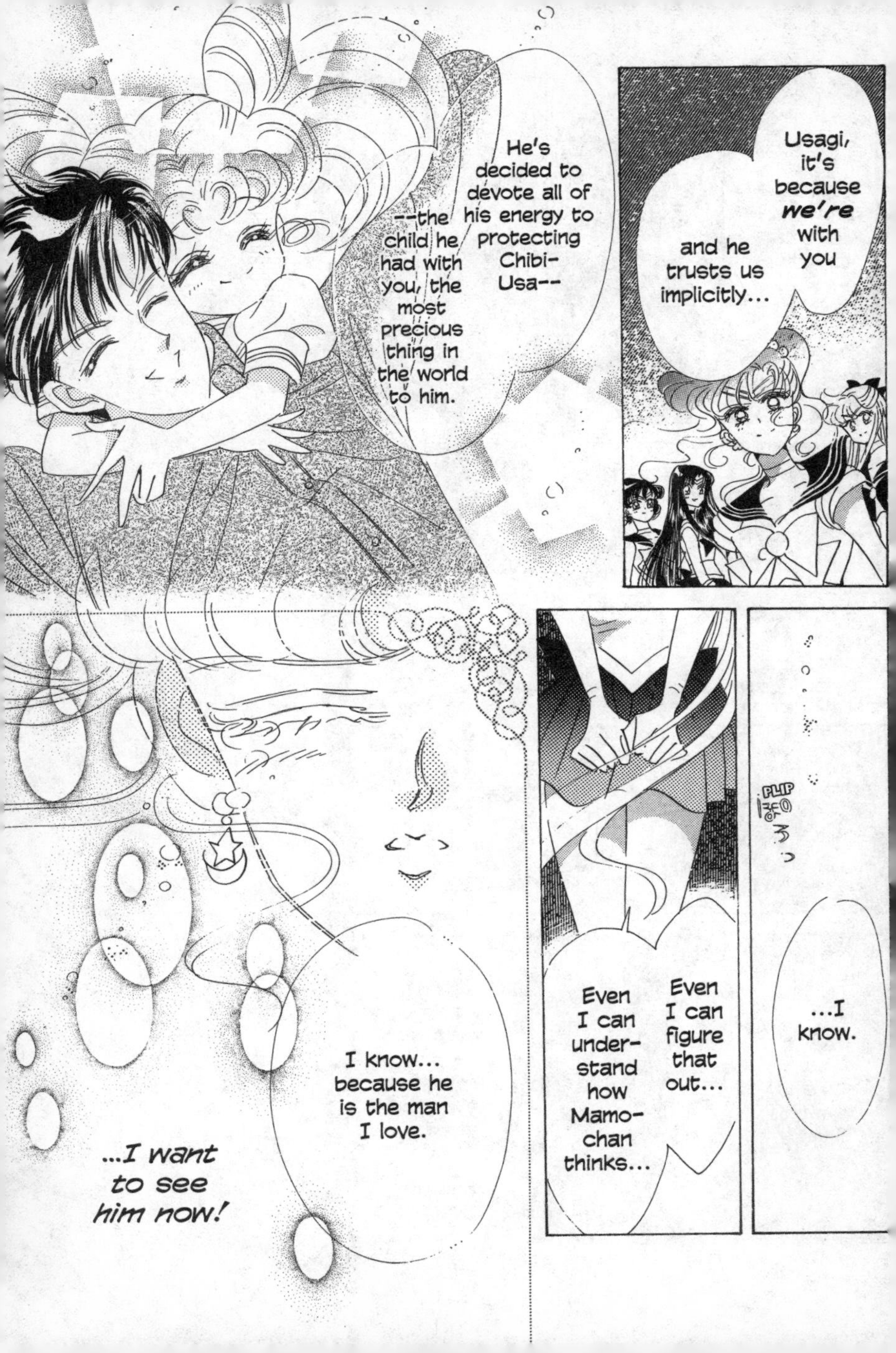

Usagi, it's because *we're* with you
and he trusts us implicitly...
He's decided to devote all of his energy to protecting Chibi-Usa--
--the child he had with you, the most precious thing in the world to him.
PLIP
...I know.
Even I can figure that out...
Even I can understand how Mamo-chan thinks...
I know... because he is the man I love.
...I want to see him now!

*God is so mean!*

*I want to be with him so much!*

*I thought we'd finally see each other...*

*...and we're torn apart again...*

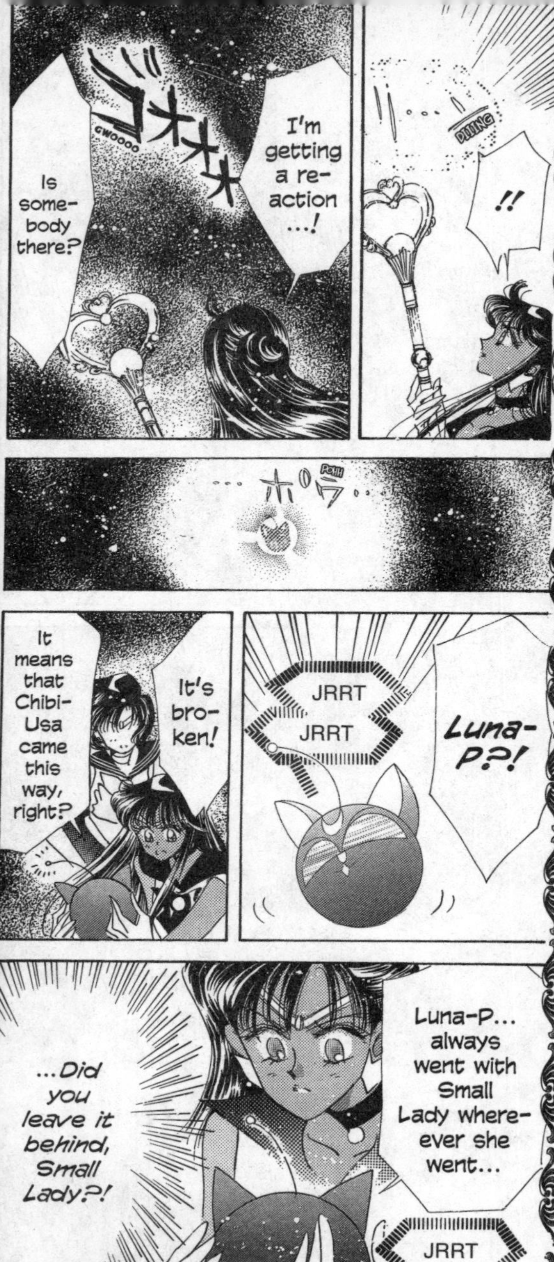
DIIING
!!
I'm getting a re-action...!
GWOOOO
Is some-body there?
PCHH
JRRT
JRRT
Luna-P?!
It's bro-ken!
It means that Chibi-Usa came this way, right?
Luna-P... always went with Small Lady where-ever she went...
JRRT
...Did you leave it behind, Small Lady?!

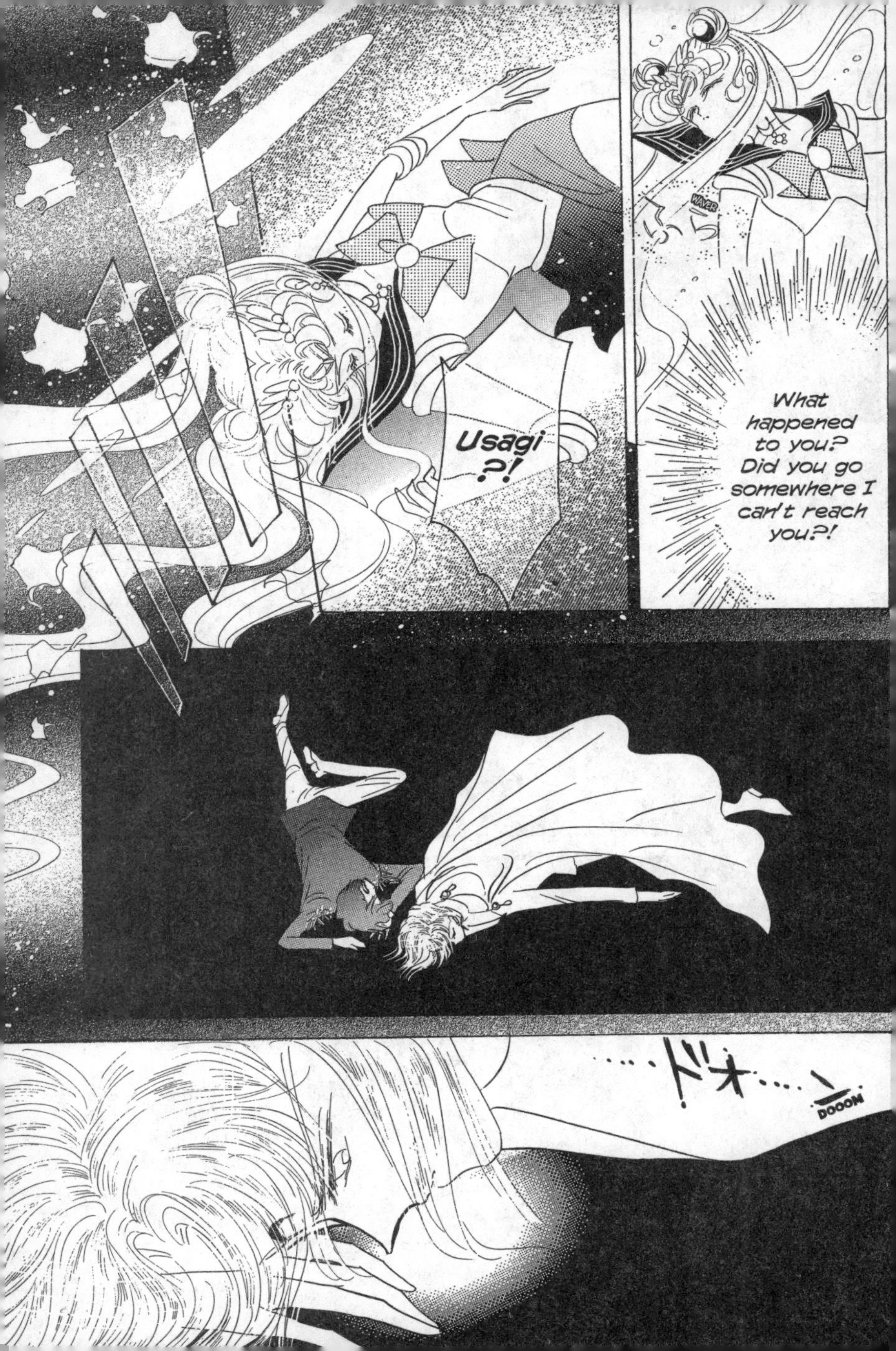
WAVER
What happened to you? Did you go somewhere I can't reach you?!
Usagi ?!
DOOOM

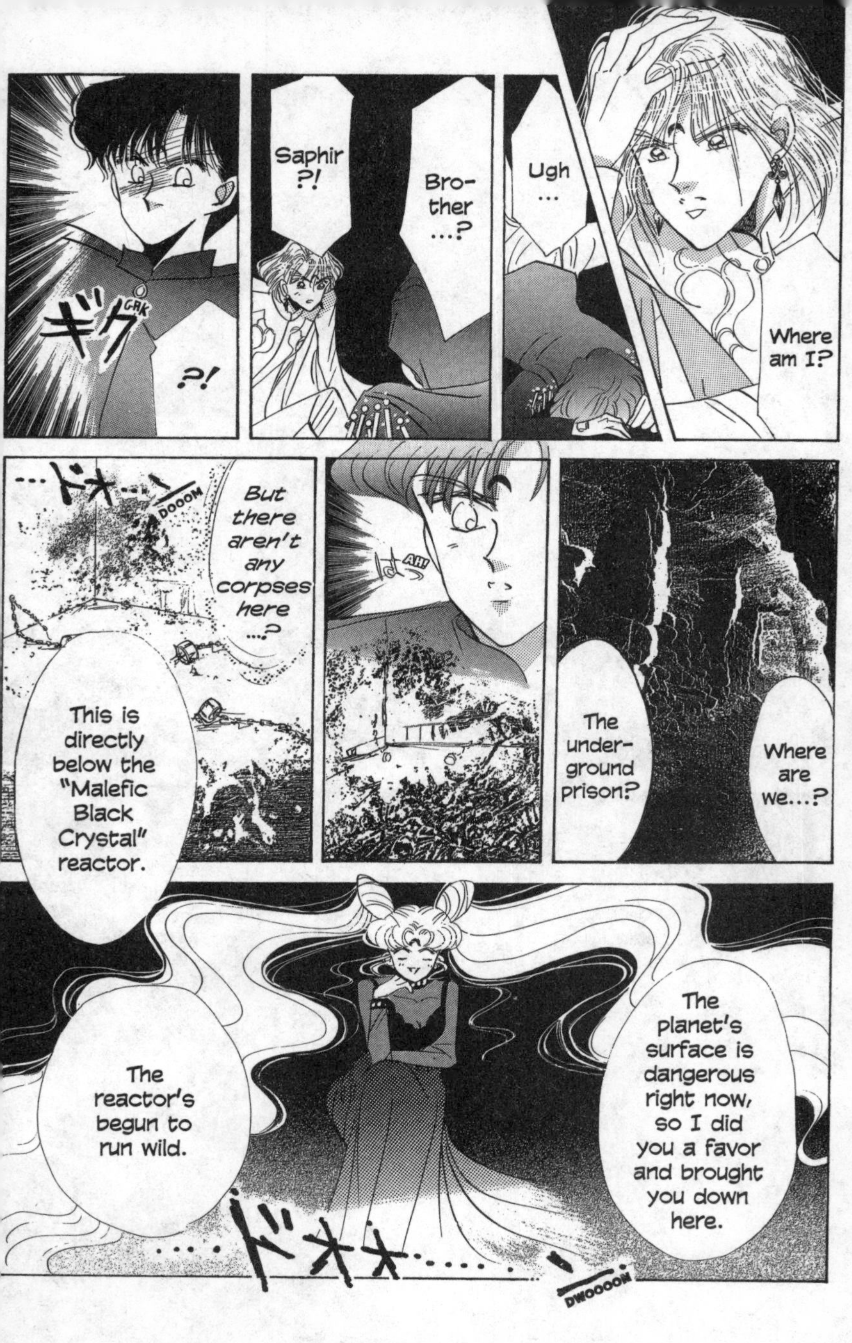
Ugh
...
Where am I?
Bro-ther ...?
Saphir ?!
GAK
?!
Where are we...?
The under-ground prison?
AH!
But there aren't any corpses here ...?
DOOOM
This is directly below the "Malefic Black Crystal" reactor.
The planet's surface is dangerous right now, so I did you a favor and brought you down here.
The reactor's begun to run wild.
DWOOOON

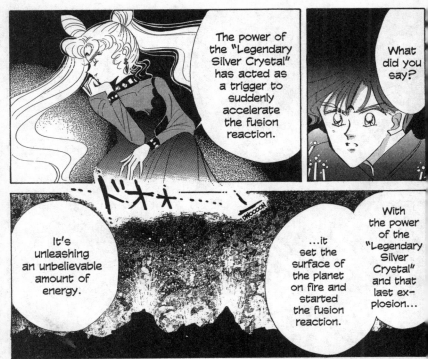

What did you say?
The power of the "Legendary Silver Crystal" has acted as a trigger to suddenly accelerate the fusion reaction.
ドオオ――ン
DWOOOON
With the power of the "Legendary Silver Crystal" and that last ex-plosion...
...it set the surface of the planet on fire and started the fusion reaction.
It's unleashing an unbelievable amount of energy.
It's all thanks to you, Saphir.
All because you built both the reactor and the system that regulates the "Malefic Black Crystal's" fusion reaction.
Thanks to them, this planet has been able to mature so much.
And now, Nemesis is an unbeatable planet.

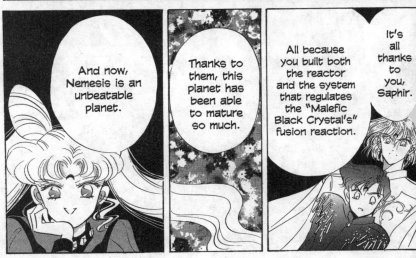

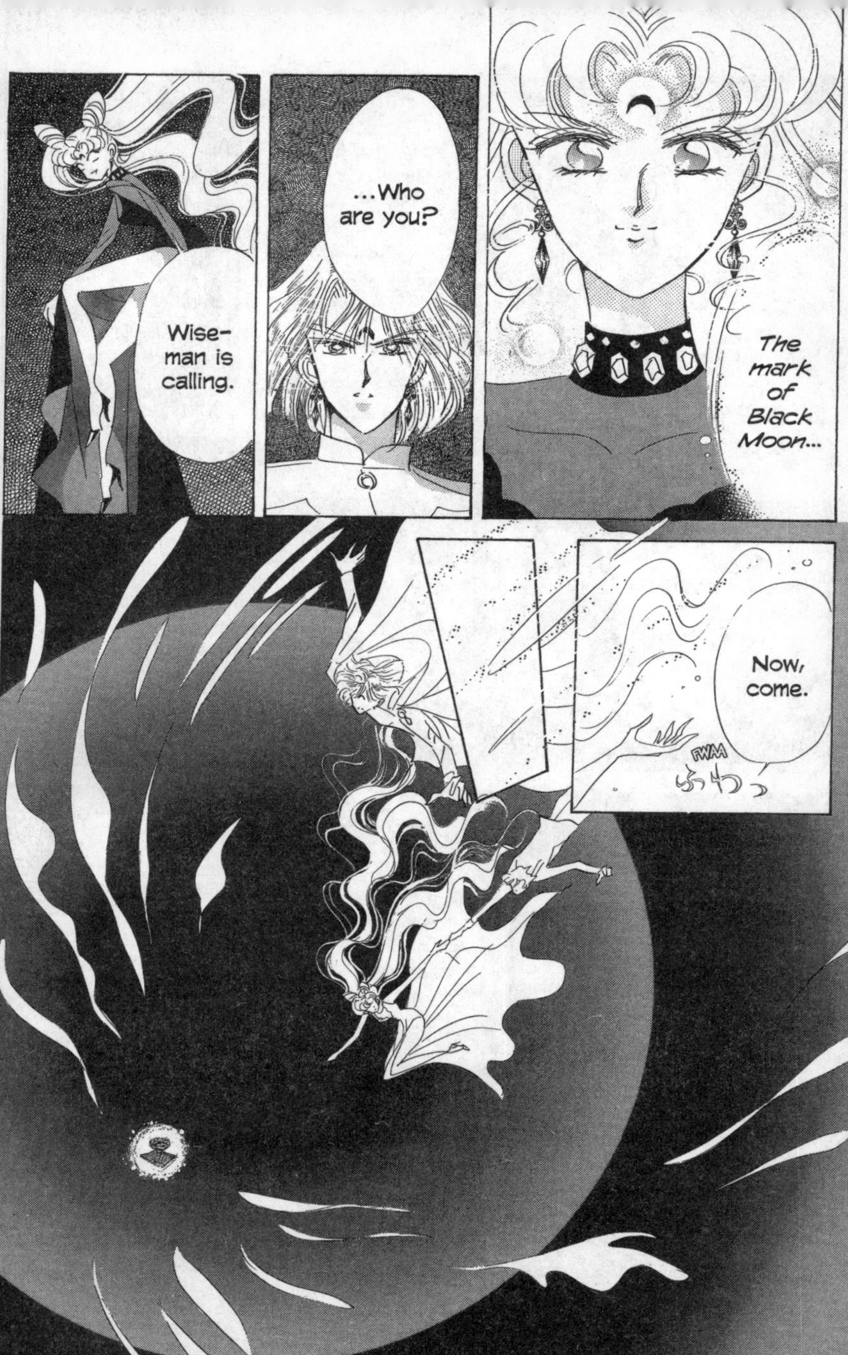
The mark of Black Moon...
...Who are you?
Wise-man is calling.
Now, come.
FWAA
ふわっ

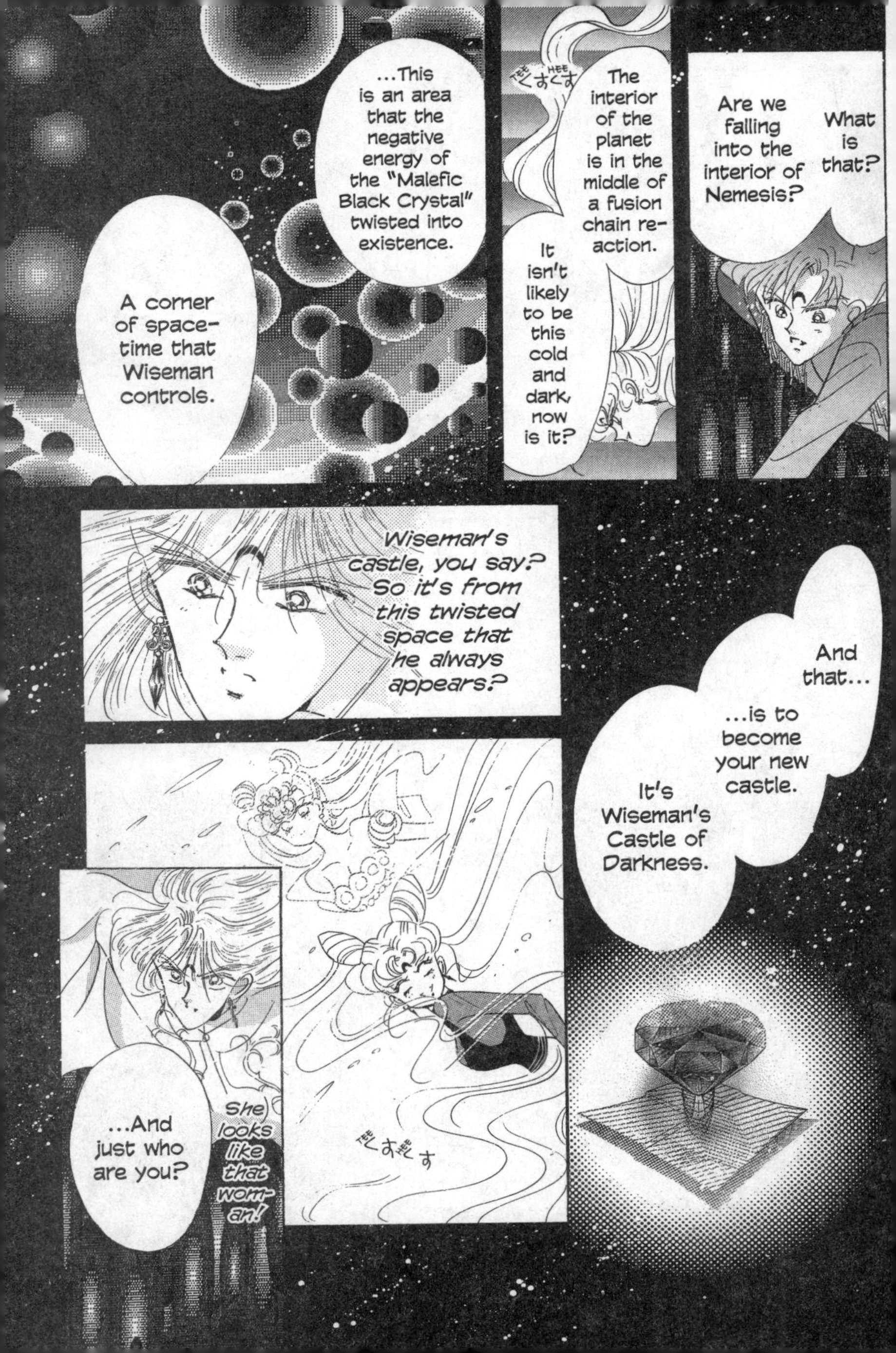
What is that?
Are we falling into the interior of Nemesis?
TEE HEE
The interior of the planet is in the middle of a fusion chain reaction.
It isn't likely to be this cold and dark, now is it?
...This is an area that the negative energy of the "Malefic Black Crystal" twisted into existence.
A corner of space-time that Wiseman controls.
It's Wiseman's Castle of Darkness.
And that...
...is to become your new castle.
Wiseman's castle, you say? So it's from this twisted space that he always appears?
TEE HEE
She looks like that woman!
...And just who are you?

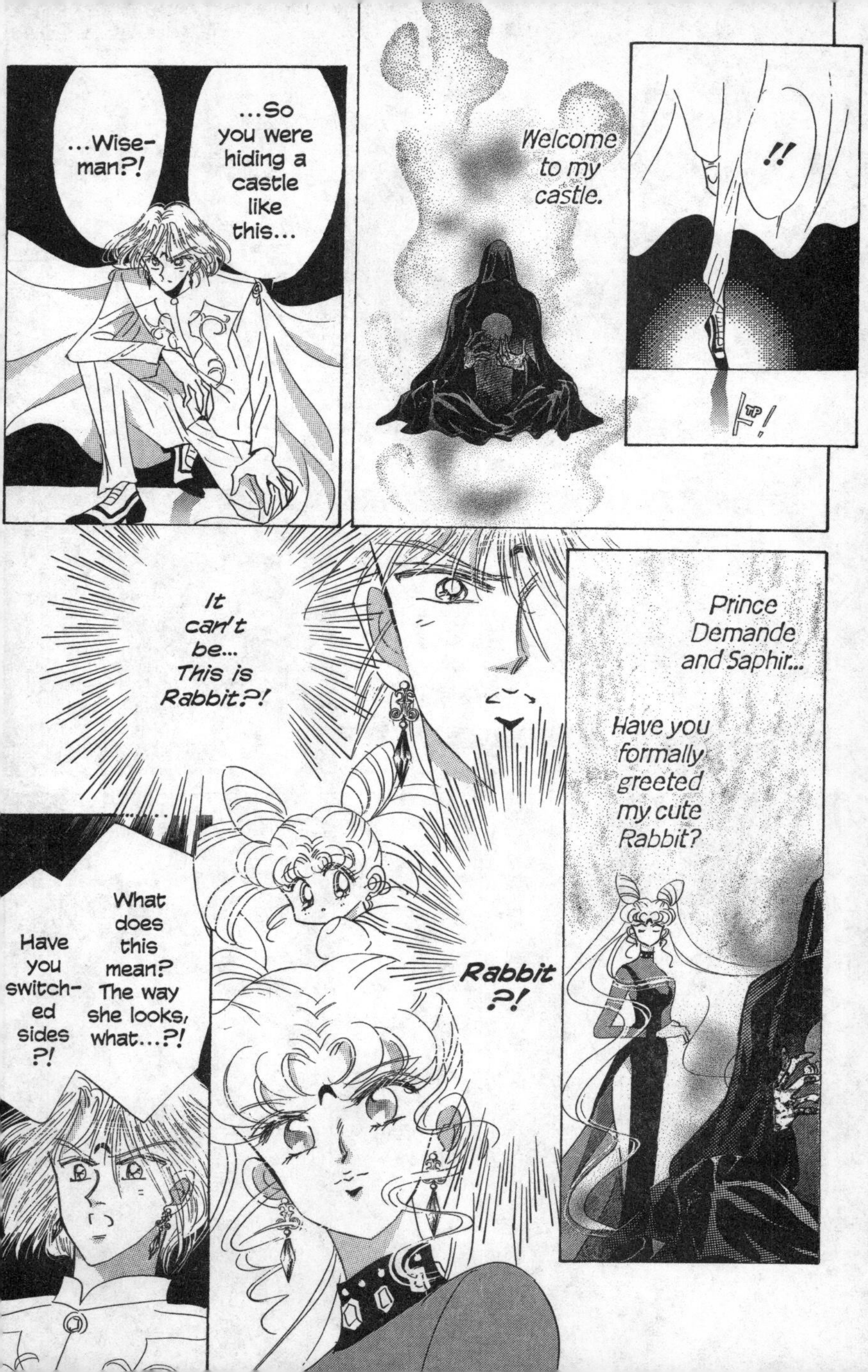
!!
TP!
Welcome to my castle.
...So you were hiding a castle like this...
...Wise-man?!
Prince Demande and Saphir...
Have you formally greeted my cute Rabbit?
It can't be... This is Rabbit?!
Rabbit ?!
......
What does this mean? The way she looks, what...?!
Have you switch-ed sides ?!

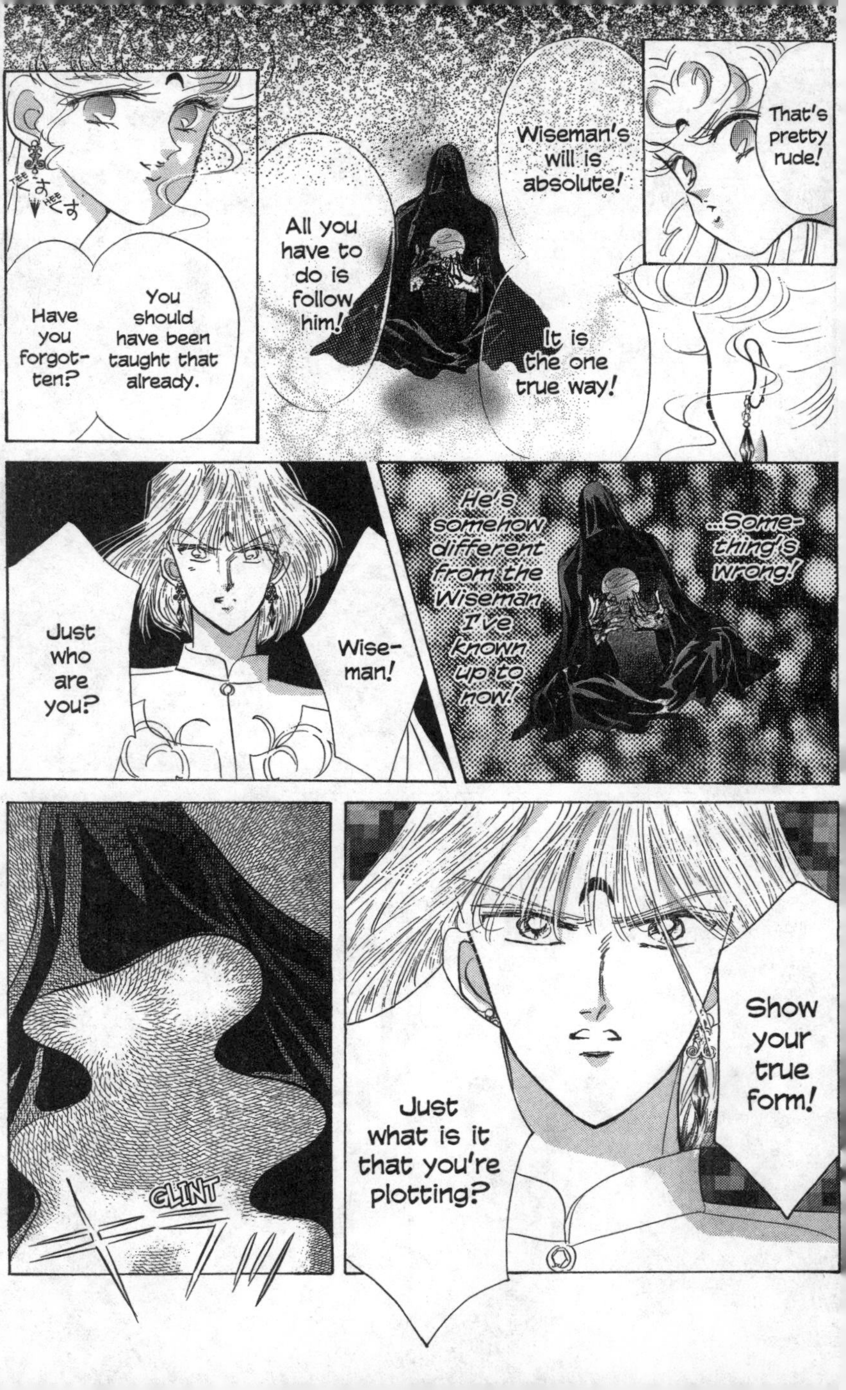

That's pretty rude!
Wiseman's will is absolute!
All you have to do is follow him!
It is the one true way!
くすくす TEE HEE
Have you forgotten?
You should have been taught that already.
...Something's wrong!
He's somehow different from the Wiseman I've known up to now!
Wise-man!
Just who are you?
Show your true form!
Just what is it that you're plotting?
CLINT

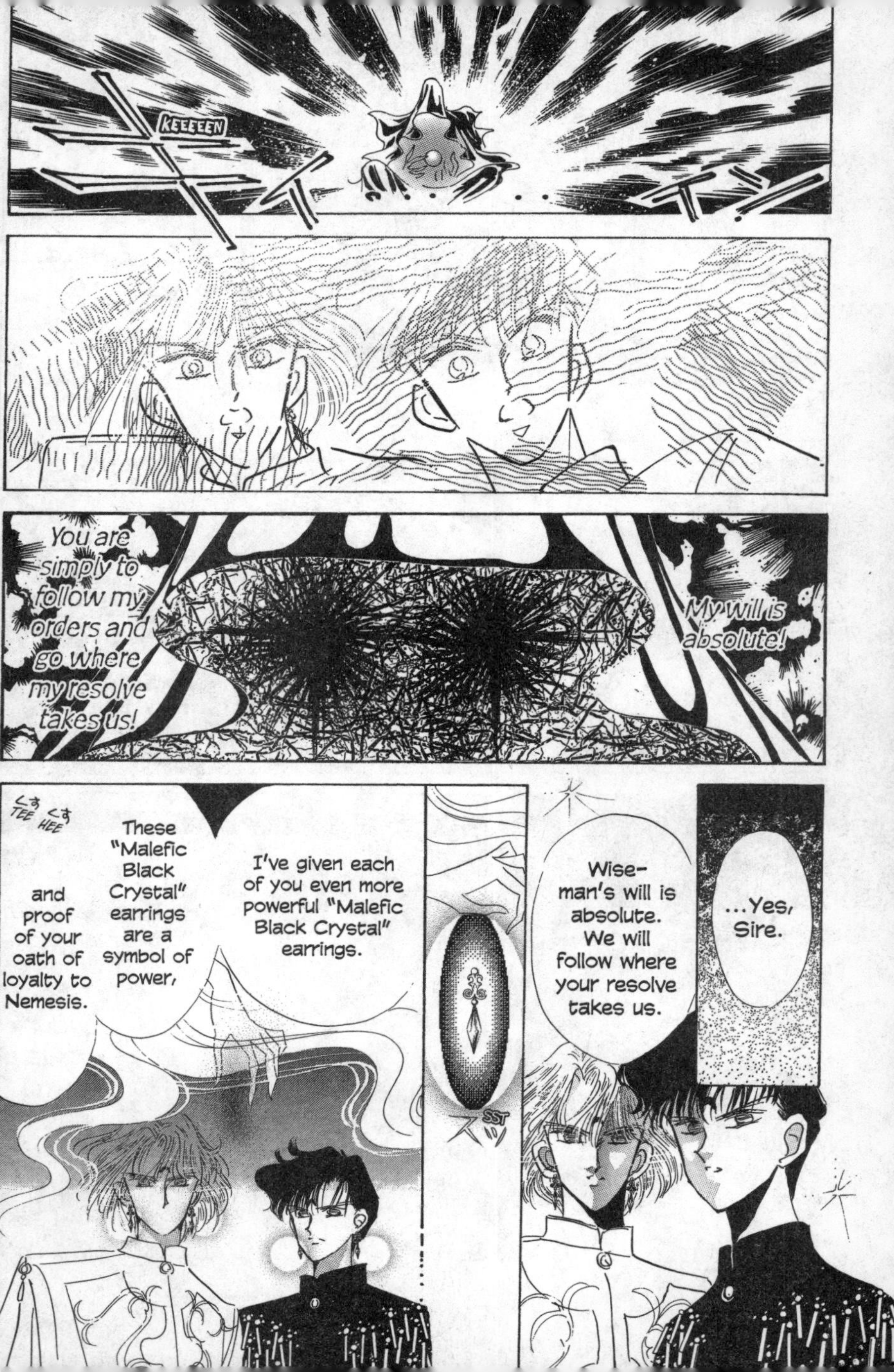
KEEEEEN
My will is absolute!
You are simply to follow my orders and go where my resolve takes us!
...Yes, Sire.
Wise-man's will is absolute. We will follow where your resolve takes us.
SST
I've given each of you even more powerful "Malefic Black Crystal" earrings.
These "Malefic Black Crystal" earrings are a symbol of power,
and proof of your oath of loyalty to Nemesis.
くす TEE くす HEE

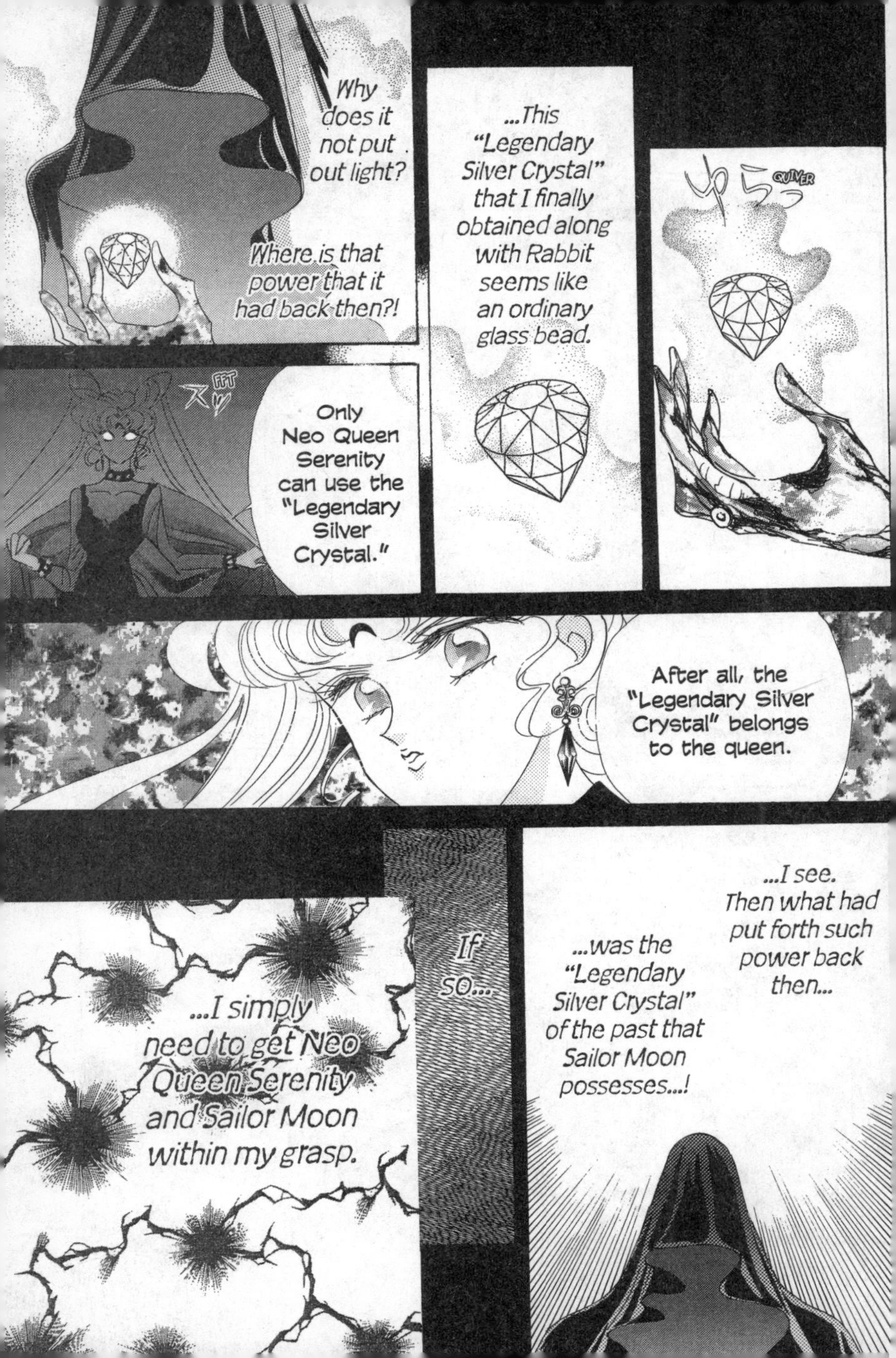
ゆらっ
QUIVER
...This "Legendary Silver Crystal" that I finally obtained along with Rabbit seems like an ordinary glass bead.
Why does it not put out light?
Where is that power that it had back then?!
スッ
FFT
Only Neo Queen Serenity can use the "Legendary Silver Crystal."
After all, the "Legendary Silver Crystal" belongs to the queen.
...I see. Then what had put forth such power back then...
...was the "Legendary Silver Crystal" of the past that Sailor Moon possesses...!
If so...
...I simply need to get Neo Queen Serenity and Sailor Moon within my grasp.

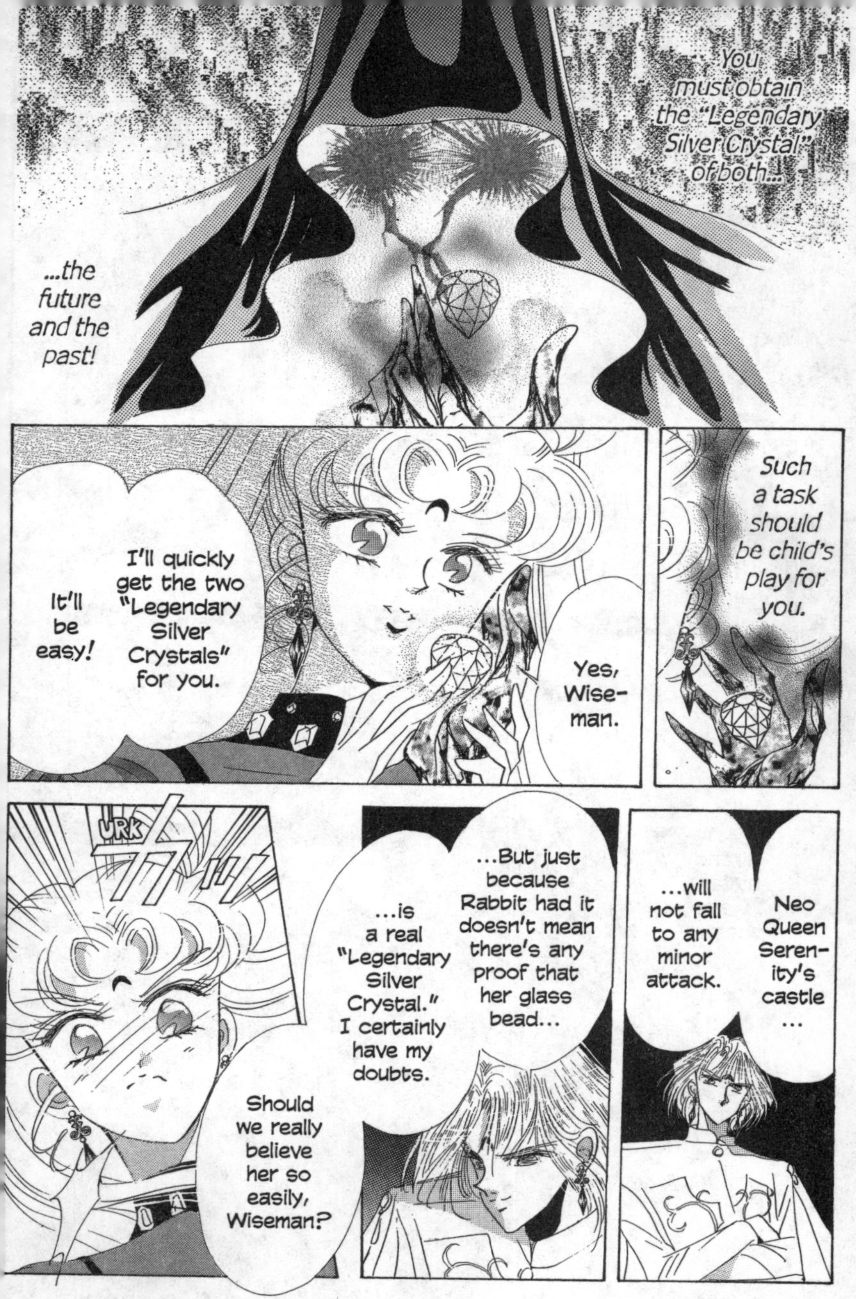
You must obtain the "Legendary Silver Crystal" of both...
...the future and the past!
Such a task should be child's play for you.
Yes, Wiseman.
I'll quickly get the two "Legendary Silver Crystals" for you.
It'll be easy!
Neo Queen Serenity's castle...
...will not fall to any minor attack.
...But just because Rabbit had it doesn't mean there's any proof that her glass bead...
...is a real "Legendary Silver Crystal." I certainly have my doubts.
URK
Should we really believe her so easily, Wiseman?

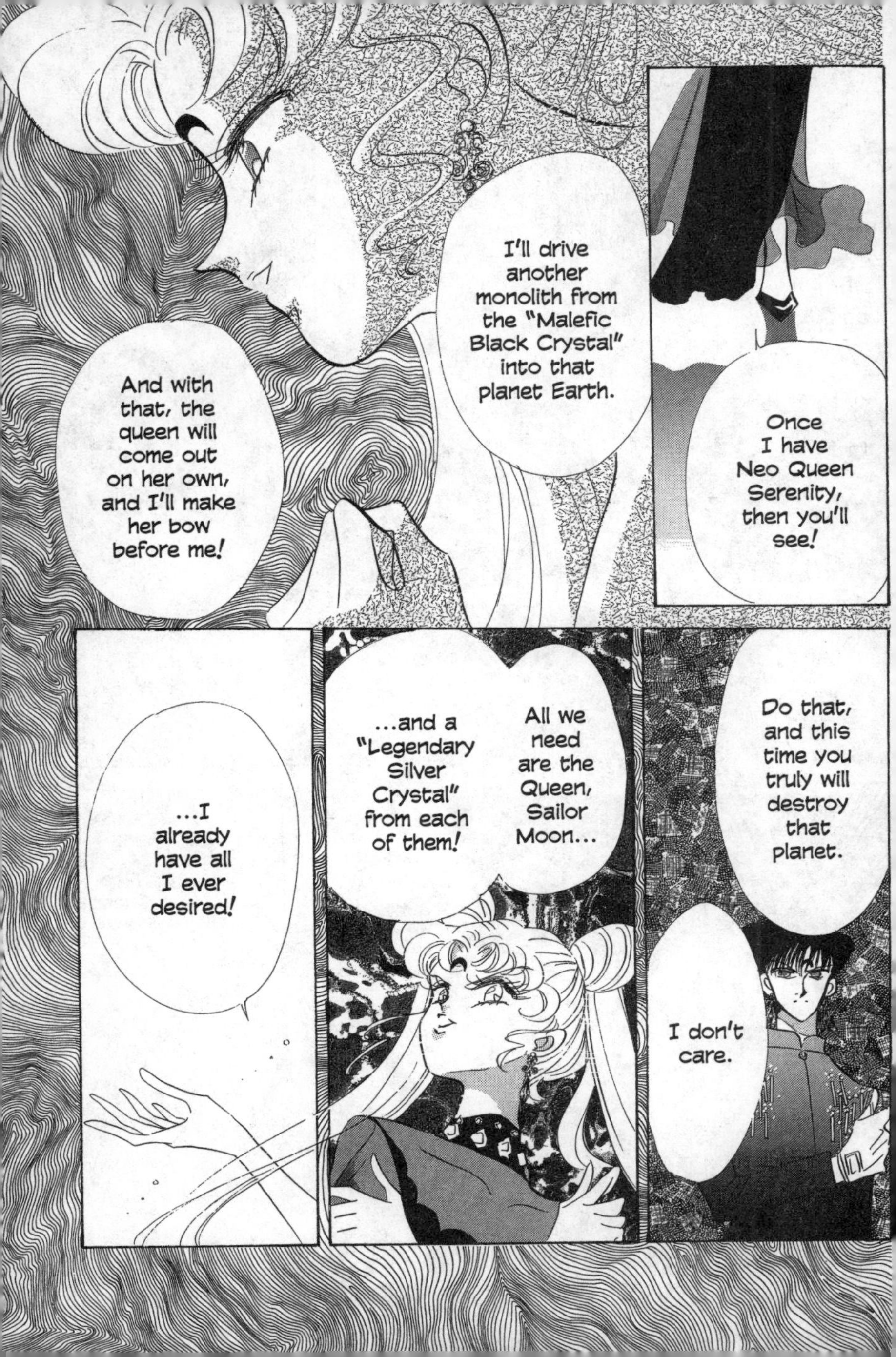
Once I have Neo Queen Serenity, then you'll see!
I'll drive another monolith from the "Malefic Black Crystal" into that planet Earth.
And with that, the queen will come out on her own, and I'll make her bow before me!
Do that, and this time you truly will destroy that planet.
I don't care.
All we need are the Queen, Sailor Moon...
...and a "Legendary Silver Crystal" from each of them!
...I already have all I ever desired!

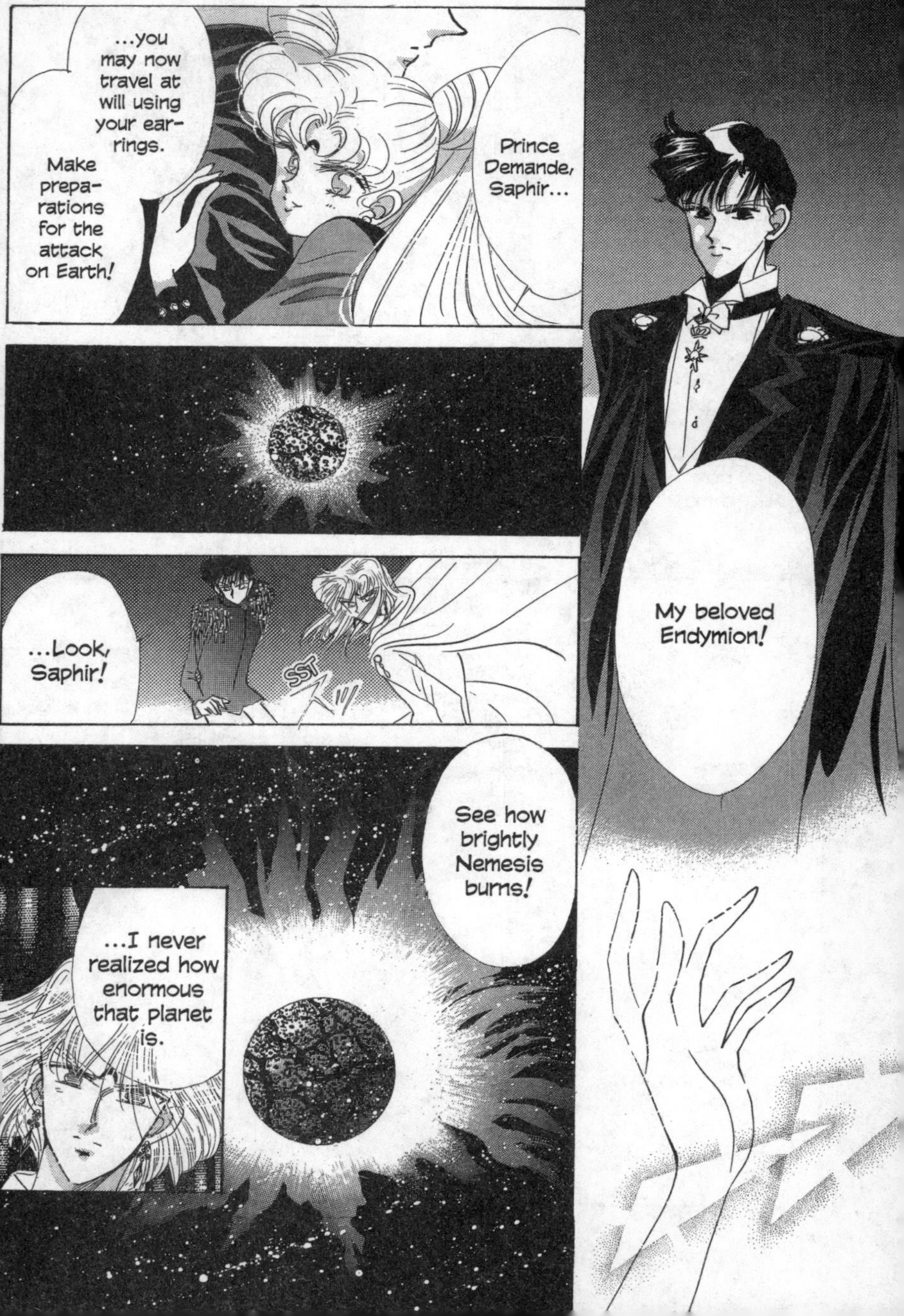
My beloved Endymion!
Prince Demande, Saphir...
...you may now travel at will using your ear-rings.
Make prepa-rations for the attack on Earth!
...Look, Saphir!
SST
See how brightly Nemesis burns!
...I never realized how enormous that planet is.

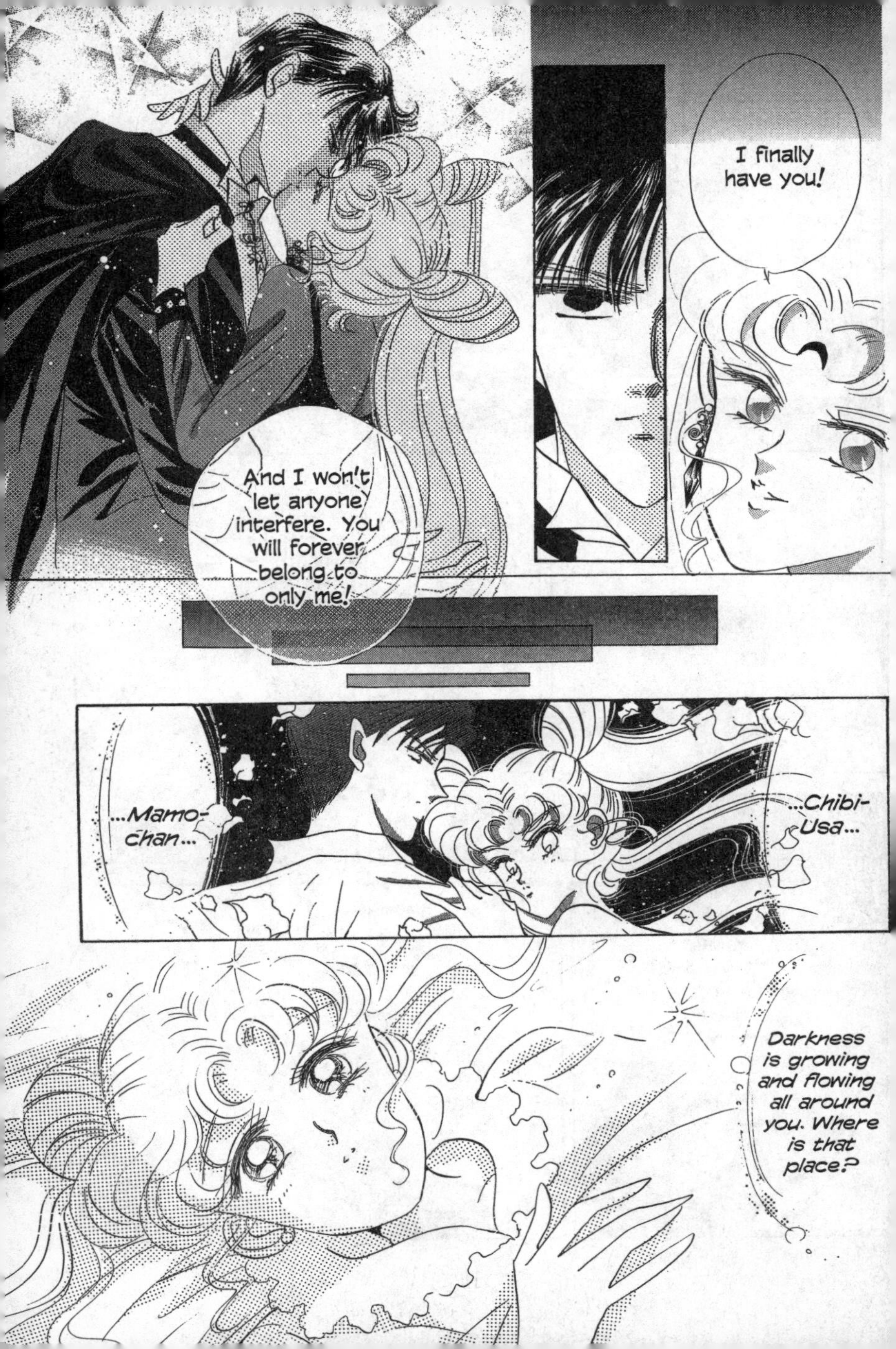
I finally have you!
And I won't let anyone interfere. You will forever belong to only me!
...Chibi-Usa...
...Mamo-chan...
Darkness is growing and flowing all around you. Where is that place?

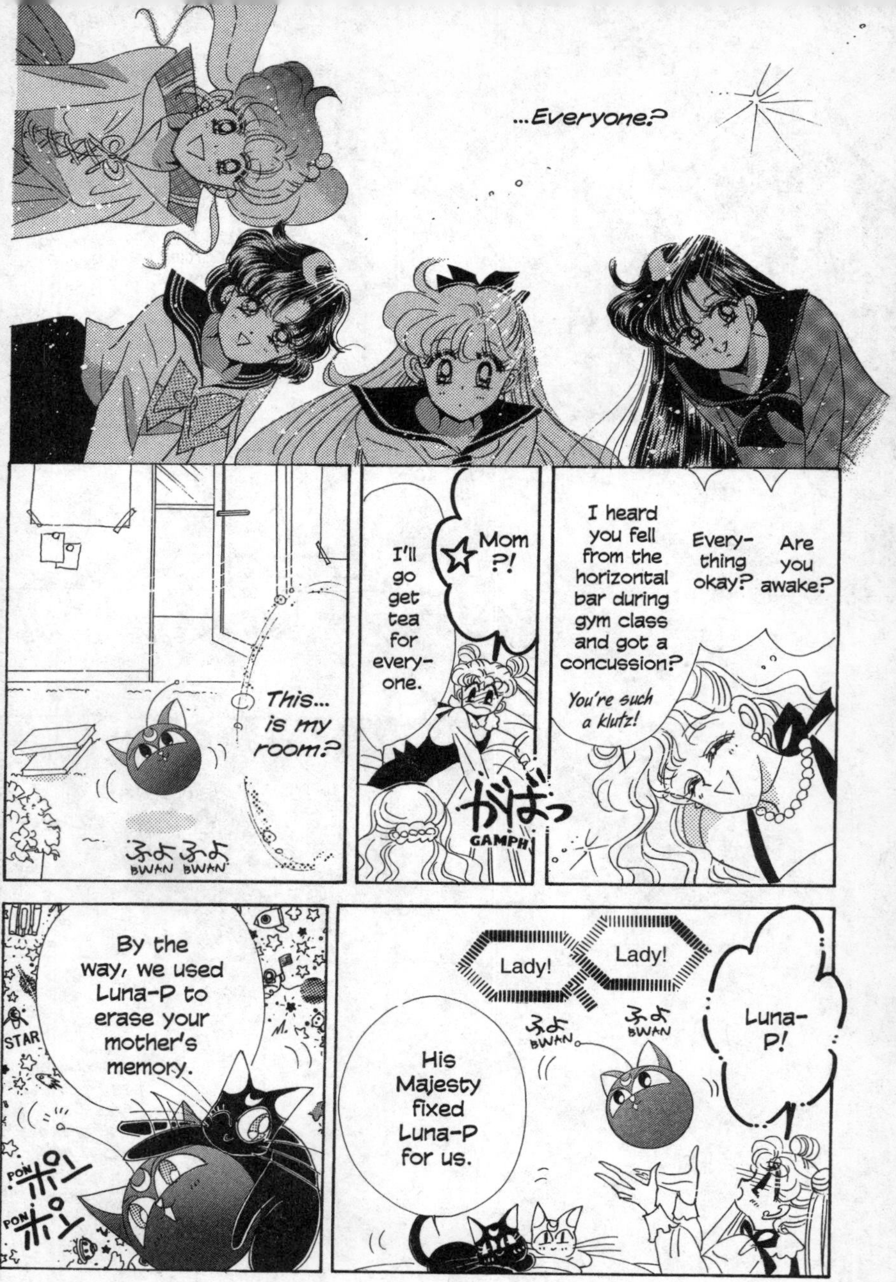
...Everyone?
Are you awake?
Every-thing okay?
I heard you fell from the horizontal bar during gym class and got a concussion?
You're such a klutz!
Mom?!
I'll go get tea for every-one.
がばっ
GAMPH
This... is my room?
ふよふよ
BWAN BWAN
Luna-P!
Lady!
Lady!
ふよ
BWAN
ふよ
BWAN
His Majesty fixed Luna-P for us.
By the way, we used Luna-P to erase your mother's memory.
STAR
ポン
PON
ポン
PON

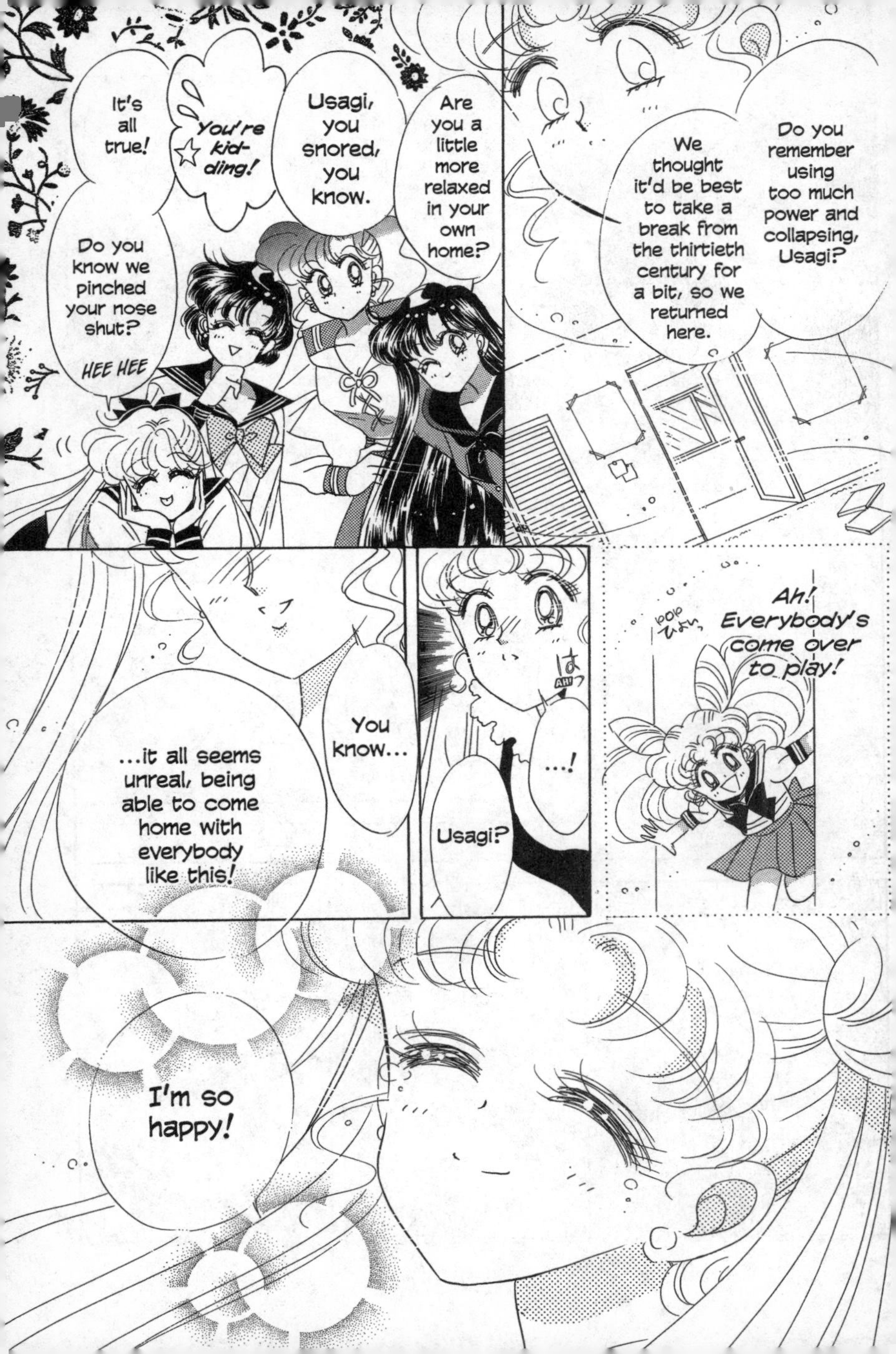
Do you remember using too much power and collapsing, Usagi?
We thought it'd be best to take a break from the thirtieth century for a bit, so we returned here.
Are you a little more relaxed in your own home?
Usagi, you snored, you know.
You're kidding!
It's all true!
Do you know we pinched your nose shut?
HEE HEE
Ah! Everybody's come over to play!
はっ
AH!
...!
Usagi?
You know...
...it all seems unreal, being able to come home with everybody like this!
I'm so happy!

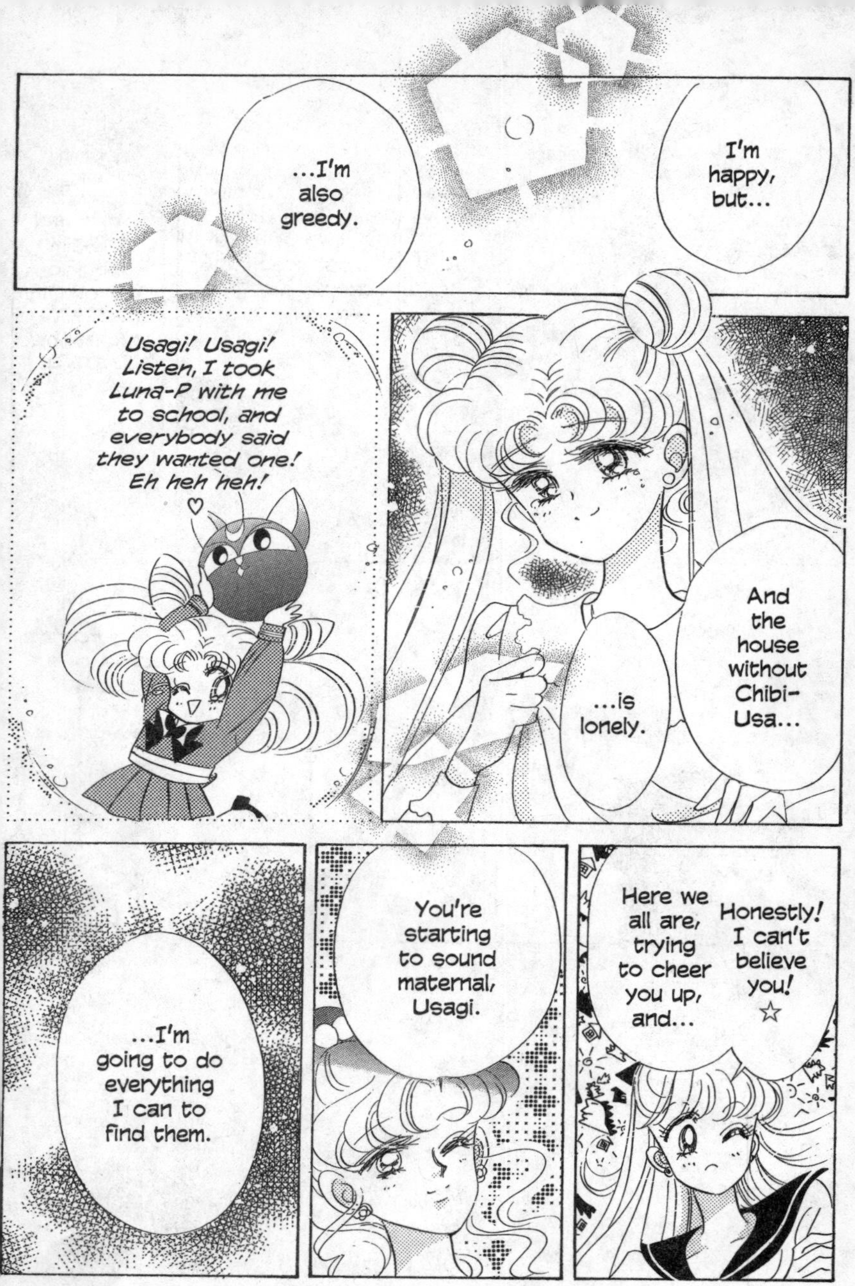
I'm happy, but...
...I'm also greedy.
And the house without Chibi-Usa...
...is lonely.
Usagi! Usagi! Listen, I took Luna-P with me to school, and everybody said they wanted one! Eh heh heh!
Honestly! I can't believe you! ☆
Here we all are, trying to cheer you up, and...
You're starting to sound maternal, Usagi.
...I'm going to do everything I can to find them.

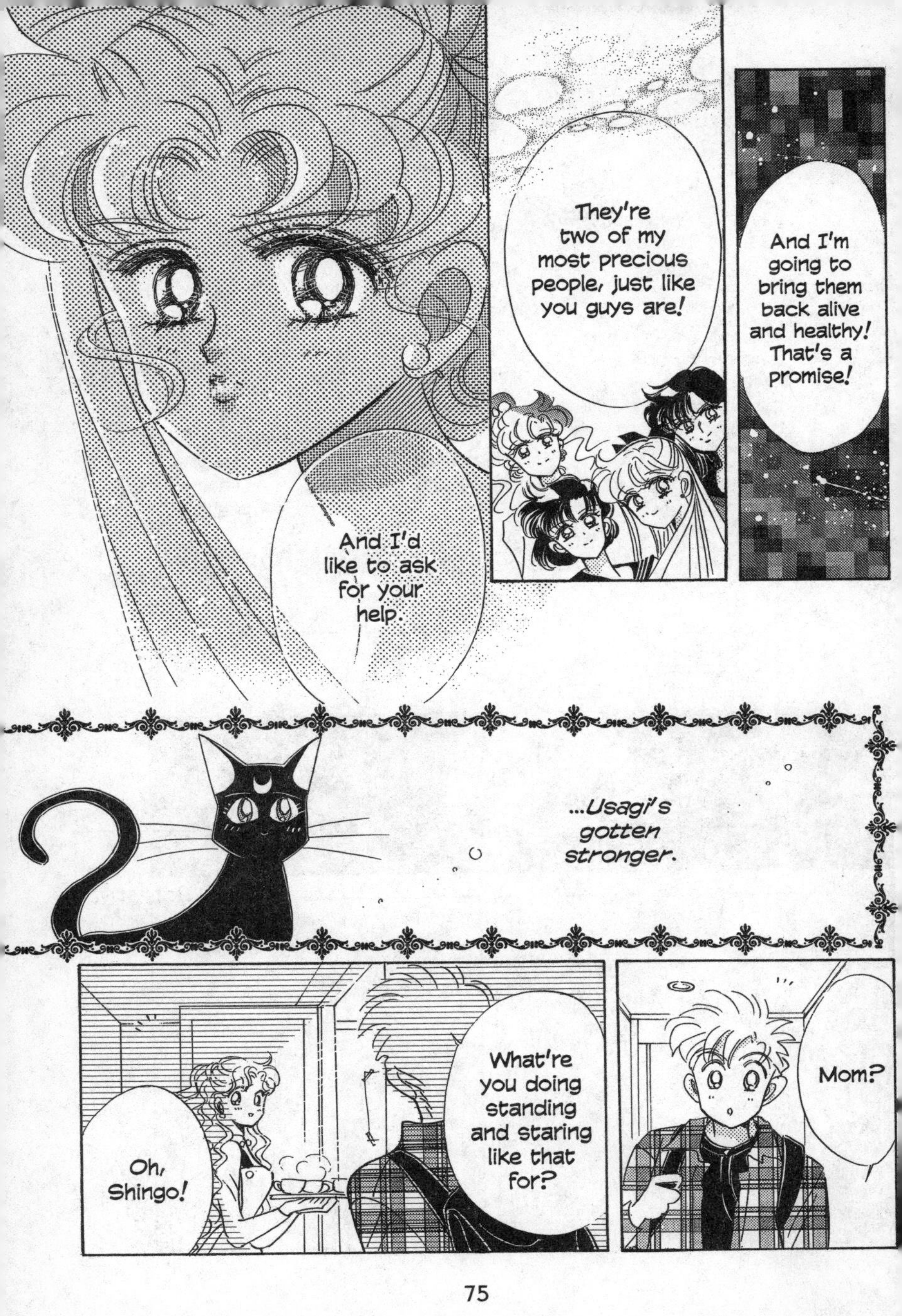
And I'm going to bring them back alive and healthy! That's a promise!
They're two of my most precious people, just like you guys are!
And I'd like to ask for your help.
...Usagi's gotten stronger.
Mom?
What're you doing standing and staring like that for?
Oh, Shingo!

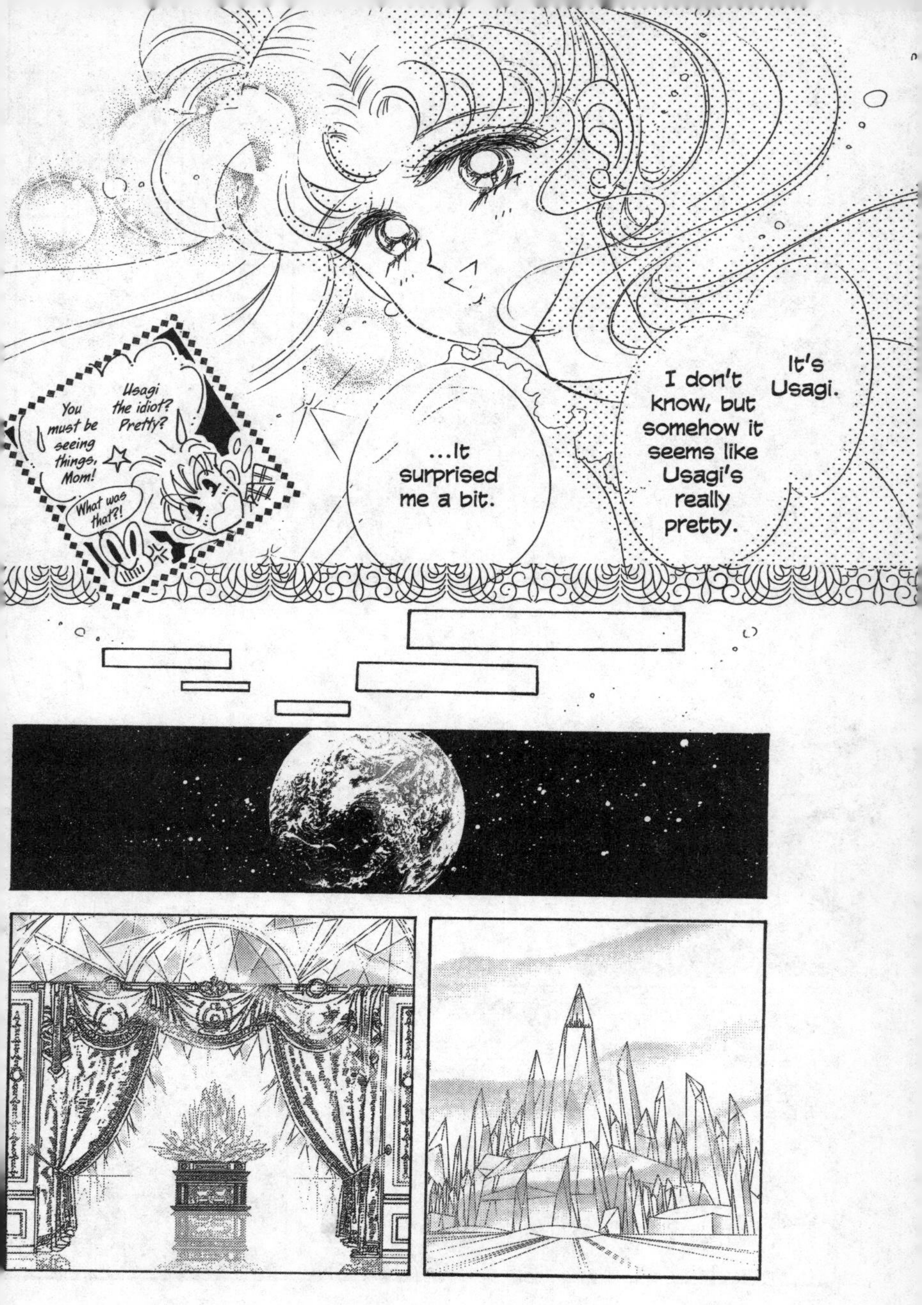
It's Usagi.
I don't know, but somehow it seems like Usagi's really pretty.
...It surprised me a bit.
Usagi the idiot? Pretty?
You must be seeing things, Mom!
What was that?!

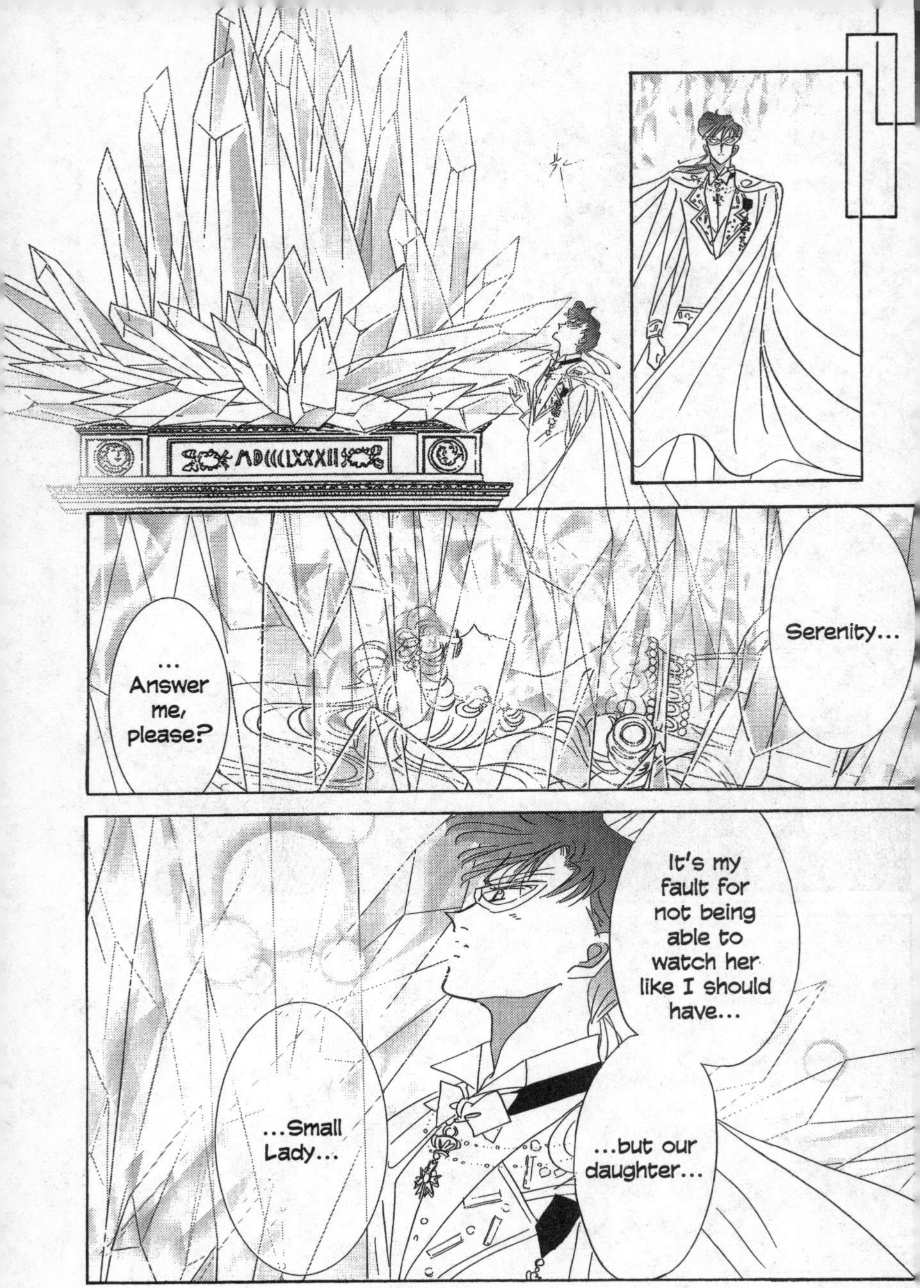
Serenity...
... Answer me, please?
It's my fault for not being able to watch her like I should have...
...but our daughter...
...Small Lady...

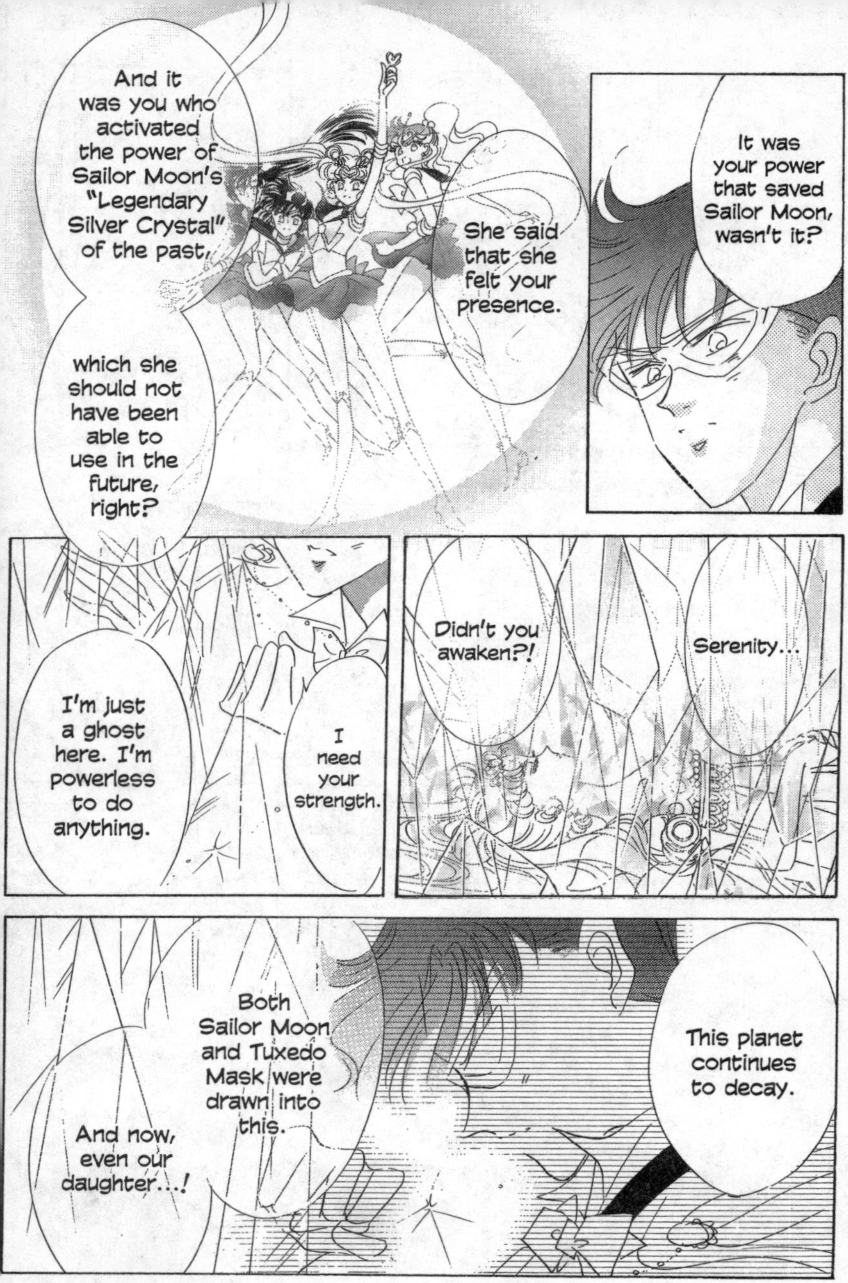
It was your power that saved Sailor Moon, wasn't it?
She said that she felt your presence.
And it was you who activated the power of Sailor Moon's "Legendary Silver Crystal" of the past,
which she should not have been able to use in the future, right?
Serenity...
Didn't you awaken?!
I need your strength.
I'm just a ghost here. I'm powerless to do anything.
This planet continues to decay.
Both Sailor Moon and Tuxedo Mask were drawn into this.
And now, even our daughter...!

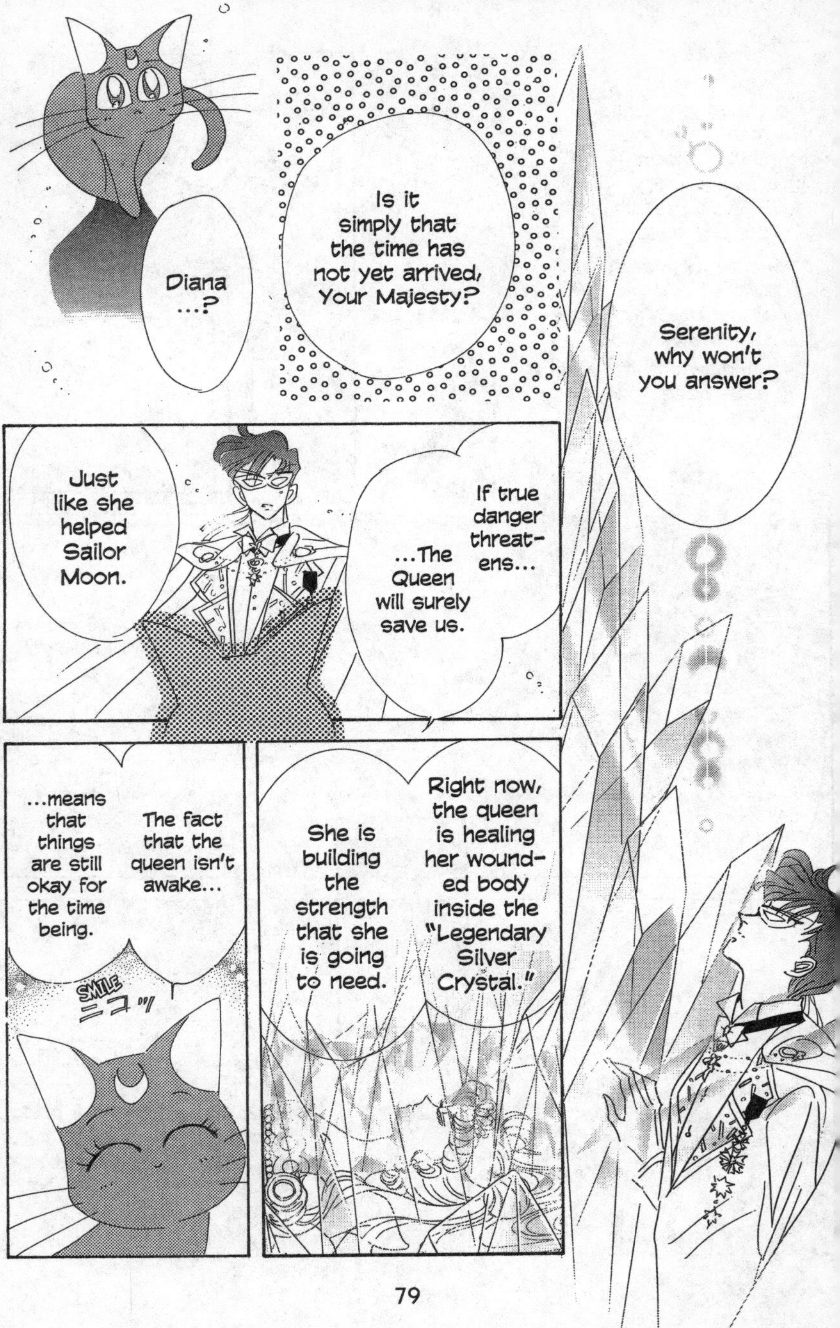
Serenity, why won't you answer?
Is it simply that the time has not yet arrived, Your Majesty?
Diana ...?
If true danger threat-ens...
...The Queen will surely save us.
Just like she helped Sailor Moon.
Right now, the queen is healing her wound-ed body inside the "Legendary Silver Crystal."
She is building the strength that she is going to need.
The fact that the queen isn't awake...
...means that things are still okay for the time being.
SMILE
ニコッ

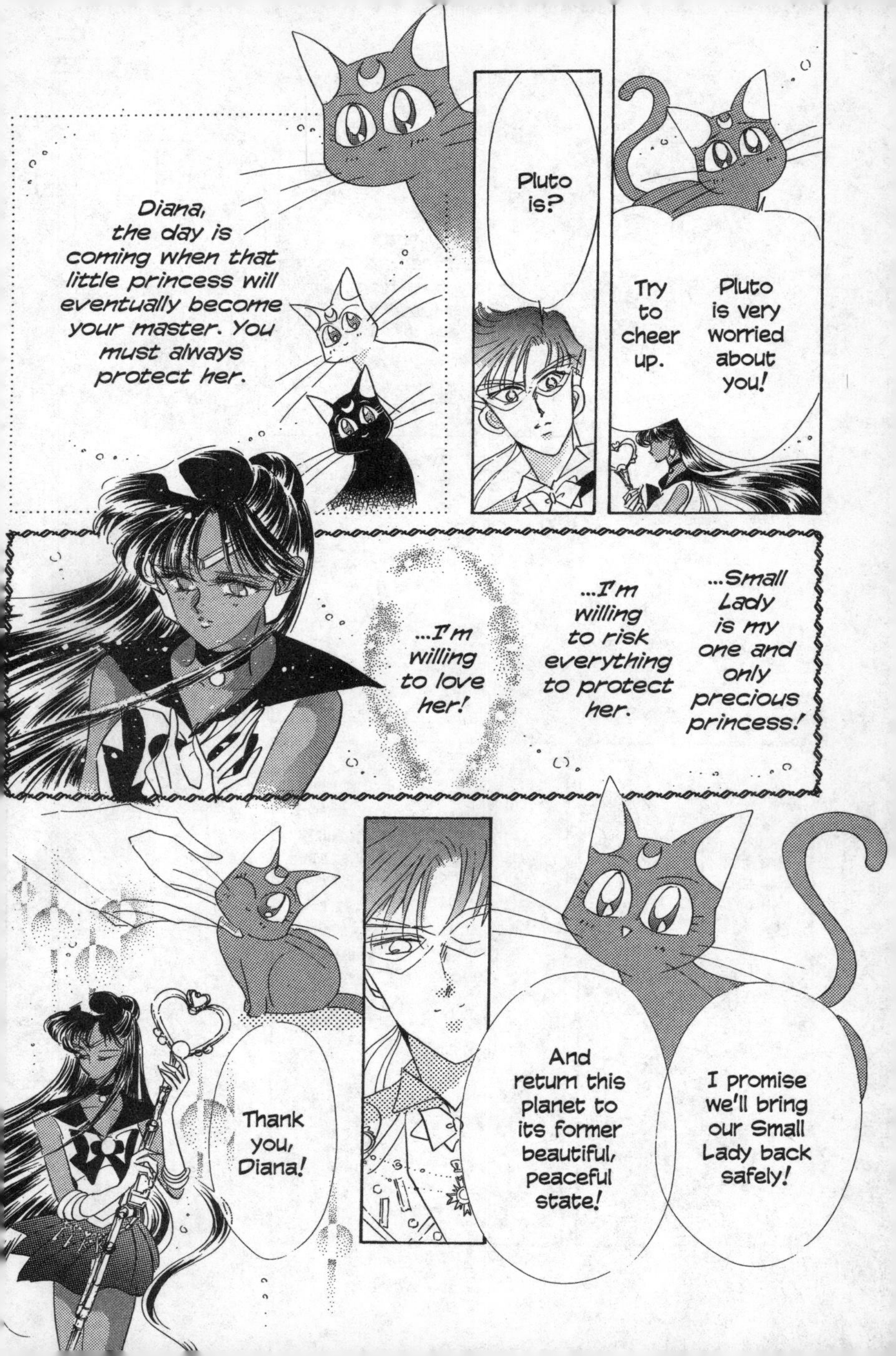
Pluto is very worried about you!
Try to cheer up.
Pluto is?
Diana, the day is coming when that little princess will eventually become your master. You must always protect her.
...Small Lady is my one and only precious princess!
...I'm willing to risk everything to protect her.
...I'm willing to love her!
I promise we'll bring our Small Lady back safely!
And return this planet to its former beautiful, peaceful state!
Thank you, Diana!

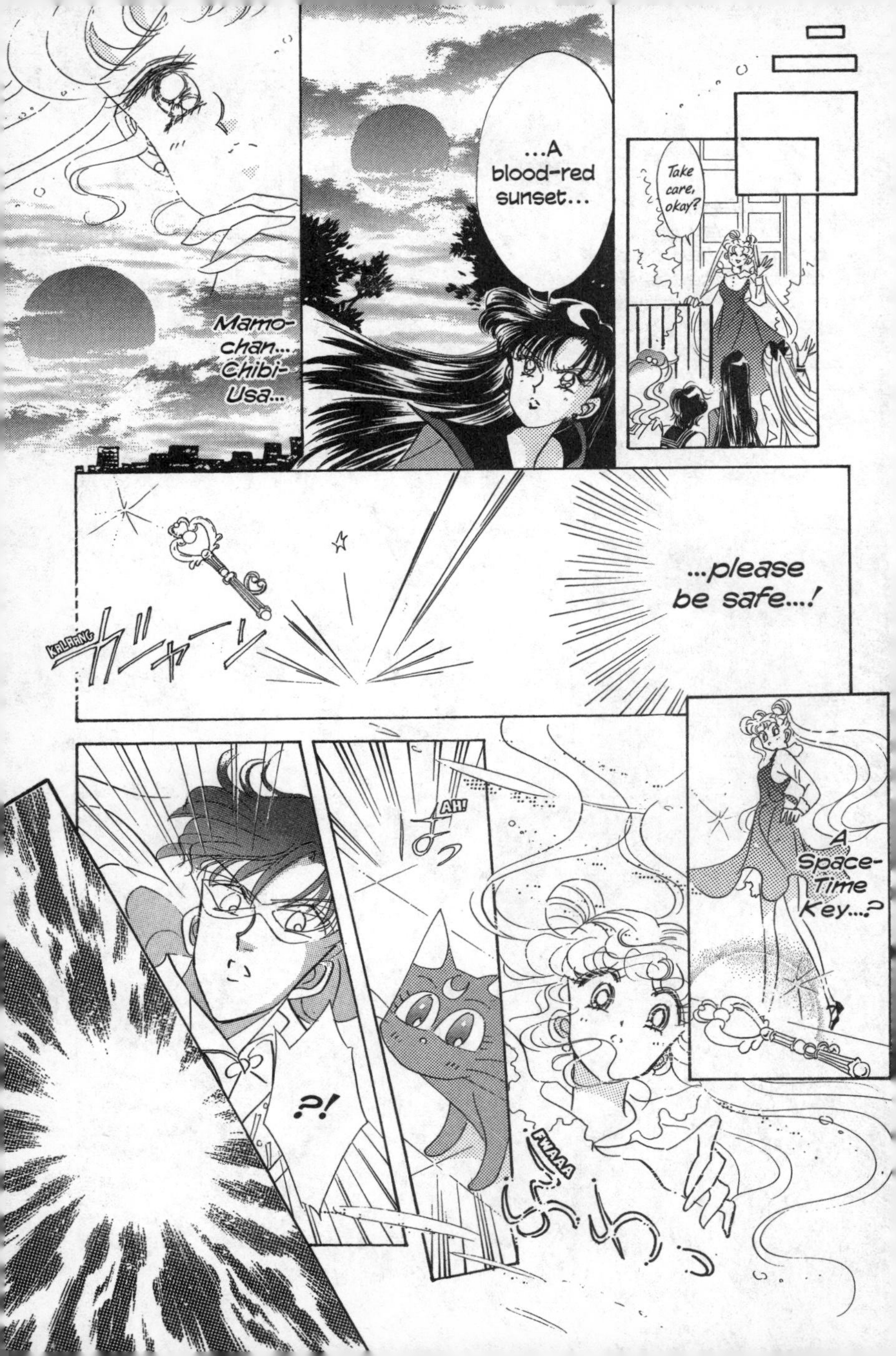
Take care, okay?
...A blood-red sunset...
Mamo-chan... Chibi-Usa...
...please be safe...!
KALAANG
A Space-Time Key...?
AH!
FWAAA
?!

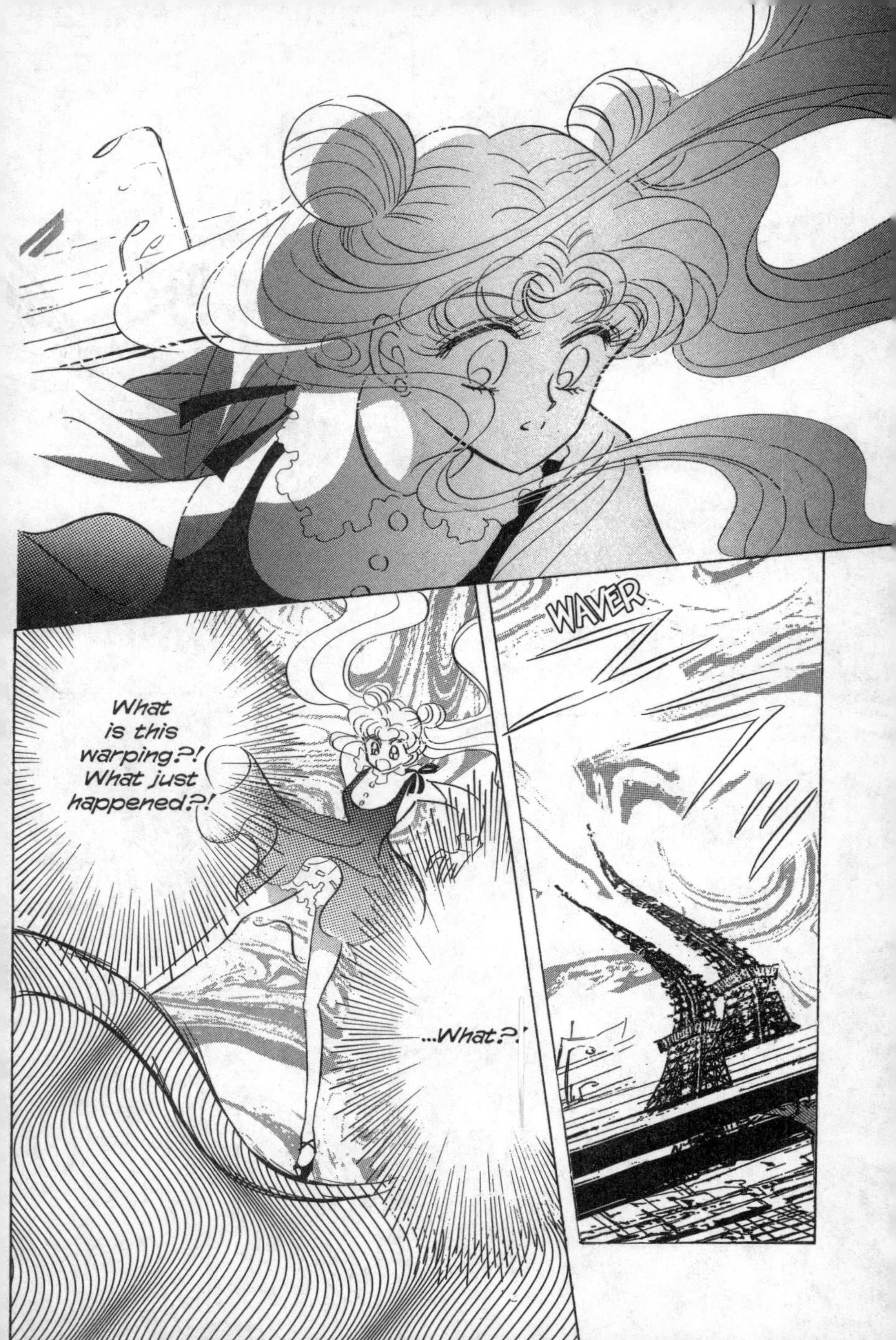
WAVER
What is this warping?! What just happened?!
...What?!

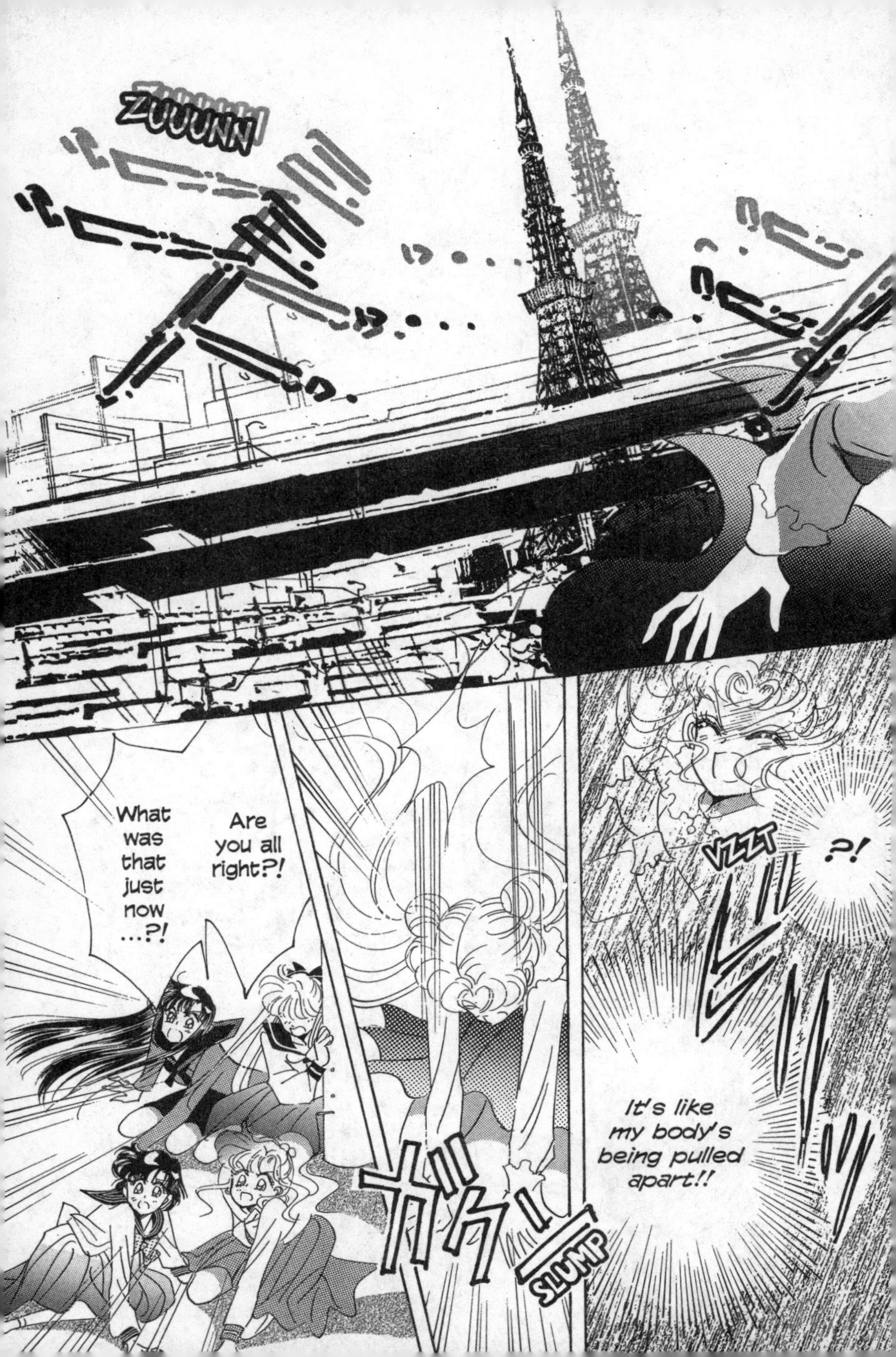
ZUUUNN
?!
VZZT
It's like my body's being pulled apart!!
SLUMP
Are you all right?!
What was that just now ...?!

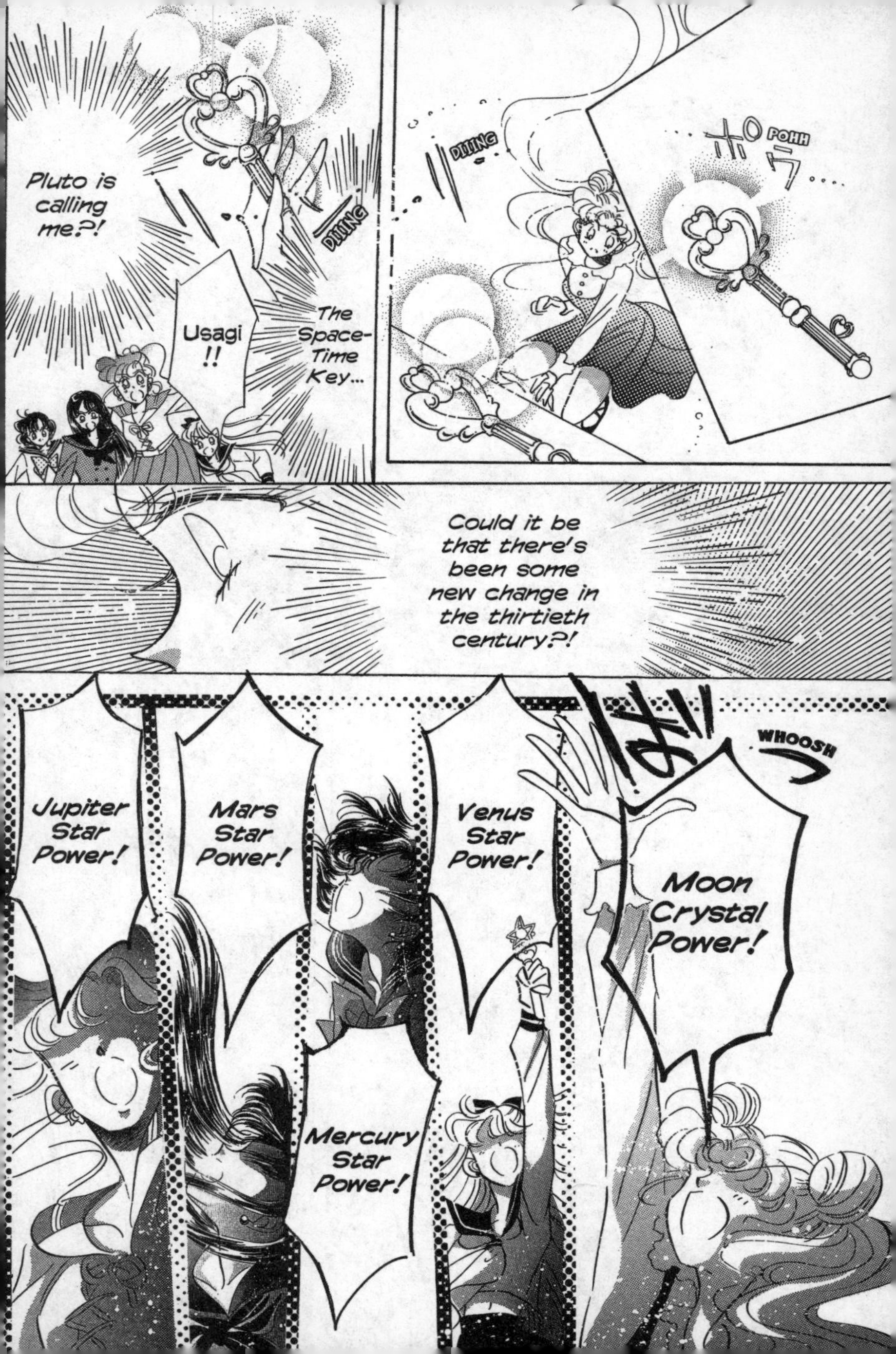
POHH
DIIING
DIIING
The Space-Time Key...
Usagi !!
Pluto is calling me?!
Could it be that there's been some new change in the thirtieth century?!
WHOOSH
Moon Crystal Power!
Venus Star Power!
Mercury Star Power!
Mars Star Power!
Jupiter Star Power!

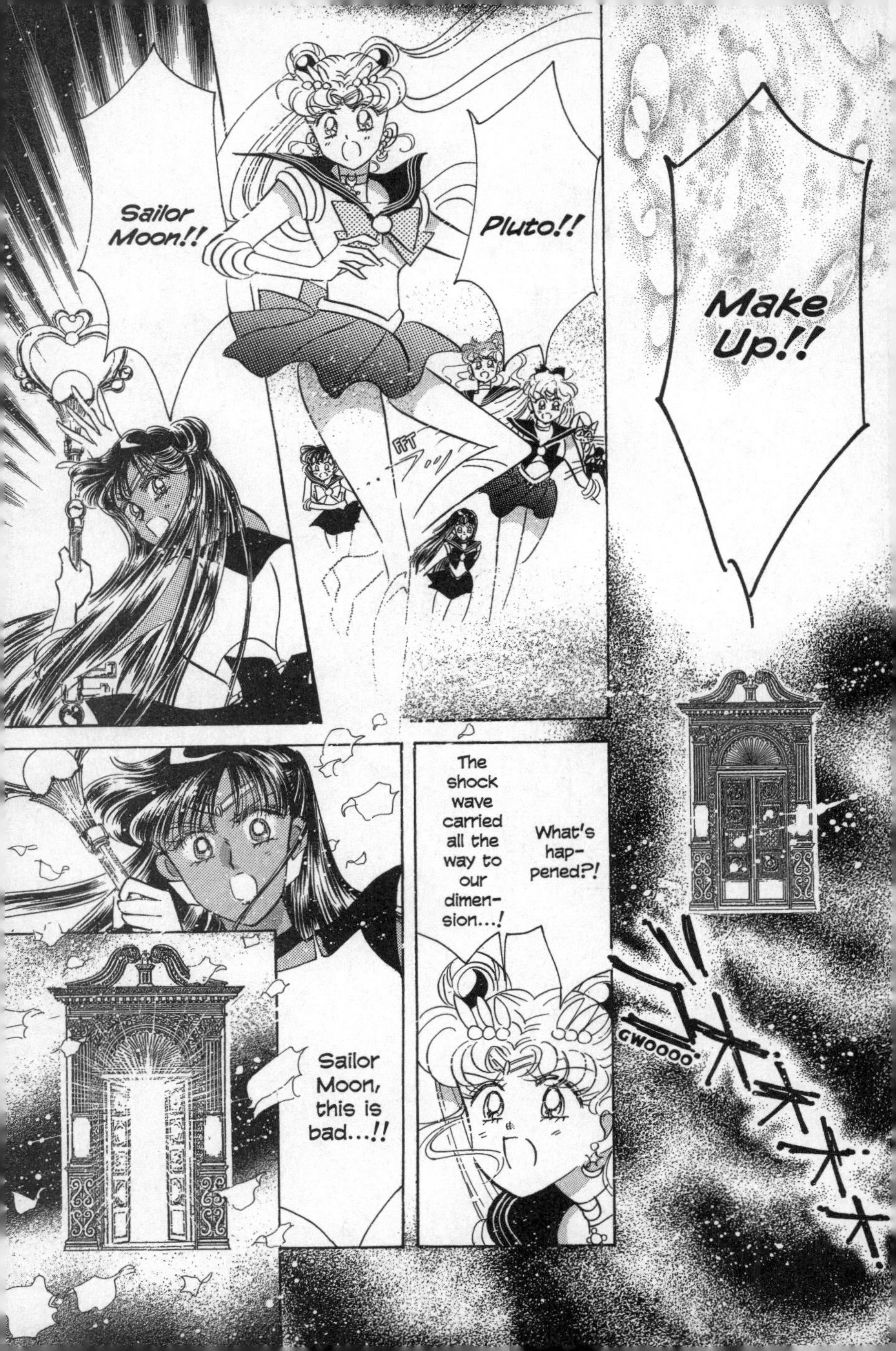

Make Up!!
GWOOOO
Pluto!!
Sailor Moon!!
FFT
What's hap-pened?!
The shock wave carried all the way to our dimen-sion...!
Sailor Moon, this is bad...!!

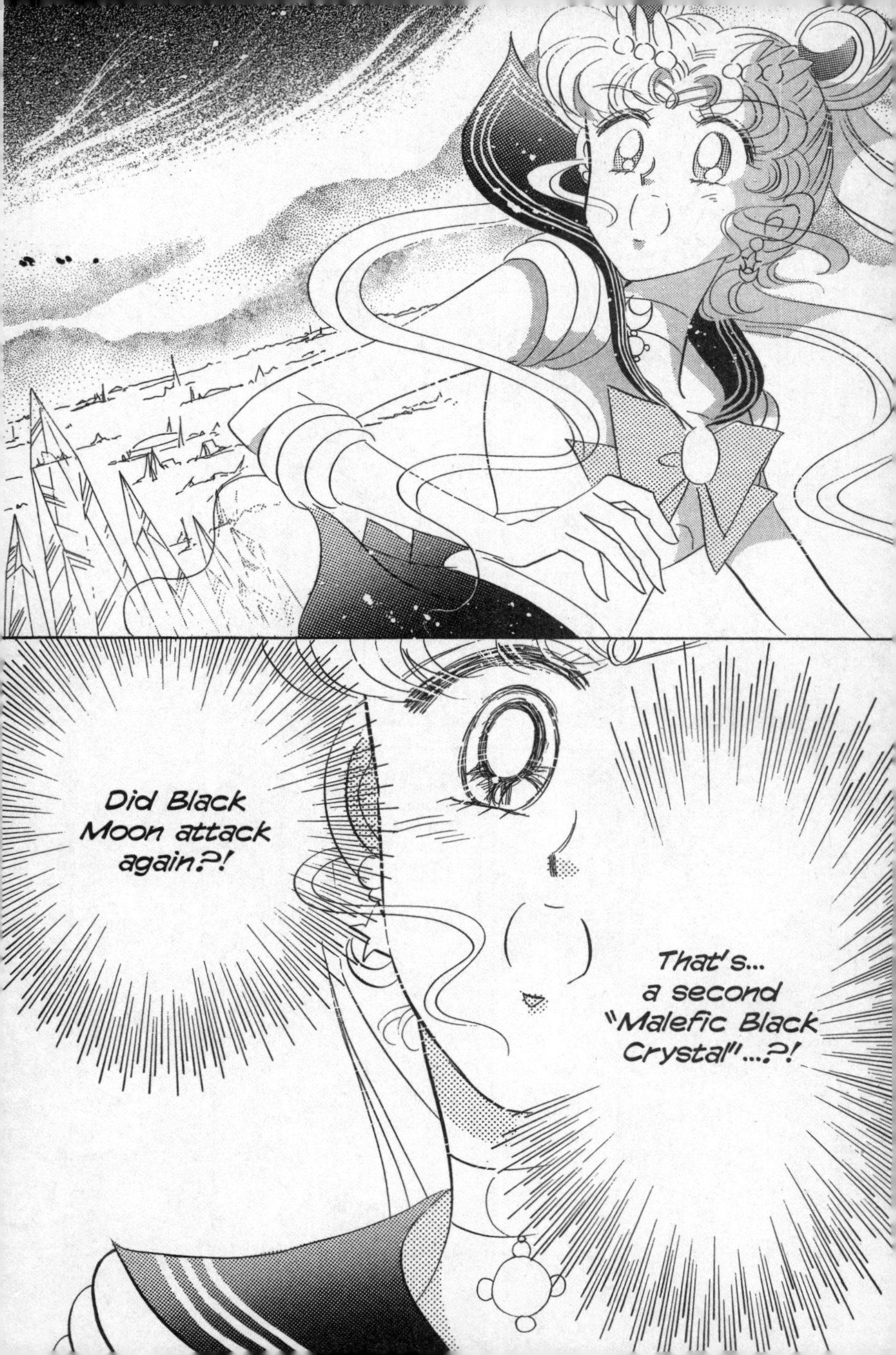
That's... a second "Malefic Black Crystal"...?!
Did Black Moon attack again?!

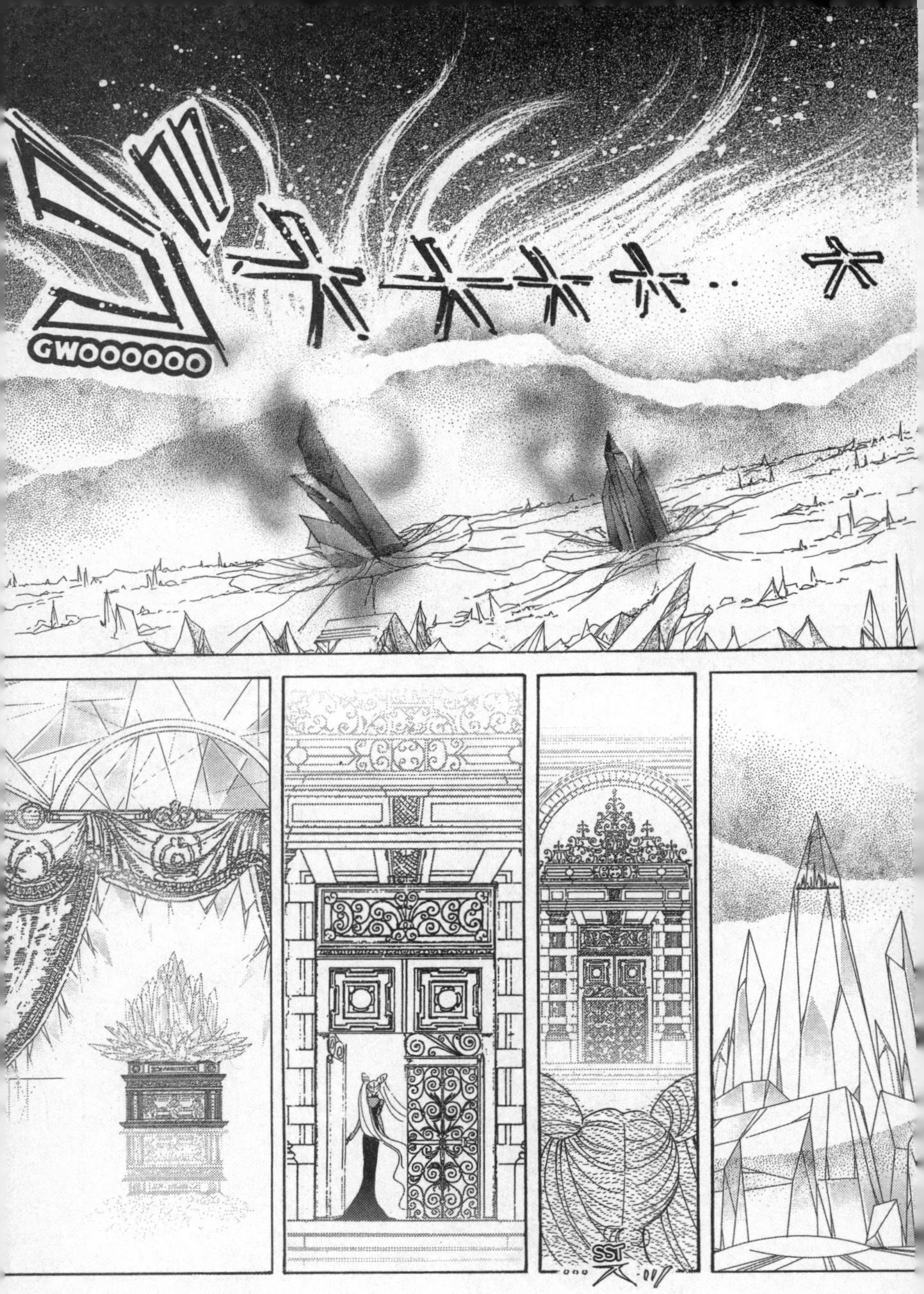
GWOOOOOO
SST

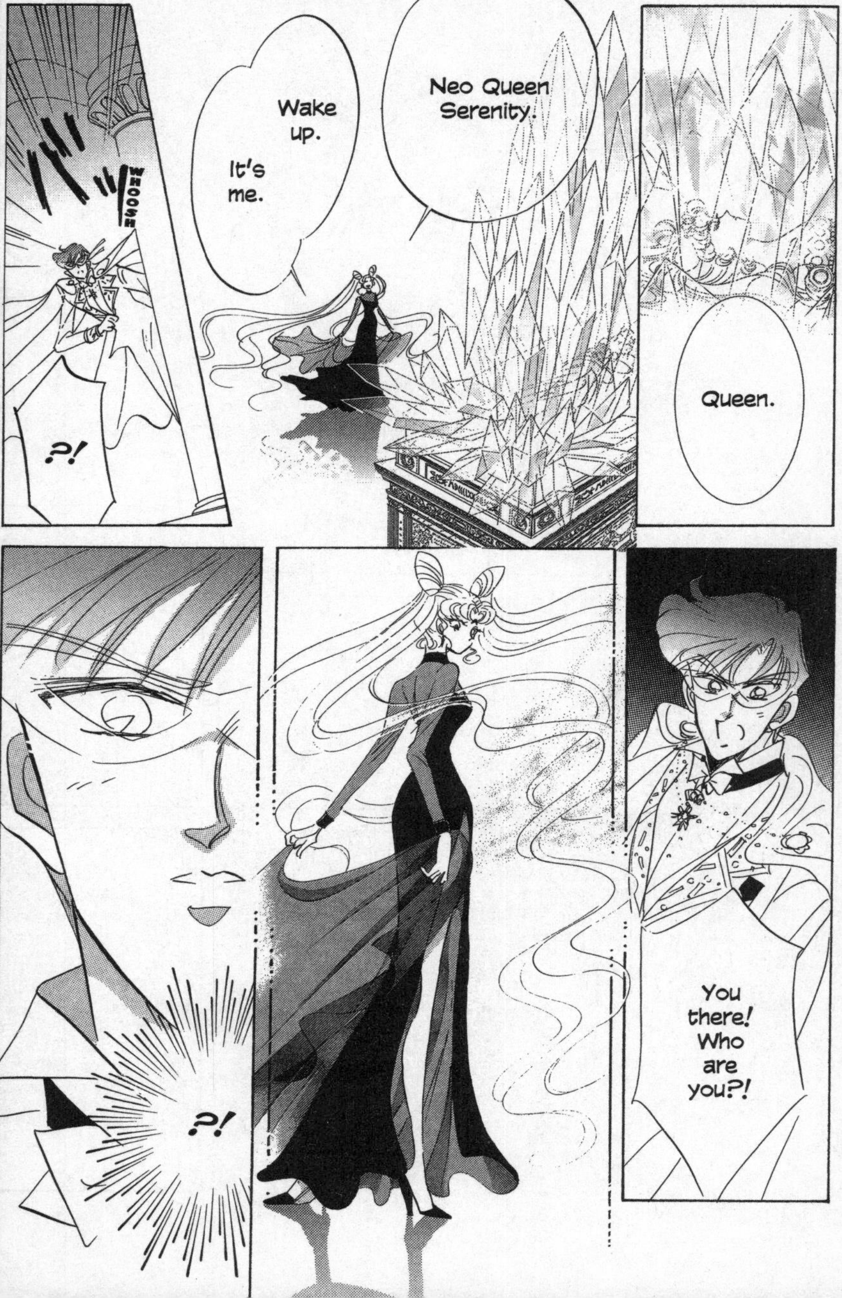
Queen.
Neo Queen Serenity.
Wake up.
It's me.
WHOOSH
?!
You there! Who are you?!
?!

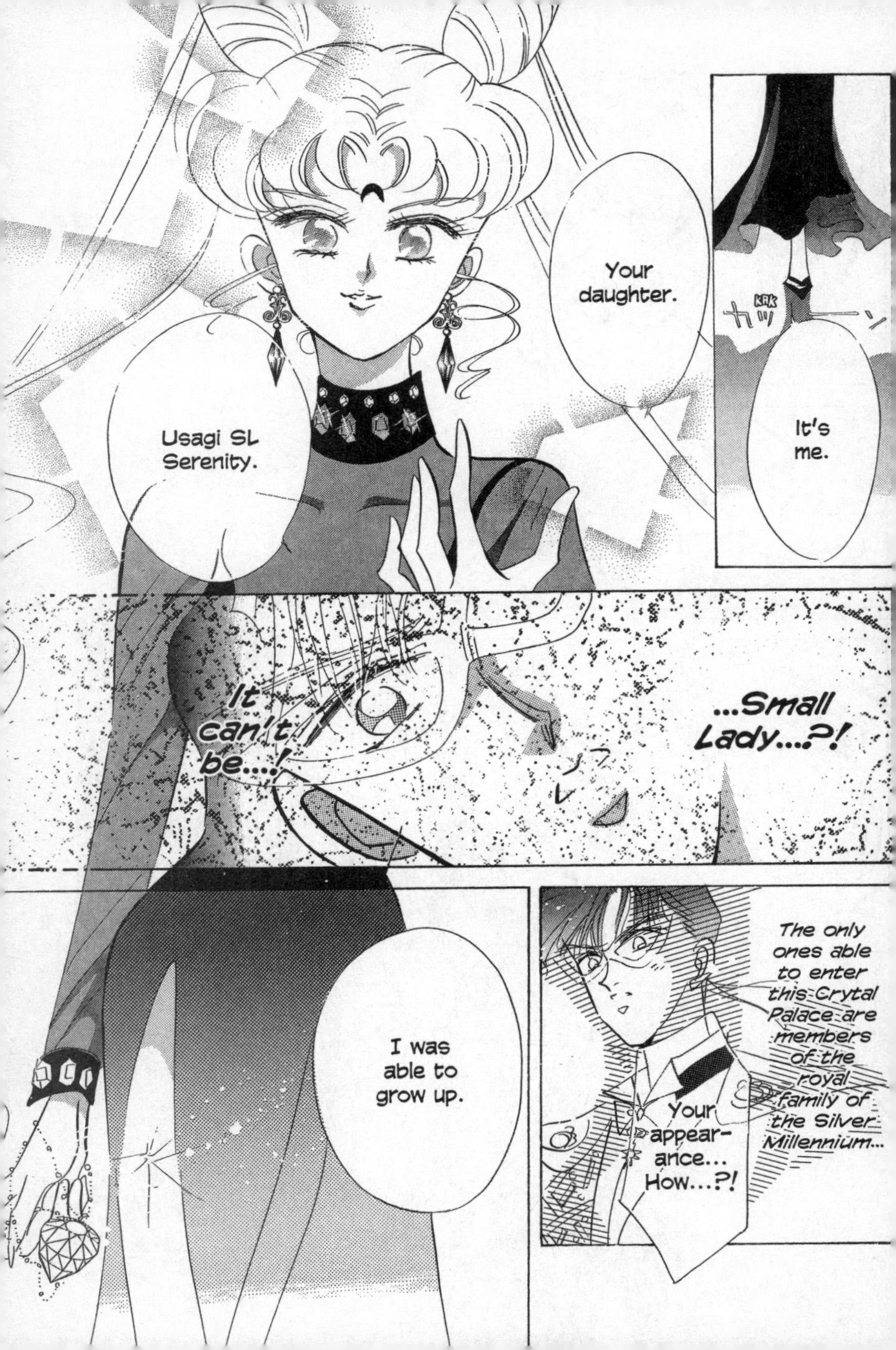
KRK
It's me.
Your daughter.
Usagi SL Serenity.
...Small Lady...?!
It can't be...!
The only ones able to enter this Crytal Palace are members of the royal family of the Silver Millennium...
Your appear-ance... How...?!
I was able to grow up.

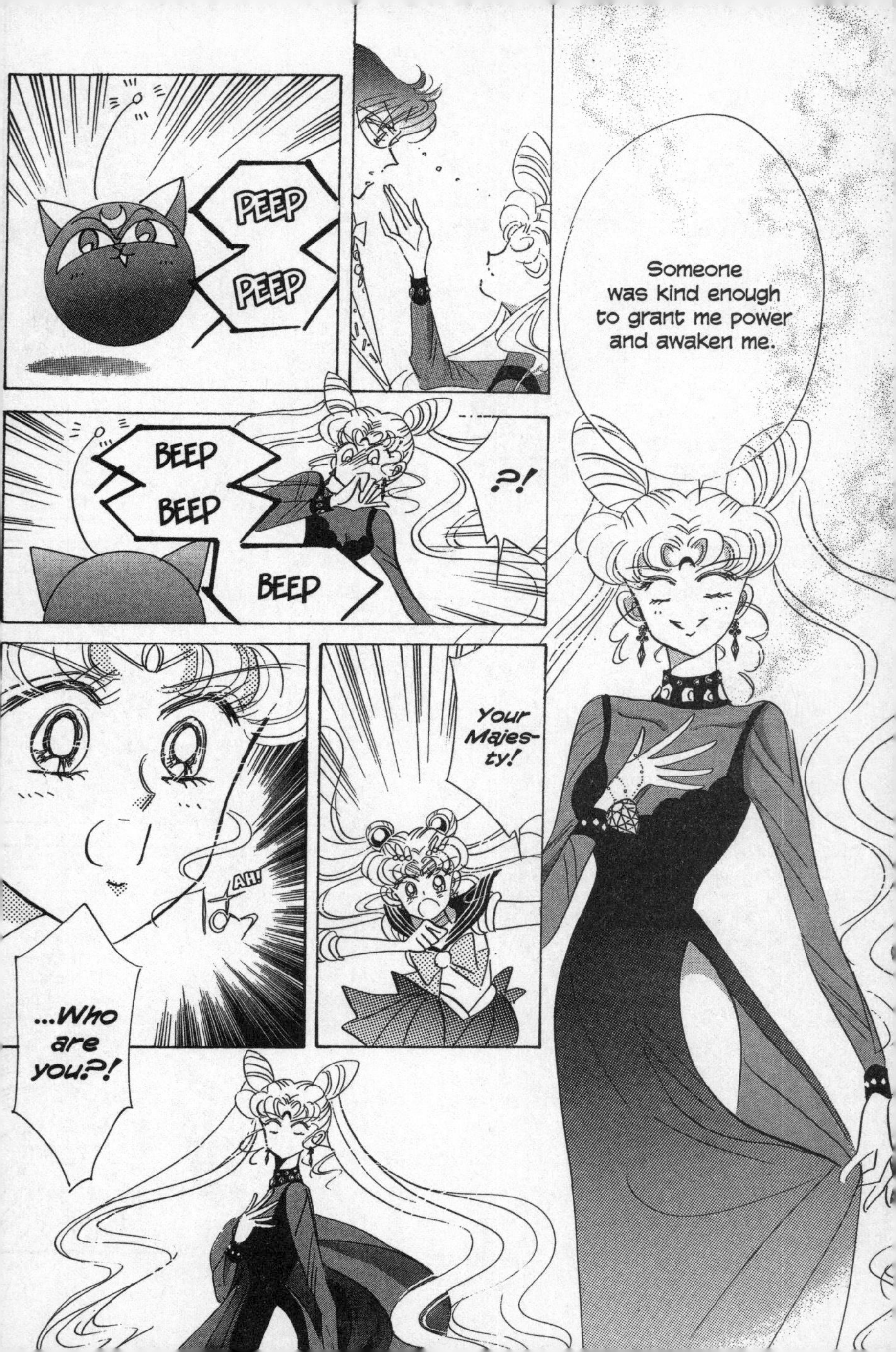

PEEP
PEEP
?!
BEEP
BEEP
BEEP
Your Majes-ty!
AH!
...Who are you?!
Someone was kind enough to grant me power and awaken me.

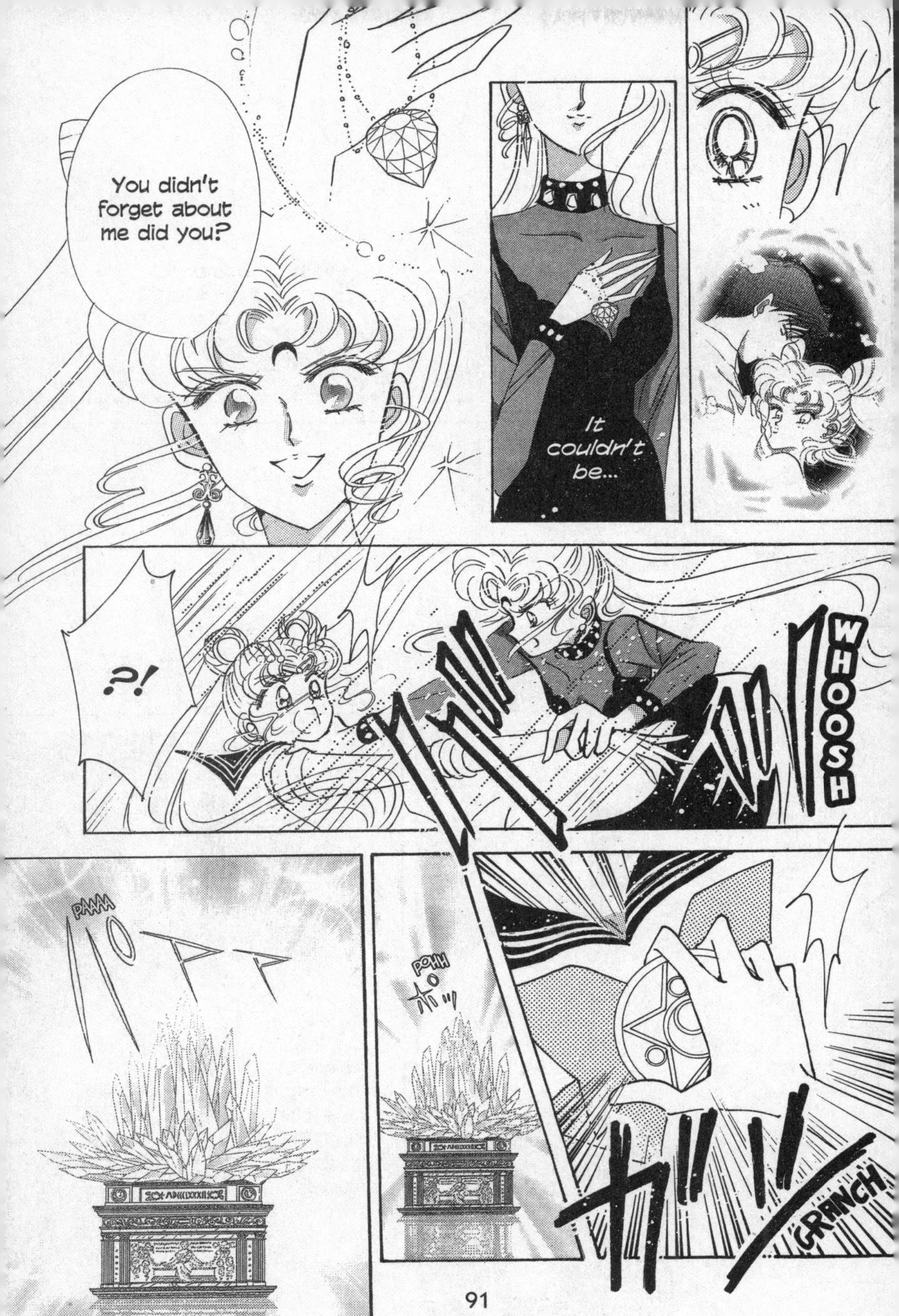
...
It couldn't be...
You didn't forget about me did you?
WHOOSH
?!
GRANCH
POHH
PAAAA

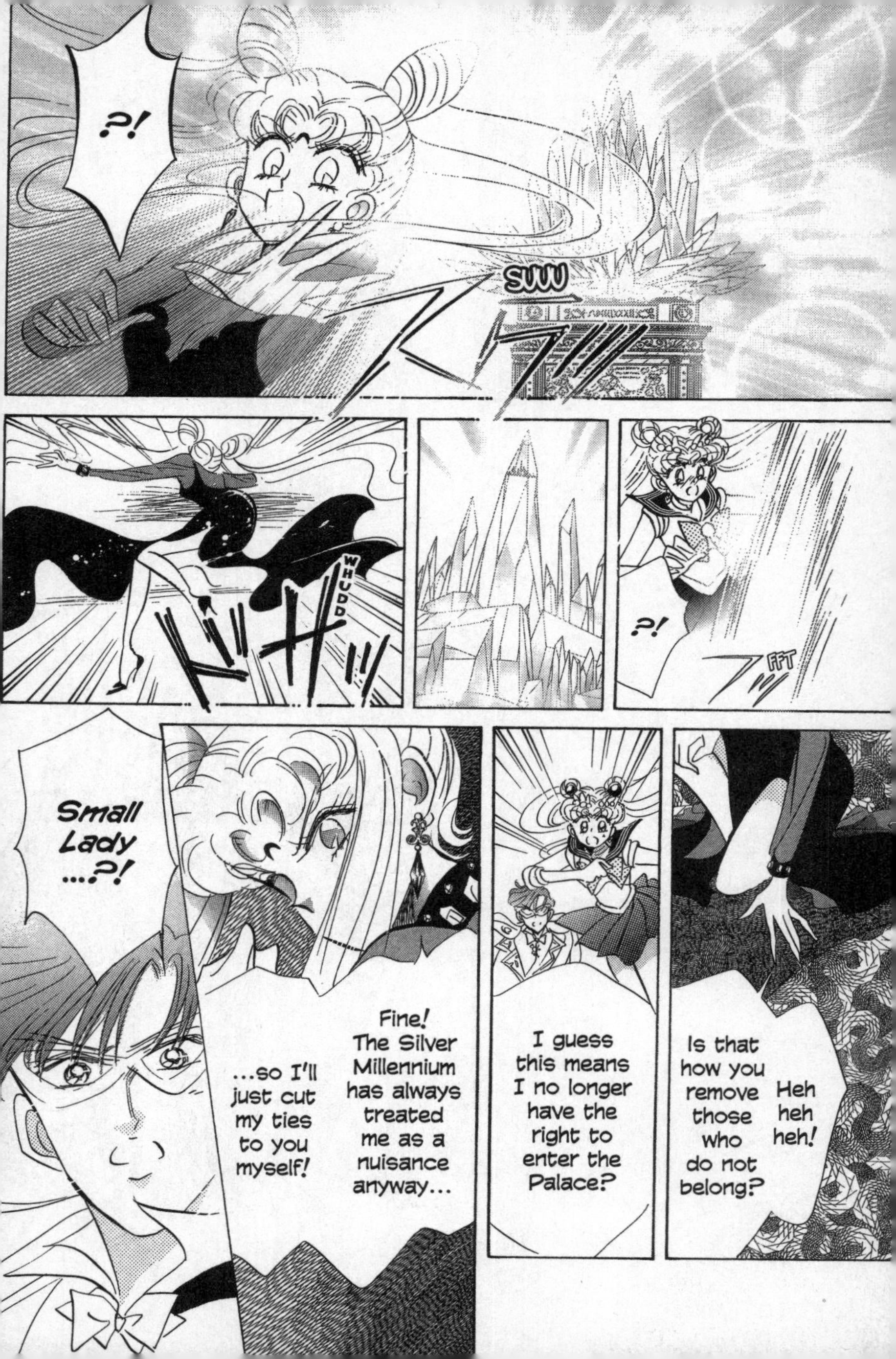
?!
SUUU
?!
FFT
WHUDD
Heh heh heh!
Is that how you remove those who do not belong?
I guess this means I no longer have the right to enter the Palace?
Fine! The Silver Millennium has always treated me as a nuisance anyway...
...so I'll just cut my ties to you myself!
Small Lady ...?!

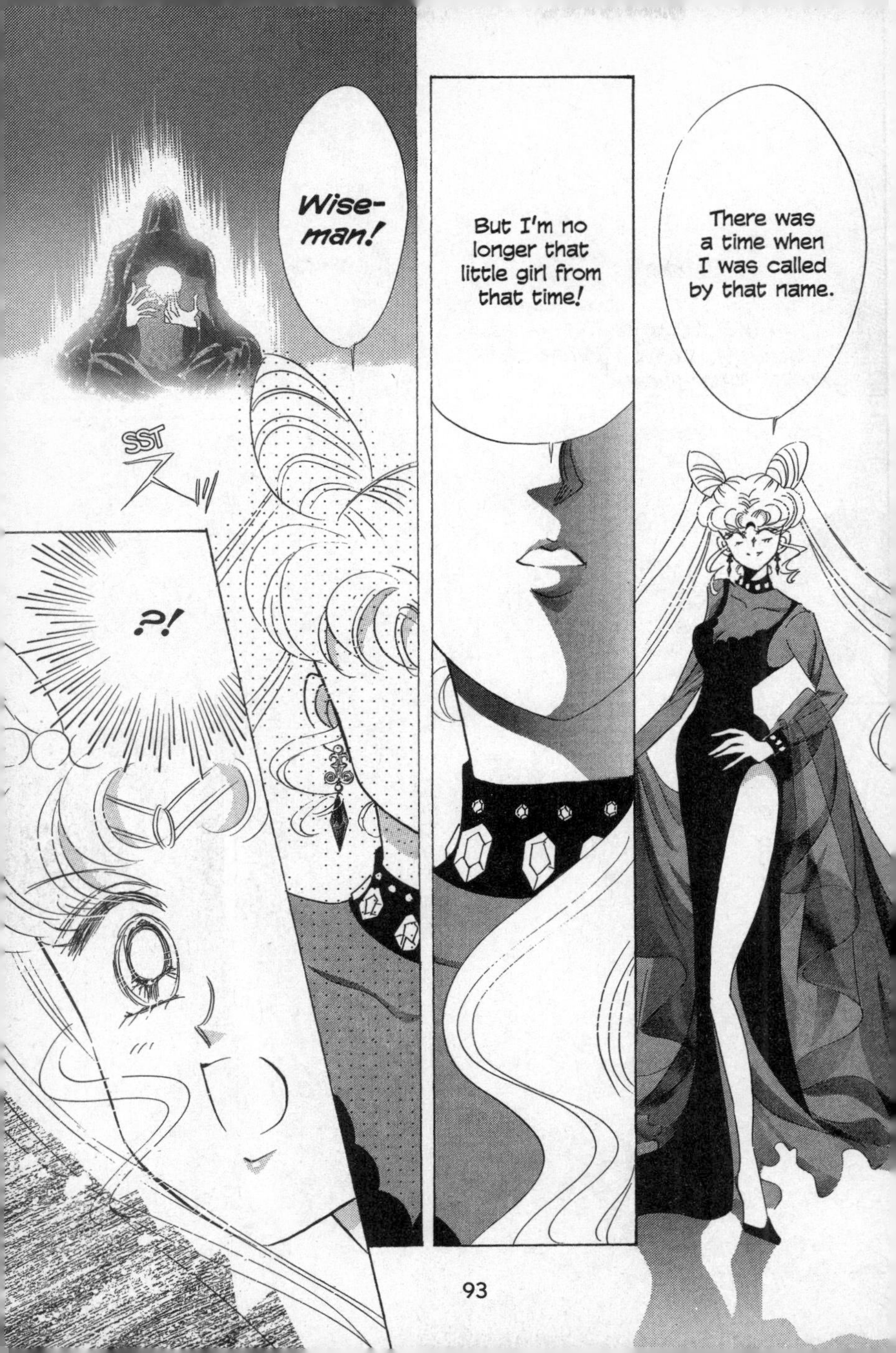
There was a time when I was called by that name.
But I'm no longer that little girl from that time!
Wise-man!
SST
?!

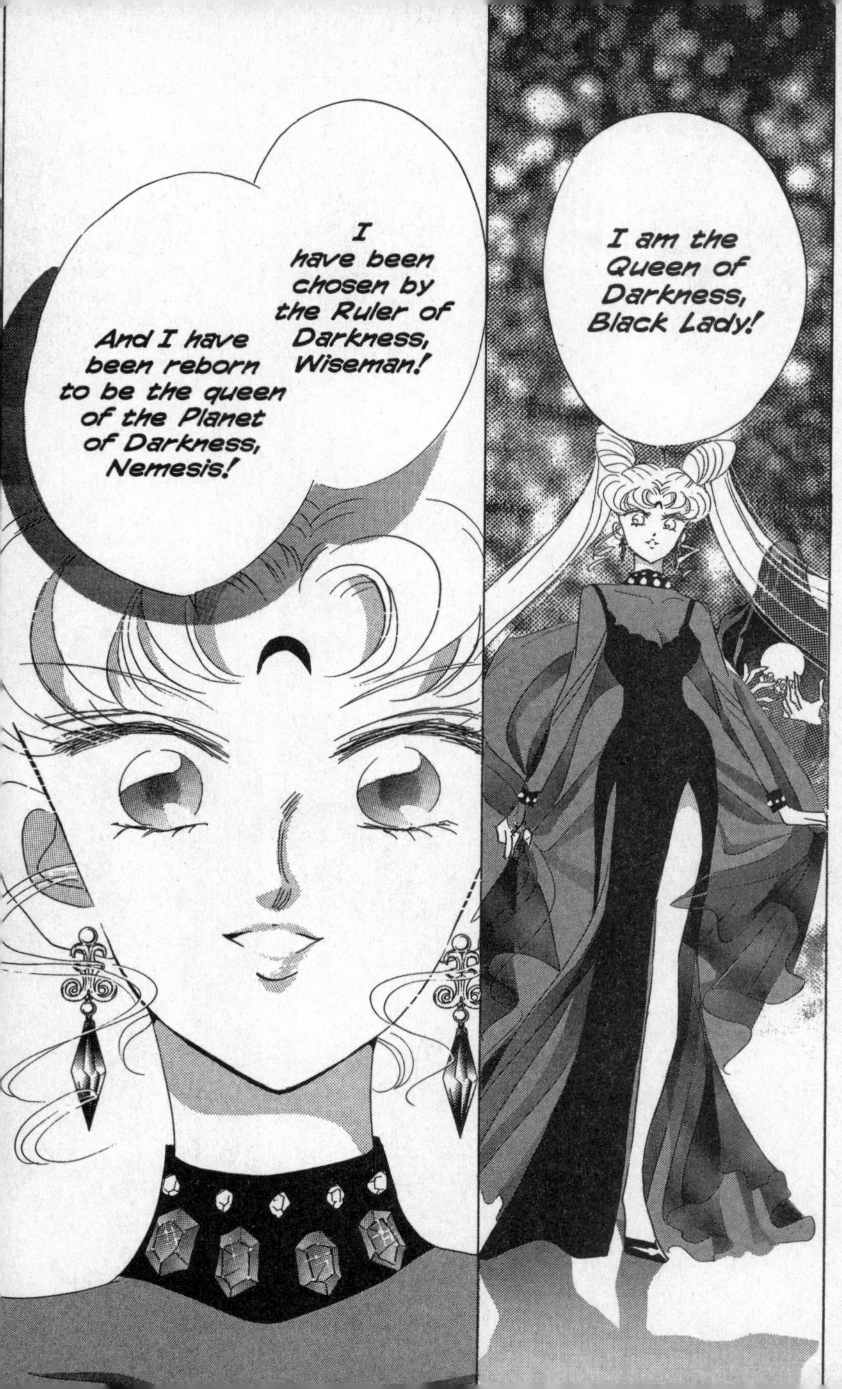
I am the Queen of Darkness, Black Lady!
I have been chosen by the Ruler of Darkness, Wiseman!
And I have been reborn to be the queen of the Planet of Darkness, Nemesis!

## Act 24
## Attack, Black Lady

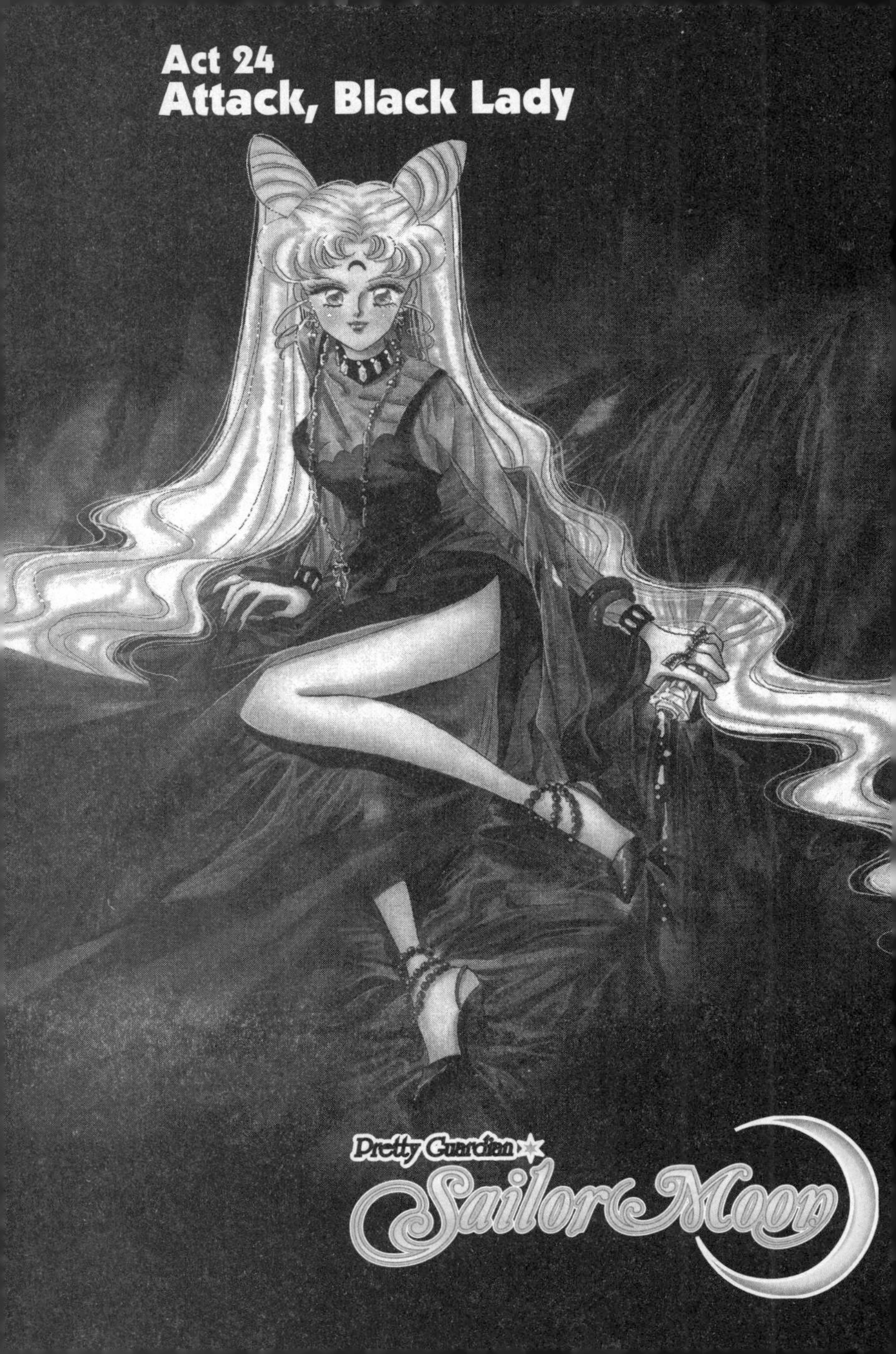
Pretty Guardian
Sailor Moon

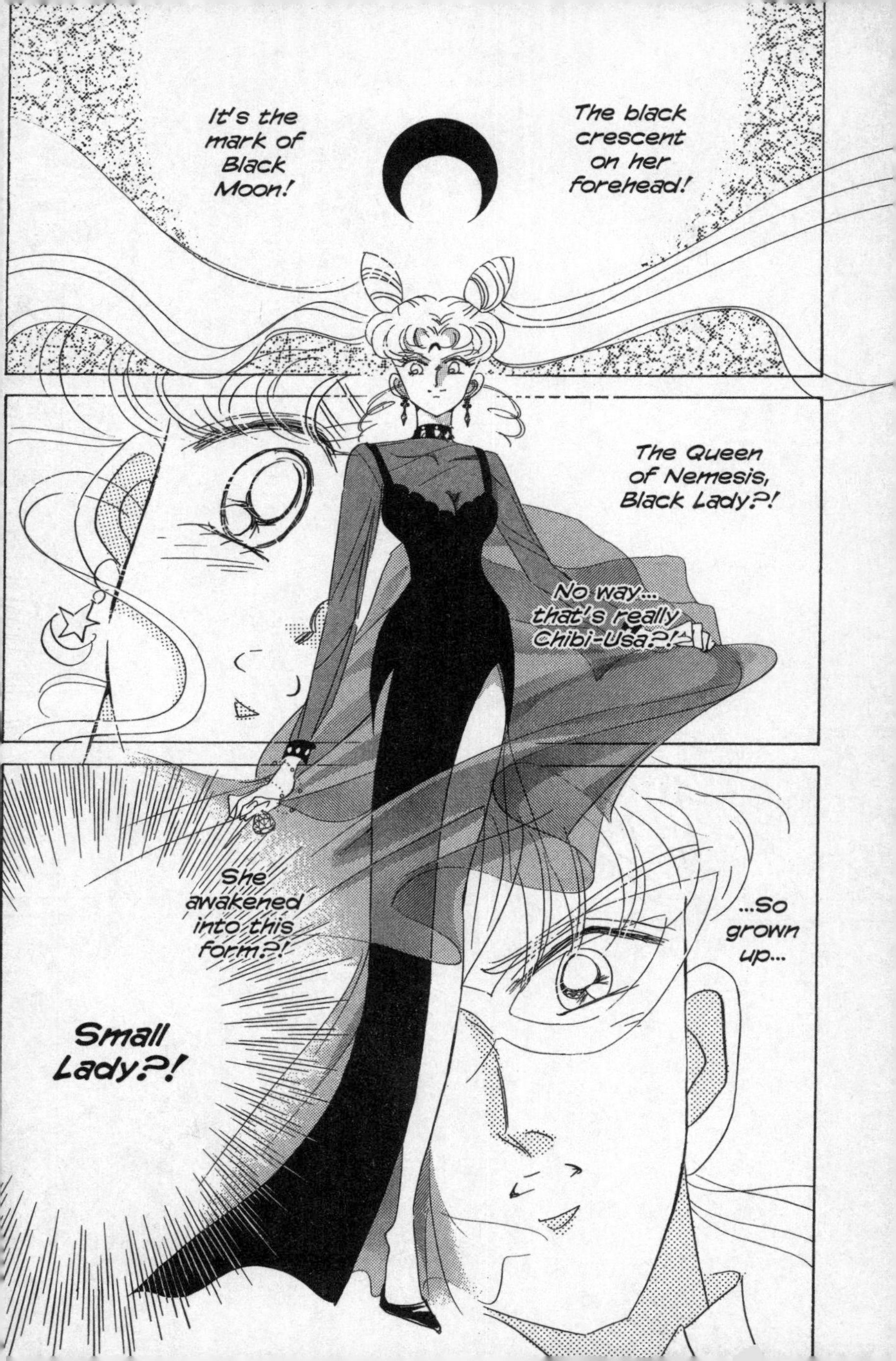
The black crescent on her forehead!
It's the mark of Black Moon!
The Queen of Nemesis, Black Lady?!
No way... that's really Chibi-Usa?!
...So grown up...
She awakened into this form?!
Small Lady?!

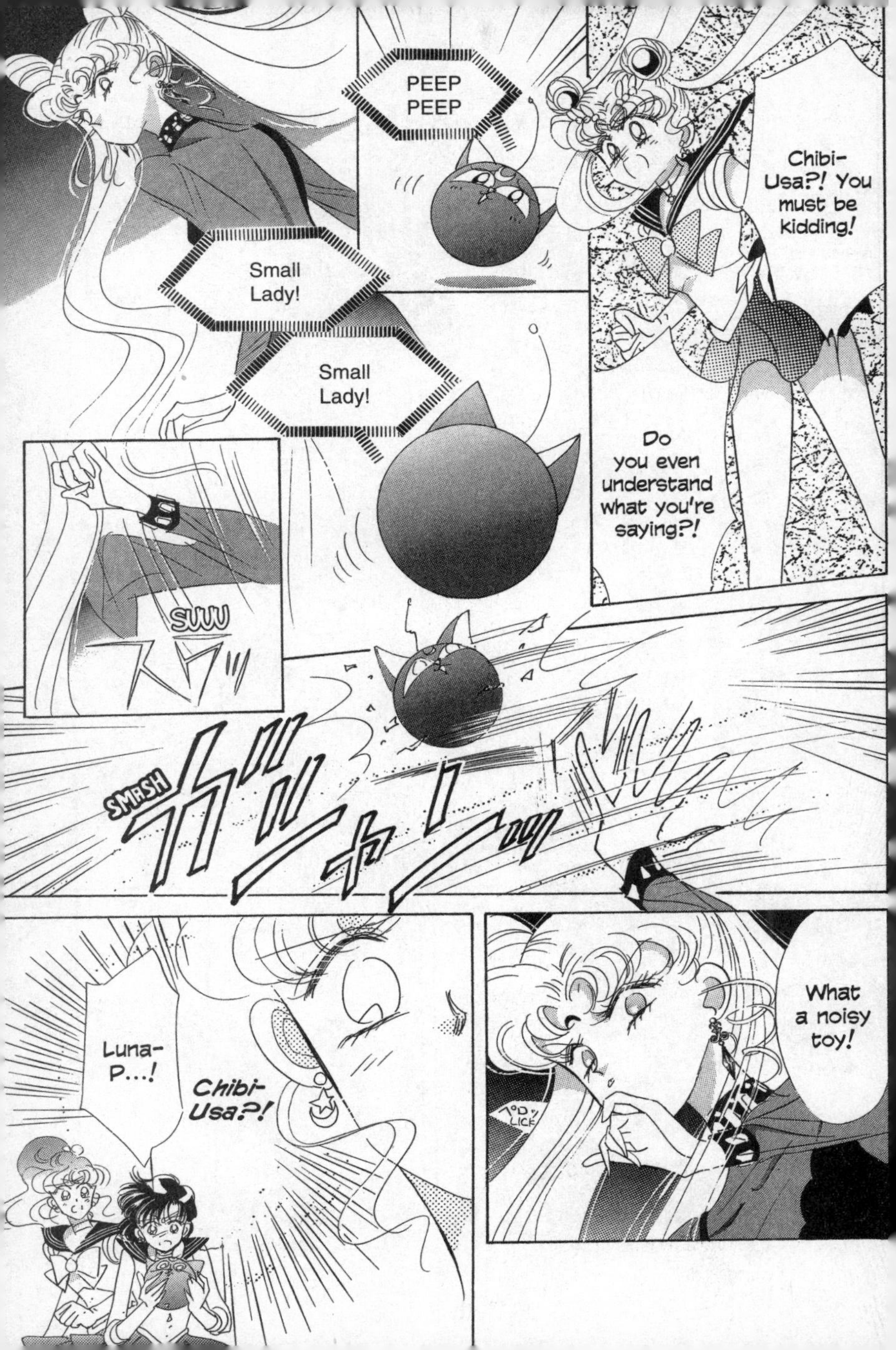
Chibi-Usa?! You must be kidding!
Do you even understand what you're saying?!
PEEP PEEP
Small Lady!
Small Lady!
SUUU
SMASH
What a noisy toy!
LICK
Chibi-Usa?!
Luna-P...!

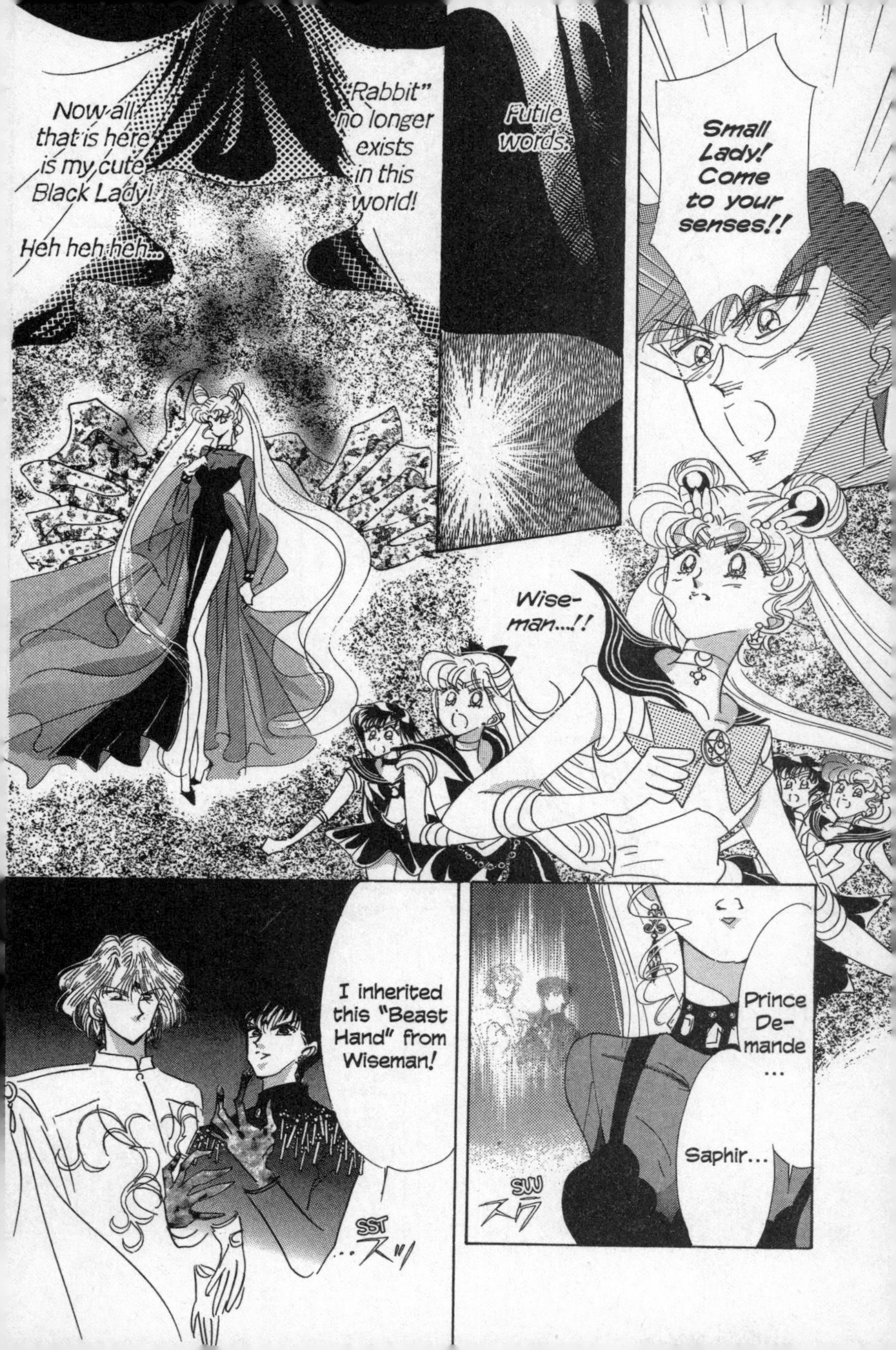
Small Lady! Come to your senses!!
Futile words.
"Rabbit" no longer exists in this world!
Now all that is here is my cute Black Lady!
Heh heh heh...
Wise-man...!!
Prince De-mande...
Saphir...
SWU
スウ
I inherited this "Beast Hand" from Wiseman!
SST
...スッ

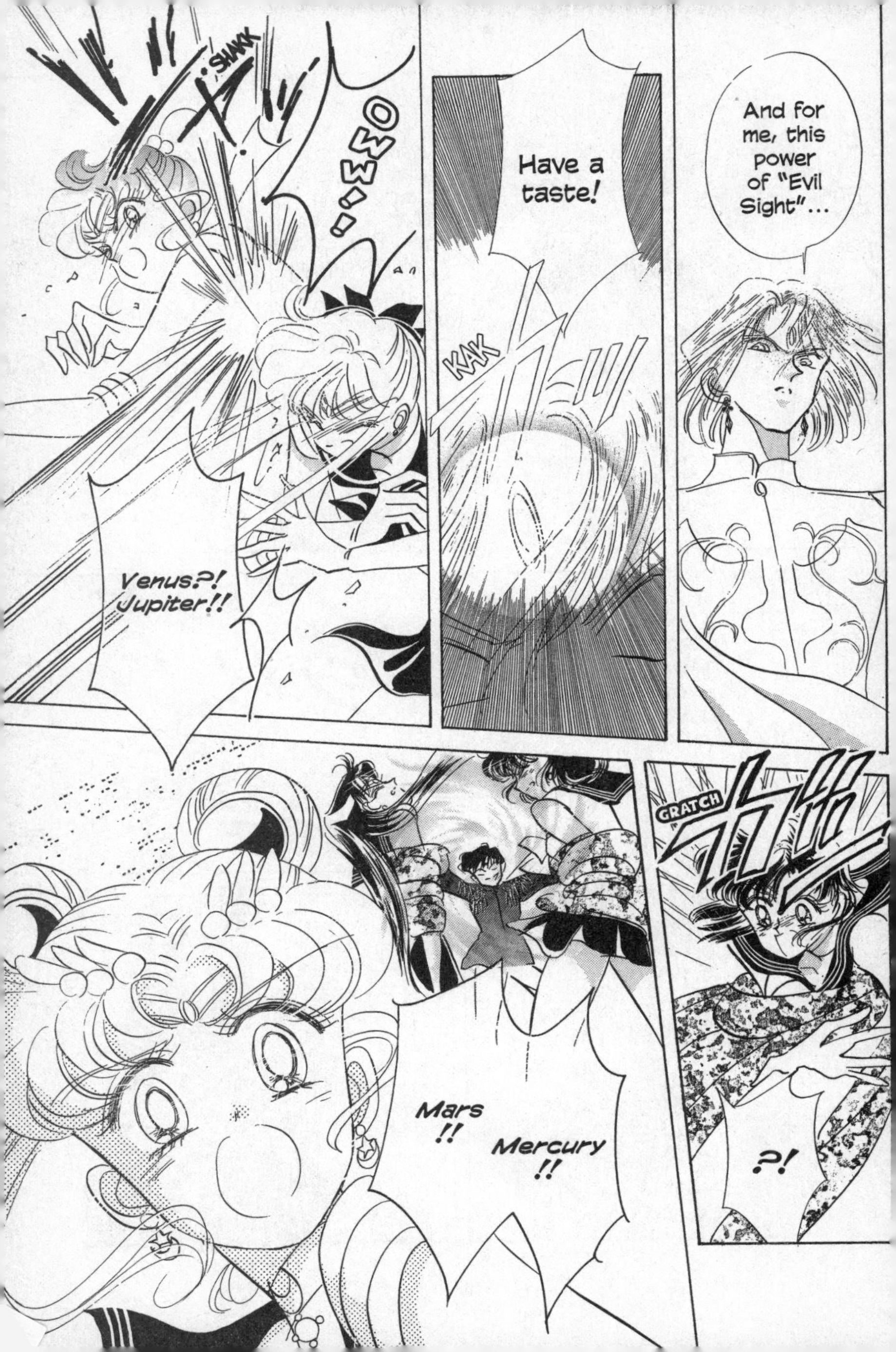

And for me, this power of "Evil Sight"...
Have a taste!
KAK
SHAKK
OWW!!
Venus?! Jupiter!!
GRATCH
?!
Mars!!
Mercury!!

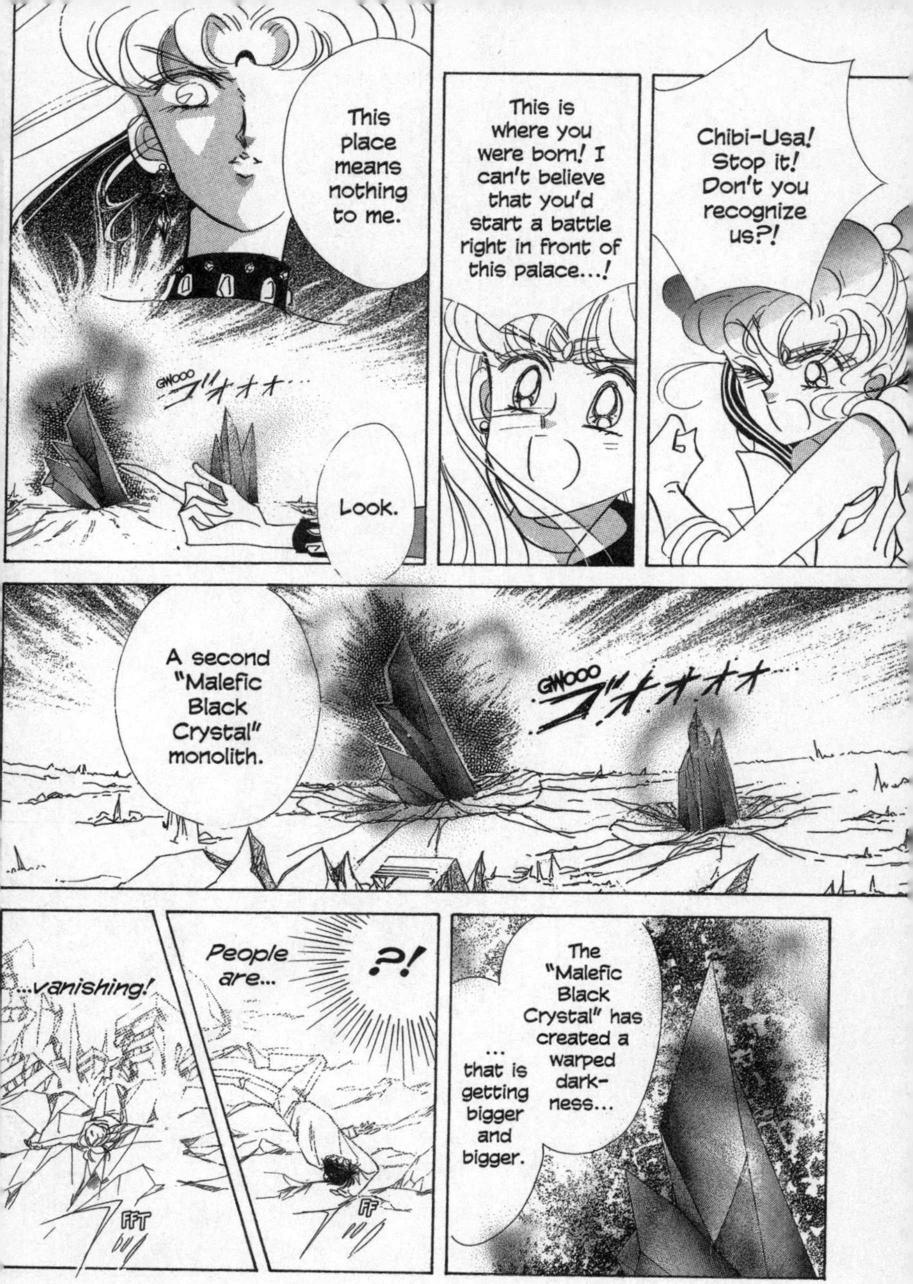
Chibi-Usa! Stop it! Don't you recognize us?!
This is where you were born! I can't believe that you'd start a battle right in front of this palace...!
This place means nothing to me.
GWOOO
ゴオオオ…
Look.
A second "Malefic Black Crystal" monolith.
GWOOO
ゴオオオオ…
The "Malefic Black Crystal" has created a warped darkness...
... that is getting bigger and bigger.
?!
People are...
FF
...vanishing!
FFT

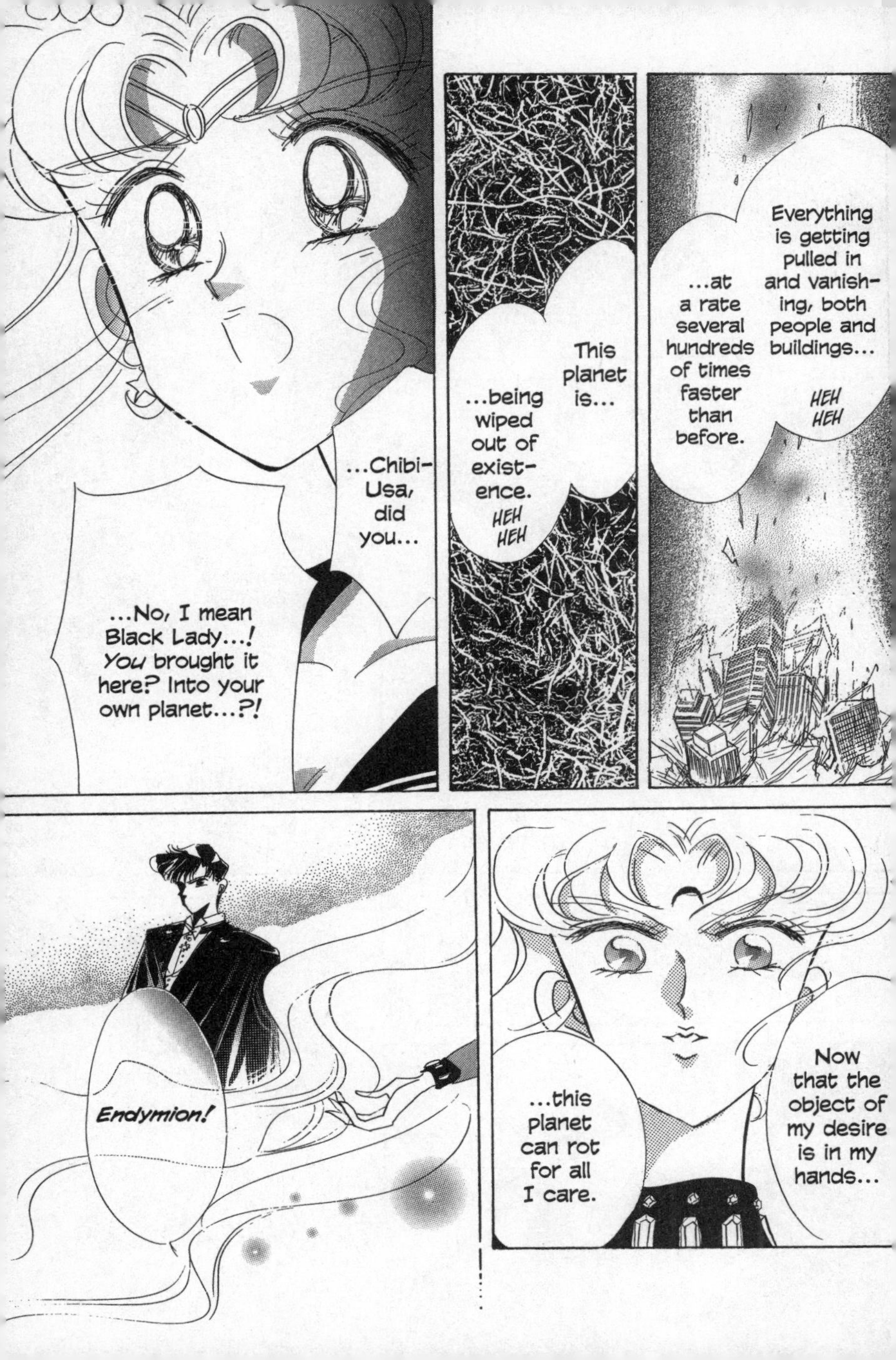

Everything is getting pulled in and vanishing, both people and buildings...
HEH HEH
...at a rate several hundreds of times faster than before.
This planet is...
...being wiped out of existence.
HEH HEH
...Chibi-Usa, did you...
...No, I mean Black Lady...! *You* brought it here? Into your own planet...?!
Now that the object of my desire is in my hands...
...this planet can rot for all I care.
*Endymion!*

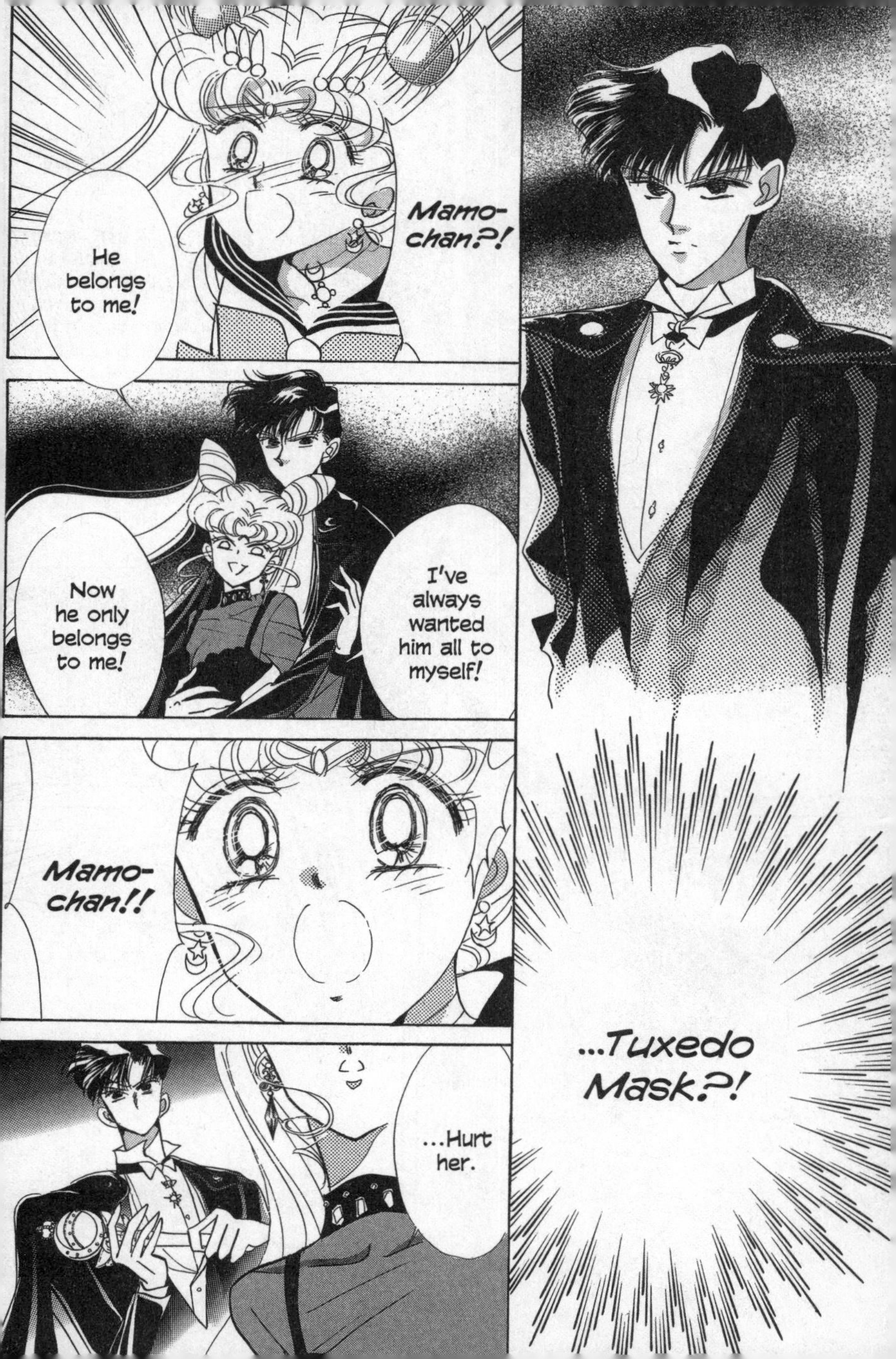

...Tuxedo Mask?!
Mamo-chan?!
He belongs to me!
I've always wanted him all to myself!
Now he only belongs to me!
Mamo-chan!!
...Hurt her.

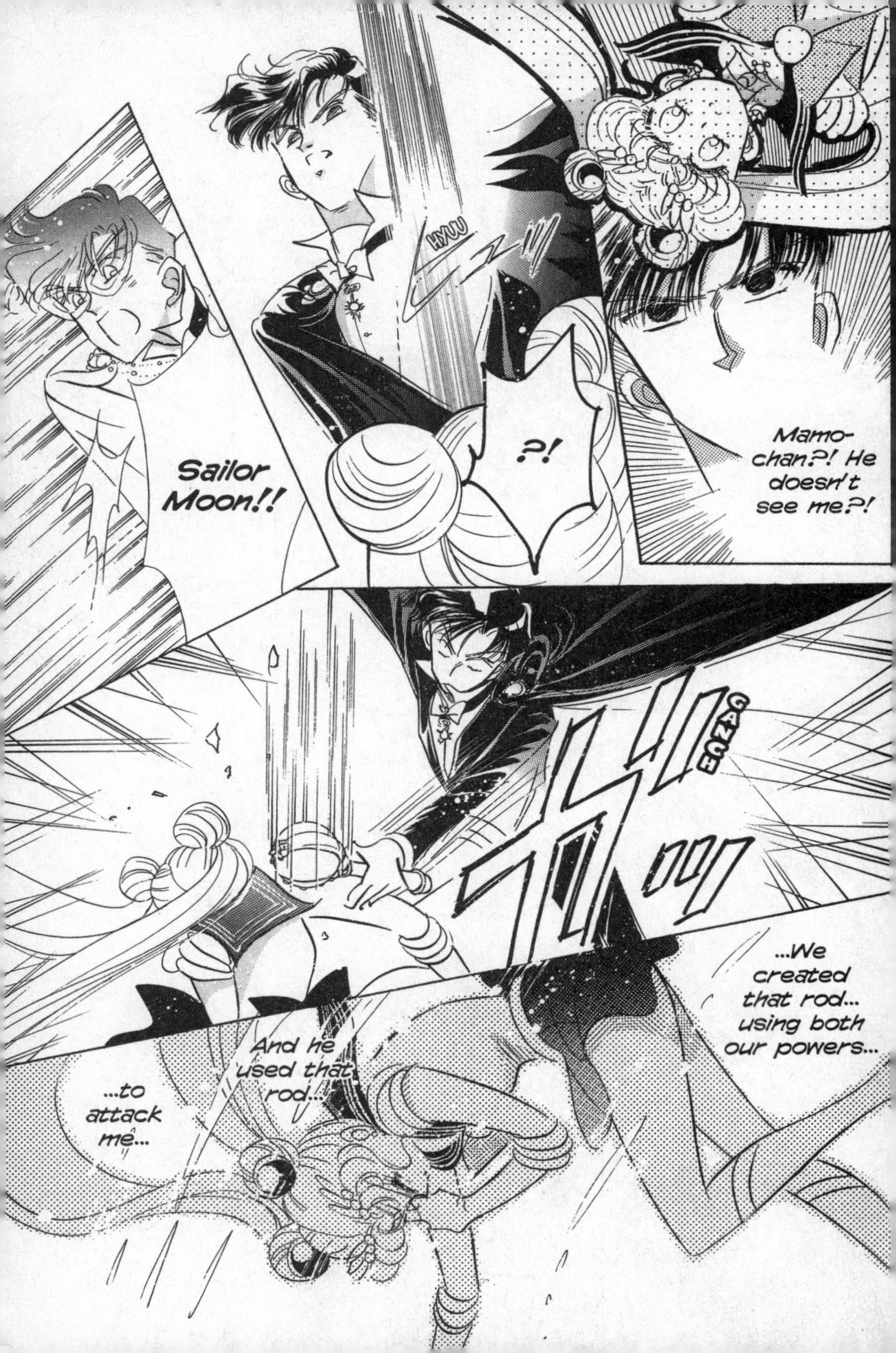

Mamo-chan?! He doesn't see me?!
HYUU
?!
Sailor Moon!!
GANCH
...We created that rod... using both our powers...
And he used that rod...
...to attack me...

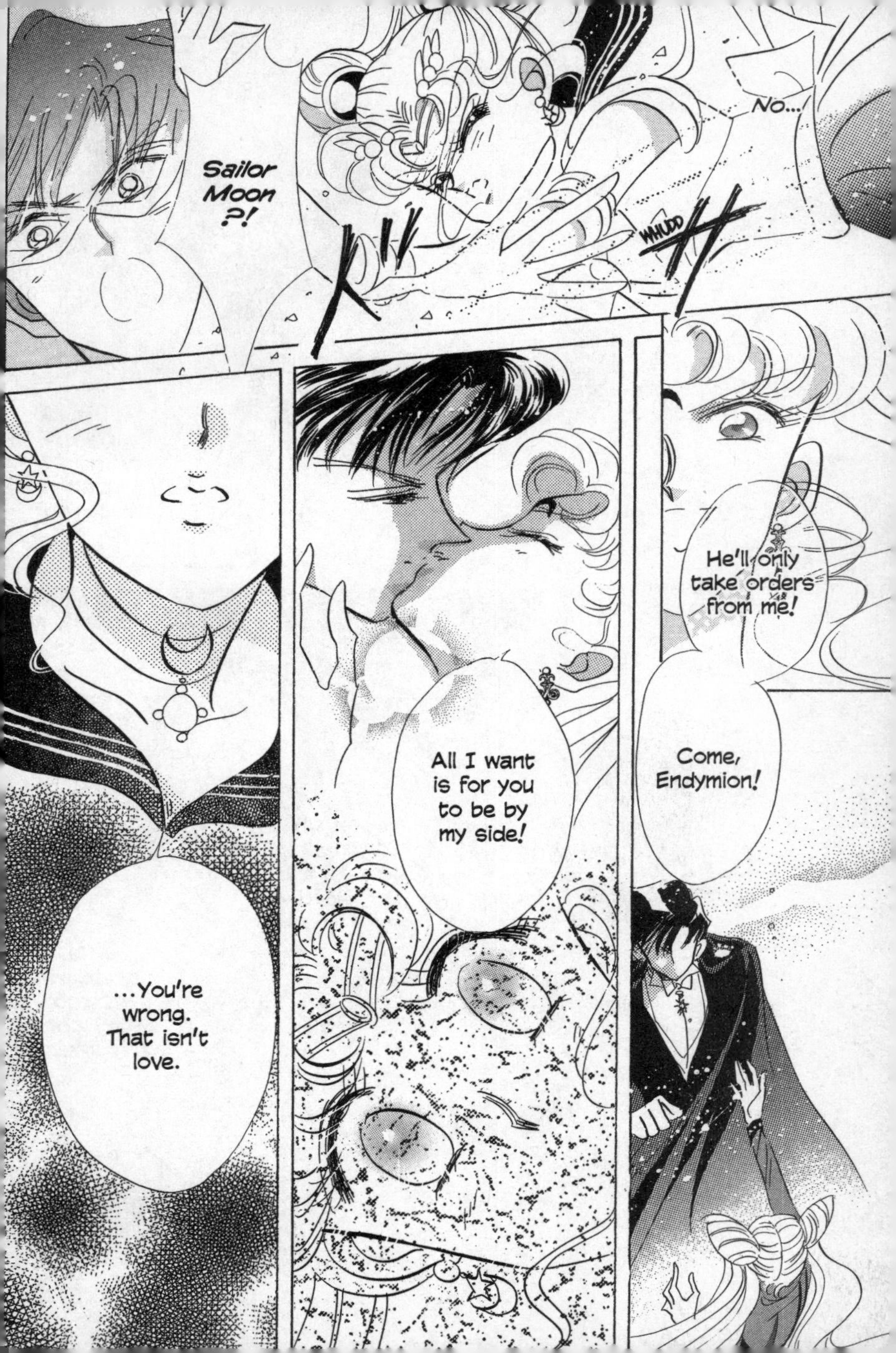
No...
WHUDD
Sailor Moon ?!
He'll only take orders from me!
Come, Endymion!
All I want is for you to be by my side!
...You're wrong. That isn't love.

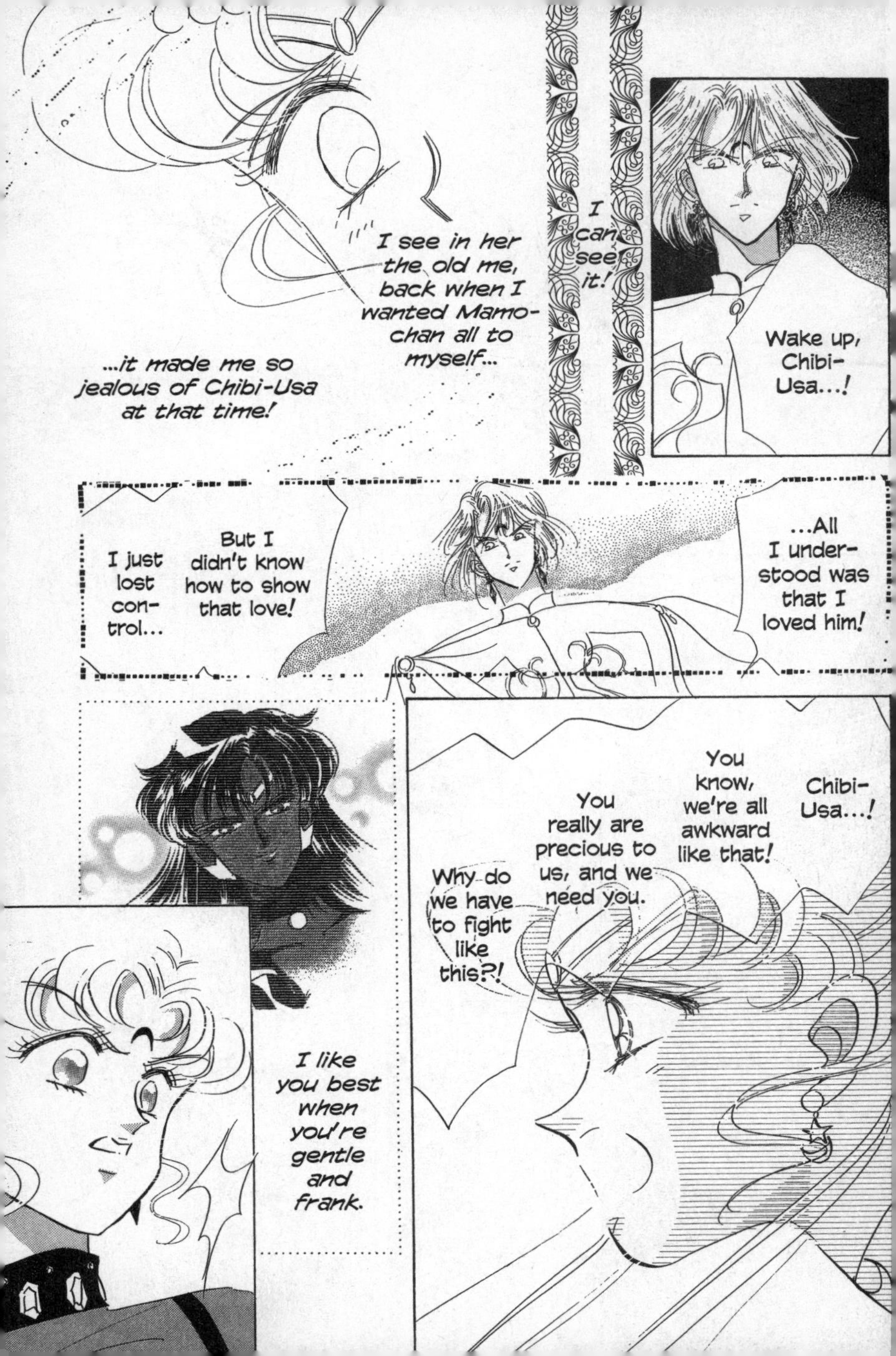
Wake up, Chibi-Usa...!
I can see it!
I see in her the old me, back when I wanted Mamo-chan all to myself...
...it made me so jealous of Chibi-Usa at that time!
...All I understood was that I loved him!
But I didn't know how to show that love!
I just lost control...
Chibi-Usa...!
You know, we're all awkward like that!
You really are precious to us, and we need you.
Why do we have to fight like this?!
I like you best when you're gentle and frank.

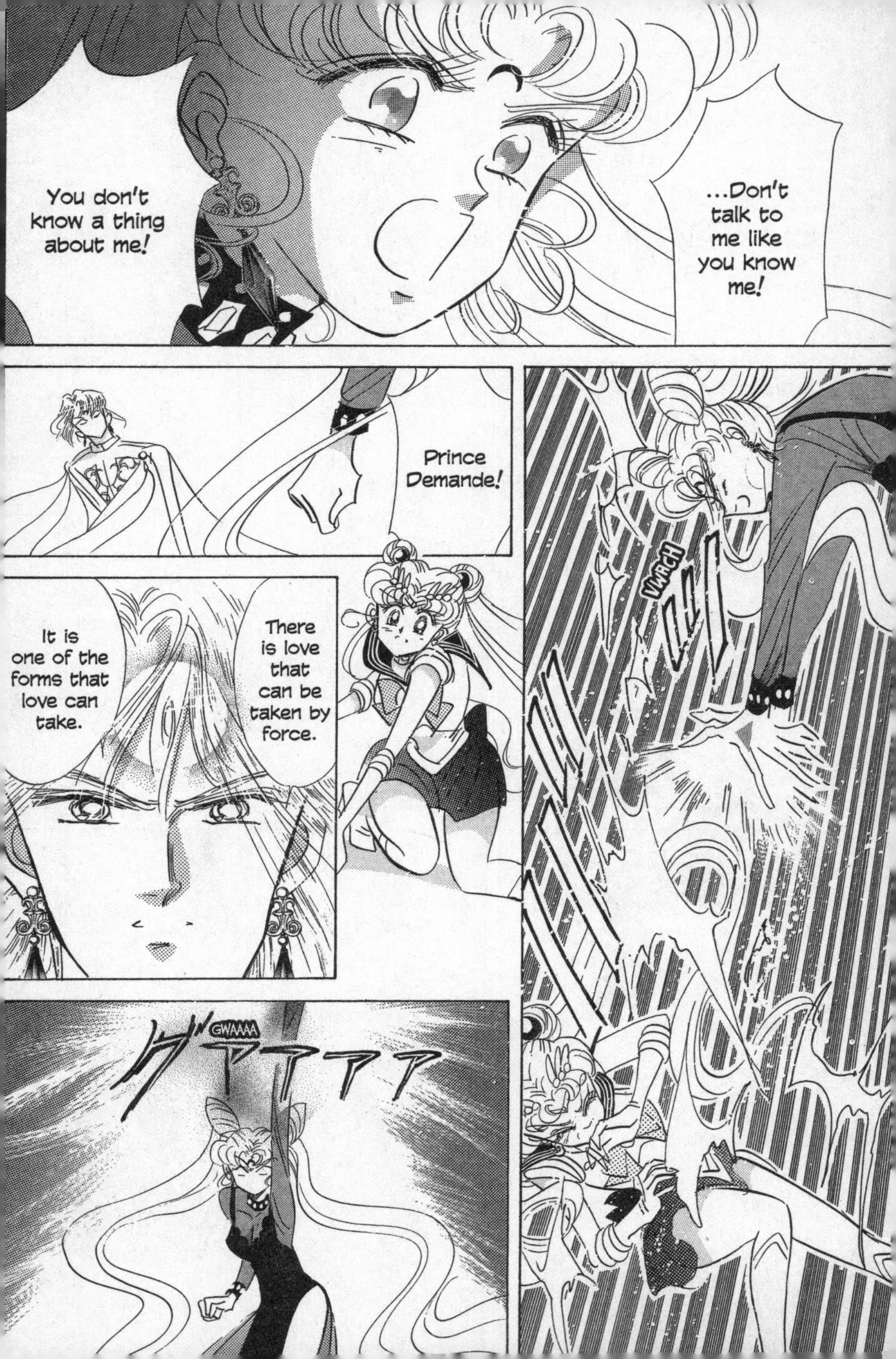
...Don't talk to me like you know me!
You don't know a thing about me!
VWACH
Prince Demande!
There is love that can be taken by force.
It is one of the forms that love can take.
GWAAAA

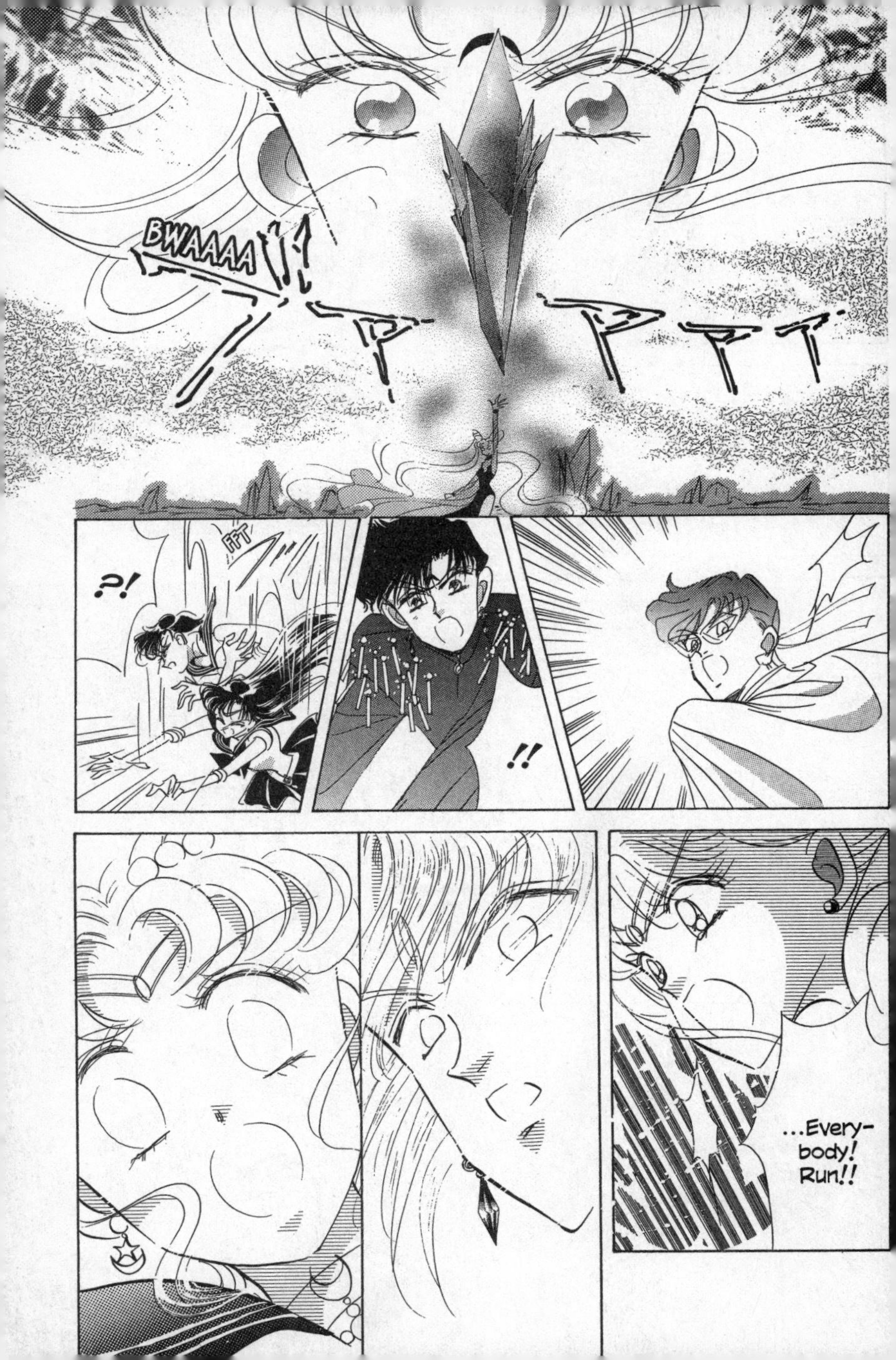
BWAAAA!!
!!
FFT
?!
...Every-
body!
Run!!

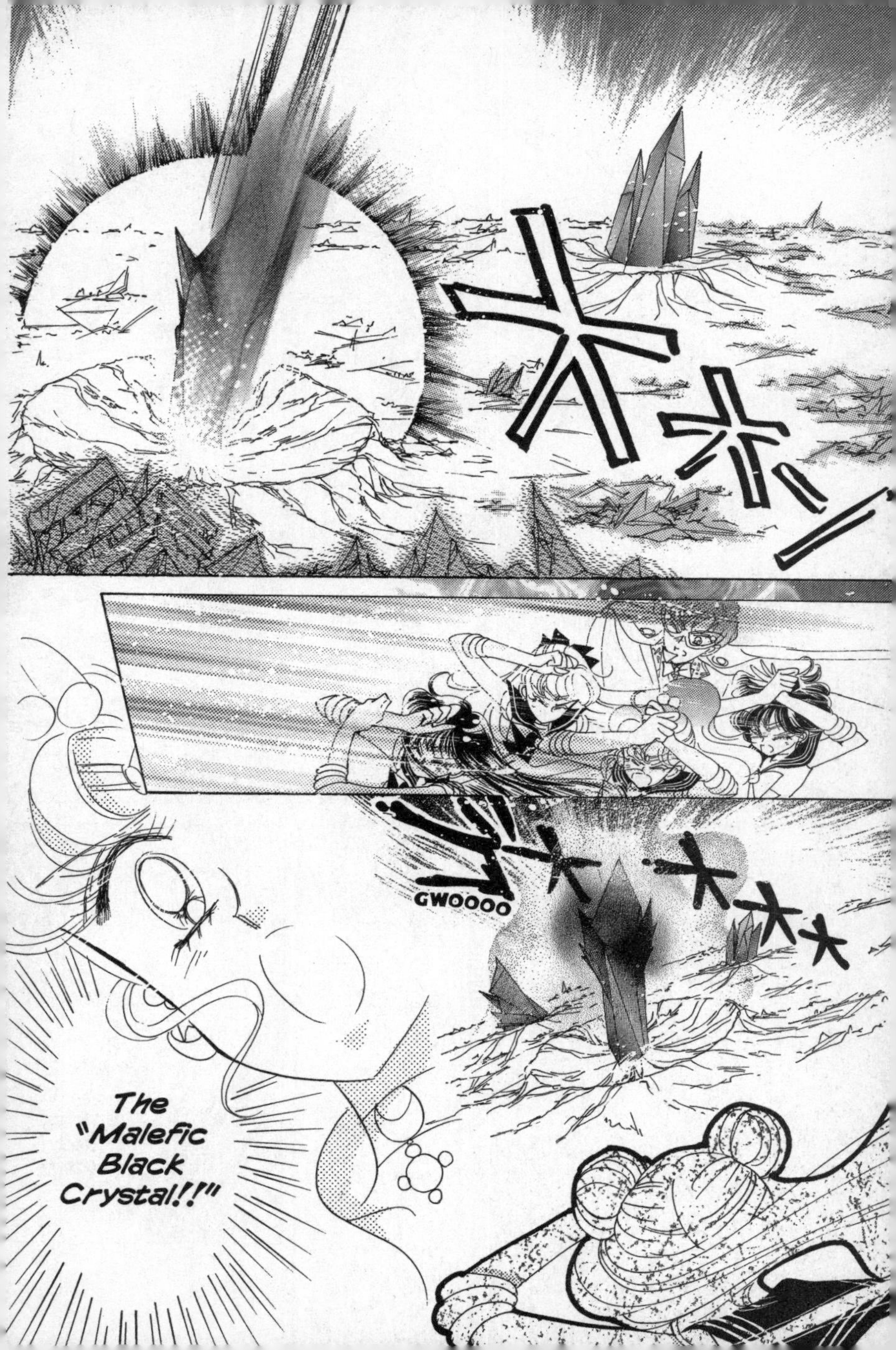
GWOOOO
The "Malefic Black Crystal!!"

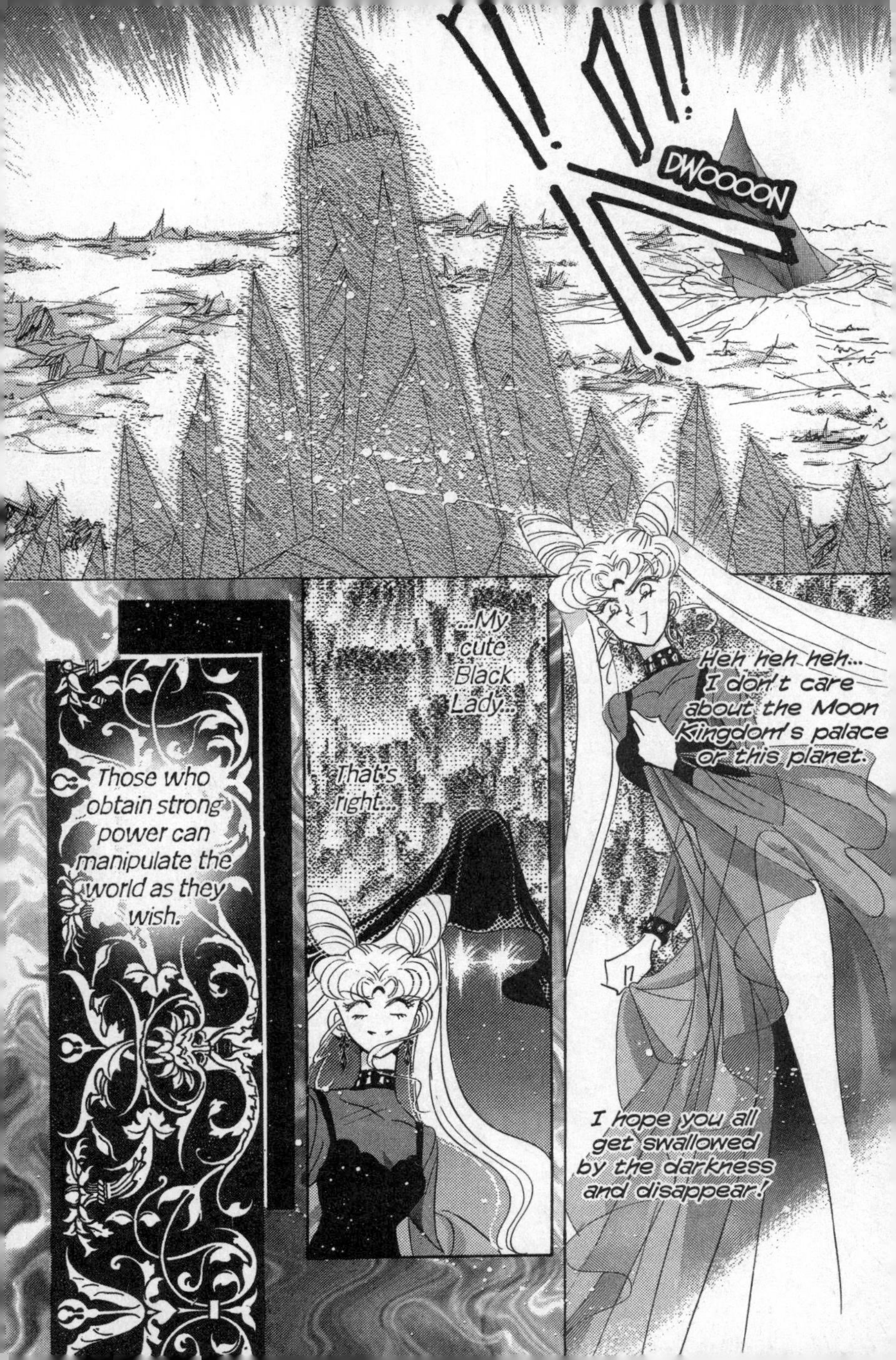
DWOOOOON
Heh heh heh... I don't care about the Moon Kingdom's palace or this planet.
I hope you all get swallowed by the darkness and disappear!
...My cute Black Lady...
That's right...
Those who obtain strong power can manipulate the world as they wish.

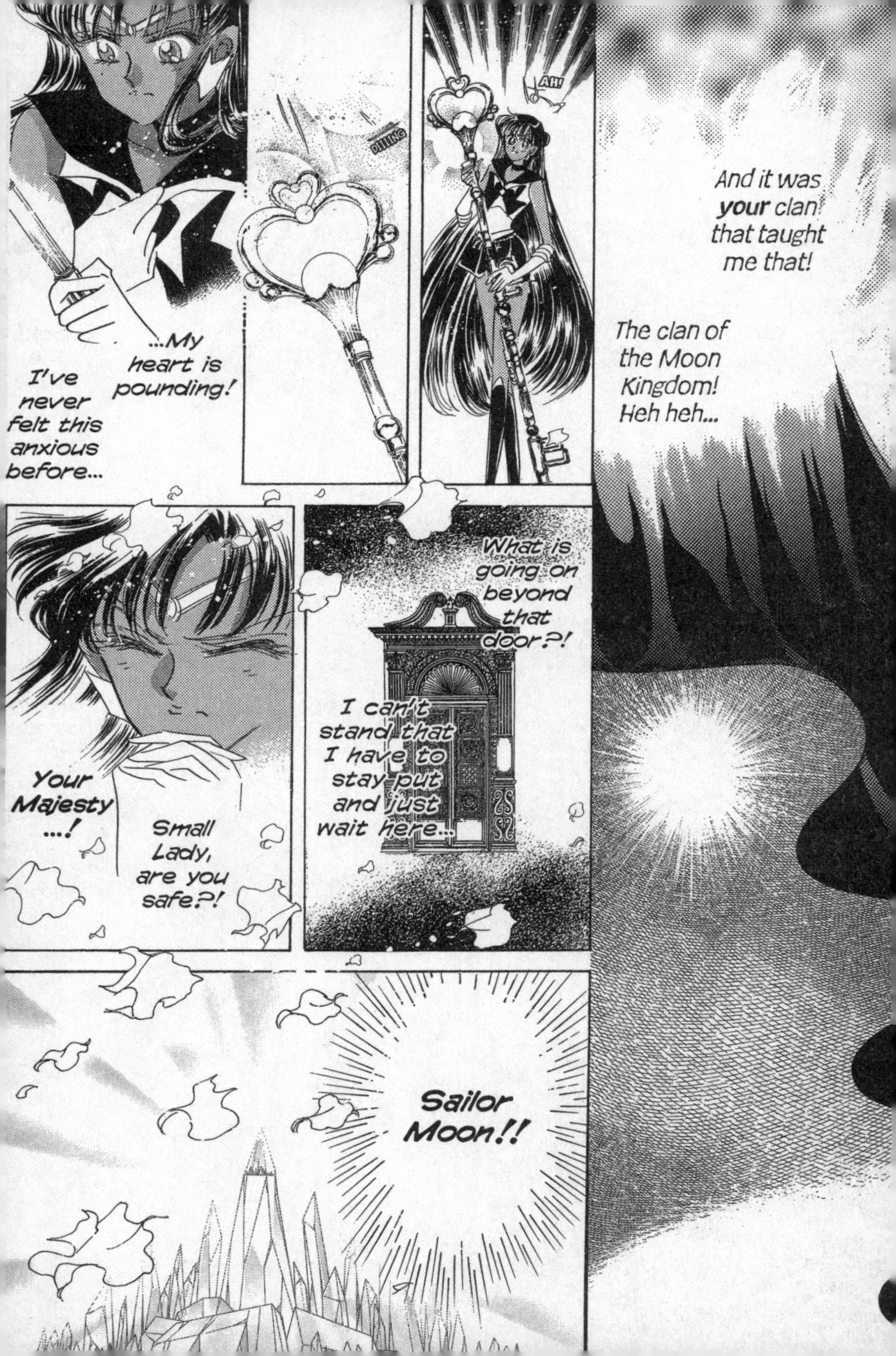
And it was **your** clan that taught me that!
The clan of the Moon Kingdom! Heh heh...
AH!
DIIING
...My heart is pounding!
I've never felt this anxious before...
What is going on beyond that door?!
I can't stand that I have to stay put and just wait here...
Small Lady, are you safe?!
Your Majesty ...!
Sailor Moon!!

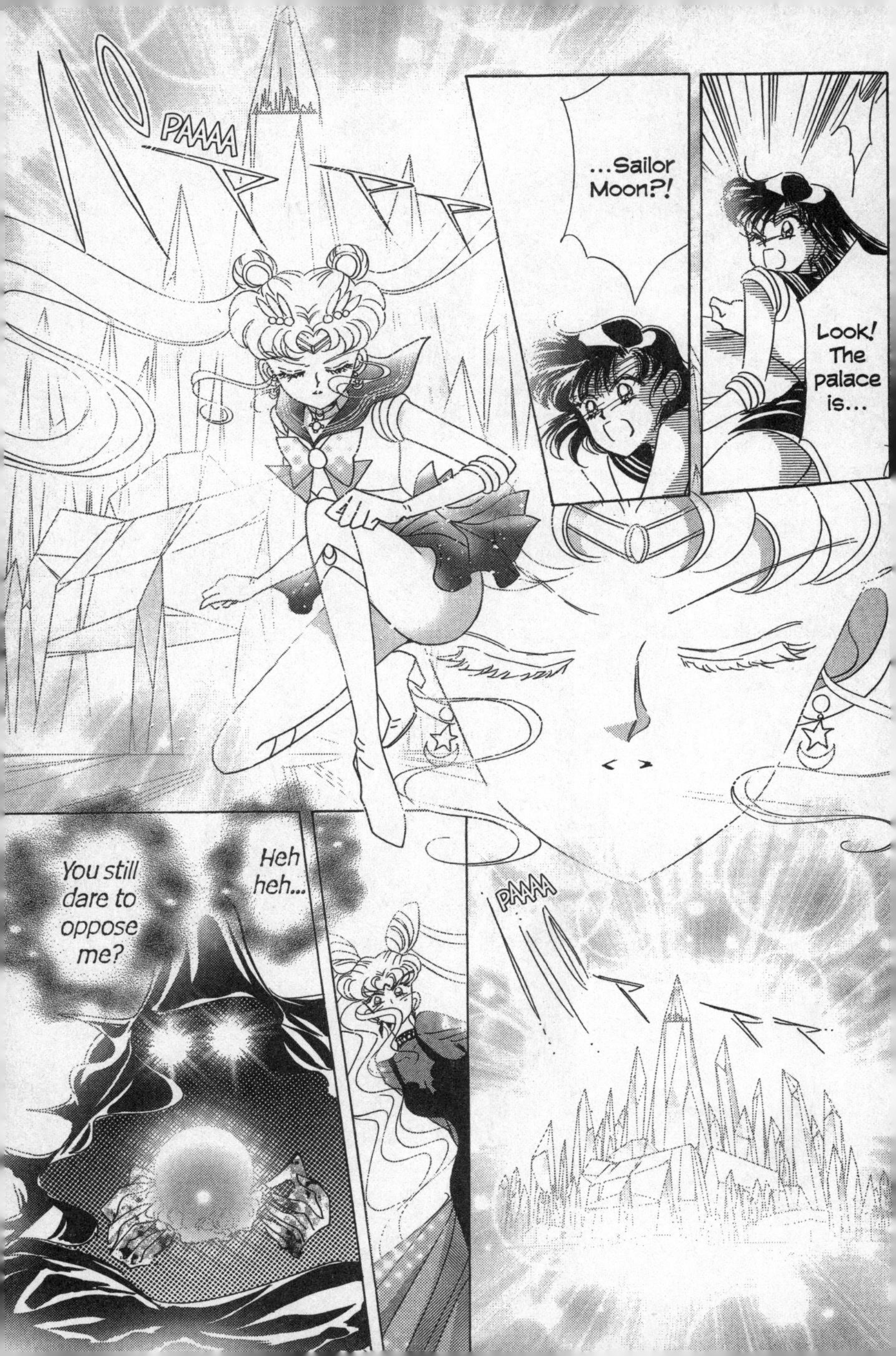
Look! The palace is...
...Sailor Moon?!
PAAAA
PAAAA
Heh heh...
You still dare to oppose me?

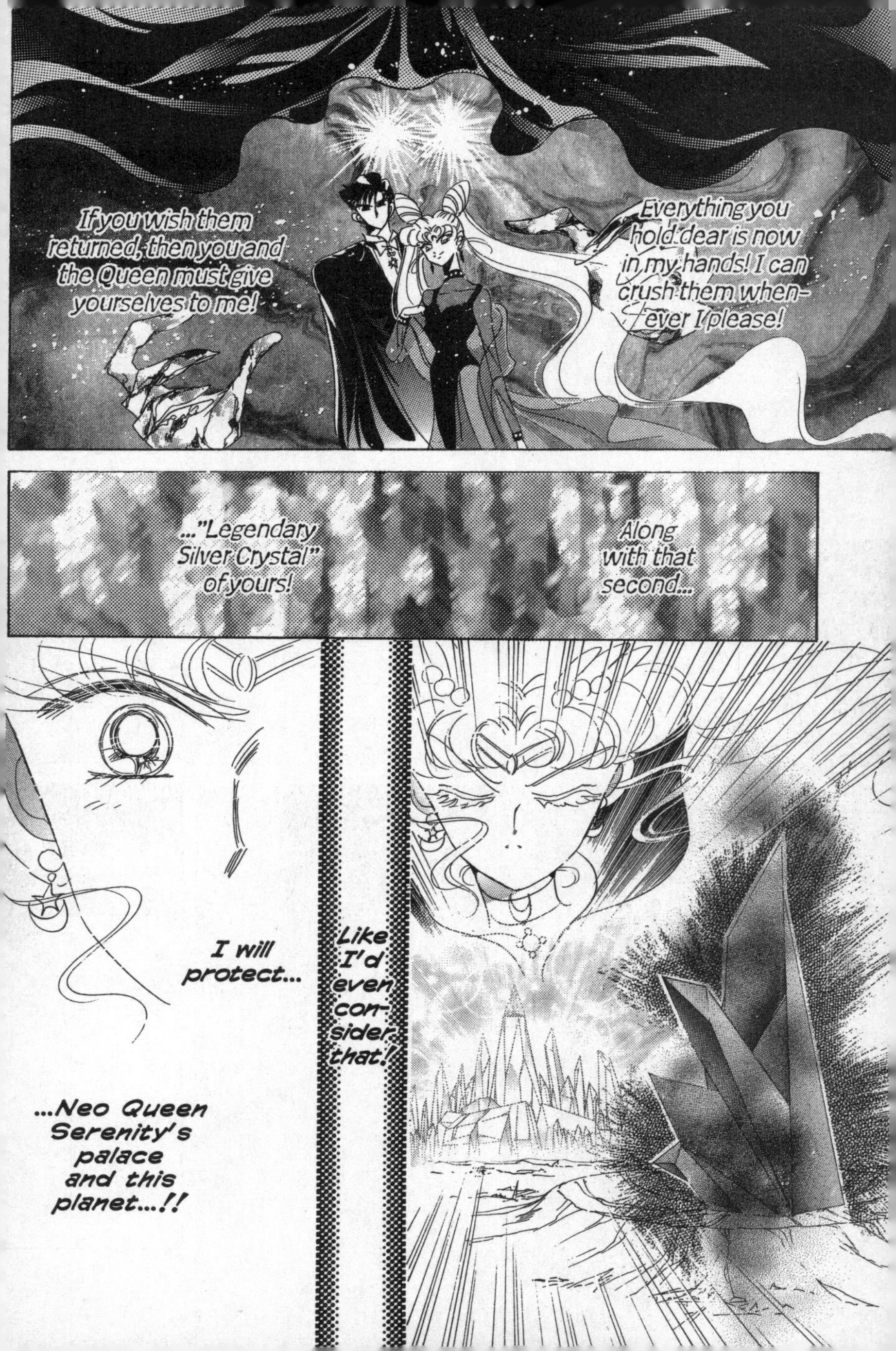
Everything you hold dear is now in my hands! I can crush them when-ever I please!
If you wish them returned, then you and the Queen must give yourselves to me!
Along with that second...
..."Legendary Silver Crystal" of yours!
Like I'd even con-sider that!
I will protect...
...Neo Queen Serenity's palace and this planet...!!

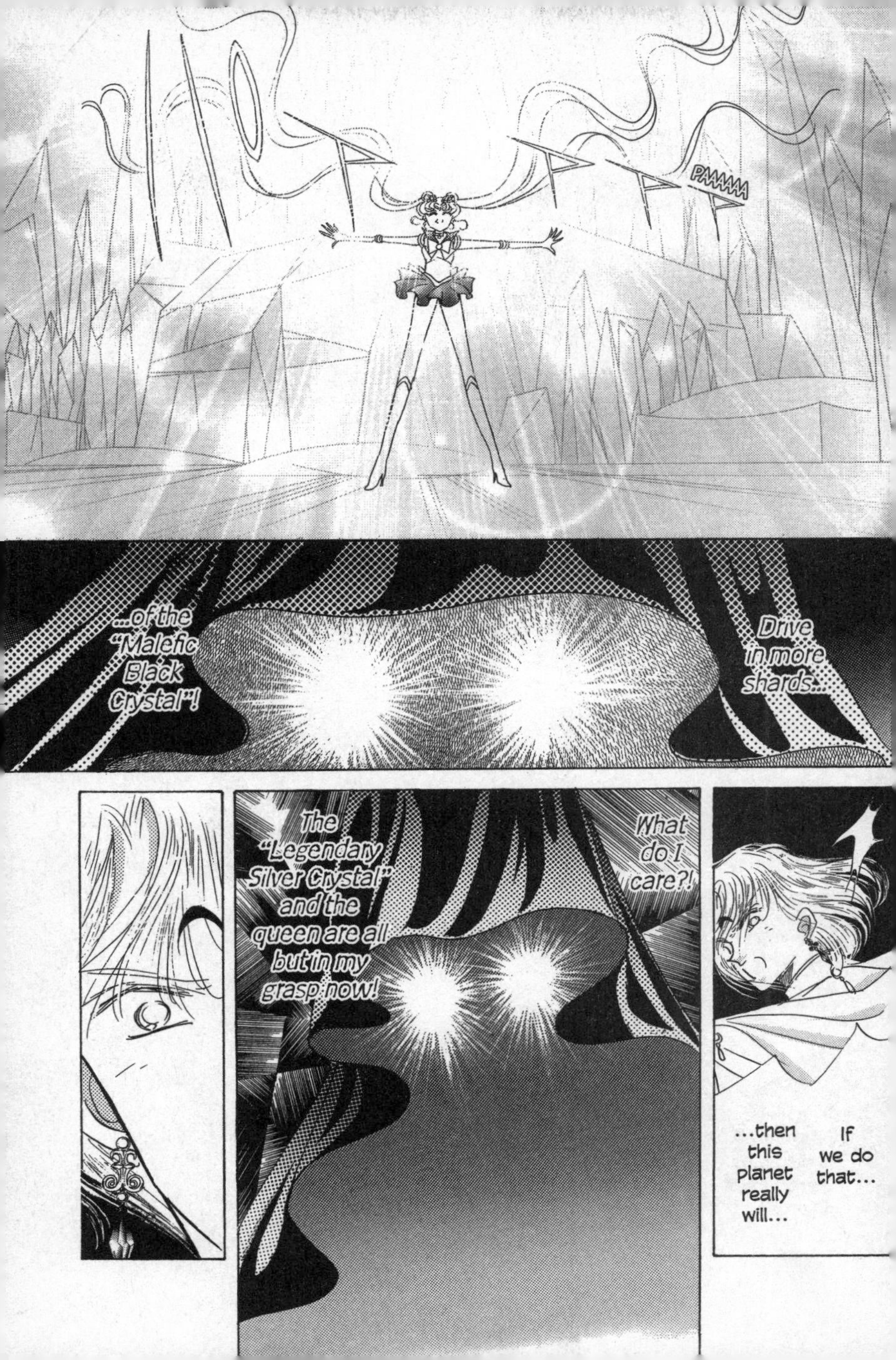
PAAAAAA
Drive in more shards...
...of the "Malefic Black Crystal"!
If we do that...
...then this planet really will...
What do I care?!
The "Legendary Silver Crystal" and the queen are all but in my grasp now!

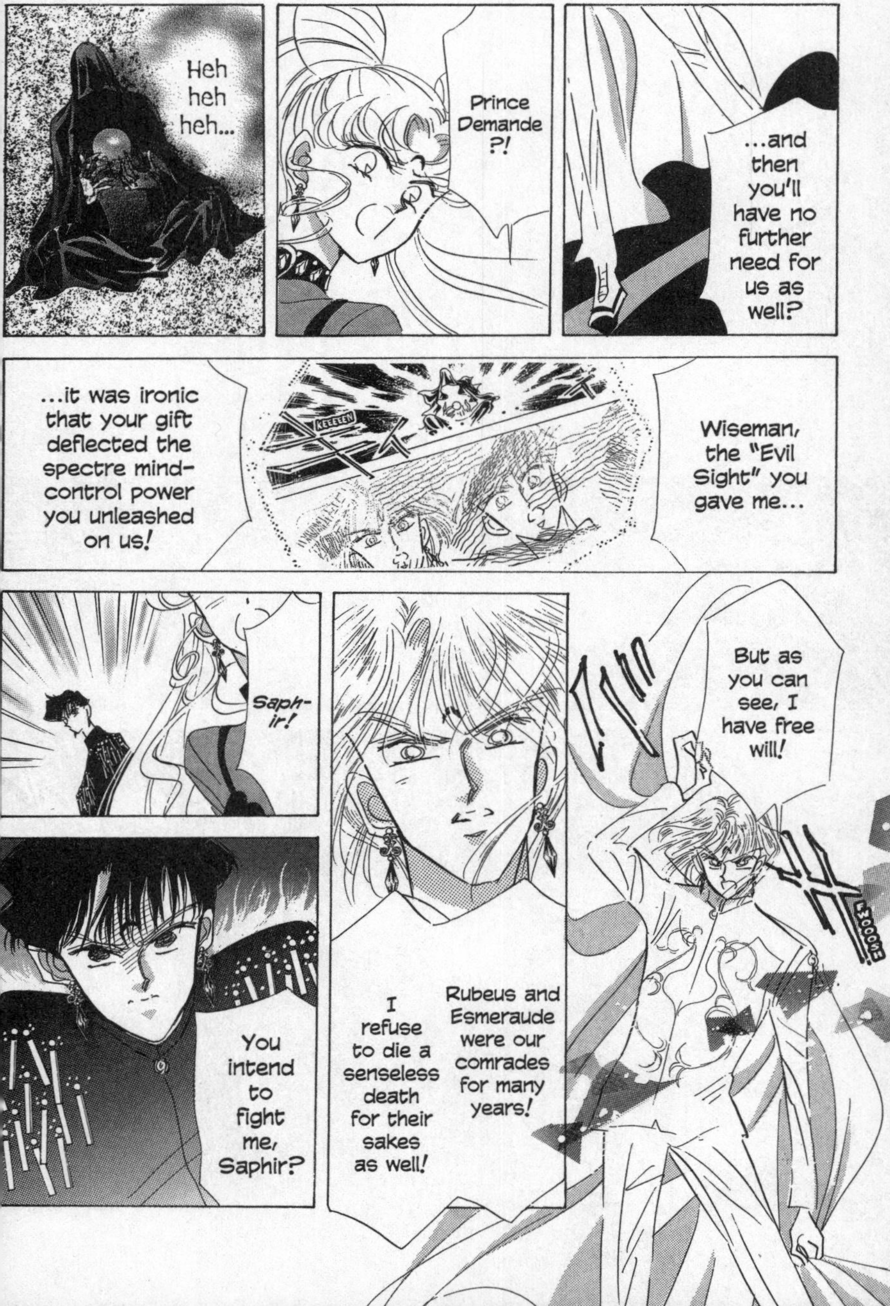
...and then you'll have no further need for us as well?
Prince Demande ?!
Heh heh heh...
Wiseman, the "Evil Sight" you gave me...
KEEEEEN
...it was ironic that your gift deflected the spectre mind-control power you unleashed on us!
But as you can see, I have free will!
FWOOOSH
Rubeus and Esmeraude were our comrades for many years!
I refuse to die a senseless death for their sakes as well!
Saph-ir!
You intend to fight me, Saphir?

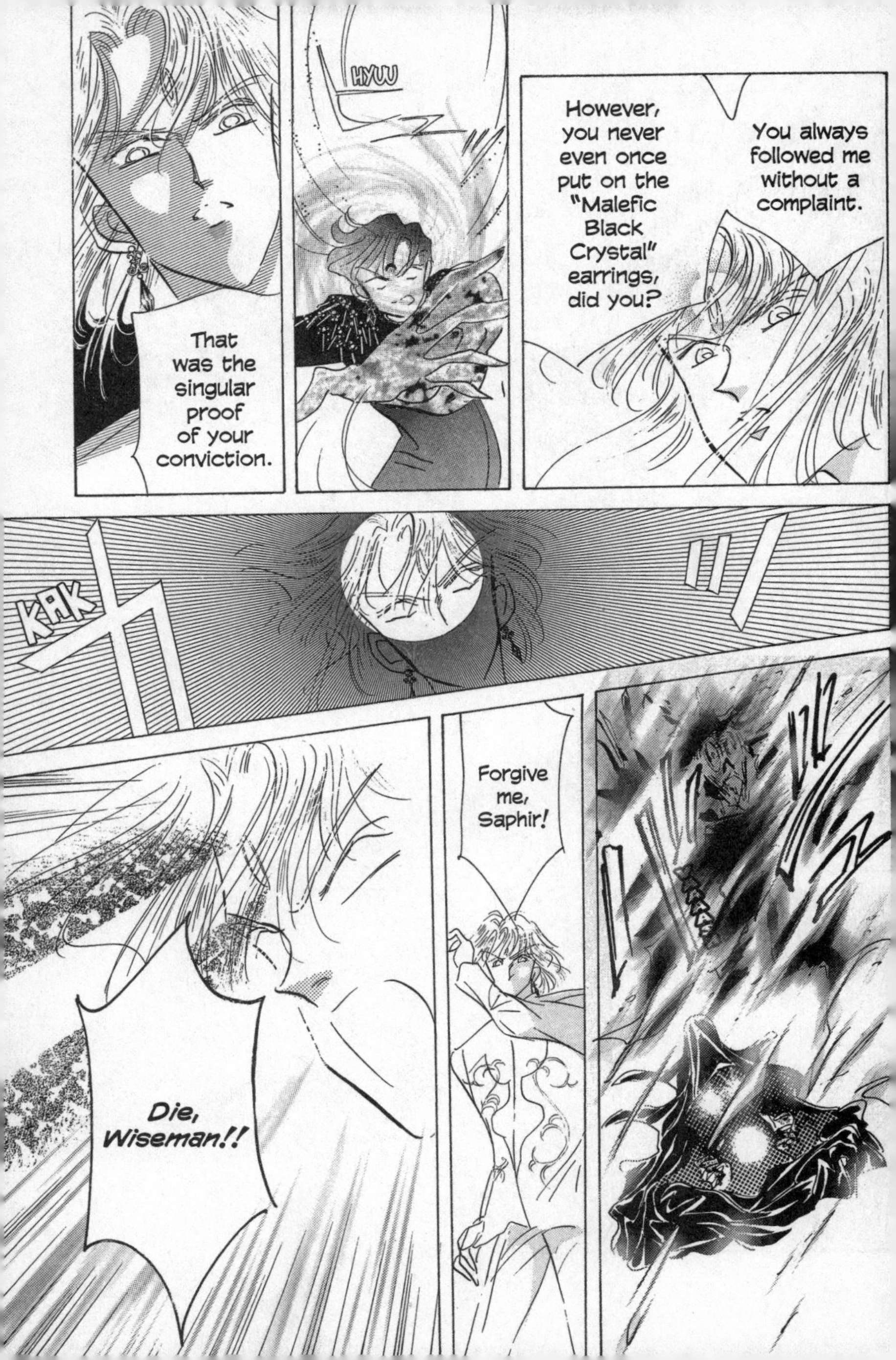
You always followed me without a complaint.
However, you never even once put on the "Malefic Black Crystal" earrings, did you?
HYUU
That was the singular proof of your conviction.
KAK
Forgive me, Saphir!
Die, Wiseman!!

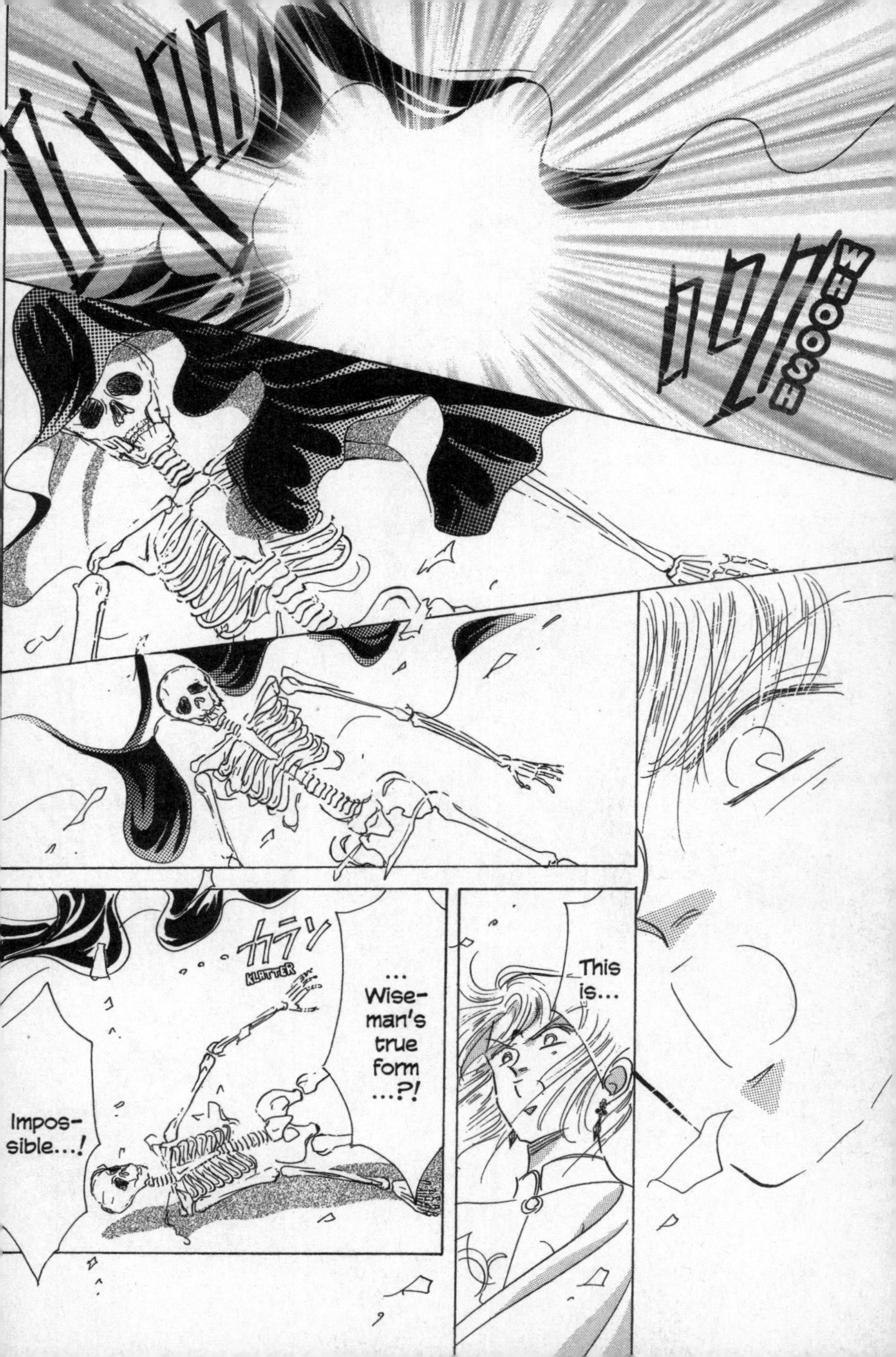
WHOOSH
This is...
... Wiseman's true form ...?!
カラン
KLATTER
Impossible...!

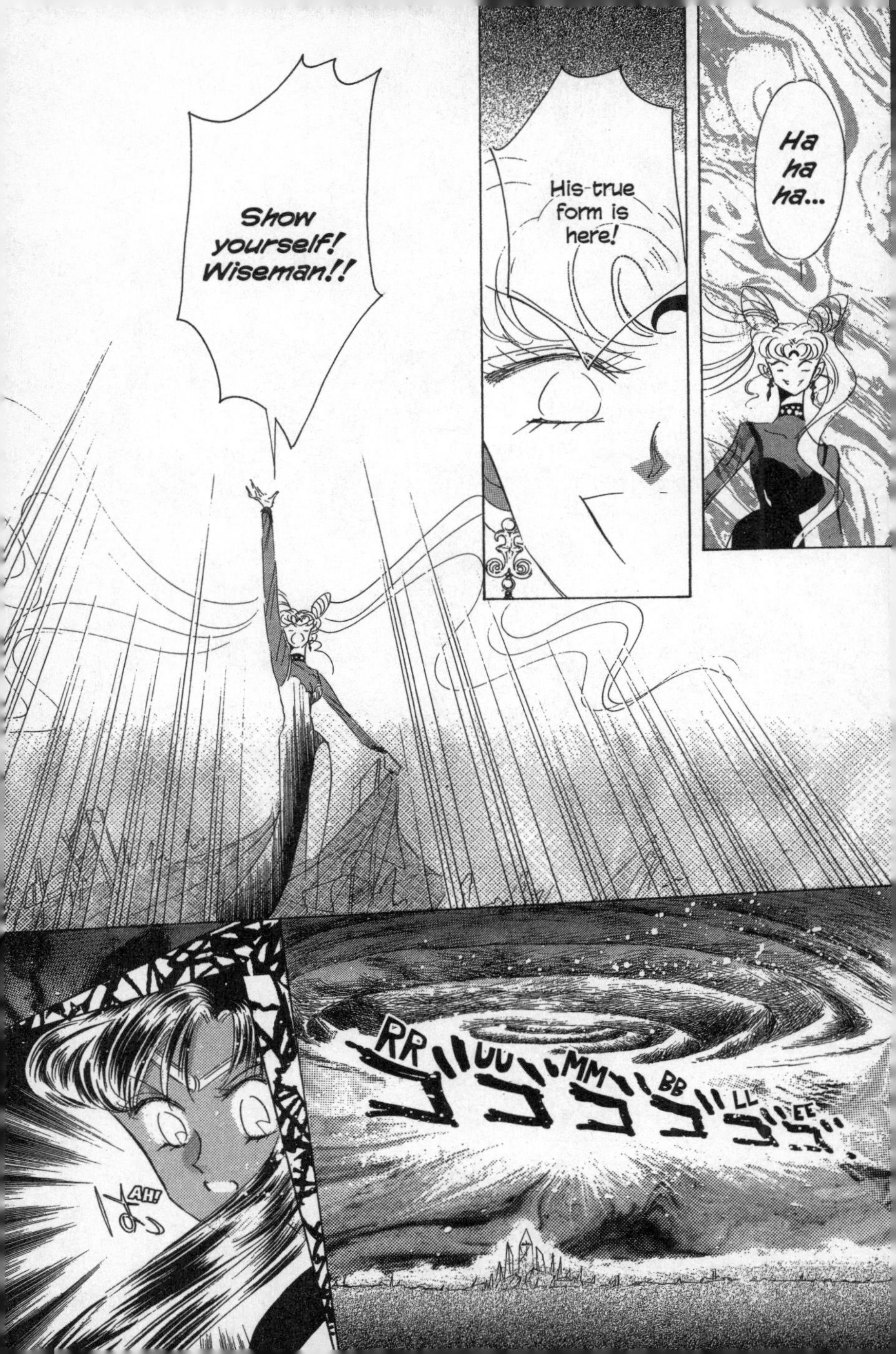
Ha ha ha...
His-true form is here!
Show yourself! Wiseman!!
RRUUMMBBLLEE
AH!

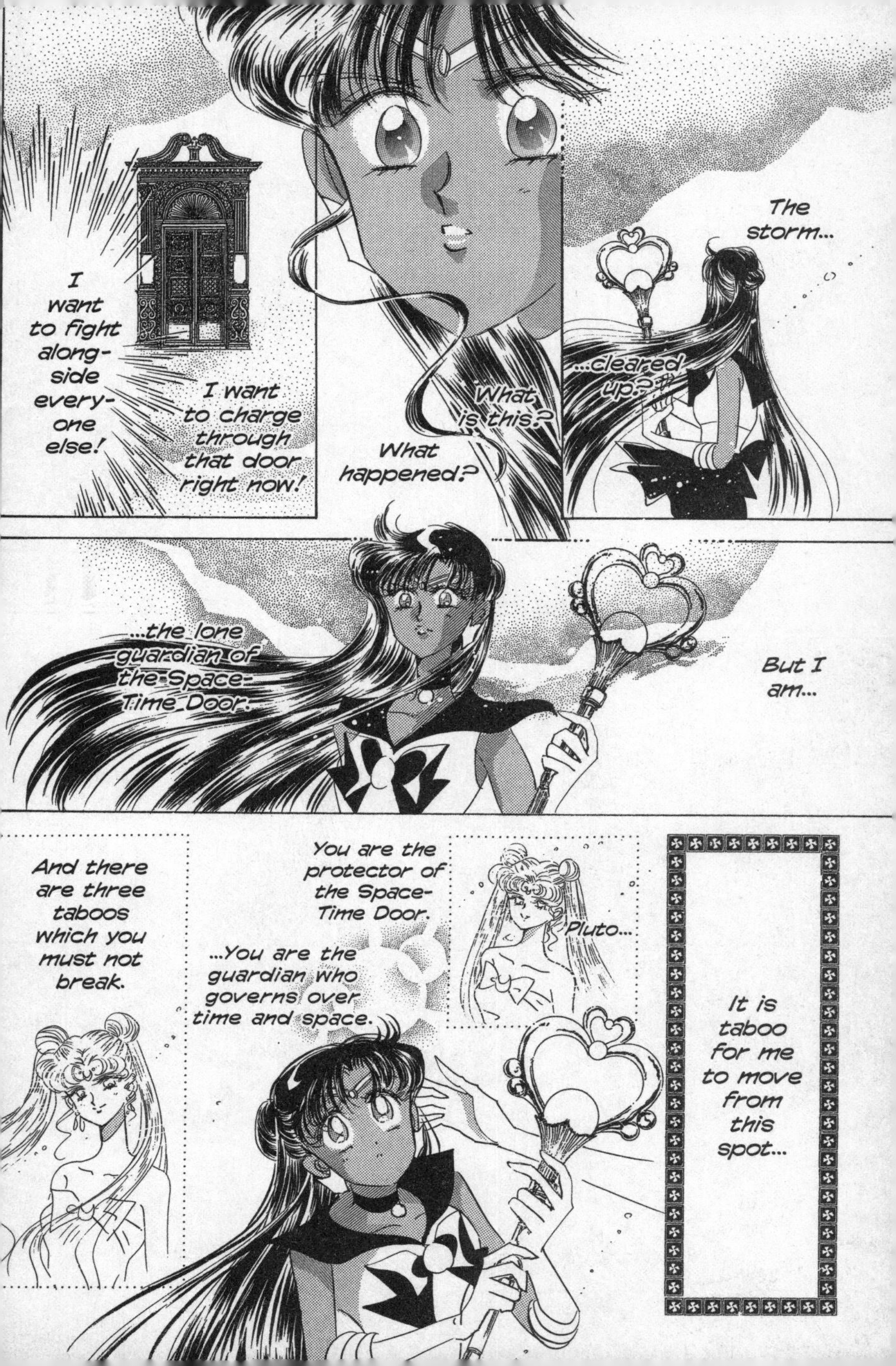
The storm...
...cleared up?
What is this?
What happened?
I want to charge through that door right now!
I want to fight alongside everyone else!
But I am...
...the lone guardian of the Space-Time Door.
It is taboo for me to move from this spot...
Pluto...
You are the protector of the Space-Time Door.
...You are the guardian who governs over time and space.
And there are three taboos which you must not break.

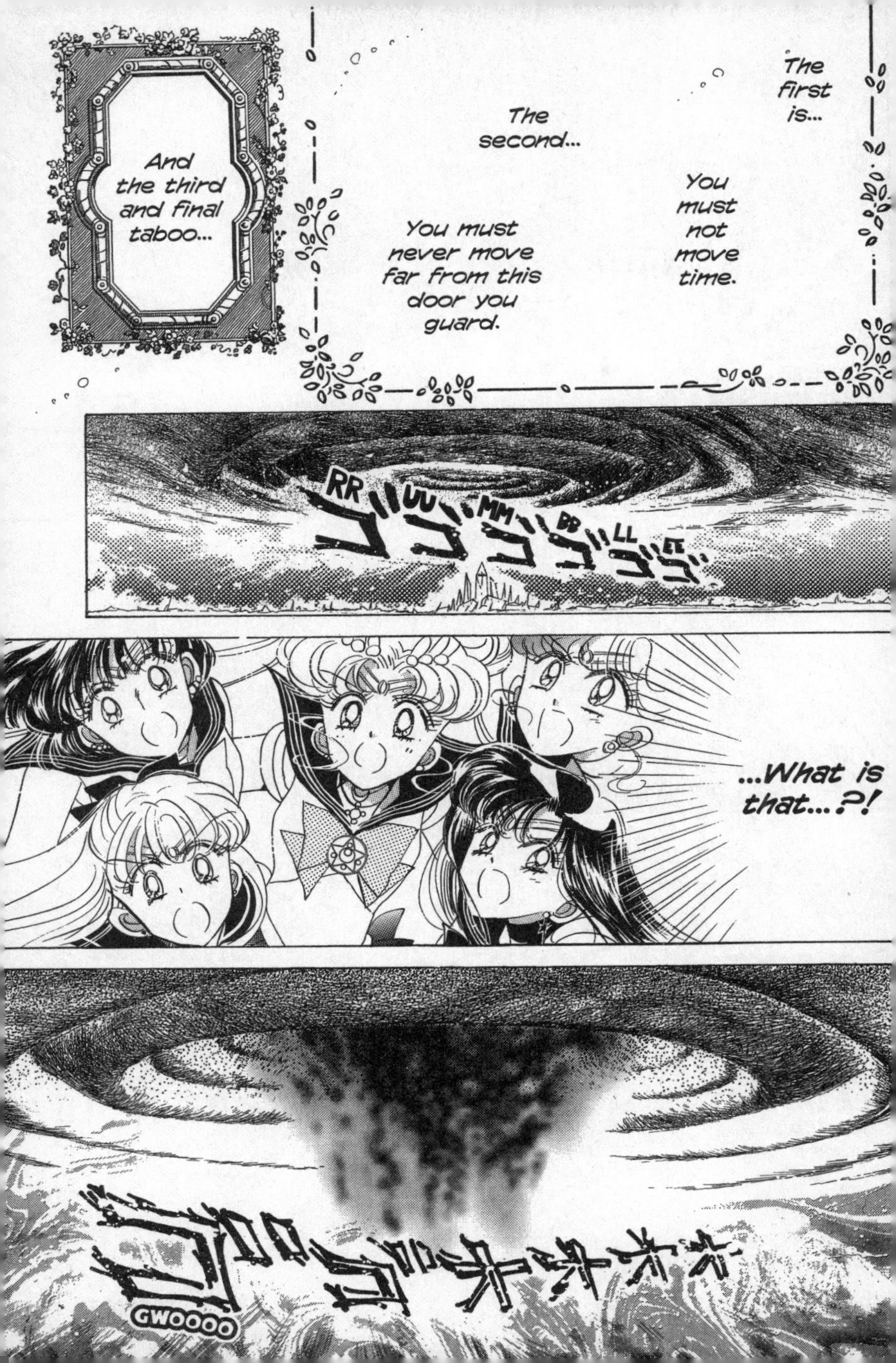
The first is...
You must not move time.
The second...
You must never move far from this door you guard.
And the third and final taboo...
RRUUMMBBLLEE
...What is that...?!
GWOOOO

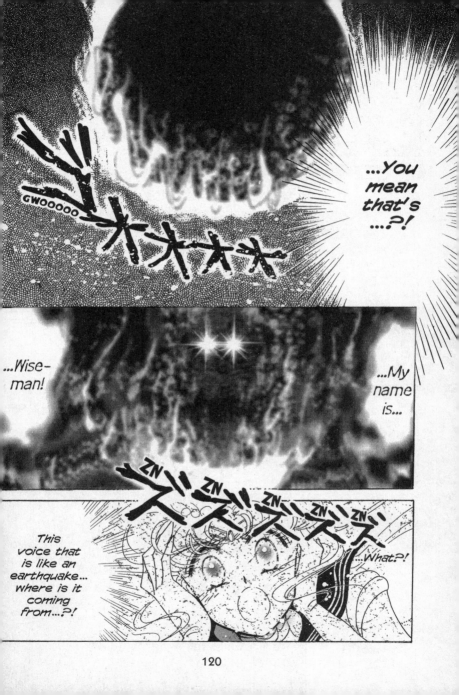

...You mean that's ...?!

GWOOOOO

...Wise-man!

...My name is...

ZN ZN ZN ZN ZN

This voice that is like an earthquake... where is it coming from...?!

...What?!

120

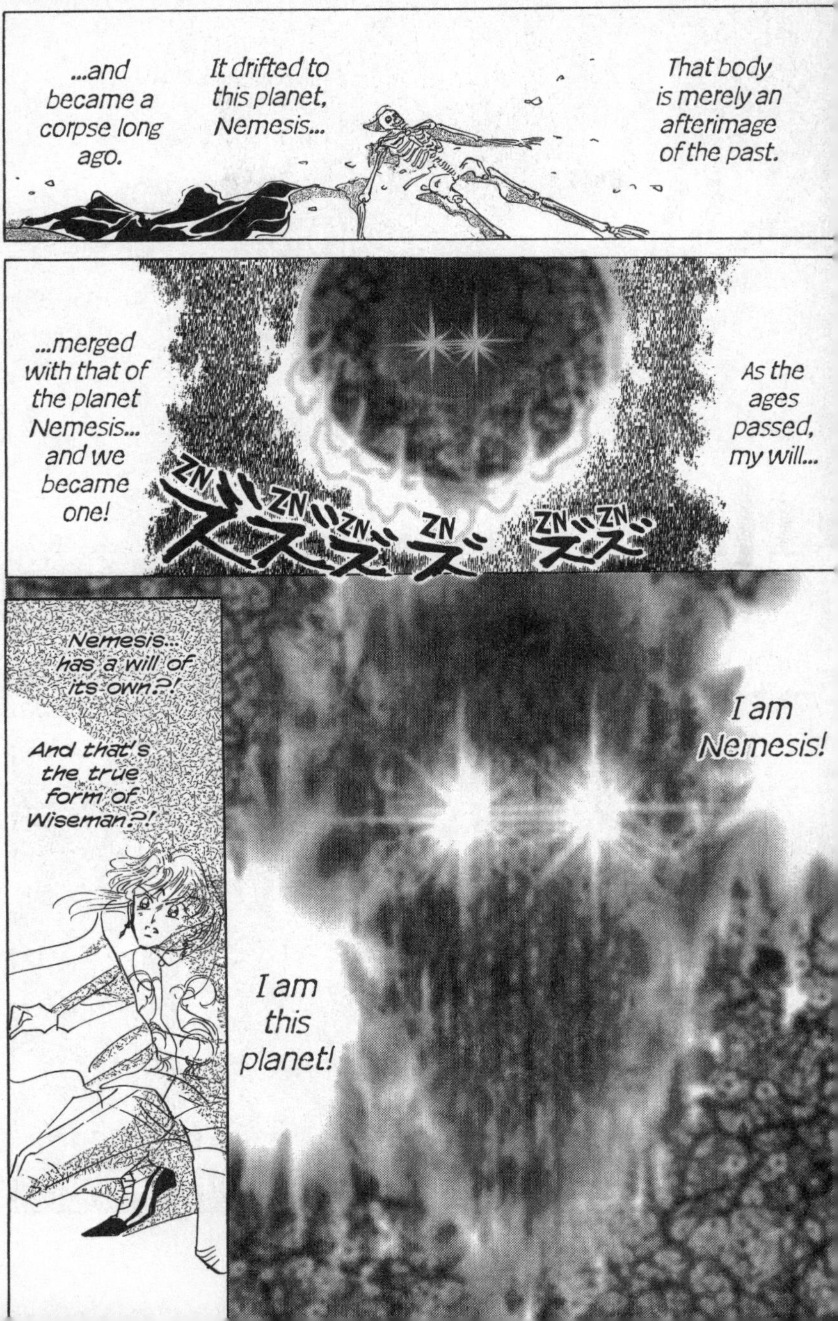
That body is merely an afterimage of the past.
It drifted to this planet, Nemesis...
...and became a corpse long ago.
As the ages passed, my will...
...merged with that of the planet Nemesis... and we became one!
ZN ZN ZN ZN ZN ZN
ズズズズ ズズ
I am Nemesis!
I am this planet!
Nemesis... has a will of its own?!
And that's the true form of Wiseman?!

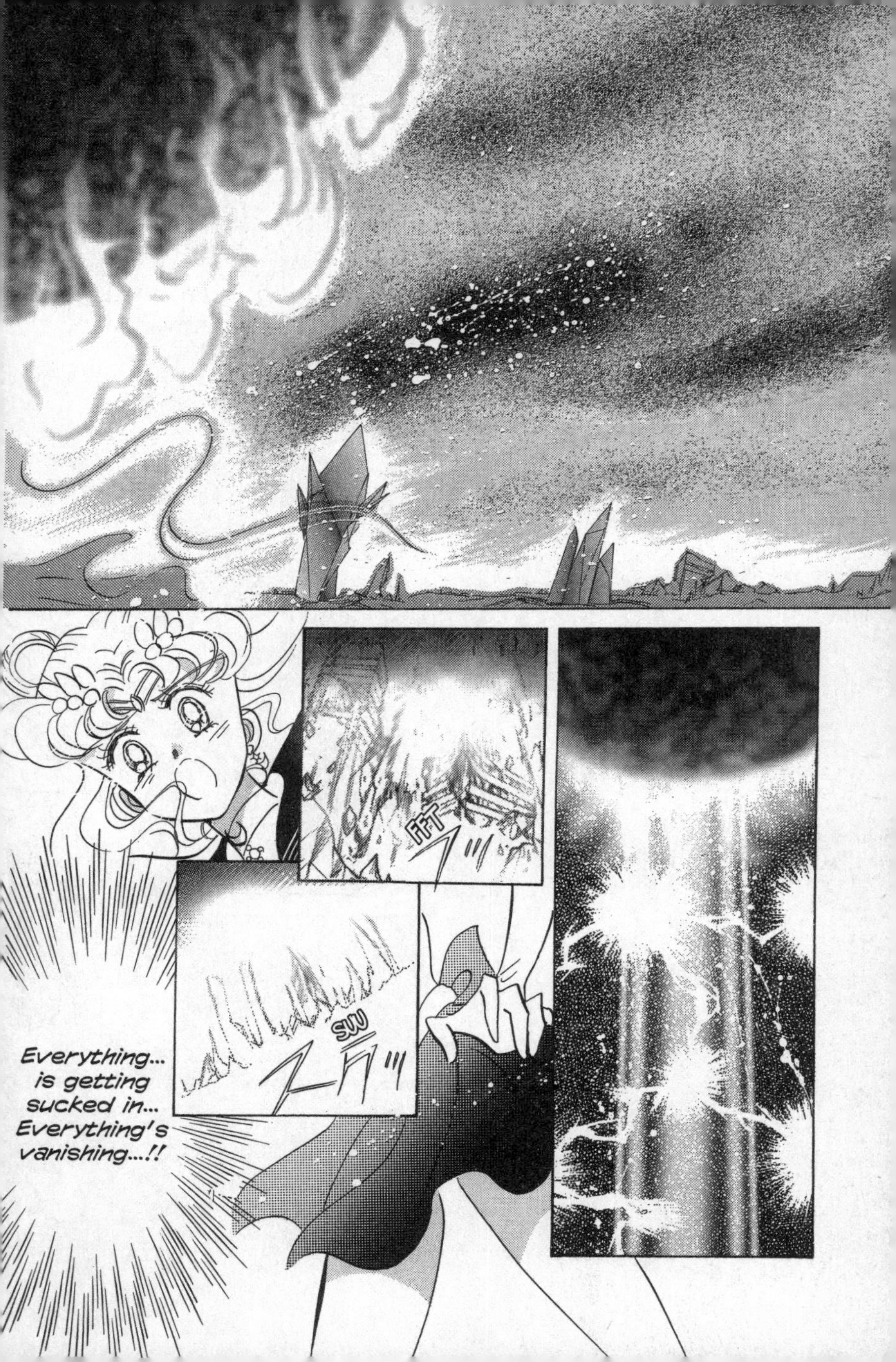
FFT
SUU
Everything... is getting sucked in... Everything's vanishing...!!

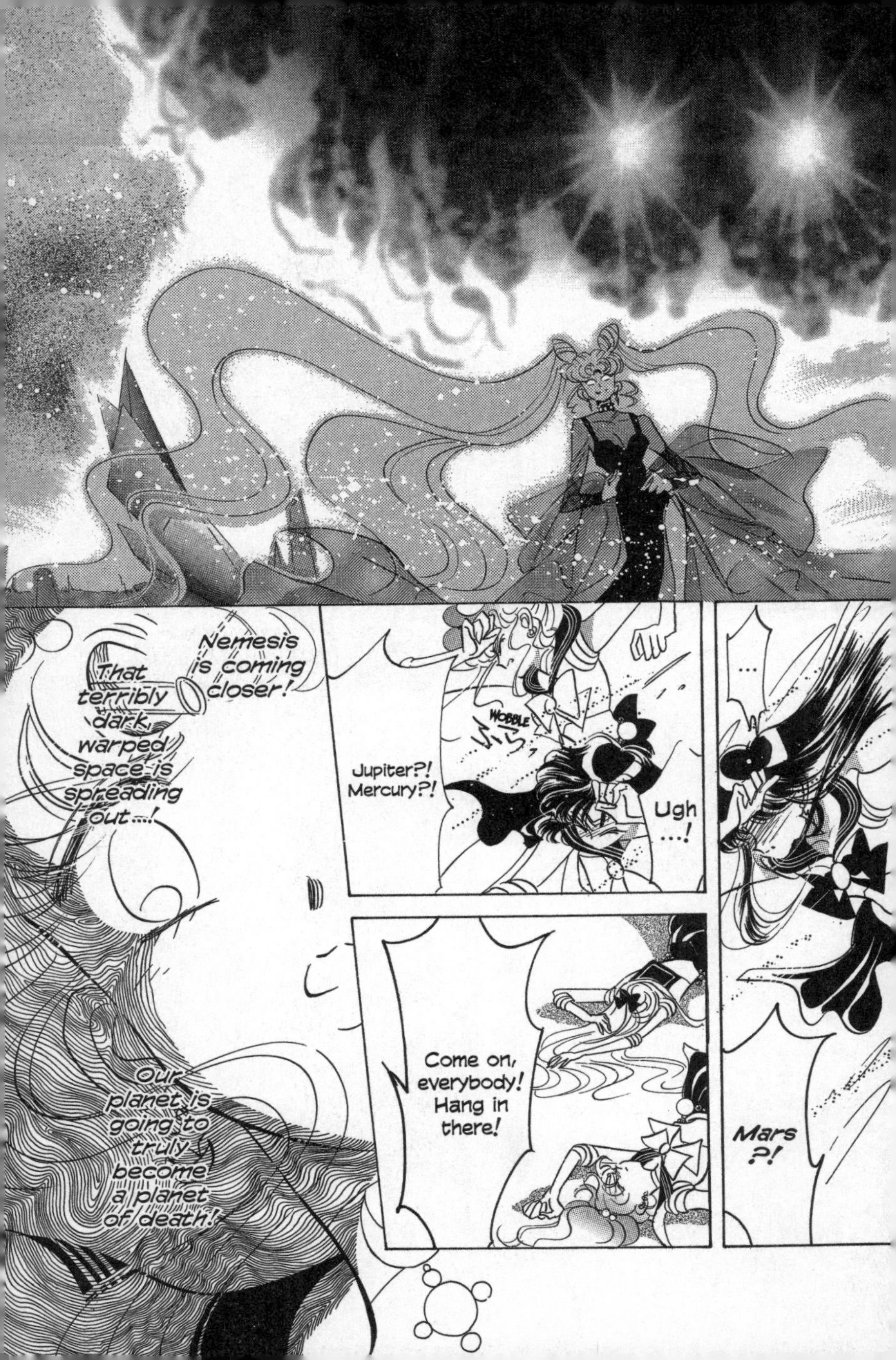
...
Mars ?!
Jupiter?! Mercury?!
WOBBLE
ふら
Ugh ...!
Come on, everybody! Hang in there!
Nemesis is coming closer!
That terribly dark warped space is spreading out...!
Our planet is going to truly become a planet of death!

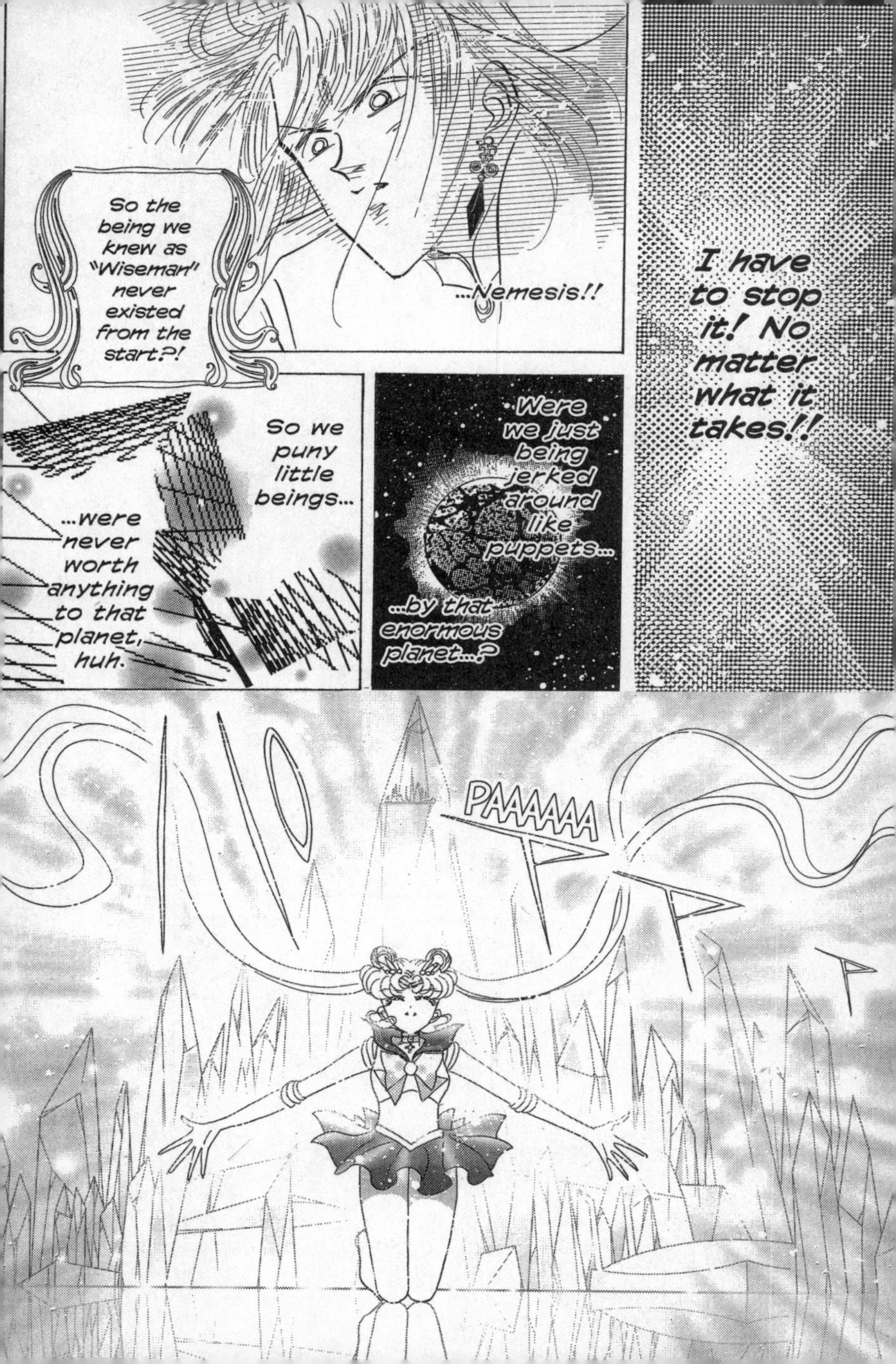

I have to stop it! No matter what it takes!!
So the being we knew as "Wiseman" never existed from the start?!
...Nemesis!!
Were we just being jerked around like puppets...
...by that enormous planet...?
So we puny little beings...
...were never worth anything to that planet, huh.
PAAAAAA

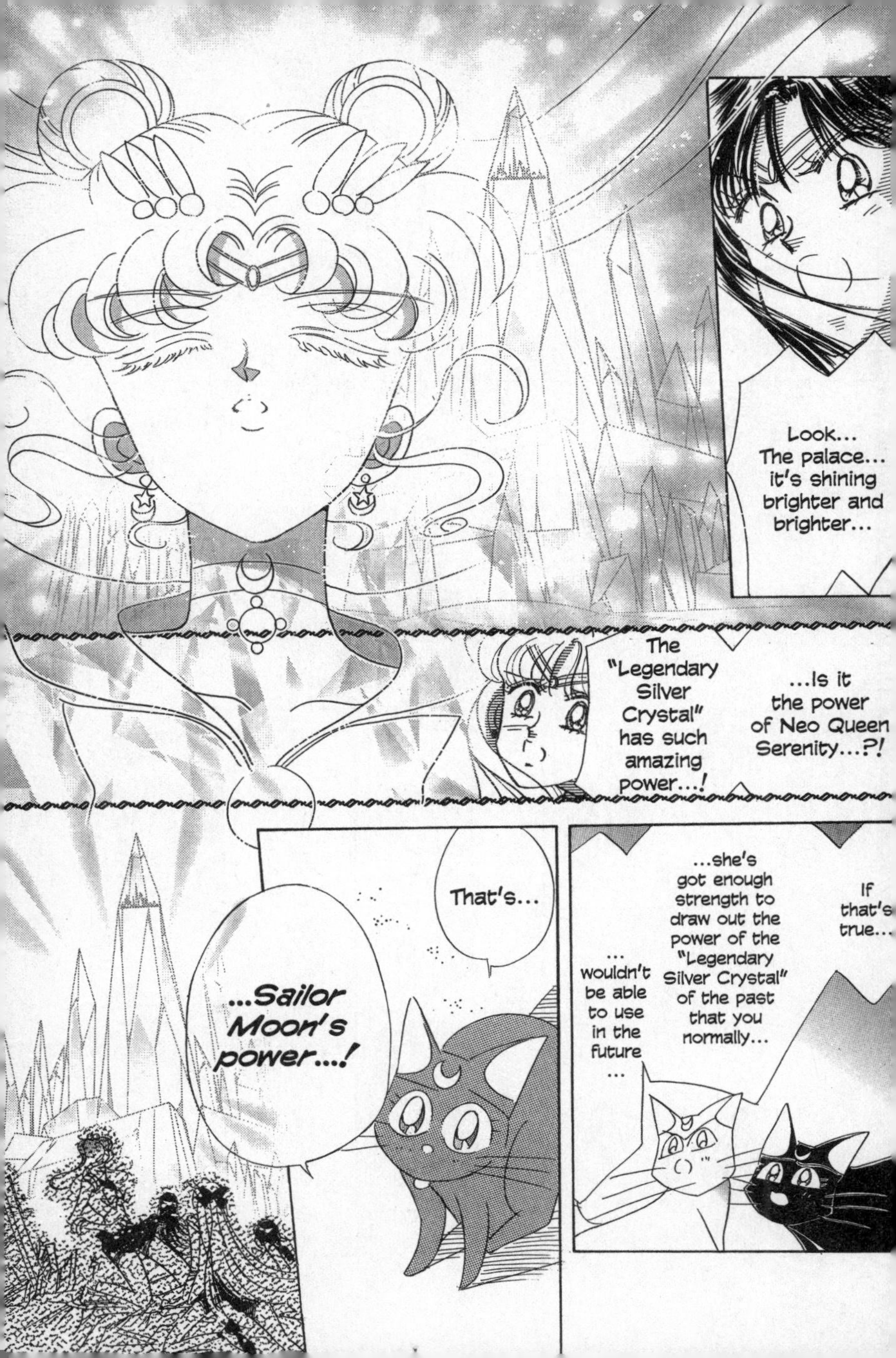
Look... The palace... it's shining brighter and brighter...
...Is it the power of Neo Queen Serenity...?!
The "Legendary Silver Crystal" has such amazing power...!
If that's true...
...she's got enough strength to draw out the power of the "Legendary Silver Crystal" of the past that you normally...
...wouldn't be able to use in the future...
That's...
...Sailor Moon's power...!

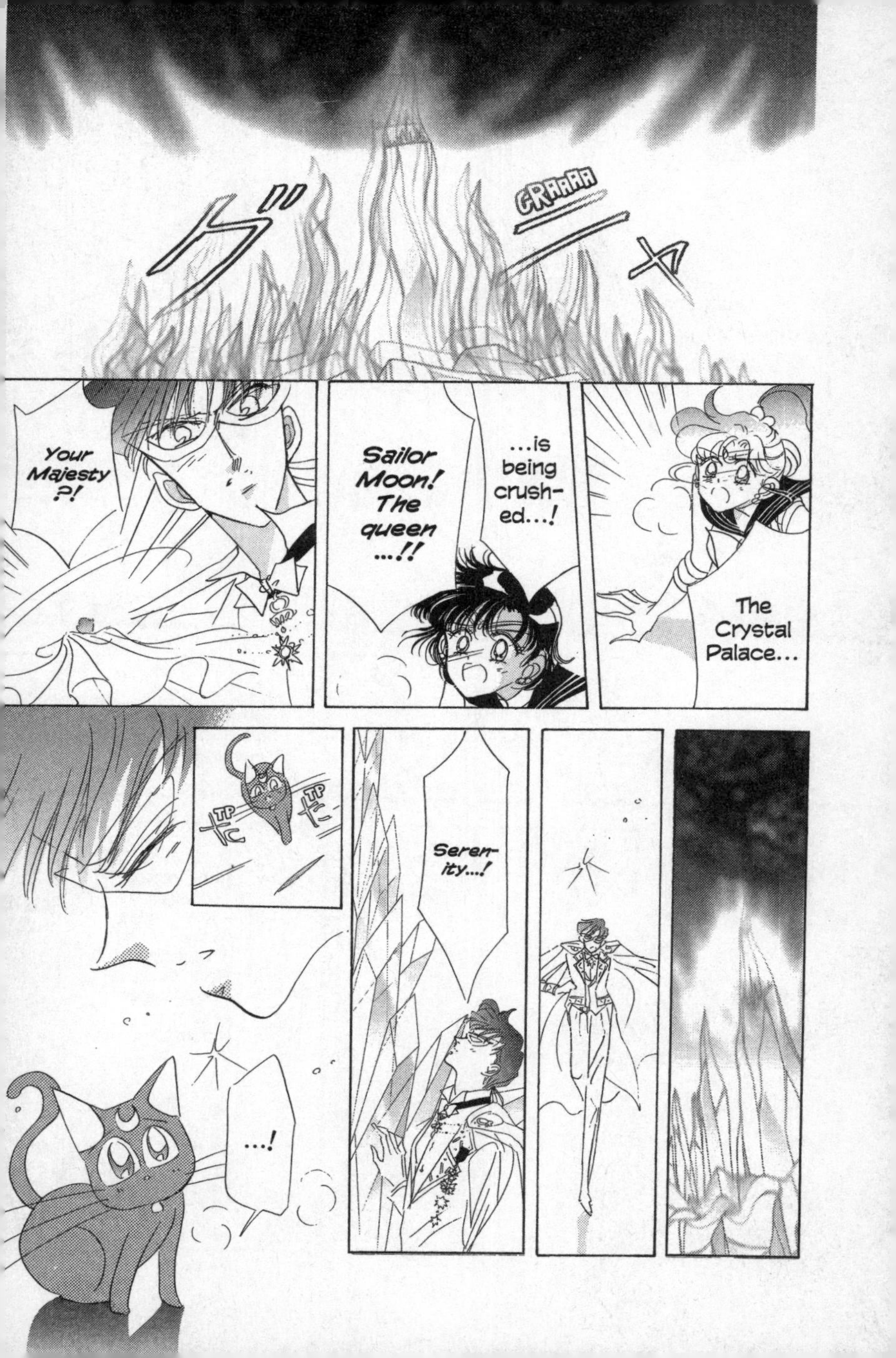
CRAAAA
The Crystal Palace...
Sailor Moon! The queen ...!!
...is being crush-ed...!
Your Majesty ?!
Seren-ity...!
TP
TP
...!

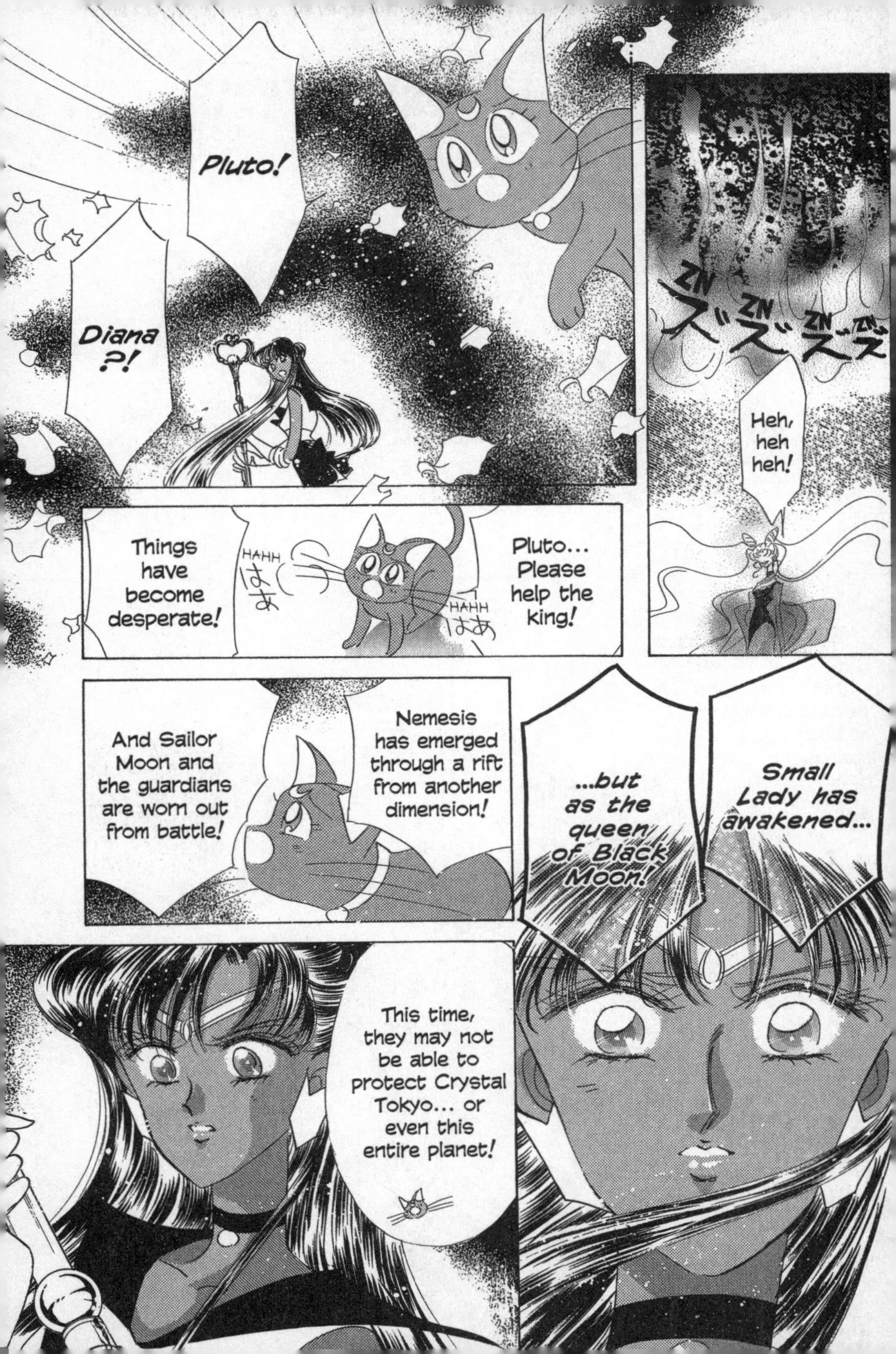
ZN ズ ZN ズ ZN ズ ZN ズ
Heh, heh heh!
Pluto!
Diana?!
Pluto... Please help the king!
HAHH はあ
HAHH はあ
Things have become desperate!
Small Lady has awakened...
...but as the queen of Black Moon!
Nemesis has emerged through a rift from another dimension!
And Sailor Moon and the guardians are worn out from battle!
This time, they may not be able to protect Crystal Tokyo... or even this entire planet!

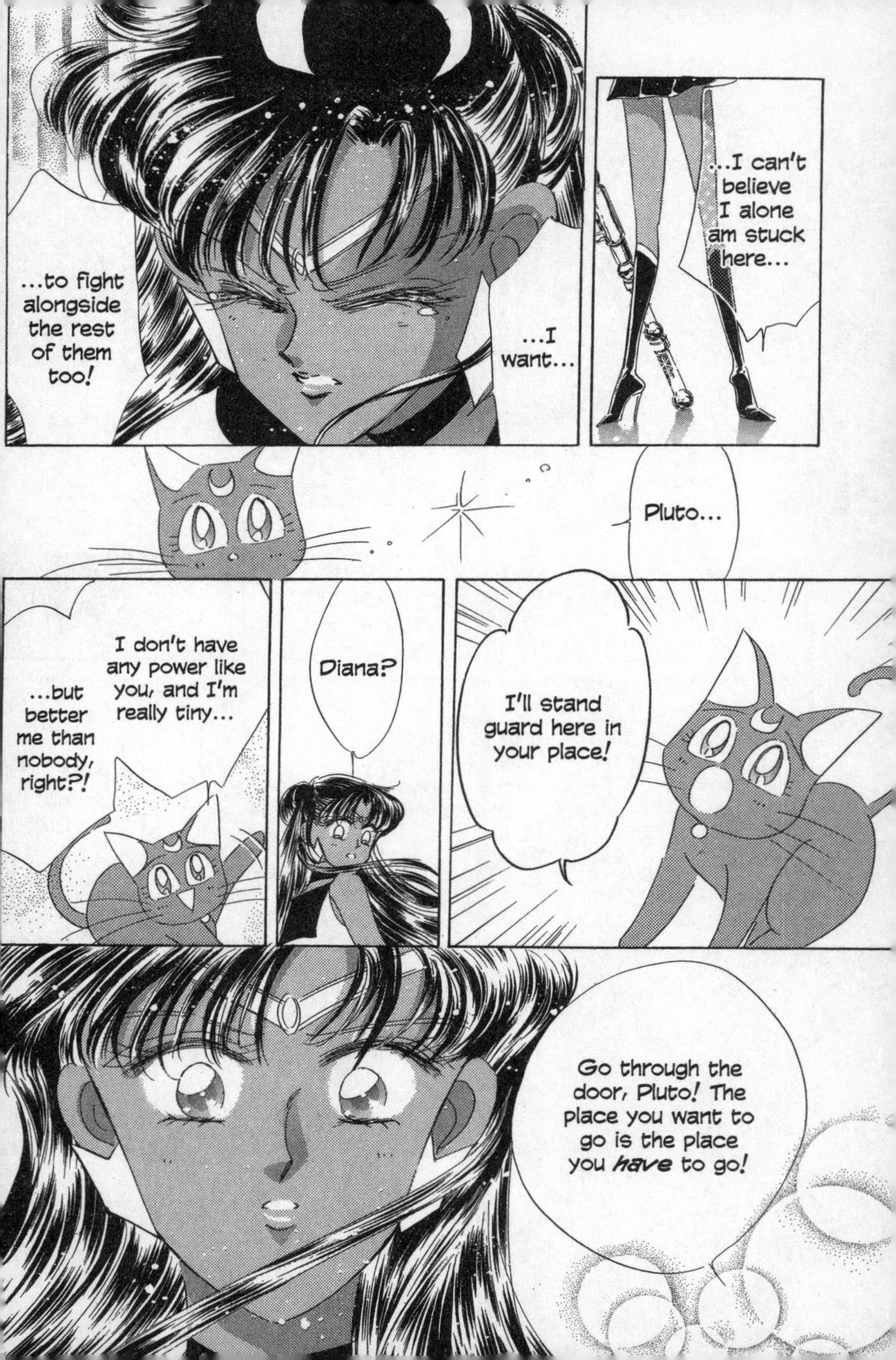
...I can't believe I alone am stuck here...
...I want...
...to fight alongside the rest of them too!
Pluto...
I'll stand guard here in your place!
Diana?
I don't have any power like you, and I'm really tiny...
...but better me than nobody, right?!
Go through the door, Pluto! The place you want to go is the place you *have* to go!

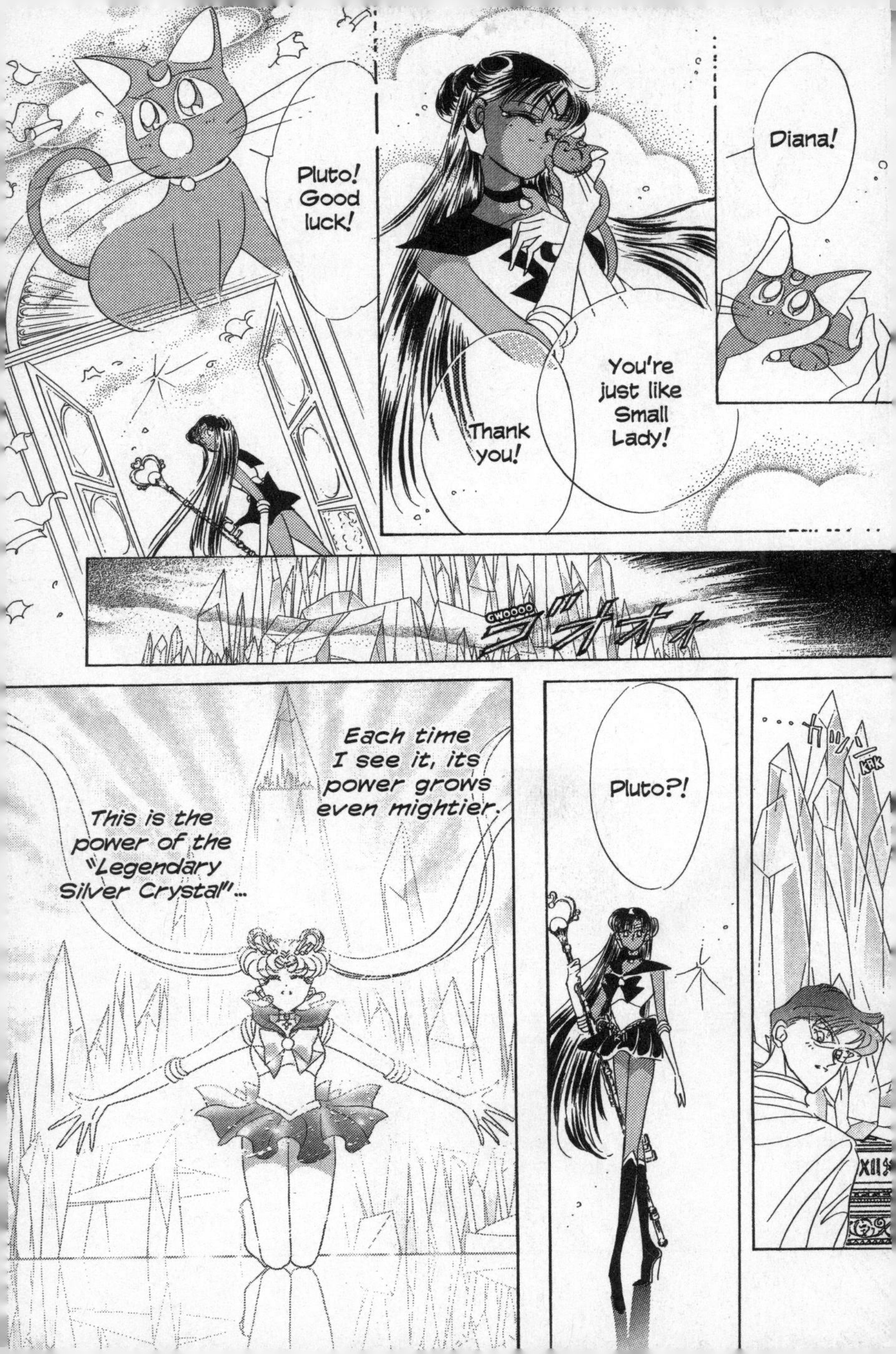
Diana!
You're just like Small Lady!
Thank you!
Pluto! Good luck!
GWOOOO
KRK
Pluto?!
Each time I see it, its power grows even mightier.
This is the power of the "Legendary Silver Crystal"...

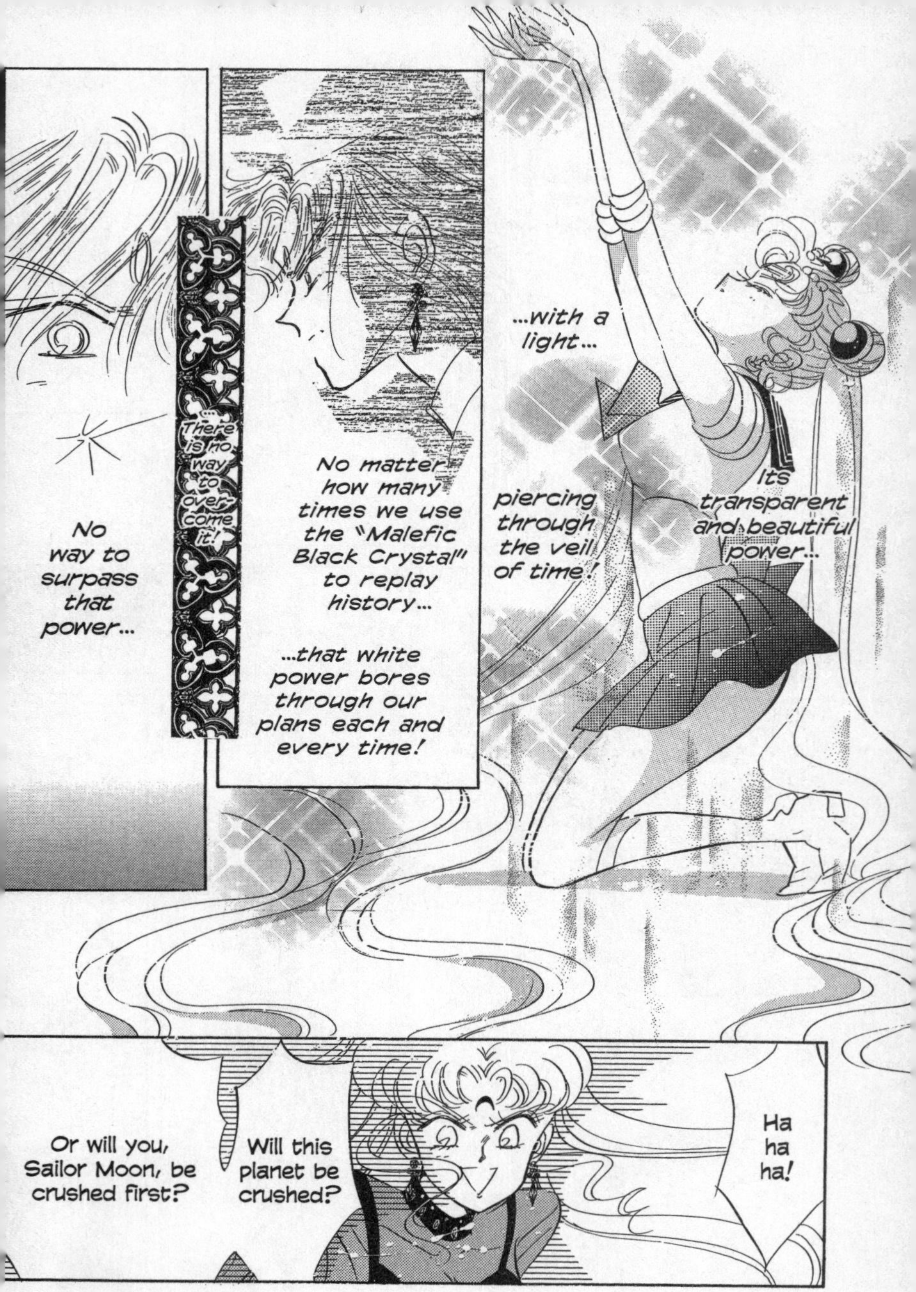
Its transparent and beautiful power...
...with a light...
piercing through the veil of time!
No matter how many times we use the "Malefic Black Crystal" to replay history...
...that white power bores through our plans each and every time!
...There is no way to over-come it!
No way to surpass that power...
Ha ha ha!
Will this planet be crushed?
Or will you, Sailor Moon, be crushed first?

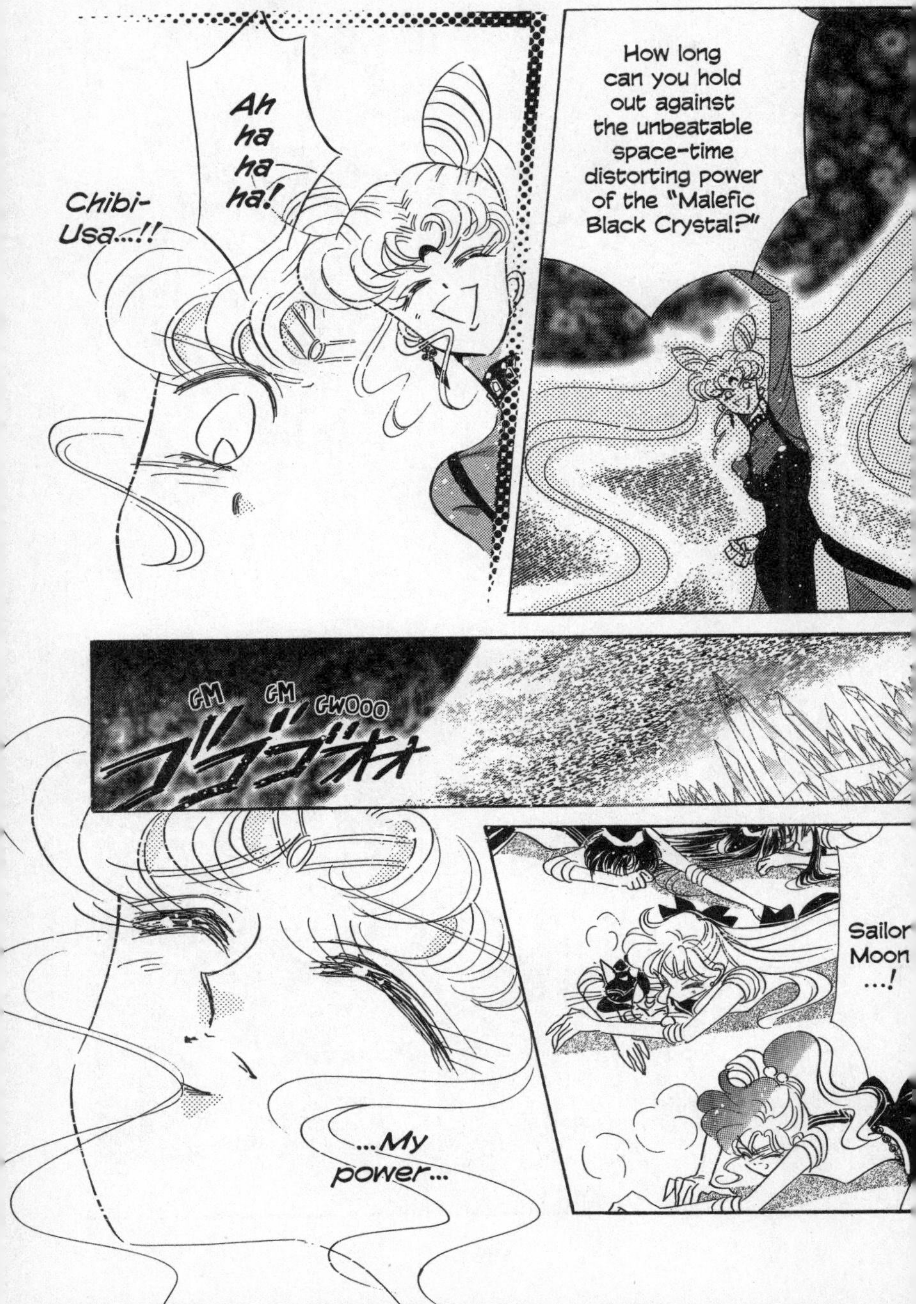
How long can you hold out against the unbeatable space-time distorting power of the "Malefic Black Crystal?"
Ah ha ha ha!
Chibi-Usa...!!
GM GM GWOOO
ゴゴゴオオ
Sailor Moon ...!
...My power...

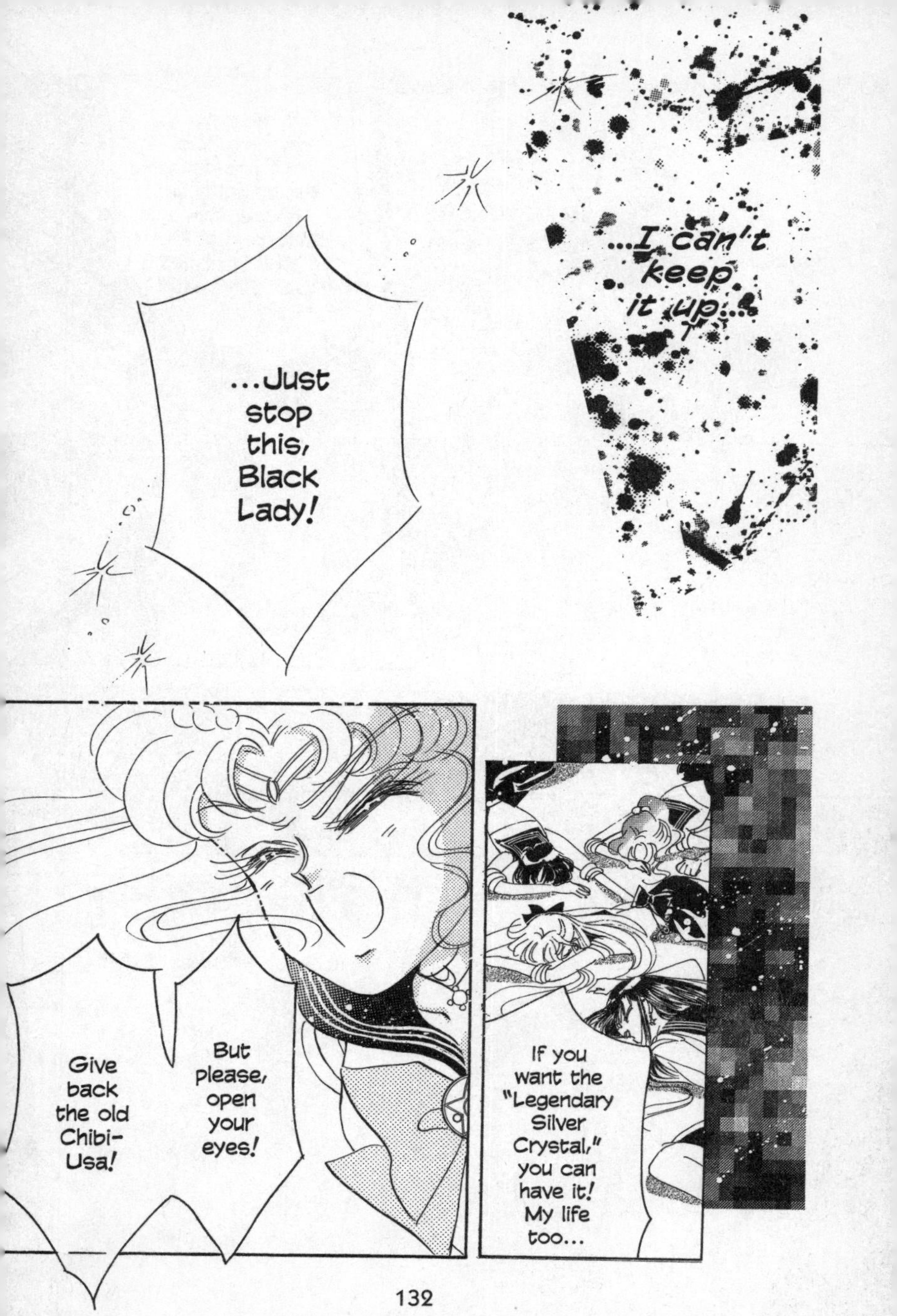
...I can't keep it up...
...Just stop this, Black Lady!
If you want the "Legendary Silver Crystal," you can have it! My life too...
But please, open your eyes!
Give back the old Chibi-Usa!

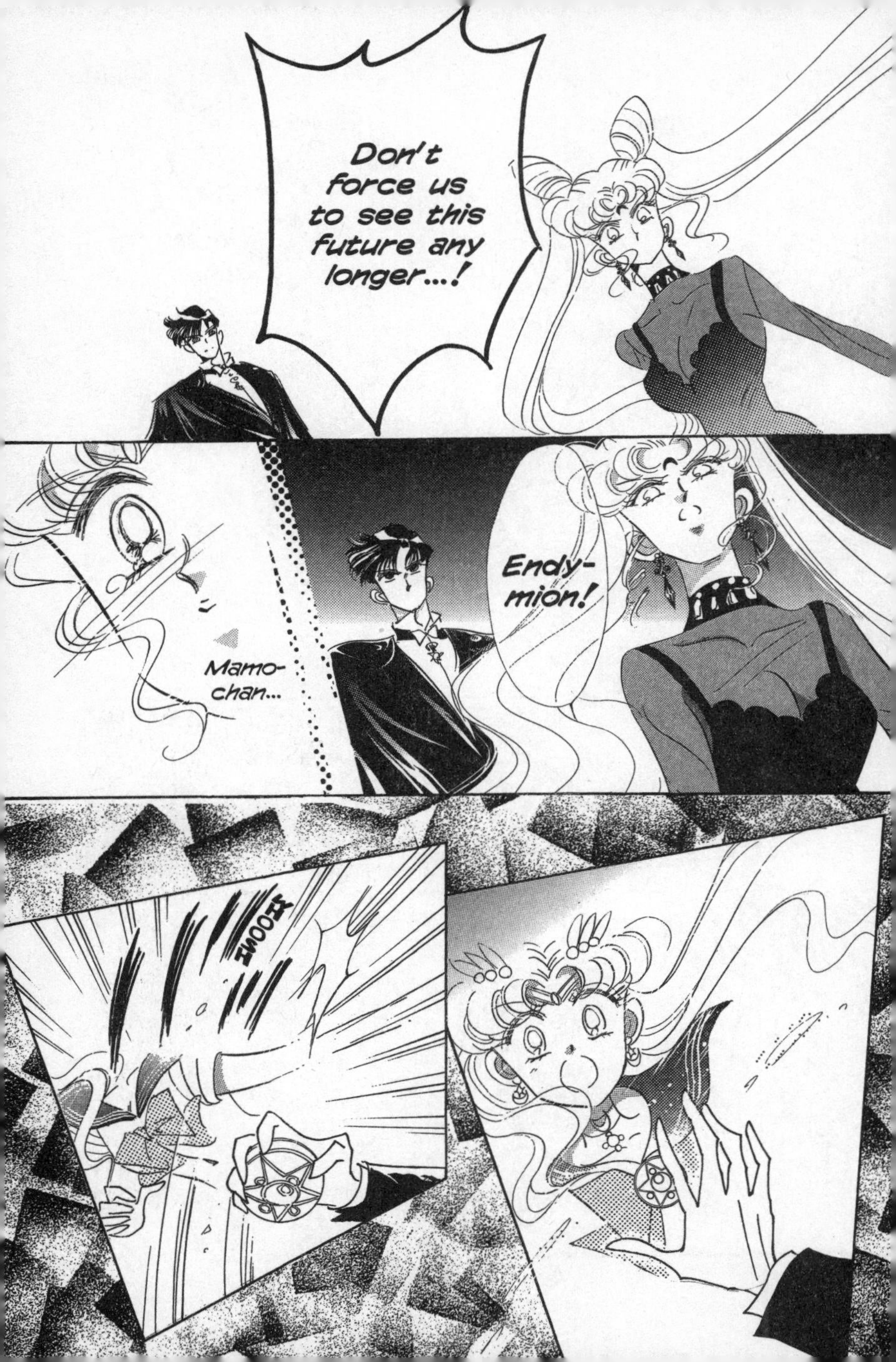
Don't force us to see this future any longer...!
Endy-mion!
Mamo-chan...

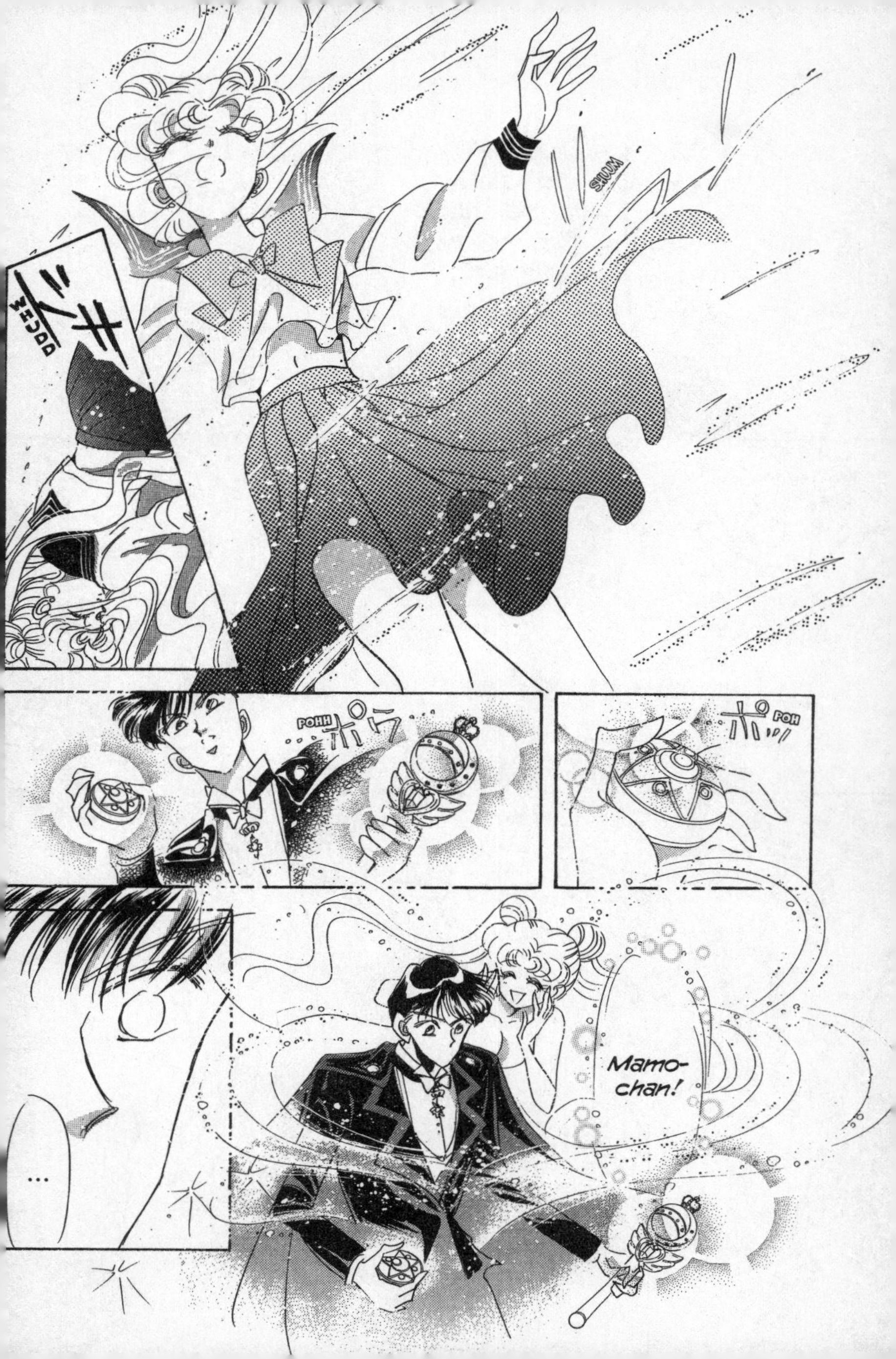
SHUUM
WHUDD
POH
POHH
Mamo-chan!
...

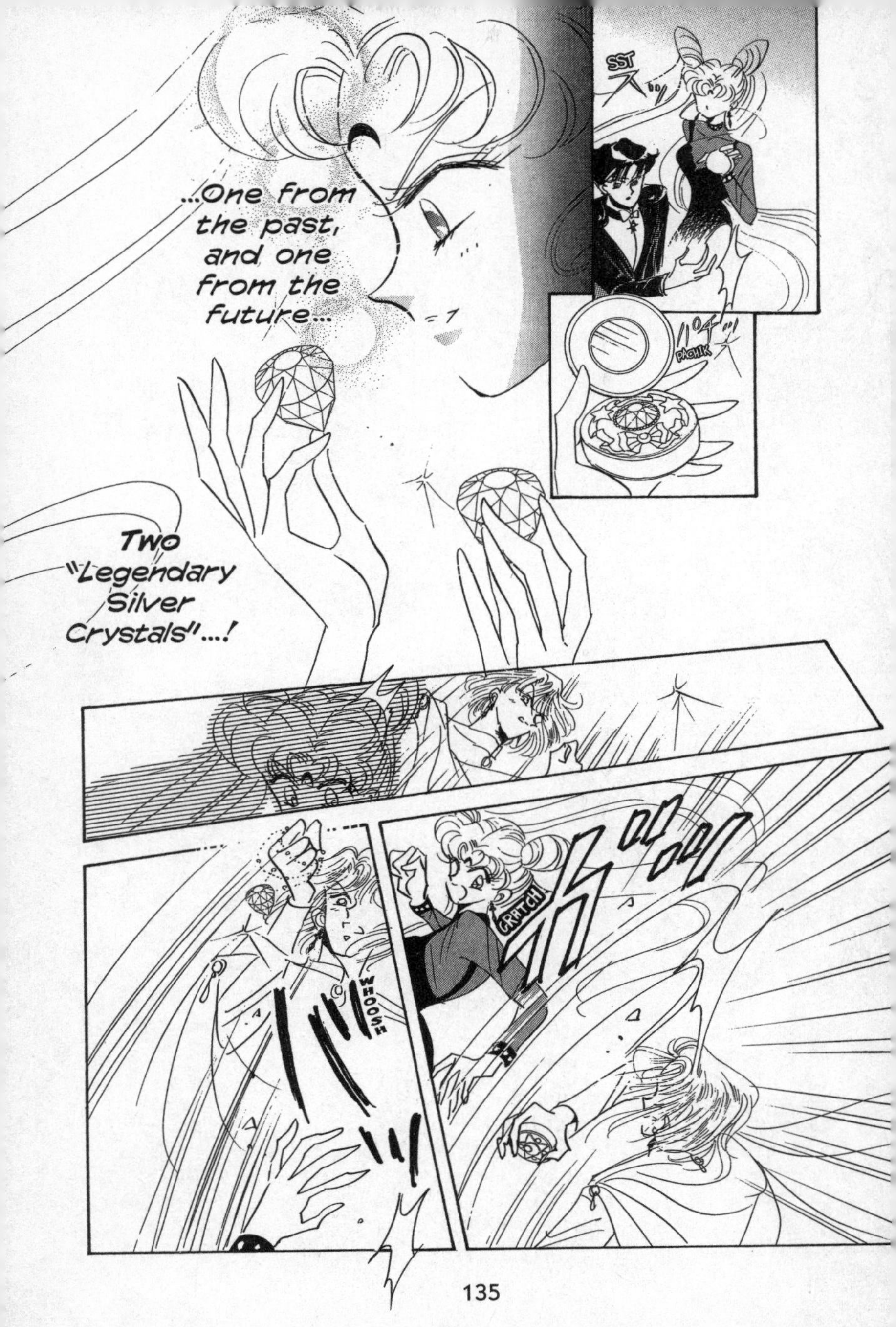
SST
PACHIK
...One from the past, and one from the future...
Two "Legendary Silver Crystals"...!
GRATCH
WHOOSH

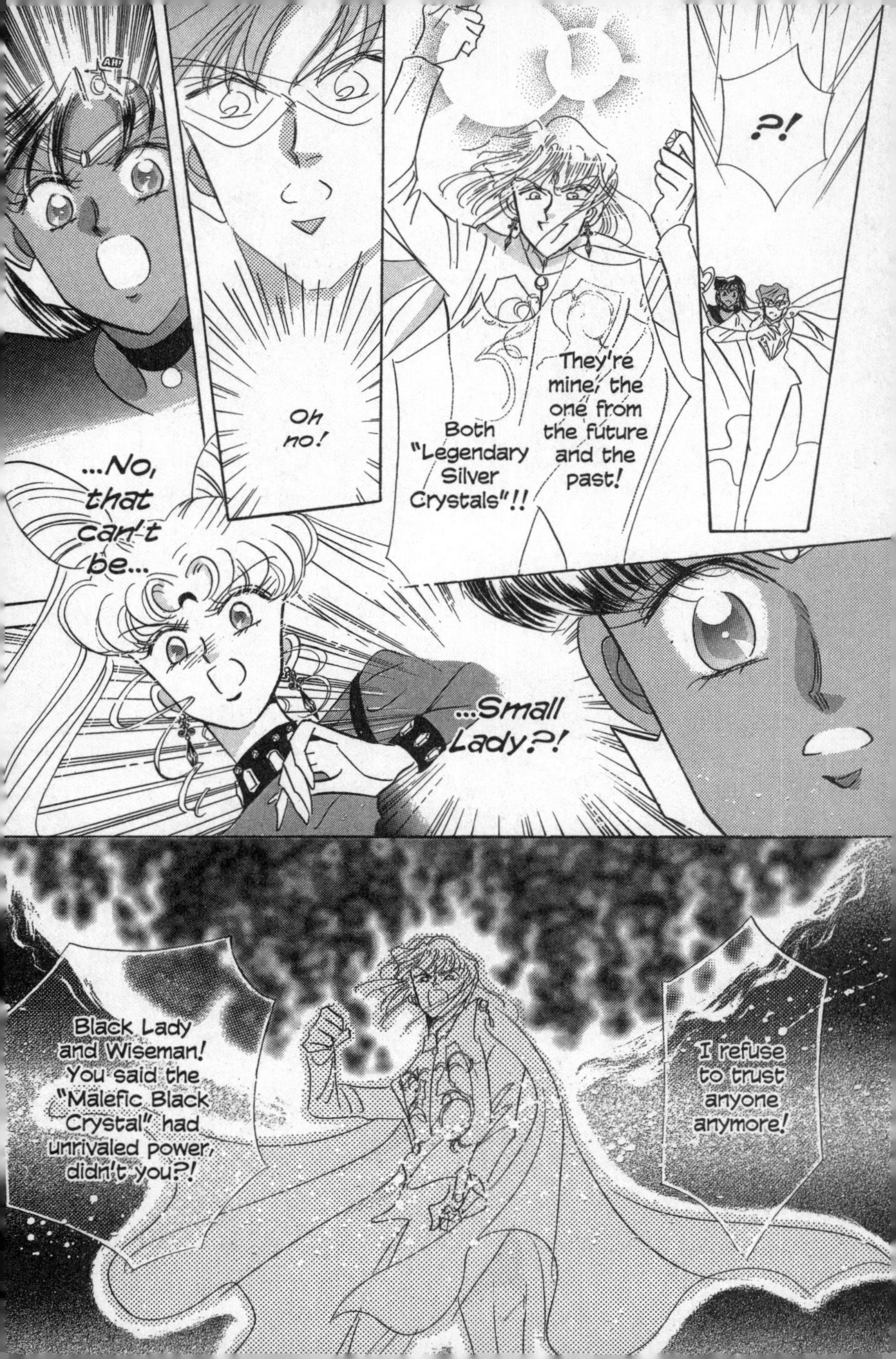
?!
They're mine, the one from the future and the past!
Both "Legendary Silver Crystals"!!
Oh no!
AH!
...Small Lady?!
...No, that can't be...
I refuse to trust anyone anymore!
Black Lady and Wiseman! You said the "Malefic Black Crystal" had unrivaled power, didn't you?!

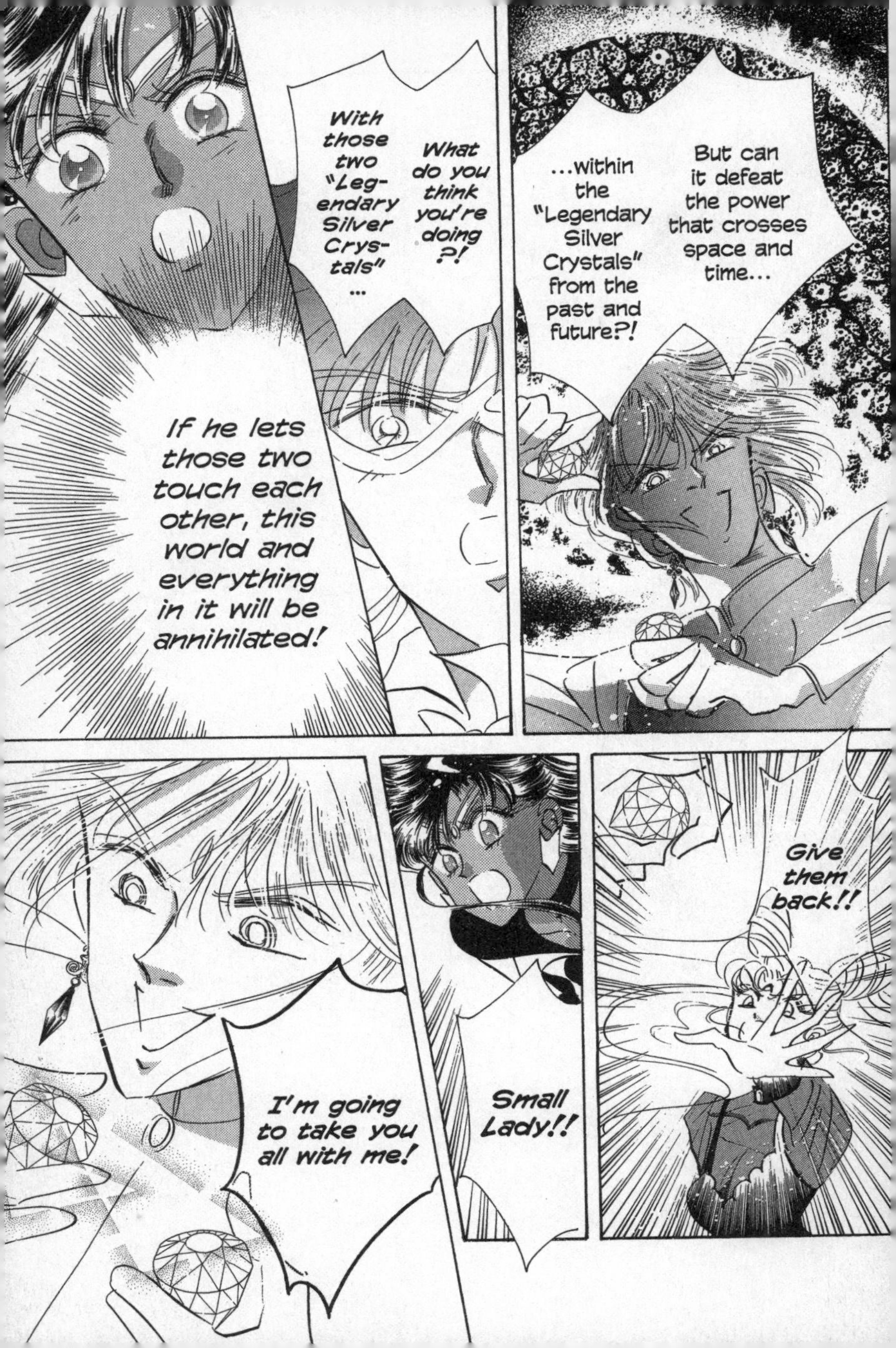
But can it defeat the power that crosses space and time...
...within the "Legendary Silver Crystals" from the past and future?!
What do you think you're doing?!
With those two "Legendary Silver Crystals"...
If he lets those two touch each other, this world and everything in it will be annihilated!
Give them back!!
Small Lady!!
I'm going to take you all with me!

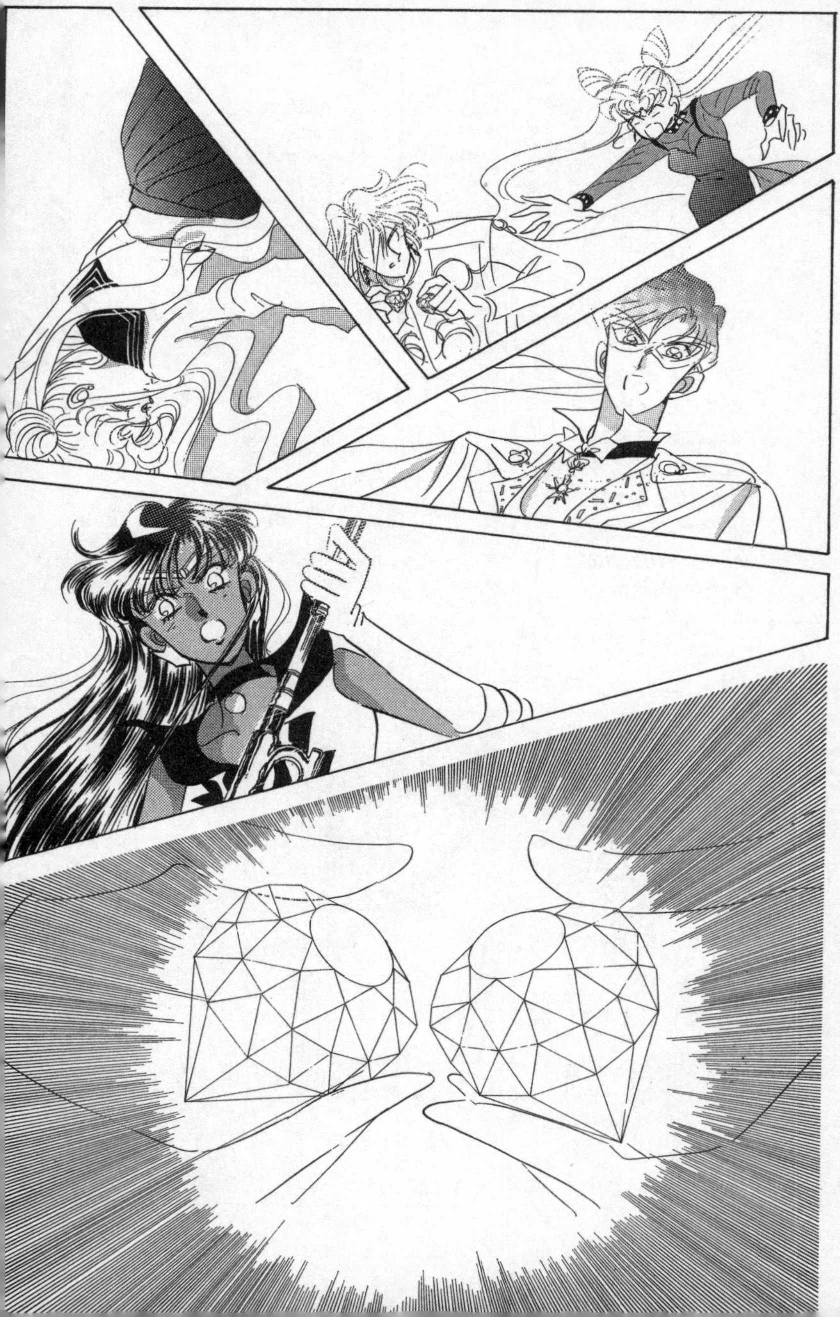

# Act 25
# Showdown, Death Phantom

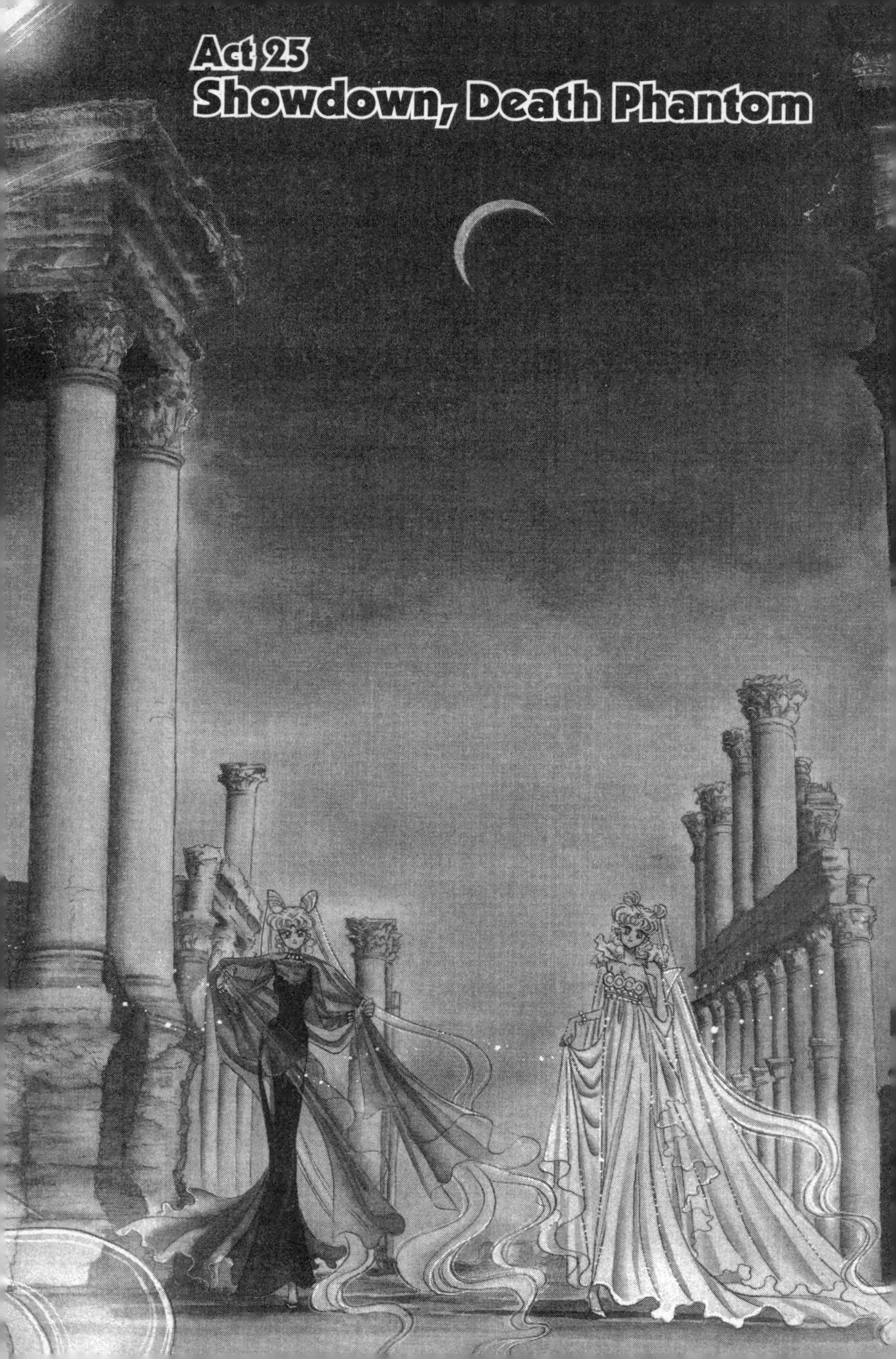

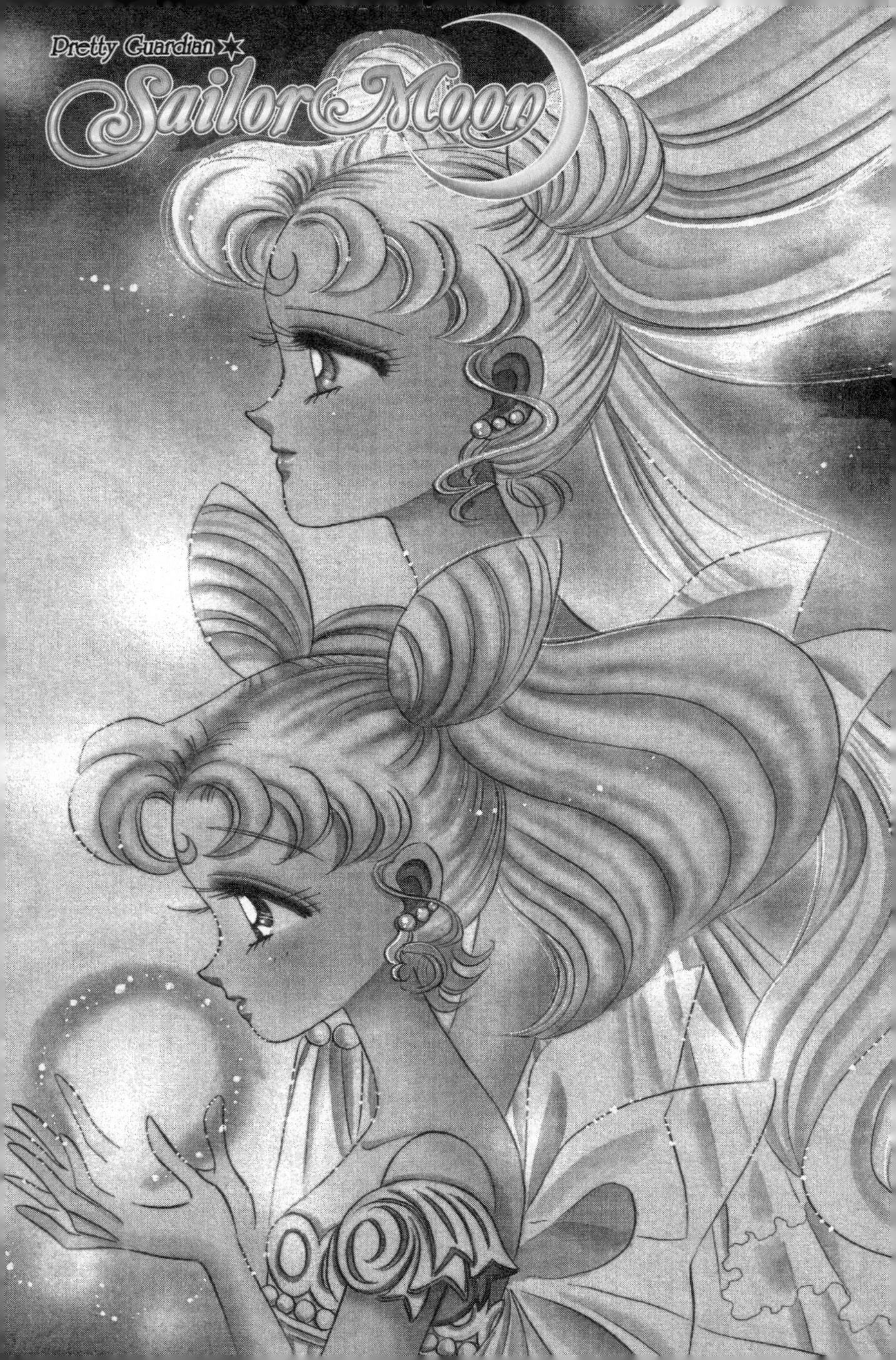
Pretty Guardian ★
Sailor Moon

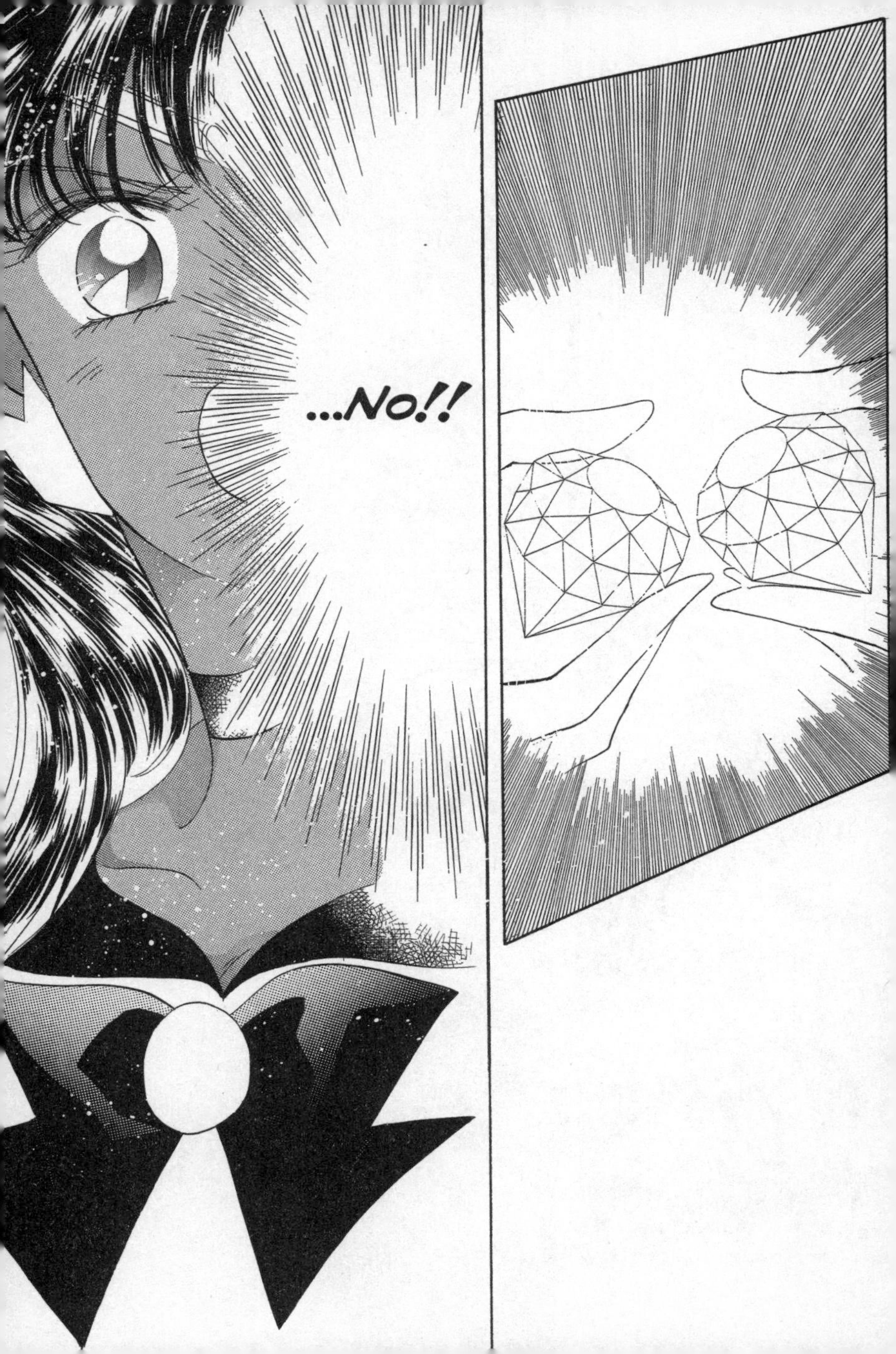
...No!!

...This is the end! Everything is going to be destroyed...!!

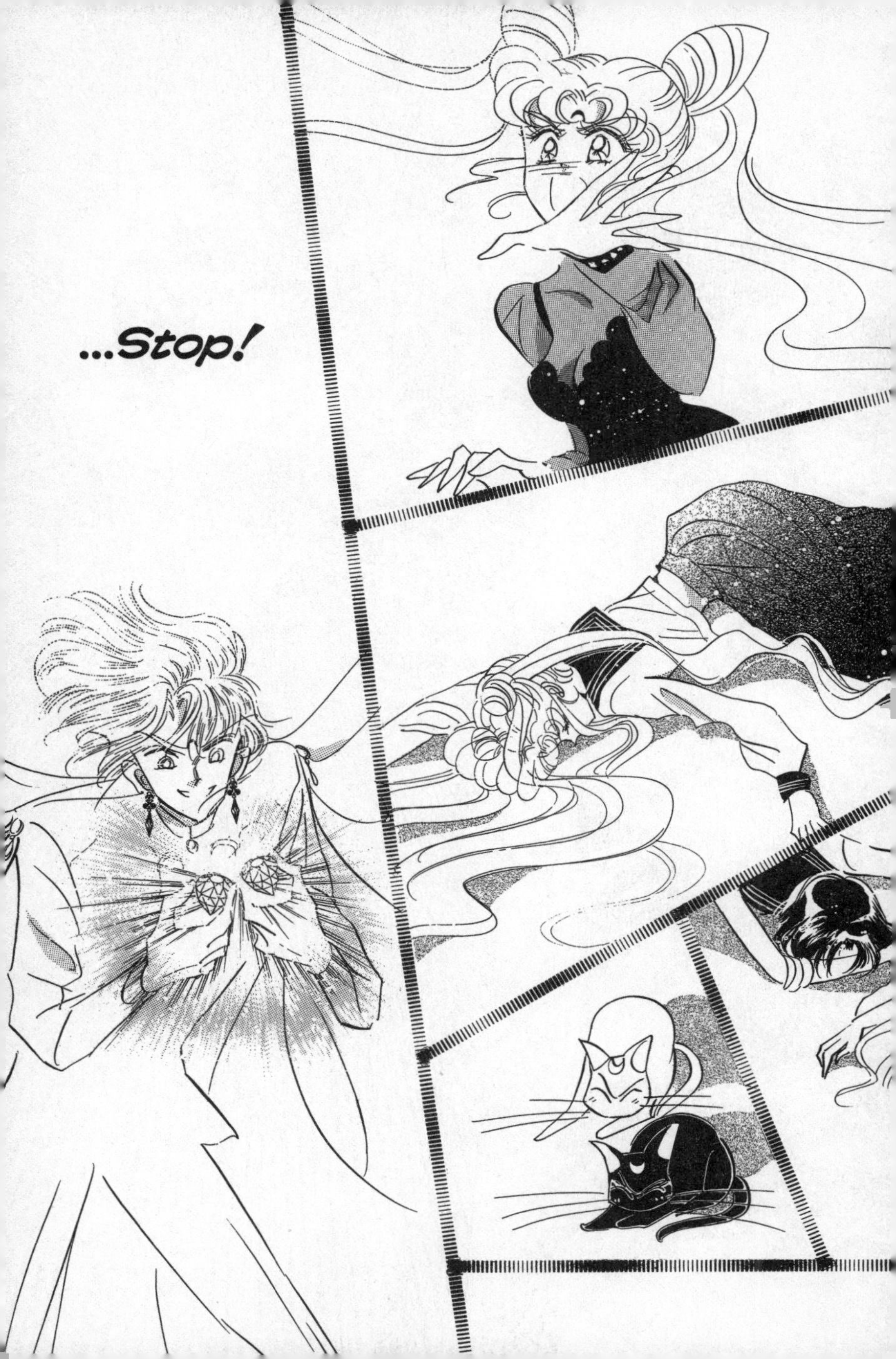
...Stop!

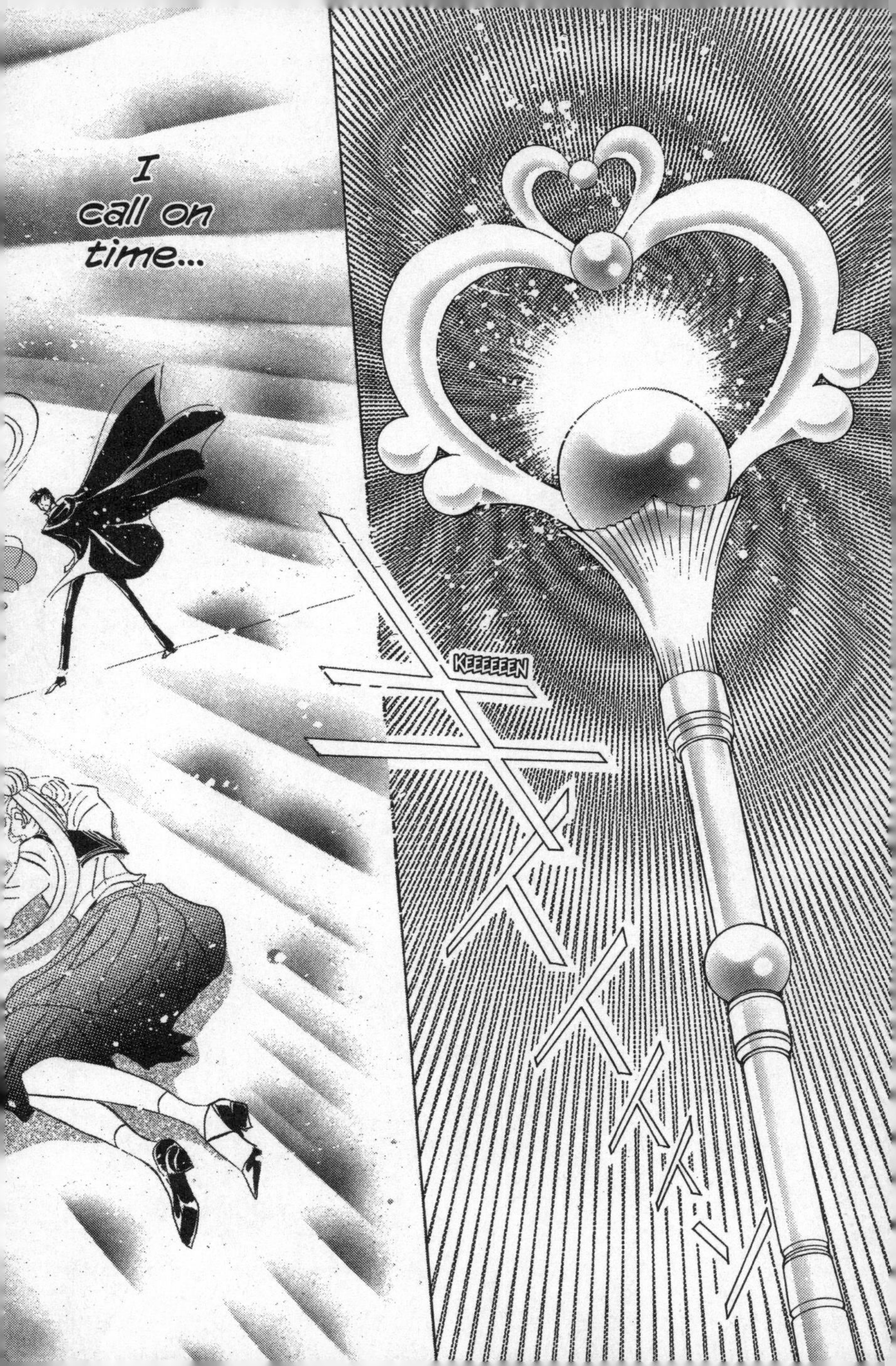
KEEEEEEN
I call on time...

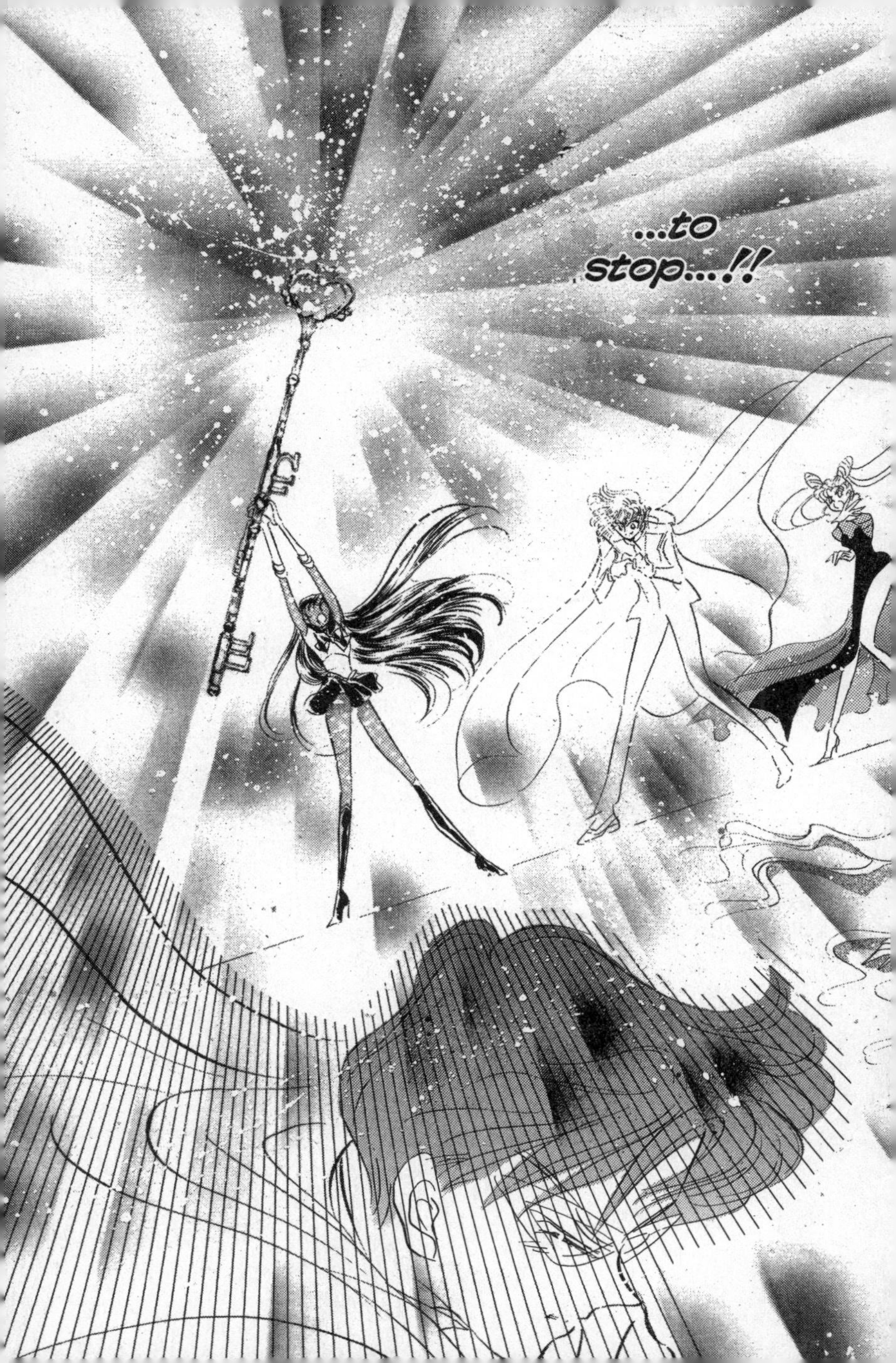
...to
stop...!!

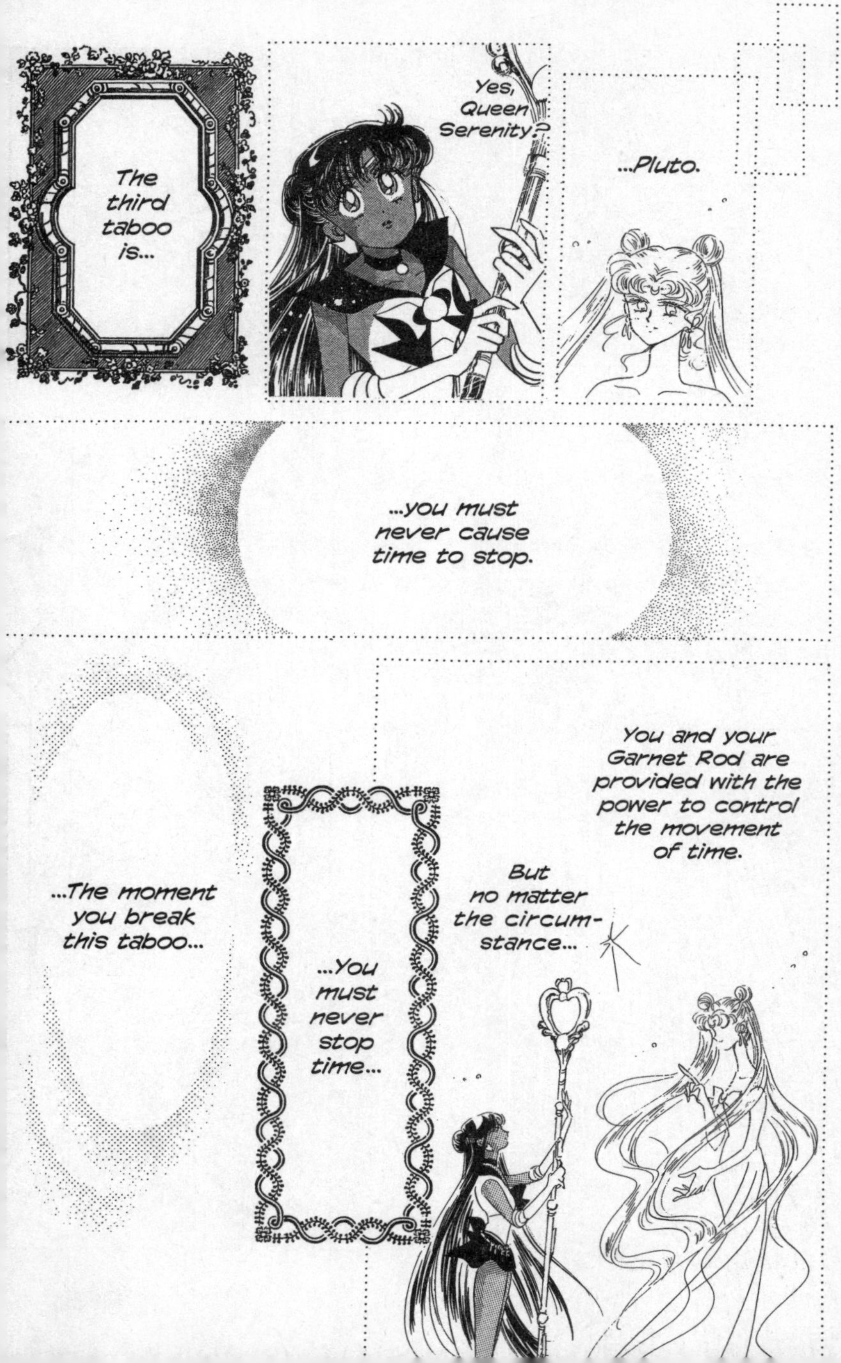
...Pluto.
Yes, Queen Serenity?
The third taboo is...
...you must never cause time to stop.
You and your Garnet Rod are provided with the power to control the movement of time.
But no matter the circum-stance...
...You must never stop time...
...The moment you break this taboo...

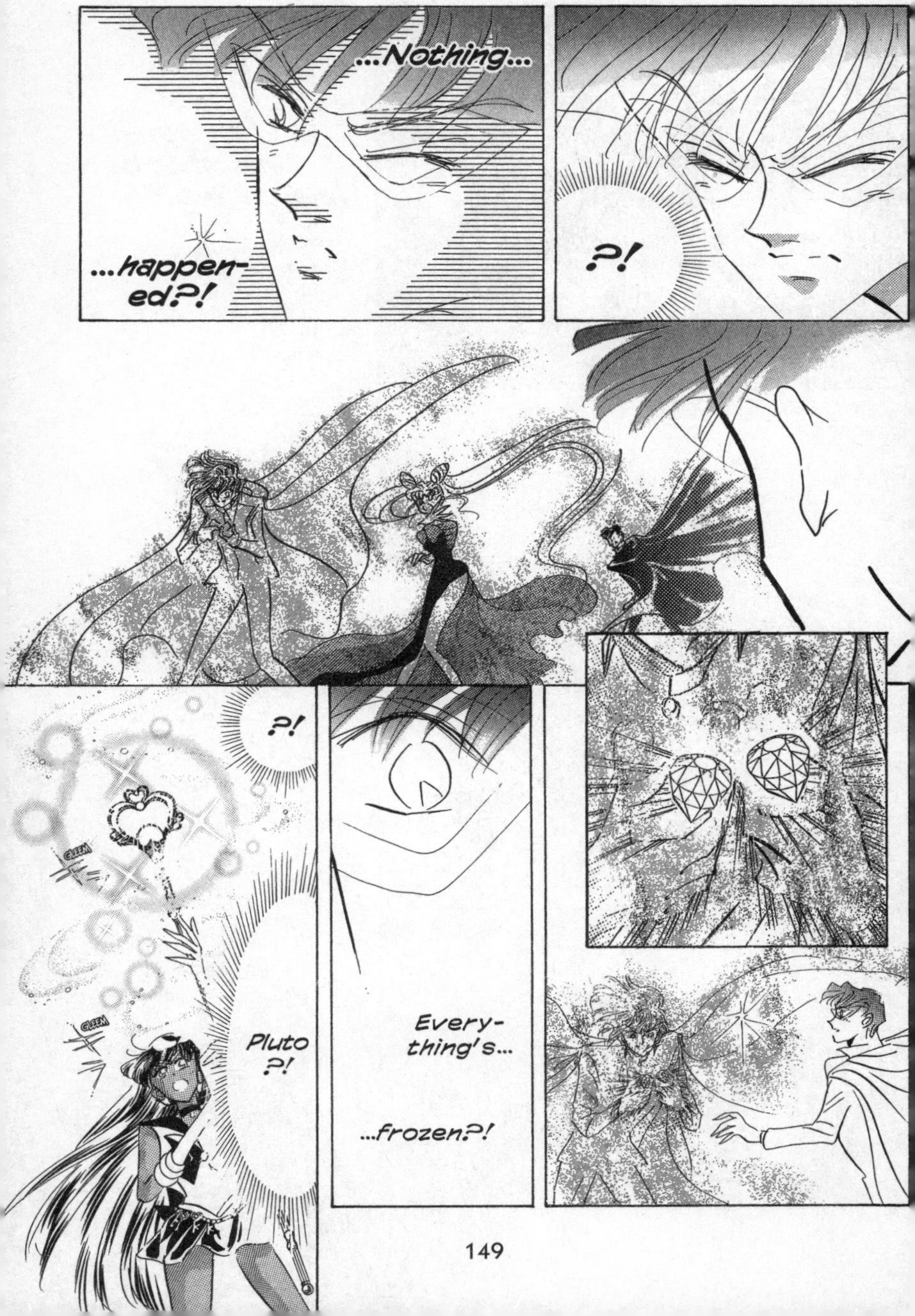
?!
...Nothing...
...happen-
ed?!
Every-
thing's...
...frozen?!
GLEEM
?!
GLEEM
Pluto
?!

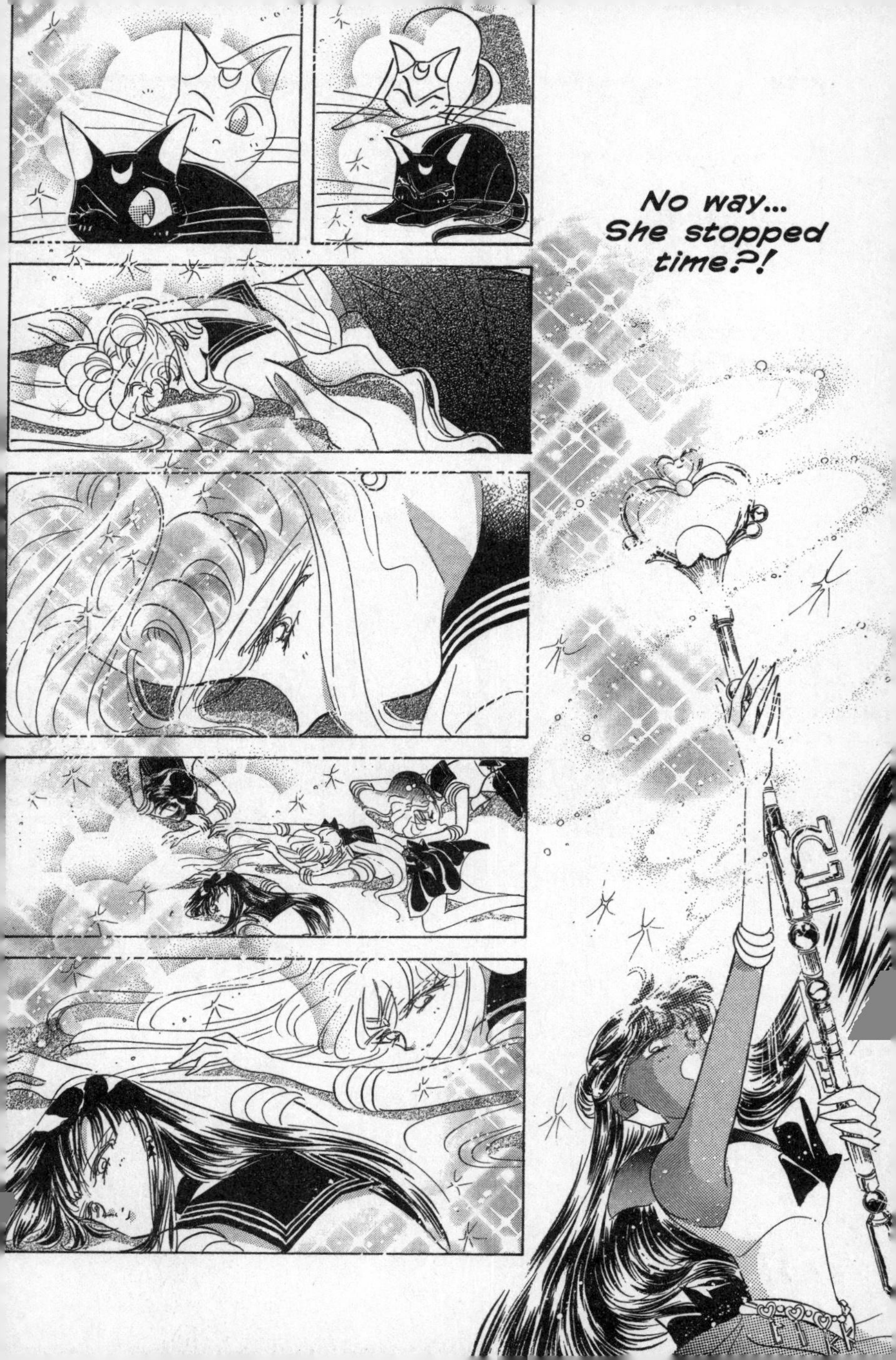
No way...
She stopped
time?!

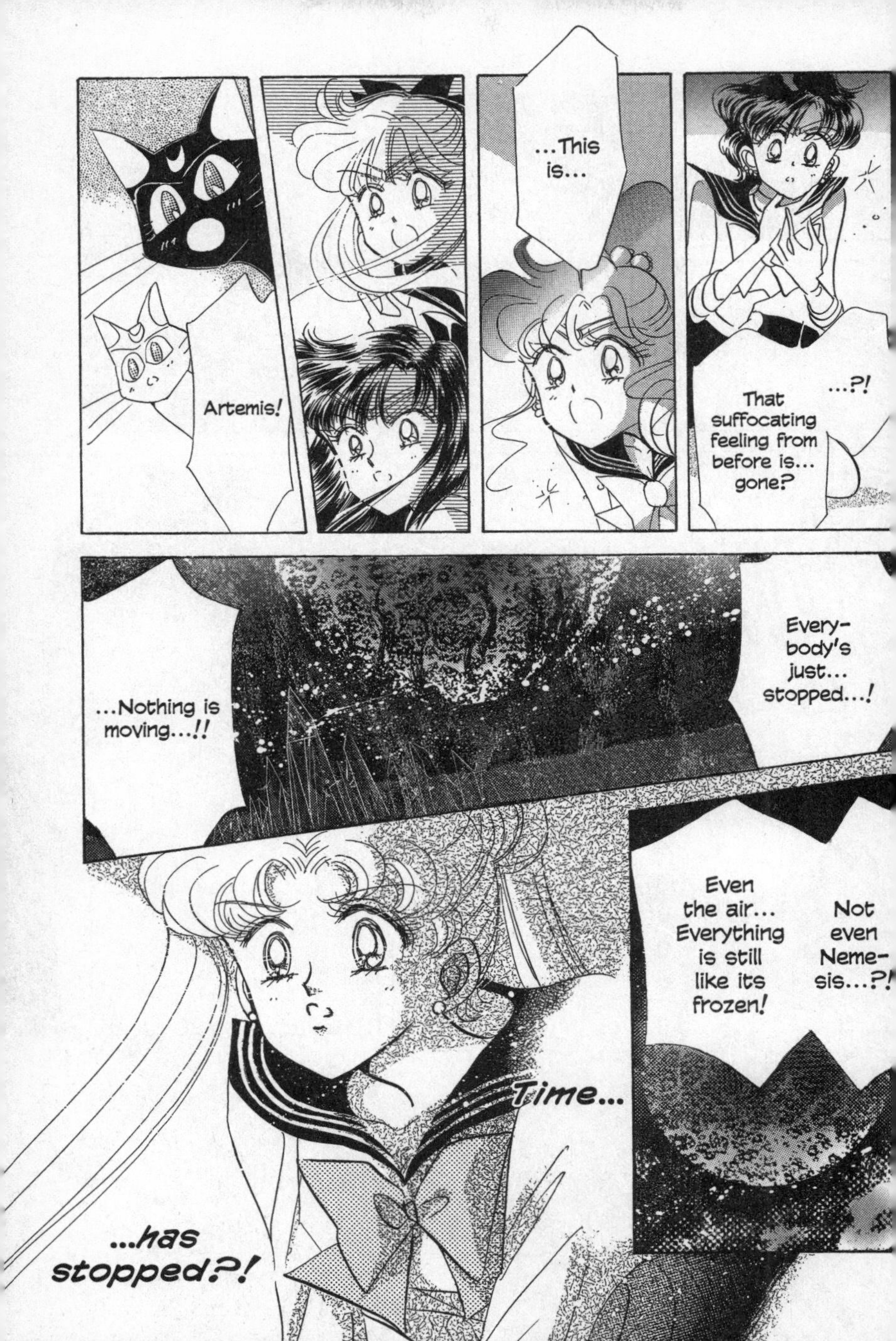

...?!
That suffocating feeling from before is... gone?
...This is...
Artemis!
Every-body's just... stopped...!
...Nothing is moving...!!
Not even Neme-sis...?!
Even the air... Everything is still like its frozen!
Time...
...has stopped?!

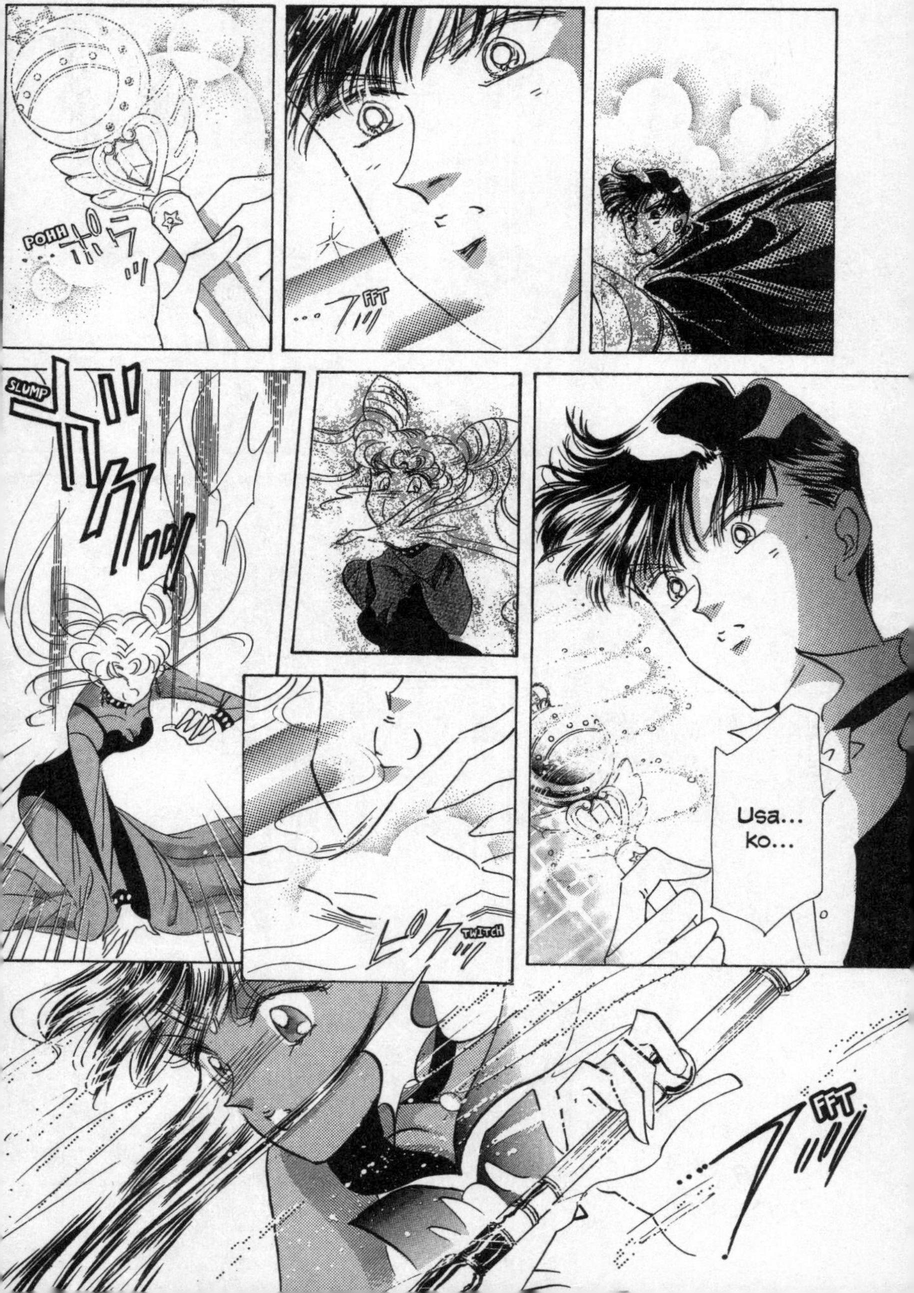
FFT
POHH
Usa...
ko...
TWITCH
SLUMP
FFT

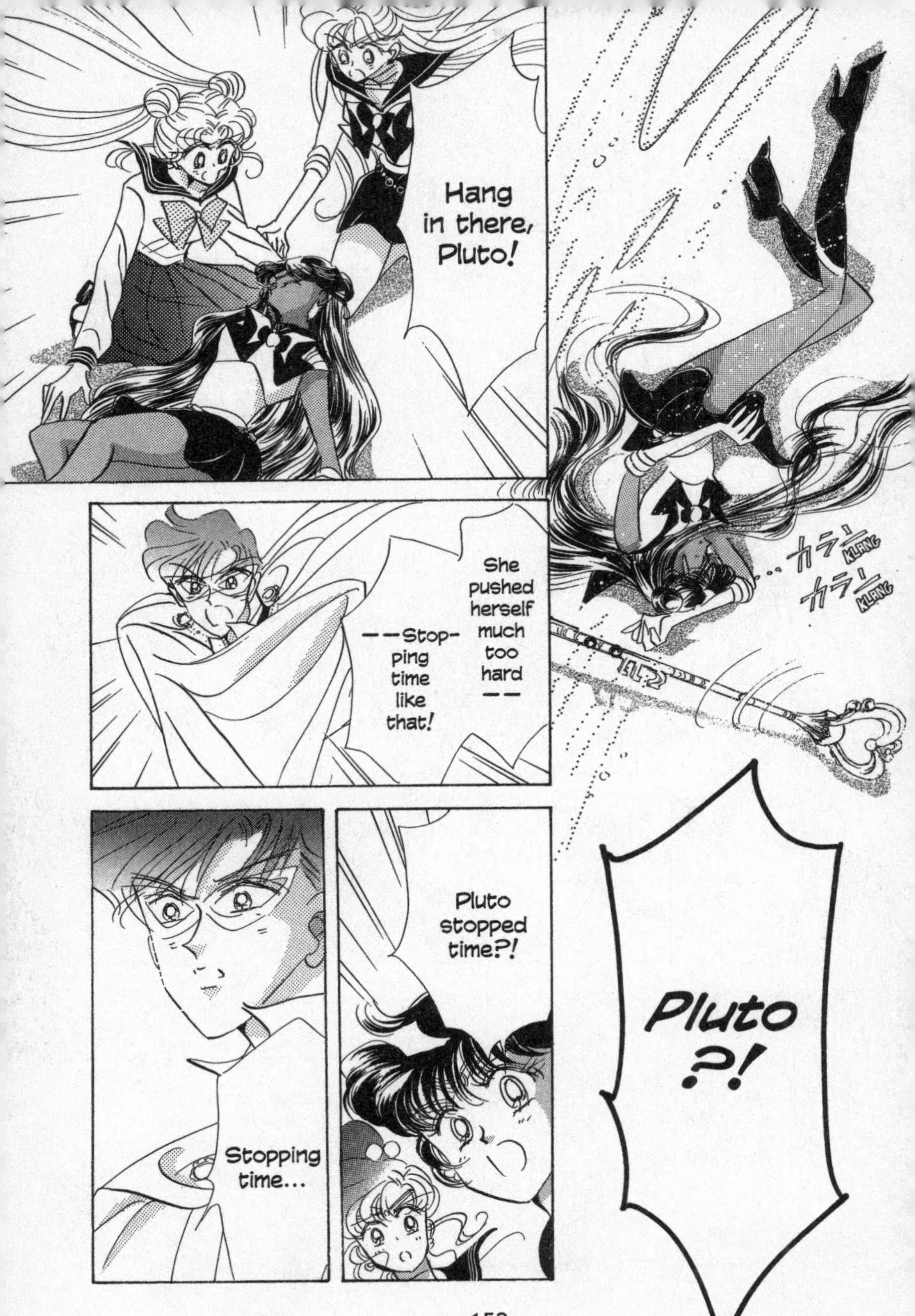
カラン KLANG
カラン KLANG
Pluto ?!
Hang in there, Pluto!
She pushed herself much too hard ——
——Stopping time like that!
Pluto stopped time?!
Stopping time...

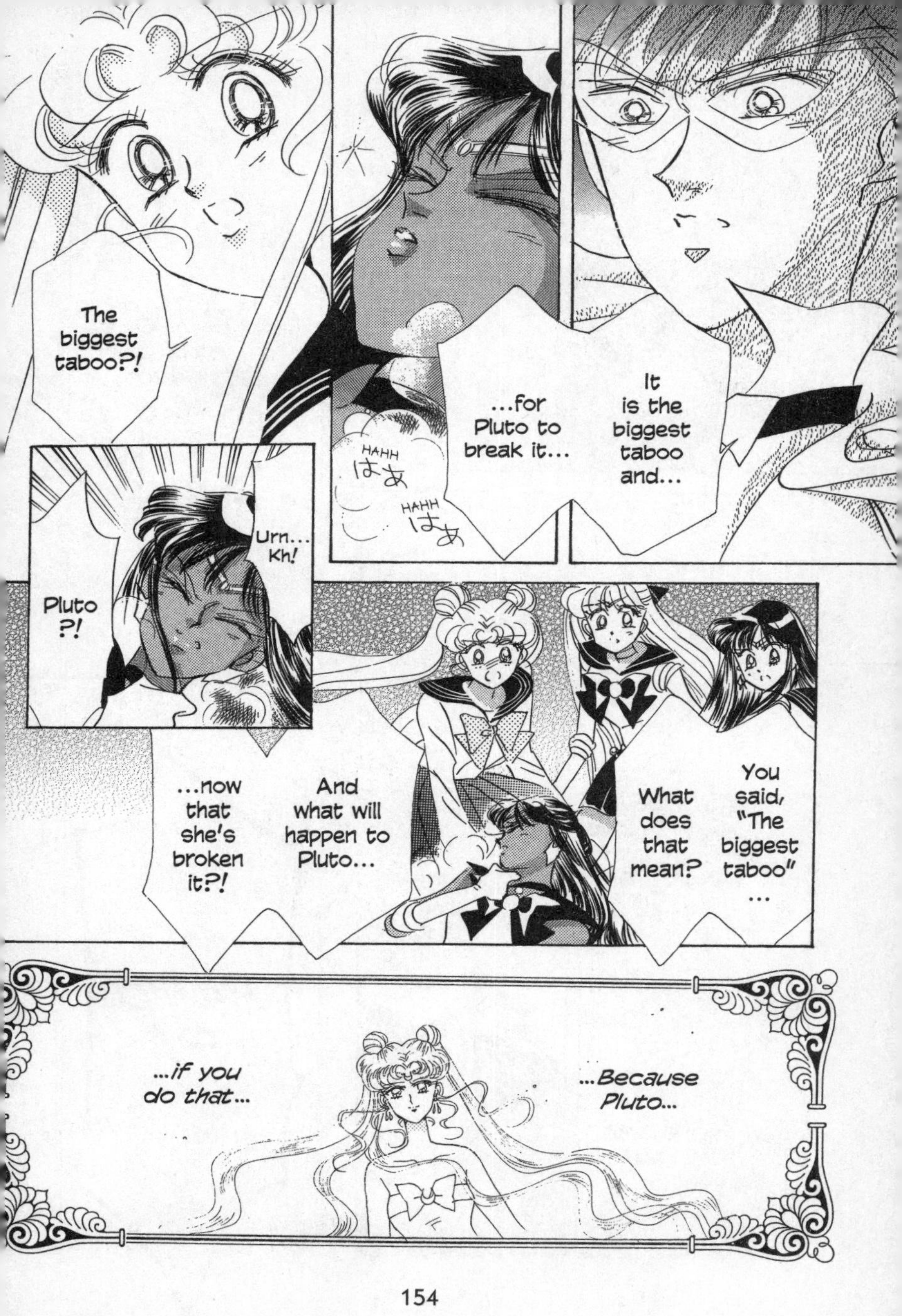
It is the biggest taboo and...
...for Pluto to break it...
HAHH はあ
HAHH はあ
The biggest taboo?!
You said, "The biggest taboo" ...
What does that mean?
And what will happen to Pluto...
...now that she's broken it?!
Urn... Kh!
Pluto ?!
...Because Pluto...
...if you do that...

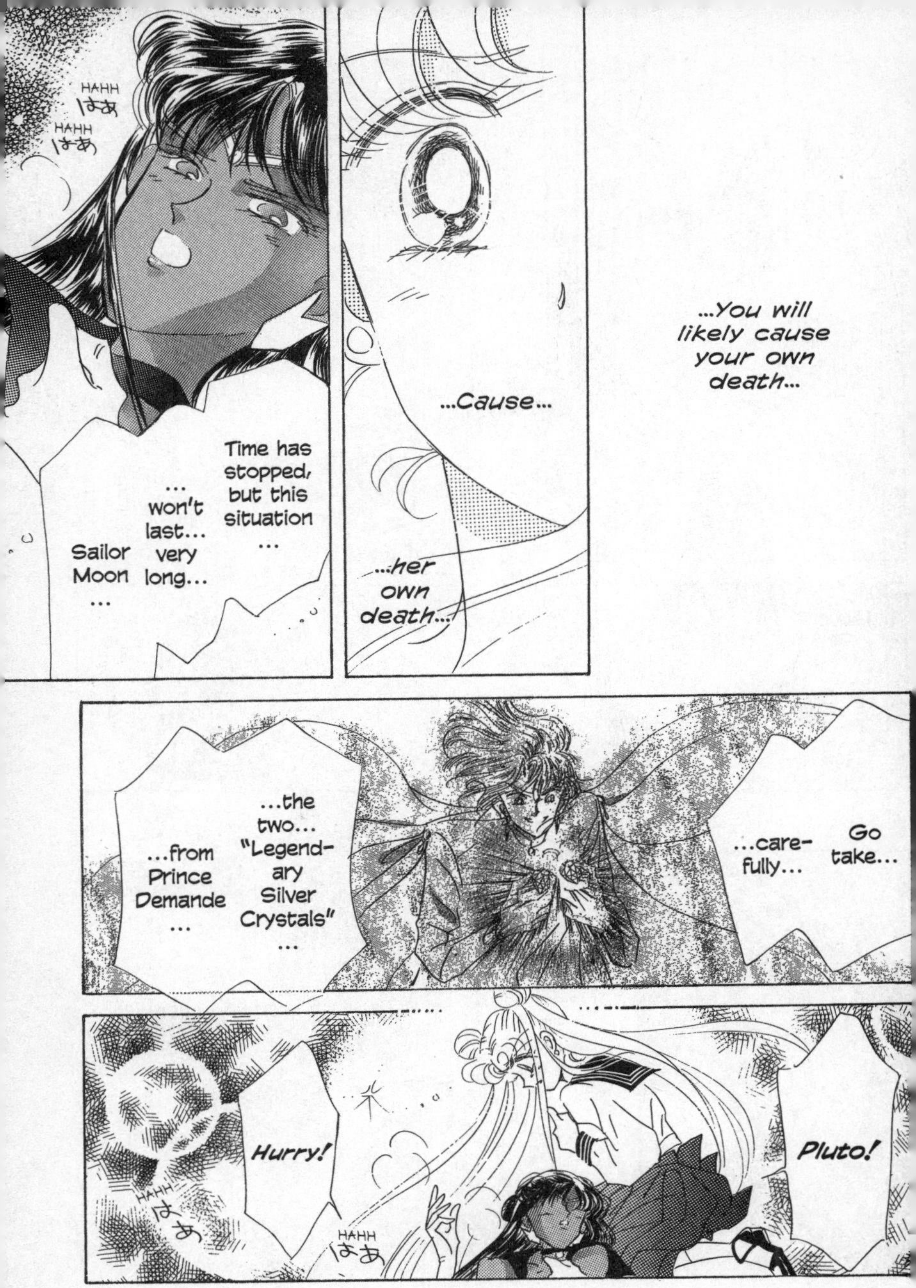
...You will likely cause your own death...
...Cause...
...her own death...
HAHH はあ
HAHH はあ
Time has stopped, but this situation...
...won't last... very long...
Sailor Moon...
Go take...
...care-fully...
...the two... "Legend-ary Silver Crystals"...
...from Prince Demande...
Pluto!
HAHH はあ
Hurry!
HAHH はあ

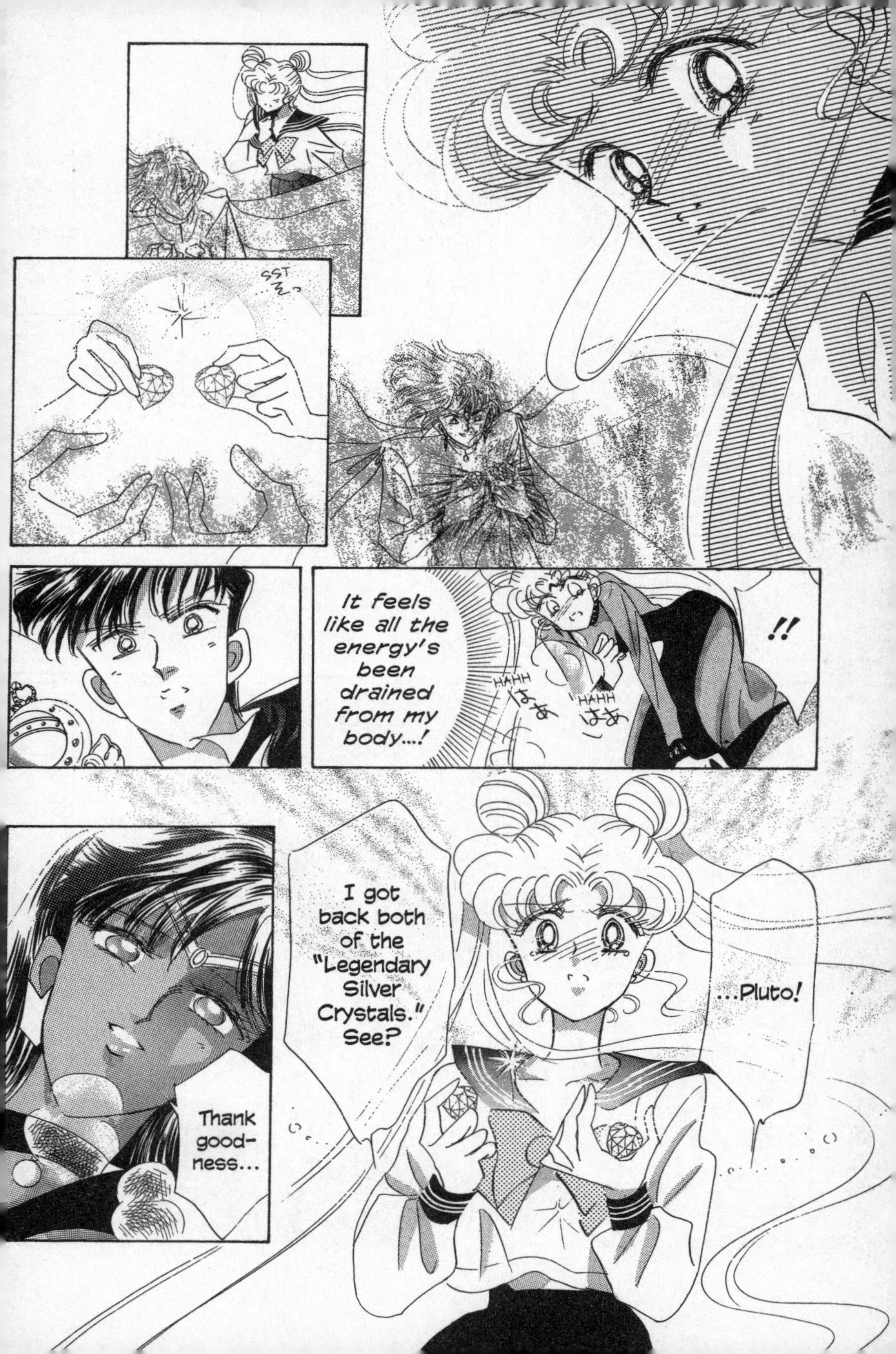
SST
!!
It feels like all the energy's been drained from my body...!
HAHH はあ
HAHH はあ
...Pluto!
I got back both of the "Legendary Silver Crystals." See?
Thank goodness...

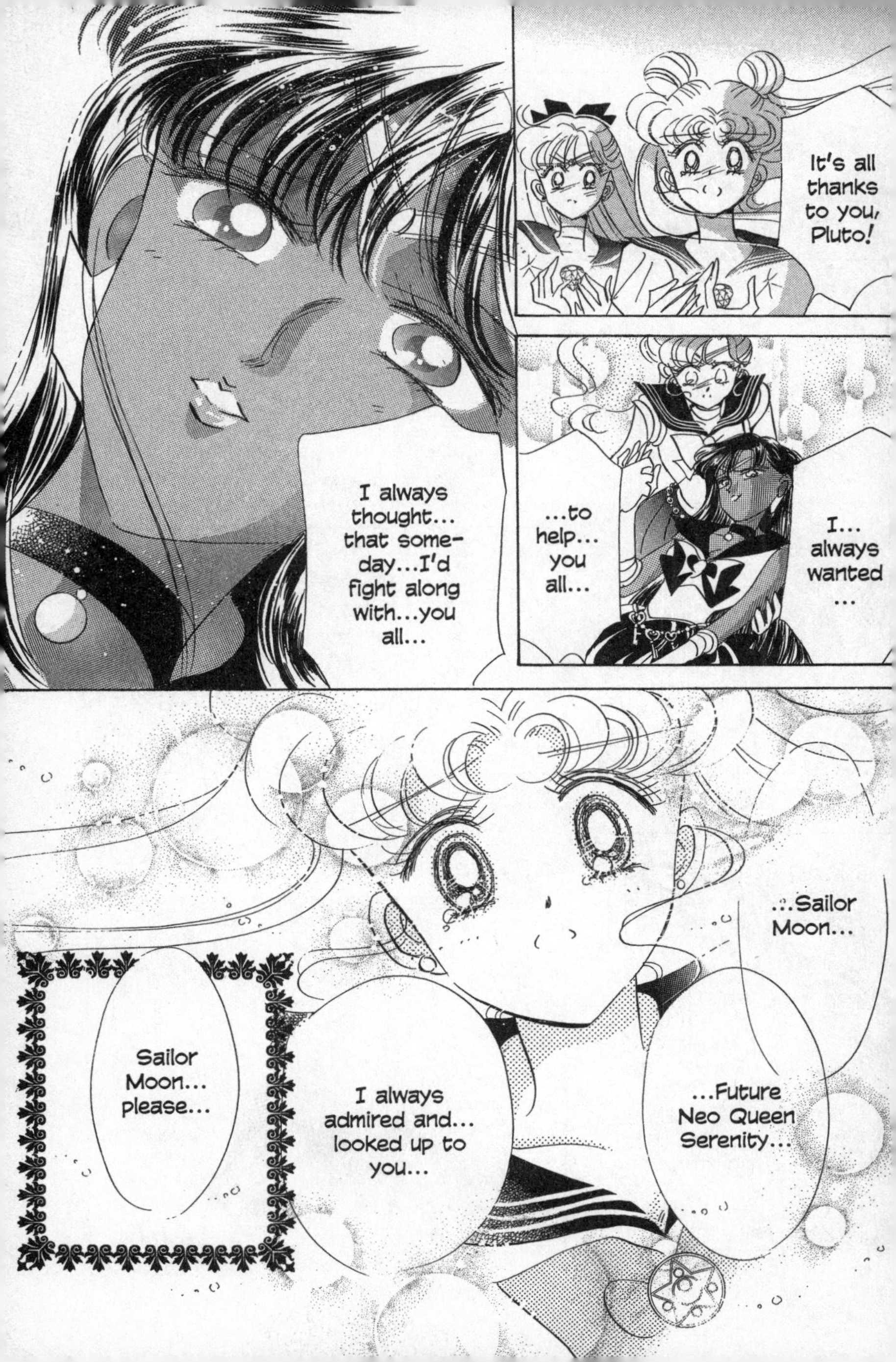
It's all thanks to you, Pluto!
I... always wanted ...
...to help... you all...
I always thought... that some-day...I'd fight along with...you all...
...Sailor Moon...
...Future Neo Queen Serenity...
I always admired and... looked up to you...
Sailor Moon... please...

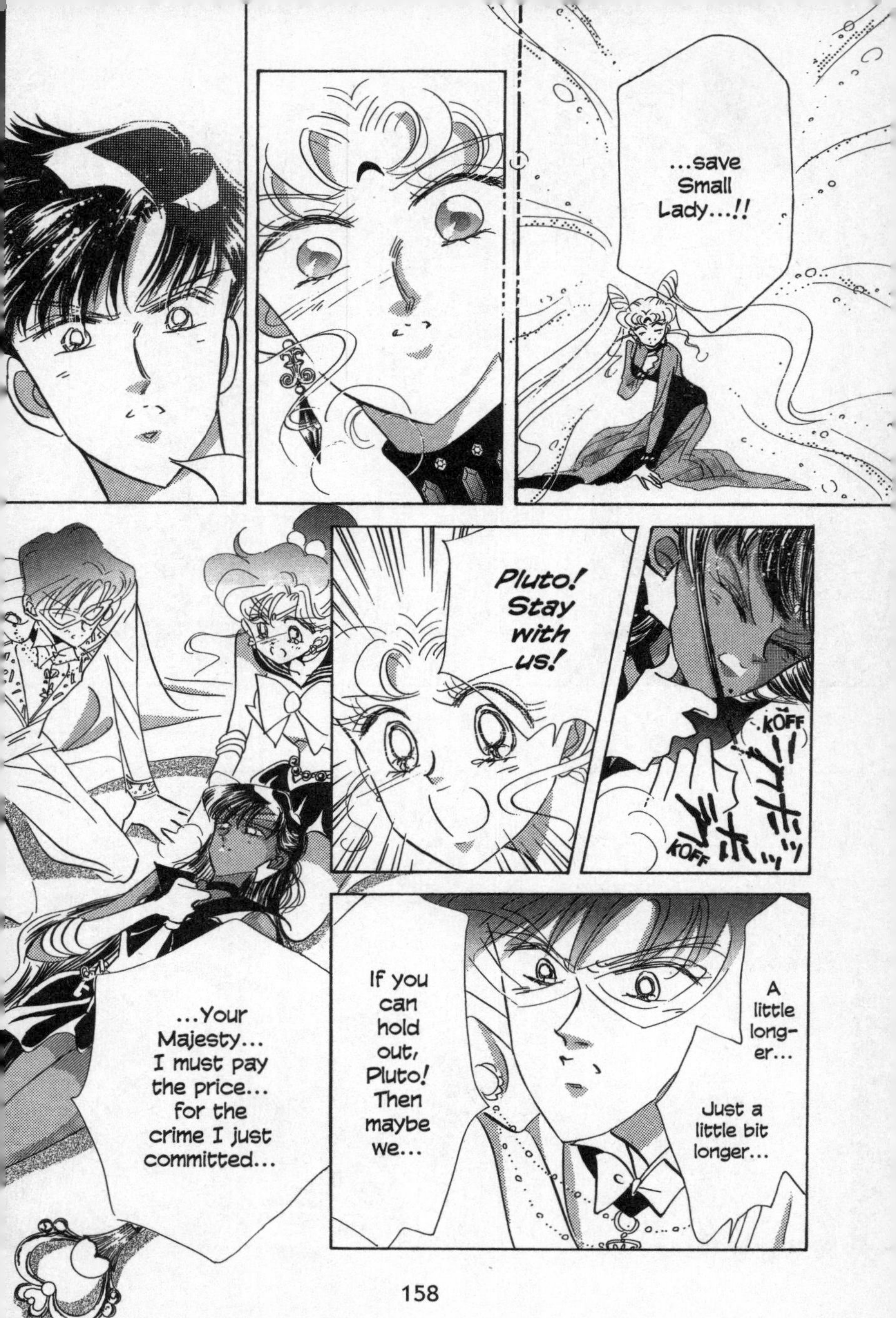
...save Small Lady...!!
KOFF
KOFF
Pluto! Stay with us!
A little longer...
Just a little bit longer...
If you can hold out, Pluto! Then maybe we...
...Your Majesty... I must pay the price... for the crime I just committed...

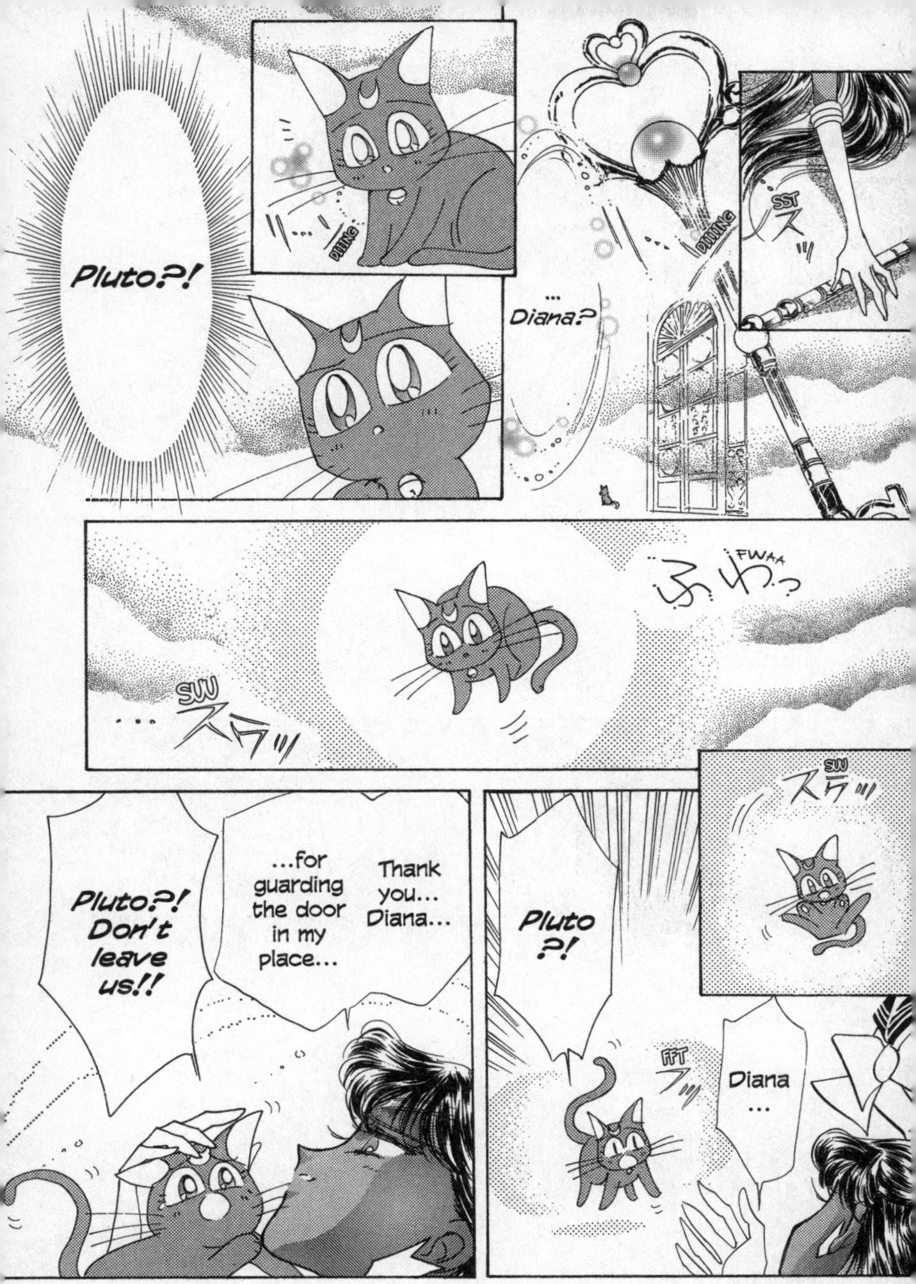
SST
スッ
DIIING
... Diana?
DIIING
Pluto?!
FWAA
ふわっ
SUU
スウッ
...
SUU
スウッ
Diana ...
FFT
フッ
Pluto ?!
Thank you... Diana...
...for guarding the door in my place...
Pluto?! Don't leave us!!

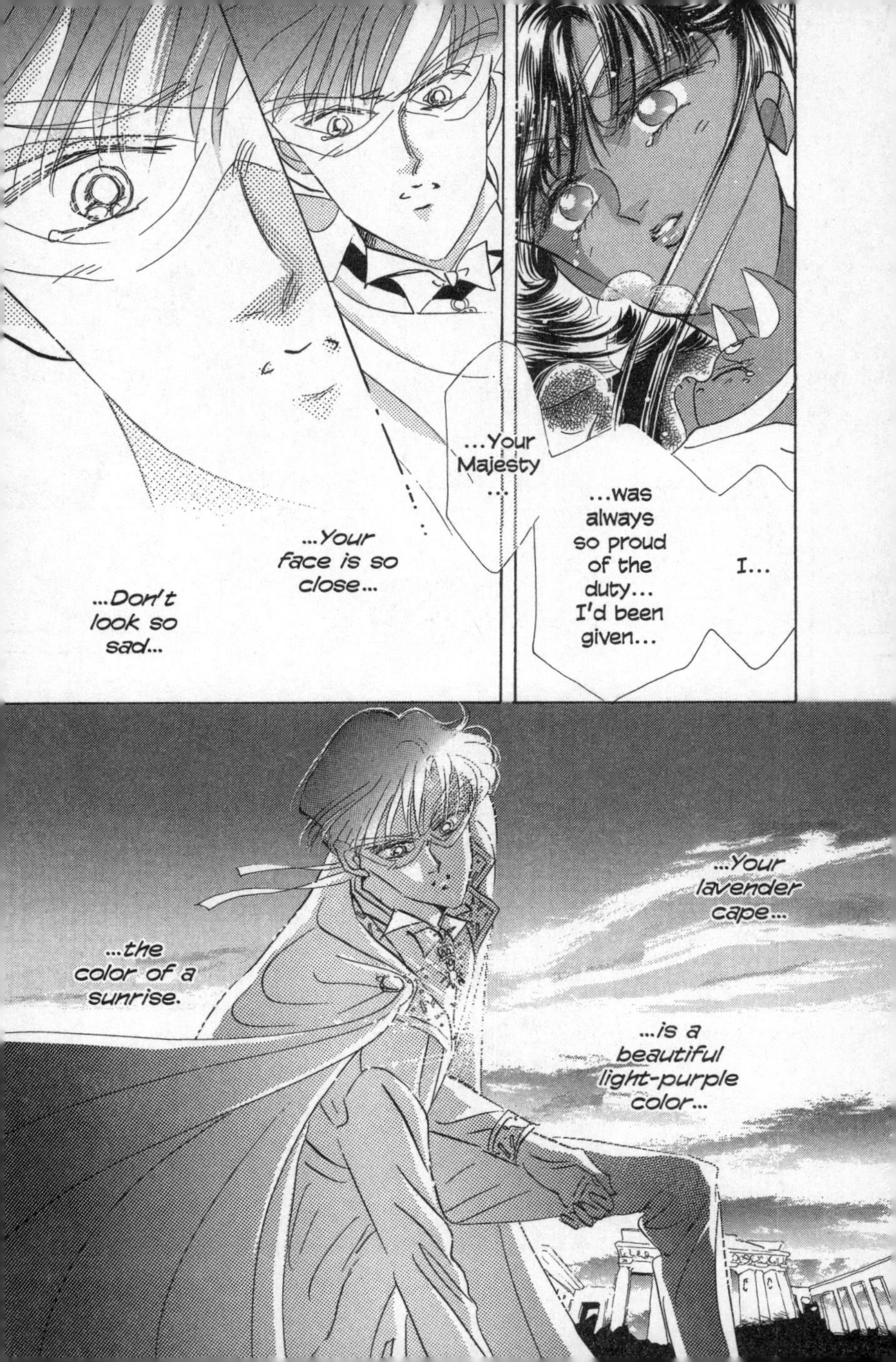

I...
...Your Majesty...
...was always so proud of the duty... I'd been given...
...Your face is so close...
...Don't look so sad...
...Your lavender cape...
...is a beautiful light-purple color...
...the color of a sunrise.

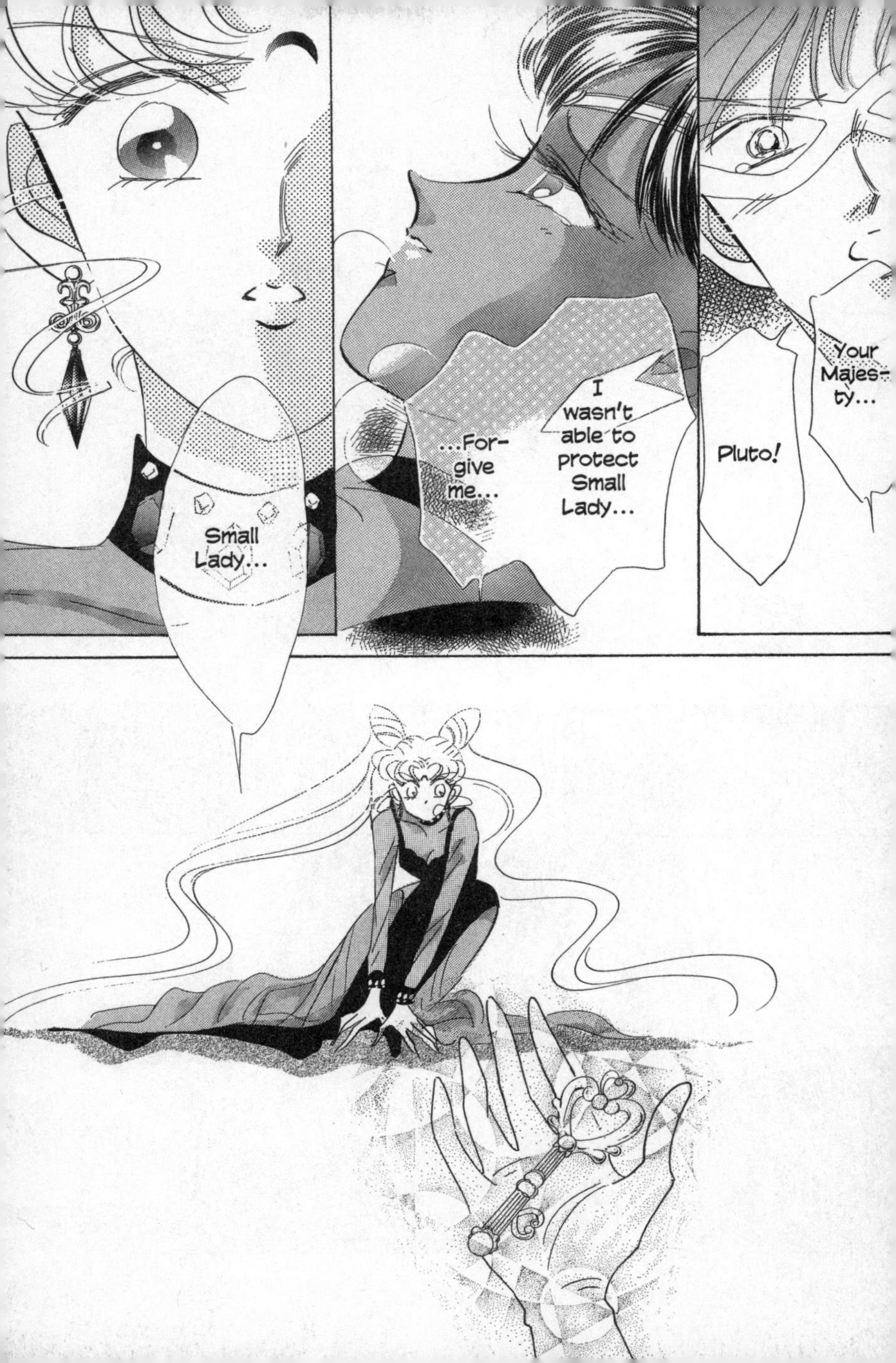
Your Majes-ty...
Pluto!
I wasn't able to protect Small Lady...
...For-give me...
Small Lady...

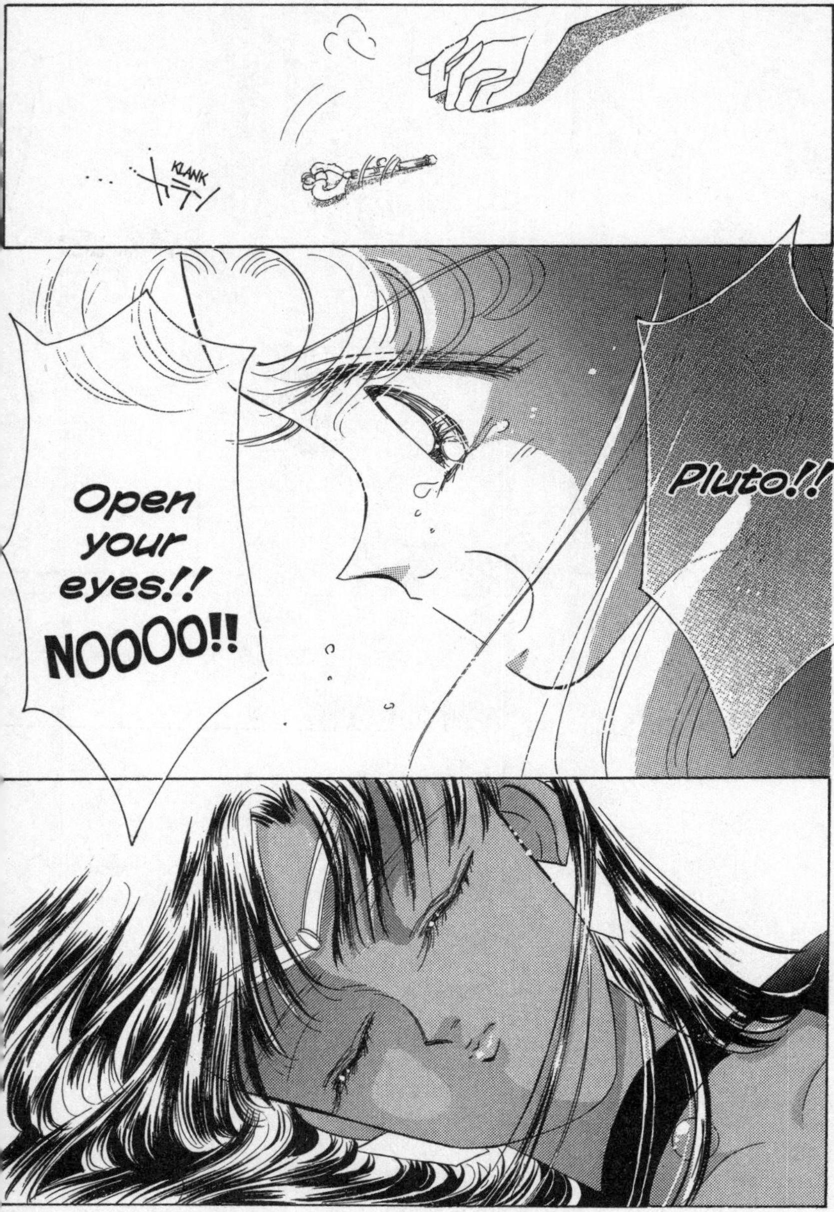
KLANK
Pluto!!
Open your eyes!! NOOOO!!

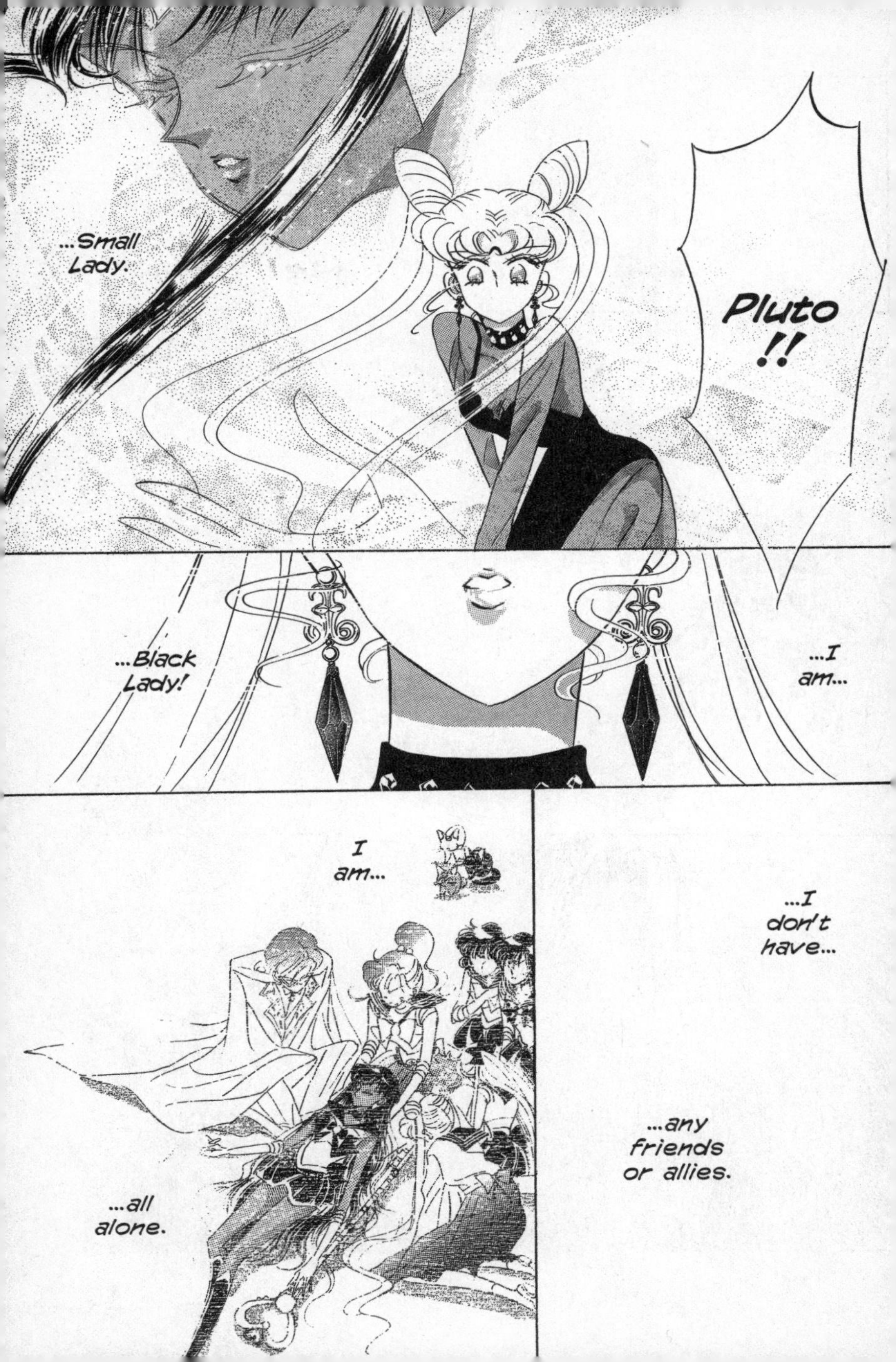
Pluto !!
...Small Lady.
...I am...
...Black Lady!
...I don't have...
...any friends or allies.
I am...
...all alone.

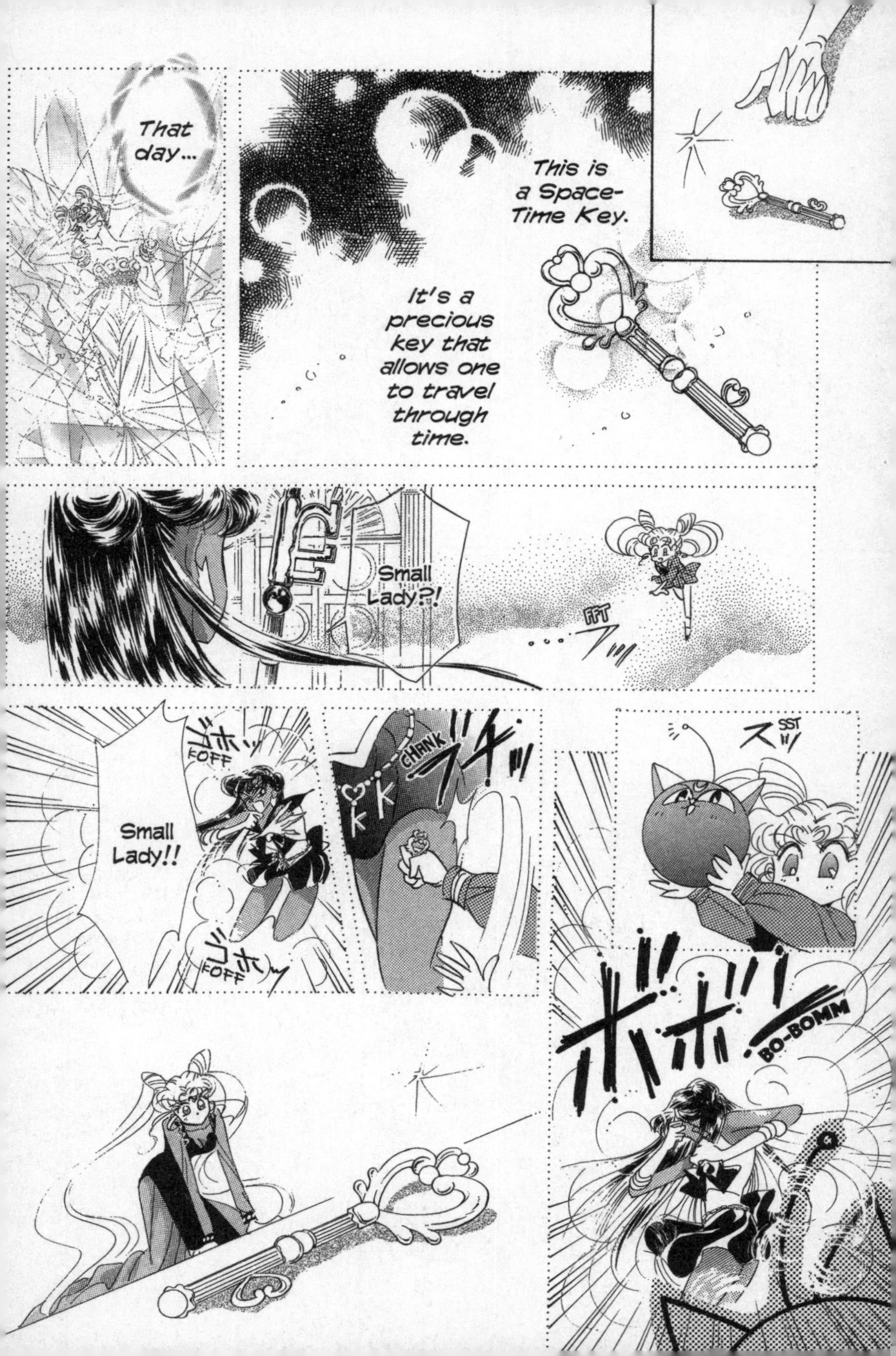
This is a Space-Time Key.
It's a precious key that allows one to travel through time.
That day...
Small Lady?!
FFT
SST
BO-BOMM
CHANK
Small Lady!!
KOFF
KOFF

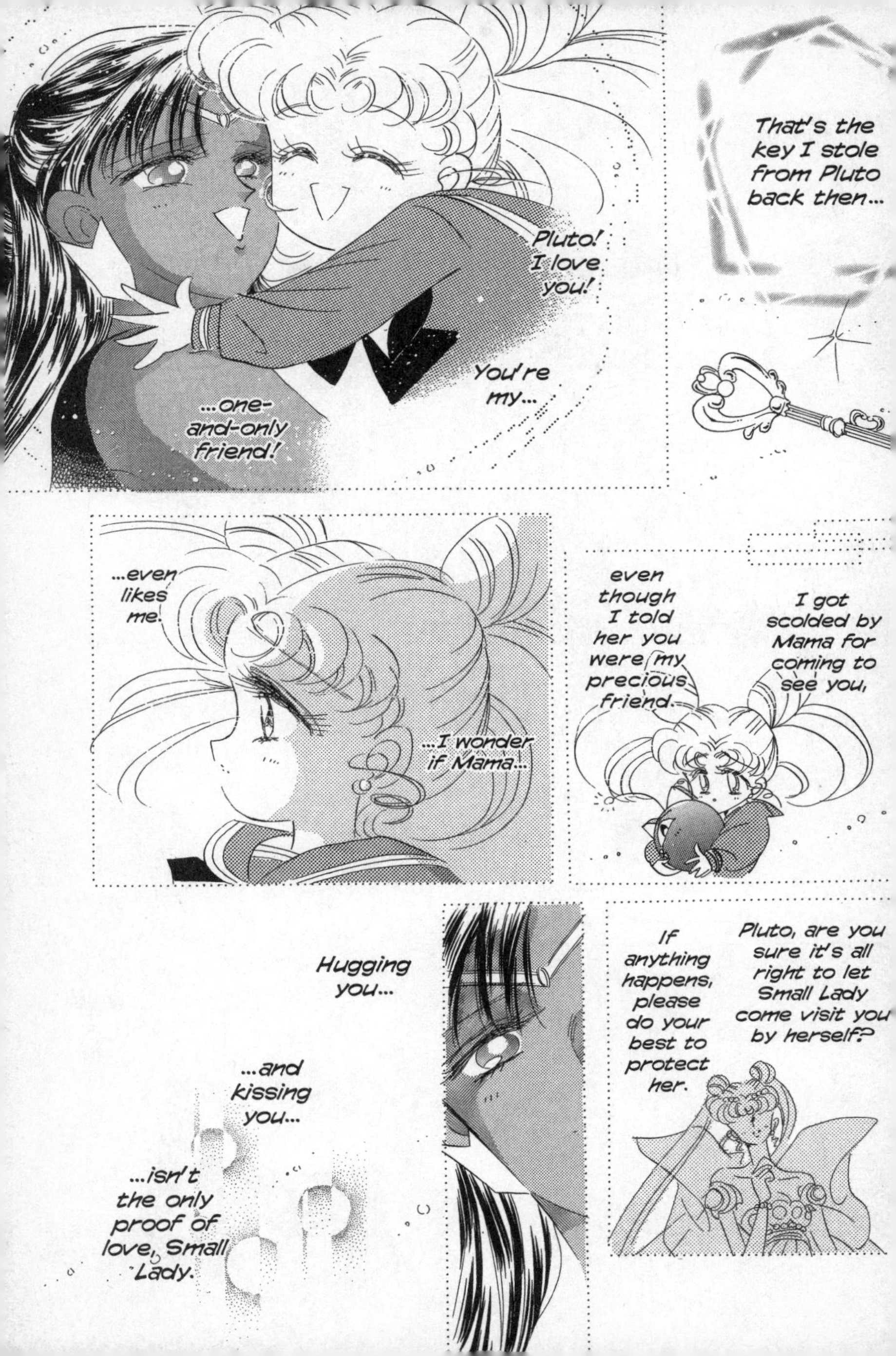
That's the key I stole from Pluto back then...
Pluto! I love you!
You're my...
...one-and-only friend!
I got scolded by Mama for coming to see you,
even though I told her you were my precious friend.
...I wonder if Mama...
...even likes me.
Pluto, are you sure it's all right to let Small Lady come visit you by herself?
If anything happens, please do your best to protect her.
Hugging you...
...and kissing you...
...isn't the only proof of love, Small Lady.

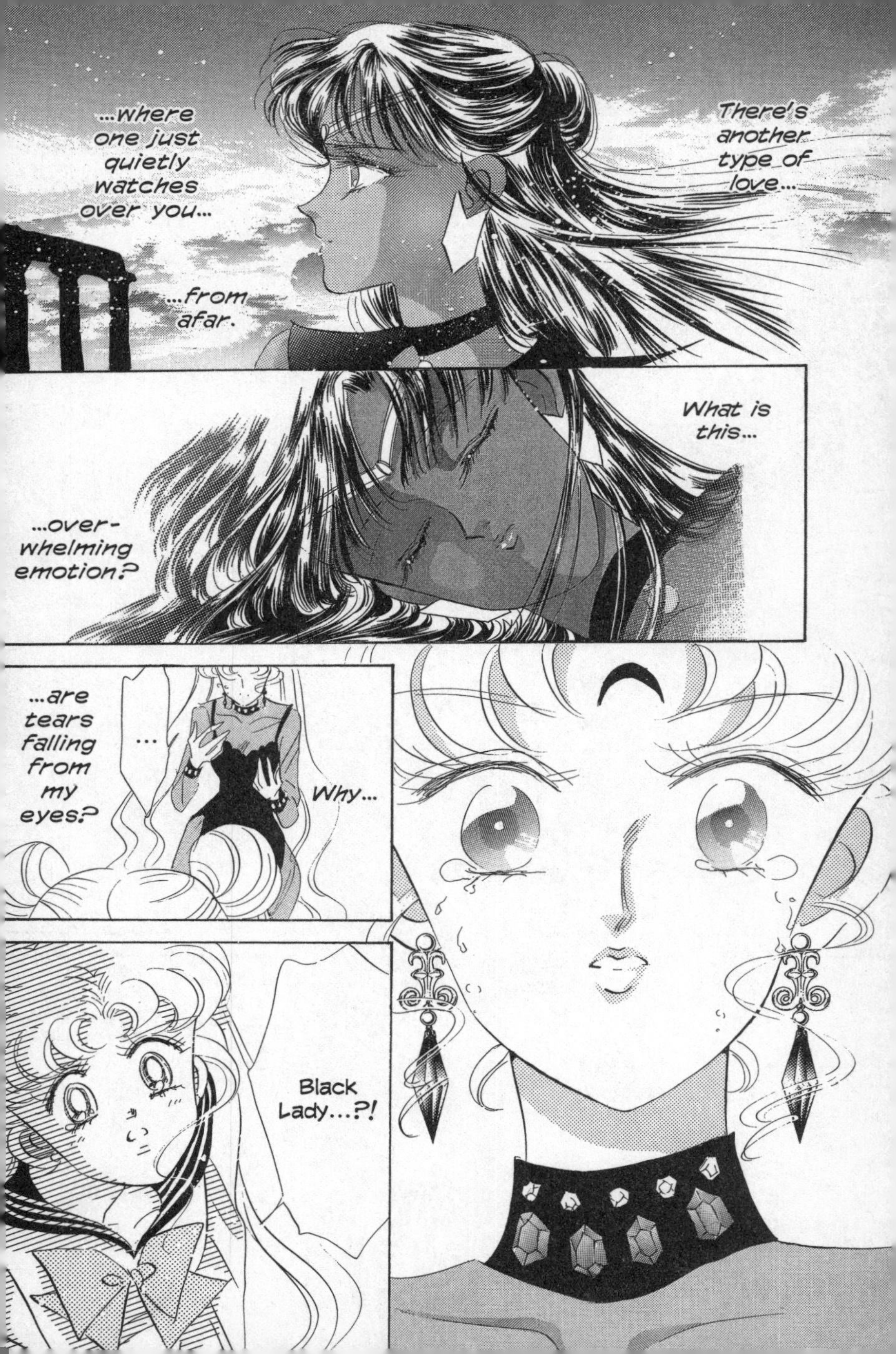
There's another type of love...
...where one just quietly watches over you...
...from afar.
What is this...
...over-whelming emotion?
Why...
...
...are tears falling from my eyes?
Black Lady...?!

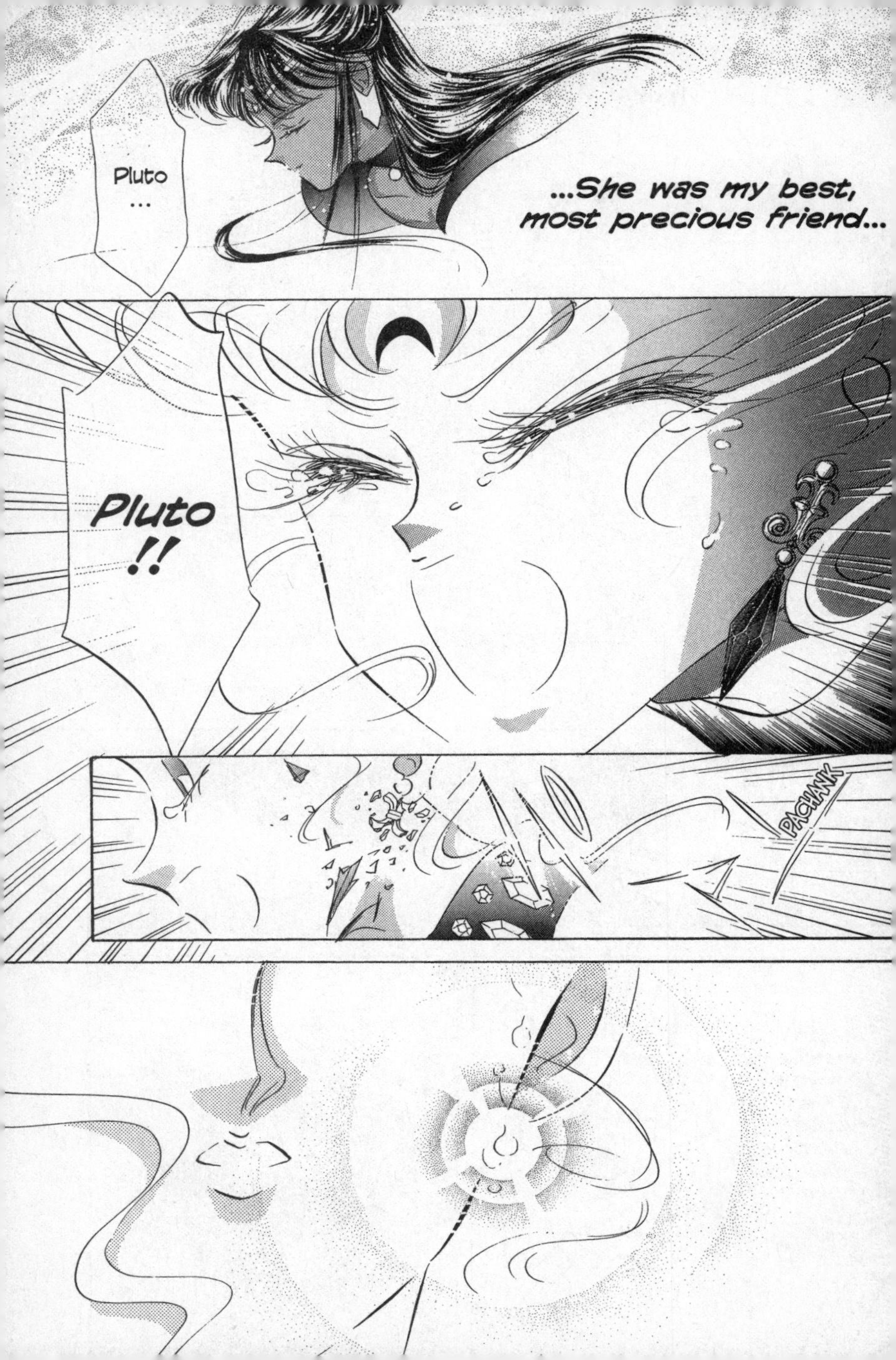
...She was my best, most precious friend...
Pluto ...
Pluto !!
PACHANK

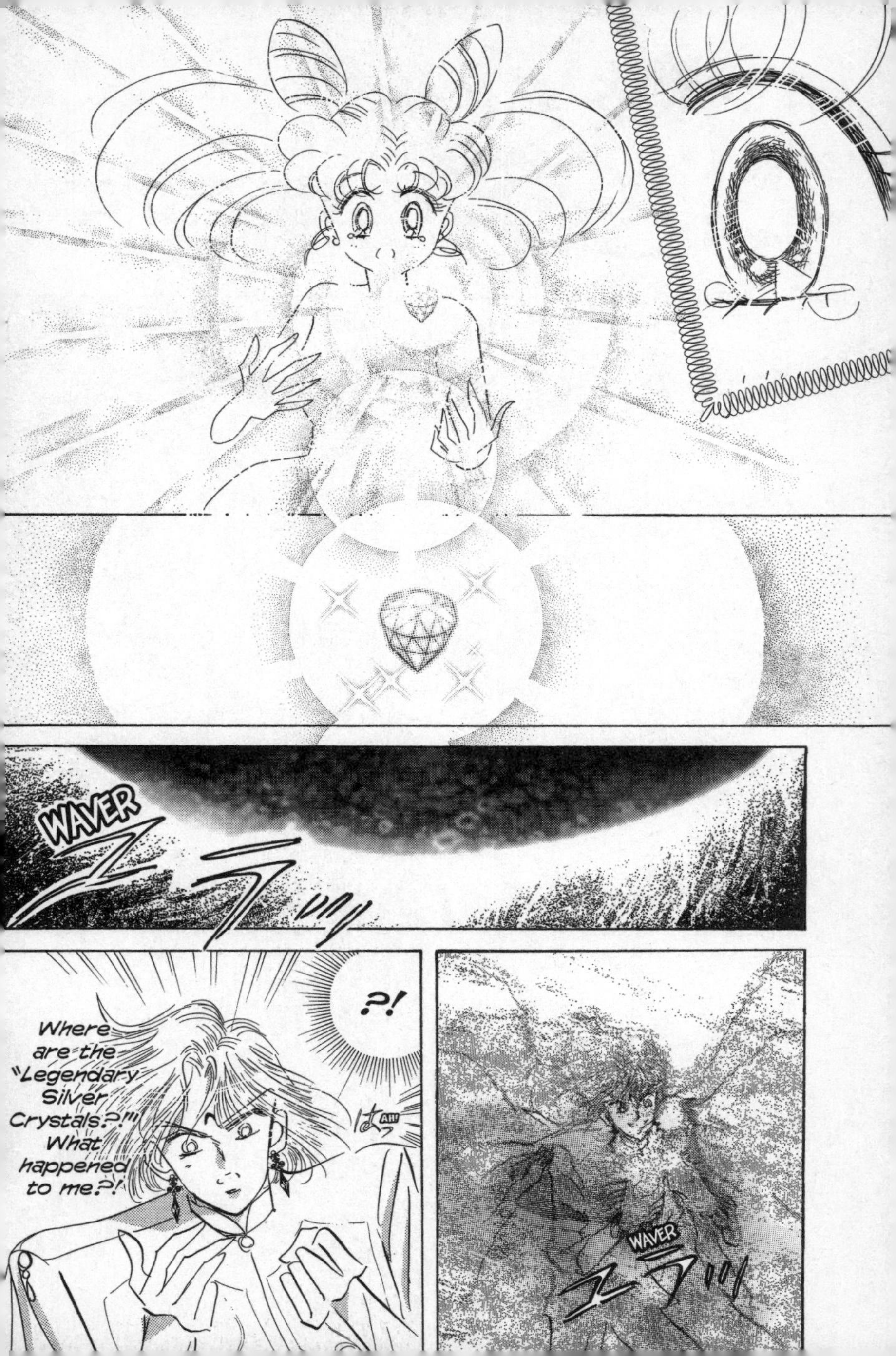
WAVER
WAVER
?!
Where are the "Legendary Silver Crystals?!" What happened to me?!
AH!

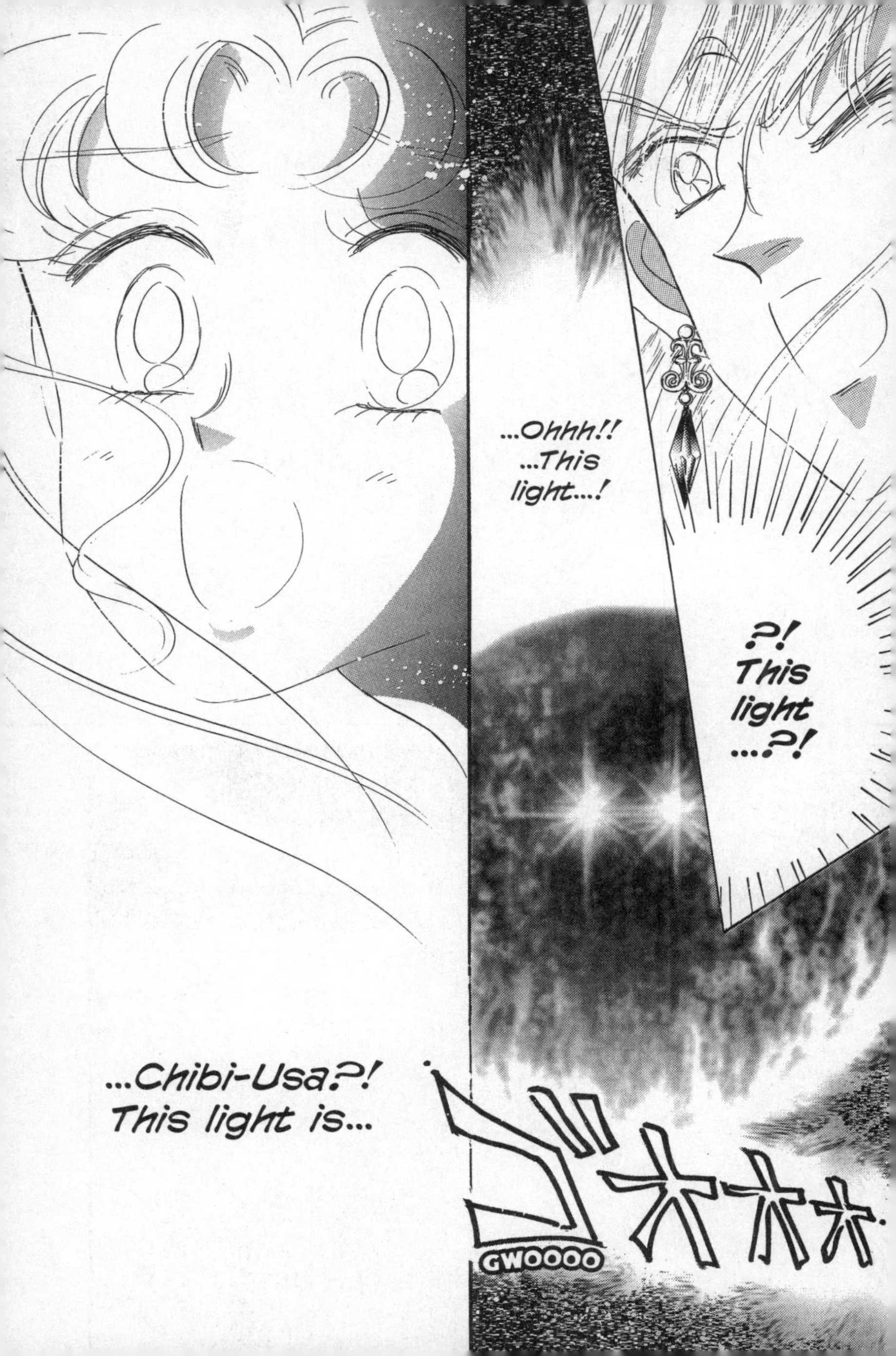
?! This light ...?!
...Ohhh!! ...This light...!
ゴォオォ
GWOOOO
...Chibi-Usa?! This light is...

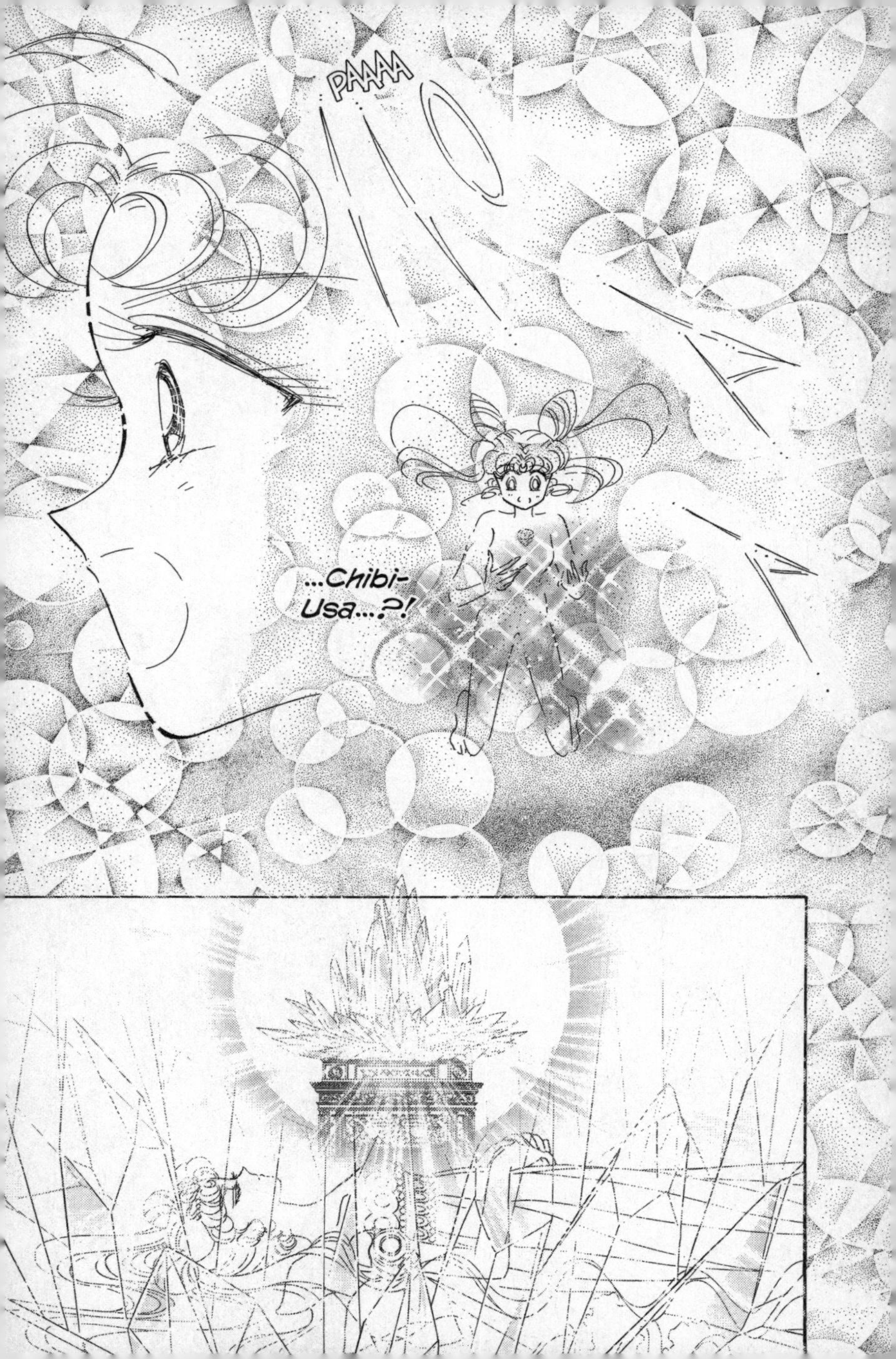
PAAAA
...Chibi-Usa...?!

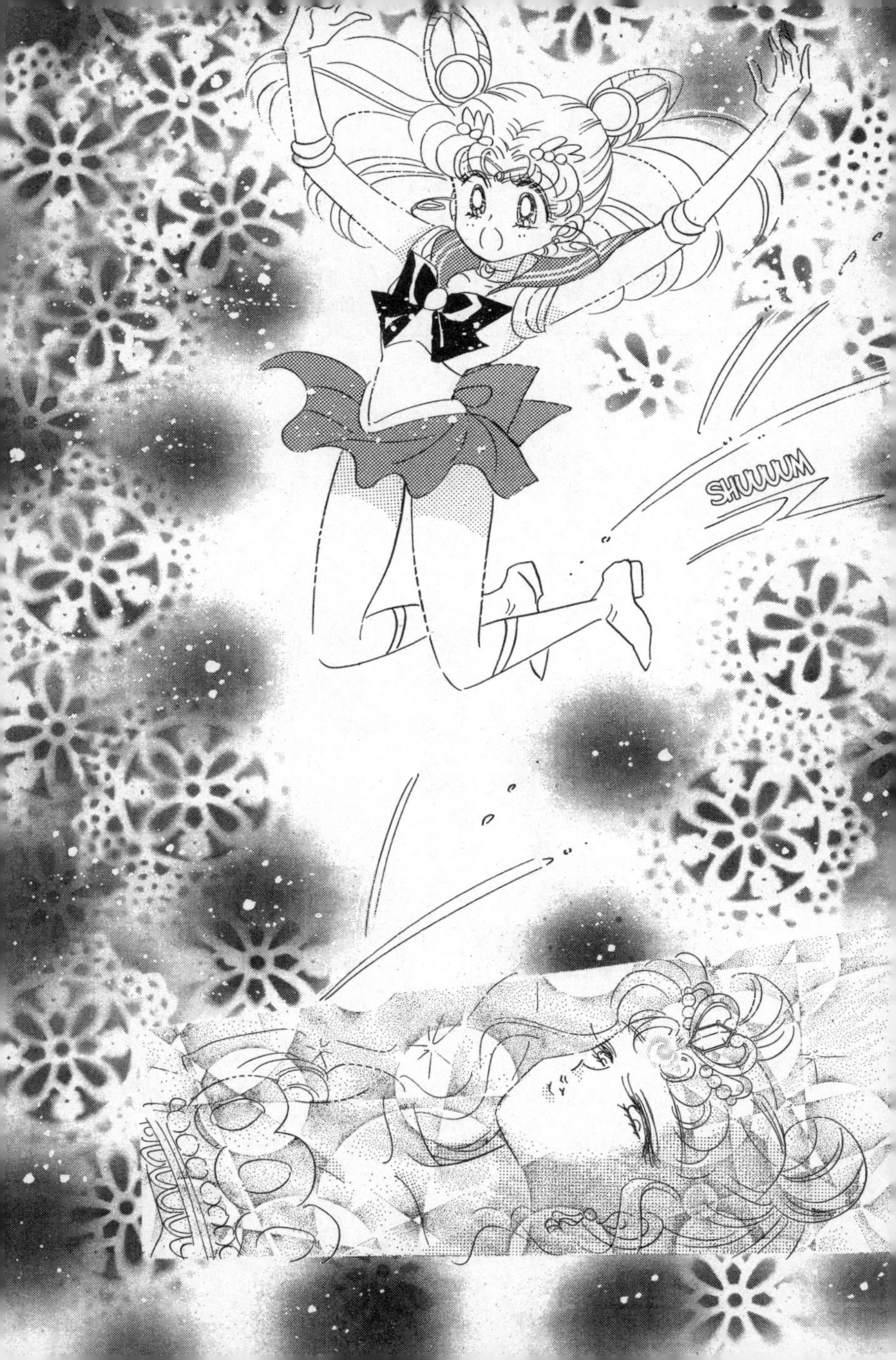
SHUUUUM

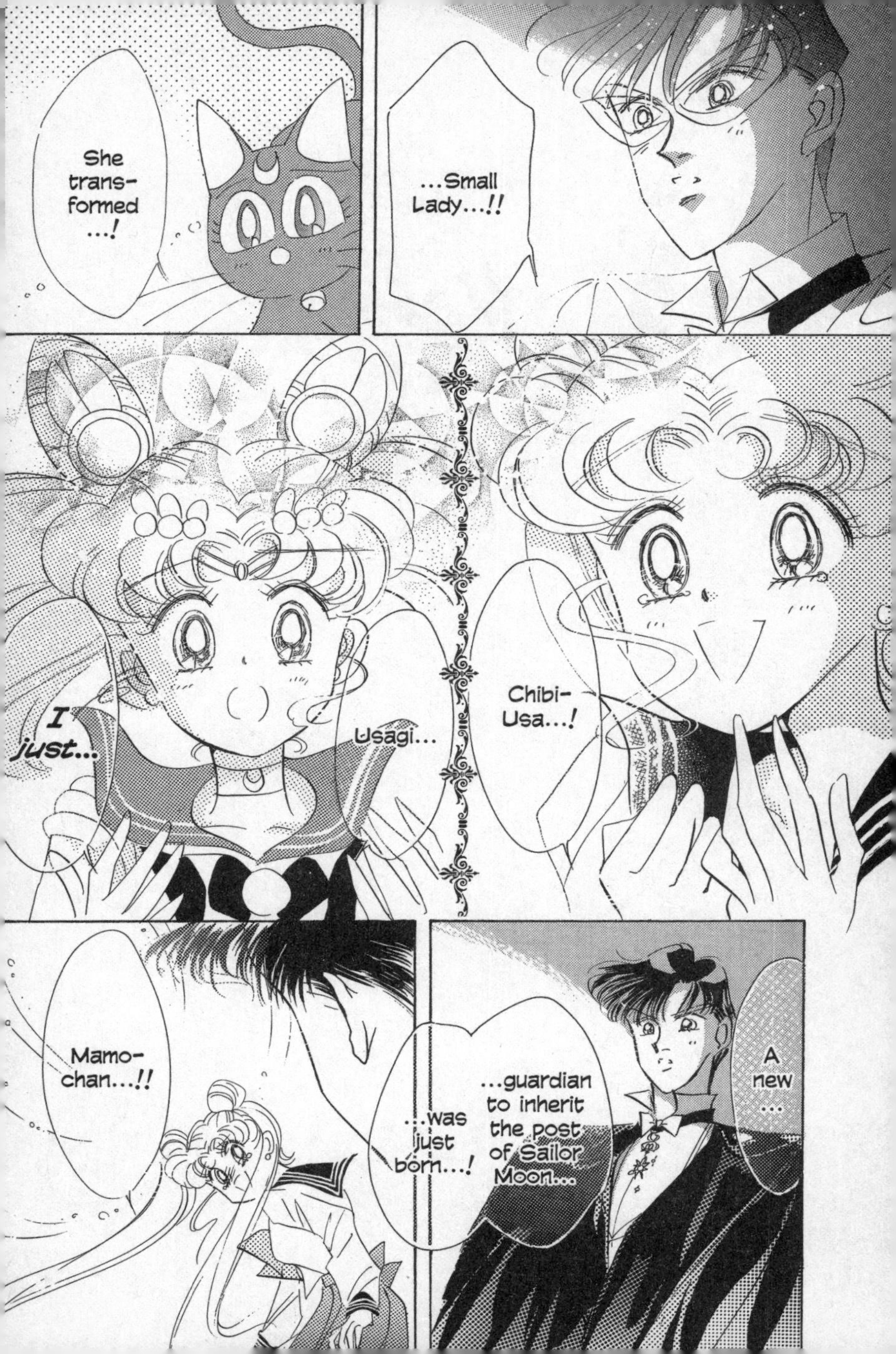
...Small Lady...!!
She transformed...!
Chibi-Usa...!
Usagi...
I just...
A new...
...guardian to inherit the post of Sailor Moon...
...was just born...!
Mamo-chan...!!

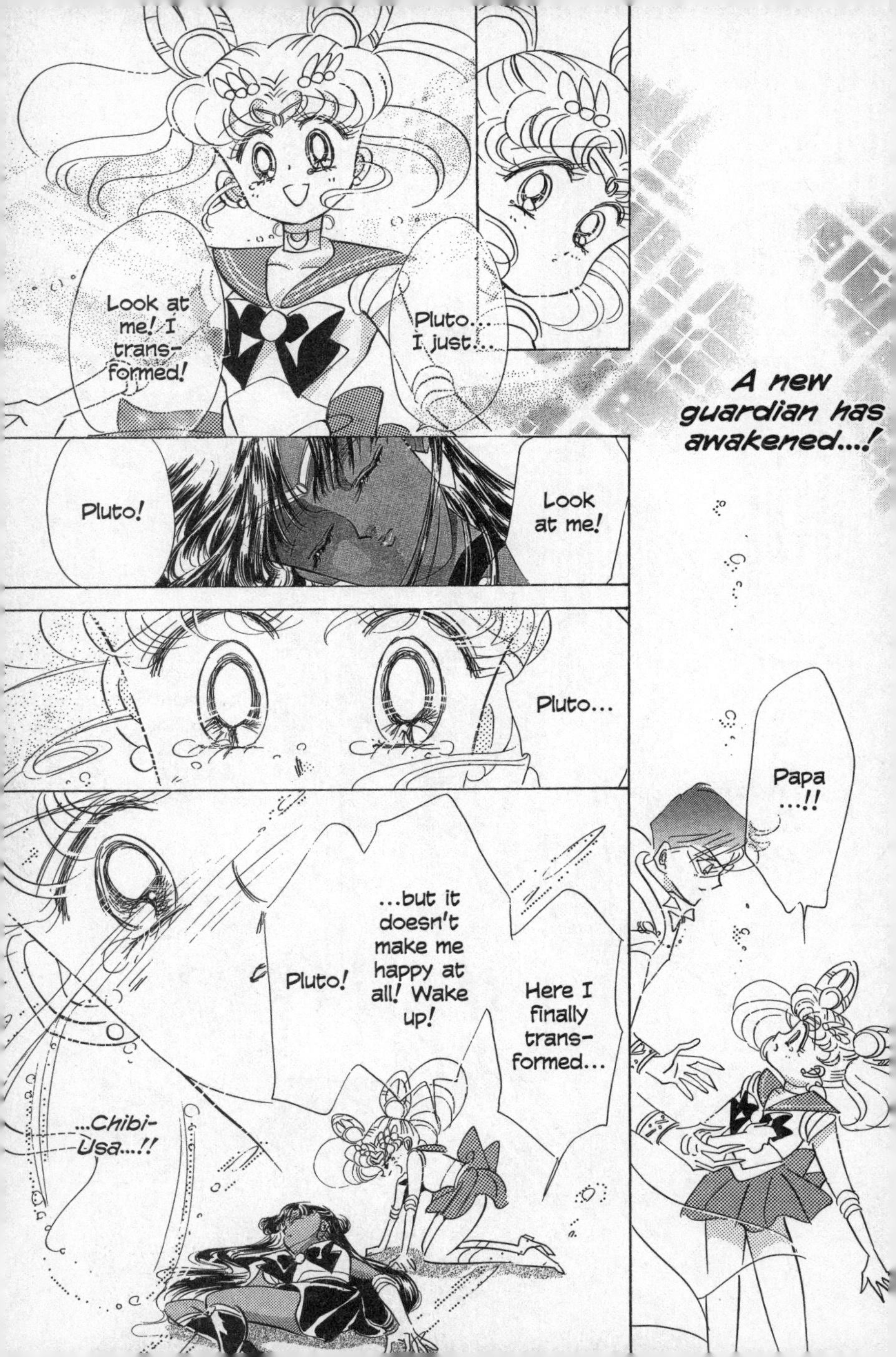
A new guardian has awakened...!
Papa ...!!
Pluto... I just...
Look at me! I trans-formed!
Look at me!
Pluto!
Pluto...
Here I finally trans-formed...
...but it doesn't make me happy at all! Wake up!
Pluto!
...Chibi-Usa...!!

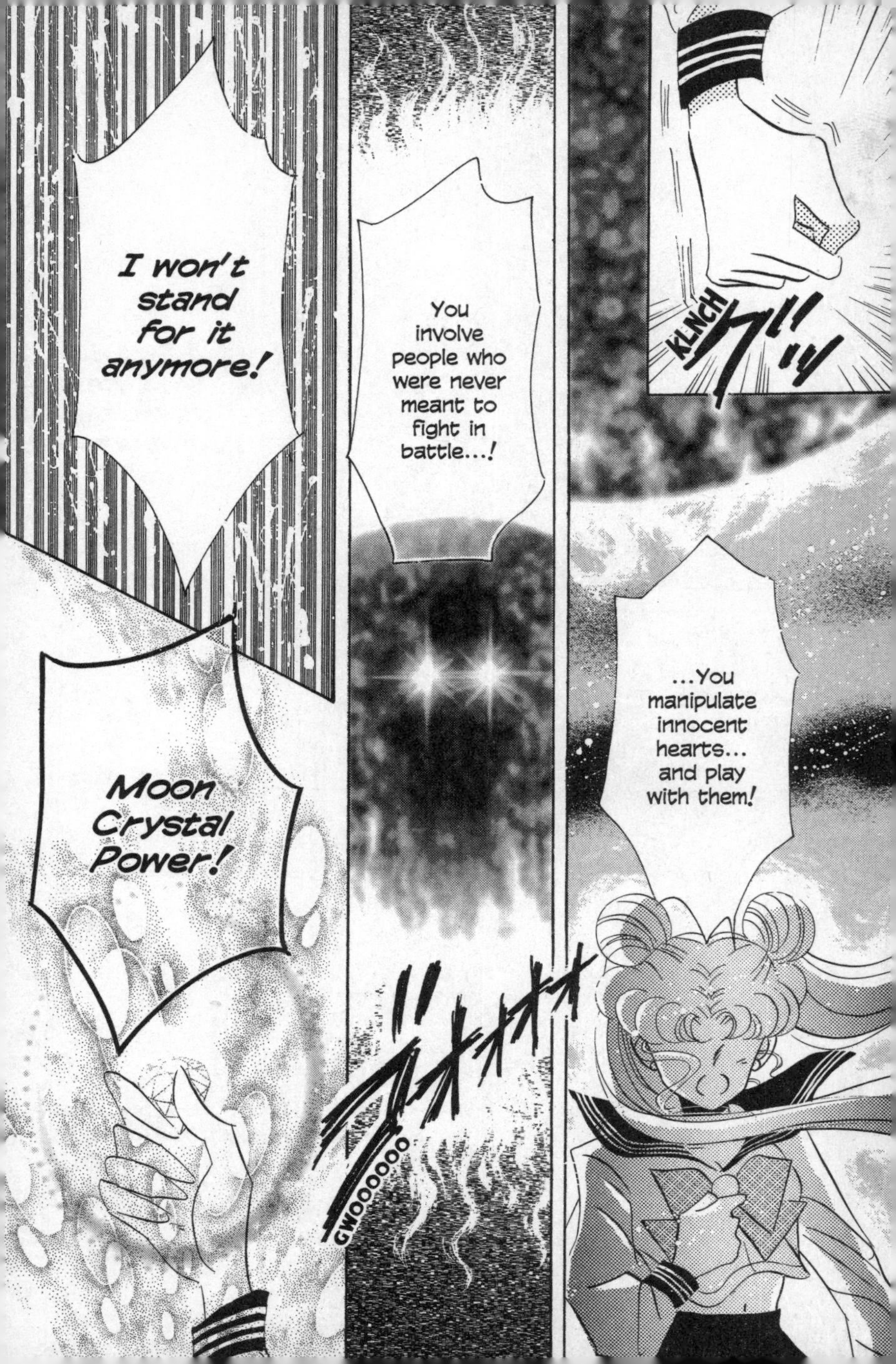
KLNCH
...You manipulate innocent hearts... and play with them!
You involve people who were never meant to fight in battle...!
GWOOOOOO
I won't stand for it anymore!
Moon Crystal Power!

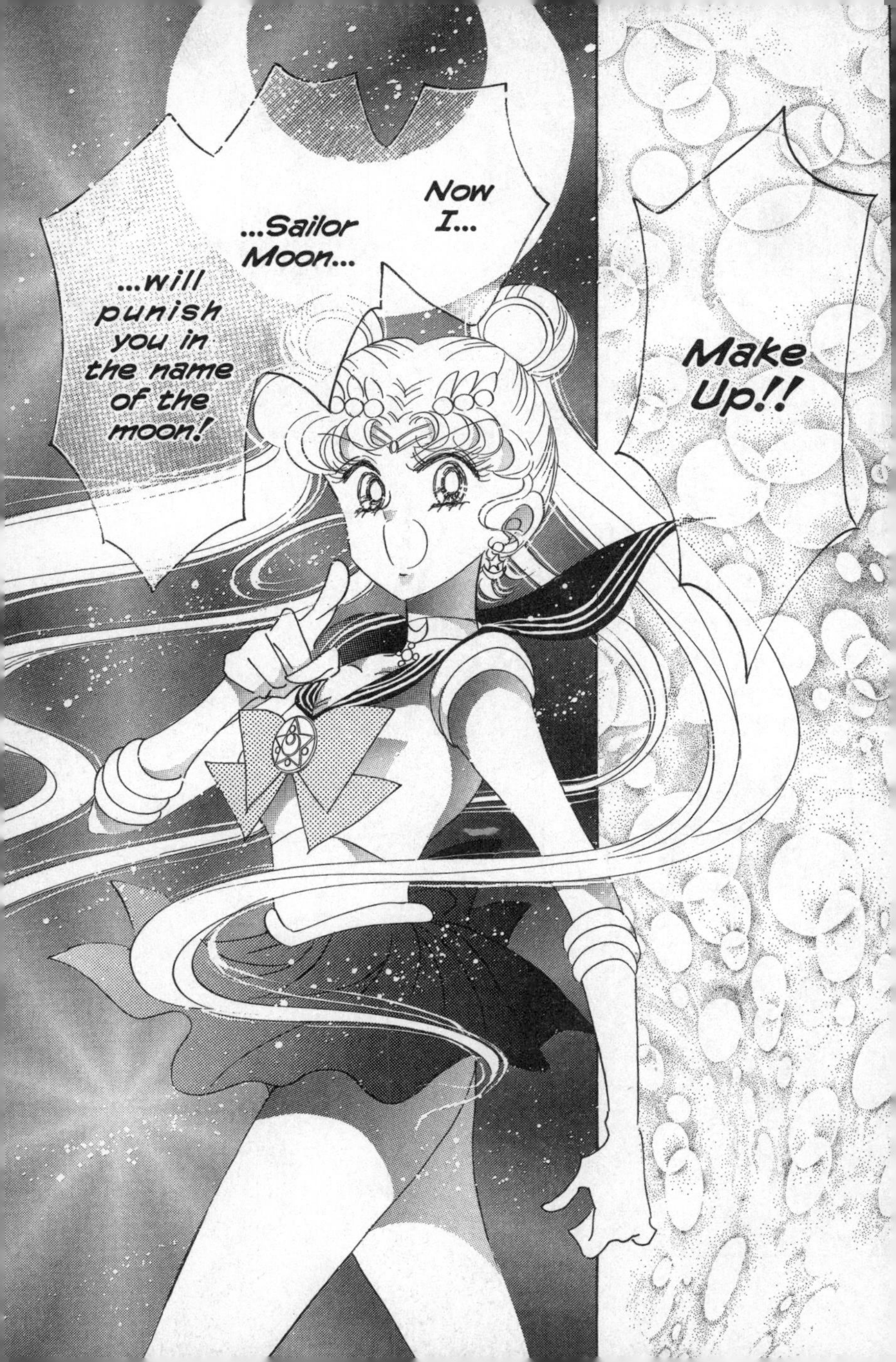

Make Up!!
Now I...
...Sailor Moon...
...will punish you in the name of the moon!

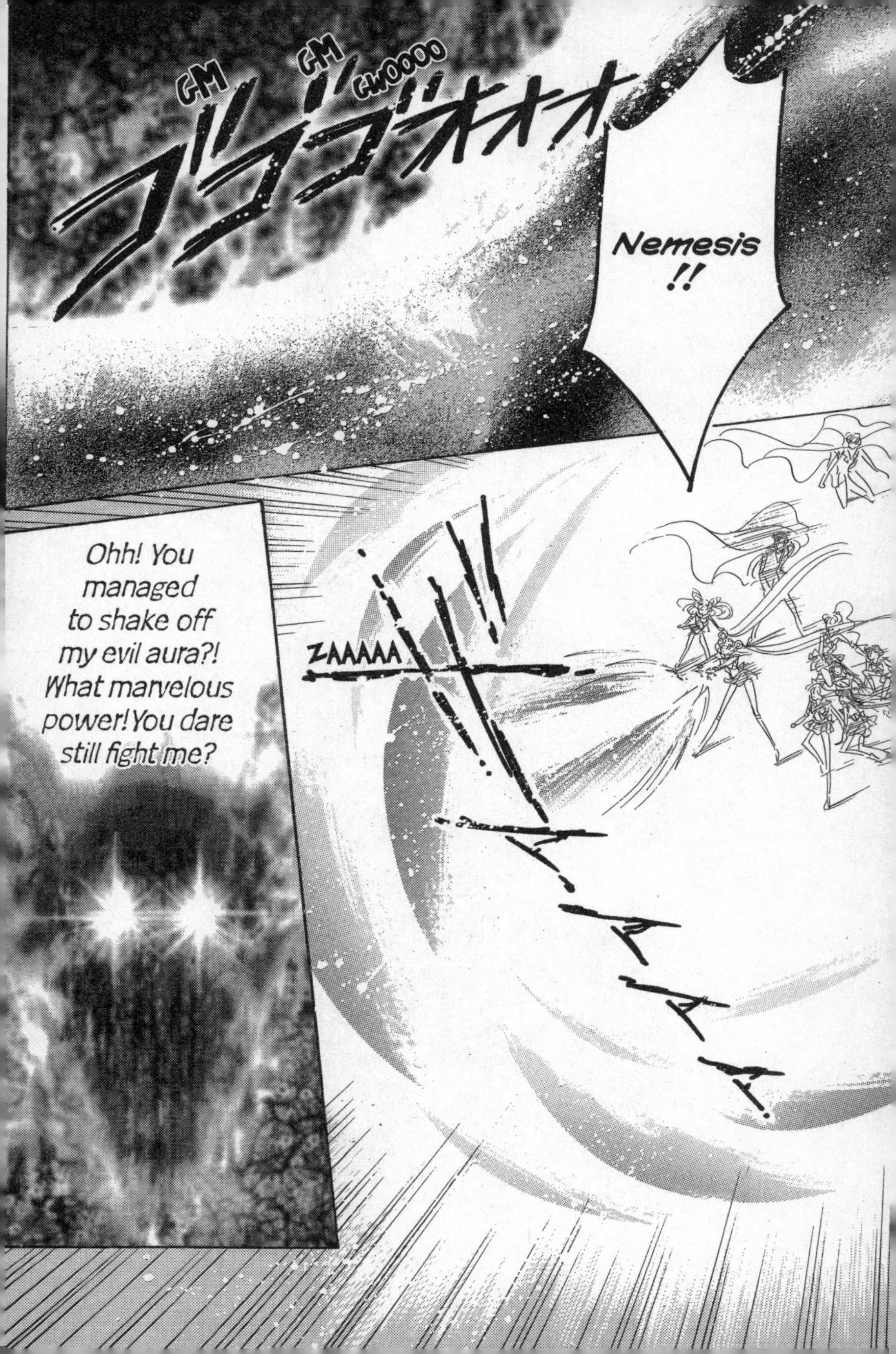
Nemesis !!
GM
GM
GWOOOO
ゴゴゴオオオ
ZAAAAA
Ohh! You managed to shake off my evil aura?! What marvelous power! You dare still fight me?

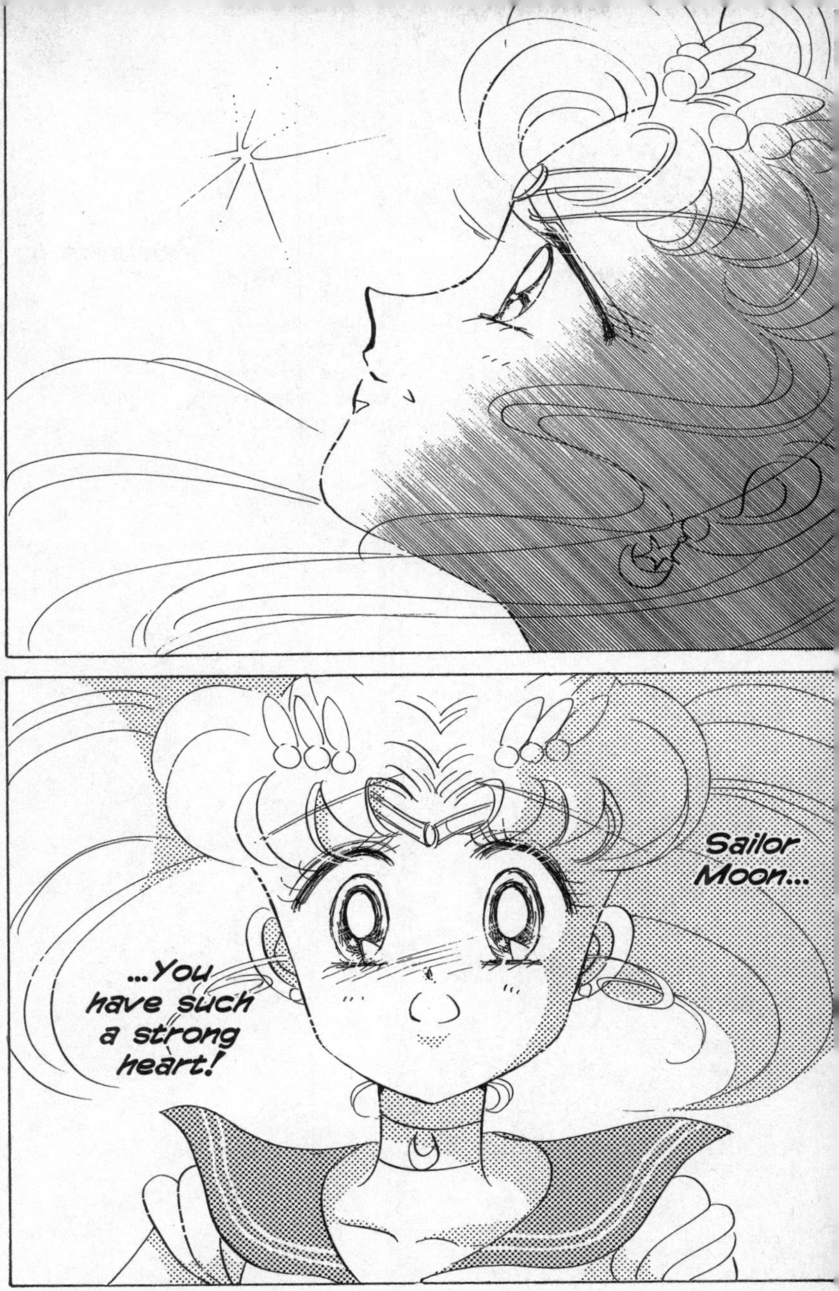
Sailor Moon...
...You have such a strong heart!

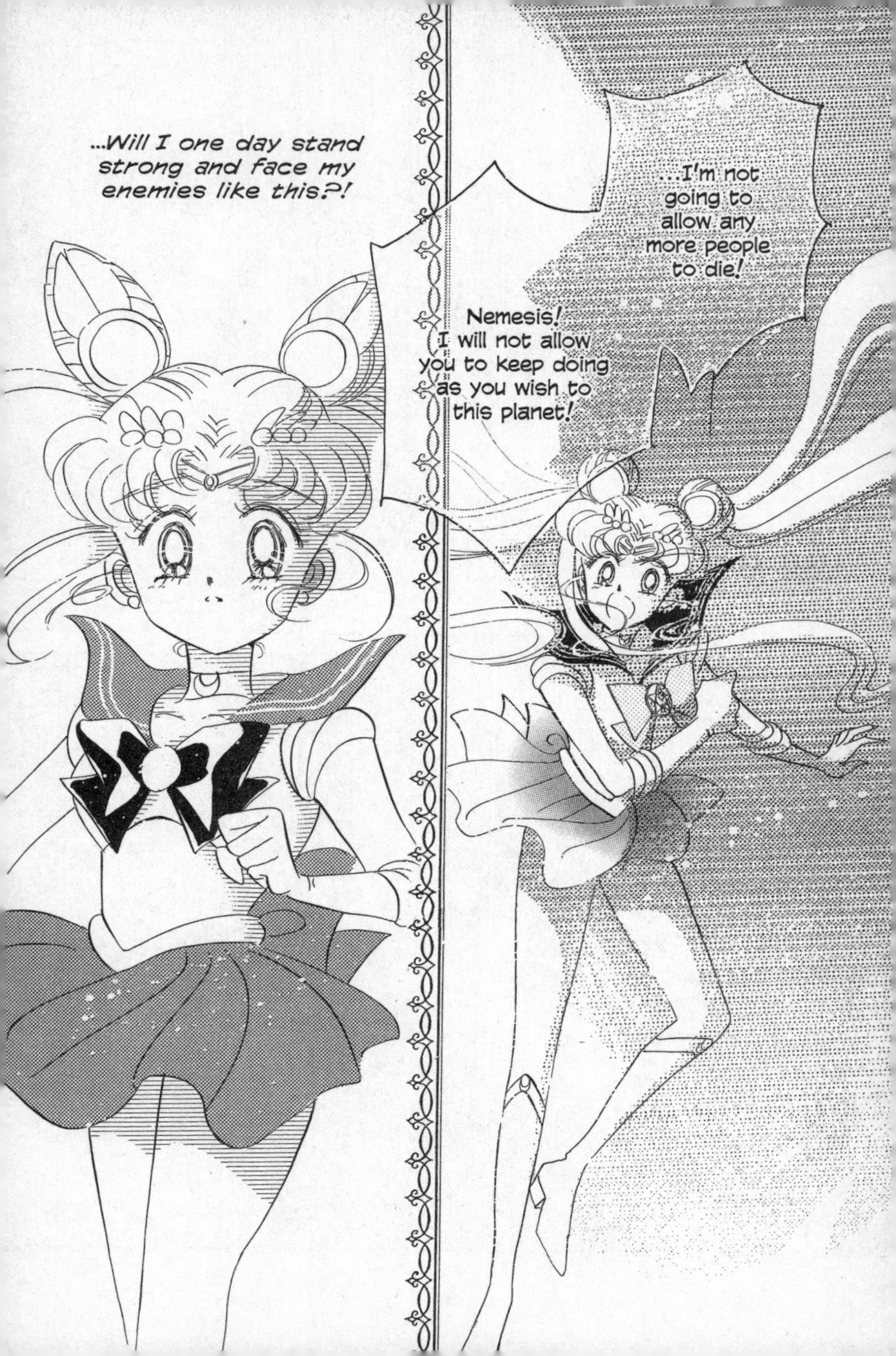
...I'm not going to allow any more people to die!
Nemesis! I will not allow you to keep doing as you wish to this planet!
...Will I one day stand strong and face my enemies like this?!

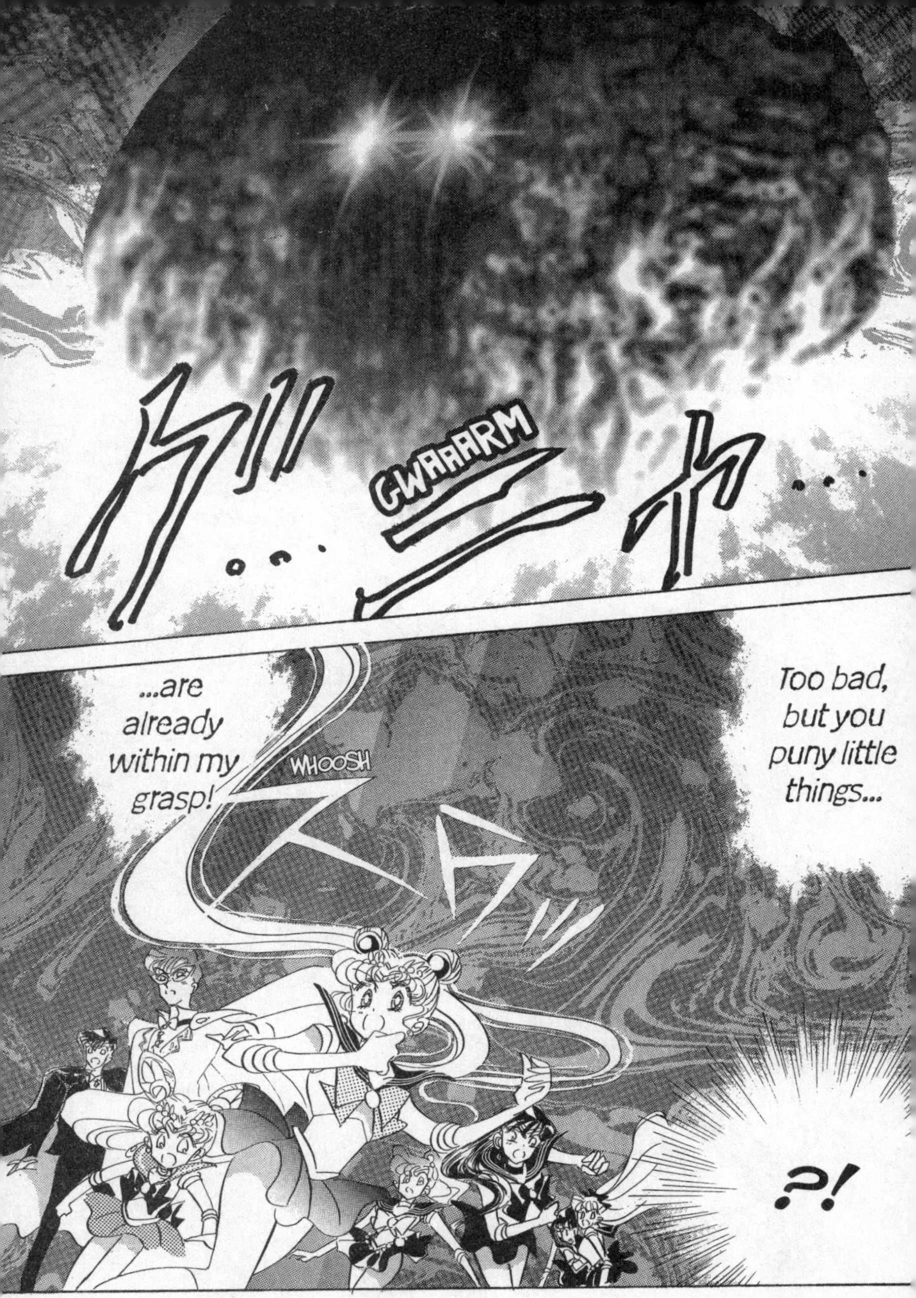
GWAAARM
Too bad, but you puny little things...
...are already within my grasp!
WHOOSH
?!

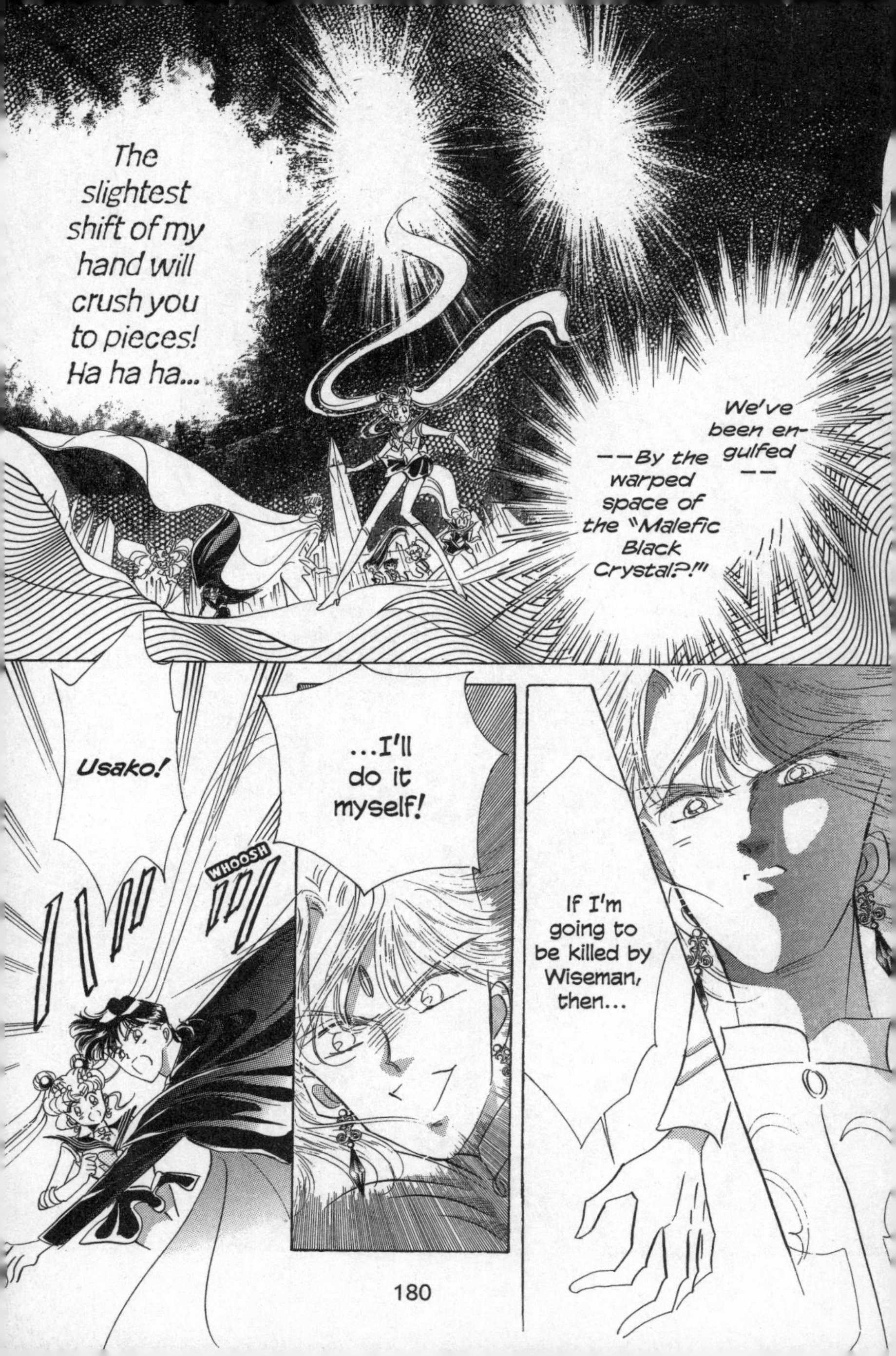
The slightest shift of my hand will crush you to pieces! Ha ha ha...
We've been en-gulfed --
--By the warped space of the "Malefic Black Crystal?!"
If I'm going to be killed by Wiseman, then...
...I'll do it myself!
Usako!
WHOOSH

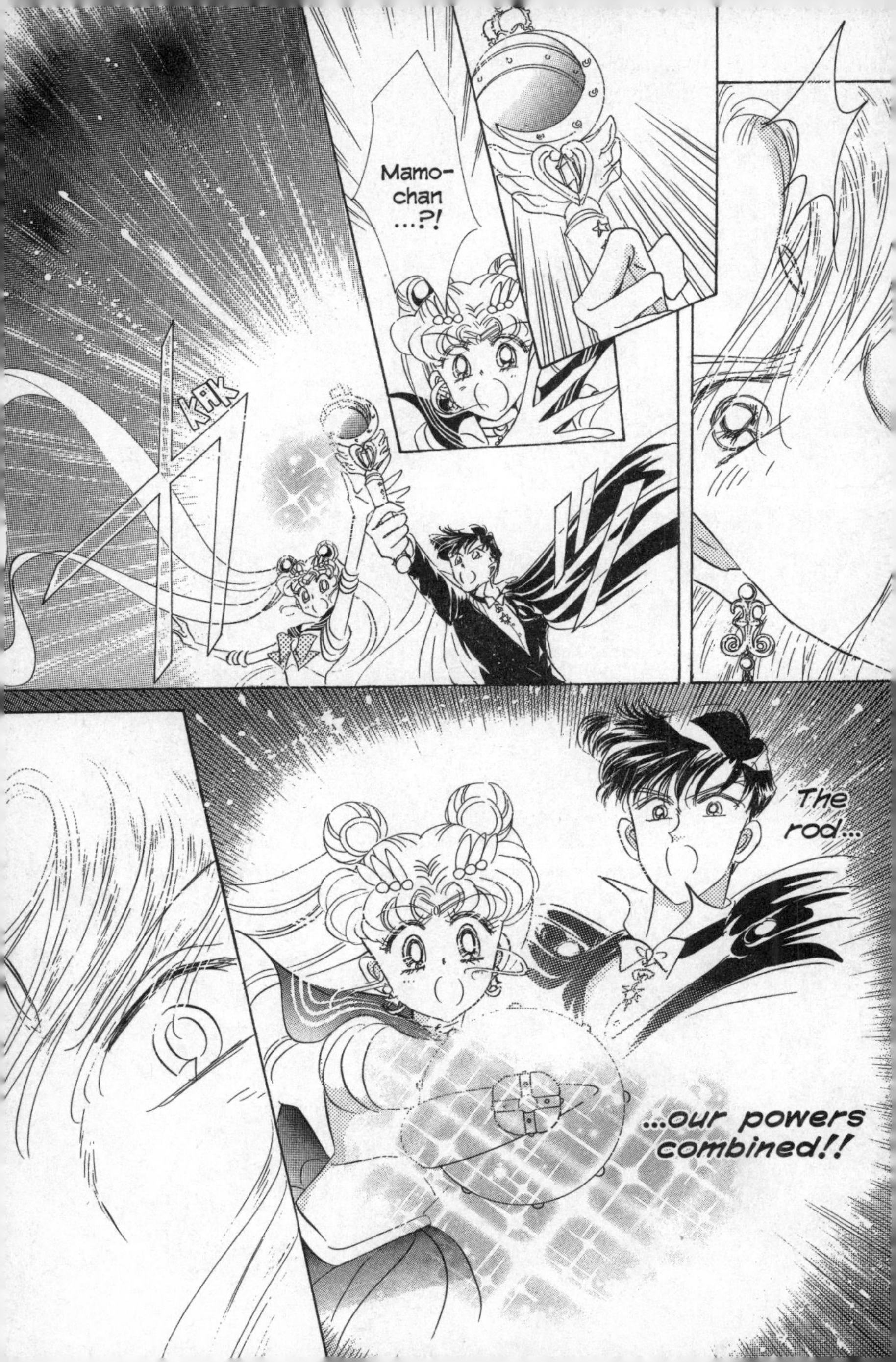
Mamo-chan ...?!
KRAK
The rod...
...our powers combined!!

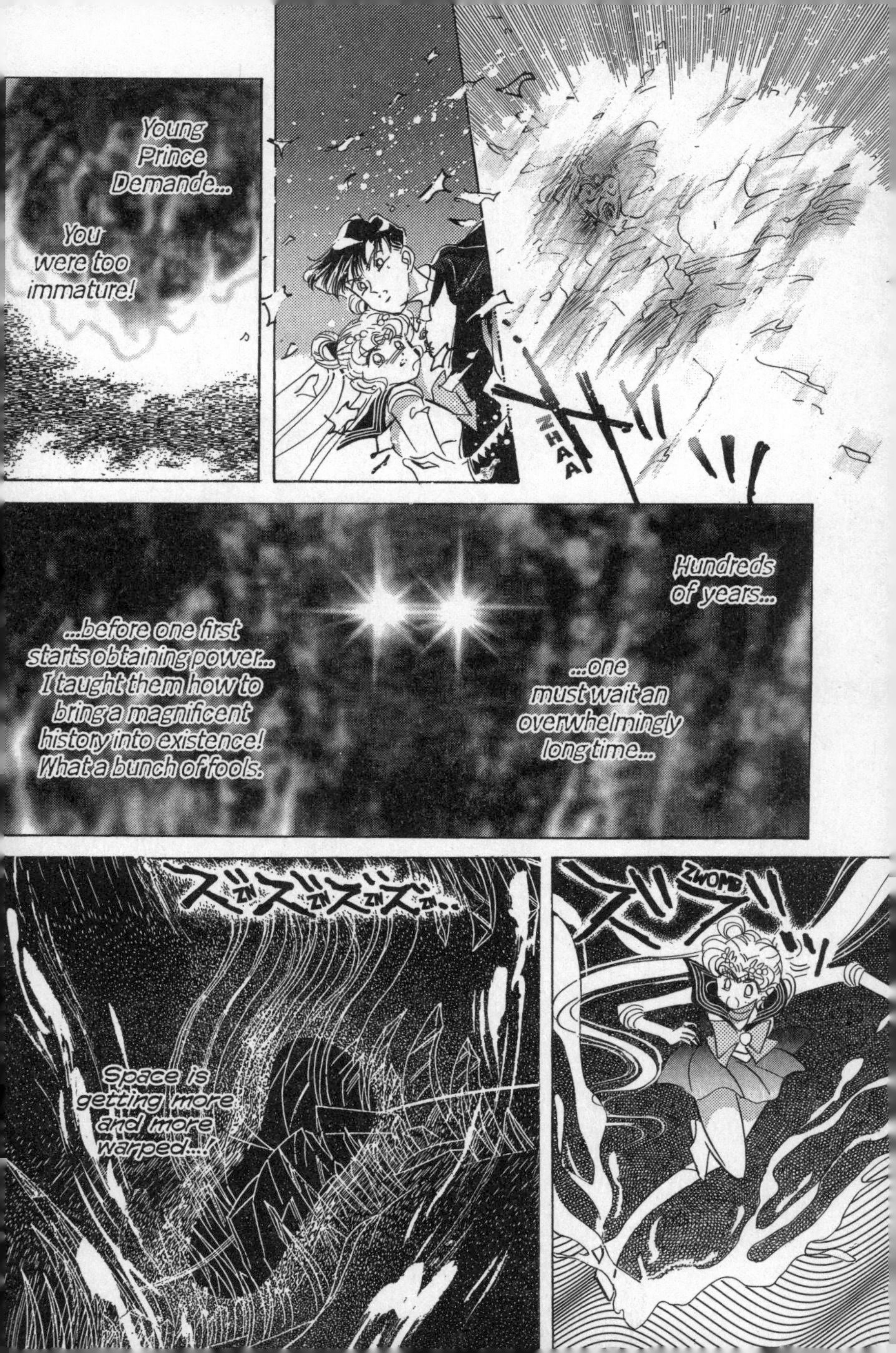
ZHAA
Young Prince Demande...
You were too immature!
Hundreds of years...
...one must wait an overwhelmingly long time...
...before one first starts obtaining power... I taught them how to bring a magnificent history into existence! What a bunch of fools.
ZWOMB
ZN ZN ZN ZN..
Space is getting more and more warped...!

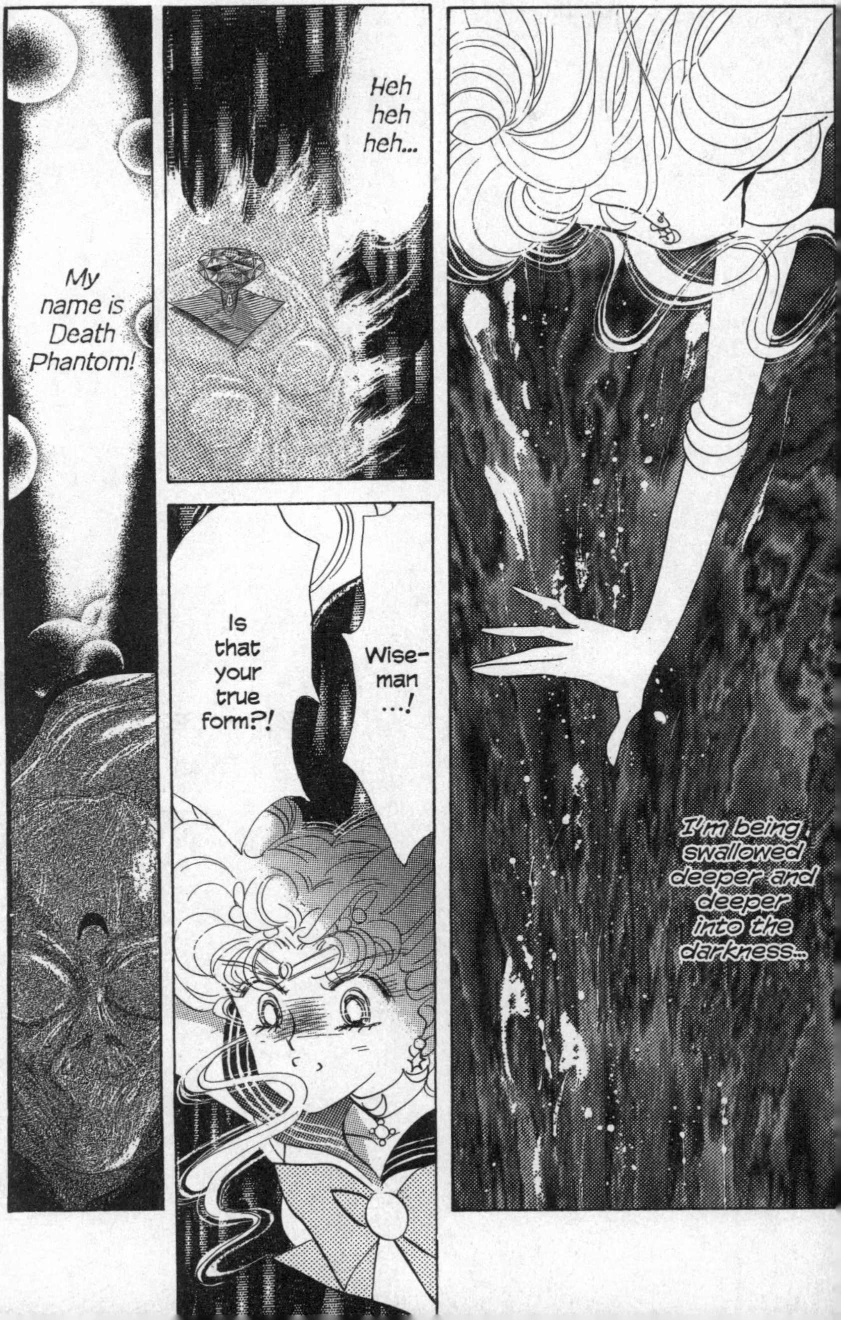
I'm being swallowed deeper and deeper into the darkness...
Heh heh heh...
Wise-man ...!
Is that your true form?!
My name is Death Phantom!

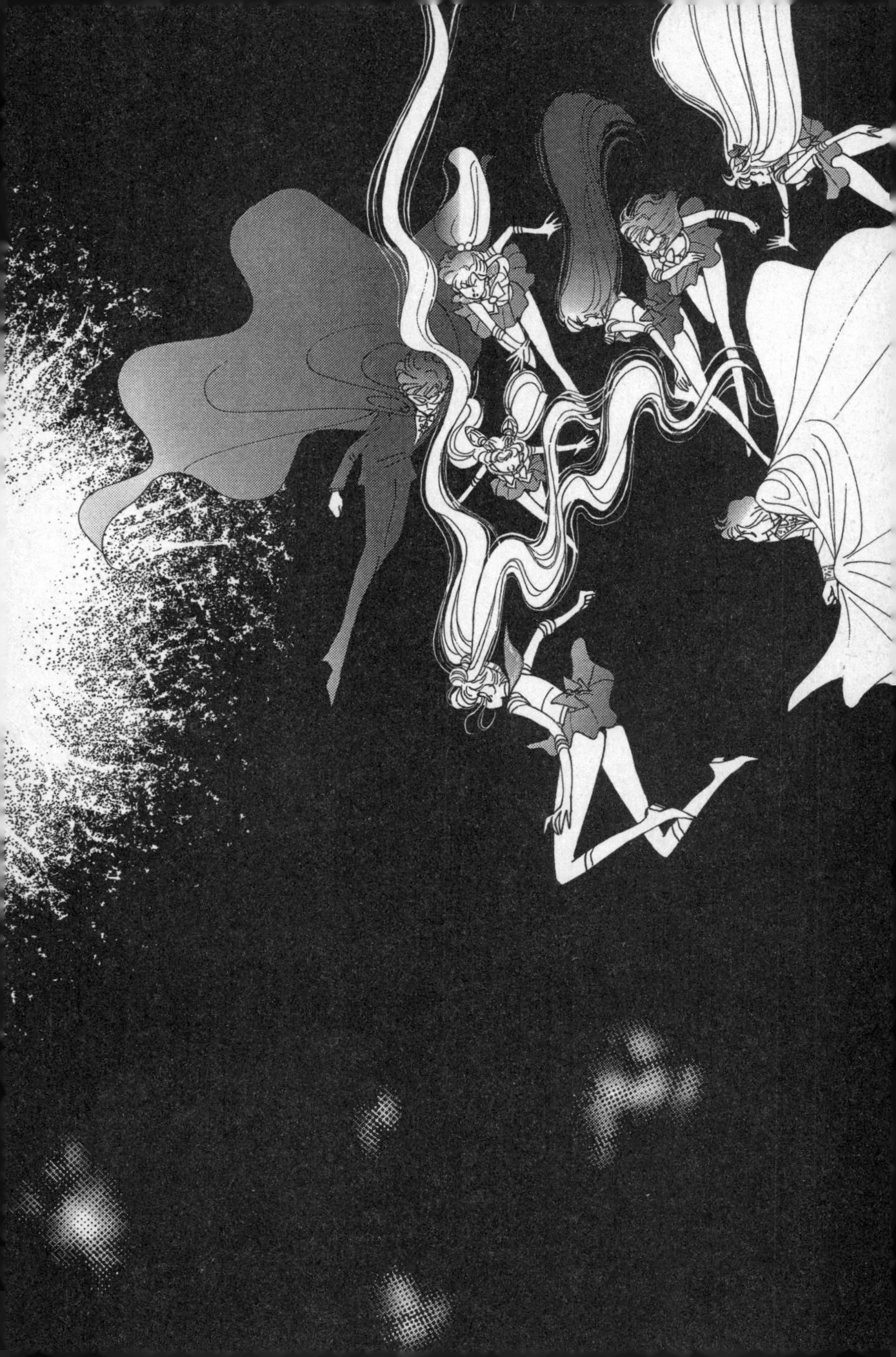

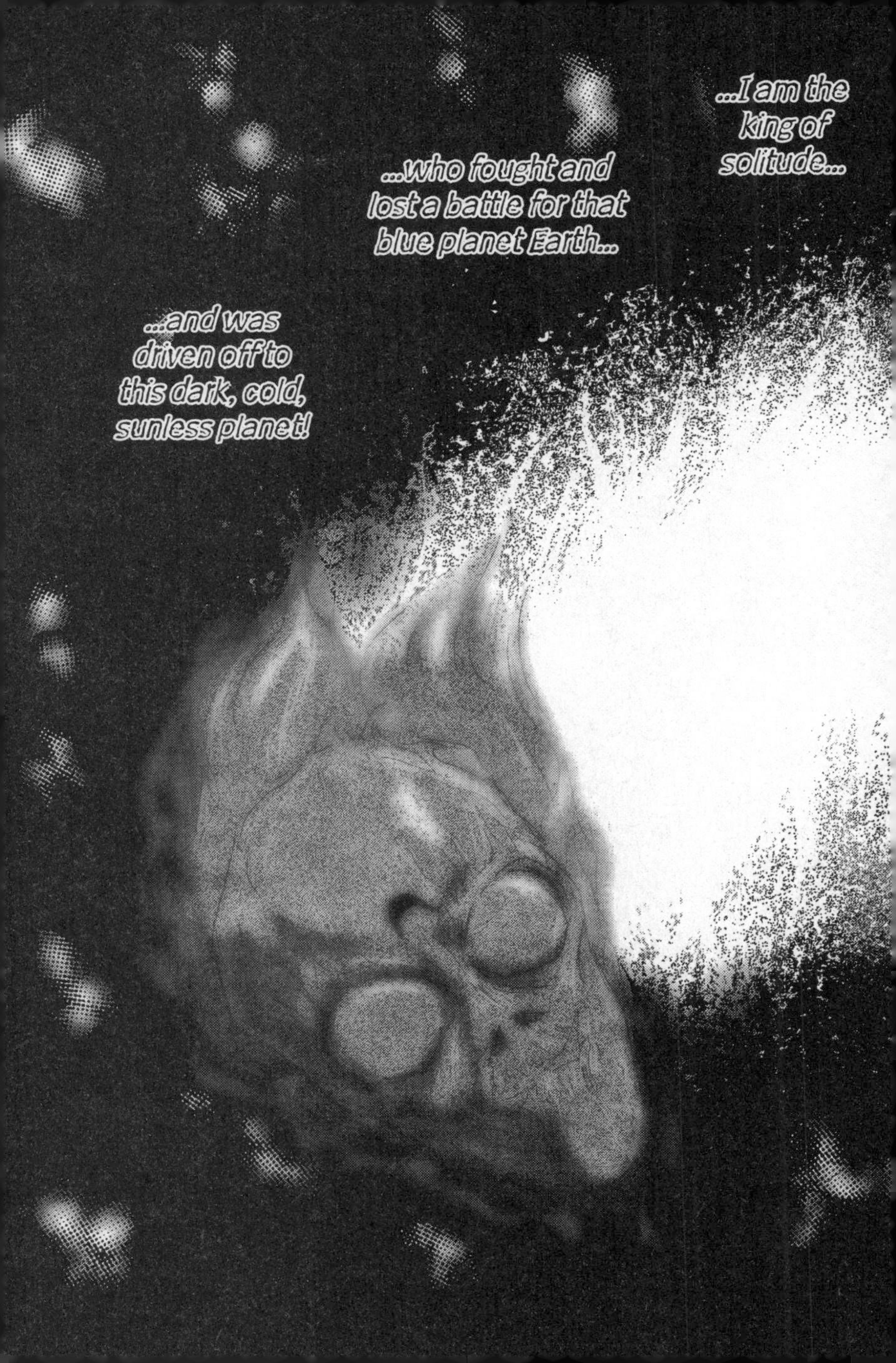
...I am the king of solitude...
...who fought and lost a battle for that blue planet Earth...
...and was driven off to this dark, cold, sunless planet!

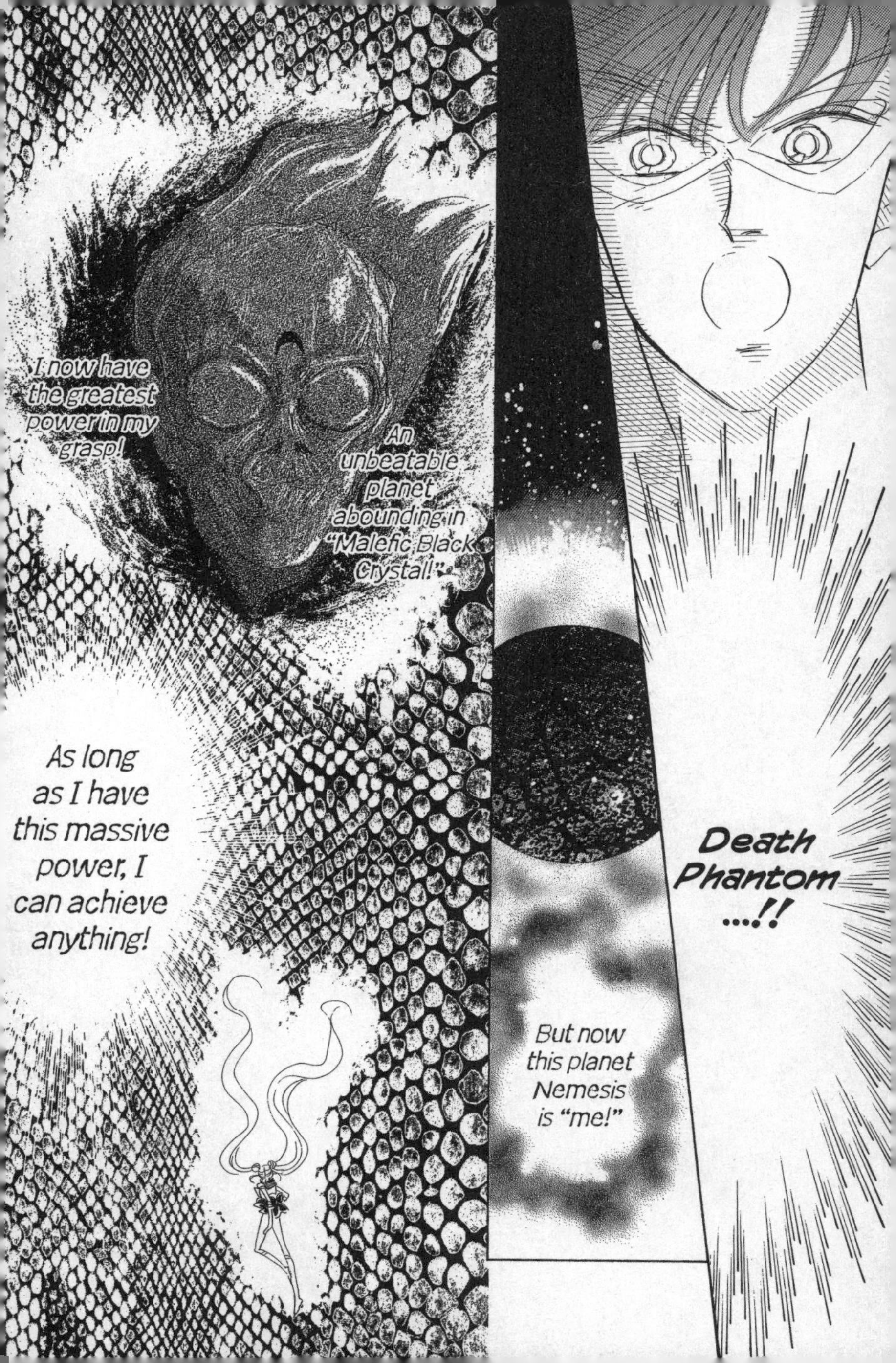

Death Phantom ...!!
But now this planet Nemesis is "me!"
I now have the greatest power in my grasp!
An unbeatable planet abounding in "Malefic Black Crystal!"
As long as I have this massive power, I can achieve anything!

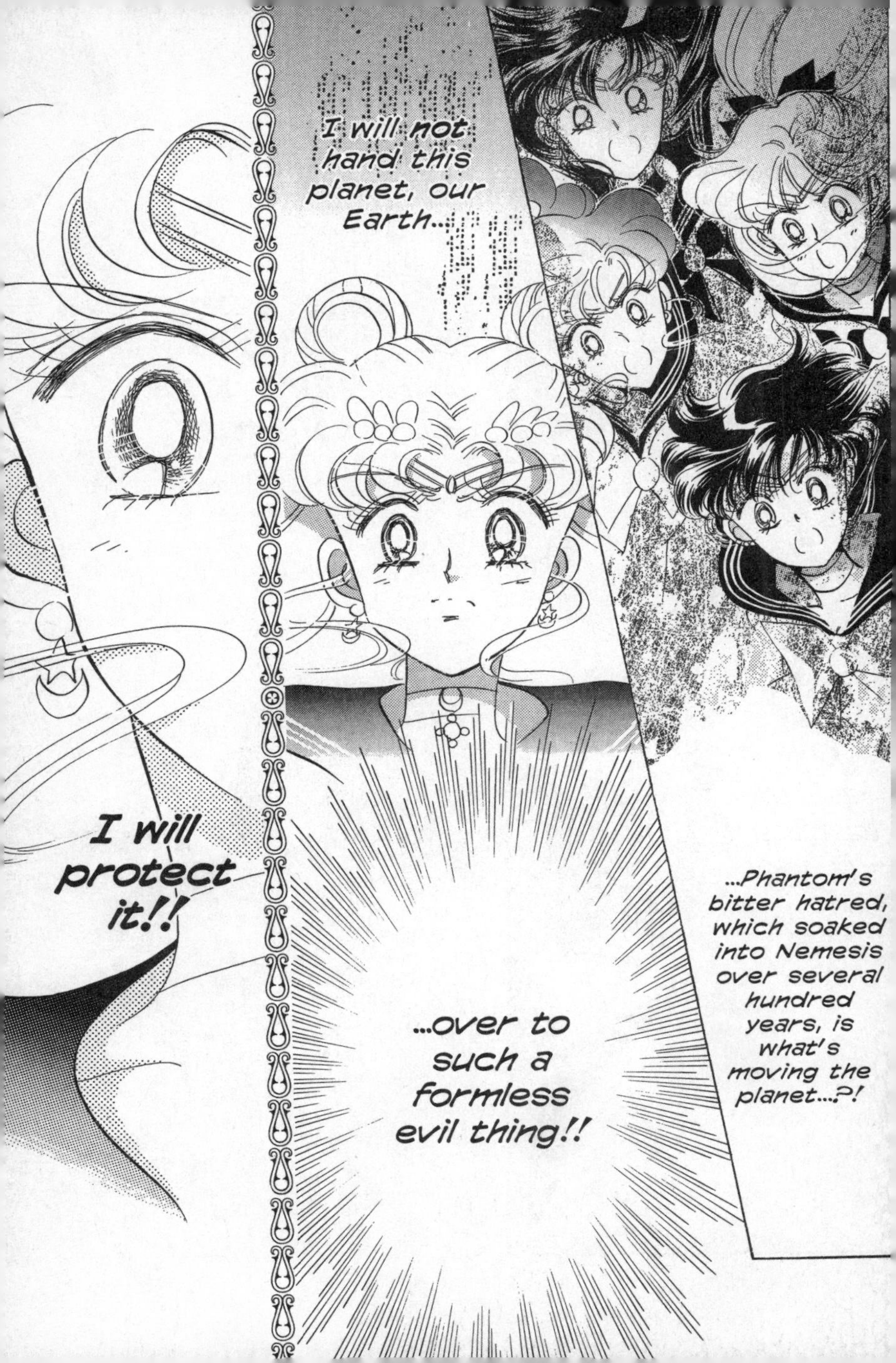
...Phantom's bitter hatred, which soaked into Nemesis over several hundred years, is what's moving the planet...?!
I will not hand this planet, our Earth...
...over to such a formless evil thing!!
I will protect it!!

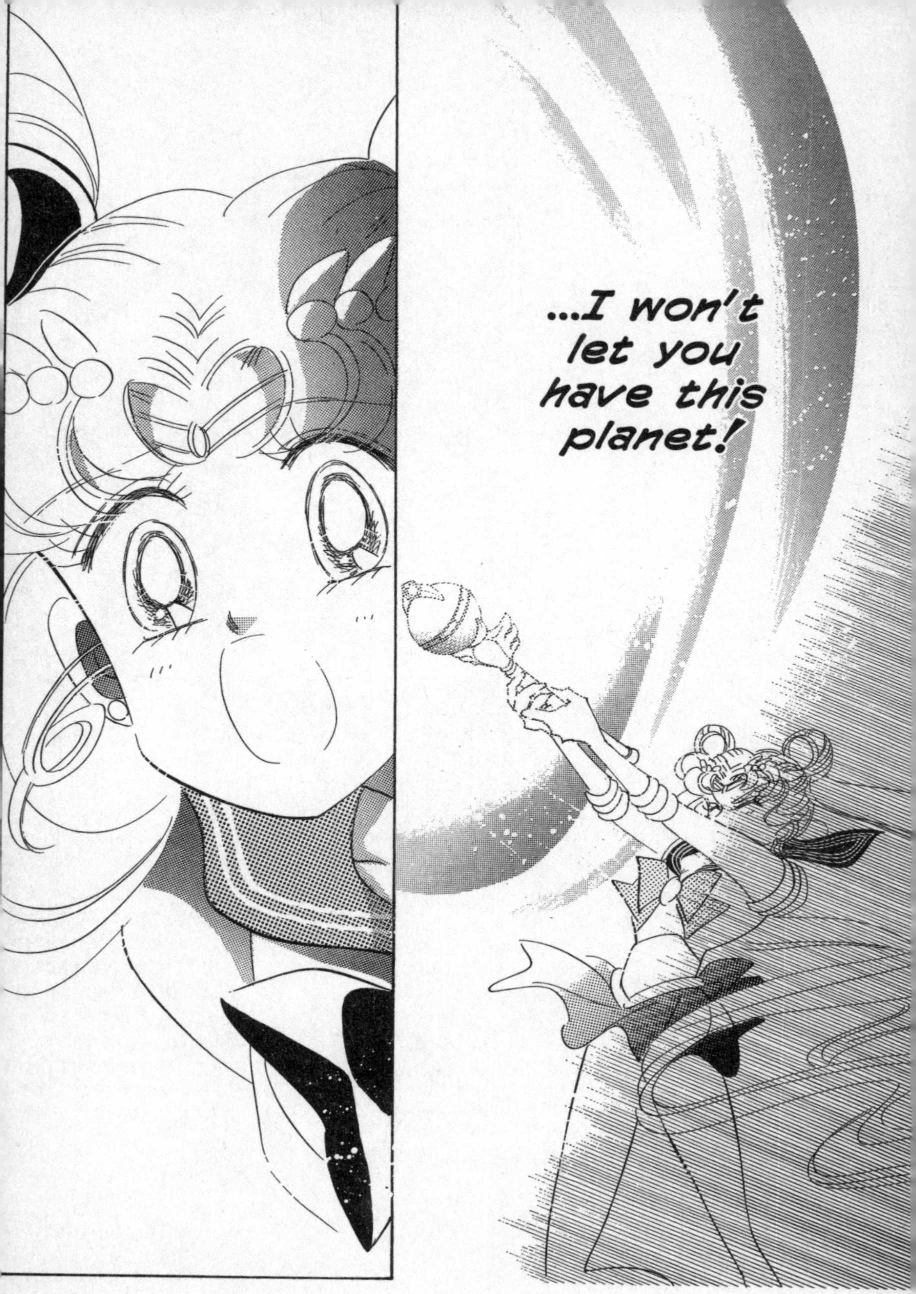
...I won't let you have this planet!

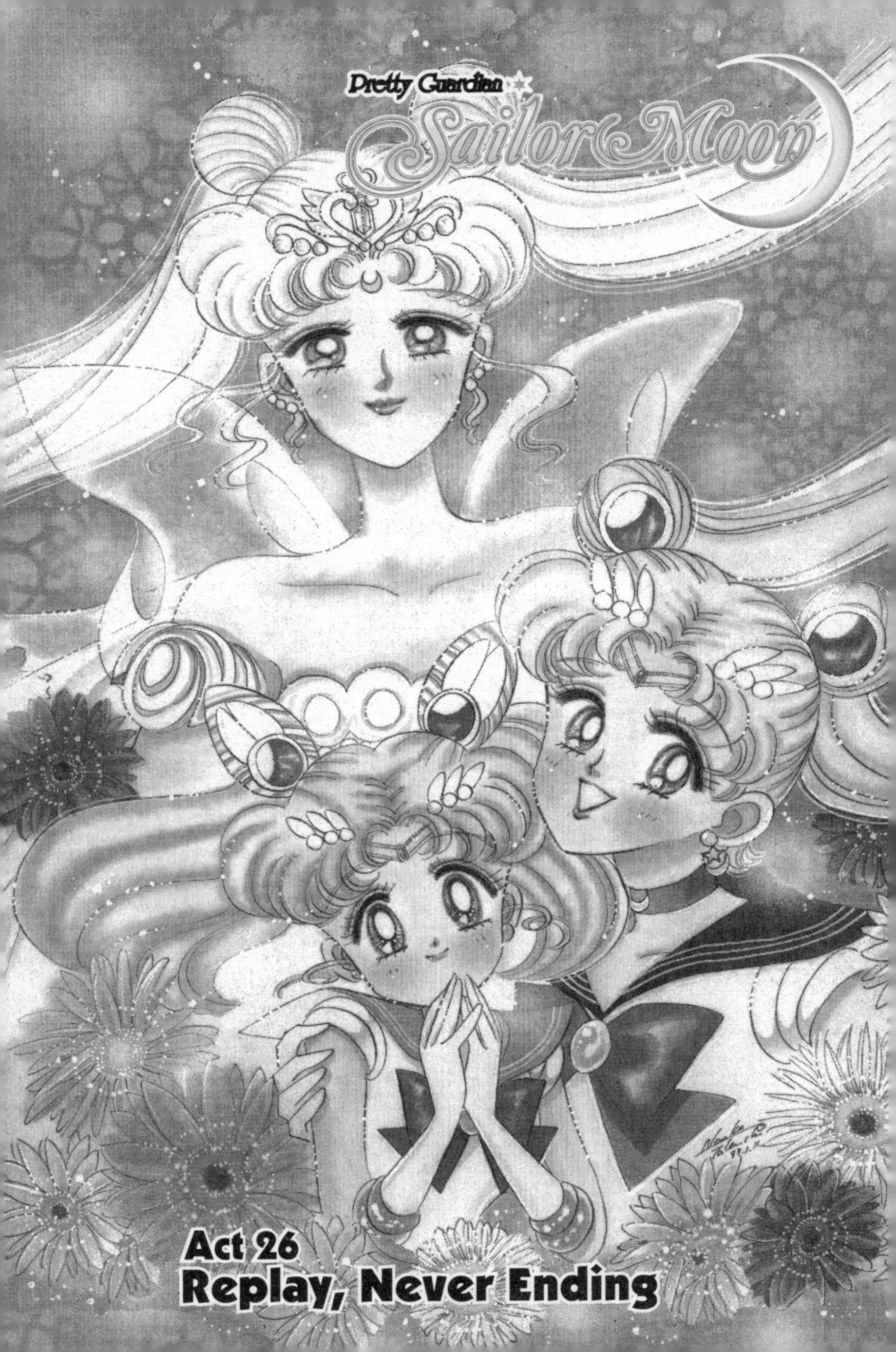
Pretty Guardian
Sailor Moon
Act 26
Replay, Never Ending

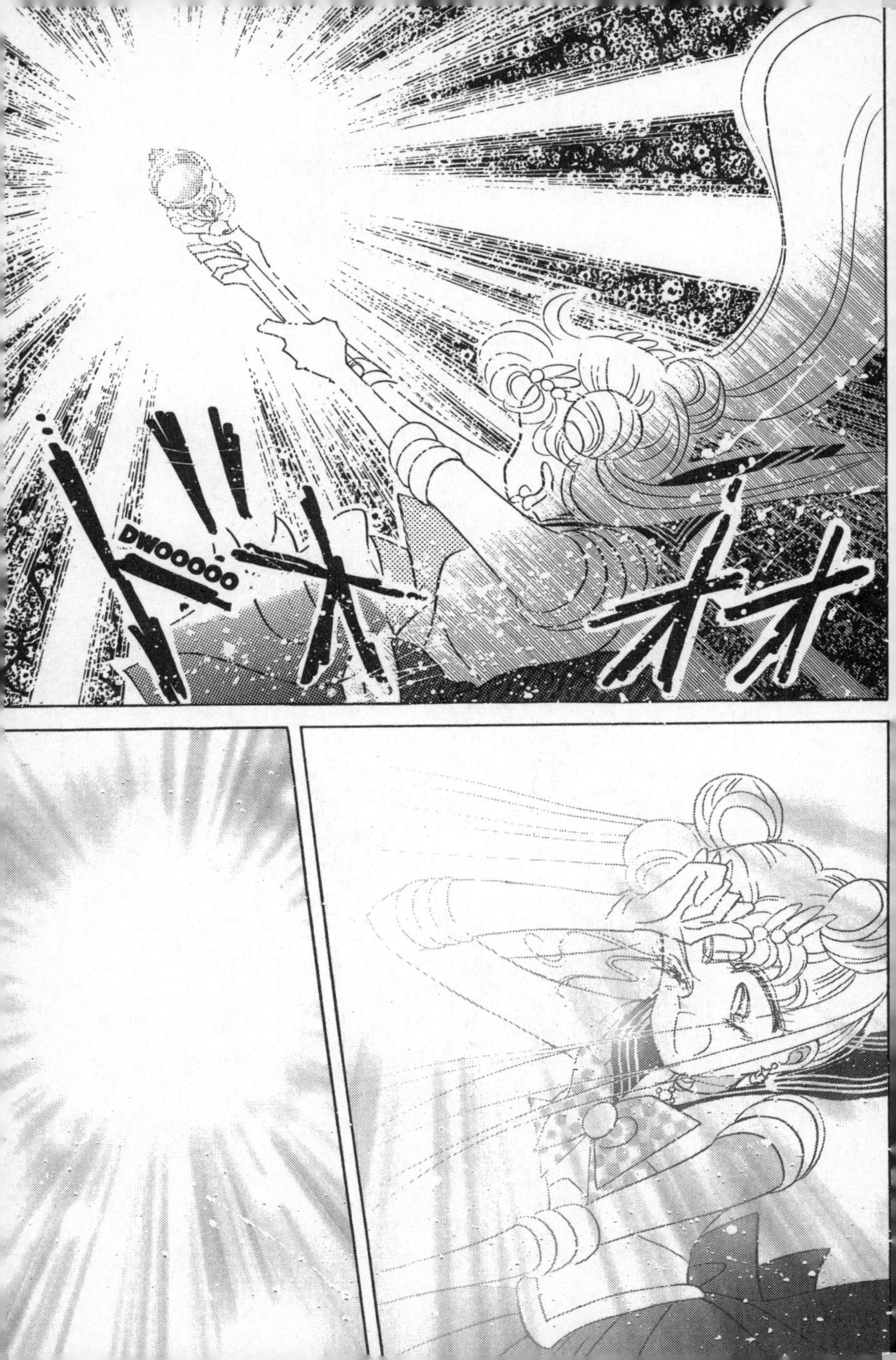
ドオオオ
DWOOOOO

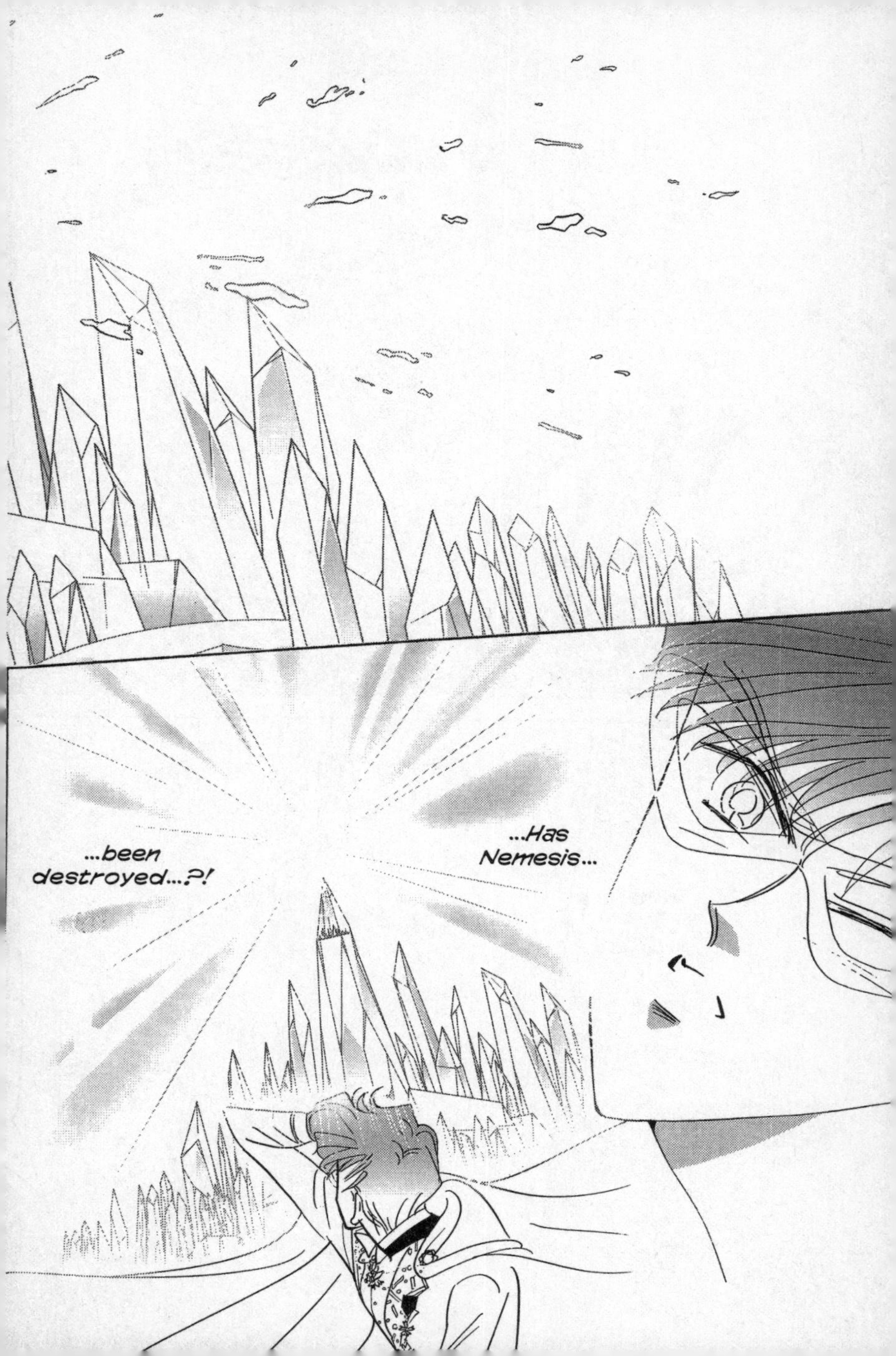
...Has Nemesis...
...been destroyed...?!

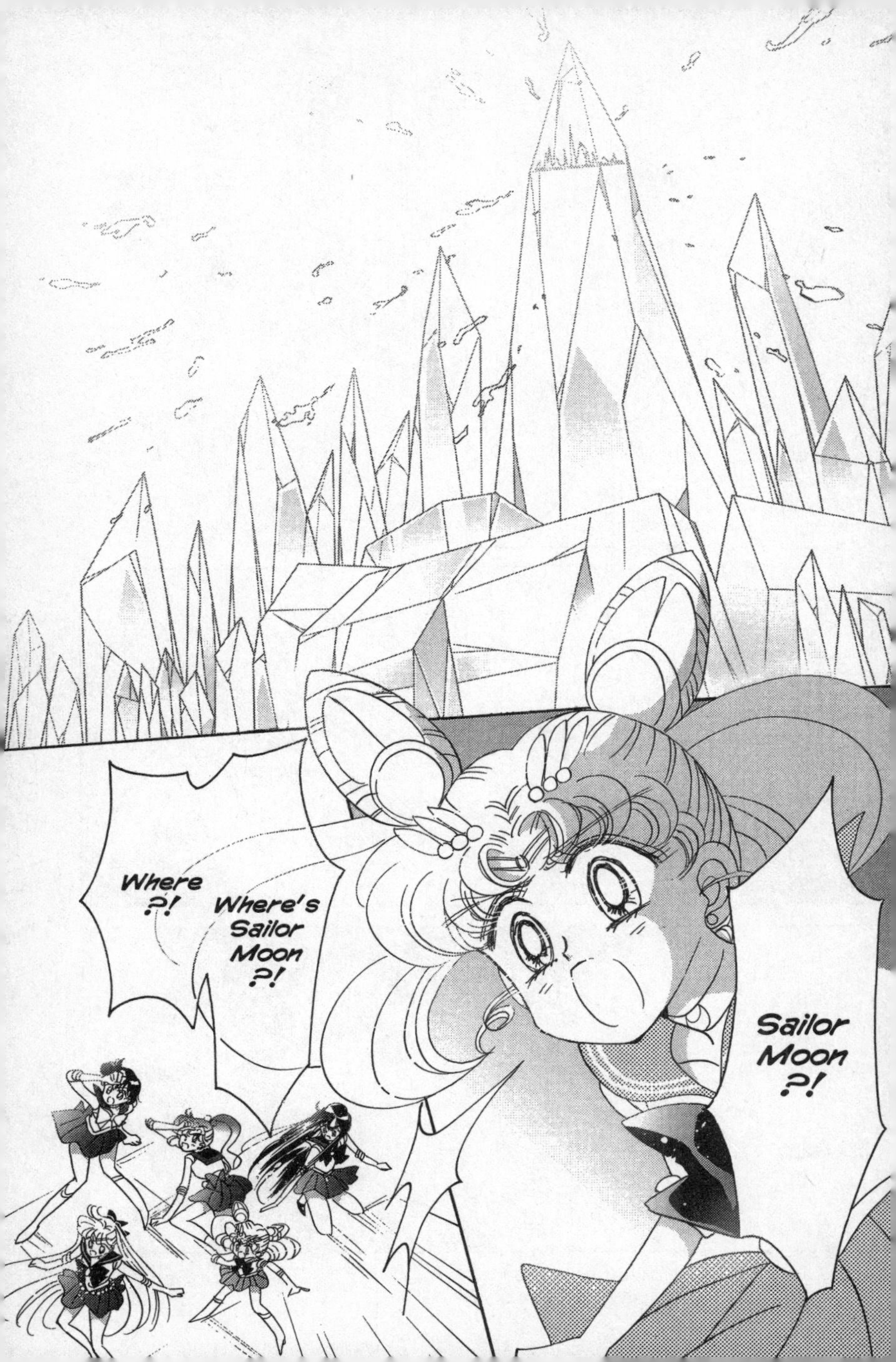
Sailor Moon ?!
Where ?!
Where's Sailor Moon ?!

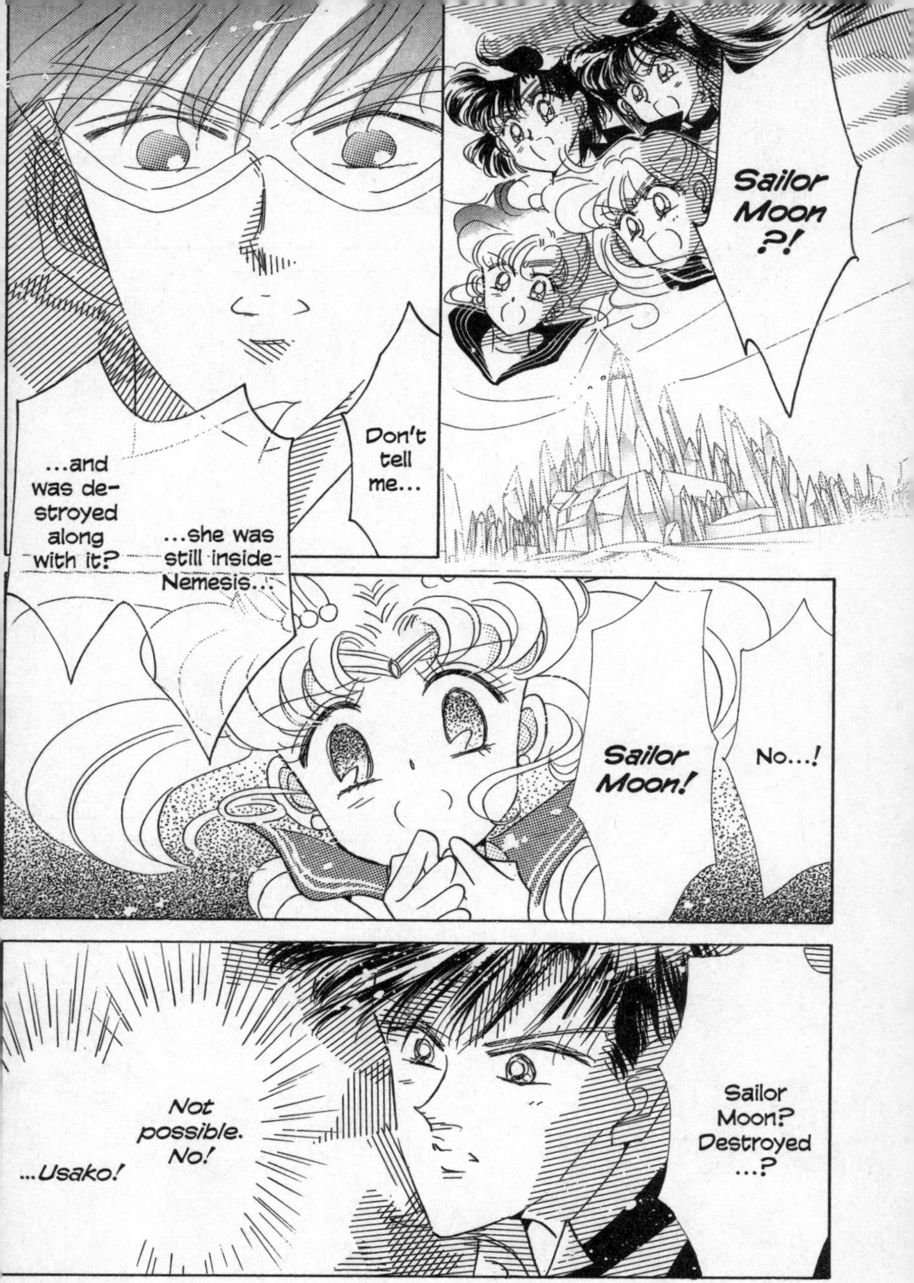
Sailor Moon ?!
Don't tell me...
...she was still inside Nemesis...
...and was de-stroyed along with it?
No...!
Sailor Moon!
Sailor Moon? Destroyed ...?
Not possible. No!
...Usako!

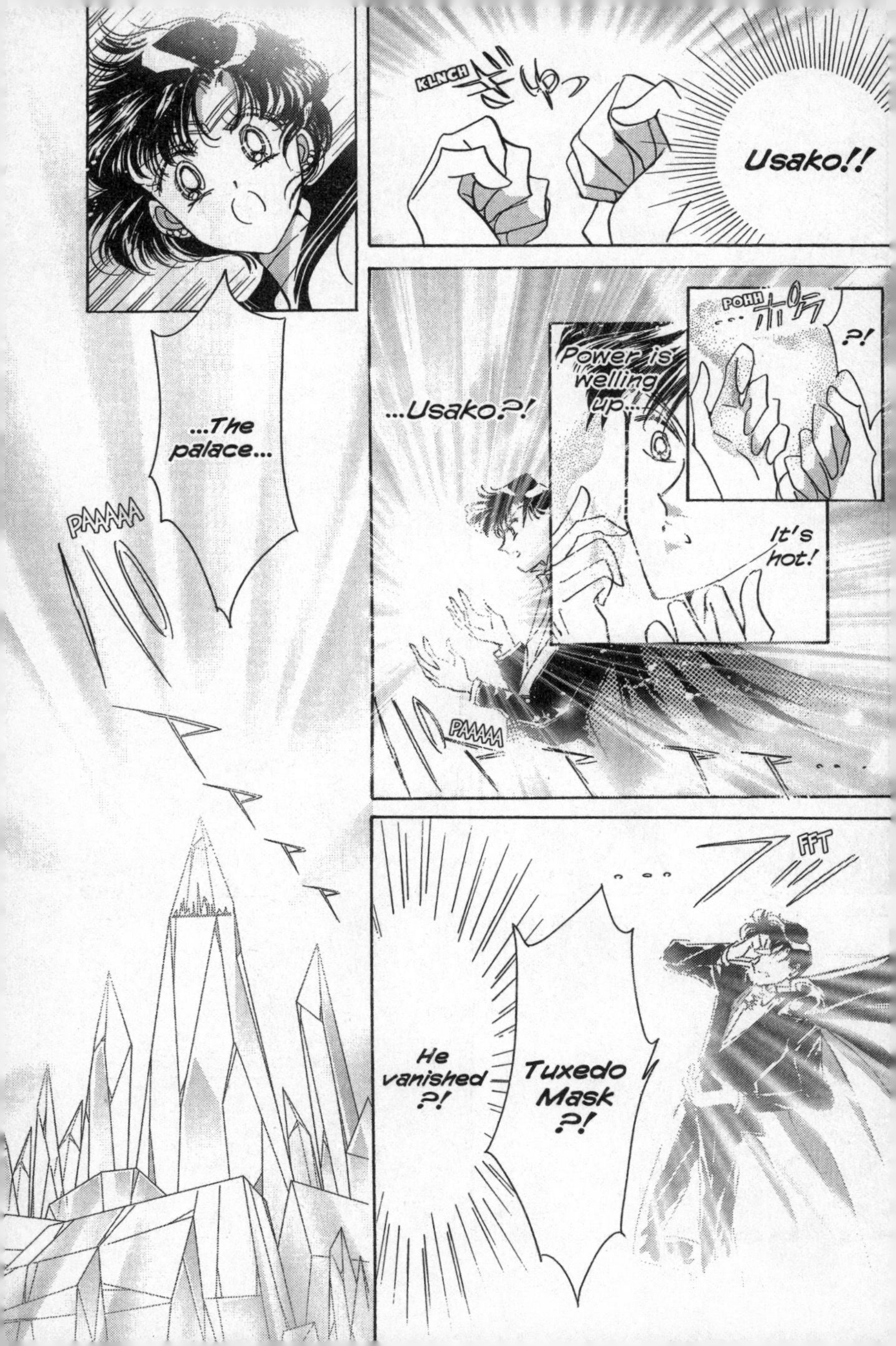
Usako!!
KLNCH
POHH
?!
Power is welling up...
It's hot!
...Usako?!
PAAAA
FFT
Tuxedo Mask ?!
He vanished ?!
...The palace...
PAAAAA

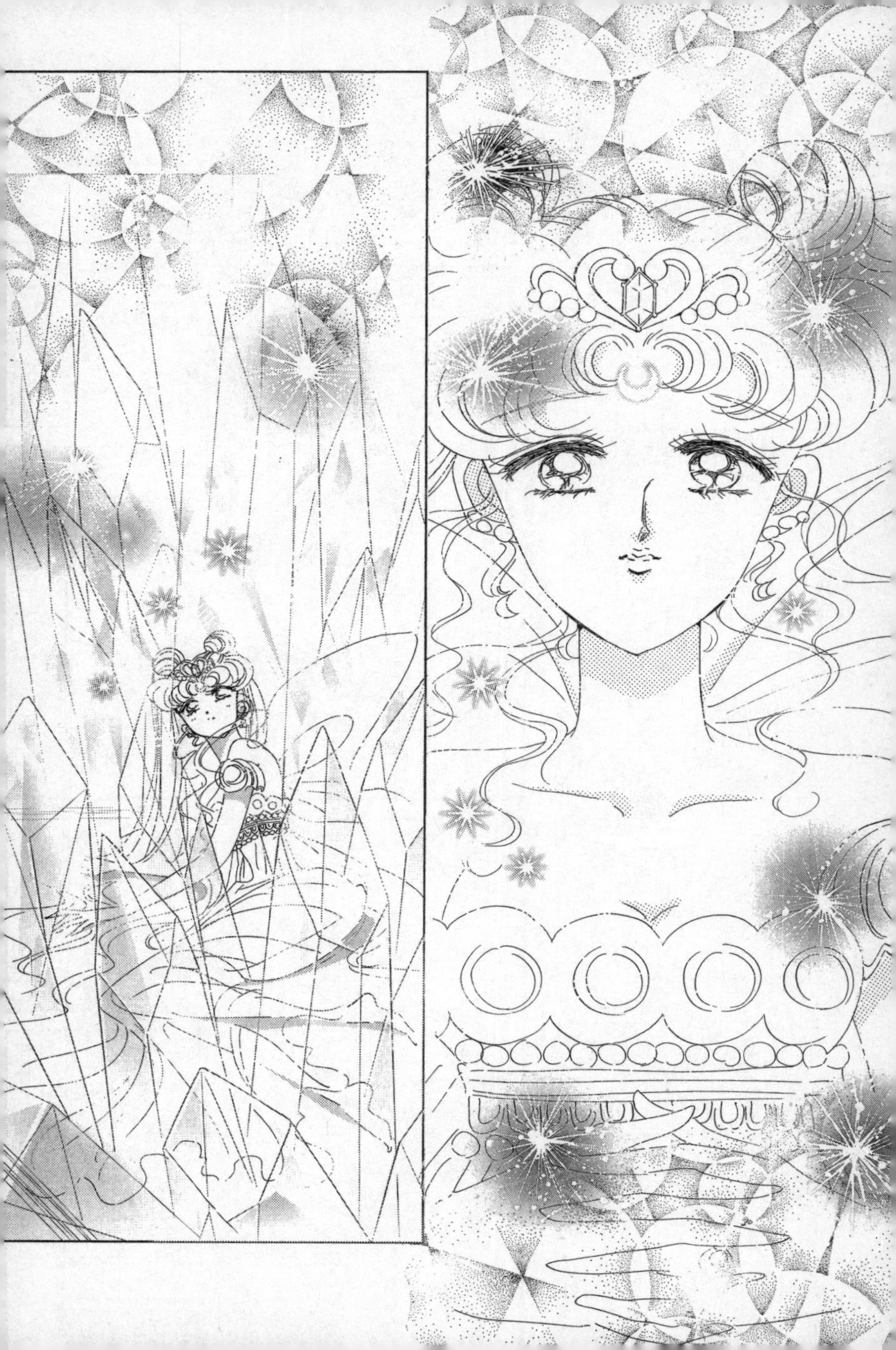

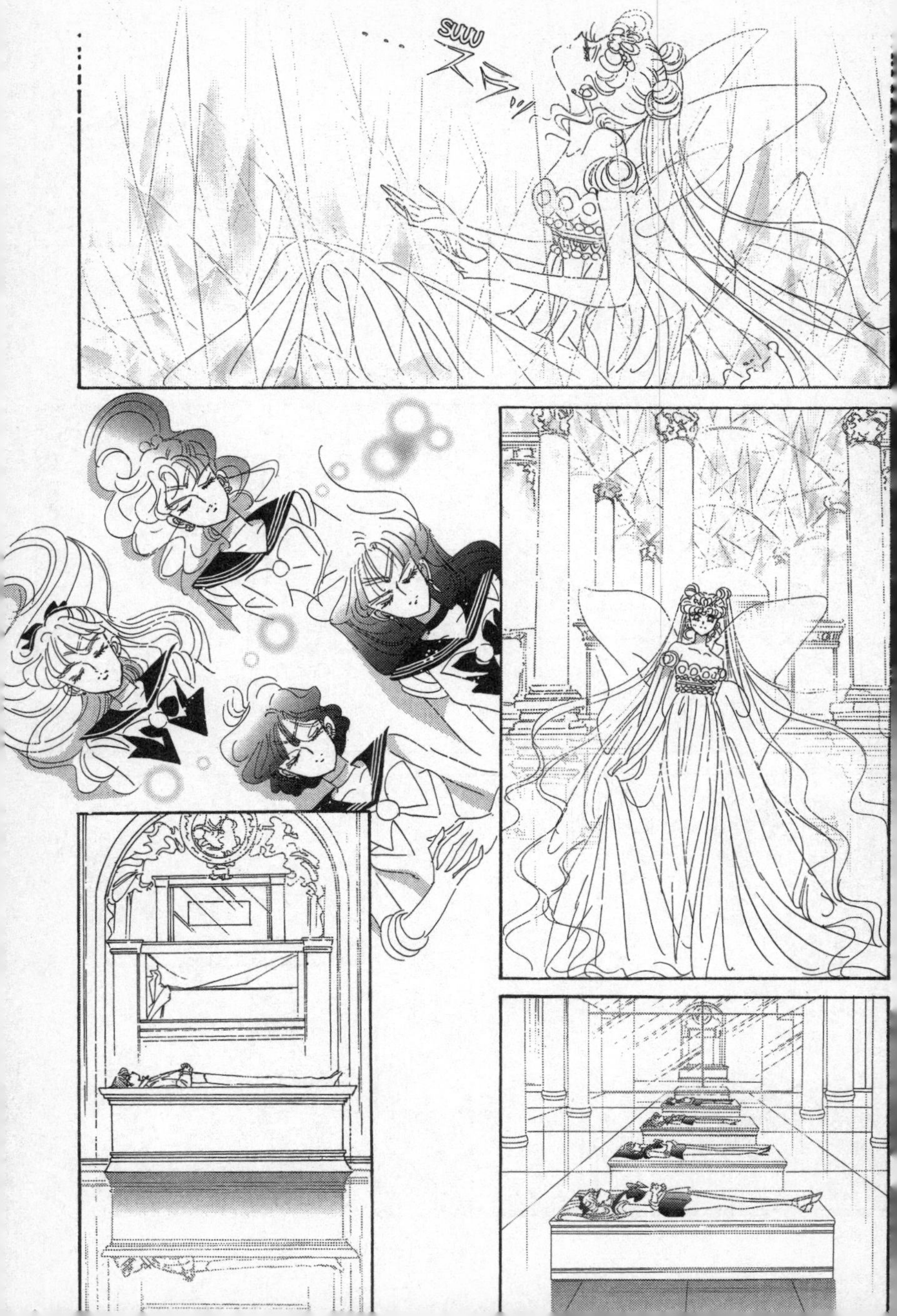

. . .
SUUU
スラッ

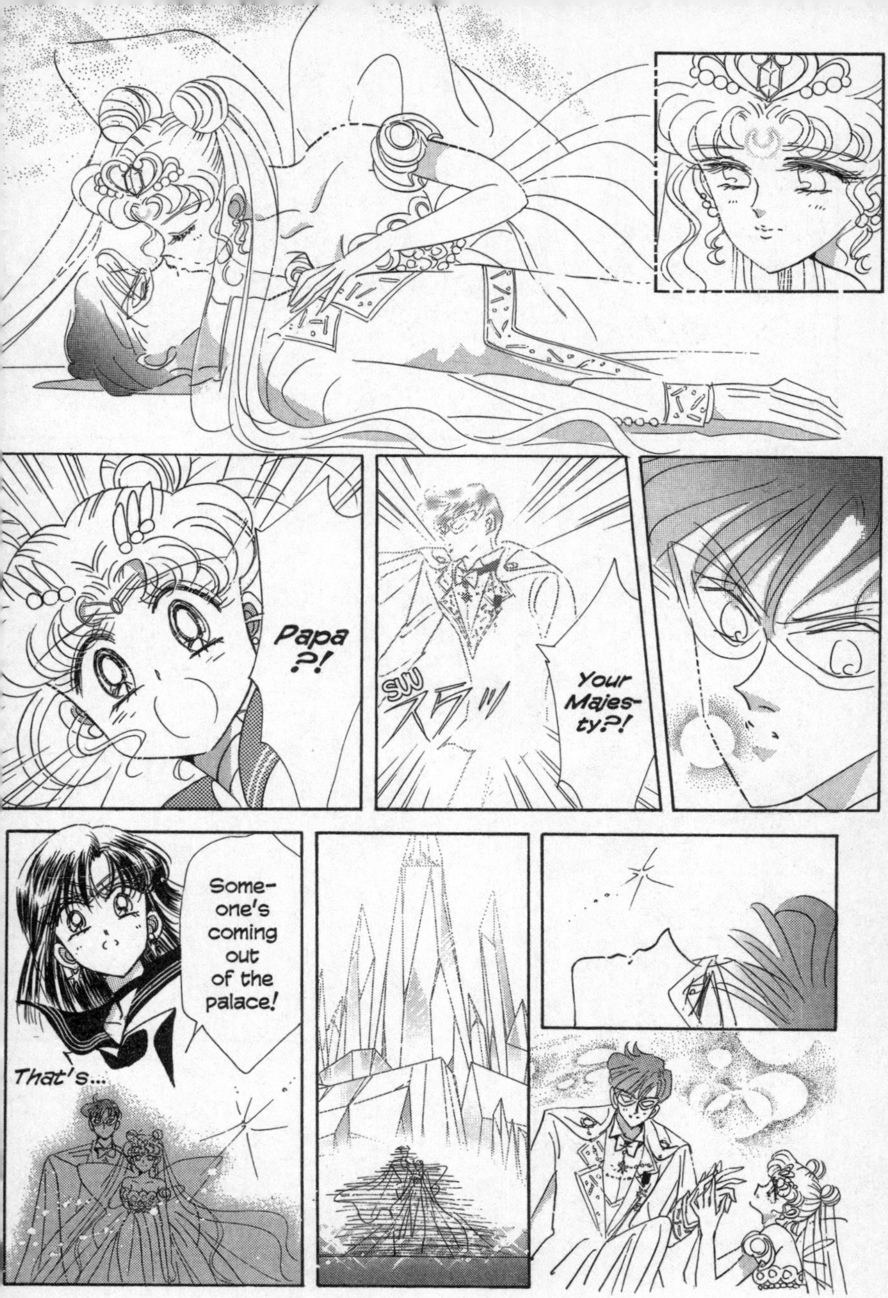

Your Majes-ty?!
SUU
スラッ
Papa ?!
Some-one's coming out of the palace!
That's...

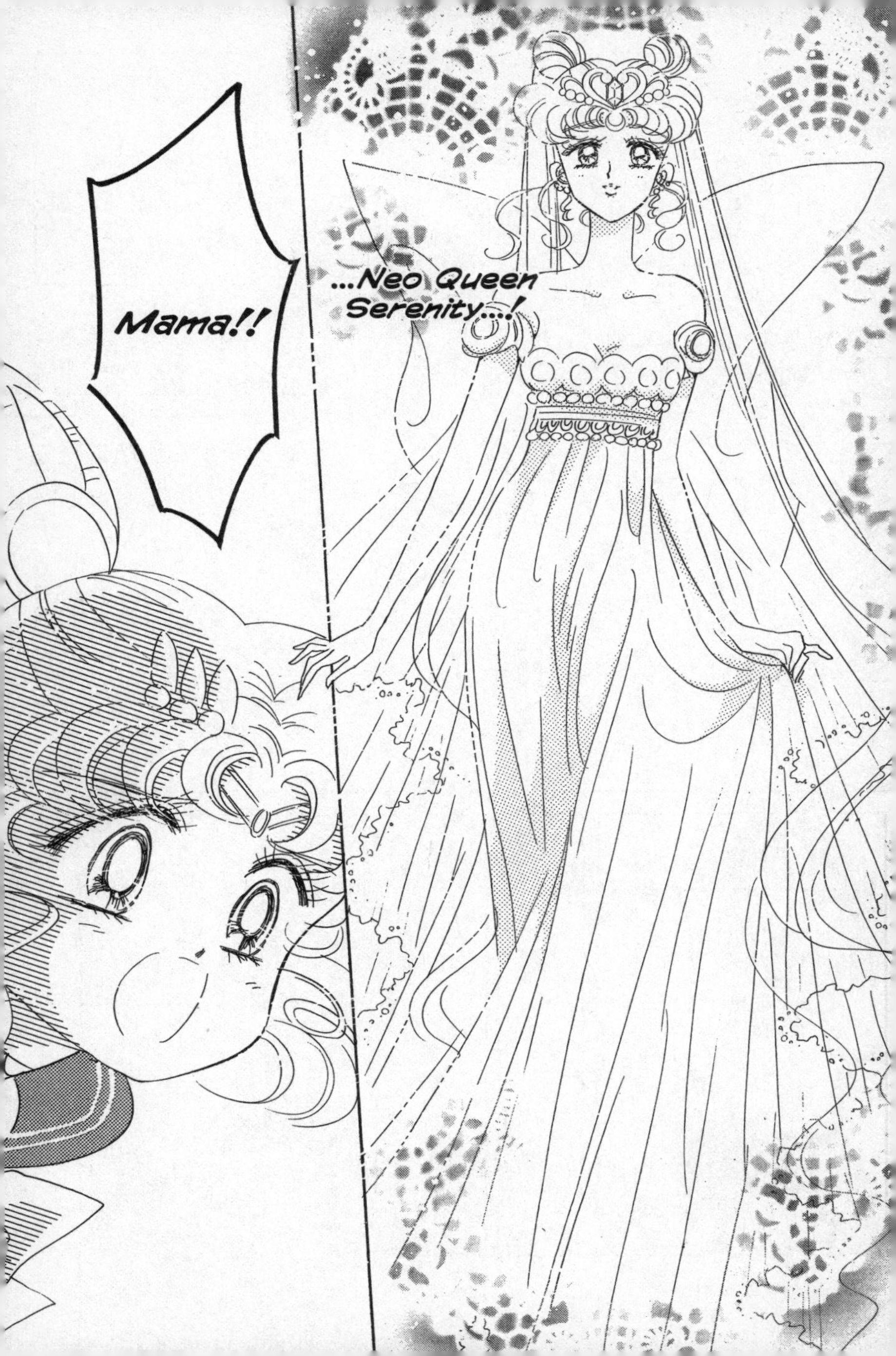
...Neo Queen Serenity...!
Mama!!

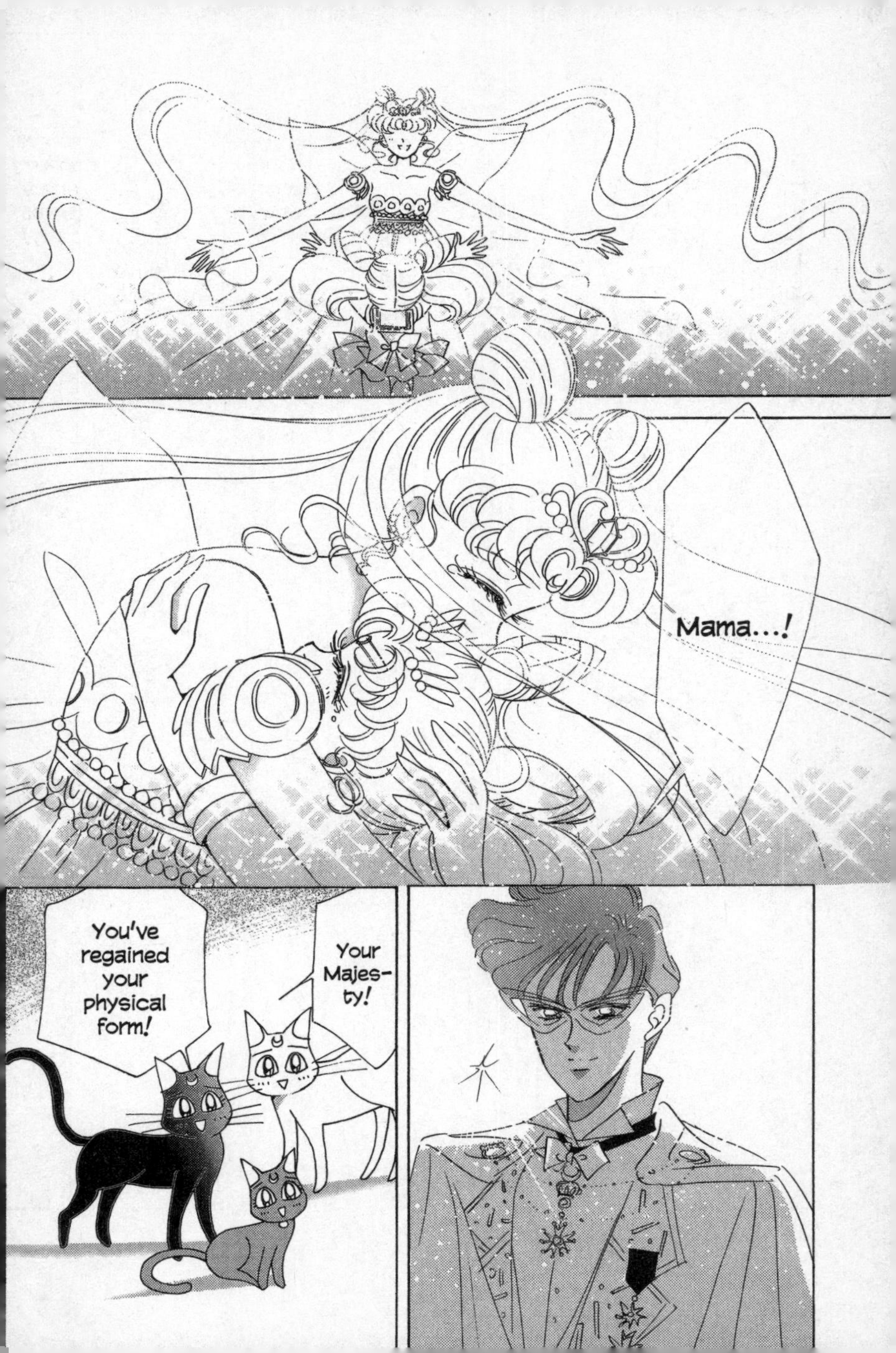
Mama...!
Your Majes-ty!
You've regained your physical form!

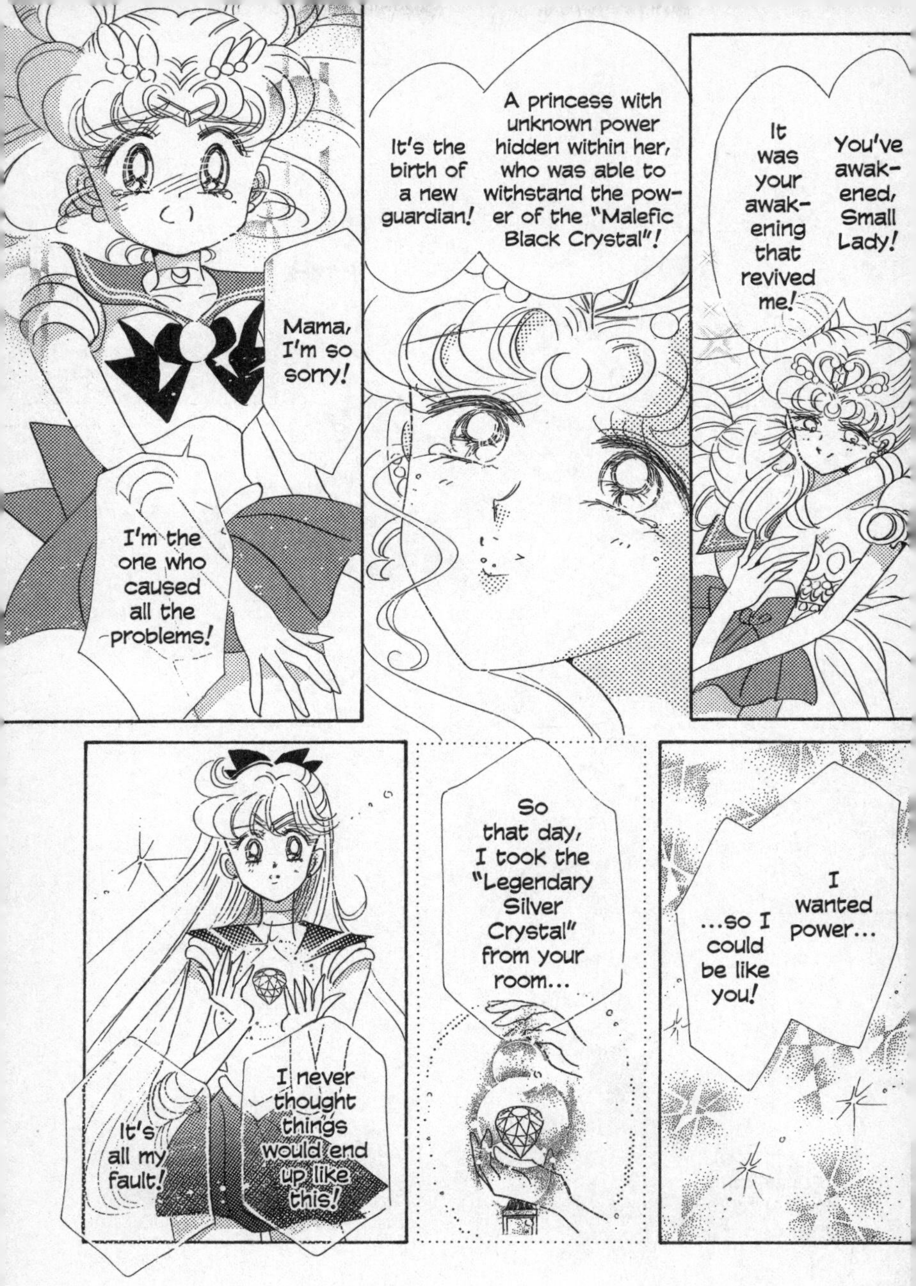
You've awak-ened, Small Lady!
It was your awak-ening that revived me!
A princess with unknown power hidden within her, who was able to withstand the pow-er of the "Malefic Black Crystal"!
It's the birth of a new guardian!
Mama, I'm so sorry!
I'm the one who caused all the problems!
I wanted power...
...so I could be like you!
So that day, I took the "Legendary Silver Crystal" from your room...
I never thought things would end up like this!
It's all my fault!

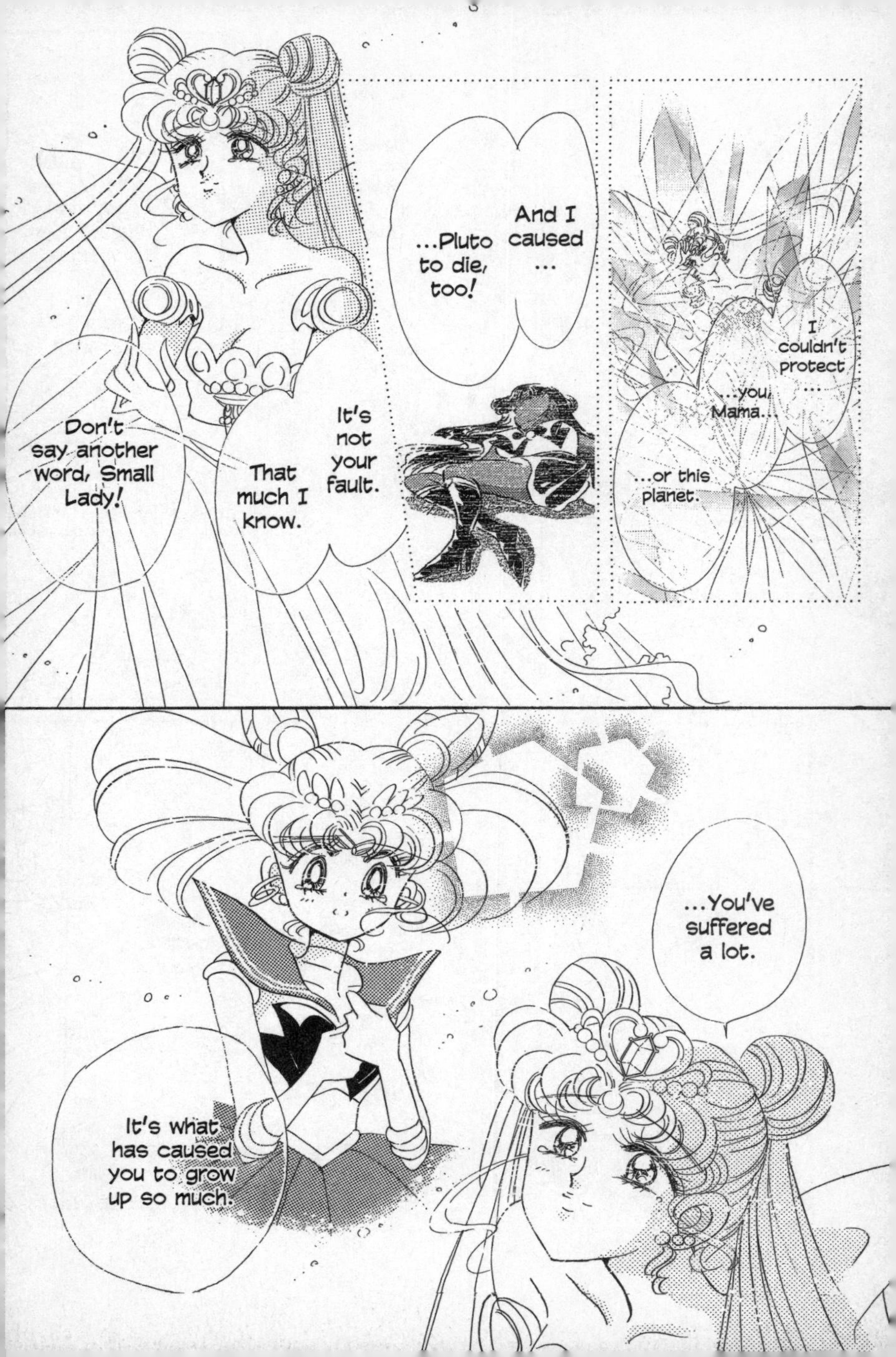
I couldn't protect ...
...you, Mama...
...or this planet.
And I caused ...
...Pluto to die, too!
It's not your fault.
That much I know.
Don't say another word, Small Lady!
...You've suffered a lot.
It's what has caused you to grow up so much.

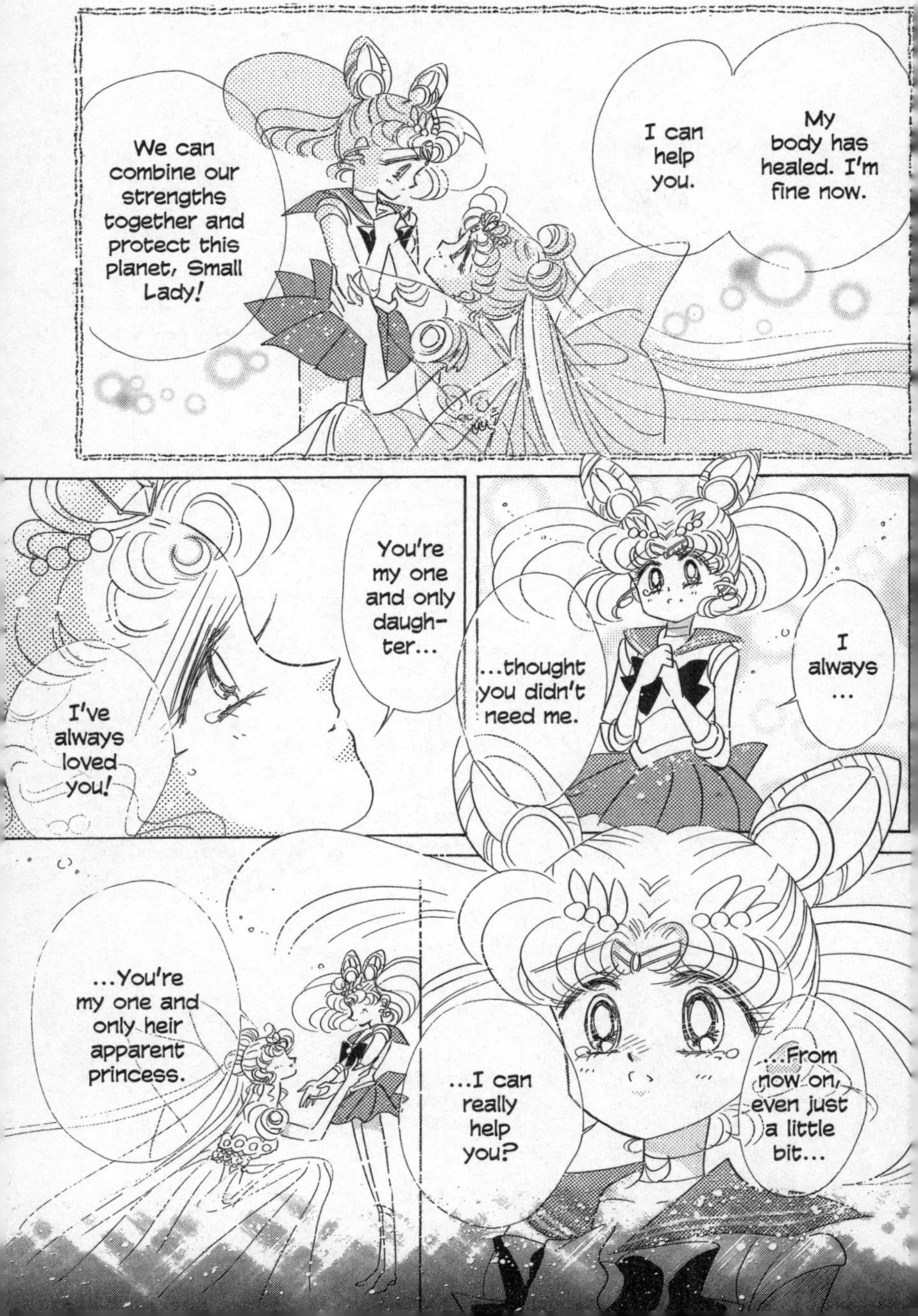
My body has healed. I'm fine now.
I can help you.
We can combine our strengths together and protect this planet, Small Lady!
I always...
...thought you didn't need me.
You're my one and only daughter...
I've always loved you!
...From now on, even just a little bit...
...I can really help you?
...You're my one and only heir apparent princess.

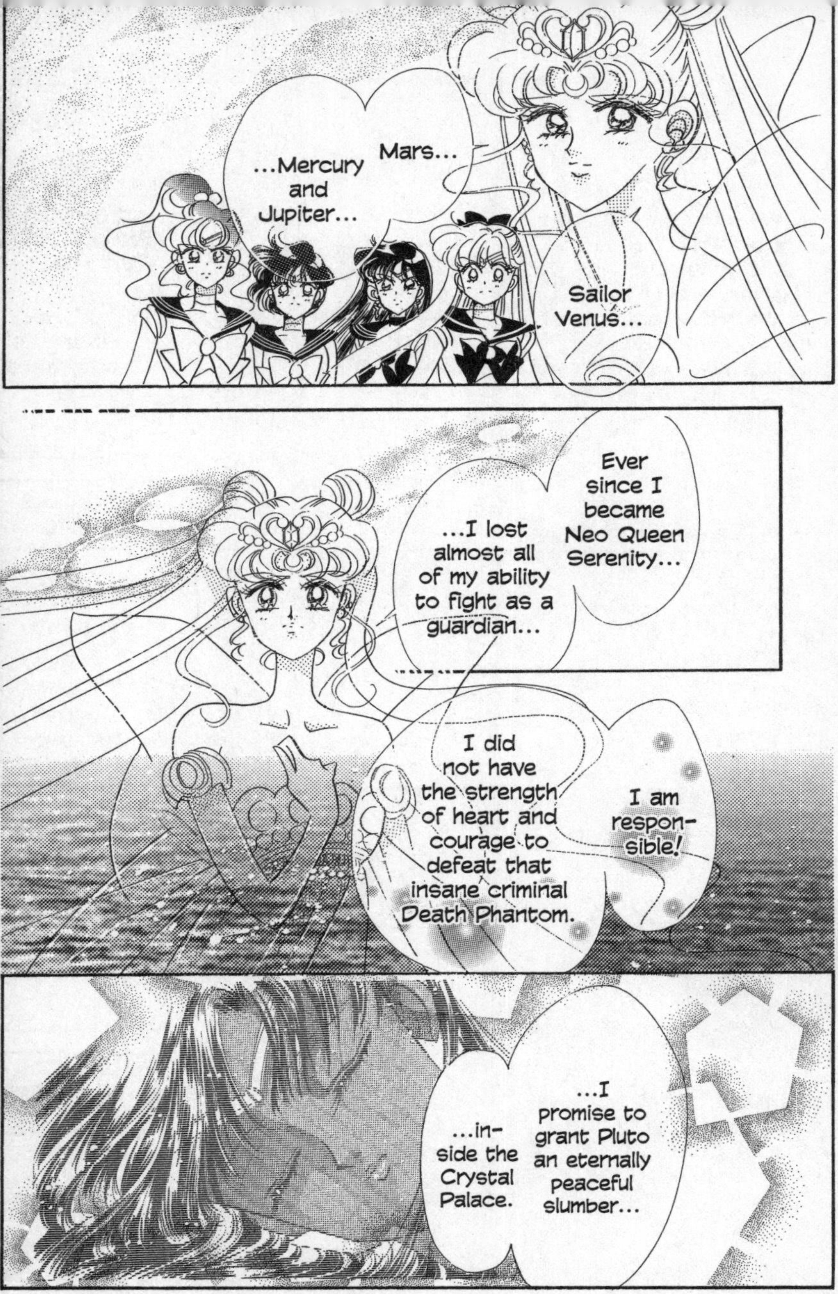
Sailor Venus...
Mars...
...Mercury and Jupiter...
Ever since I became Neo Queen Serenity...
...I lost almost all of my ability to fight as a guardian...
I am respon-sible!
I did not have the strength of heart and courage to defeat that insane criminal Death Phantom.
...I promise to grant Pluto an eternally peaceful slumber...
...in-side the Crystal Palace.

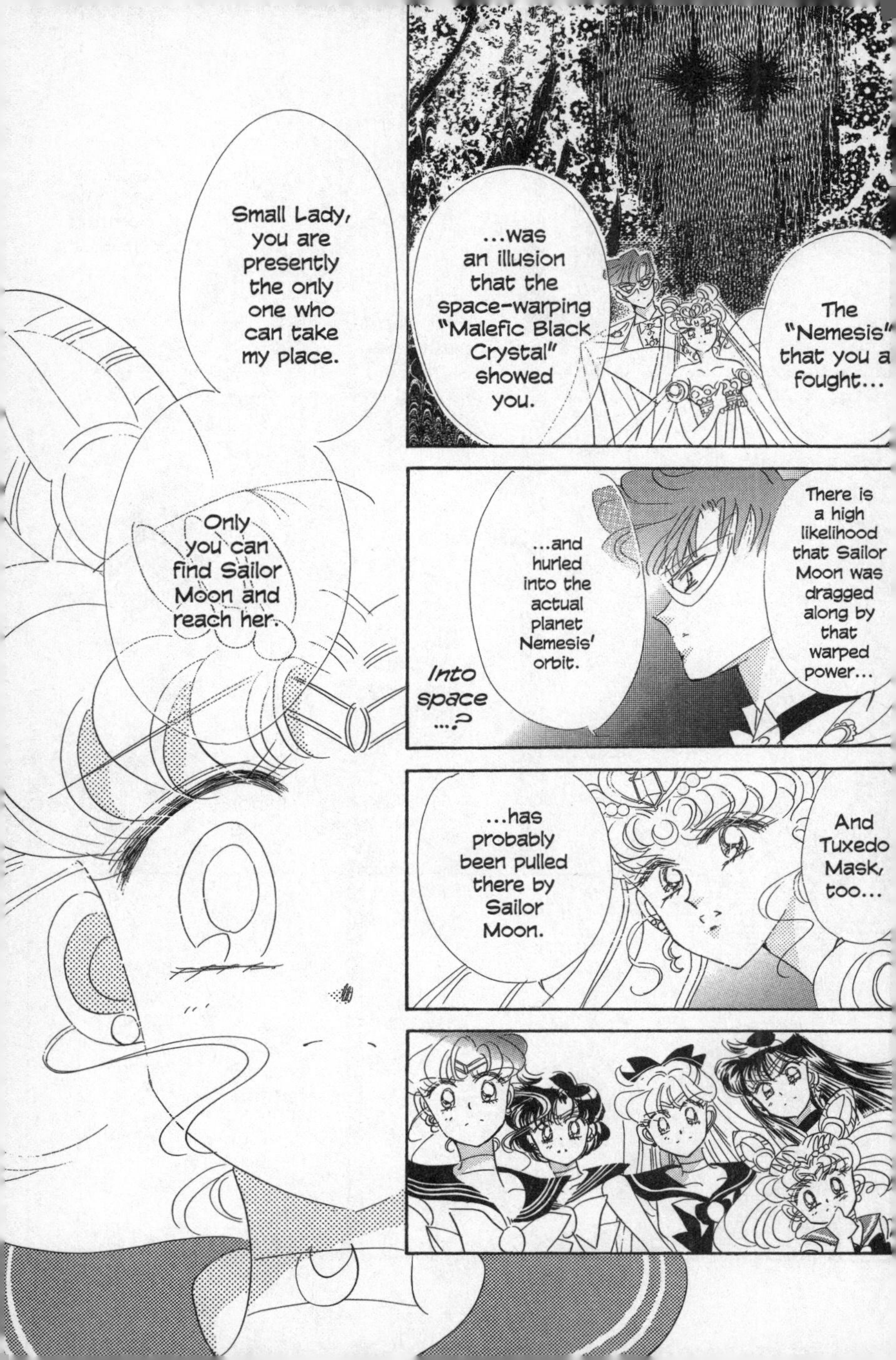
The "Nemesis" that you a fought...
...was an illusion that the space-warping "Malefic Black Crystal" showed you.
There is a high likelihood that Sailor Moon was dragged along by that warped power...
...and hurled into the actual planet Nemesis' orbit.
Into space ...?
And Tuxedo Mask, too...
...has probably been pulled there by Sailor Moon.
Small Lady, you are presently the only one who can take my place.
Only you can find Sailor Moon and reach her.

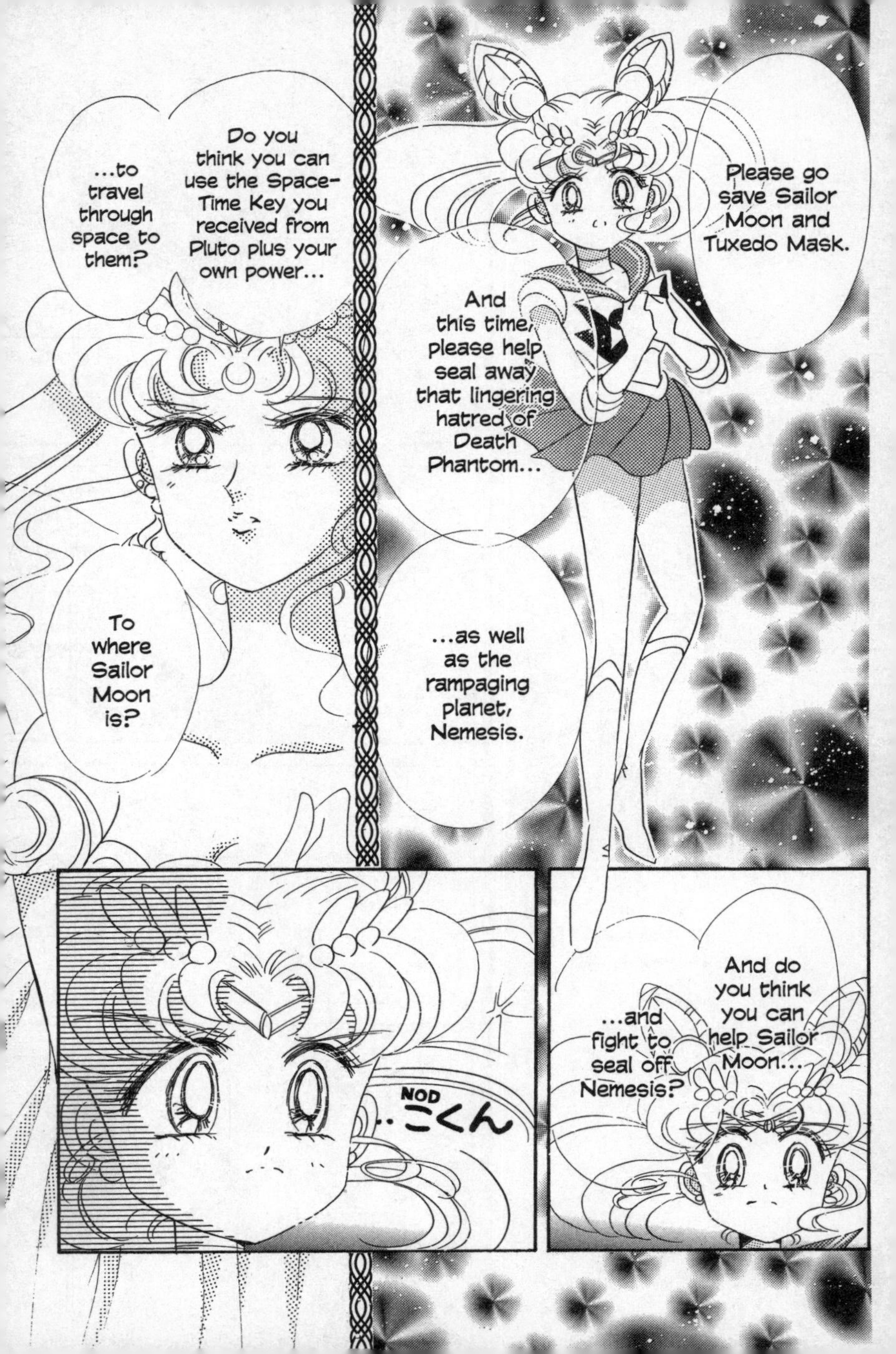
Please go save Sailor Moon and Tuxedo Mask.
And this time, please help seal away that lingering hatred of Death Phantom...
...as well as the rampaging planet, Nemesis.
Do you think you can use the Space-Time Key you received from Pluto plus your own power...
...to travel through space to them?
To where Sailor Moon is?
And do you think you can help Sailor Moon...
...and fight to seal off Nemesis?
NOD
...こくん

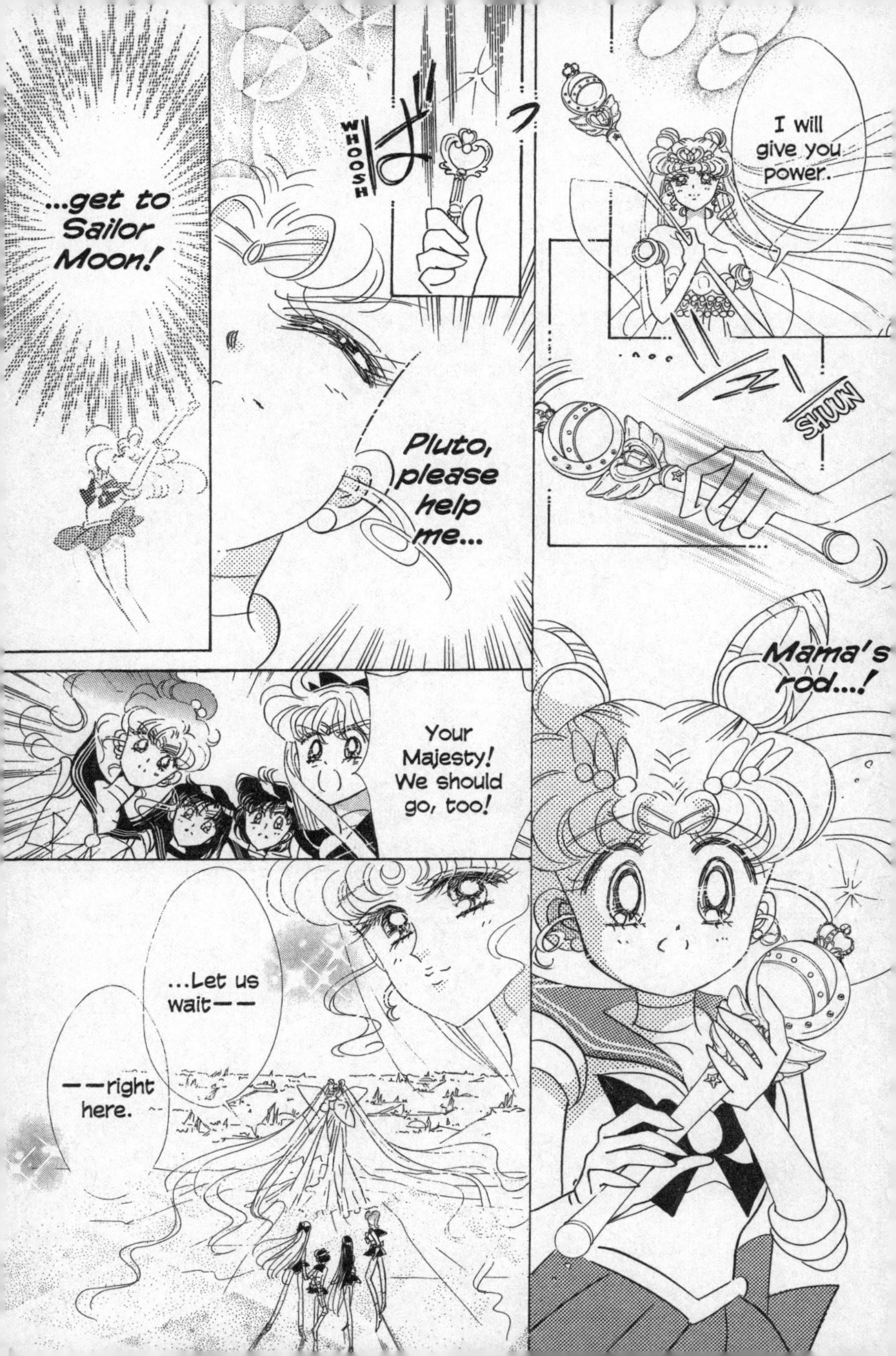

I will give you power.
SHUUN
Mama's rod...!
WHOOSH
Pluto, please help me...
...get to Sailor Moon!
Your Majesty! We should go, too!
...Let us wait——
——right here.

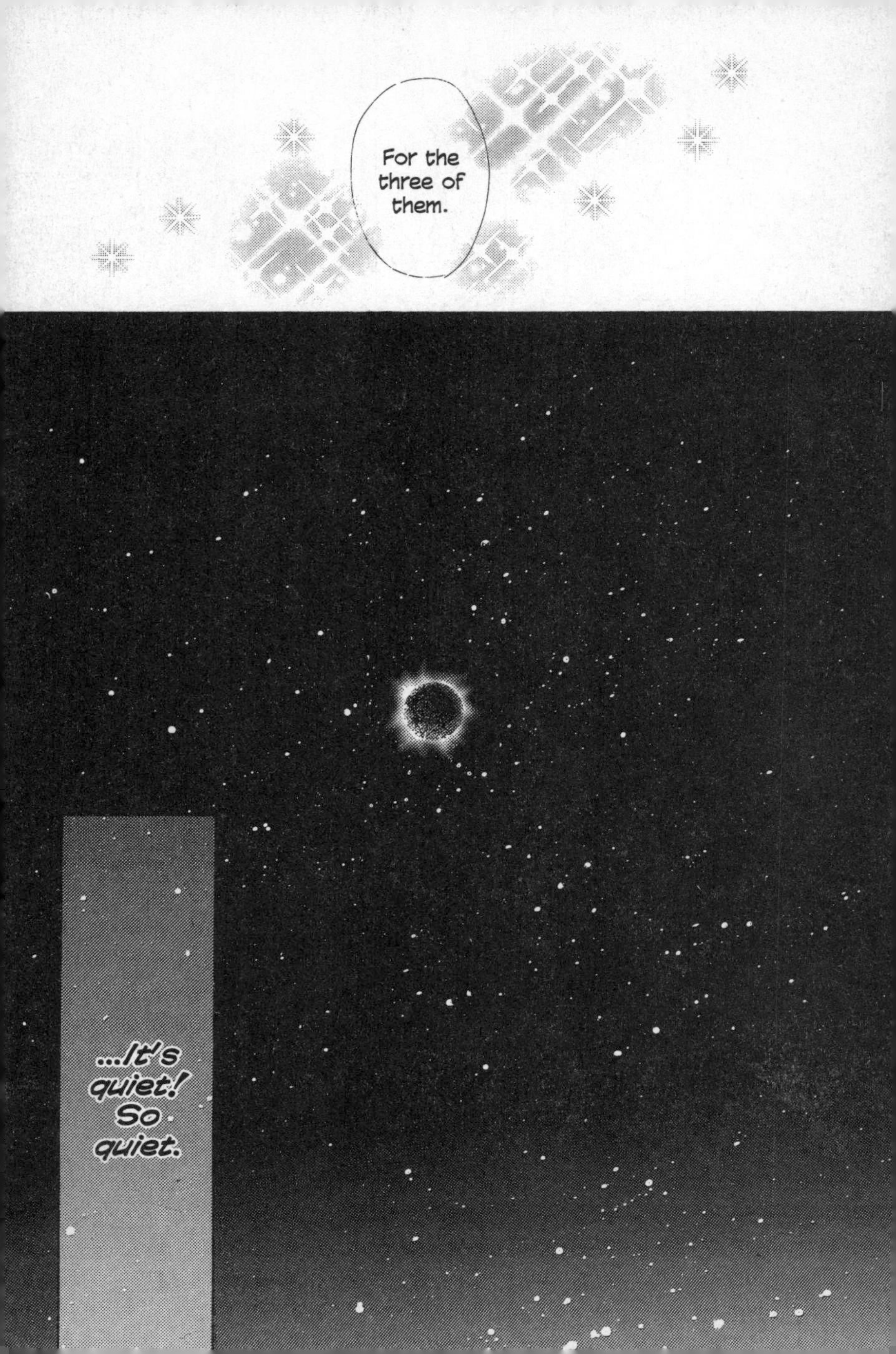
For the three of them.
...It's quiet! So quiet.

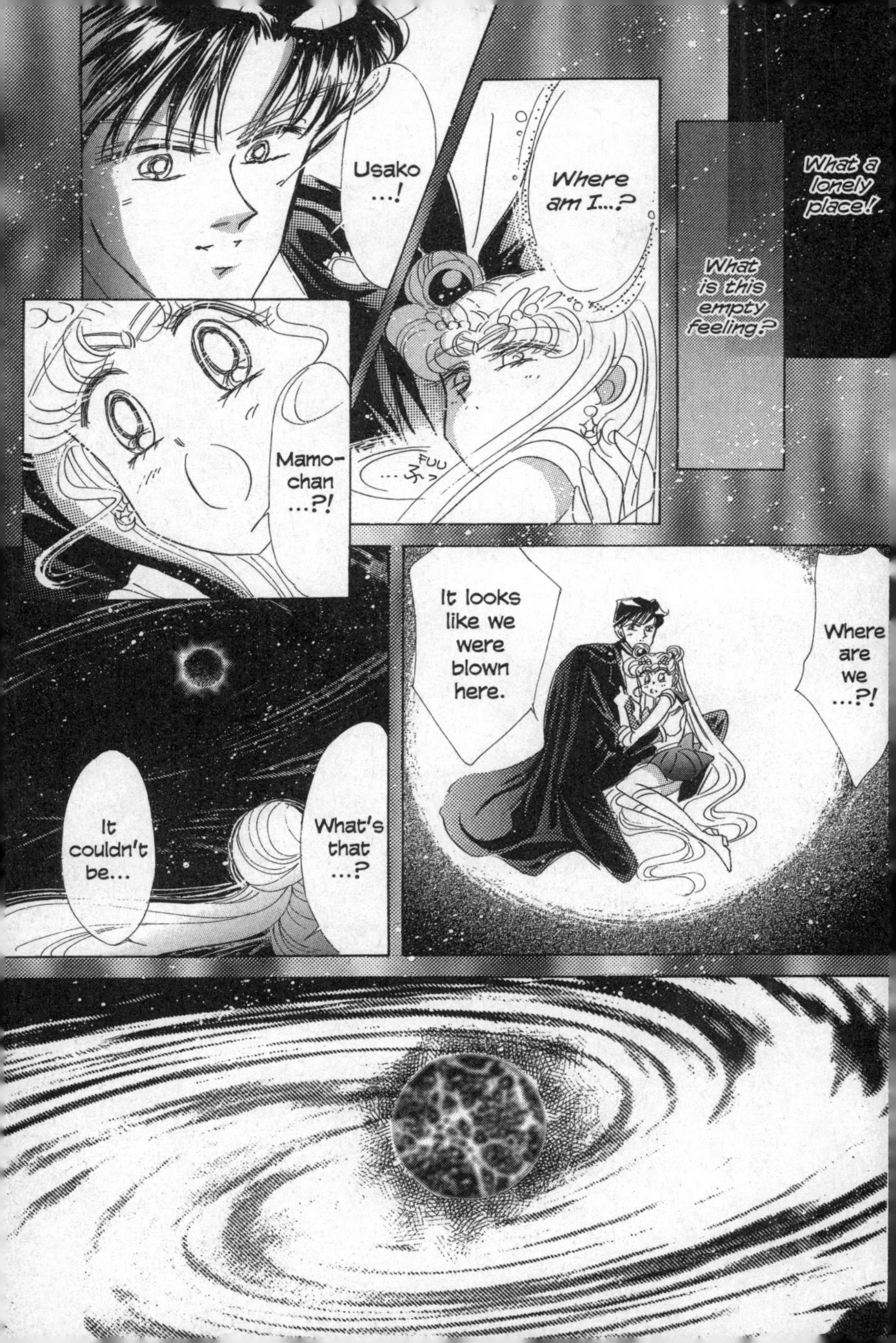
What a lonely place!
What is this empty feeling?
Where am I...?
FUU
Usako ...!
Mamo-chan ...?!
Where are we ...?!
It looks like we were blown here.
What's that ...?
It couldn't be...

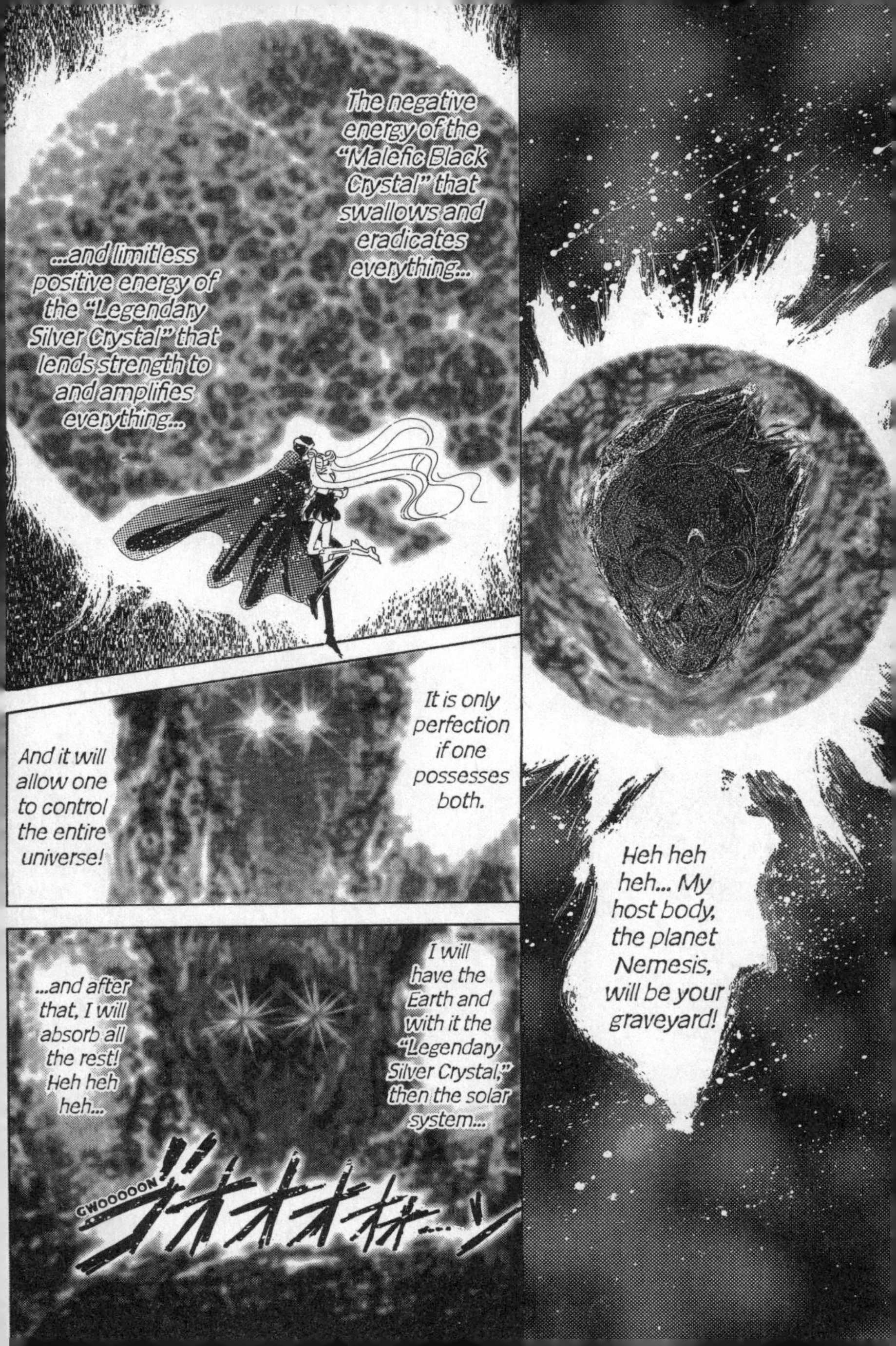
Heh heh heh... My host body, the planet Nemesis, will be your graveyard!
The negative energy of the "Malefic Black Crystal" that swallows and eradicates everything...
...and limitless positive energy of the "Legendary Silver Crystal" that lends strength to and amplifies everything...
It is only perfection if one possesses both.
And it will allow one to control the entire universe!
I will have the Earth and with it the "Legendary Silver Crystal," then the solar system...
...and after that, I will absorb all the rest! Heh heh heh...
GWOOOOON

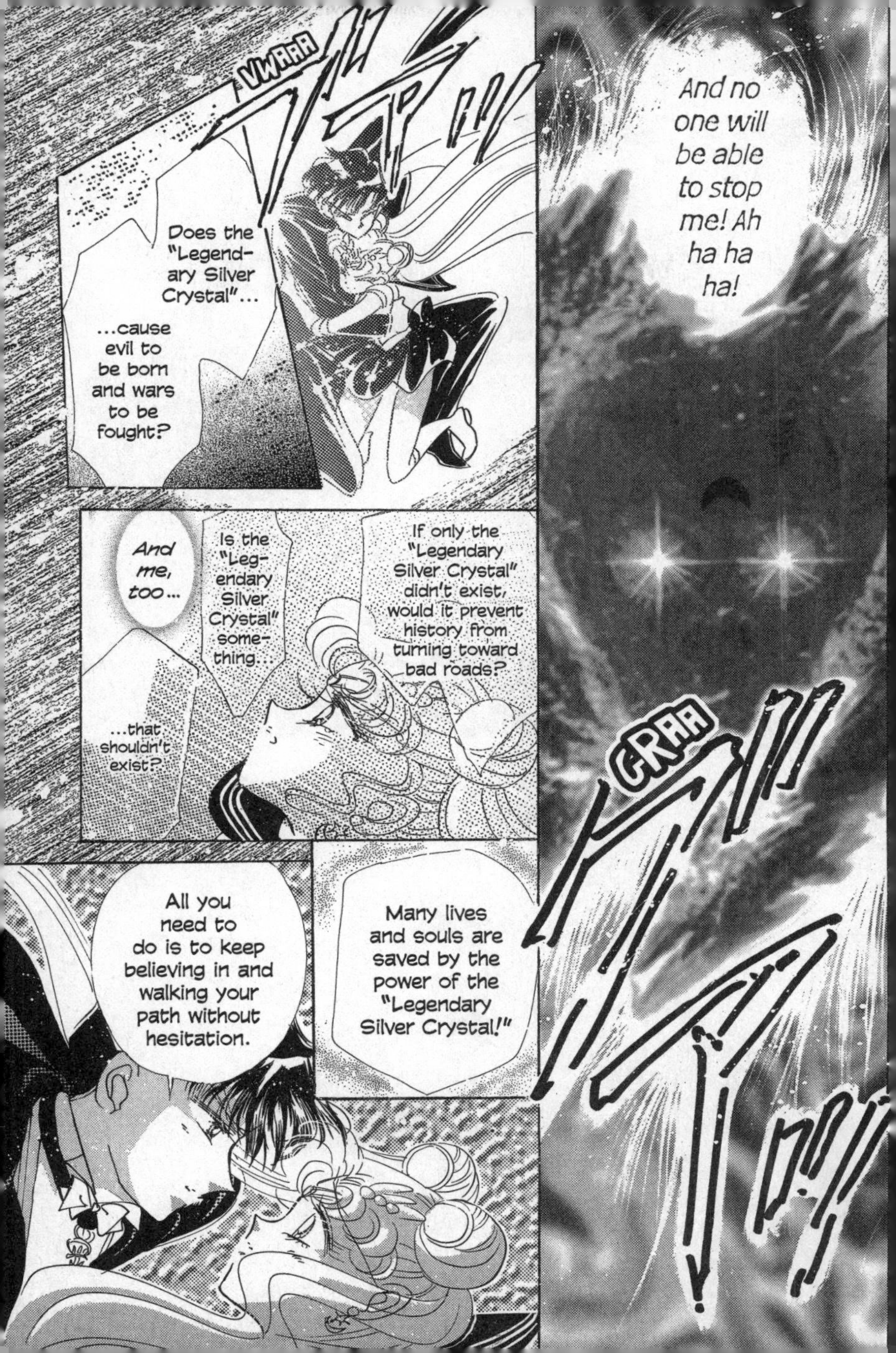

And no one will be able to stop me! Ah ha ha ha!
CRAA
VWAAA
Does the "Legendary Silver Crystal"...
...cause evil to be born and wars to be fought?
If only the "Legendary Silver Crystal" didn't exist, would it prevent history from turning toward bad roads?
Is the "Legendary Silver Crystal" something...
...that shouldn't exist?
And me, too...
Many lives and souls are saved by the power of the "Legendary Silver Crystal!"
All you need to do is to keep believing in and walking your path without hesitation.

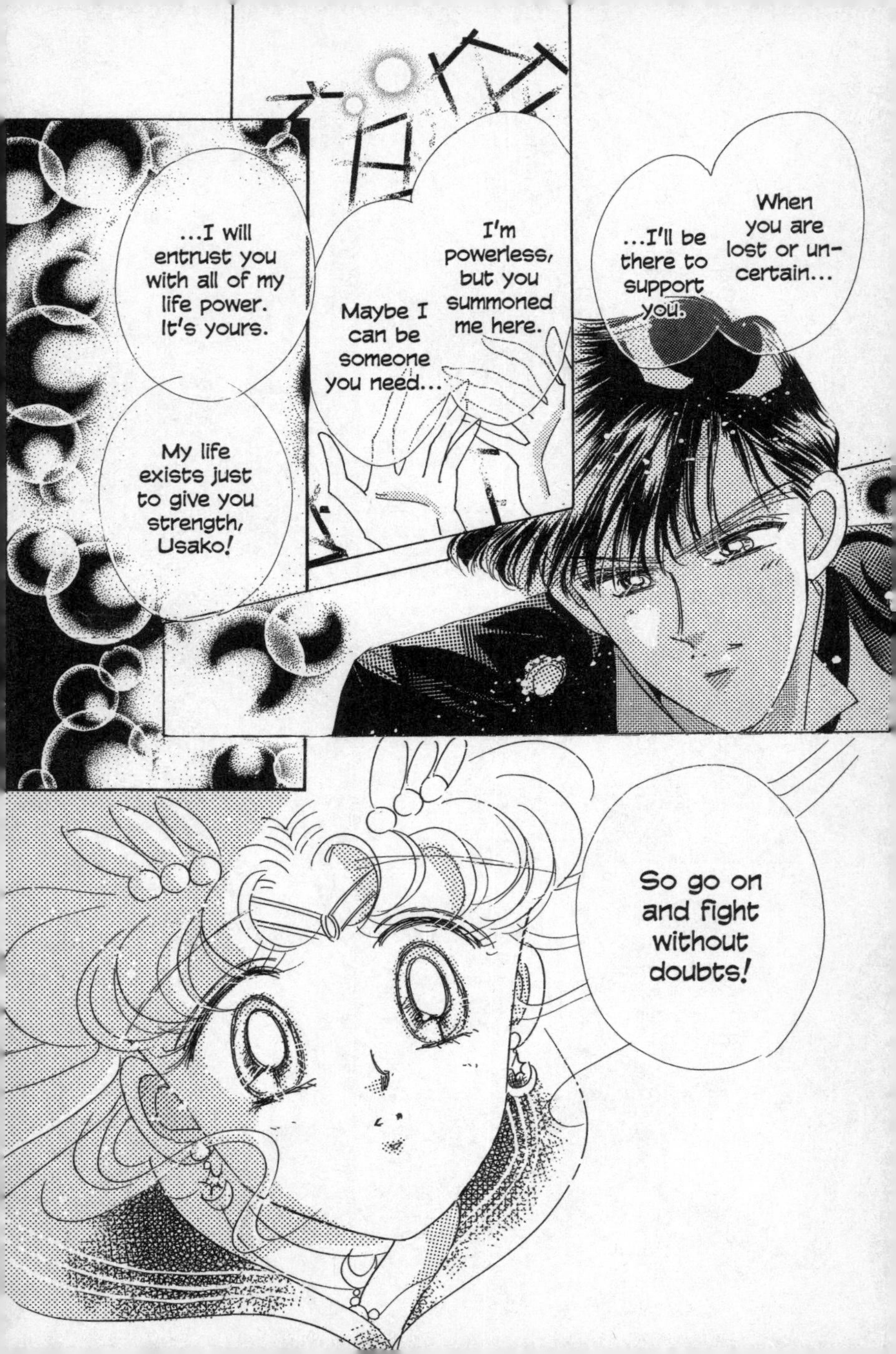
When you are lost or uncertain...
...I'll be there to support you.
I'm powerless, but you summoned me here.
Maybe I can be someone you need...
...I will entrust you with all of my life power. It's yours.
My life exists just to give you strength, Usako!
So go on and fight without doubts!

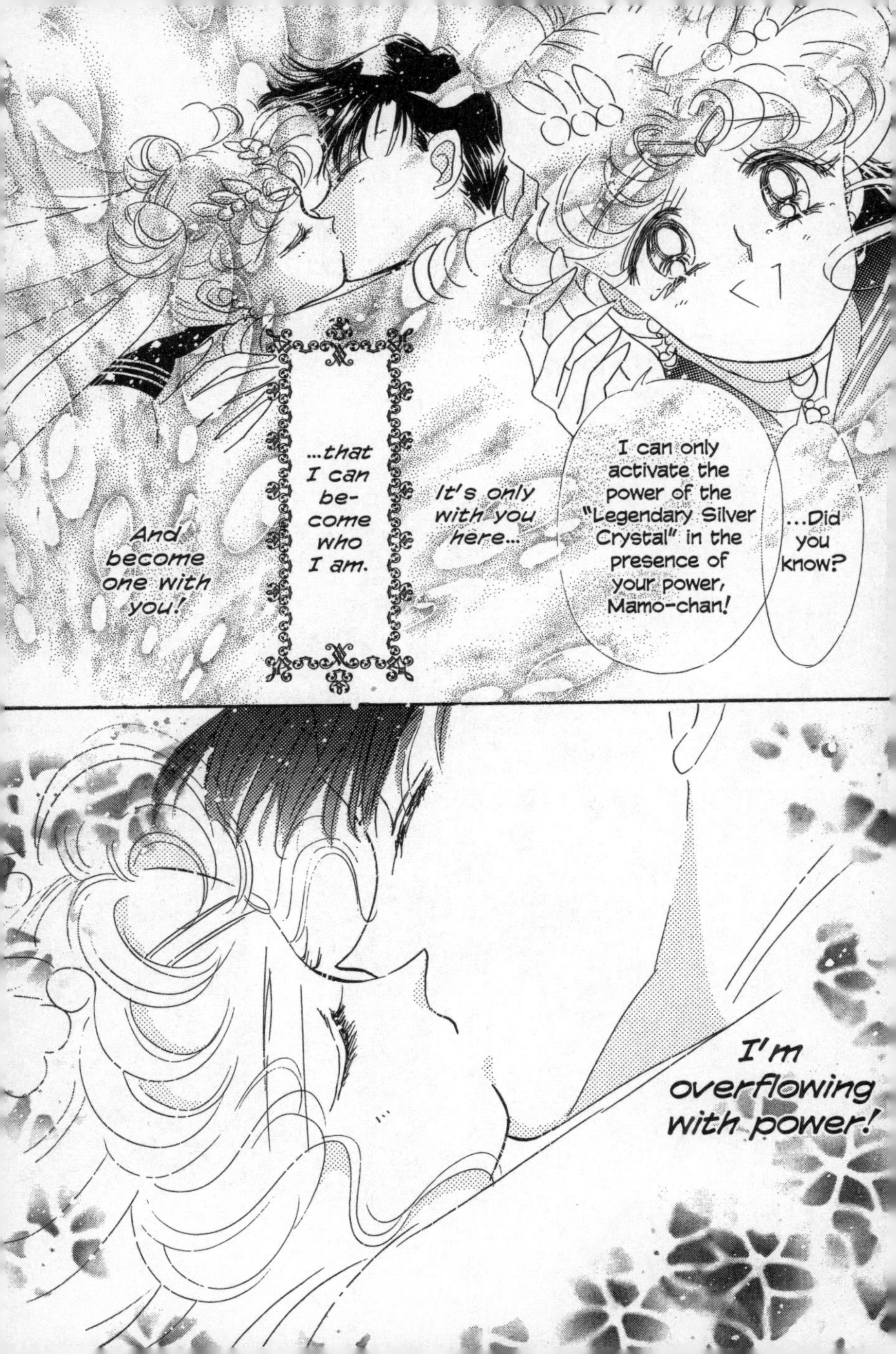
...Did you know?
I can only activate the power of the "Legendary Silver Crystal" in the presence of your power, Mamo-chan!
It's only with you here...
...that I can be-come who I am.
And become one with you!
I'm overflowing with power!

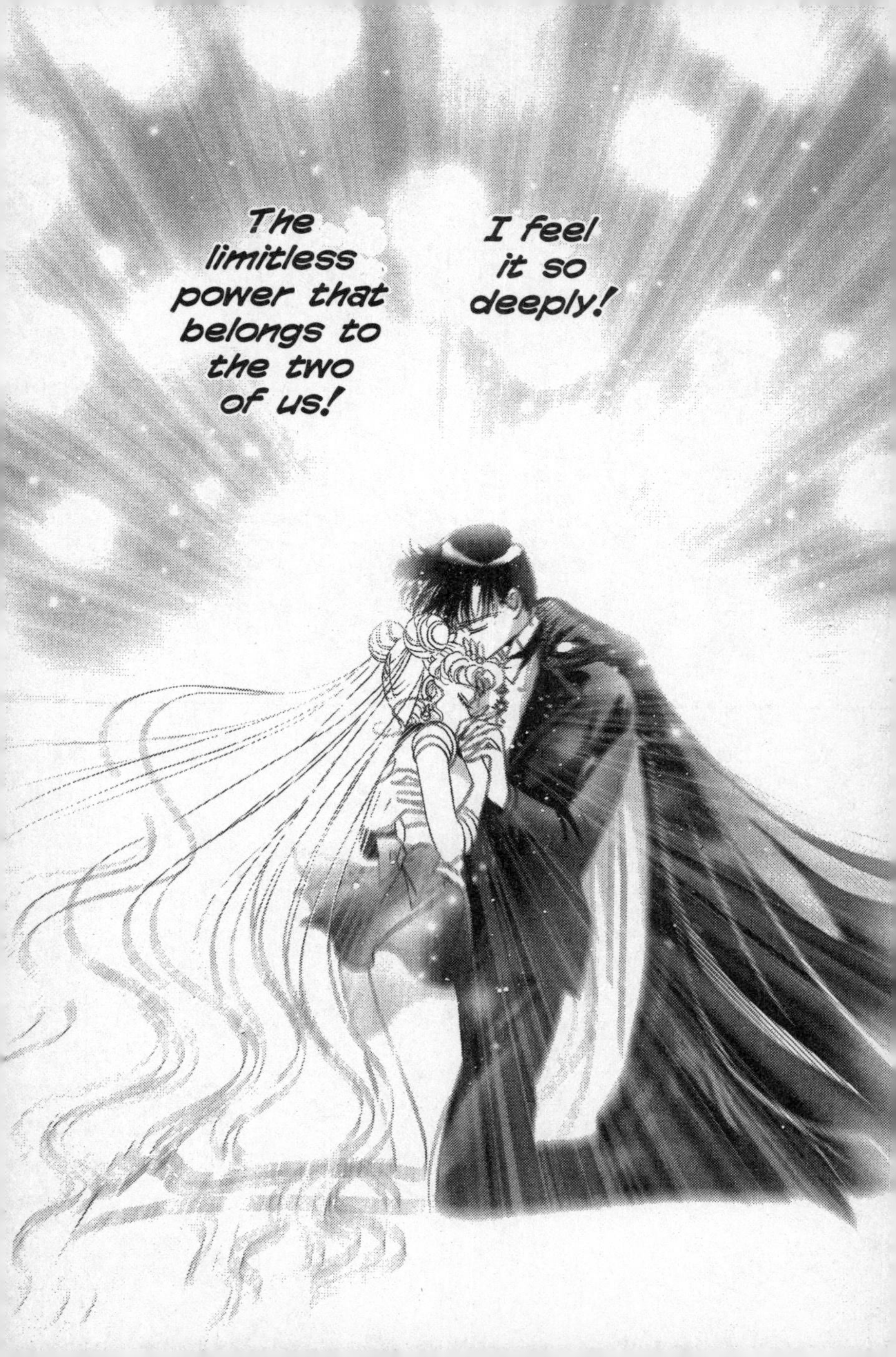
I feel it so deeply!
The limitless power that belongs to the two of us!

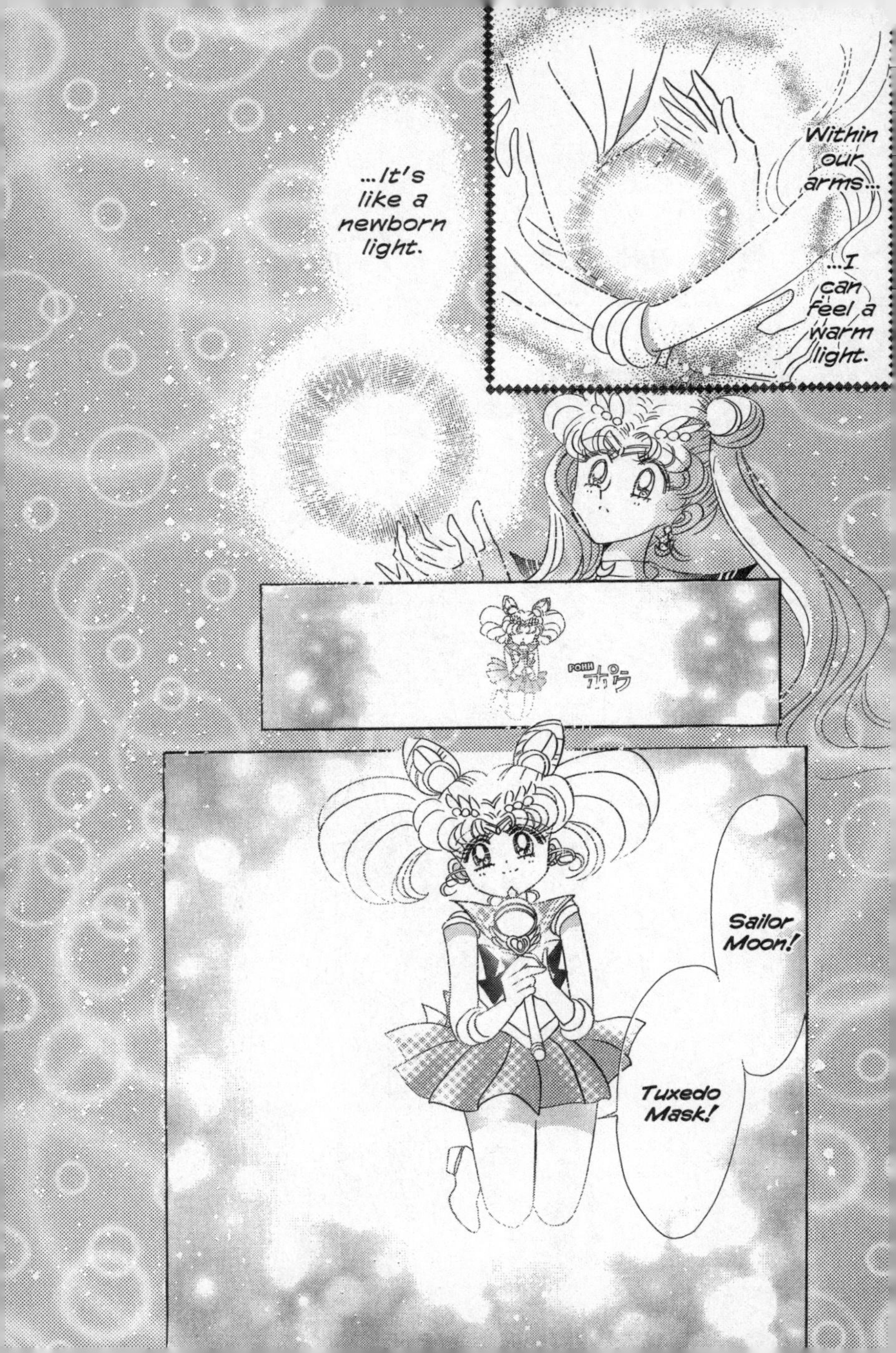
Within our arms...
...I can feel a warm light.
...It's like a newborn light.
POHH
ポウ
Sailor Moon!
Tuxedo Mask!

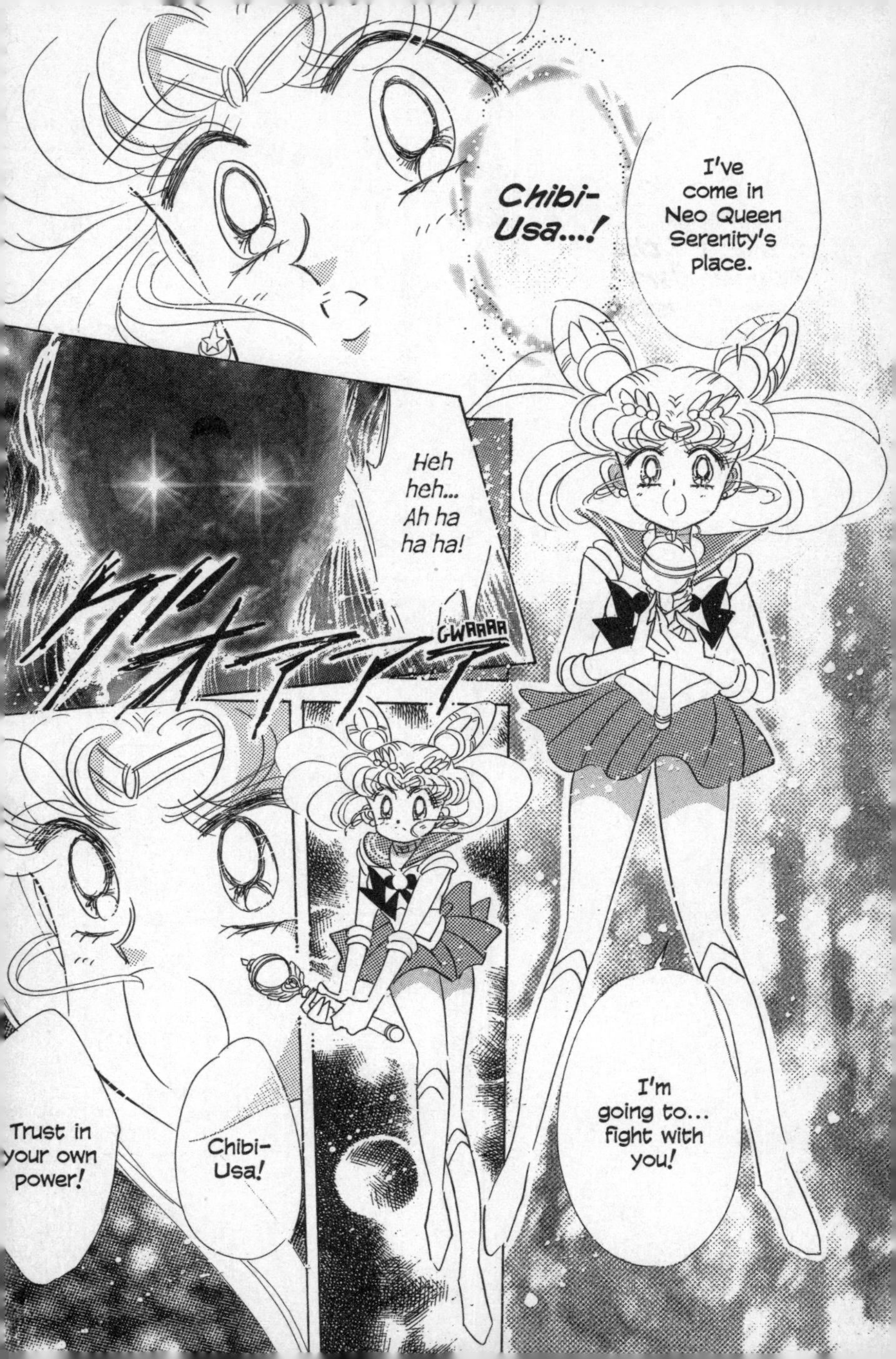
I've come in Neo Queen Serenity's place.
Chibi-Usa...!
Heh heh... Ah ha ha ha!
GWAAAA
I'm going to... fight with you!
Chibi-Usa!
Trust in your own power!

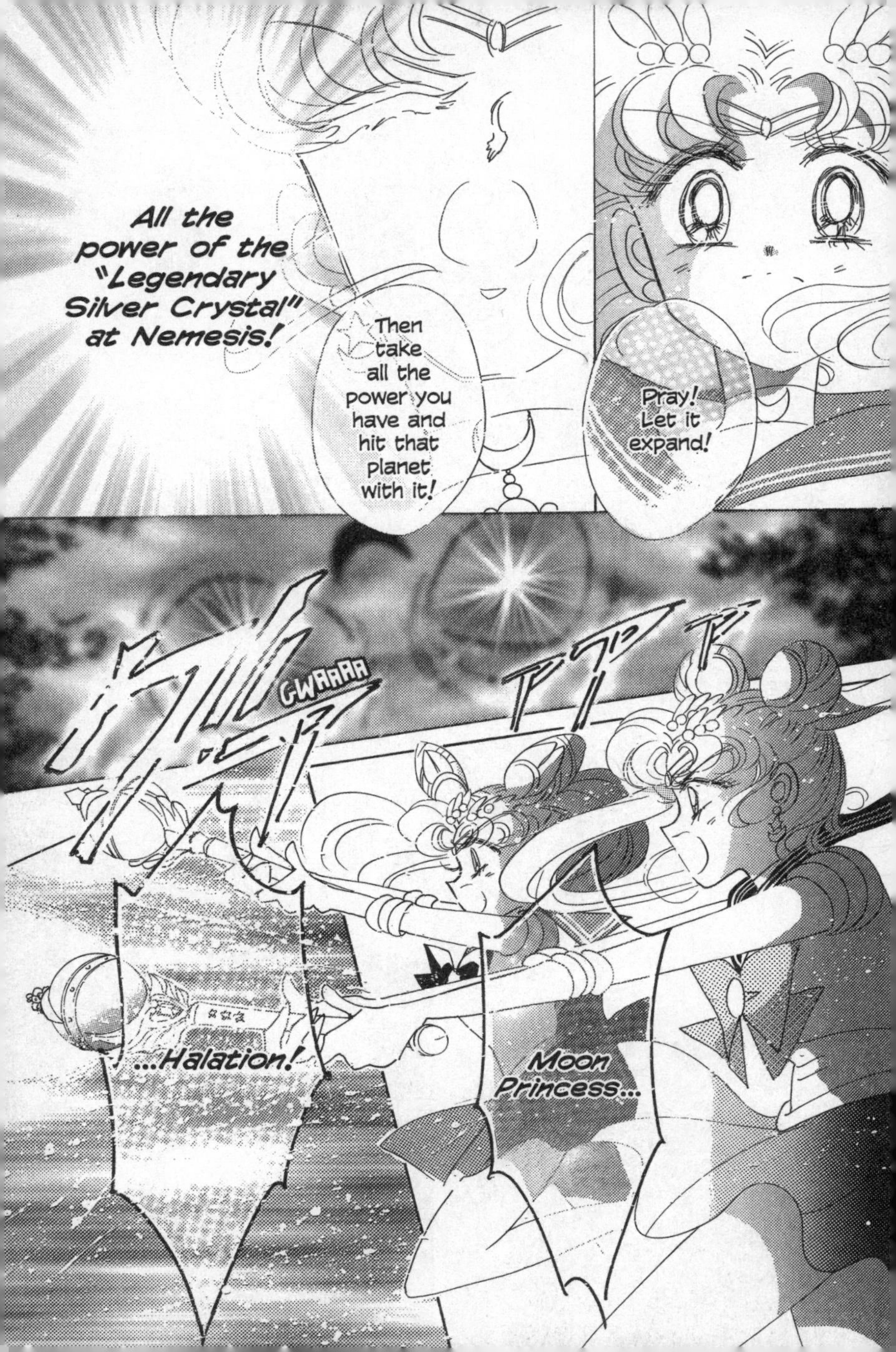
Pray! Let it expand!
Then take all the power you have and hit that planet with it!
All the power of the "Legendary Silver Crystal" at Nemesis!
GWAAAA
Moon Princess...
...Halation!

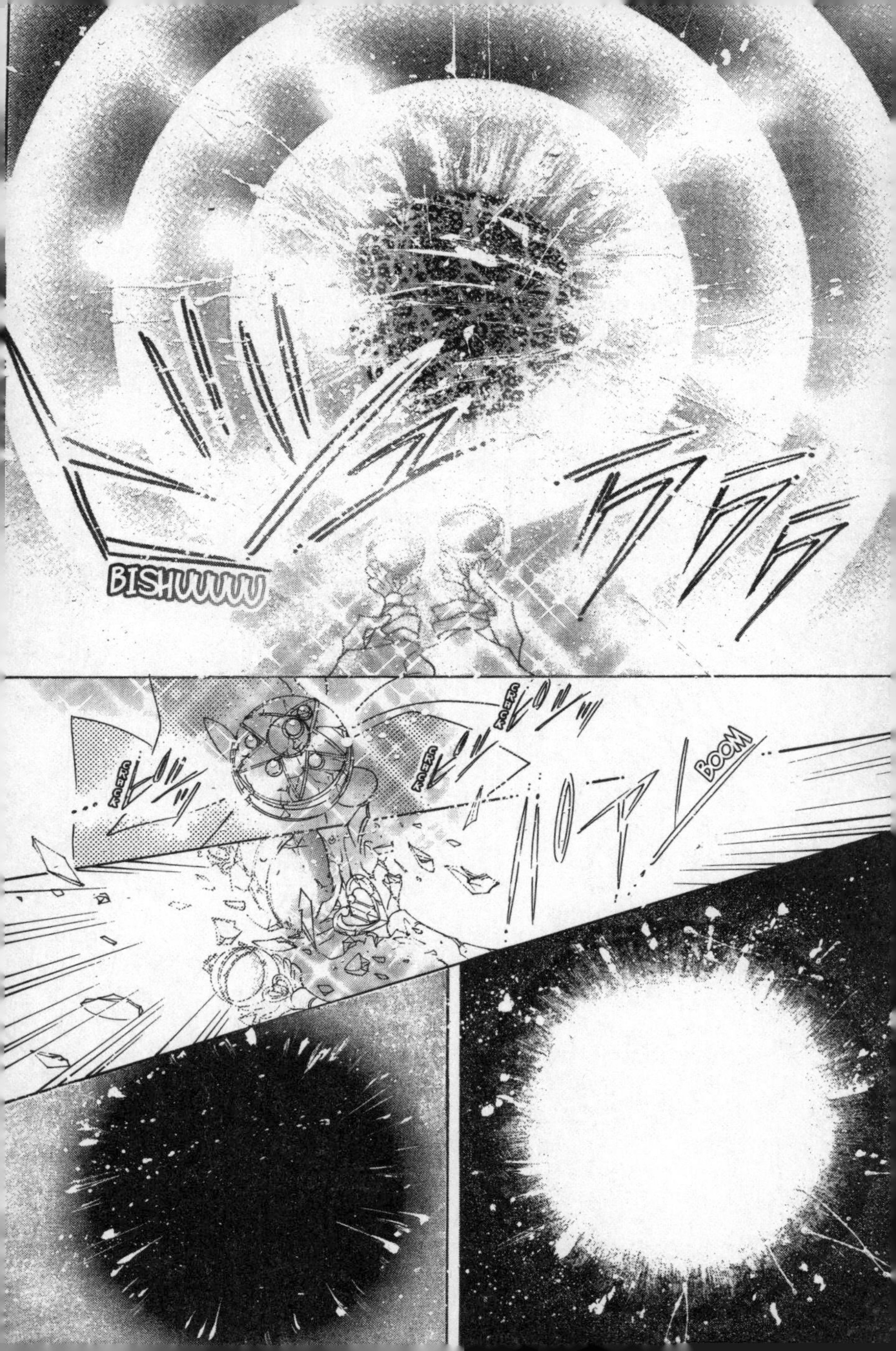
BISHUUUUU
BOOM
CRACK
CRACK
CRACK

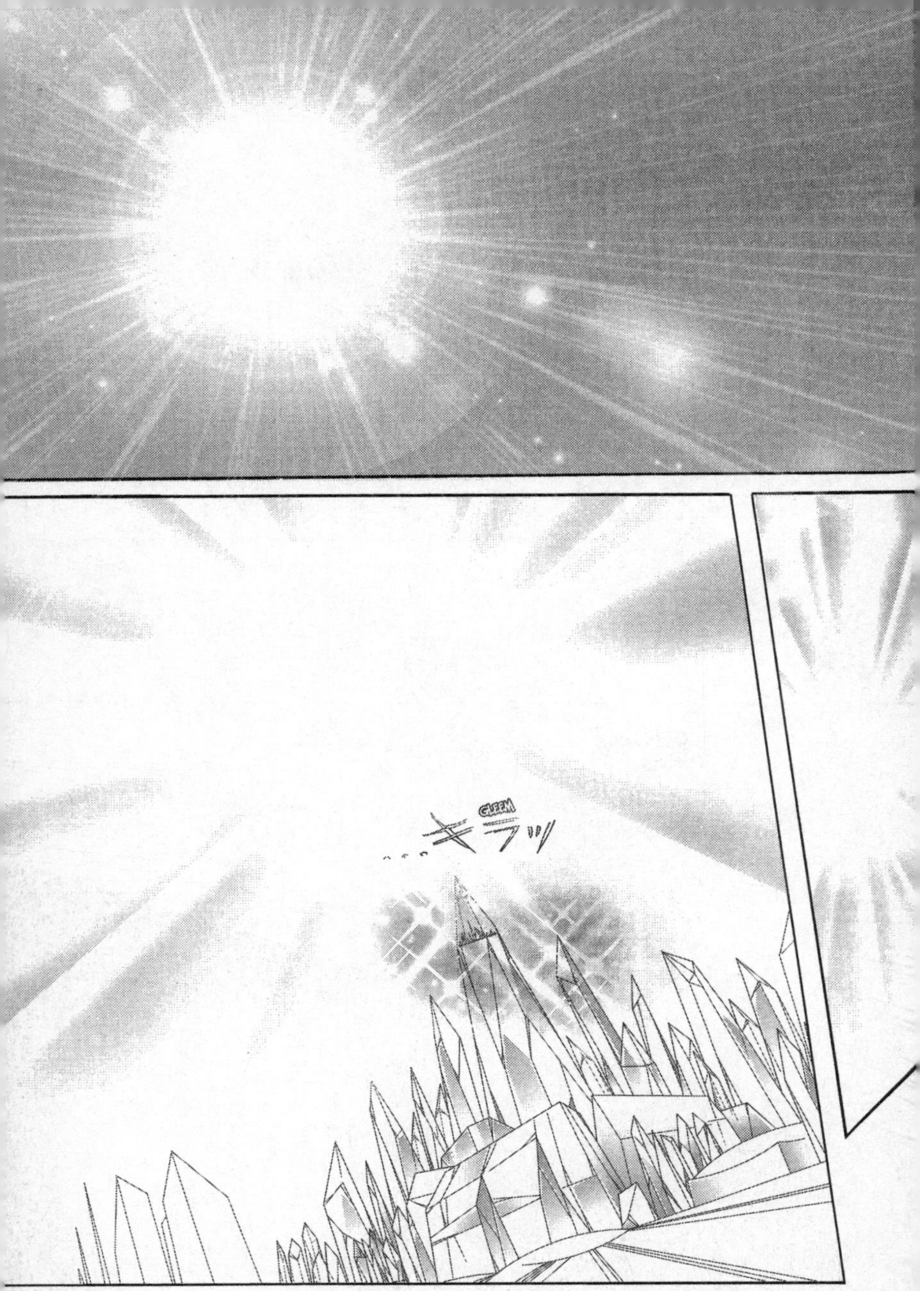
...キラッ
GLEEM

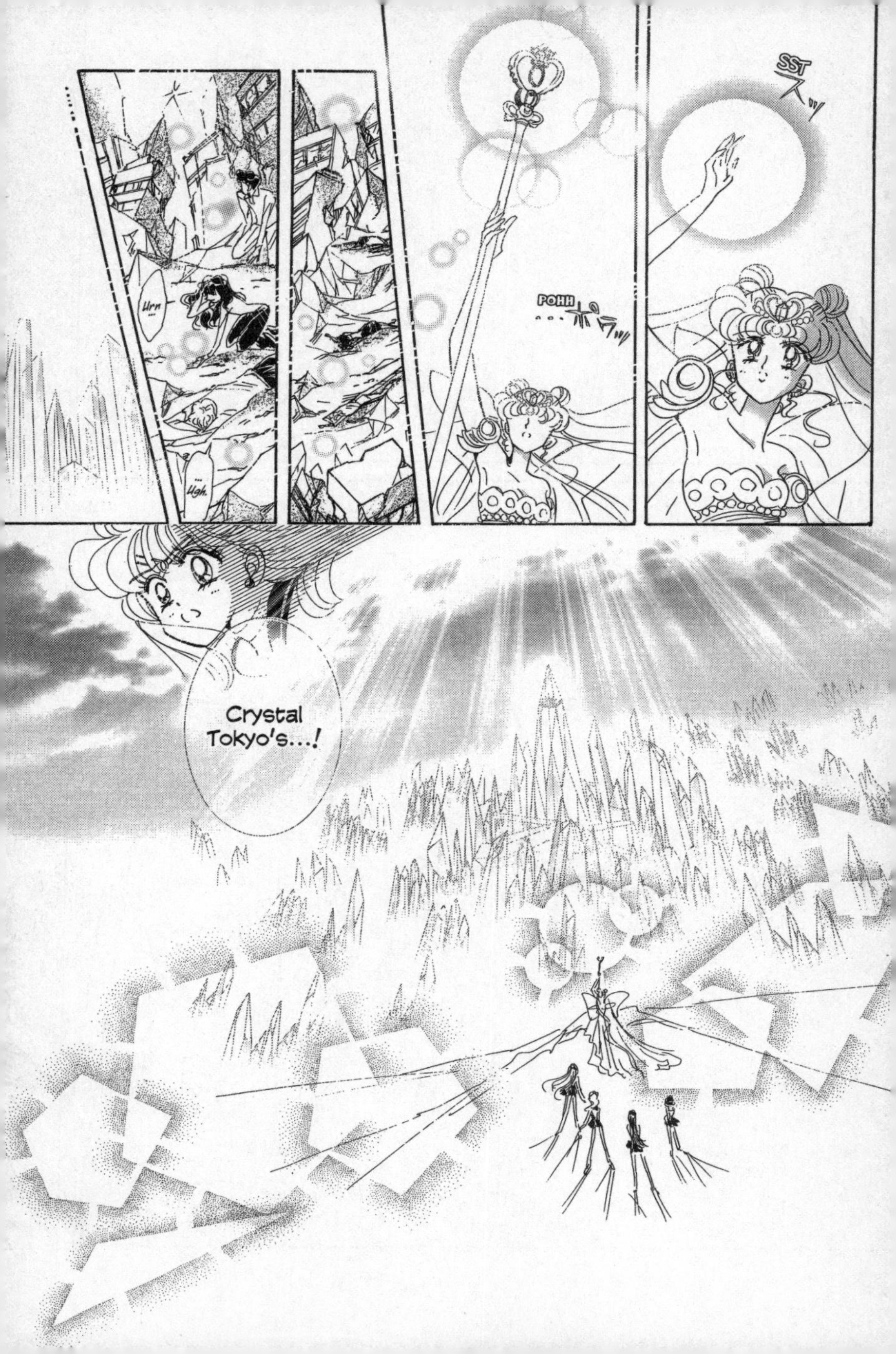
SST
POHH
Urn...
...Ugh.
Crystal Tokyo's...!

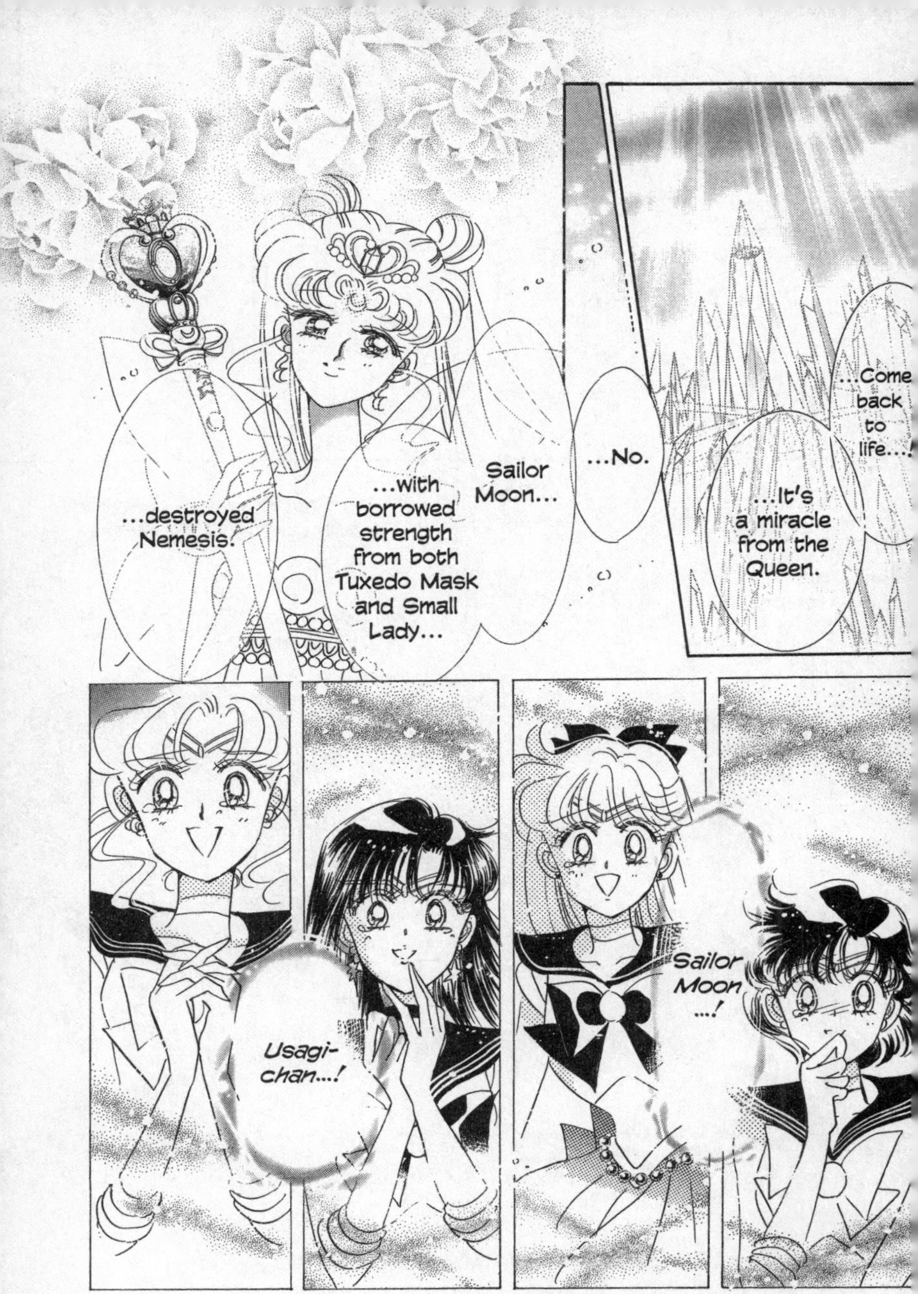
...Come back to life....
...It's a miracle from the Queen.
...No.
Sailor Moon...
...with borrowed strength from both Tuxedo Mask and Small Lady...
...destroyed Nemesis.
Sailor Moon ...!
Usagi-chan...!

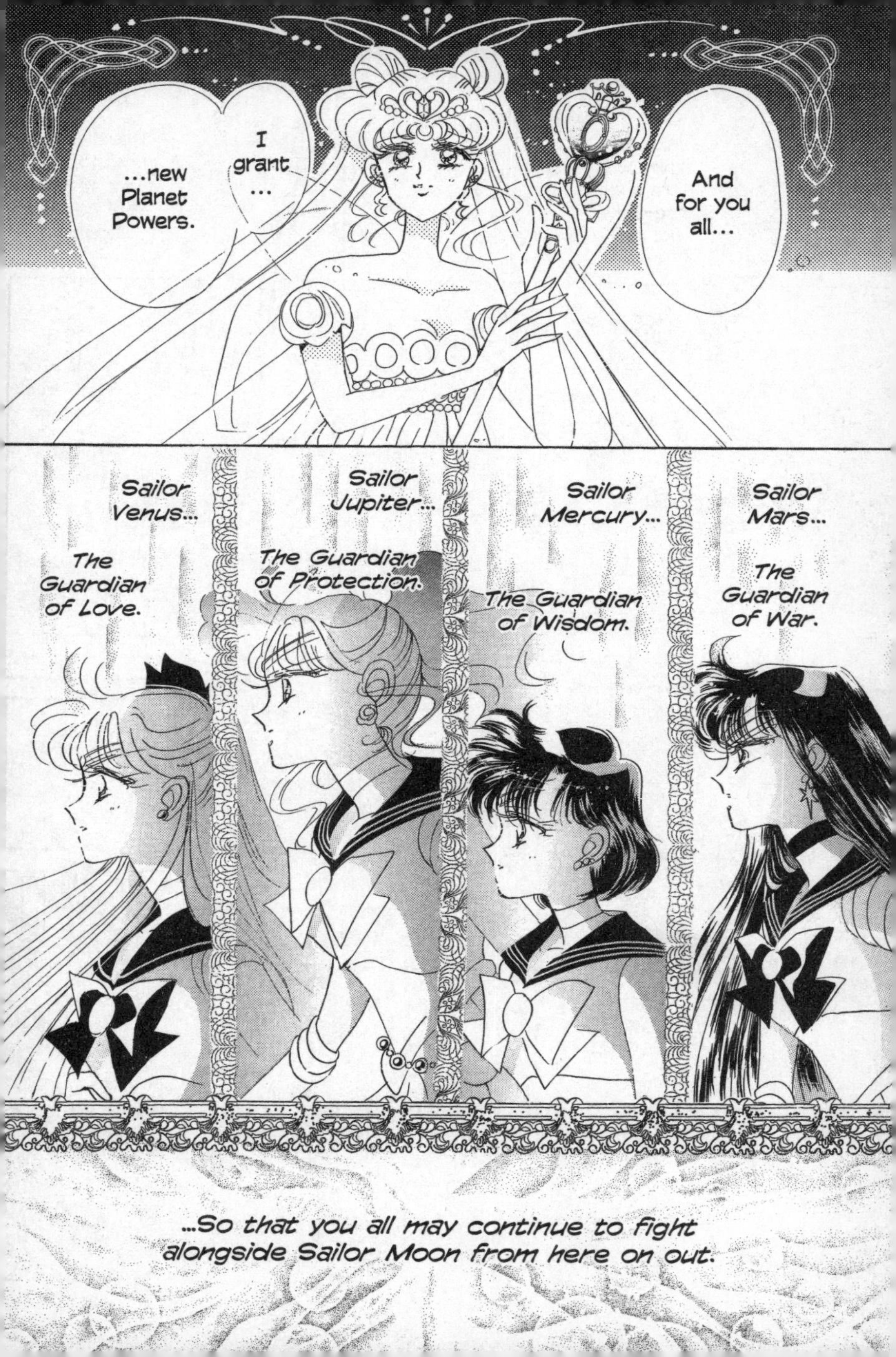

And for you all...
I grant...
...new Planet Powers.
Sailor Mars...
The Guardian of War.
Sailor Mercury...
The Guardian of Wisdom.
Sailor Jupiter...
The Guardian of Protection.
Sailor Venus...
The Guardian of Love.
...So that you all may continue to fight alongside Sailor Moon from here on out.

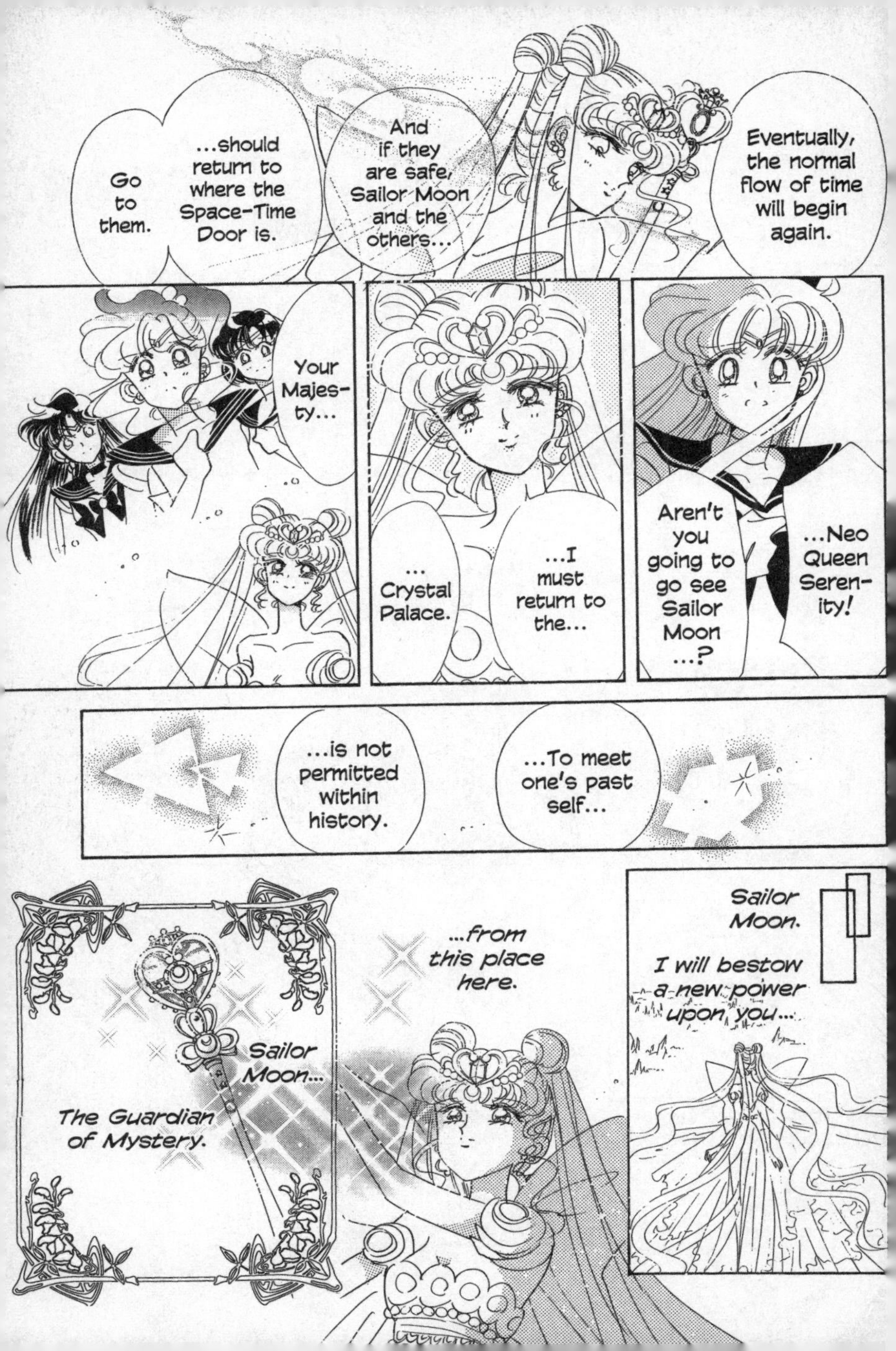
Eventually, the normal flow of time will begin again.
And if they are safe, Sailor Moon and the others...
...should return to where the Space-Time Door is.
Go to them.
...Neo Queen Seren-ity!
Aren't you going to go see Sailor Moon ...?
...I must return to the...
...Crystal Palace.
Your Majes-ty...
...To meet one's past self...
...is not permitted within history.
Sailor Moon.
I will bestow a new power upon you...
...from this place here.
Sailor Moon...
The Guardian of Mystery.

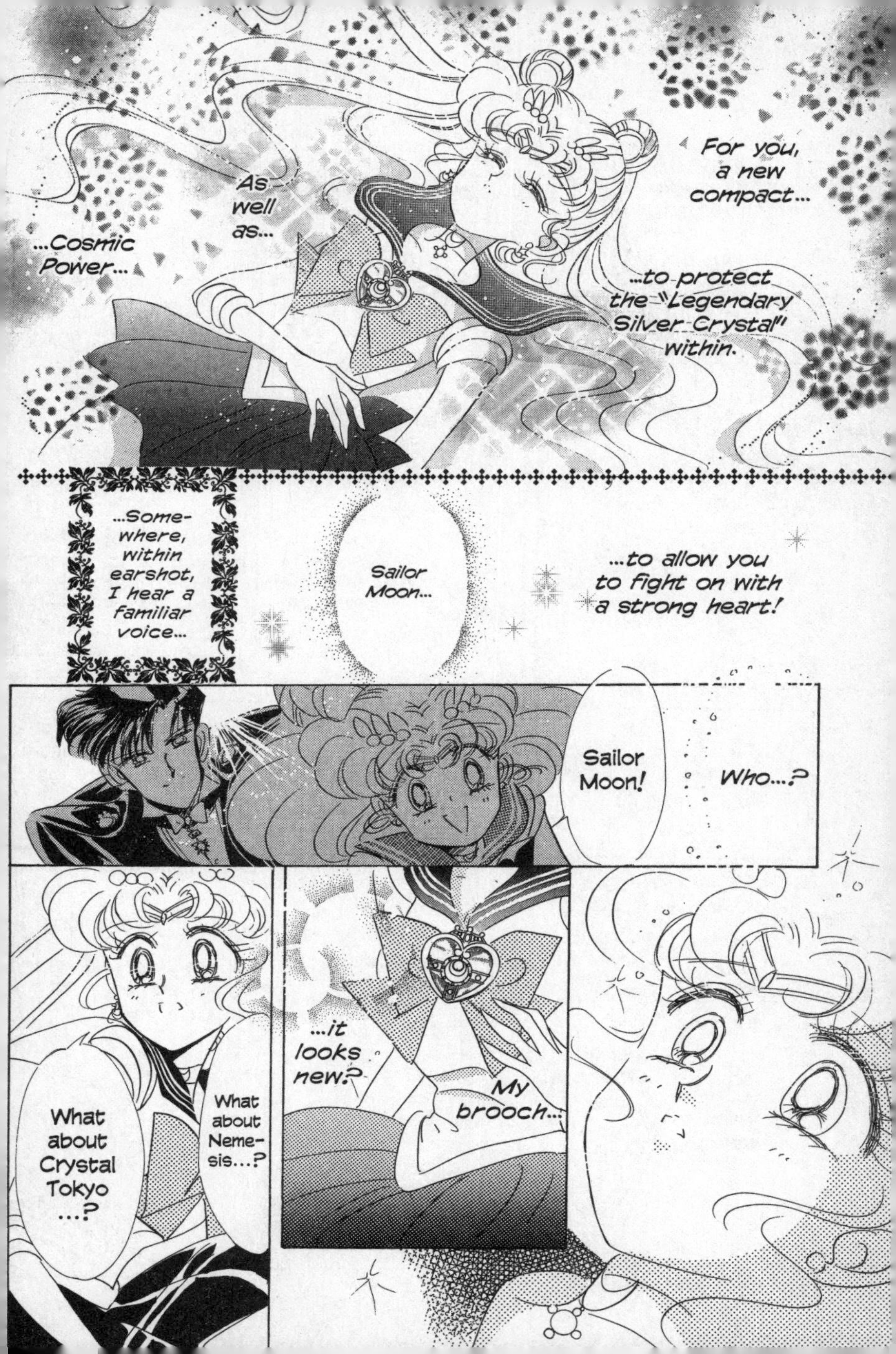
For you, a new compact...
...to protect the "Legendary Silver Crystal" within.
As well as...
...Cosmic Power...
...to allow you to fight on with a strong heart!
Sailor Moon...
...Some-where, within earshot, I hear a familiar voice...
Who...?
Sailor Moon!
My brooch...
...it looks new?
What about Nemesis...?
What about Crystal Tokyo ...?

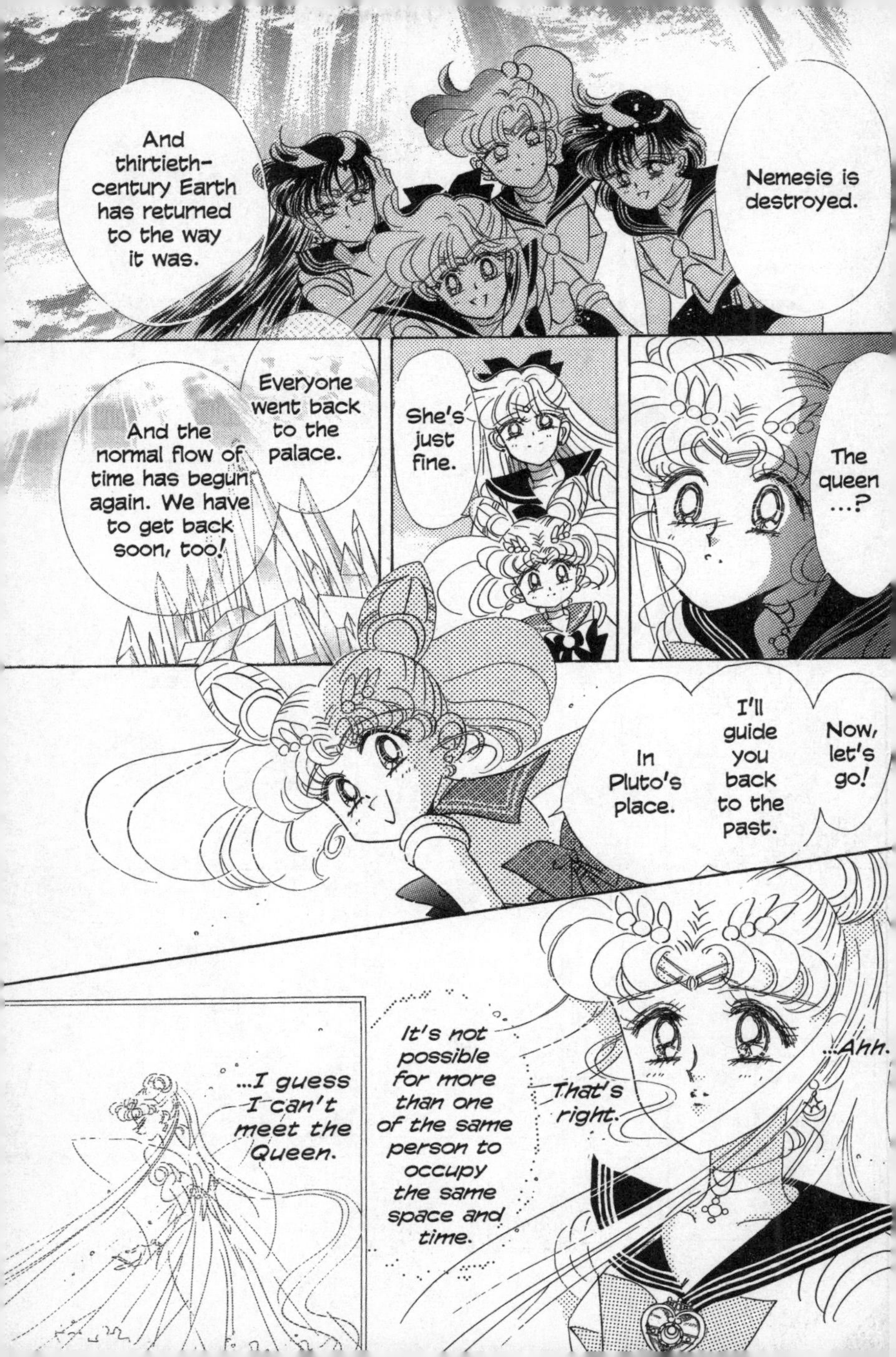
Nemesis is destroyed.
And thirtieth-century Earth has returned to the way it was.
The queen ...?
She's just fine.
Everyone went back to the palace.
And the normal flow of time has begun again. We have to get back soon, too!
Now, let's go!
I'll guide you back to the past.
In Pluto's place.
...Ahh.
That's right.
It's not possible for more than one of the same person to occupy the same space and time.
...I guess I can't meet the Queen.

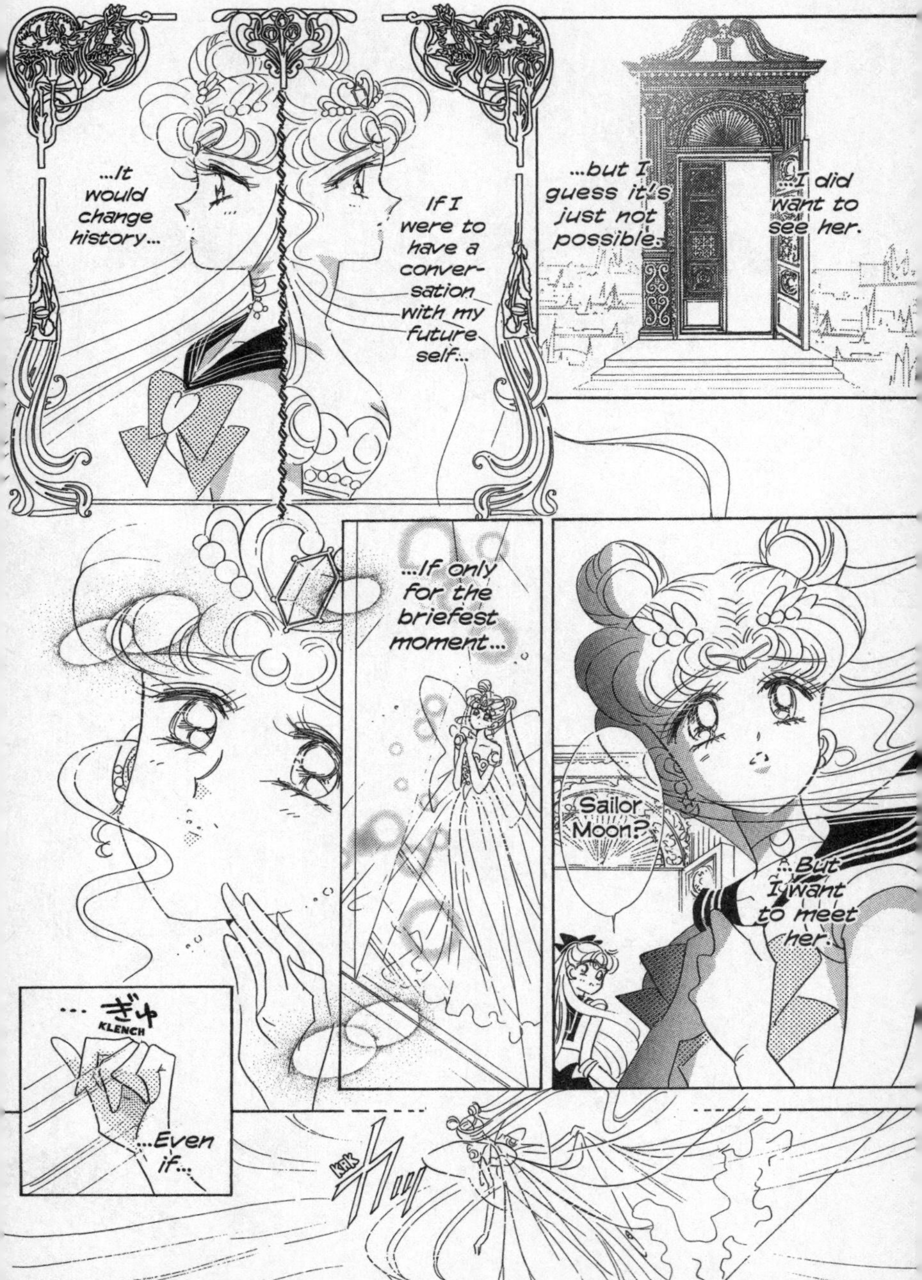
...I did want to see her.
...but I guess it's just not possible.
If I were to have a conversation with my future self...
...It would change history...
Sailor Moon?
...But I want to meet her.
...If only for the briefest moment...
... ぎゅ
KLENCH
...Even if...
KAK

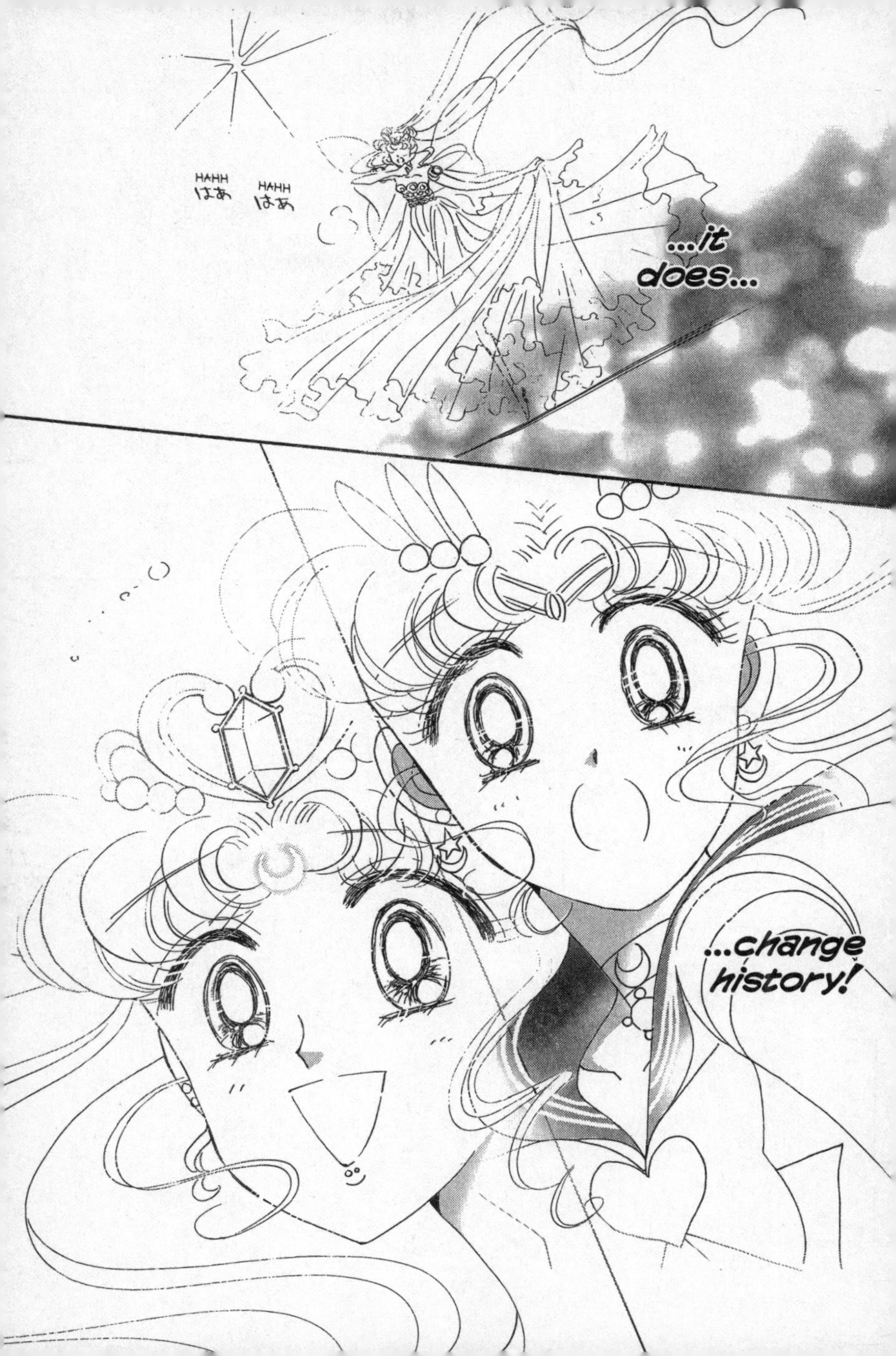
...it does...
HAHH はあ
HAHH はあ
...change history!

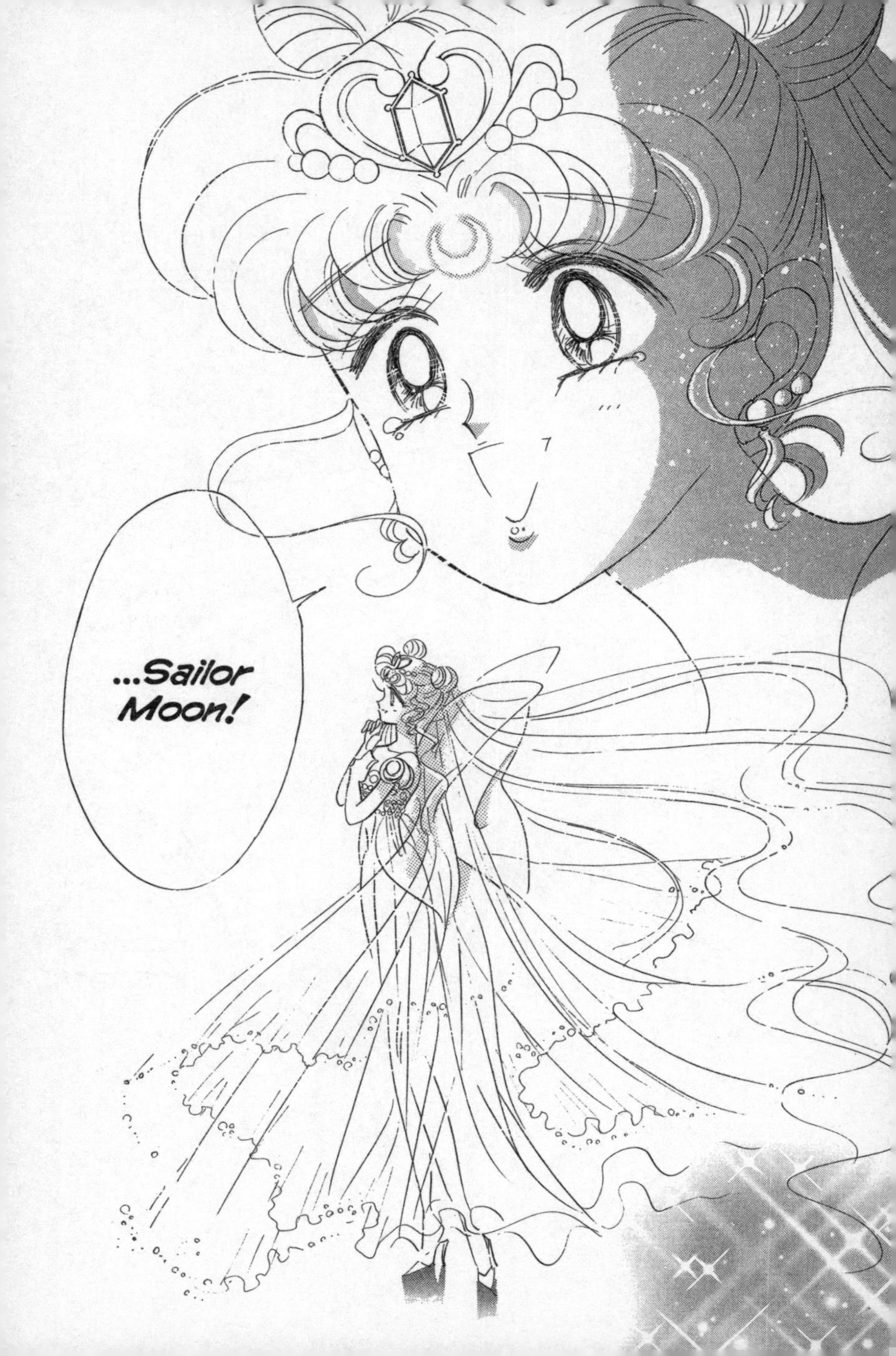
...Sailor Moon!

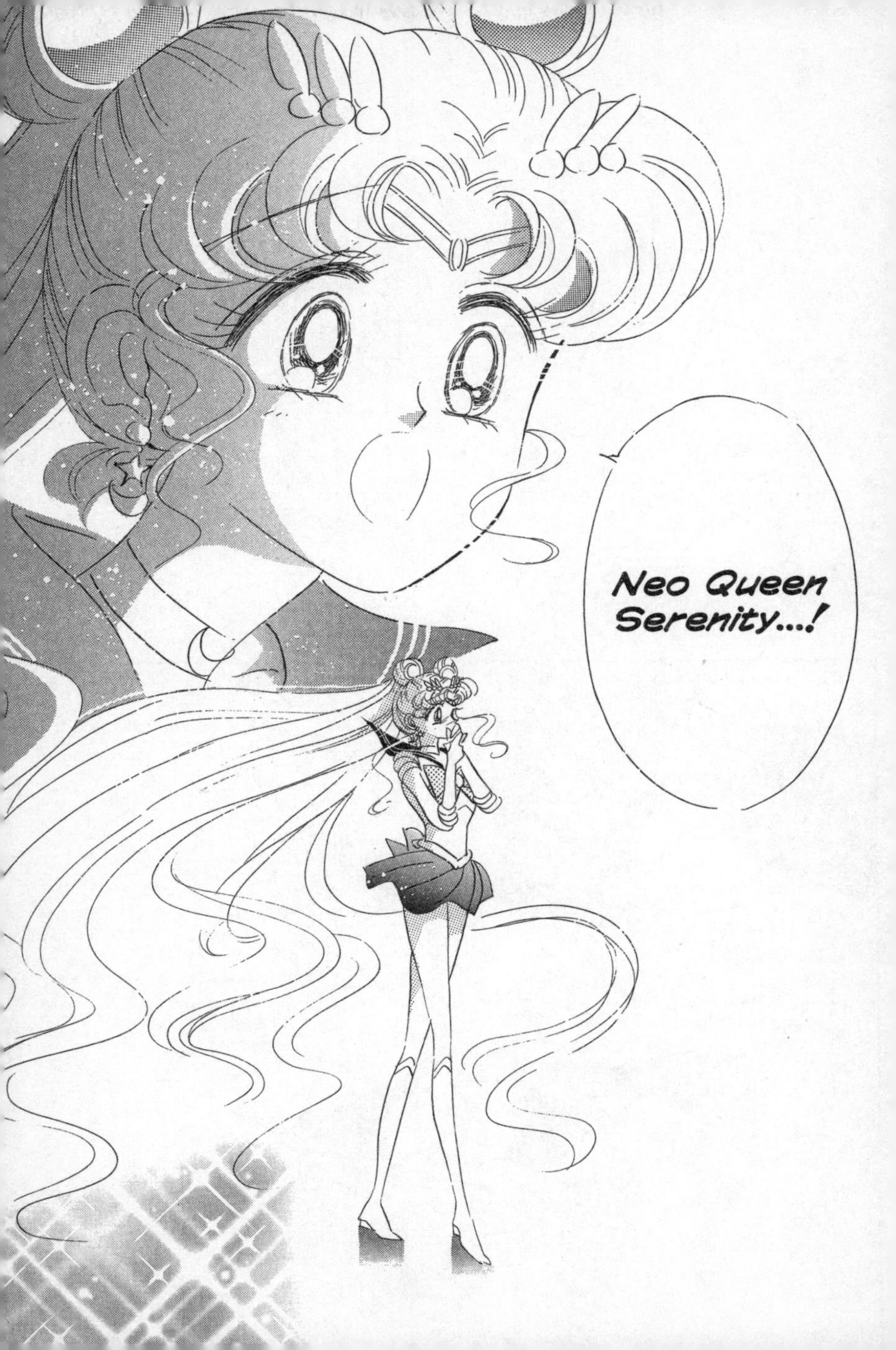
Neo Queen Serenity...!

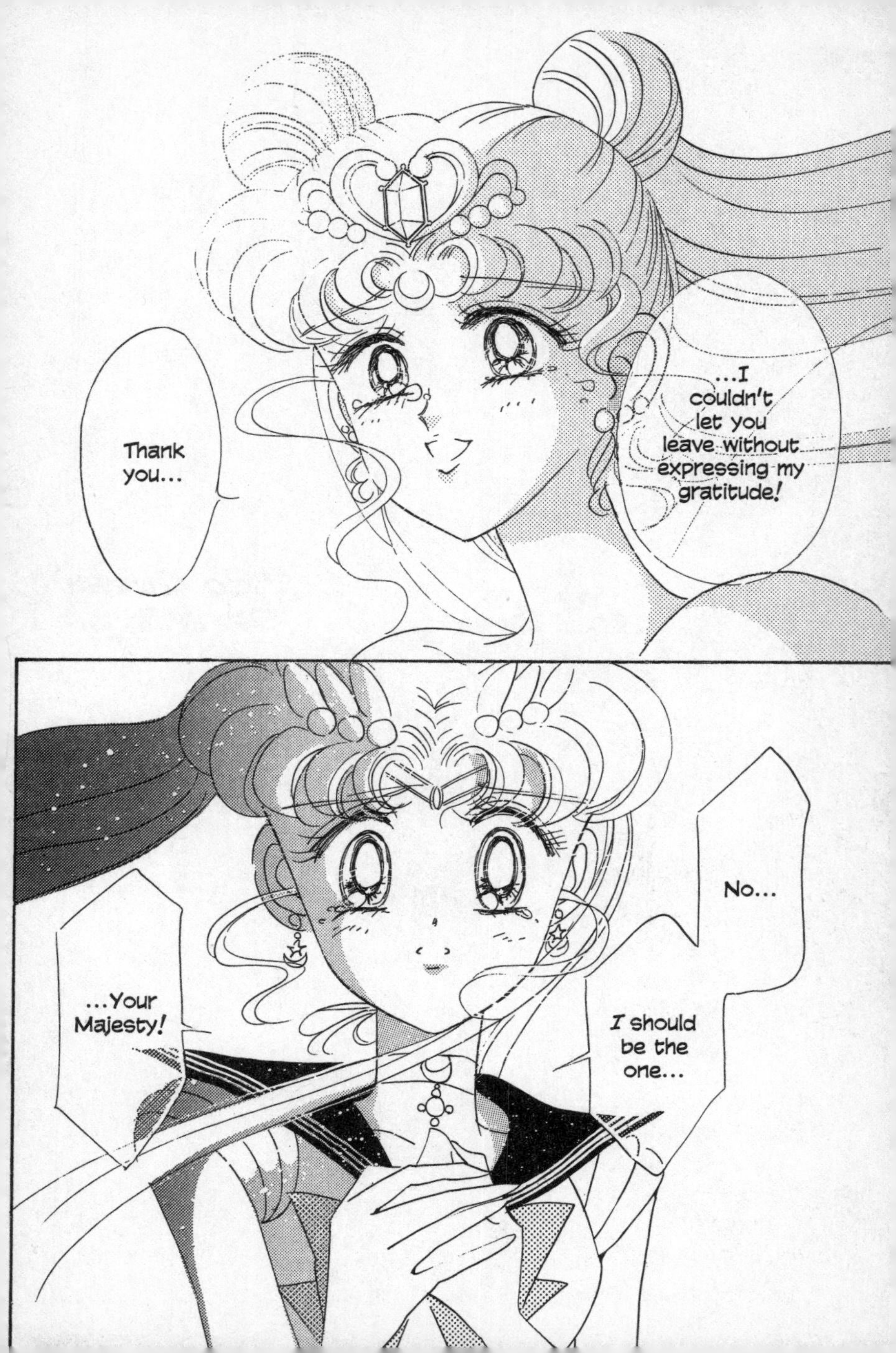
...I couldn't let you leave without expressing my gratitude!
Thank you...
No...
I should be the one...
...Your Majesty!

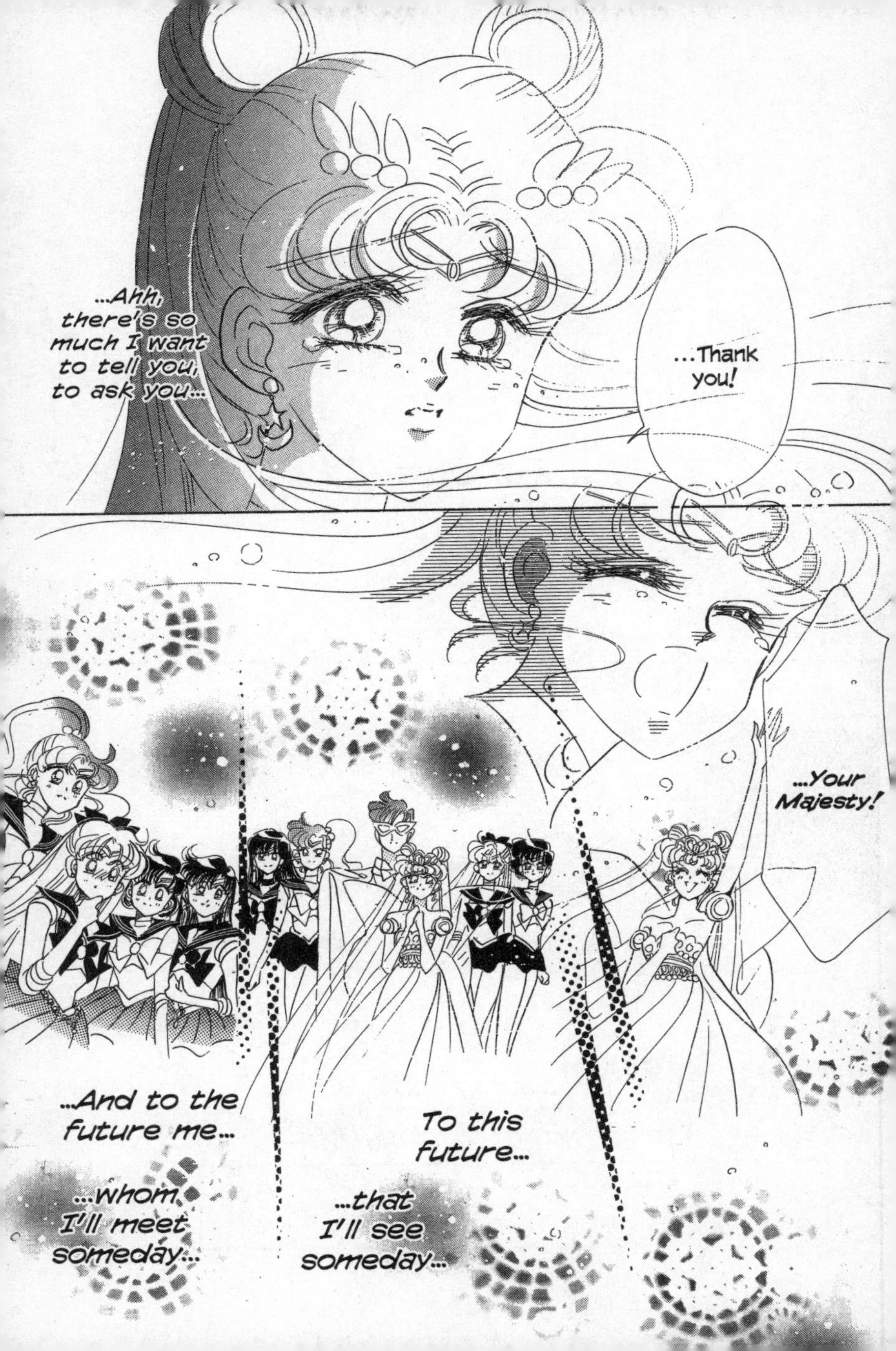
...Thank you!
...Ahh, there's so much I want to tell you, to ask you...
...Your Majesty!
To this future...
...that I'll see someday...
...And to the future me...
...whom I'll meet someday...

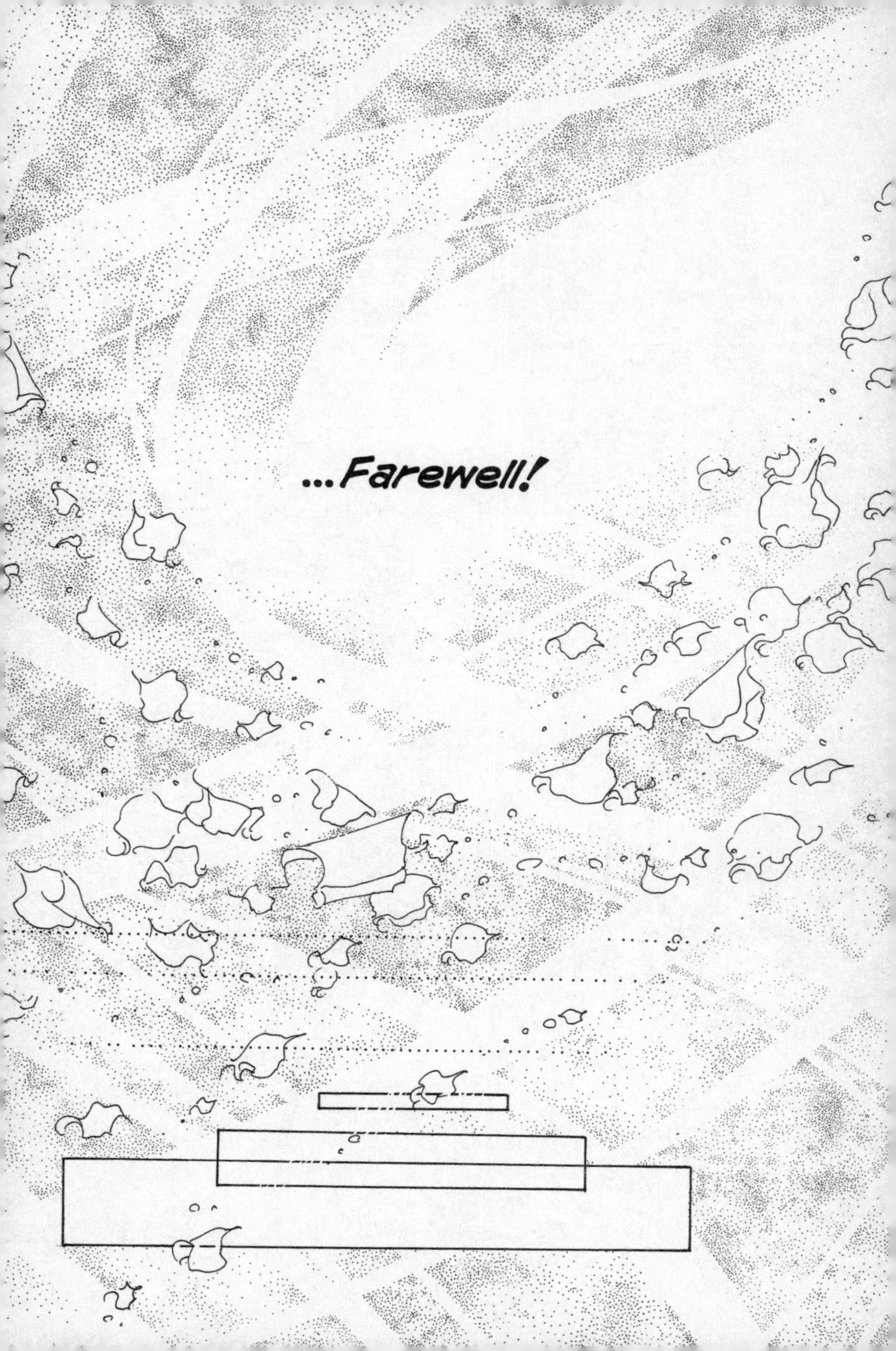
...Farewell!

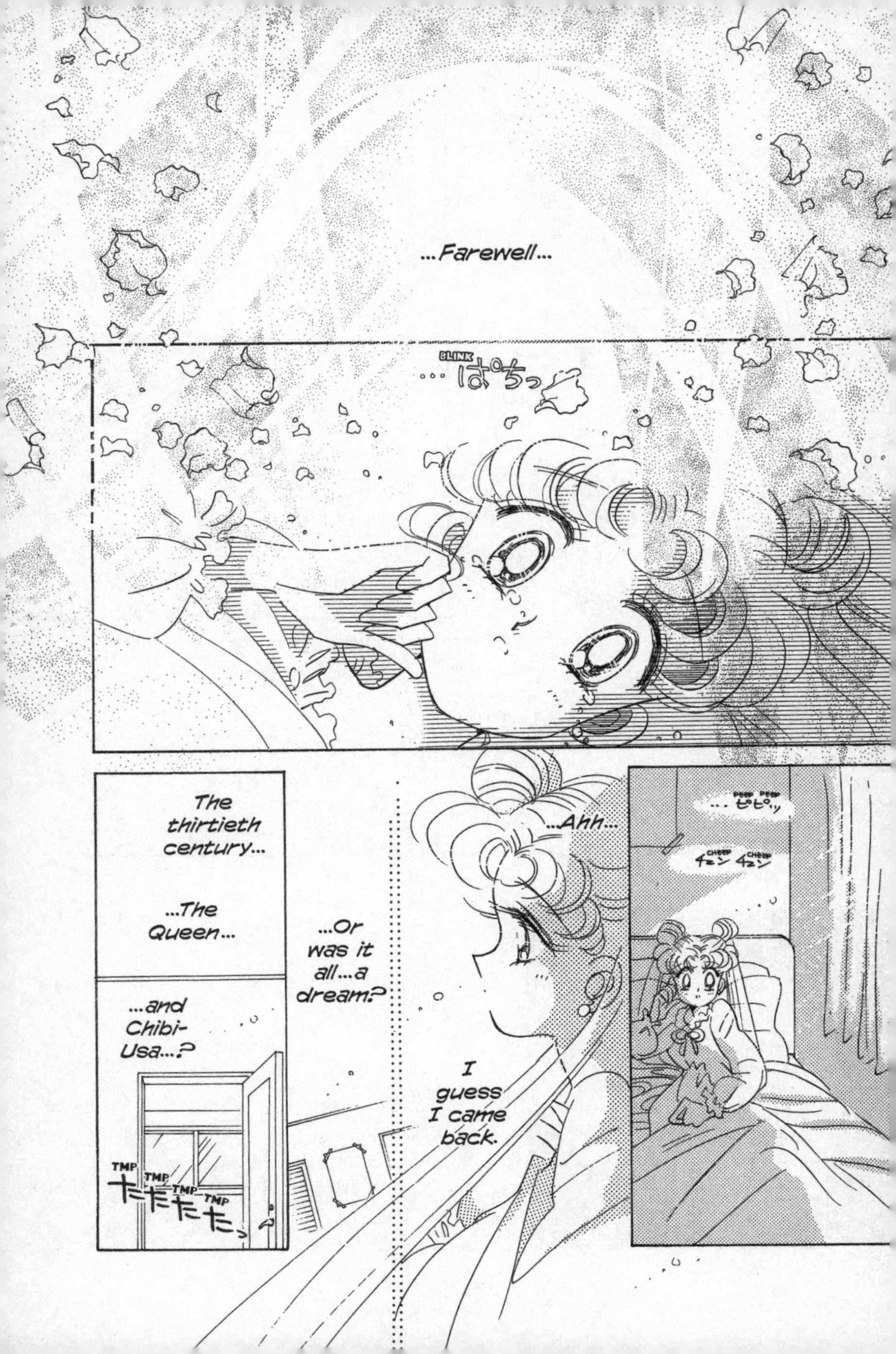

...Farewell...
BLINK
...ぱちっ
PEEP PEEP
...ピピッ
CHEEP CHEEP
チュン チュン
...Ahh...
...Or was it all...a dream?
I guess I came back.
The thirtieth century...
...The Queen...
...and Chibi-Usa...?
TMP TMP TMP TMP
たたたたっ

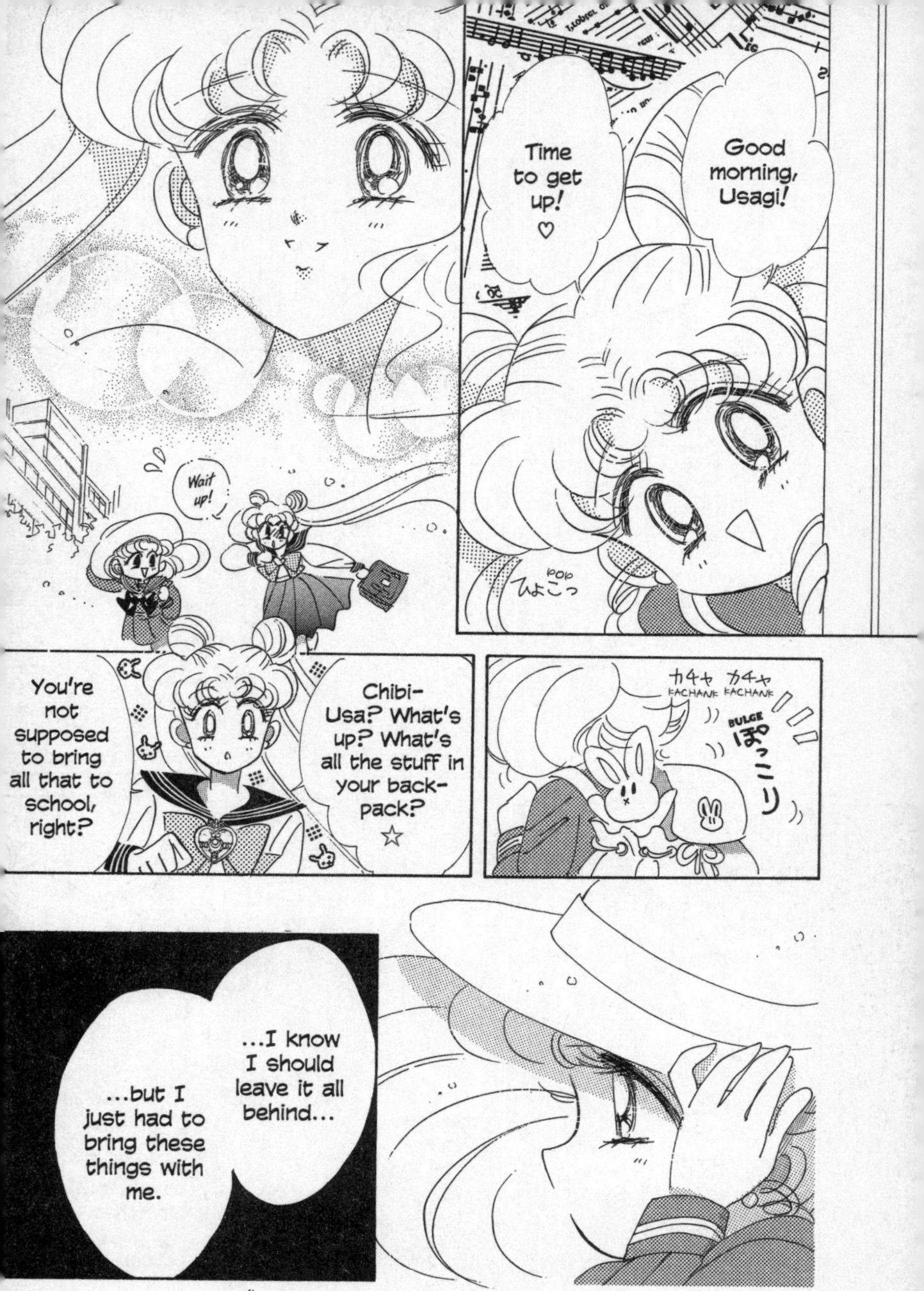
Good morning, Usagi!
Time to get up! ♡
ひよこっ
Wait up!
カチャ カチャ
KACHANK KACHANK
BULGE
ぽっこり
Chibi-Usa? What's up? What's all the stuff in your back-pack? ☆
You're not supposed to bring all that to school, right?
...I know I should leave it all behind...
...but I just had to bring these things with me.

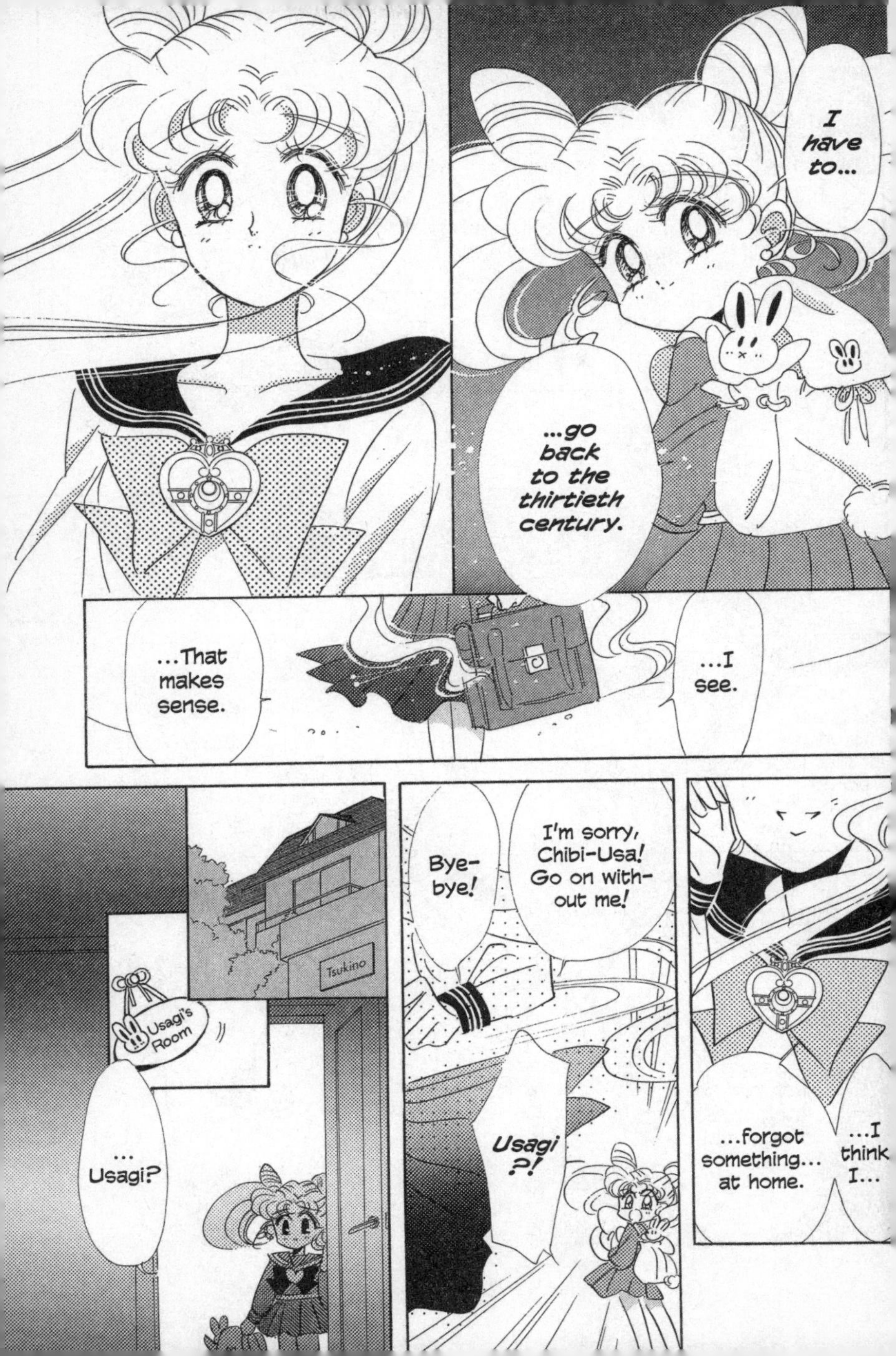

I have to...
...go back to the thirtieth century.
...I see.
...That makes sense.
...I think I...
...forgot something... at home.
I'm sorry, Chibi-Usa! Go on with-out me!
Bye-bye!
Usagi ?!
Tsukino
Usagi's Room
... Usagi?

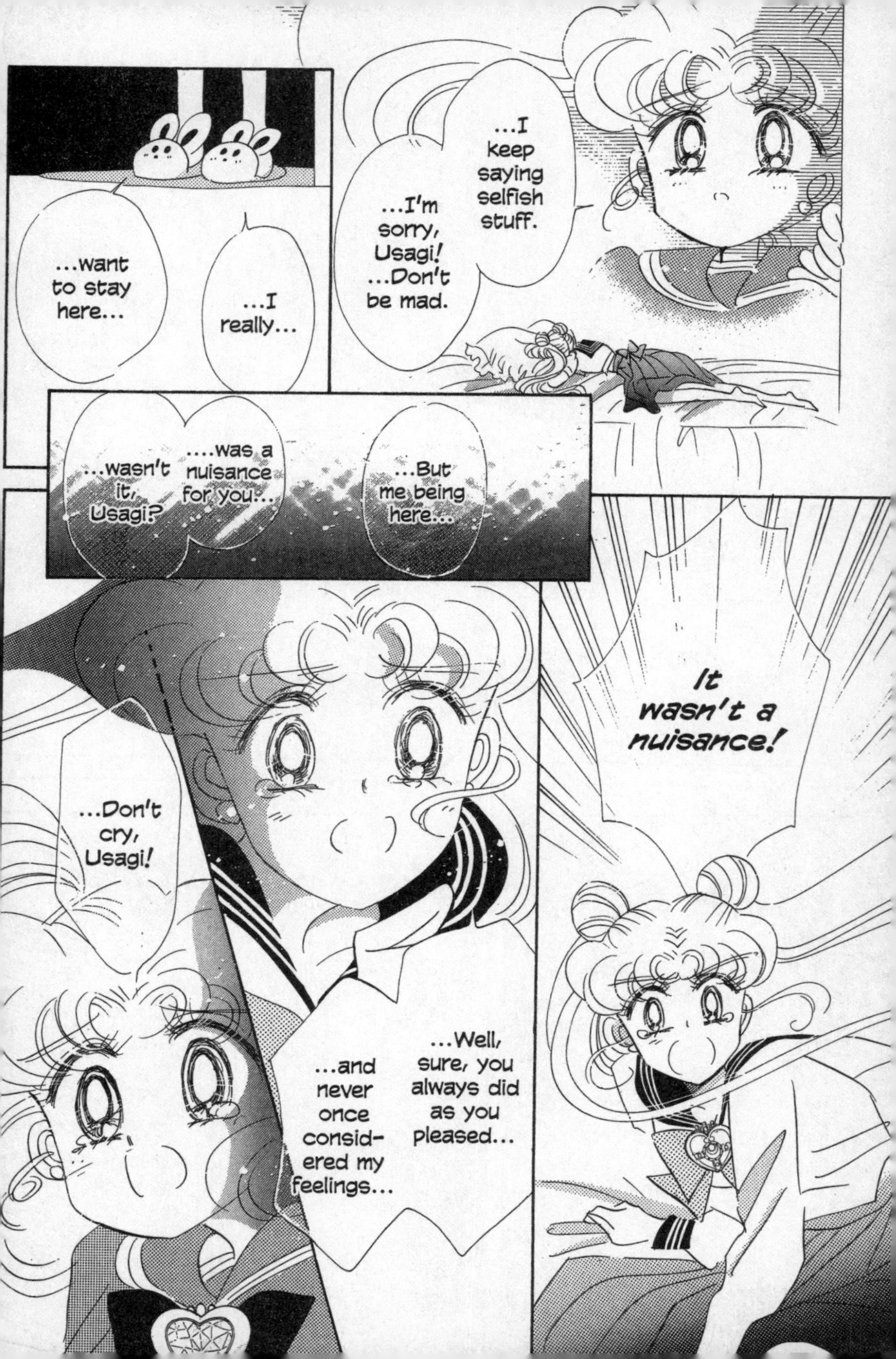
...I keep saying selfish stuff.
...I'm sorry, Usagi! ...Don't be mad.
...I really...
...want to stay here...
...But me being here...
....was a nuisance for you...
...wasn't it, Usagi?
It wasn't a nuisance!
...Well, sure, you always did as you pleased...
...and never once consid-ered my feelings...
...Don't cry, Usagi!

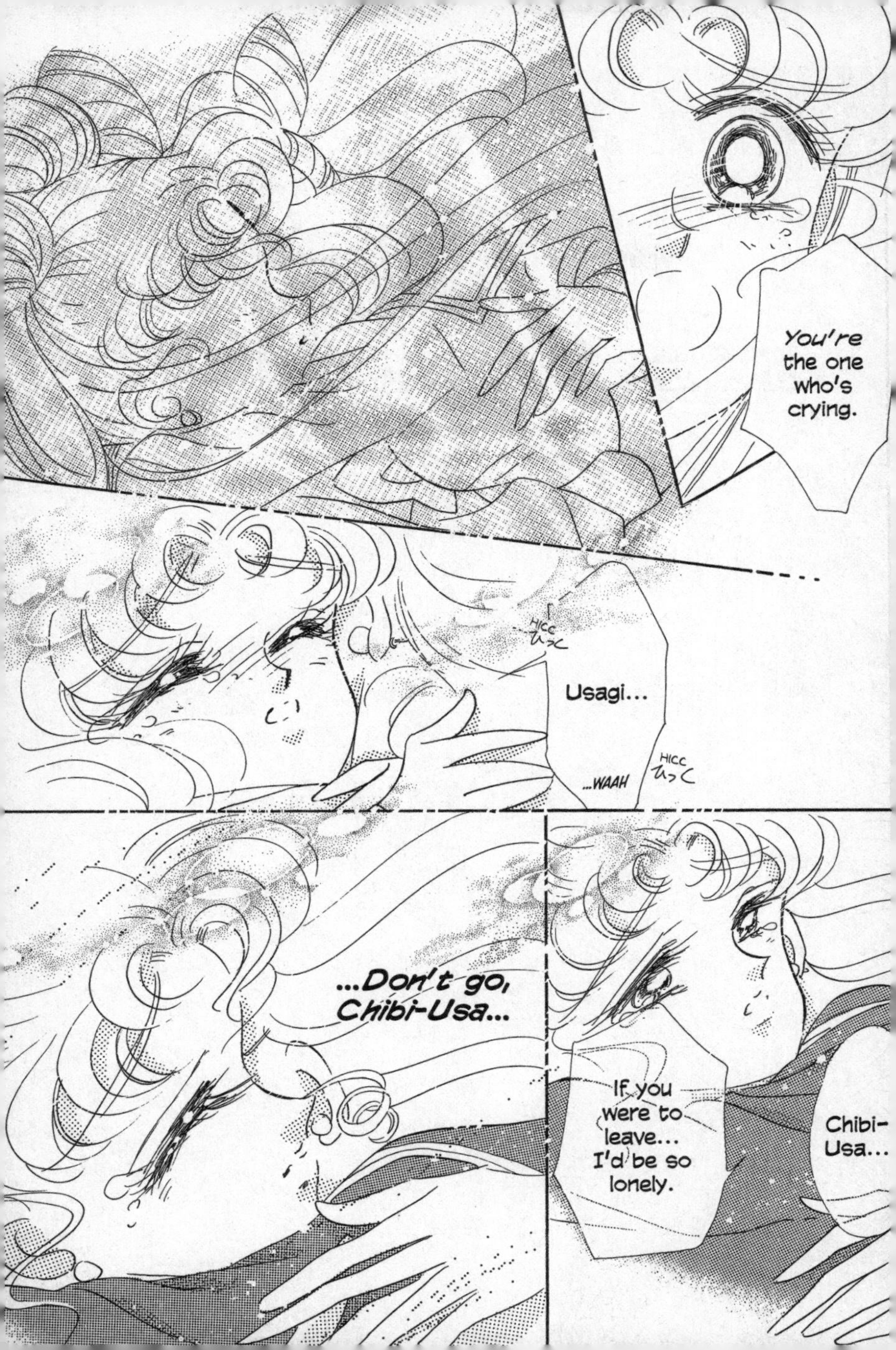
You're the one who's crying.
HICC ひっく
Usagi...
HICC ひっく
...WAAH
Chibi-Usa...
If you were to leave... I'd be so lonely.
...Don't go, Chibi-Usa...

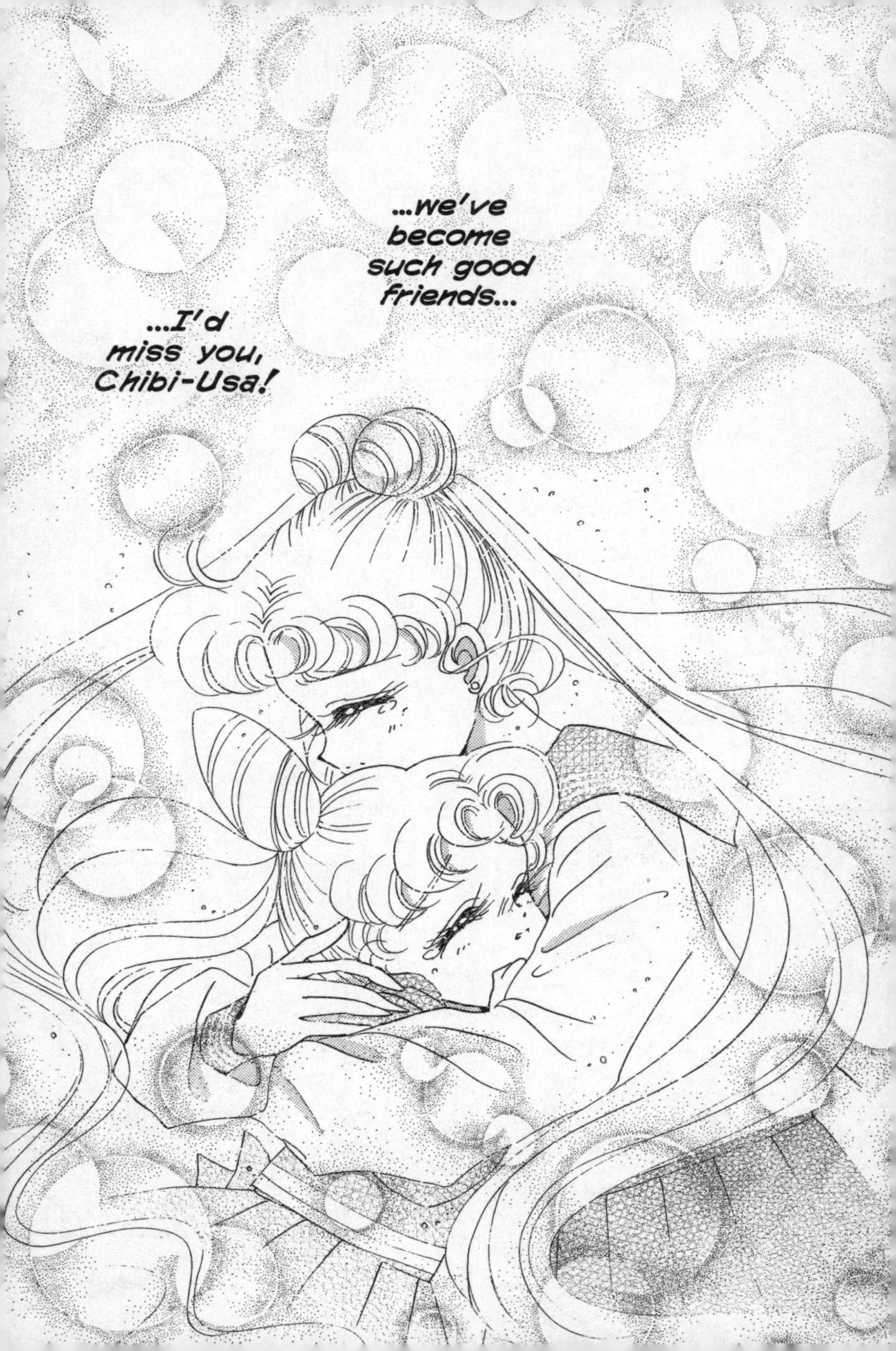
...we've become such good friends...
...I'd miss you, Chibi-Usa!

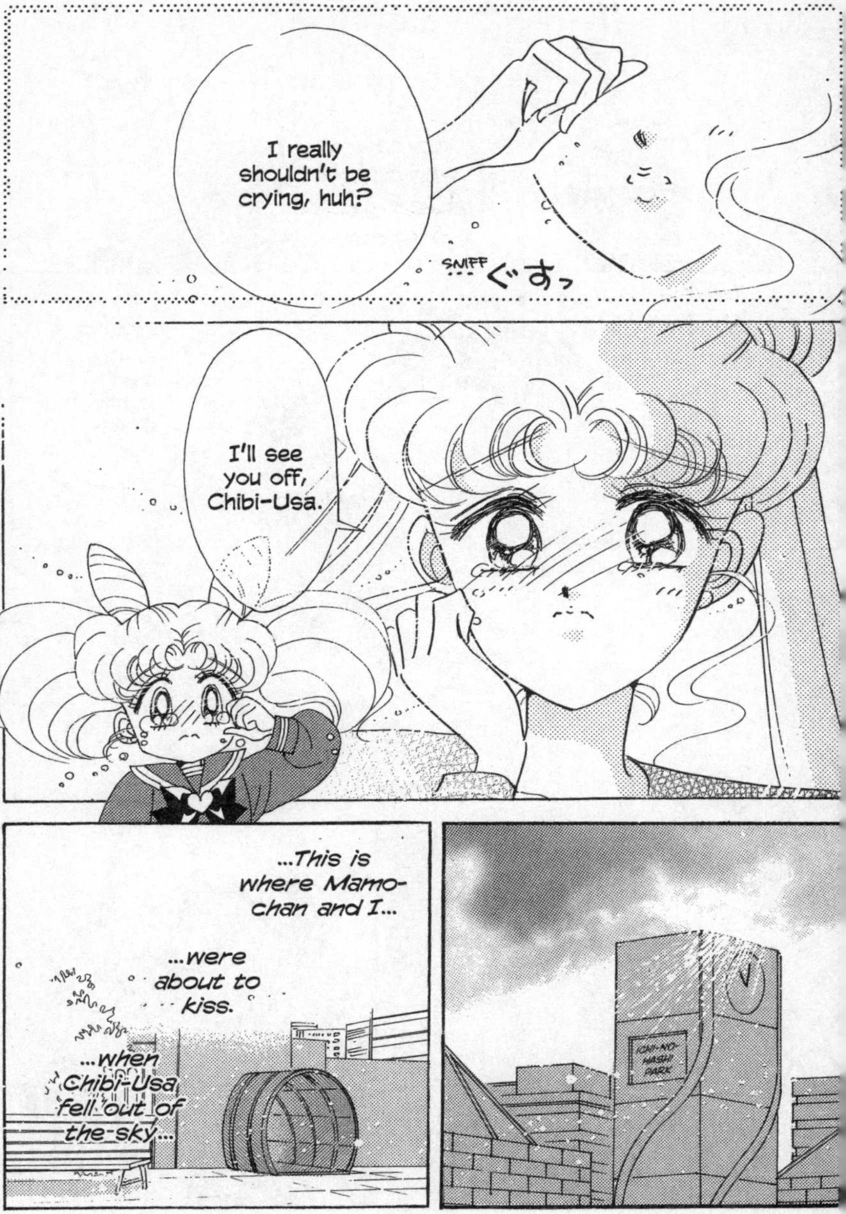
I really shouldn't be crying, huh?
SNIFF
ぐすっ
I'll see you off, Chibi-Usa.
ICHI-NO-HASHI PARK
...This is where Mamo-chan and I...
...were about to kiss.
...when Chibi-Usa fell out of the sky...

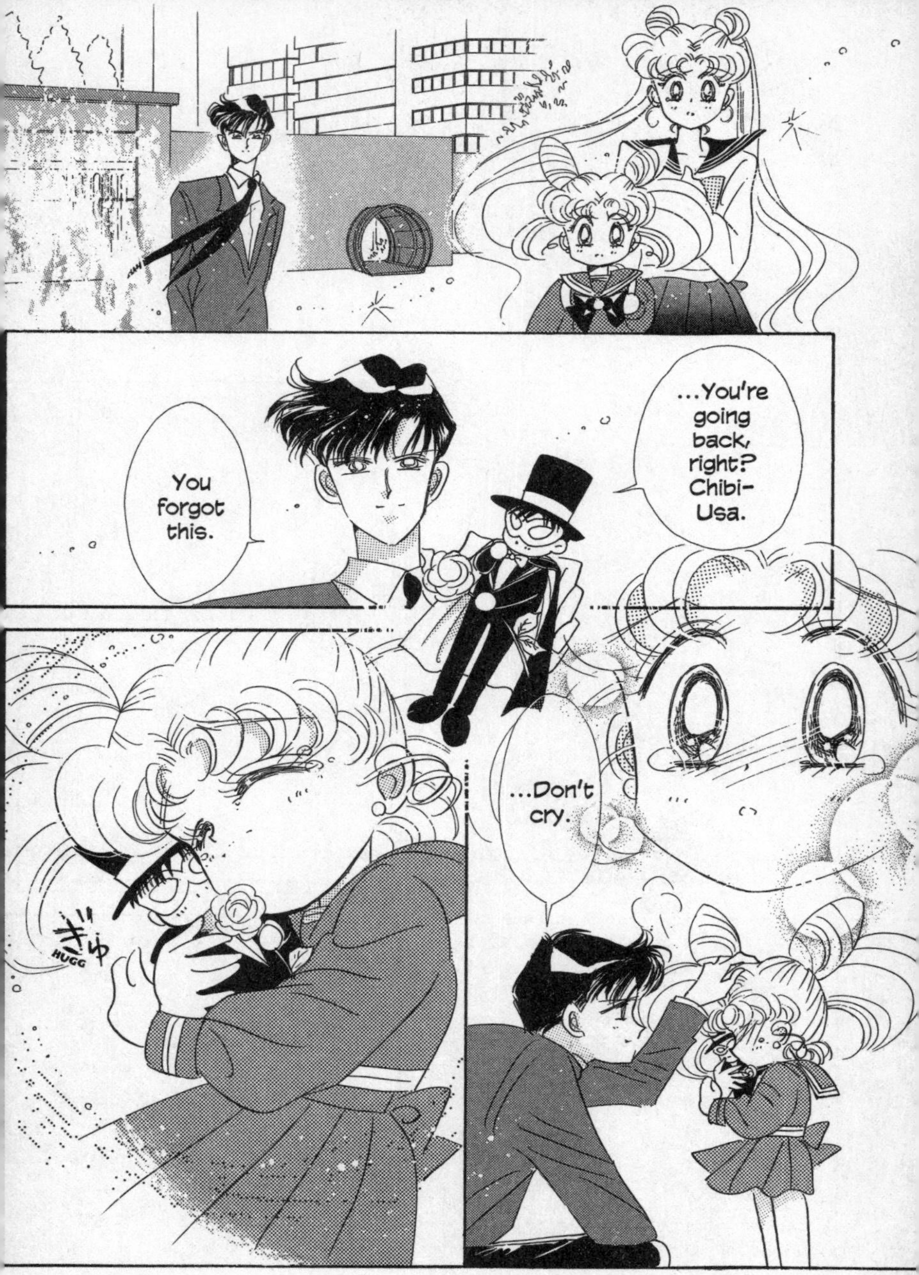
...You're going back, right? Chibi-Usa.
You forgot this.
...Don't cry.
ぎゅ
HUGG

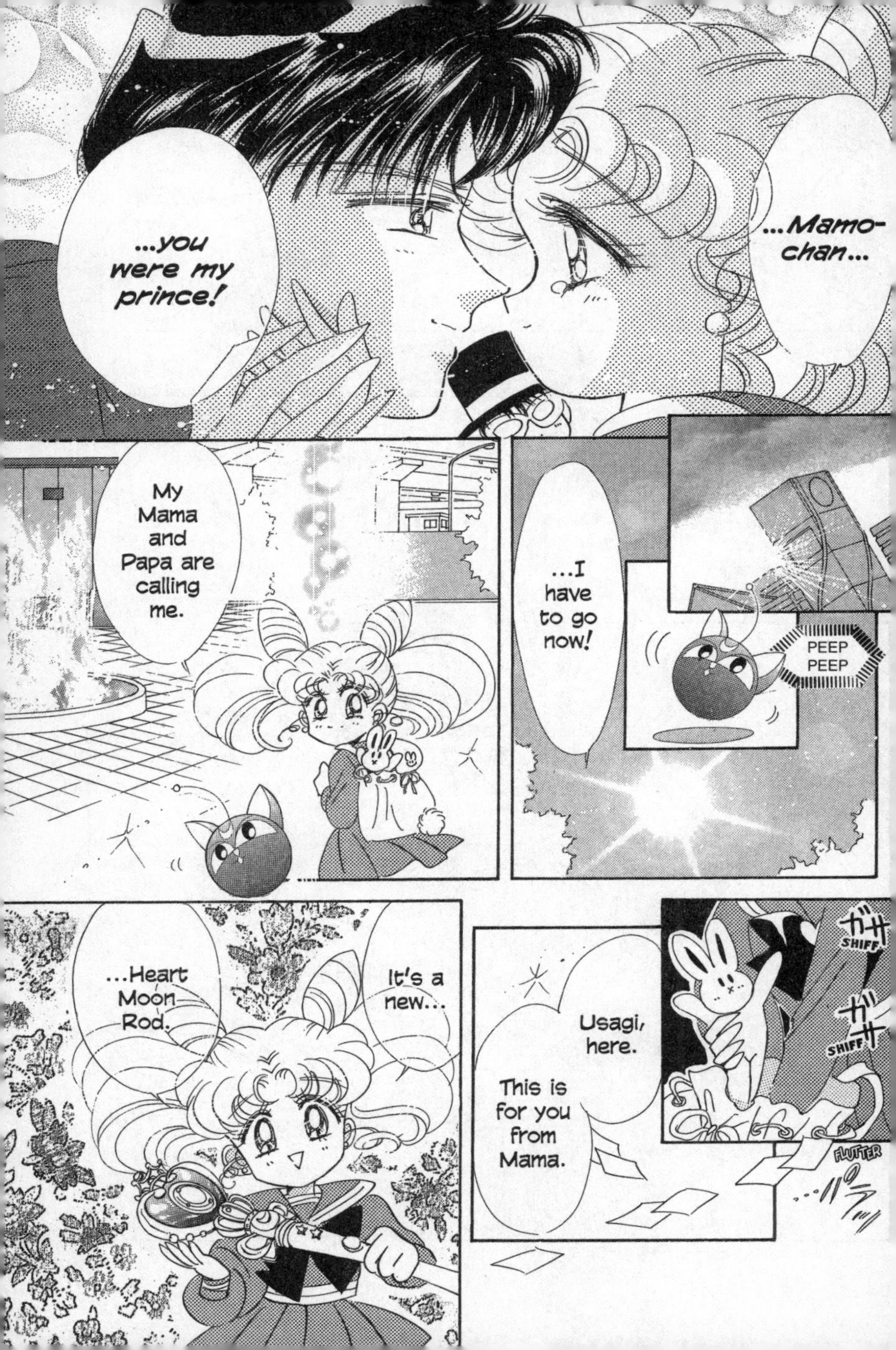
...Mamo-chan...
...you were my prince!
PEEP PEEP
...I have to go now!
My Mama and Papa are calling me.
SHIFF
SHIFF
FLUTTER
Usagi, here.
This is for you from Mama.
It's a new...
...Heart Moon Rod.

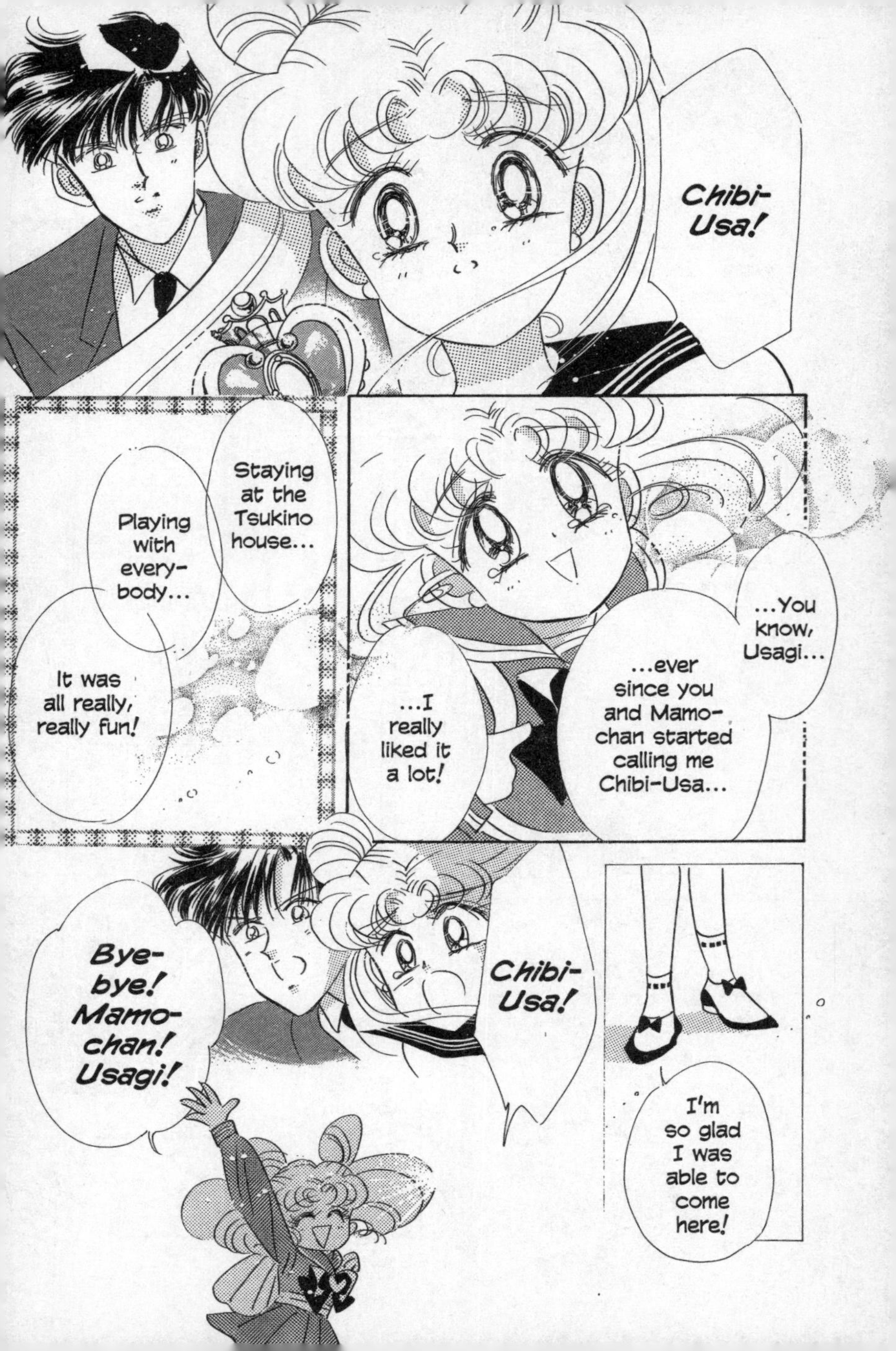
Chibi-Usa!
...You know, Usagi...
...ever since you and Mamo-chan started calling me Chibi-Usa...
...I really liked it a lot!
Staying at the Tsukino house...
Playing with every-body...
It was all really, really fun!
I'm so glad I was able to come here!
Chibi-Usa!
Bye-bye! Mamo-chan! Usagi!

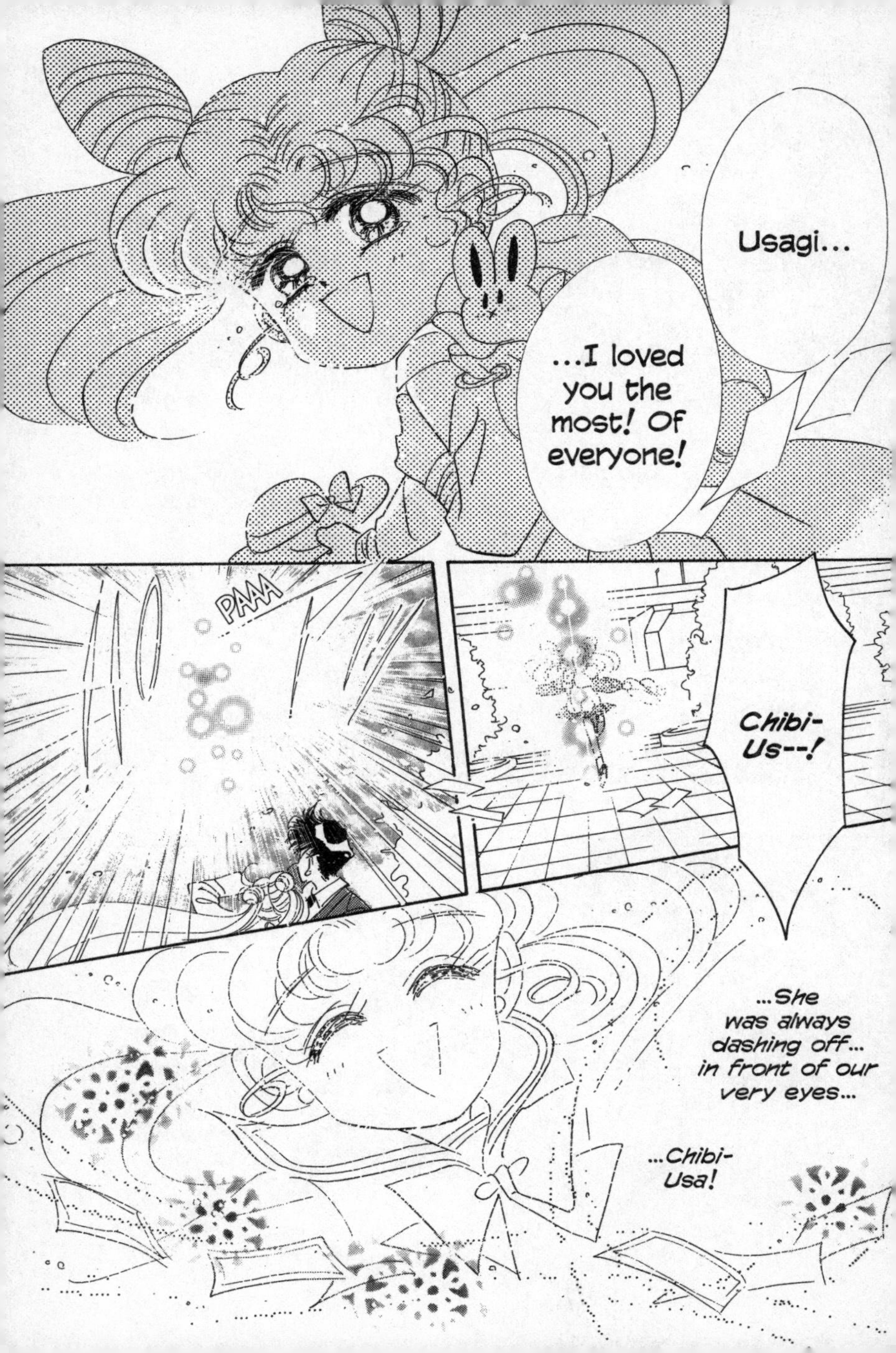
Usagi...
...I loved you the most! Of everyone!
Chibi-Us--!
PAAA
...She was always dashing off... in front of our very eyes...
...Chibi-Usa!

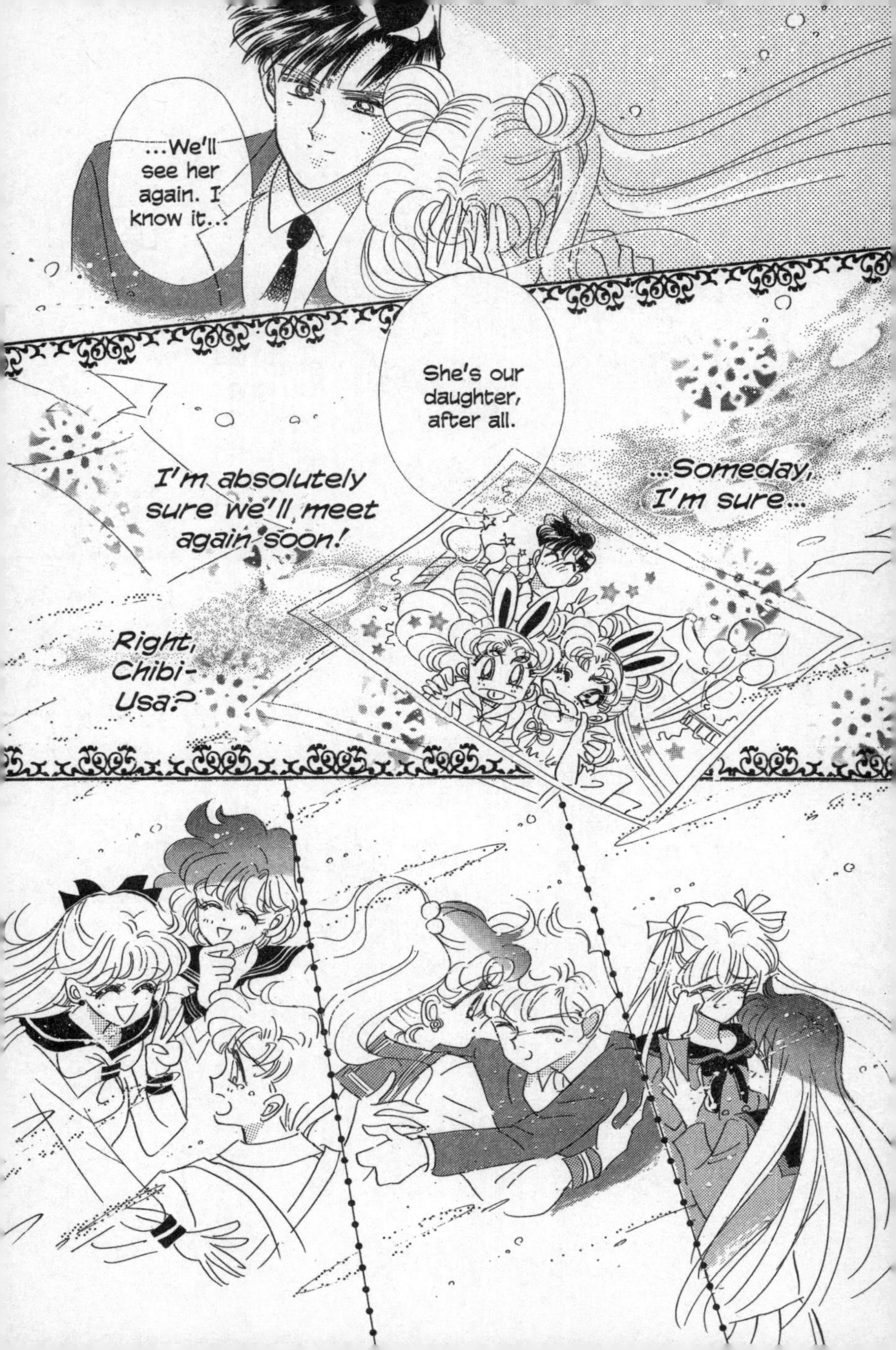
...We'll see her again. I know it...
She's our daughter, after all.
...Someday, I'm sure...
I'm absolutely sure we'll meet again soon!
Right, Chibi-Usa?

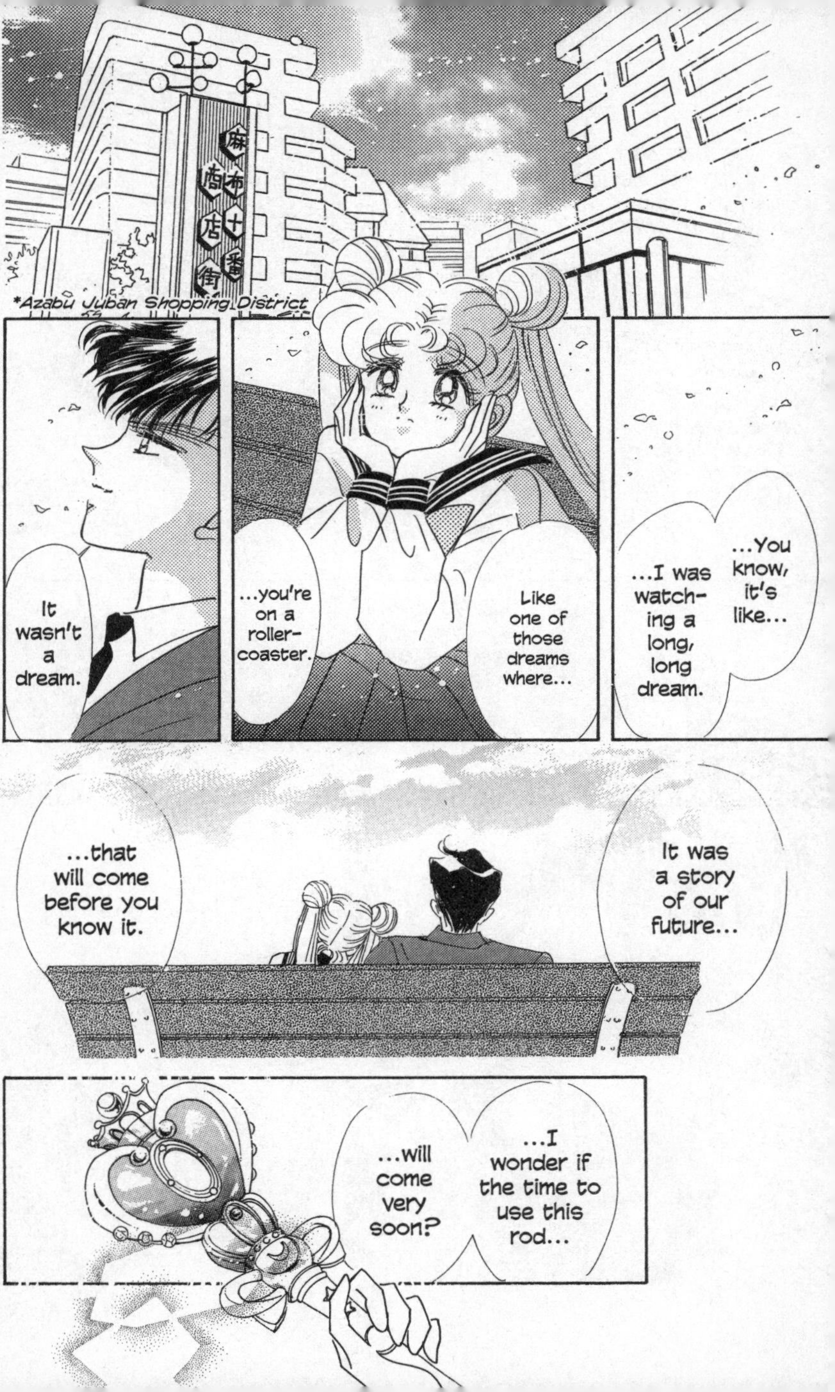
麻布十番商店街
*Azabu Juban Shopping District
...You know, it's like...
...I was watching a long, long dream.
Like one of those dreams where...
...you're on a roller-coaster.
It wasn't a dream.
It was a story of our future...
...that will come before you know it.
...I wonder if the time to use this rod...
...will come very soon?

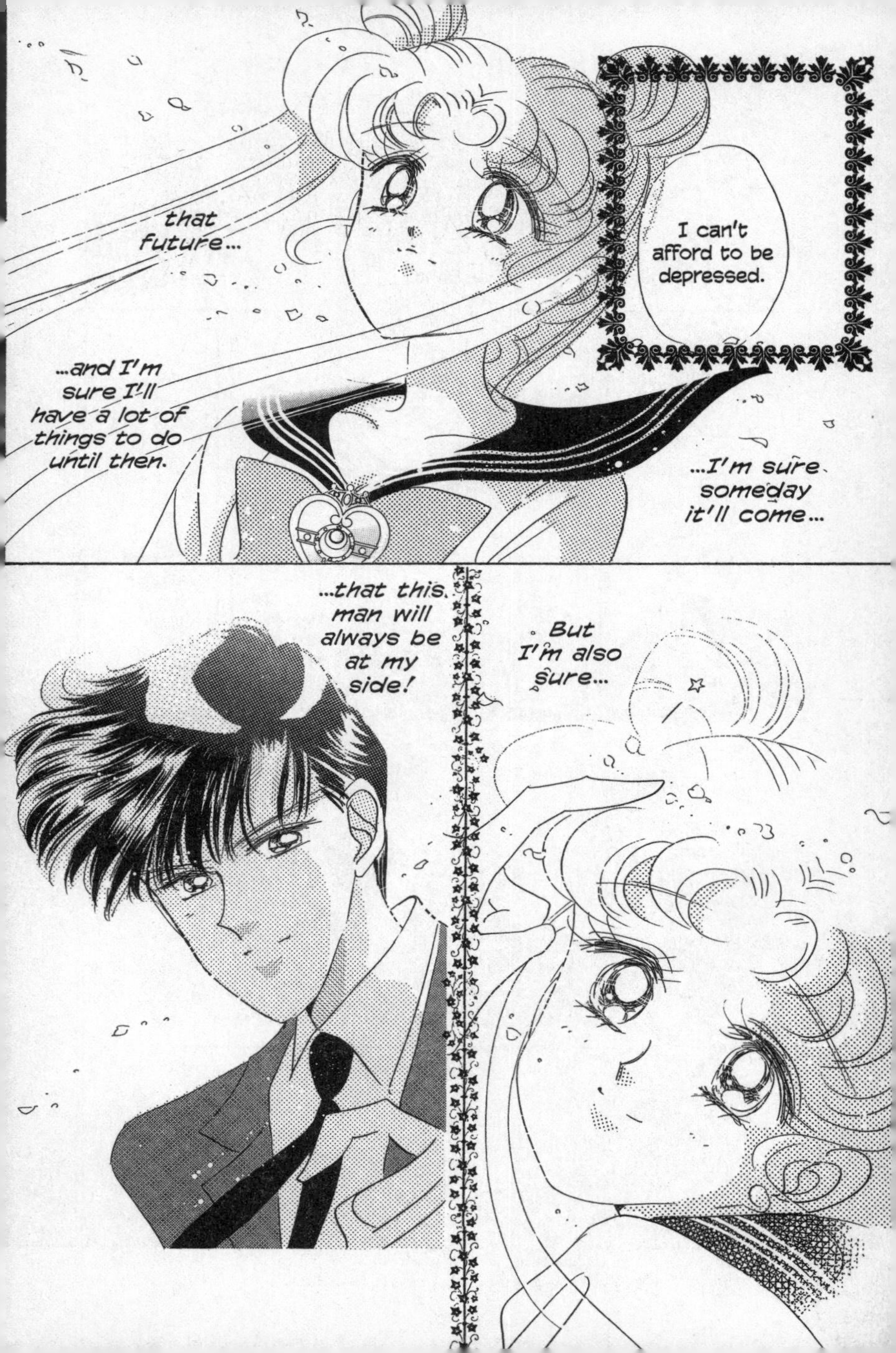
I can't afford to be depressed.
...I'm sure someday it'll come...
that future...
...and I'm sure I'll have a lot of things to do until then.
But I'm also sure...
...that this man will always be at my side!

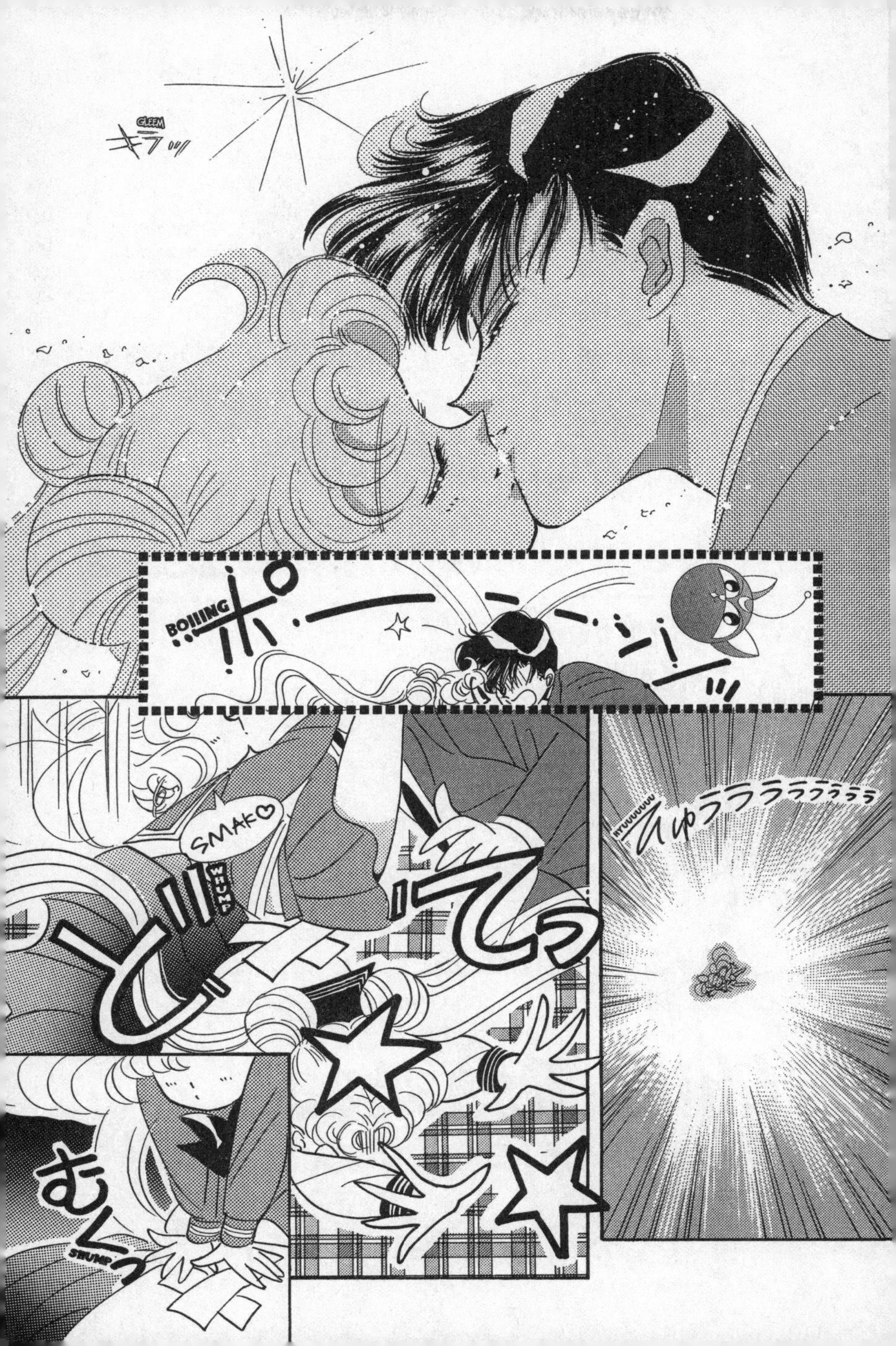
GLEEM
キラッ
BOIIING
HYUUUUUU
SMAK♡
WHUMP
どてっ
SHUMP
むくっ

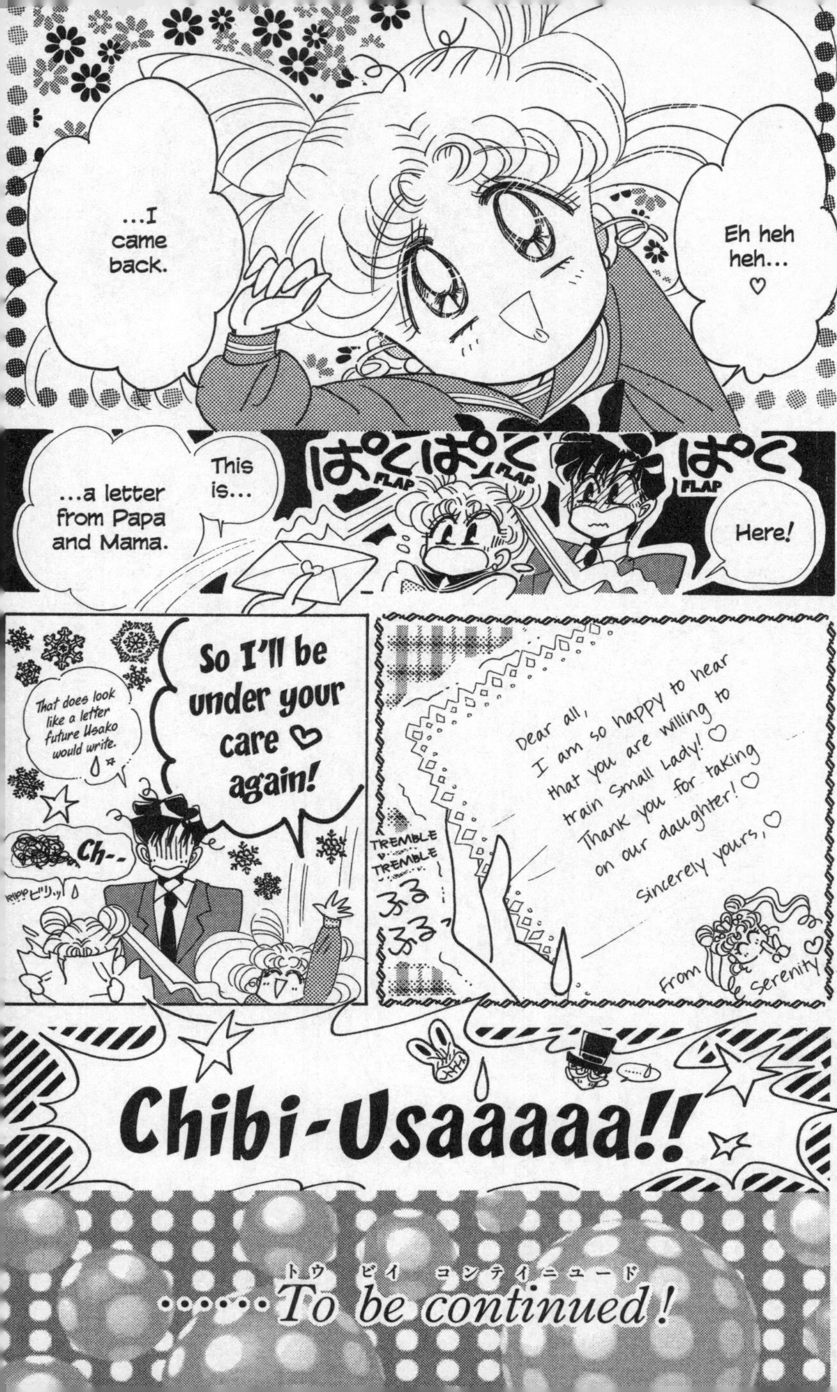
Eh heh heh... ♡
...I came back.
Here!
ぱくぱくぱく FLAP FLAP FLAP
This is...
...a letter from Papa and Mama.
TREMBLE TREMBLE ふるふるっ
Dear all,
I am so happy to hear that you are willing to train Small Lady! ♡
Thank you for taking on our daughter! ♡
Sincerely yours, ♡
From Serenity
So I'll be under your care ♡ again!
That does look like a letter future Usako would write.
Ch--
RIP ビリッ
.....
Chibi-Usaaaaaa!!
......To be continued!

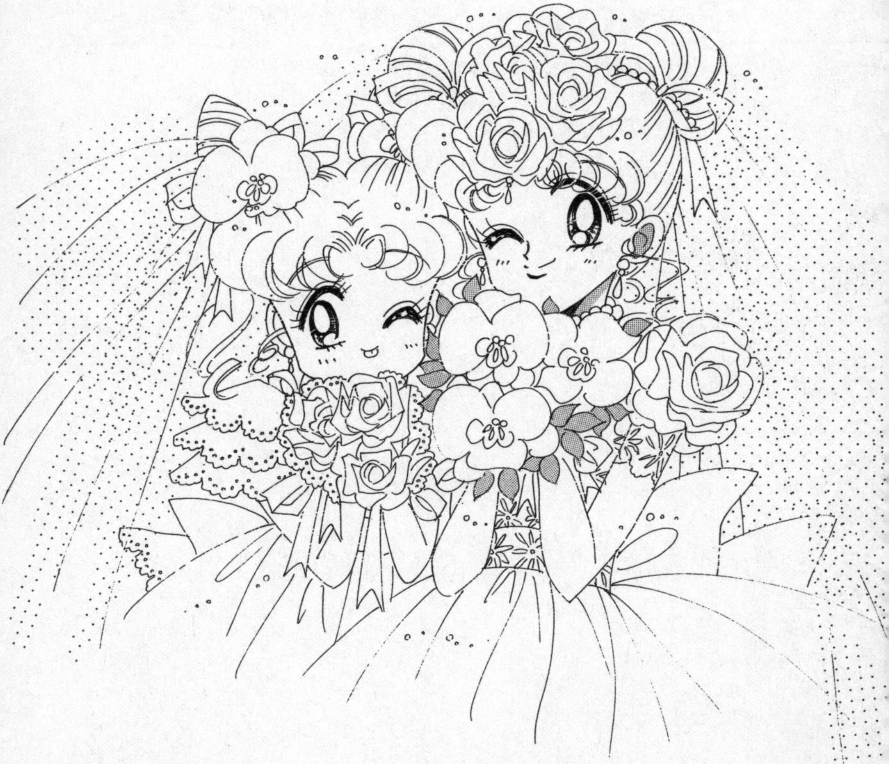

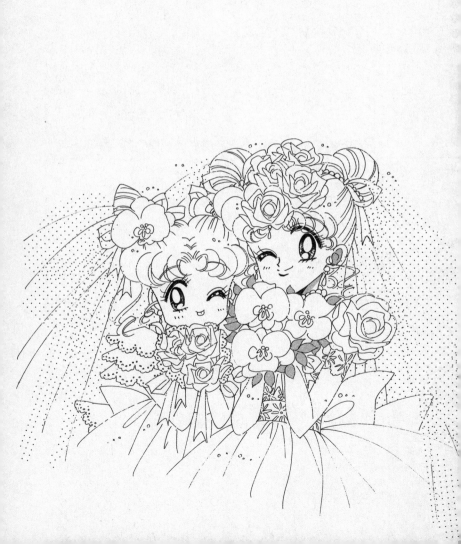

# Preview of *Sailor Moon 6*

We're pleased to present you a preview from
*Sailor Moon 6*. Please check our website
(www.kodanshacomics.com) to see when
this volume will be available.

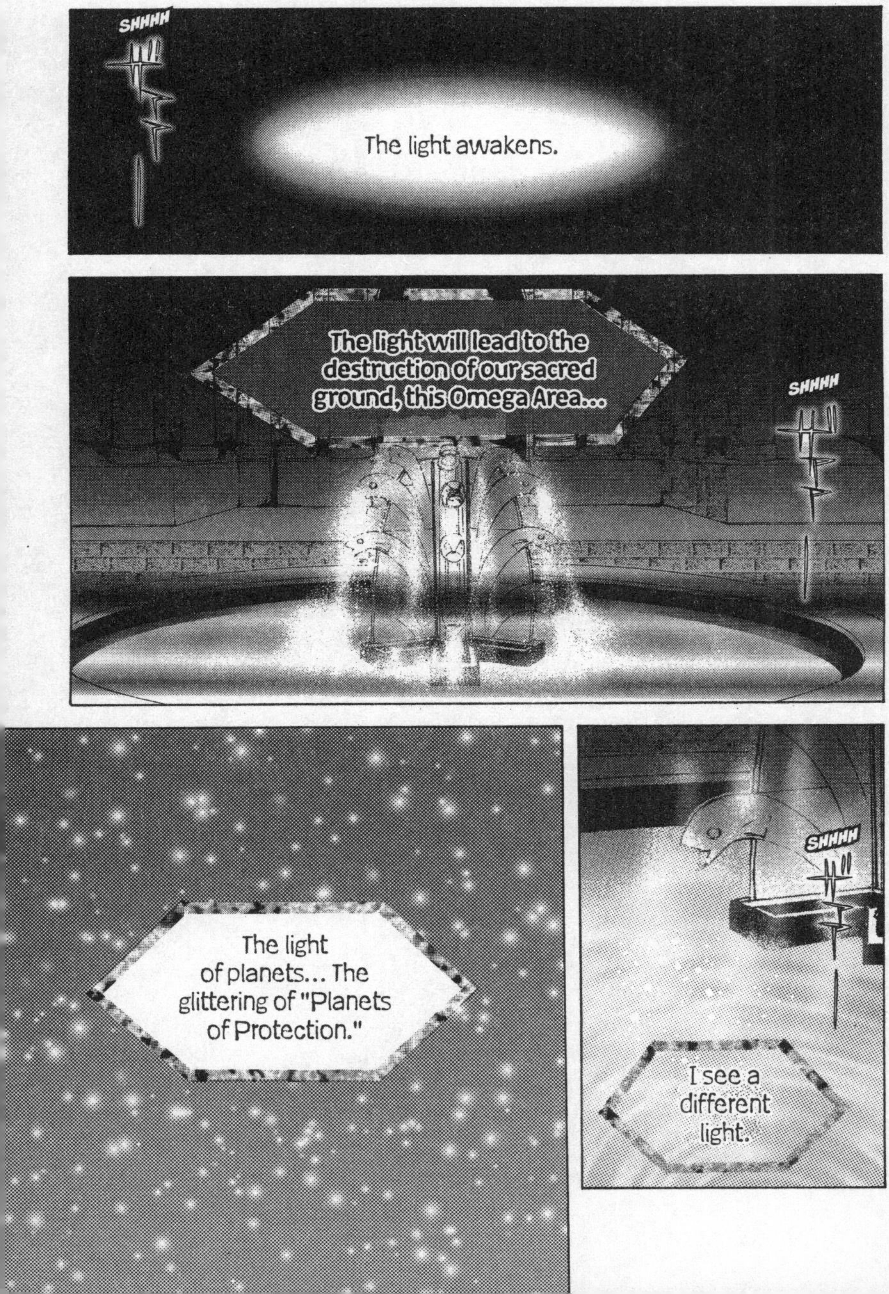
SHHHH
The light awakens.
The light will lead to the destruction of our sacred ground, this Omega Area...
SHHHH
SHHHH
I see a different light.
The light of planets... The glittering of "Planets of Protection."

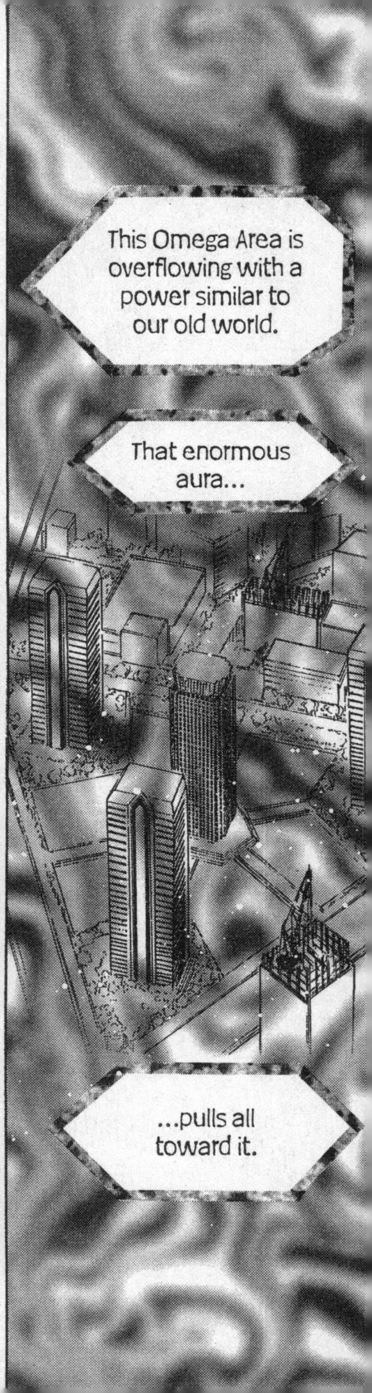
This Omega Area is overflowing with a power similar to our old world.
That enormous aura...
...pulls all toward it.

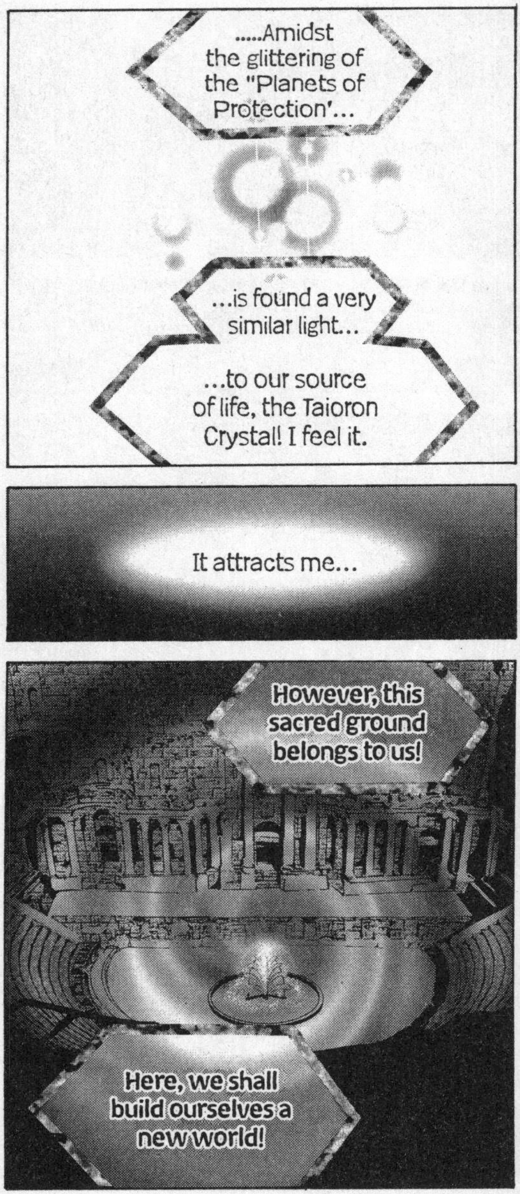
.....Amidst the glittering of the "Planets of Protection'...
...is found a very similar light...
...to our source of life, the Taioron Crystal! I feel it.
It attracts me...
However, this sacred ground belongs to us!
Here, we shall build ourselves a new world!

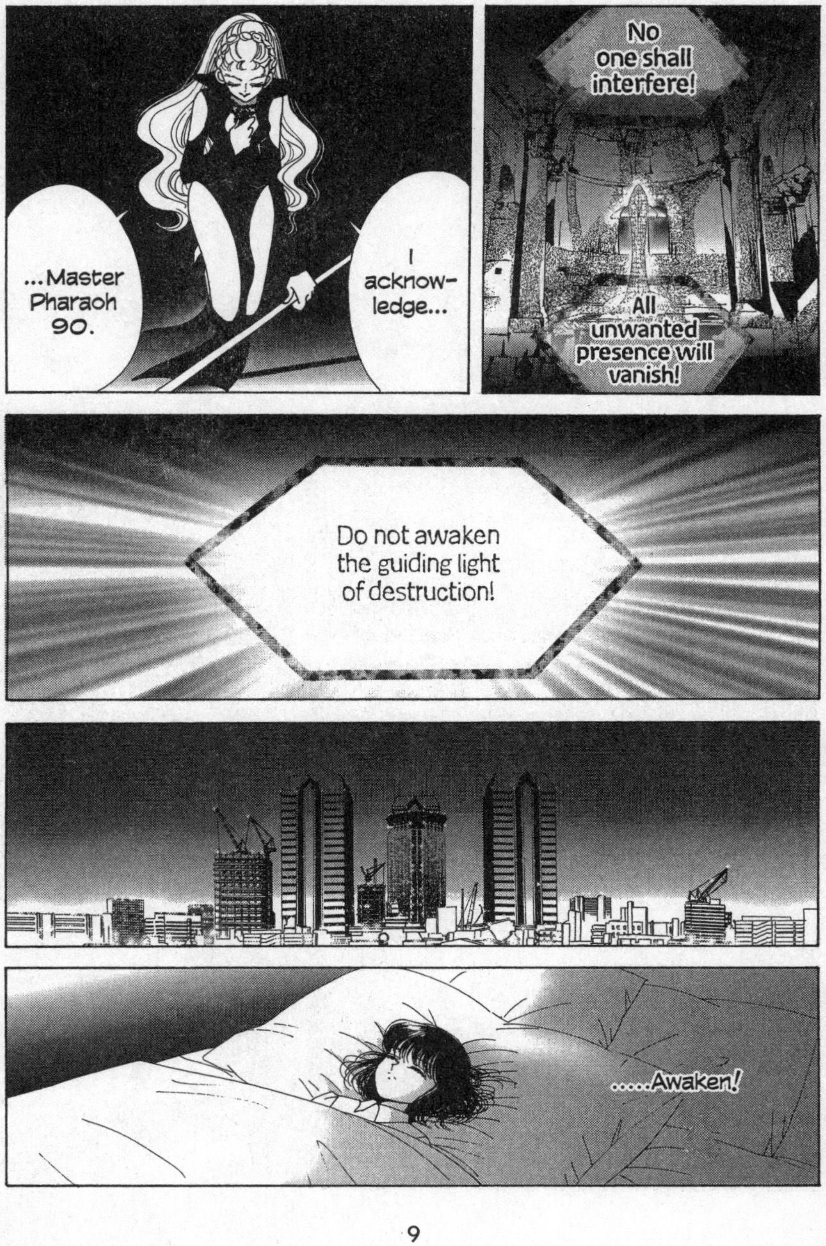
No one shall interfere!
All unwanted presence will vanish!
I acknowledge...
...Master Pharaoh 90.
Do not awaken the guiding light of destruction!
.....Awaken!

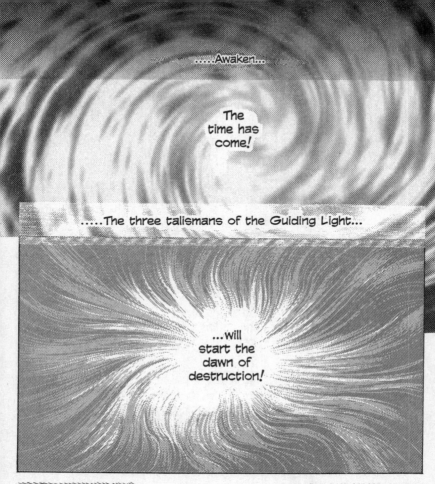

.....Awaken...

The
time has
come!

.....The three talismans of the Guiding Light...

...will
start the
dawn of
destruction!

10

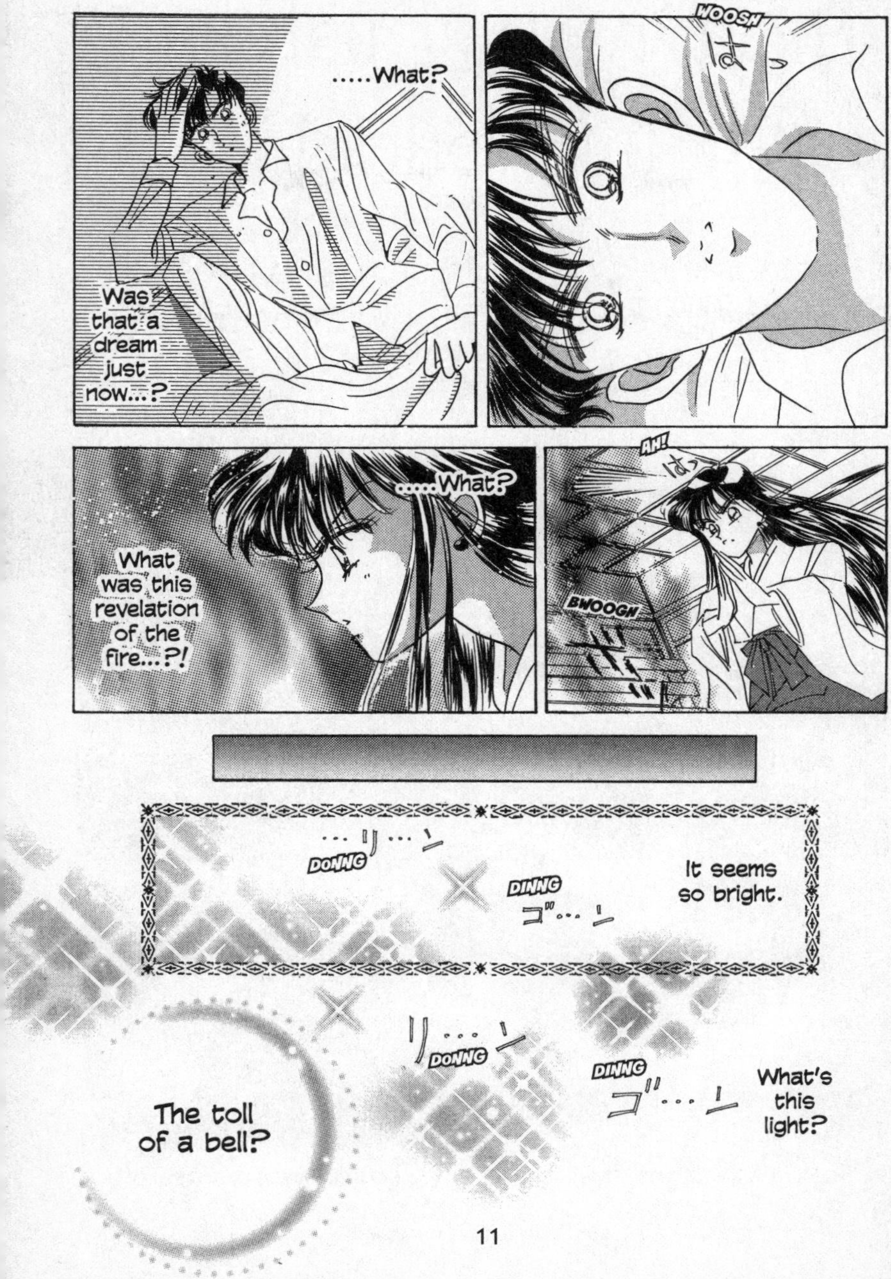
WOOSH
.....What?
Was that a dream just now...?
AH!
BWOOGH
......What?
What was this revelation of the fire...?!
It seems so bright.
DINNG
DONNG
What's this light?
DINNG
DONNG
The toll of a bell?

# The Pretty Guardians are back!

---

★

---

Kodansha Comics is proud to present *Sailor Moon* with all new translations.

For more information, go to **www.kodanshacomics.com**

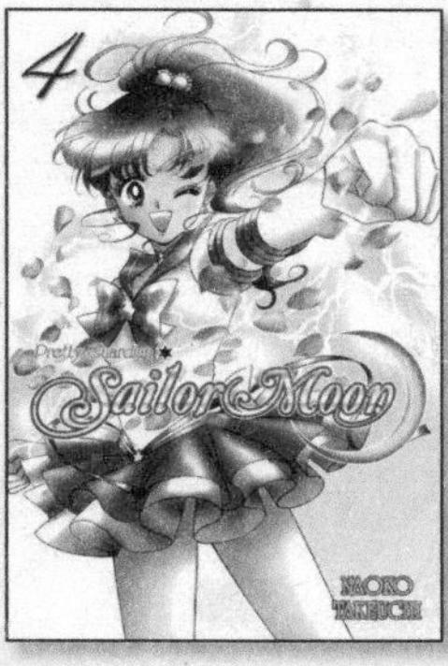
4
Pretty Guardian
Sailor Moon
NAOKO TAKEUCHI
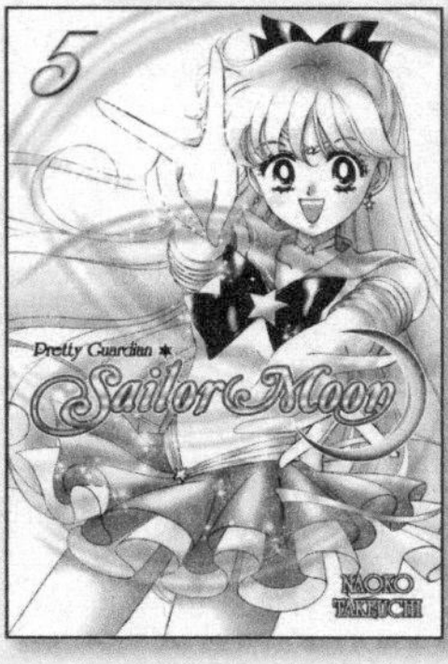
5
Pretty Guardian
Sailor Moon
NAOKO TAKEUCHI
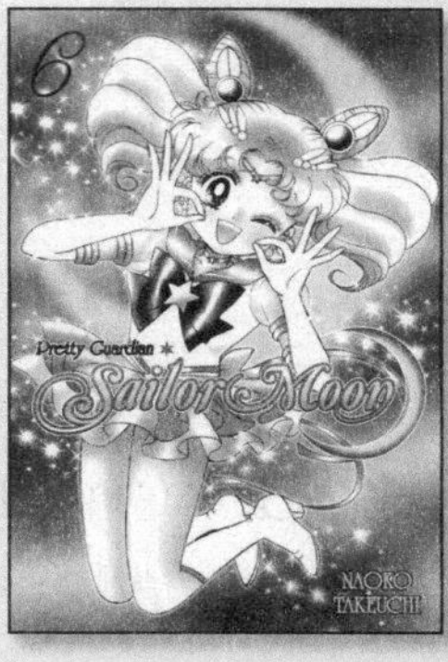
6
Pretty Guardian
Sailor Moon
NAOKO TAKEUCHI
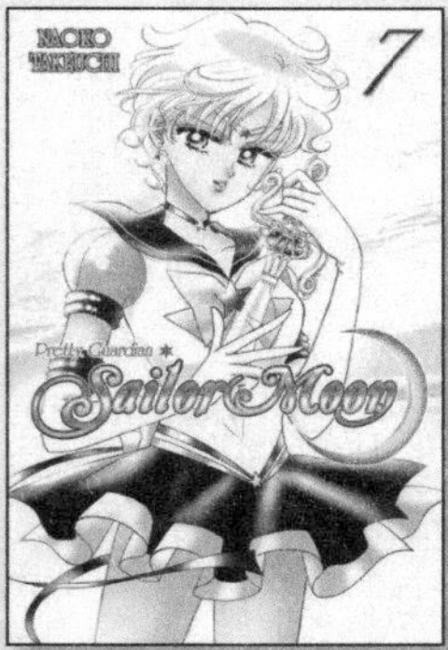
NAOKO TAKEUCHI
7
Pretty Guardian
Sailor Moon
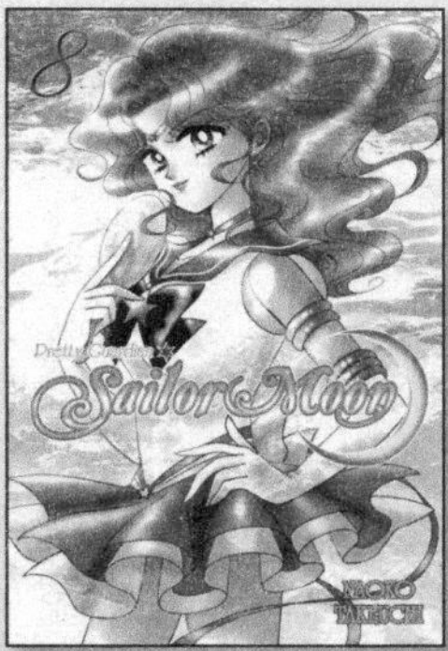
8
Pretty Guardian
Sailor Moon
NAOKO TAKEUCHI
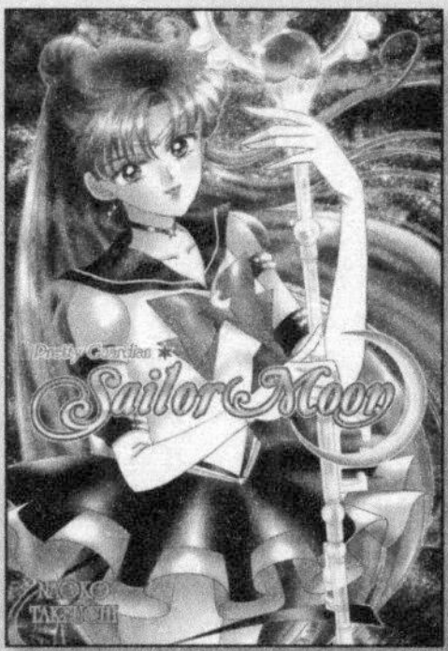
Pretty Guardian
Sailor Moon
NAOKO TAKEUCHI
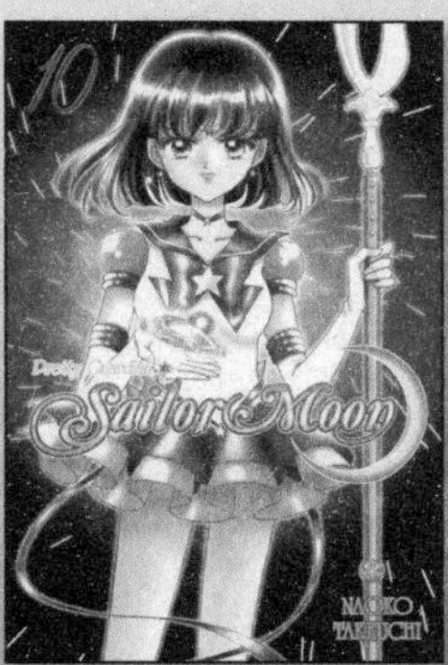
10
Pretty Guardian
Sailor Moon
NAOKO TAKEUCHI
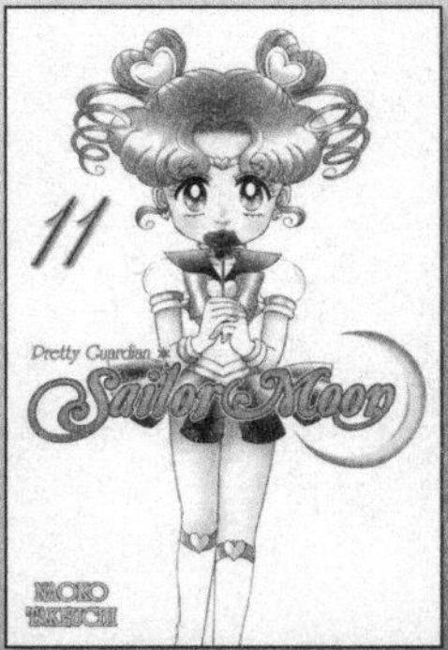
11
Pretty Guardian
Sailor Moon
NAOKO TAKEUCHI
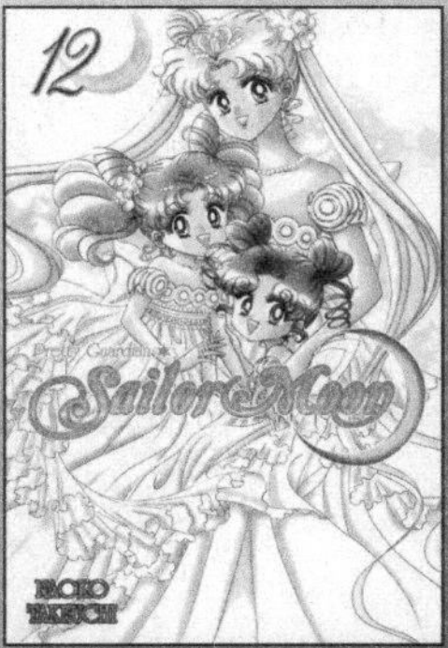
12
Pretty Guardian
Sailor Moon
NAOKO TAKEUCHI

KC KODANSHA COMICS